Also by

CHAPMAN PINCHER

TREACHERY

RANDOM HOUSE

NEW YORK

TREACHERY

Betrayals, Blunders,
and Cover-ups:
Six Decades of Espionage Against
America and Great Britain

CHAPMAN PINCHER

Published in the United States by Random House,
an imprint of The Random House Publishing Group,
a division of Random House, Inc., New York.

RANDOM HOUSE and colophon are registered
trademarks of Random House, Inc.

LIBRARY OF CONGRESS
CATALOGING-IN-PUBLICATION DATA
Pincher, Chapman.
Treachery: betrayals, blunders, and cover-ups: six decades of
espionage against America and Great Britain
/ Chapman Pincher.
p. cm.
Includes bibliographical references and index.
ISBN 978-1-4000-6807-4
eBook ISBN 978-1-58836-859-1
1. Espionage, British—History—20th century. 2. Espionage,
Soviet—United States—History. 3. Espionage, Soviet—
Great Britain—History. 4. Espionage—United States—
History—20th century. I. Title.
UB271.G7P565 2009   327.124707309'045—dc22
2008033875

Printed in the United States of America on acid-free paper

www.atrandom.com

2 4 6 8 9 7 5 3 1

FIRST EDITION

Book design by Barbara M. Bachman

CONTENTS

Admission

—

AFTER SIXTY YEARS OF INVESTIGATING THE MASSIVE RUS-
sian espionage assault on Great Britain and the United States—currently
in dangerous resurgence with a militant Kremlin regime intent on
restoring nuclear superpower status—I have become increasingly incensed and ashamed, as the detailed truth continues to emerge, by the
daily peril cold-bloodedly imposed on the people of both countries by
British traitors. Throughout time, there has been general agreement
that the foulest brand of treachery is the betrayal of a close, confiding,
and protective friend. In view of Britain's eternal debt to the American
people for their crucial assistance in preserving its liberty in two world
wars and throughout the forty-five years of the cold war, their betrayal
on such a staggering scale is cause for national remorse.

It is now apparent that the treachery not only threatened the British
and American forces during World War II, but placed the whole free
world in gravest jeopardy, when, for more than thirty years, Soviet nuclear missiles, perpetually aimed at British and American cities, could
have paralyzed both nations in minutes, with colossal loss of life.

The chilling content of documents unexpectedly released in Russia
since the collapse of the Soviet Union has revealed that updated copies
of Britain's most secret defense plans, including details of American intentions confided to the United Kingdom in joint interests, hemor-
rhaged regularly to Moscow. The Kremlin's continued access to the

evolving British and American defense strategy substantially increased the danger of a Soviet preemptive nuclear strike. As will be seen, some of the traitors exulted in their knowledge that the damage they were inflicting affected the security of the United States—the archopponent of their Communist creed.

Additionally, as intriguing new releases continue to reveal, an avalanche of ancillary secret information reached Moscow, year after year, on a scale that would never have been credible had not records of it become available.

Regrettably, the outrage we should all have felt has never expressed itself because a continuous conspiracy of deception by officials, assisted by politicians, ensured that the true extent of the evil that these traitors had perpetrated has been suppressed or systematically diluted to diminish its impact. Partly to conceal the ineffectiveness of the British secret services and their appalling penetration by Soviet "moles," and especially to preserve relations with the United States, the responsible authorities have consistently ensured that the full truth should be withheld, being abetted by successive governments in doing so. All those involved in covering up the traitors' treachery, protecting many of them from prosecution and public censure, thoroughly deserve to share their ignominy.

With the current political practice of apologizing for national crimes against humanity, such a shameful record cries out for full admission and sincere public apology, but such statesmanship is never likely to be forthcoming from any British authority now. No existing politician is aware, or wishes to be told, of the mass of detailed evidence that continues to accrue from both Russian and British sources. Officials of the British secret services are constitutionally averse to any avoidable admissions of their past incompetence and misdemeanors. I have therefore decided to place all the relevant facts so far exposed on record in this book, which, while presenting a fuller and more finely focused survey than has been possible before, also constitutes my personal apology.

I feel urged to make it as a World War II soldier who later developed close links with the American armed forces over half a century of defense reporting, involving expeditions with the U.S. Air Force, Navy, and Army, in which I developed friendships with men whom I admired for their dedicated professionalism. I also feel qualified to make it as an investigator who covered each espionage case as it occurred. Being now in a position to see the villainy in historical perspective, I feel particularly aggrieved as the treachery was committed by compatriots of my generation, those who deliberately covered up their crimes. Those who regard such a gesture as excessive may change their minds as they see the evidence unfold.

The current rise in Russian espionage activity in Great Britain and the United States, involving the recruitment of new traitors, and the evident danger of a new post-Soviet East-West nuclear arms race make all that is recorded in this book much more than academic history. Regarding human sources—spies and agents on the ground, who will always remain essential in the intelligence war—basic Russian practice has not changed, as the British security authorities have publicly warned. So the disclosures presented here expose lessons to be learned in preserving today's Anglo-American partnership and tightening the bond between us for the hazardous period ahead.

The whole espionage debacle, now so starkly visible, prompts two crucial questions. Could ineptitude on such a scale by the British Security Service, known as MI5, in failing to detect so many traitors before they inflicted so much damage be due entirely to sheer incompetence? Or was there at least one long-serving penetration agent—a "supermole"—inside MI5, not only supplying the Kremlin with British and American defense and intelligence secrets, but protecting its other spies and agents, whenever practicable, by preventing effective action against them? The British people, the Americans, Canadians, and other allies whose security was also treacherously undermined, have a right to know how their life-threatening predicament arose, what was done about it, and especially what was not done. So this book also addresses one question in particular: If there was a supermole inside MI5 over many years, who was it?

This book is not an attack on MI5 as it currently behaves, but solely with respect to its suspiciously dismal performance against the intelligence assault by the Soviet Union. In view of its brilliant record against the wartime German threat, it seems pertinent to ask why that was so. In its attempts to conceal its failures, the extent to which MI5 blatantly exploited its license to lie, as now disclosed by its own documents and sponsored books, is astonishing.

Such serious charges, against a major department of state, and especially against deceased individuals, require the evidence to be presented in detail. The claim that such people should be immune to exposure because they are no longer here to defend themselves has never been acceptable and is now expunged by the passage of time.

Perceptive readers may appreciate my frustration at having been unaware of the extent of the criminality and incompetence when, as a national journalist, I could have exposed it while the perpetrators and those who covered up for them were still alive. Anyone who doubts that I would have done so should consult the many recently declassified prime ministerial, cabinet, and Defense Ministry papers recording the long series of secret efforts to stifle my activities, with one infuriated prime minister (Harold Macmillan) even urging—in writing—that I should be "suppressed" or "got rid of."

I have intruded some personal experiences, as I encountered so many of the players. This may attract criticism that the book is self-serving, but the sole purpose is to enhance its authority. Details of relevant works mentioned in the text can be found in the references section, which also includes the British National Archives codes for files concerning the main cases. I have also inserted dates, whenever significant, since chronology can be so revealing, especially concerning relationships. My substantial collection of papers will be deposited at King's College, London, where I have been a Life Fellow for many years.

The whole experience has been like attempting to construct a giant jigsaw puzzle with all the missing pieces hidden, many concealed in officially inaccessible places or even deliberately destroyed. I hope that readers will share my excitement at filling in the gaps, replacing many probabilities by certainties to present a wider, more vivid, and ever more amazing picture than has been possible before, while trying to resolve the last major espionage mysteries of the twentieth century.

The picture I can now display is horrific and intensely shaming but is clearly visible for all who dare to look. Still more of it is likely to accrue, but the time for public outrage has already arrived.

TREACHERY

CHAPTER 1

A Momentous Message

——

LATE IN THE YEAR 2000, VLADIMIR PUTIN, PRESIDENT OF THE Russian Federation, awarded the posthumous title "Superagent of Military Intelligence" to Ursula Beurton, a former British housewife who is better known in the annals of espionage by her Soviet code name, Sonia. It was an unprecedented honor for a woman who had already held two Orders of the Red Banner for her treacherous activities in several countries, especially in Great Britain, where she had been deeply involved in the theft of both British and American atomic bomb secrets during World War II. Shortly after she died, in Berlin in 2000 at the age of ninety-three, some of her other exploits were released from the Moscow archives for publication in Russian books. One of them, which had occurred in Oxford in 1943 under the noses of MI5, then located nearby, involved information so politically explosive that it was regarded by the British prime minister, Winston Churchill, as requiring the utmost secrecy.

In August 1943, Churchill and President Franklin D. Roosevelt, accompanied by senior aides, met in Quebec to decide about the date and details of the invasion of Italy from North Africa and, later, of France from Great Britain. In addition, on August 19, they signed a separate agreement concerning collaboration between Britain and the United States on the production of an atomic bomb. The American atomic project was progressing so rapidly that Churchill wanted British scientists to join it there, but the U.S. government had objected to such a move. Previously, in June 1942, at a meeting in Washington, D.C., Churchill and Roosevelt had made a loose arrangement to pool atomic information and develop a bomb together, but with the setting up of the vast Manhattan Project, the United States was contributing so much more money and effort that the will to share the proceeds had seriously declined. At Quebec, Churchill was determined to exploit his friendship with Roosevelt to resurrect the partnership and enshrine it in a formal treaty.

The old warrior's persistence resulted in a separate two-page document, usually referred to as the Quebec Agreement. In it, the two leaders stated that Great Britain and the United States would collaborate to produce an atomic weapon and would never use it against each other or against any other country without mutual consent. It also declared that neither would ever communicate any information about it to any third party without joint consent. There was also agreement about continuing atomic collaboration in the postwar situation.

The Quebec Agreement was an exceptionally sensitive document because the very existence of any work on the bomb was supposedly so secret that it referred to the project only as "Tube Alloys." Also, Churchill and Roosevelt were most anxious to avoid offending the Soviet leader, Joseph Stalin, by making him aware that he would not be given any information about the new weapon, which could devastatingly weaken the Soviet Union's military position in the postwar world. Having been forced into becoming allies by Adolf Hitler's attack on them in 1941, the Russians were bearing the brunt of the fighting.

Churchill therefore kept the Quebec Agreement and its details secret to himself, a few trusted aides, and the Chiefs of Staff of the British Armed Forces. The distribution list—those to whom a copy was sent for information—is therefore likely to have been very restricted indeed. Several documents now in the British National Archives testify to the extraordinary extent of the measures taken to prevent unauthorized persons from having any knowledge of its details. As late as June 1949, the prime minister, then Clement Attlee, expressed his deep concern that details of the Quebec Agreement and subsequent secret accords might be revealed to a U.S. Senate committee, from which they might leak. Even in 1951, both Attlee and President Harry Truman were still insisting that details of the agreement should remain secret. A statement about the Quebec Agreement made in Robert Norris's heavily researched biography of the American general Leslie Groves, *Racing for the Bomb*, provides further evidence of the desired secrecy: "Only a few senior officials on each side of the Atlantic knew of the highly secret arrangement. For several years after the war the existence of the agreement was not known either to the American Congress or the British Parliament."

Yet the Russian archives have now shown that on Saturday, September 4, 1943—only sixteen days after the signing—Sonia, sitting in Oxford, supplied the Red Army Intelligence Center with an account of all the essential aspects of the Quebec Agreement, along with ancillary details, sending them directly to Moscow by radio.

The scene for this astonishing achievement was a cottage, 50a George Street in Oxford's Summertown district, once occupied by the coachman serving a large house from which it was separated by a stone wall. Having taken her miniature high-tech radio transmitter from a cavity in the wall, in which it was normally hidden, Sonia, then thirty-six, was sitting at a table downstairs. It was late at night, and the obligatory blackout curtains, required to eliminate the smallest chink of light observable by a German bomber, ensured her total privacy. Laboriously, she had already converted the document she had surreptitiously acquired, letter by letter, into a code believed to be unbreakable. Having completed the encoding and rechecked it, she began to tap it out in Morse.

The high aerial she had strung up with the permission of the owner of the big house—ostensibly to service her large conventional radio set—ensured that her efforts reached Red Army intelligence, generally known as the GRU. There, her masters and Stalin himself quickly rated her coup as "of the greatest value" because "for the first time" the military and political leadership of the Soviet Union knew that the United States and Great Britain were creating an atomic military alliance and were going to hide it from its wartime ally. The GRU archives record, "On 19 August 1943, in a secret personal message to Marshal Stalin, Roosevelt and Churchill reported about their agreed plans for the surrender of Italy and other matters but there was no word about the fact that they had also made an additional secret agreement about the use of nuclear weapons."

What Stalin regarded as his allies' perfidy inevitably affected his attitude when, on November 28, he met Churchill and Roosevelt in

Tehran to discuss both the war and the postwar situation. The Western leaders were hoping to establish better relations with the Soviet dictator, who, according to newspapers, had arrived in a "prickly, suspicious mood." Historians may wonder to what extent his suspicion was fortified—and his later behavior conditioned—by deep resentment generated by his knowledge that his country had just been secretly excluded from a project likely to change the military parameters forever, as he already knew from his atomic spies. Did Stalin interpret his exclusion as the first icy gust of the cold war to come? To this day, Russian writers regard it as an inexcusable British-American "dirty trick" on a gallant ally that had absorbed the impact of the German savagery with tremendous losses.

In 2006, the release of the private papers of Vyacheslav Molotov, Stalin's most trusted deputy, revealed that on October 15, 1943, a British spy had also supplied details of the early plans for Operation Overlord, the Anglo-American assault on Normandy. These, too, had been agreed upon at Quebec. Stalin's array of British traitors, serving both the GRU and the other arm of Soviet intelligence, most commonly known as the KGB, had been instructed to seek out the secret results of the conference. One of them—described in a GRU report to Molotov as "our source of trusted credibility"—had quickly responded with plans and maps of landing beaches. They included the estimate that this "second front," which should reduce German pressure on the Soviet forces, was unlikely to be attempted before the spring of 1944. Small wonder that Stalin was "prickly and suspicious" at Tehran.

There were potentially more dangerous consequences. Once the plans for Overlord were in Soviet hands, there was always the risk that they might leak to Germany, through a spy in the Kremlin, a defector, or a captured Russian general. In view of Stalin's dream of a totally Communist Europe, there was even the possibility that if, by the spring of 1944, the German forces were in full retreat out of the Soviet Union, it might suit him to leak the plans deliberately.

Whether Sonia appreciated the scale of her achievement is unknown because she never mentioned it to anyone and, probably on Soviet orders, withheld it from her memoirs. Her son Michael Hamburger, with whom I am in regular contact, was astonished when I told him about it in 2003. That she experienced a glow of satisfaction cannot be doubted, because in the previous month, after managing to make an espionage assignment in London in a violent storm, she had received special praise from her Moscow chief in a message stating that if he had more Sonias, the war would be over much sooner. Her Quebec coup was extraordinary for another reason: She was so heavily pregnant that she gave birth only four days later. In a letter to her mother written on September 8, she announced the birth of her second son.

The GRU archives show that Sonia also included the fact that some senior Americans, both military and scientific, had reservations about any atomic partnership with Britain. So she had clearly been given a summary of all the atomic aspects of the Quebec Agreement, which had been circulated in secrecy in some British government department and abstracted by some high-level traitor.

How did this diminutive woman obtain this so secret document so soon? As Sonia was already the mother of two children, it is unlikely that she would have strayed far from her cottage so shortly before going into labor, especially as she had booked a private room in a nursing home nearby. It is also clear from her letters that she had not visited London since mid-August. While she had continued to shop locally and might have risked a short train journey, it is unlikely that she would have visited any distant hiding place to pick up a document concealed there, especially if it involved a bicycle ride. She had no automobile.

Because of rigid Soviet espionage rules and the risk of wartime letter censorship, such precious and sensitive information would not have been sent to her by mail. Nor, for security's sake, was any additional courier likely to have been involved. So whoever gave her the details of the Quebec Agreement delivered them either to her home or to a nearby hiding place that Sonia monitored and emptied. It seems certain that the information was delivered to her in documentary form rather than verbally, because on September 4 she also transmitted a complete list of the fifteen British scientists who had already been selected to move to America.

Sonia's historic achievement is tantalizing proof that she had some prime, high-level British source whose name has still been withheld by the Russian authorities. When her coup was made public in 2002, in a GRU-sponsored book, *The GRU and the Atomic Bomb,* GRU colonel general Alexander Pavlov, who vouched for its authenticity in a foreword, was at pains to point out that "the time has not yet arrived when still unsuspected or unproven wartime sources can safely be named."

Had Churchill, a supreme patriot and the son of an American mother, ever known about this historic betrayal, his anger and amazement that any Briton could have behaved so treacherously, not only to his own country, but to the ally he had pressured into the agreement only through joint goodwill, may be imagined. The first hard evidence regarding the possible identity of the traitor who had purloined the information and somehow transferred it to Sonia surfaced almost exactly two years after the event—on September 5, 1945—in faraway Ottawa, so widely flung was the network of Soviet espionage.

CHAPTER 2

Duplicity Exposed

IN APRIL 2004, DISTINGUISHED HISTORIANS AND SECURITY officials from Great Britain, the United States, and Canada, along with representatives of the Canadian government, met in Ottawa to pay tribute to a young Russian soldier who had changed history. While ruthless Soviet espionage against Western democracies had been waged since the early 1930s and throughout World War II, the first public exposure of its enormousness had not occurred until 1945. On September 5 of that year, Lieutenant Igor Gouzenko, a twenty-six-year-old Red Army cipher clerk, left his office in the Soviet embassy in Ottawa with 109 secret telegrams hidden in his clothing and a mass of information in his head.

Gouzenko was a member not of the KGB (*Komityet Gosudarstvennoy Bezopasnosti*), the widely known and much feared Soviet intelligence and security service, but of the GRU, which specialized in military intelligence. The GRU—short for *Glavnoye Razvedyvatelnoye Upravleniye*—had been founded in 1926 as the Chief Intelligence Directorate of the Red Army. Unlike the KGB, which descended from previous organizations with different names, the GRU retained its old title. (For simplicity's sake, I will refer to the KGB by those initials throughout its existence.)

The GRU—the organization to which Sonia also belonged—was one of the main engines of Soviet power, its prime purpose being the prevention of the collapse of the Soviet Union by outside enemies, while the main original remit of the KGB was to prevent its collapse from enemies within. Although the USSR did not set up its diplomatic mission in Canada until the summer of 1943, it was quickly staffed and equipped for espionage. Within months, both the GRU and the KGB were operating in force out of the Soviet embassy in Ottawa to recruit local Communist agents, as they were from most of their other Western embassies. They worked strictly independently and in rivalry, mutual secrecy between the GRU and the KGB being required by the Kremlin in the interests of efficiency, security, and reliability. Recently released Russian documents found by the independent Russian historian Dr. Svetlana Chervonnaya, such as the archives of Molotov, have revealed that Stalin was suspicious of information provided by only one of the agencies and so required separate confirmation from the other.

A continuing appreciation of their fierce independence throughout the time dealt with in this study is essential to an understanding of Soviet espionage. As a KGB document states, it was not until 1981 that the Politburo decided that, for the first time, the KGB and the GRU were required to cooperate in a worldwide intelligence operation, code-named Ryan, to penetrate what it (wrongly) believed to be joint American-British plans for a preemptive nuclear strike against the Soviet Union. The fact that this had never happened before, even during the highly dangerous Cuban missile crisis, suggests that there had been no need for it because the Politburo was already being supplied with the necessary information.

After two years in Canada, with its freedom, high living standards, and open society, Gouzenko and his wife, Svetlana, had hated the thought of their imminent return to Moscow. Igor had been under criticism for some minor lapse of duty and faced unduly severe disciplinary action. Though both he and his wife were judged in Moscow to be traitors who betrayed their motherland for economic gain, they seemed to be genuinely horrified by the underhanded Russian behavior to such a friendly and well-intentioned people as the Canadians, who, like the British and the Americans, had been wartime allies of the Soviet Union.

Gouzenko was the first defector to provide documentary proof of the scale and purpose of the Soviet Union's espionage and subversion activities against its allies. His evidence revealed that what came to be called the cold war between East and West, which was to affect the whole world for forty-five years, was already being waged by the Soviet

Union in anticipation of an eventual military showdown between communism and capitalism. However, if historians need to fix one day when both sides consciously became embroiled in the cold war, then September 5, 1945, is probably it. That was the general view of the academics who attended the two-day conference convened to make "the first ever historical examination of the Gouzenko affair" in April 2004. A memorial plaque erected by the Canadian government to Gouzenko's memory at the end of that conference states, "The Gouzenko Affair brought the realities of the emerging Cold War to the attention of the Canadian public." It also brought it to the public attention of the rest of the world.

At first, the seventy-year-old Canadian prime minister, Mackenzie King, was so concerned about offending the Russians, who had helped to save the West from fascism, that he favored handing Gouzenko back to the Soviet embassy and certain death. He wrote in his diary, "He had enough evidence to prove that instead of being friends, the Russians were really enemies. The forces it will arouse are more terrific than any of us begin to comprehend."

Only a month previously, the Japanese had been forced to surrender to the United States after two of its cities had been destroyed by atomic bombs, and Mackenzie King knew that the Soviet Union had been deliberately excluded from the atomic revolution that had transformed both major warfare and international politics forever. He was also aware that Stalin and his people deeply resented it when they had suffered so much to defeat the mutual German enemy and realized that the Canadian public, which had been strongly pro-Russian during the war, would be deeply shocked if they learned of the Soviet espionage duplicity.

Fortunately for Gouzenko, the chief of British Security Coordination, William Stephenson (later Sir), a Canadian who was based in New York, as he had been since 1940, happened to be in Ottawa and was instrumental in reversing the view that the defector should be handed back to the Russians. Instead, he was granted asylum, with the entire incident being concealed from the public. Secret MI5 documents on the Gouzenko affair, released in 2004, revealed that Stephenson's intervention was to give him a major role in the whole ensuing saga.

When Mackenzie King saw all Gouzenko's evidence, he was staggered, recording in his diary that Stalin's apparently friendly gesture in 1943 of abolishing the Comintern—the Soviet-controlled international organization to foment world revolution—had been a fraud. It was one of history's most significant moments of truth, as was quickly appreciated in Washington and London. President Truman was deeply shocked when, on September 12, J. Edgar Hoover, chief of the Federal Bureau of Investigation, informed him that information supplied by the Royal Canadian Mounted Police (RCMP) had revealed that "the Soviets have made the obtaining of complete information regarding the atomic bomb the number one project of Soviet espionage."

The Canadian prime minister flew to Washington and discussed the threat in detail with Truman and selected officials. He then sailed to London to see the newly installed British prime minister, Clement Attlee, arriving on the *Queen Mary* on October 7. Both Truman and Attlee were dismayed by the Soviet duplicity, which entirely changed the Western leaders' attitudes to future dealings with Stalin. Effectively, these and later summit meetings initiated the postwar nuclear arms race. (Shortly after the Gouzenko defection, while I was still in the wartime army involved with secret weapons, I received a top-secret War Office document categorizing classified information that might safely be passed to Allied countries. The Soviet Union had already been placed in a class of its own to which no such information of any category could be passed.)

While in London, Mackenzie King also sought out Winston Churchill, and the details of the Gouzenko defection confirmed the former prime minister's view that the Soviet Union was the new opponent of the democracies. Churchill was to make this clear a few months later, in his historic speech at Fulton, Missouri, in which he introduced the concept of an "iron curtain" imprisoning many European countries and called for a special defensive relationship between Great Britain and the United States.

Gouzenko, who was highly intelligent, with a promising academic background, proved to be an excellent witness when he gave his evidence in secret to the RCMP on the morning of September 7. With the Russians using every means to recover their traitor, by force if necessary, Gouzenko and his wife were spirited out of Ottawa. They were hidden in various cottages for three weeks, with armed guards, until safer accommodations could be found at a secret military training base—Camp X—near Whitby, on Lake Ontario, about two hundred miles away, where the defector was subjected to prolonged questioning. Still, no hint of his defection leaked to the media.

Gouzenko exposed more than twenty Canadians who appeared to be working as agents for the GRU, which had taken over the Canadian Communist Party, using it as an intelligence tool. He also named a British scientist, Alan Nunn May, who was working on the Allied atomic bomb project in Canada and had supplied the GRU with details of the first atomic bomb test in America, along with samples of uranium explosive and other information. This was the first proof that the Russians had been actively trying to penetrate Western atomic secrets, and it caused particular concern, as both the United States and Great Britain were hoping that their atomic monopoly would last substantially longer than it eventually did.

Faces had fallen in MI5 at the exposure of May's treachery because inquiries quickly showed that he had been among the first to be recruited to the British bomb project. So his knowledge had not been limited to the secrets he had learned in Canada. He had also paid several visits to an important atomic laboratory in Chicago, where he had been told a great deal in the belief that MI5 had cleared him for security. Events would show that May had done little more than confirm for the Russians technical information that had already been supplied in much greater detail by other spies, but because of the chance timing of his exposure, the effect of his treachery on Anglo-American relations would quickly prove to be catastrophic.

Sonia's provision of the Quebec Agreement, two years previously, was to be of considerable significance to the Gouzenko affair, because according to the GRU archives, it had alerted the GRU headquarters—and Stalin—to the part Canada was to play in the development of the atomic bomb. Though Canada had not been a signatory to the Quebec Agreement, it was a member of influential bodies set up as a result of it and was participating heavily in the atomic research project. This had eventually led the GRU to order its contingent in the Ottawa embassy to activate May, who had already been recruited to GRU service in England, as will be seen.

Among several spies working for the GRU in America, Gouzenko fingered "the assistant to [Edward] Stettinius," the U.S. secretary of state. After inquiries, he was believed to be Alger Hiss, who worked at the heart of the American government, being head of the State Department's political affairs office, and had attended the Yalta conference in February 1945. With impressive family credentials, Hiss was being considered as the U.S. candidate to become secretary general of the United Nations.

Gouzenko reported having seen evidence of a leak to Moscow concerning a forthcoming visit to Ottawa by British counterintelligence officers. This almost certainly referred to a visit paid by the senior MI5 officer Guy Liddell, to advise the RCMP in 1944 concerning German espionage. Gouzenko later suggested that this leak meant that Moscow "had an inside track in MI5."

He provided the first proof that the Soviet military chiefs were already making contingency plans for possible war to achieve world communism. They were seeking details of America's plans for demobilization, its future strategy, troop dispositions, and details of advances in weapons design, radar, and any other secret information that would assist their purpose. Gouzenko also provided details of the GRU's structure, size, and leading personnel.

His defection remained secret for five months and became public knowledge only after the news was deliberately leaked by the FBI. The story broke on the radio and in U.S. newspapers on February 3, 1946, revealing that Ottawa was a major GRU base for espionage in the whole of North America. Two days later, the Canadian government set up a royal commission to examine Gouzenko's evidence. Though not all the owners of the code names in his documents were identified, twenty who were named comprised two Canadian members of Parliament (MPs), scientists, academics, and civil servants, including a cipher expert.

Gouzenko proved to be an articulate witness with exceptional recall. He never contradicted himself or, like so many defectors, exaggerated his claims to improve his value. Lawyers who tried to ambush him all failed. The royal commission's eventual report stated that it was impressed by his sincerity and had no hesitation in accepting his statements and that Canada was in debt to him. Further proof of his veracity has been provided by GRU archives, released as recently as 2002 in the officially sponsored Russian book *The GRU and the Atomic Bomb* by Vladimir Lota, a former GRU officer granted special access. Twelve of those Canadians who were arrested were convicted and sentenced to prison terms, with two more having their sentences overturned on appeal. The rest were acquitted for various legal reasons, but in no case had Gouzenko's information or memory been at fault.

Meanwhile, the defection had such an impact in Moscow that Stalin set up a damage limitation commission that included the KGB chief, Lavrenti Beria, as the GRU archives have recently disclosed. Both the GRU and KGB leaderships in Moscow exercised a ruthless response to such a disaster to protect their intelligence officers from exposure. They immediately severed all contact with their spies and agents without explanation to them, and their controlling officers were instructed to suspend or severely limit operations until further order. This meant that the services of the sources were suspended, perhaps for months until the danger had passed, but the Centers, as the Moscow headquarters were called, regarded a slump in intelligence as worthwhile to protect the sources and to avoid any diplomatic incident that might lead to the expulsion of an embassy officer, with consequent adverse publicity.

The timing of the defection could not have been worse for the Soviet Union. The destruction of Hiroshima and Nagasaki had convinced Stalin that his country must become an atomic power with all speed, and at that time, the Soviet scientists were greatly dependent on atomic information being provided by GRU and KGB spies. Though the GRU chief, General Ivan Ilichev, escaped execution or imprisonment because he had already demanded Gouzenko's return to Moscow, he was dismissed from the army.

The Soviet reaction underlined the extent to which the GRU and KGB operated independently. Evidence resulting from Gouzenko's defection showed that the KGB and the GRU were organized as quite separate espionage networks in each major country, each with its own controlling "Center" in Moscow. They recruited agents separately and secretly. Each was required to protect its own patch, and they were forbidden to consult each other without permission from the top intelligence authority in Moscow, the State Defense Committee. While they did not share agents or raw intelligence, information of special interest to each other could be shared through the State Defense Committee without sources being revealed.

Before he had defected, Gouzenko, with whom I was to correspond and converse by telephone over many months, had told his wife that if he were to be captured by his Russian colleagues, she was to tell the RCMP of the existence of a GRU spy inside the British security agency, MI5. The code name of that mole was Elli.

CHAPTER 3

A Spy Called Elli

———

Among the revelations that Gouzenko rated most important was his knowledge that there was an exceptionally valuable
GRU spy inside MI5 with the code name Elli. After completing a cipher
course in April 1942, Gouzenko had been posted to a branch of the GRU
Center in Moscow and had served there for a year, deciphering messages coming in from its spies operating abroad and learning a great deal
of extremely sensitive information.

He knew that MI5 was an organization based mainly in Great
Britain, where it was concerned with countering foreign spies and saboteurs. He had never decoded messages concerning Elli, but a companion, with whom he had shared a desk before his posting to Canada in
June 1943, had done so regularly. Though it was a breach of the rules,
they sometimes gossiped if something of special interest, like an Elli
message, came through. On one occasion, Gouzenko's companion
showed him a deciphered message and explained its contents, drawing
on his memory of previous messages. As Gouzenko told me in several
long telephone conversations, he had eventually learned six details
about Elli, who had to be British-born to be an MI5 officer at that time.

1. In spite of the feminine sound of his code name in English,
Elli was male. (The Russian code names given to women usually
ended in "a," like Sonia and Tina, while the GRU agent Alexan-

der Foote later revealed that the Center occasionally "used short male and female names indiscriminately without regard to sex." Decrypts of Soviet messages have disclosed an unknown woman spy code-named Eric and a man code-named Iris.)

2. The Center rated Elli so highly that to protect his identity, personal contacts with him were forbidden unless absolutely necessary, and only then with the Center's express permission. His couriers should communicate with him through *duboks*—hiding places where messages could be left or collected, also called "dead-letter boxes" or "dead drops." Further, the Center exercised such control that it insisted on approving the *duboks*, which was why that detail had appeared in an Elli message. Such knowledge permitted the GRU to send another agent to empty a *dubok* should the usual courier become unavailable. Within the Center, Elli's identity was known to very few.

3. Elli's information was usually sent in code to the Center in Moscow by the military attaché in the Soviet embassy in London, who was always a GRU officer. So Elli had a courier who collected his written information and either had direct access to the embassy without raising suspicion and took it there or gave it to someone who did so. Recently released Russian documents showed that both the GRU and the KGB recruited two types of informant—"agents," who were active spies directed from Moscow; and "confidential contacts," who knowingly might provide valuable information when approached but were not under discipline and did not report regularly. At that stage, Elli was clearly a full-blooded agent.

4. Elli was in a position to consult and to remove those MI5 files that dealt with Russians suspected of involvement in espionage in London. In late 1942, when Gouzenko had first heard about Elli, all those files were located in the MI5 registry at Blenheim Palace, near Oxford, where most of the agency had been evacuated to escape the London bombing. It would therefore seem likely that Elli was based in Blenheim and his courier lived nearby.

Gouzenko also recalled how another GRU cipher clerk, named Koulakov, who had been sent from Moscow to Ottawa in 1945, had boasted, concerning the British security services, that

"Moscow has everything, including their secret files of agents." The renegade MI5 officer Peter Wright assured me that he had seen that statement in MI5 records of Gouzenko's interrogations, and later, Gouzenko confirmed that to me. Koulakov's evidence indicated that Elli was still in place in 1945.

5. Some of Elli's messages were so important that they were passed directly to Stalin by the GRU chief, who had direct contact with him. Declassified GRU and KGB documents have confirmed that Stalin took a personal interest in information supplied by several important spies, demanding immediate translations of their "raw" messages as they arrived. In Gouzenko's memoirs, *This Was My Choice,* he recalled that a senior GRU officer took such messages by hand to the Kremlin.

6. There was "something Russian" in Elli's background. Later, Gouzenko's wife consulted her husband's records and told me that his deskmate had said, *"Ou nego shto-to Russkoe,"* which translates as "He has something Russian in his background." As Gouzenko told me, he could not understand, particularly in view of this exceptional feature, why British security had failed to detect Elli without delay on hearing his evidence.

During the period he had mentioned, the only member of MI5 who had regular access to the relevant files about Russian intelligence officers in the course of his duties was the officer in charge of Soviet counterespionage, Roger Hollis, then based at Blenheim Palace. As will be seen, he became embroiled in the Gouzenko case in ways that should have aroused suspicion at the time but did not do so until a team of counterintelligence officers began to investigate the possibility of Soviet penetration of MI5 in the 1960s and 1970s. Clearly, if the man in charge of countering Soviet agents had been one himself, the mystery of how they had been so stunningly successful for so long would be resolved.

The possibility was horrific because Hollis remained in MI5 for twenty-seven years, heading it for nine, and a head of MI5 who was a Soviet agent would have been privy to almost every important state secret, including details of preparations for war. He would have been crucially poised to warn the Kremlin of any Anglo-American preemptive nuclear strike or assist in any attempted Russian attack. Both threats were seen as so real and constant that the British, American, French, and Soviet governments spent billions to counter them. So "supermole" would be no exaggeration for such an agent who was master of all the circumstances. The comparable position in the United States would have been the discovery that J. Edgar Hoover, the FBI chief, had been a Soviet agent throughout his long service.

The MI5 investigators therefore made strenuous efforts to find "something Russian" in Hollis's background so that they could confront him with it. In spite of all their research and resources, the best these professionals could do was to discover that he had visited Moscow in 1934, when traveling to China on the Trans-Siberian Railway. This seriously weakened the case against him, because to suggest, as some did, that Gouzenko's statement could refer simply to someone who had visited Russia briefly was like saying that anyone who has made one trip to Paris has "something French in his background."

Colonel John Lash, a Russian scholar in Government Communications Headquarters (GCHQ), the signals interception station based at Cheltenham, assured me that "something Russian" must have meant something prerevolutionary. Otherwise the statement would have been "something Soviet." Then, in 1985, while browsing through a book called *Along the Road to Frome,* one of several written by Hollis's elder brother Christopher, I made a most relevant discovery. Members of the Hollis family and other relatives believed, with genealogical evidence, that they were directly descended from the Russian czar Peter the Great and were rather proud of it. In that book, published in 1958, Christopher had stated, "I did, indeed, I suppose, share with my distant and much removed cousin, Annie Moberley, a claim to descent from Peter the Great." In another of his books, *Oxford in the Twenties,* when explaining his rather peculiar looks, Christopher stated that he was "the inheritor of a good deal of mixed blood, but it came from Eastern Europe."

Annie Moberley's father, George, had been born in St. Petersburg, where his forebears were well established as merchants before the revolution. He became bishop of Salisbury and firmly believed in his descent from the heroic czar. The Hollis brothers' mother, formerly Margaret ("Meg") Church, was related to Richard Church, a dean of St. Paul's, in London, whose wife was a direct descendant of a woman named Sarah Cayley, who allegedly derived from an illegitimate son of Peter the Great. The Moberleys also traced their connection with the czar through Sarah Cayley.

Christopher Hollis, who was highly intelligent, certainly believed in the royal relationship, however distant. Whether or not it was real or taken seriously by other members of the Hollis family, they all knew about it. If Roger had been Elli, he could directly or indirectly have revealed this Russian connection to some Soviet contact, who would have informed Moscow in one of the enciphered messages, which would explain how Gouzenko's deskmate had heard about it.

Whether Roger believed the Russian connection or not, it is inconceivable that he failed to appreciate the danger that it might make him suspect if his MI5 superiors heard about it following Gouzenko's statement. Confirmation of the Russian connection was the missing link in Gouzenko's evidence, and had it been known in MI5, Hollis should surely have been closely questioned about the "coincidence," along with the other matching features.

What better fit could there be for Gouzenko's statement—"he has something Russian in his background"? No other Elli candidate has ever fulfilled the description. Gouzenko could not possibly have known anything about Hollis or his family when, as a young cipher clerk, he had made his original statement about Elli to the Canadian authorities in 1945. It was an inexcusable gaffe by Peter Wright—later the self-styled "spycatcher"—and the other counterintelligence investigators of the Hollis case to have failed to read the biographical books by Roger's well-known brother, which were on the shelves of many libraries.

As will be seen, deciphered Soviet intelligence signals have since proved beyond all doubt that a GRU agent code-named Elli definitely existed and worked inside British counterintelligence. The Elli case is so important and has been given such derisory attention by officialdom that I decided to pursue it with every possible resource. This book contains the record of my long quest for Elli.

Many people find it hard to believe that Hollis, who was the son of a bishop, could possibly have become a Soviet agent. Yet released KGB documents, GRU admissions, and decrypts of Soviet intelligence messages have exposed in horrifying detail a large number of intelligent, privileged young Britons and Americans who dedicated their lives to Stalin's brand of communism. Some of them ended up in high places, including the secret services, where they were prepared to betray their

country, their compatriots, and their allies in the Soviet interest, whatever the risk to themselves.

By 1945, Elli had probably been given a different code name because
both the GRU and the KGB renamed most of their agents in the autumn
of 1944 after they became aware, through their spies, that their coded
messages were in danger of being deciphered by both the Americans
and the British. After Gouzenko's revelations, the name was almost certainly changed again. Until the new names become known, I will continue to refer to him as Elli. The only known suspect who fitted the
profile was Roger Hollis. Further, all the evidence concerning Hollis
suggests that if he was ever recruited by the Russians, it was by the
GRU, not the KGB.

Whether guilty or not, Hollis may well have felt a frisson when he
heard about Gouzenko's description of Elli, especially the detail about
something Russian in his background. Had he been innocent, he might
have wished to clear his name in advance of any questioning, but there
is no evidence that he ever mentioned the Russian connection to anybody in MI5 at any time. As Sherlock Holmes had wondered, in a different situation, "Why didn't the dog bark?"

Supporters of Hollis have argued that if he had been a Soviet spy
throughout such a long MI5 career, some defector would have exposed
him. It would seem that Gouzenko did exactly that, but his information
was to be studiously ignored, a convenience facilitated by the fact that,
unlike most of his allegations, his evidence about Elli was unsupported
by his stolen documents.

Another GRU source operating in Britain, a proven Soviet agent
named Oliver Green, had already indicated when interrogated by MI5
officers in 1942 that the GRU had an informant inside MI5, but he had
been disbelieved. Later, the same attitude was to be taken, again and
again, when defectors indicated the existence of an important spy inside
MI5.

It would seem to be significant that among the mass of documents
covering the Gouzenko case that MI5 has released, there are few references to Elli. There are enough to prove that MI5 made some inquiries
into Gouzenko's allegation, but there are none concerning Hollis's
eventual interview with Gouzenko or MI5's internal efforts to discover
Elli's identity. Attempts by leading British academics such as Professor
Peter Hennessy to secure the missing documents have all been rebuffed

and it is reasonable to wonder why. After more than sixty years, such documents could not conceivably threaten national security. They might, however, resurrect interest in the case against Hollis.

One MI5 statement by the officer Michael Hanley, dated December 6, 1949, which seems to have escaped censorship, contained a brief reference to Elli and also revealed that Gouzenko had said that the cover name of one of the GRU officers involved in servicing British spies in London had been Dragun. As Hanley noted, Gouzenko had, in fact, been referring to the real name of the GRU assistant military attaché in London at the time, Colonel Vassili Dragoun, but this was proof that Gouzenko had learned some details of the GRU's espionage activities in Britain.

The archival section of the Foreign and Commonwealth Office at Hanslope Park has kindly provided me with copies of its documents on Dragoun. They confirm that he had arrived in London in July 1941, serving his senior GRU officer, Major General Ivan Sklyarov, the military attaché, who was personally involved in the recruitment of at least one major British spy, as will be seen. Described as arrogant and demanding, Dragoun was promoted to major general and military attaché in September 1943, leaving in 1944. So he had definitely been involved in GRU espionage at the time Gouzenko claimed. The documents also support Gouzenko's evidence that the military attaché dealt with information provided by spies, signing the dispatches encoded from documents delivered to the embassy by their couriers.

CHAPTER 4

Inauspicious Start

IF HOLLIS WAS ELLI, HOW AND WHY HAD HE BECOME MOTIVATED to spy against his own country? To attempt to understand such treachery, it was necessary to discover everything possible about his early life.

Hollis was born in Wells, in Somerset, on December 2, 1905, and christened Roger Henry. His father, George Arthur Hollis, was vice principal of Wells Theological College and would eventually become principal as well as resident canon and chancellor of the cathedral, a building of haunting medieval beauty. In 1931, he would be promoted suffragan bishop of Taunton.

In 1898, George Hollis had married Mary Margaret Church, whose father was a canon of Wells. She was also niece of a famous dean of London's St. Paul's, so Roger's genetic and environmental background was exceptionally ecclesiastical. Meg was also the fount of the claim to descent from Czar Peter the Great. Roger's elder brother Christopher eventually converted to Roman Catholicism and taught at Stonyhurst, the Jesuit school, while the eldest brother, Michael, became Protestant bishop of Madras. As both Roger and Christopher were later to declare, religion was all-pervasive in the lives of the Hollis family.

If it might be thought that such an atmosphere and such parents constituted an unlikely environment for treachery, the background of proven traitors indicates the reverse. Several who betrayed their country came from strongly ecclesiastical beginnings. Anthony Blunt's father was a vicar in Bournemouth and, later, at the British embassy in Paris, while his grandfather had been suffragan bishop of Hull. Klaus Fuchs was the son of a German Quaker preacher who became a professor of theology. John Vassall's father was an Anglican priest. Vidkun Quisling's father was a Lutheran pastor. While Donald Maclean was not a son of the manse, he had harsh Presbyterianism and reliance on the Bible thrust on him by his parents. There are other examples indicating that such an ambience can breed rebellion against authoritarian society.

In 1909, Hollis's father was appointed vicar of St. Bartholomew's Church in Leeds, which was a marked contrast for the family, who lived in that industrial area for ten years. Roger attended Leeds Grammar School until September 1918, when he entered the Junior School (Watson's House) of Clifton College, Bristol, as a boarder. Clifton was a public school with a good reputation, though hardly to be compared with Eton, to which Christopher had made his way, with financial help from a well-wisher.

A school acquaintance (A. R. Jackson) described Roger as "a scholarly, apparently harmless individual—not a strong character." An assiduous worker, he won a classics exhibition to Worcester College, Oxford. By that time, his father had returned to Wells as principal of the Theological College there, and his four sons, including the youngest, Marcus, spent most of their holidays there. In the autumn of 1924, Roger arrived at Oxford University, a year after Christopher, who had distinguished himself as a debater, had left. Though his exhibition had been in classics, he decided to read English.

In October 1925, a person named Roger Hollis published three short poems in an anthology called *Ten Singers*. This now rare volume is significant because it also contained four poems by Cecil Day-Lewis, who was already at Wadham College when Hollis had arrived at Worcester College. Day-Lewis was to become poet laureate and, before that, one of the most ardent and prominent Communists in Great Britain. *Ten Singers* contains no details of the ten contributors, but in view of the date and the Oxford connection, it would seem most likely that Roger Hollis the poet was the same person as the subject of this study. It would also seem likely, having both succeeded in being published in one volume when so young, that he and Day-Lewis were acquainted or became so. If the poems were not by the Roger Hollis of this study, they form the first of the many alleged coincidences that dog this case. If they were, they would help to explain why Hollis decided to switch to the study of English. The poems show that at that stage of his life, the author was acutely sensitive to the sound and precise meaning of words and skill-fully evocative in their employment. They betray that he was a country-man, as Hollis always remained at heart, with observant references to birds, flowers, and weather changes. They also reveal that the author was deeply religious with an intense belief that all nature's joyous gifts, from birdsong to the glory of sunset, derive from God.

Such a facility with words would account for his capacity to make and keep Oxford friends such as Evelyn Waugh, Graham Greene, Claud Cockburn, and others who would make their names as writers.

In his biography of his father, Sean Day-Lewis records that in Cecil's second year at Oxford, in 1924, he and his friend Rex Warner started a literary society called The Jawbone in reference to the imple-ment with which Samson slew the Philistines. The members read their latest verses, and Day-Lewis "acquired some prestige in the eyes of Jawbone members" by having several poems published in the *Ten Singers* anthology in October 1925. Presumably, Hollis would have felt similar self-satisfaction. An Oxford Poetry Society had been started in the twenties and still exists. I have been unable to establish whether or not Roger Hollis was a member.

Such sensitive and imaginative young men tend to be impressionable and likely to be affected, more than most, by the freedom and indepen-dence of university life after the strictures and enforced routine of boarding school. In his later life, Hollis was to tell an MI5 interrogator that he quit Oxford early to get away from the cloying, ecclesiastical at-mosphere at home because he was not religious. If the poems were by the Roger Hollis of this study, it would seem that he lost his faith at Ox-ford, a not uncommon event among undergraduates, as I experienced myself. His brother Christopher was already an unbeliever when he ar-rived at Oxford, as he confessed in his autobiography, *The Seven Ages*. He then believed the Christian religion to be "simply untrue" and found that most of his undergraduate friends were agnostic.

While there is no specific evidence concerning Roger, he and his brother were subject to similar emotional forces both at home and at Oxford, and it would seem probable that Christopher wielded some in-fluence over his younger brother. Under such circumstances, when deep religious faith has been lost, there is often a sudden conversion to a replacement creed. With many, such as Maclean and Blunt, who had become agnostic at school, it was atheistic communism to which they gave lifelong commitment. The observant journalist Charlotte Haldane, who joined the Communist Party in 1937 and experienced what she called "a violent bout of Communist religious mania," has left a vivid description of what she called "the middle-class Communist convert." This was "the type of person who, as a result of psychological strains and stresses endured in childhood or adolescence, rebuts the discipline in which he, or she, has been brought up but, having an emotional need for direction, is compelled to seek another, still more rigorous." As Cyril Connolly put it, "Marxism satisfied the rebelliousness of youth and its craving for dogma."

A biography of Day-Lewis states that he had lost his faith early and in 1926 was already of the Far Left, being on the University Strike Committee supporting the striking coal miners. There were several similarities between Hollis and Day-Lewis. Each was the son of a Protestant clergyman, each experienced the subtle effects of World War I on young people, each won a classics exhibition to an Oxford college, and each apparently lost his faith in adolescence. Being fairly privileged members of society may have exacerbated their guilt about injustices, as it certainly did with many others. They also shared an interest in golf at the university. Both are on record as having played golf there, regularly, with the young Hugh Gaitskell, the future Labour leader, and so were probably acquaintances, if not friends. Roger took up golf seriously and became a good amateur player, though it would be tennis that would affect his career. This was in spite of the fact that at Oxford, according to his contemporary Sir Harold Acton, who was also an acquaintance of Day-Lewis's, Hollis was already noticeably round-shouldered, a spinal defect that would become progressive over the years.

Day-Lewis described his time at Oxford as years of emotional and intellectual revolt. After he left, in the 1930s, he became an important figure in the Communist Party. So the seeds may have been sown at Oxford—perhaps through the influence of various Communist friends such as Claud Cockburn, a six-foot-two-inch, gangly, bespectacled youth with a broad smile. Cockburn, who believed that any behavior was excusable if it furthered the cause, was to stress that words were not enough and that action was required of a serious Communist.

Hollis may have also been influenced politically by his brother

Christopher, who was sufficiently informed about Marxism and the Russian Revolution to write a well-documented and highly perceptive biography of Lenin, which he published in 1938 as his first major book. Though by that time he had resolved his personal need for a creed by embracing Roman Catholicism, the book was studiously objective and understanding regarding the causes of the revolution and Lenin's role in it.

Little about Hollis's university work is on record. A search of the databases of the Poetry Library in London has revealed no further published poems by Roger Hollis. Possibly, with the loss of his religious faith, he may have lost his interest in poetry, which he may have used to express his Christian belief. One certainty is that he became a heavy drinker. This further symptom of rebellion may also be indicative of an emotional crisis. Sir Dick White, his closest future colleague in MI5, who had been a remote contemporary at Oxford, told me in writing that Hollis had a reputation there for wasting his time on "wine, women and golf," sowing his wild oats as a reaction to his upbringing in a "close Church atmosphere." He became part of a bibulous, flamboyant set, which included Evelyn Waugh and Harold Acton, who described him to me as "rather hearty and young for his age." Roger Fulford, an MI5 colleague, remembered him at Oxford as "rather dissipated."

Waugh's diaries record many hard-drinking sessions such as a lunch with Roger and Cockburn where "we drank all the afternoon." Cockburn, Waugh, and Roger Hollis had one particularly alcoholic dinner, after which they went on a pub crawl, which, "after sundry, indecorous adventures, ended up at the Hypocrites Club, where another blind was going on." Next day, Waugh gave lunch to Hollis, Cockburn, and others at the New Reform Club, with "more solid drinking." Oddly, Christopher Hollis, in his book *Oxford in the Twenties,* made only one reference to his brother. He describes how Waugh had picked Roger up from his home in Wells by motorcycle to go drinking, and Roger had ended up so drunk that he had fallen off the pillion seat several times on the way back, with Waugh leaving him propped up outside his home. Christopher hid the fact that it was Roger by calling him Henry, his middle name, but whoever compiled the index revealed that it was Sir Roger, who was dead when the book was published in 1976. (Perhaps in deference to the secrecy surrounding Roger, Christopher made no reference to him in any of his other books.)

Getting so drunk so often may not have been unusual for an Oxford undergraduate of the 1920s. However, it is worth noting that many of the young men of the time who became Soviet spies—Kim Philby, Guy Burgess, Donald Maclean, Anthony Blunt, and others, including several Soviet defectors to the West—were addicted to alcohol from an early age. Heavy drinking is frequently a symptom of secret internal pressures.

In his diaries, Waugh described Hollis as "a good bottle man." At one lunch they were joined by Tom Driberg, a future Labour MP, who was a student at Oxford's Christ Church. Driberg was already a member of the Communist Party, became leader of its Oxford branch, and would eventually become a proven paid agent for the KGB with the code name Lepage, and for Czech intelligence, where his code name was Crocodile. Waugh also described a dinner with Roger Hollis and Claud Cockburn, who was to fight with the Communists in the Spanish Civil War, become involved with leading international Communist subversives in Europe, and write regularly for the *Daily Worker* and even for *Pravda*.

Those who did not witness the ardor of Communists in Britain between the two great wars, as I did, can never fully appreciate their fervency, which was born of a semireligious assurance that their belief was the only way forward. Many highly intelligent young men were certain that within a few years there would be a workers' revolution, with the establishment of a British Communist state. The Cambridge don Anthony Blunt, for example, stated he was confident that when the revolution came, he would be made commissar for the arts!

It was a Communist's duty to recruit others and promote the "party line." So both Day-Lewis and Hollis are likely to have been "worked on" by friends who were established Communists, such as Cockburn, Driberg, and the future novelist Graham Greene, in their Oxford days. In the process, Hollis may have become a Soviet sympathizer and admirer of the Communist experiment. He certainly became anti-American, which was a Communist requirement, the United States being seen as the archcapitalist state.

Greene was a conservative by inclination when he first went to Oxford, but he joined the Communist Party in the autumn of 1924, showing what contact with a proselytizing revolutionary like Cockburn could do to a bright young man. Greene was to join MI6, where his chief was the traitor Kim Philby, whom he continued to admire when he was exposed as a KGB spy for the "sincerity of his beliefs."

Another left-wing activist and Marxist who eventually joined the Communist Party was Maurice Richardson, then a student at New College. He was coeditor with Cockburn of a short-lived Communist weekly called *Seven Days*. Hollis was so influenced by this impractical dreamer that he was prepared to go with him to Mexico, ostensibly for literary reasons, though Stalin had selected Mexico as a center for activity on behalf of the Comintern, the vast, conspiratorial apparatus dedicated to spreading world revolution. Mexico had been chosen because it was politically unstable and geographically convenient for infiltrating the United States and South American countries considered ripe for revolution. Both the KGB and the GRU rated it second only to China for subversive work, and many senior agitators and spies were posted there. The Mexican venture never materialized. Instead, Hollis was to choose China.

The Oxford friend likely to have been most influential on Hollis was Cockburn, a cousin of Evelyn Waugh's, who had been born in Peking in 1904, the son of a diplomat known as "Chinese Harry." He entered Keble College and joined the Communist Party in the autumn of 1924, the term when Hollis appeared. Cockburn became the diplomatic and foreign correspondent for Britain's Communist national newspaper, the *Daily Worker*, which he served from 1935 until 1946. Writing under the pseudonym Frank Pitcairn, he also concocted many of the anonymous leader columns for the paper, always promoting the Soviet party line and its anti-American stance. Cockburn was to reappear in extraordinary ways in the professional life of Hollis, who would come to be regarded as MI5's expert on communism. Hollis would also resume contact with Driberg.

Hollis could well have mentioned the Peter the Great connection to his Communist friends, possibly in jest, or he might have believed it, in which case he could have felt an emotional attachment to Russia. This could have provided an additional personal reason for a lifelong feeling for Russia, which may have increased his interest in Soviet communism and the interest of Communists in him. Emotional attachment to "Mother Russia" seems to have been a major factor in compelling several proven traitors to spy for the Soviet Union though they had not been born there. The American Soviet agents Theodore Hall, Harry

Gold, the Cohens, Julius Rosenberg, Kitty Harris, and William Weis-band, who all figure later in this book, were born of Russian immigrants to the United States, while the German spy Richard Sorge had a Russian mother. Though any connection was rather distant in Hollis's case, Peter the Great was an exceptionally romantic link.

Hollis's failure to join the Communist Party is of small consequence. Neither did Anthony Blunt, who, while describing himself as "only a paper Marxist," agreed to "work for the Comintern," which in his case really meant for the KGB. Nor did Philby, who was always a covert Communist and, when under suspicion, could sustain himself with the knowledge that nobody could pin on him any link with Communist organizations because he had never been a member of any, as he recorded in *My Silent War.* Converts to communism who were talent-spotted as possible future agents were advised not to join the party or to voice their beliefs. The traitor John Cairncross, who was recruited to the KGB while at Cambridge, never joined. Neither did the GRU agent and radio operator Alexander Foote.

In later life, I was surprised by London University contemporaries of mine who turned out to have been secret Communists. They had been advised that their chances of securing an influential post of value to the party would be greater if their commitment was unknown, and some, who were already members, were advised to leave the party. Looking back, I believe the only open symptom of their belief had been their anti-Americanism.

In March–April 1926, aged twenty, Hollis left Oxford a year and two terms short of the time when he should have taken his degree examinations. The family explanation of this premature departure, which has been projected by various supporters of Hollis, claims that he realized that with no intellectual ambitions, being too fond of drink, and with his father finding it hard to support his wayward son, he would be doing everyone a kindness by dropping something he did not want to do anyway. It was not uncommon for young men, especially "black sheep," to abandon thoughts of an academic career. Hollis was later to tell the MI5 committee that investigated him that he had left because he was bored with Oxford, did not think he had done enough work to secure a good degree, and wanted "to get away from the family and the Church."

This view was generally accepted until 1995, when the meticulous author Tom Bower published the official biography of Sir Dick White, former director general of MI5 and, later, chief of MI6, who had been Hollis's closest friend in the British intelligence world. The book, titled *The Perfect English Spy,* referred to Hollis's "abrupt rustication," which ended his time at Oxford, as a "penalty" for using his time as "an interlude of wine and roses" instead of studying. But what did "rustication" mean? I consulted Bower, who had spent much time with White over several years. After looking at his notes of the relevant interview, he assured me that when White said that Hollis had been "rusticated," he definitely meant that he had been "thrown out of the University." The statement that Hollis had been expelled, which entirely conflicted with the account he was to give when interrogated, was evidence that he was capable of lying when it suited him.

Possibly, Hollis really was merely "rusticated" for a few weeks and then decided to rebel and not return. If the university authorities had left it to him to explain to his parents why he had been sent home, he may have covered his disgrace by claiming to have left of his own accord because he was wasting their money and wanted to go abroad and earn his living. Christopher makes no mention of his brother's departure in his autobiographical books. The parents are likely to have been disappointed, because the Hollis family name was held in respect at Oxford.

Nor did Roger moderate his behavior on returning home. In a diary entry for Tuesday, April 13, 1926, Waugh recorded how he had visited Wells, where he and Roger lunched at a hotel and "drank champagne and brandy mixed" until they were "turned out," then went on to a village pub, where they had "heaps more to drink," ending up in a field.

It seems that Roger quickly decided that he wanted to seek his fortune in China, a decision that has mystified students of his behavior and which he could never explain satisfactorily to his interrogators. It may be that the China-born Cockburn fired his interest. It seems improbable that Hollis was recruited by Soviet intelligence while at Oxford and ordered to China. However, the GRU was active in Oxford, as the KGB was, later, at Cambridge, and, as will be seen, promising subjects were directed to Shanghai for training.

Whatever the reason, Hollis was determined to go, assuring his parents that he could make a living in China as a journalist, a profession in which he had no experience. To save money for his fare, he worked for the Standard Chartered Bank in London as a clerk, being embarrassed when another Old Cliftonian encountered him posting a pile of letters into a City mailbox.

Though he had many months in which to ponder the difficulties of earning a living in such a different country, Hollis had made a firm decision. It was a measure of the young man's determination that once he had decided on a course of action, he would fulfill it. It was also a demonstration of considerable courage at a time when young men without resources did not travel far, as they do now.

CHAPTER 5

Cosmopolitan Comrades

WHEN HOLLIS WAS INTERROGATED ABOUT HIS TIME IN CHINA, at the age of sixty-three, he professed poor memory for events there. He had first traveled there by ship—then the usual way—arriving early in 1927. He had seriously underestimated the costs and claimed that, finding himself with only £10, he had secured a job as a part-time journalist. His first stop in China was Hong Kong, then a British colony, where he may have had an introduction to a newspaper.

He moved to Shanghai and continued to earn his living by journalism. How precarious this was can be seen from the memoirs of an American newsman, Hallett Abend, who was there at the time. Referring to British correspondents, he recalled, "They were usually meagerly paid at a low rate per column inch or received very small monthly retainers." Also, Shanghai was swarming with competing journalists, with whom Hollis, as a cub reporter, was likely to have consorted in his daily quest for stories, contacts, and advice from experienced hands. So he probably lived hand to mouth unless he had been able to find some other source of income.

In letters home, Hollis indicated that he was writing for the prestigious London *Times*, but he seems to have served only as a legman for the official *Times* correspondent, who may have paid him but gave him no credit in the newspaper.

Like other Europeans, he lived in the International Settlement, described by Abend as "a cosmopolitan conglomeration of businessmen, fortune-seekers, political refugees, secret agents, Chinese mobsters, purveyors of every kind of vice and journalists covering the ever-changing collision of cultures, which was frequently marked by violence." There was an International Press Club and a large Foreign YMCA, which had splendid social and recreational facilities. These included a golf club, which could have been a special attraction to Hollis, who is known to have played his favorite game while in Shanghai. Both the Press Club and the YMCA were reasonably cheap to join, and Hollis probably did much of his social drinking at the former. The YMCA also had women members, who used the facilities like the gym and tennis courts—a further attraction for a twenty-two-year-old, alone in an environment so strange that, in December 1927, General Chiang Kai-shek had hundreds of Communists decapitated on the streets of Shanghai.

Unable to earn enough from writing, Hollis replied to an advertisement for a modest post in the British American Tobacco Company (BAT), which had widespread interests in China. He started work there, in Shanghai, on April 1, 1928, in the advertising department, probably on the public relations side, for which his journalism would have been a qualification. He remained based in Shanghai, before being transferred to Peking (now Beijing) in late 1930, from where he often visited Shanghai.

Hollis told his MI5 interrogators that, apart from golfing friends and colleagues in BAT, his acquaintances in Shanghai and other parts of China were mainly in the press world, as he continued with occasional freelance journalism. An American, Admiral William C. Mott, who remembered meeting Hollis when he visited Shanghai as a young officer, portrayed him to me as something of a socialite in both European and Chinese circles. Being the son of a bishop, as he was from 1931, would have been helpful in that respect.

Among the prominent journalists whom Hollis is likely to have met professionally or socially in what has been described as "the small goldfish bowl of the international community in Shanghai," which was immensely social, were several who were to make international names for themselves, though not mainly for their reportage. The only one of these whom he later acknowledged as an acquaintance was the American journalist Agnes Smedley. She was an overt revolutionary, burning with class hatred, who arrived in Shanghai in May 1929, aged thirty-four, after attending the Sixth World Congress of the Comintern in Moscow. Having lived in Berlin, Agnes was working as the Far East correspondent of the *Frankfurter Zeitung* and dedicated her life to helping the Chinese Communist Party achieve control of China, where she is still revered. An ardent supporter of Stalin, as well as of Mao Tse-tung, the Chinese Communist leader, she also served the GRU, which had close links with the Comintern. Her various homes were salons for other journalists of like political persuasion and for Soviet agents.

In his book *Secret War in Shanghai*, Bernard Wasserstein has described that city as "the intelligence capital of the Far East," with Soviet agents of several nationalities being there in force. As at least six of them, and possibly eight, were to impact on Hollis's subsequent intelligence career—an unusual statistic by any standard—they all need to be, briefly, noted here.

Earlier, in 1927, an American female Communist of English origin, Kitty Harris, had been posted to Shanghai to begin her espionage career, along with her partner, Earl Browder, who would become leader of the Communist Party of the United States of America. As recently released KGB records reveal, they had been sent there to develop an espionage and subversion network called the China Bureau, which had close links to Mao, and to hone their conspiratorial skills. At that time, both the KGB and the GRU were using Shanghai as a recruiting and training ground for spies because there were so many well-connected but impecunious young men and women from Europe, Great Britain, and the United States seeking their fortunes who might be recruited to the cause. Kitty Harris was a KGB agent who would eventually impinge on Hollis's counterespionage career by playing a crucial role in enabling Donald Maclean to spy so successfully inside the British Foreign Office. There is no evidence that she met Hollis in Shanghai, but archives show that they shared friends there, like Smedley, who are known to have been important Soviet agents.

In June 1925, another active recruiter, unknown to espionage researchers until recently, had been posted to Shanghai by the GRU: Karl Säre, a ruthless Stalinist from the Baltic state of Estonia. Säre, who is well documented as a traitor in Estonia today, was born in 1903. Because the Estonian police were after him for Communist subversion, he had been ordered to Leningrad when only eighteen to be trained as a spy and conspirator, remaining there for three years and becoming fluent in English and Russian. In Shanghai he posed as a journalist, a cover that offered access to important people and to other journalists and provided a reasonable excuse for clandestine investigative activity. Later, he would become first secretary—effectively the puppet boss—of Soviet Estonia and be photographed waving to the cheering rent-a-crowds before being captured and interrogated when the Germans overran Estonia in 1941. Suffice it to say, at this stage, Säre's activities in Shanghai in recruiting journalists and other likely people to "the cause of peace" would prove to be of exceptional importance in Hollis's career.

As several Soviet agents have recorded, or admitted when interrogated, it was standard practice to recruit young people to "the cause of peace" or to undercover work for the "Communist ideal" or the Comintern. Only later, when they were committed, would they discover that they were working for Soviet intelligence. By then, it was hoped that they would be motivated by the semireligious belief that in the cause of communism any action, however treacherous by normal moral standards, was not only permissible but required as duty.

The most unforgettable of the Shanghai journalists, whose espionage for Stalin, later in Japan, would change the course of World War II, was the German journalist Richard Sorge. After being wounded in World War I, he was trained as an agent of the Comintern; later, he was transferred to the GRU, which posted him to Shanghai early in 1930, when he was thirty-five. Shortly before that, he had been called to Moscow for a special briefing on his task by experienced GRU China hands, allegedly including Säre, who had then left China permanently. If the two men did meet then, or at any time during Sorge's later visits to Moscow, the encounter would prove to have been catastrophic for the German, who would later be hailed worldwide as a master spy.

Sorge's immediate remit was to consolidate and expand the GRU's China network. A forceful, tough, hard-drinking personality with the code name Ramsay, he contacted Smedley by previous arrangement, and she became his assistant and mistress. With her help and under cover of working for a German magazine, he created a local spy ring formed of agents who would later render crucial services for the Soviet Union in other countries. There have been many books about Sorge, and one of them, a semiofficial biography by Julius Mader, an East German, lists British journalists and British firms as among the sources he targeted. The firms included the British American Tobacco Company, which the GRU believed, whether rightly or wrongly, was helping to finance Chiang Kai-shek, the anti-Communist warlord. So the Sorge ring was required to penetrate the company and tap or recruit possible informants there. Hollis's position in BAT would have been of interest to the GRU.

In the summer of 1930, Sorge acquired a new recruit in the form of a twenty-three-year-old, slim, dark-haired German girl, Ursula Hamburger, who had arrived in Shanghai, traveling via Moscow on the Trans-Siberian Railway. Her father, Dr. Robert Kuczynski, was a Jewish demographer of some distinction. She had joined the Communist Youth Union in Germany in 1924, when she was seventeen. Like many others, she would later claim that she became a Communist because of Hitler's treatment of the Jews, but she was committed to Soviet communism for its ideological sake before that. In 1929, she had married a twenty-six-year-old Jewish Sudeten German, Rudolf (Rudi) Hamburger, who then secured a post as an architect in the International Settlement in Shanghai. Ursula was fluent in English because she had lived in America for two years, mainly in New York, where she had worked in a bookstore. She soon met Smedley and, as a result, received a visit from Sorge in November 1930. He recruited her to his network, with the code name Sonya or Sonia, the form I shall use. As her espionage coup in securing the Quebec Agreement has already shown, she was destined to play a truly historic role and become, in my view, the most influential female secret agent of all time, with lasting impact on British, American, and Soviet defense strategy. In that process, her conspiratorial activities and those of other members of her family who took refuge from Hitler in Great Britain would significantly impinge on Hollis's future career.

Sonia worked for Sorge for two years in Shanghai, under cover of being a freelance journalist, acting as a courier and talent spotter. In her memoirs (published under her pen name, Ruth Werner), she would recall the excitement of being recruited to an international conspiracy and how the "conspiratorial way of life" became second nature. Her husband was also keen on "social justice" and was recruited as a GRU agent.

After Sorge had visited the GRU Center in Moscow, Sonia accepted an invitation to undergo six months' professional training there to learn wireless telegraphy, including the construction of clandestine transmitters and microphotography. When qualified, she was told that she was on the regimental strength of the Red Army with the rank of captain. Sorge told her that he was leaving Shanghai in mid-December 1932 and predicted that "much lay ahead for her." He did not exaggerate. "Sonia's Station," as her transmitter was known at the GRU Center, would render crucial service in several countries, especially in Britain.

While in Shanghai, Sonia lived with Rudi, and their baby son, Michael, but they were required by the GRU to part and pursue separate espionage operations in different countries, which they did, apparently, without demur. Rudi's activities in Persia and elsewhere would later be brought to Hollis's attention.

Hollis, who became an admirer of the Chinese with a hatred for Fascist Japanese, was friendly with pro-Soviet Communists who were not journalists. One such was a New Zealander named Rewi Alley, a close friend of Agnes Smedley's whom Hollis met in Peking. Alley was so strongly pro-Communist that he became domiciled in Peking and ended his days there. In letters to me, he confirmed his friendship with Hollis.

Of much greater significance was the arrival in Shanghai in 1931 of a German, Arthur Ewert, a very senior Comintern official and an active agent and recruiter who frequently attended the Smedley gatherings and became a close friend of Sonia's. Ewert and his wife, also a seasoned revolutionary, had been posted there as undercover emissaries to the Chinese Communist Party.

As Jung Chang's meticulously researched book *Mao* records, Ewert, who had many aliases, was Moscow's chief man in Shanghai charged with keeping Mao in control of the Chinese Communist forces.

The Ewerts moved to Peking, where Hollis was then sharing an apartment with a British Army officer, Captain Anthony Stables, who was there to learn Chinese and became a first-class interpreter, as I have established from army records. In 1966, when the MI5 officer Peter Wright was making inquiries about Hollis, he visited Stables, then a retired lieutenant colonel living in the Cotswolds. Stables confirmed that he had shared an apartment with Hollis in Peking for at least a year in the early 1930s. When discussing Hollis's friends such as Agnes Smedley, Stables remembered them as being left-wing and expressed particular concern about one of them, whose name was Arthur Ewert and whom he described as an "international Socialist." He recalled meeting Ewert, whom he correctly described as a big, shambling man with powerful shoulders and a large head with red hair who spoke good English. He said that Ewert had visited their apartment to see Hollis on several occasions and Stables had found the relationship difficult to understand. He did not suggest that Hollis had been meeting Ewert for journalistic purposes, which was most unlikely because the German was operating under cover as a most senior Comintern official, sent by the Soviet leadership to continue negotiations with the Chinese Communist Party and to keep them "on line."

Peter Wright confirmed this account to me when I visited him in Tasmania in 1980 and, later, in his book *Spycatcher*, but he did not develop it there because he had made an amateurish hash of his interview with Stables. Wright told me that he wrote Ewert's name down as Ewart, believing him to be British, and after the MI5 registry had failed to find any trace of him in its records, he took no further action. He agreed that he had made a bad mistake because it meant that Hollis was never questioned about Ewert. Recently released records show that MI5 had a file on Ewert stretching back to 1919 and continuing until 1950. Of all the Soviet agents then in China, Hollis could not have consorted with a Communist of greater eminence.

There can be little doubt that on his visits to Moscow, Ewert, an inveterate talent spotter, would have reported his association with Hollis, then the son of a bishop and likely to return to Great Britain, because that was routine practice for Comintern officials, who had close contact with the GRU rather than the KGB.

In view of Hollis's choice of friends, both at Oxford and in China, to claim that he left no Communist "spoor," as his supporters have, is patently untrue. Ewert was famed in the Communist world, as many books record. He was a far more formidable figure than any Communist encountered by Philby in his early days.

Hollis went home to Britain, to spend the summer of 1934 on leave from BAT, and returned to China in the autumn. He traveled back on the Trans-Siberian Railway, breaking the journey in Moscow on the way. One of his surviving letters to his mother describes how he and an English companion were met by an Intourist guide, who accompanied them in a "very luxurious Lincoln car" to the National Hotel, where they stayed. Intourist, the Soviet tourism board, which was under KGB control, then put them into another Lincoln, with a charming young lady as a guide, to visit the "sights." He described Moscow as "a huge drab slum," which depressed him "unutterably," a statement that has been construed as evidence that he could not possibly have been a Communist. In fact, such comments were common among Stalin's supporters, and even the totally dedicated Sonia described the deplorable condition of family homes in Moscow, including some of those housing high-level officials. Philby was to make similar remarks.

In a further letter, Hollis complained to his mother about the behavior of his companion, a schoolmaster named Tebbs, teaching at the Cathedral School in Shanghai. He wrote that on their return to Shanghai, Tebbs was putting around false stories about what they had done on the trip. Hollis seemed particularly anxious about the impression Tebbs was giving that they had visited so many tourist sites that they must have stayed in Moscow for more than the one day he had described. He seemed so irritated by this seemingly trivial matter that he banged on, in his letter, about honesty, claiming to be "generally truthful," while most other people "lie blatantly." Was it because the two did, in fact, spend more than one day there? The GRU agent Karl Säre, who was back in Moscow at that time, is alleged to have stated, when interrogated in 1941, that Hollis spent "a few days" in Moscow and that they met there by arrangement.

It is odd that Hollis should have labored the point with his mother, to whom it could hardly have been significant. Maybe he was reflecting his concern that his BAT colleagues in Shanghai might hear Tebbs's version and wonder why Hollis had told them that he had spent only one day there, as he eventually reiterated at his interrogation by MI5 in 1969.

If Hollis was already sympathetic to communism at Oxford, the murderous internecine strife in China against the Communists there could have had a severe political impact similar to that exerted on others later by the street fighting in Vienna and the Spanish Civil War. He saw people, especially Communists, hanged from trees and severed heads suspended from lampposts. The far less horrific conditions of poverty and unemployment in Britain at that time had induced his Oxford friend Day-Lewis to become a firebrand Communist and recruiter to the cause, forever stressing the need to do something rather than just talk. The conditions for the poor in China were particularly searing for anyone as sensitive as Hollis appeared to have been, when young.

Much has been made of the letters written by Hollis from China, mainly to his mother, because they give no indication of any Communist interest and portray him as a conservative given to wearing his Old Cliftonian tie and requiring new ones. Donald Maclean also avoided offending his parents by hiding his conversion to communism, taking special care to conceal his school friendship with the young Communist James Klugman, who was also to become a Soviet agent of eventual interest to Hollis. As for Hollis's old school tie, Burgess wore his Old Etonian tie with pride while exiled in Moscow—a soothing link with his faraway home.

In December 1934, Hollis suffered a hemorrhage, which X-rays revealed to be due to tuberculosis of the left lung, a frightening diagnosis in those days when there was no effective drug treatment. After bed rest in Hankow and convalescence, he continued to work, but the illness recurred more seriously, and when his employers decided that he needed better treatment in a sanatorium, he was invalided out of China in July 1936 and never returned. The place where he was then treated is in doubt. One of his old BAT colleagues told me that it was Switzerland, but I could find nothing in the existing records of the major sanatoriums there. The Hollis family believes that he went from China by boat to Canada and was treated there. Wherever it happened, the treatment, if any, must have been short because he was certainly in England in August.

CHAPTER 6

Strange Interlude

—

Hᴏᴡ ʜᴏʟʟɪꜱ ʀᴇᴛᴜʀɴᴇᴅ ᴛᴏ ɢʀᴇᴀᴛ ʙʀɪᴛᴀɪɴ ꜰʀᴏᴍ ᴄʜɪɴᴀ ɪꜱ in doubt. Peter Wright, who heard and recorded the eventual interrogation of Hollis in 1969, insisted that he had said he had traveled via the Trans-Siberian Railway again. Professor Anthony Glees of Brunel University, however, claims that he has seen proof, in the form of letters and discussions with the Hollis family, that he had returned by sea across the Pacific and via Canada. A sea voyage might seem to have been better suited to a sick man, but the journey across Canada and another sea voyage to Britain meant that the route through Russia would have been quicker. The question is of some importance because, as will be seen, a new source has allegedly claimed that Hollis did return by train, breaking his journey in Moscow for a few days and renewing his acquaintance there with a Soviet agent from Shanghai named Luise Rimm.

Whatever the route, he could hardly have remained in Canada for treatment because he was soon back in Somerset, living with his parents, and had met Evelyn Swayne, who was his age, staying with her family at Burnham-on-Sea on August 31, 1936. With his brother Christopher, Hollis visited Evelyn Waugh, whose diary for September 16, 1936, recorded that the two "came to dinner."

Hollis would have saved some money in China because his letters indicate that in his later years there, especially when he was ill, there had been little to spend it on, and he also had some shared investments. But with marriage in mind, he needed assured employment, and in November, he visited London to discuss his career with BAT. He was offered a small accounts job and declined it. On the same day, he saw the journalist Peter Fleming, whom he had met in China, at *The Times* in the hope of securing a post there. It may again be pure coincidence, but *The Times* was one of the job targets specially recommended to recruits by Soviet controllers, because it not only gave access to useful informants and was a good qualification for moving to a more influential post, but was also recommended as a way into a secret service. Both Cockburn and Philby began serious journalism on *The Times*. While he had been in China, Hollis had claimed to be writing for *The Times* occasionally, but a search made for me by an editor of that newspaper proved negative.

Later, he went to see an old Oxford friend, Roger Fulford, who was also working at *The Times*, but that, too, came to nothing. Hollis does not seem to have tried any other newspaper, which was odd for a would-be Fleet Street journalist in need of a living. It would have been natural for him to have restored his connection with Cockburn, not only to relate his experiences in China, but in his search for journalistic employment. Cockburn had many contacts with newspapers and magazines. In March 1933, having left *The Times* because its policy conflicted with his political principles, Cockburn had started *The Week*, a scurrilous, widely read newsletter that achieved a surprisingly influential circulation much quoted by newspapers. He was also writing regularly for the Communist *Daily Worker* and was in contact with other prominent journalists who might have been helpful to Hollis.

In December 1936, Hollis wrote to Eve Swayne about the abdication of Edward VIII, describing himself as a "staunch Conservative" and monarchist. Yet Jack Swayne, a cousin of Eve's who knew Hollis well, told the late Francis Fisher, who was one of Hollis's golfing friends and a neighbor of mine, "When Roger returned from China he was rather Red." Perhaps Hollis's letter was written to impress Eve's Conservative parents.

He was interviewed by the Wills tobacco company without success and remained unemployed until January 14, 1937, when he approached BAT again and was offered and accepted a job in the London office of the Ardath cigarette company. On the strength of that appointment, he became engaged to Eve in February. In July, he was saddened by the news that the Japanese had attacked China, taking Peking.

During 1937, his brother Christopher was researching and writing his biography of Lenin and it seems inconceivable that he did not discuss the script with Roger, who had been to Russia, had met the leading revolutionaries Arthur Ewert and Agnes Smedley, and had witnessed Communists in action in China. Sadly, there is no record of his advice or opinion. (Christopher was to avoid listing *Lenin: Portrait of a Professional Revolutionary* among his other publications in his entry in *Who's Who* and other reference books, perhaps out of deference to his brother's position in MI5.)

In June 1937, Sonia, who was then based in Danzig, contrived to visit London before returning to Moscow for important discussions with the GRU Center. She needed a Soviet visa, and though this could have been supplied by the Soviet embassy in Warsaw, she claimed in her memoirs that she had needed to secure it from the Soviet embassy in London. This meant a long, expensive, and circuitous journey, so it seems more likely that she was required by the Center to visit London for some GRU purpose. While in London for three weeks, she saw her refugee family, including her younger sister, Brigitte, another GRU operative, and her brother, Jurgen, an active GRU agent himself. The researcher Nigel Bance has informed me that one of his Moscow intelligence sources recalled seeing an archival document stating that Sonia had alerted Jurgen Kuczynski about "the ripeness of Hollis for recruitment"—referring to his precarious finances and feelings of resentment at his circumstances. So her visit to London, after which she stayed in Moscow for three months, may have had some connection with Hollis's possible recruitment to the service of the GRU.

On Saturday, July 17, Roger married Eve in Wells Cathedral, where there was a substantial ceremony for the bishop's son, with his father officiating. His best man was Jack Swayne. *The Somerset and West of England Advertiser* described Hollis as "assistant foreign manager of the Ardath Tobacco Company," while on the marriage certificate he called himself a "Merchant."

Among the four hundred guests listed in the Wells newspaper was Major Ray "Tiny" Meldrum, a retired army officer and relative of the Swayne family, who was to change Hollis's life.

The couple honeymooned in the New Forest and moved to a modest apartment in London at 87 Gloucester Road. According to Anthony Glees, Hollis told a friend, "I didn't know about girls before I got married. She [Eve] was the first girl I ever had anything to do with." This hardly conforms with Dick White's "wine, women and golf" recollections of Hollis's behavior at Oxford or with Admiral Mott's recall of his social life in China, where as a single man and social drinker he was in demand for dinner parties. Later, his remarkable store of filthy stories hardly conformed with the image of a celibate.

The news from China angered and depressed Hollis, for in August, the Japanese had spread the war to Shanghai, where there was heavy fighting, marking the bloody climax to the first phase of the conflict. Then, in October, he quit Ardath, later claiming that he left because he hated the job. This looked like a rash extravagance, for, according to Glees, the couple had to leave their apartment and go to live with Hollis's parents, in Wells—a demeaning situation for someone who had quit that stifling atmosphere to make his own way. However, as the next chapter will show, the true circumstances may have been very different.

On October 20, 1937, by invitation of the Royal Central Asian Society in London, Hollis gave a public lecture, entitled "The Conflict in China." How he came to be invited is unknown, but he may have been a member of the society and could have volunteered to speak. (Philby was a member, having been instructed by the KGB to join the society as a venue for meeting useful sources.) Hollis gave a detailed account of the fighting, in which the Japanese were inflicting huge casualties on the poorly armed Chinese defenders. He knew the precise dates of the relevant military and political events, presumably picked up from newspapers and supplemented, perhaps, by letters from friends in China. For Hollis to have constructed such an address, and for the society to have had time to arrange and advertise it, would probably have taken some weeks.

The well-received lecture, of which I have a copy, seems to be the only firsthand documentary evidence of Hollis's real political inclinations. Understandably, he was totally on the side of China, upon which Japan "had forced a war." He believed that the Chinese military leaders were doing their best to contain the situation in the hope that the Great Powers with interests there—Great Britain, the United States, France, and Russia—would intervene. He clearly thought that his best hope of intervention was from Russia. Until then, he predicted "a China united by hatred of Japan."

Speaking with confidence, he said that eventually China would resume the leadership of Asia and that the world would be "better for so mighty an ally in the cause of peace." Some writers have attached political significance to his use of "the cause of peace"—a Communist catchphrase much used by Soviet recruiters. Coincidentally perhaps, Hollis was reflecting the Communist Party line. As Noreen Branson recorded in her *Official History of the Communist Party of Great Britain*, British Communists had reacted strongly to the Japanese offensive against China in August 1937, initiating industrial action at docks against Japanese exports.

The climax of the war in China came shortly afterward, followed by Japanese victory parades in November, even through the International Settlement in Shanghai. The British and American governments, though concerned, had done little to protect their Chinese interests and nothing to assist the Chinese people, who were repeatedly shelled and bombed by the Japanese navy and air force.

November 23, 1937, marked the beginning of a strange episode for a hard-up couple in their thirties with no apparent prospects. According to Hollis family documents examined by Anthony Glees, they drove from Wells to Bristol and sold their car. Then, presumably using that money, they traveled to Paris. After a brief stay there, they went to Loches, a small town south of Tours, where they both took French lessons. They left Loches on December 14, returned to Paris, where they spent several days, and were back in Wells in time for Christmas. This is likely to have been an expensive operation, and they could hardly have learned enough French in three weeks to qualify either of them for any job. Nor is there any indication that Eve intended to go out to work, which was uncommon and even considered degrading for a middle-class housewife in that period. So why did they go there at such a time of the year?

It may have been a totally innocent whim, though in their circumstances, it would have been an excessive luxury. It may have been part of some secretarial course to which they had committed themselves in their desperation, but there is another possible explanation, which in view of so many later suspicious events requires consideration. At that time, 1937, the GRU was expanding its British network by recruiting new agents, particularly in Paris, which was the main center for GRU operations against Great Britain—then the primary target for Soviet intelligence activity in Western Europe. For security reasons, it was the GRU practice for formal recruitment to its service to be done abroad, if possible. The Paris bureau of the Comintern was then the European focus for Communist conspiracy, as MI5 documents show, and both the KGB and the GRU were using the French capital as a recruitment and clearance center. It was also a place where British agents were introduced to their controllers, leisurely and without risk of surveillance.

When Philby had needed a letter of introduction to the subversive Communist movement in Vienna, before going there in 1933, he was obliged to visit Paris to get it. In the following year, Cockburn, who was fluent in both French and German, had been summoned to the office of the Comintern committee in Paris. Until 1933, he had been working for *The Times*, which valued him so highly as a journalist that when he decided to quit, leading figures there appealed to him not to destroy a potentially brilliant career by being an open Communist. According to an MI6 report, Cockburn replied "that he could not help himself" and felt he had to "sacrifice everything for his convictions." He then gave up a well-paid post to start what was to be a hand-to-mouth existence for the rest of his life—an example of the effect that Communist ideology could then exert on an outstanding intellect. Cockburn continued to visit Paris regularly to consult "underground contacts" in connection with the Comintern, which by then had been taken over by the GRU. As MI5 records would later show, he became closely linked to Soviet intelligence.

In April 1936, the major Cambridge spy John Cairncross had traveled to Paris to be introduced to his controller, having been recruited in London. In that year, the Soviet agent James Klugman also visited Paris to meet the illegal controller Arnold Deutsch for formal recruitment, though Deutsch was based in London.

Several well-documented GRU controllers were active in Paris in 1937. One of them was Henri Robinson, a dedicated Communist born in Belgium of a German Jewish mother and Russian father, and master of several languages. He had long been employed by the Comintern to spread world revolution. To further this process, the GRU had built up a huge conspiratorial network in Europe, which came to be known in Germany as the Rote Kapelle, usually translated as Red Orchestra. Robinson was part of a major group assisting the GRU to extend its operations in Britain. According to the CIA's two-volume survey *The Rote Kapelle,* he is believed to have taken over the U.K. network in 1937 and is known to have made many trips to London in that connection.

Robinson was arrested by the Gestapo during the German occupation of France in December 1942, when they discovered some of his papers, which found their way to MI5 in 1945. However, they then "slipped out of sight"—standard MI5 parlance for careless or willful misplacement—and did not come under scrutiny until 1947. They confirmed that Robinson had taken over the GRU networks in Great Britain in 1937. Robinson could not be questioned on the issue by the British because he had been executed by the Gestapo in 1944.

If Hollis had been suborned into working for the Comintern in "the cause of peace" while in China or on his return to Britain, Robinson or one of his staff could have required his presence in Paris for discussion about more active employment. Either Cockburn, Sonia, or her brother, Jurgen Kuczynski, could have provided the GRU with the tip that he was a ripe candidate. Jurgen is known to have visited Paris in the summer of 1937.

Nearly all the proven British spies who served the Kremlin were recruited *before* they secured access to secrets and then applied for their government posts on the advice of Soviet controllers. So if Hollis had been recruited while still unemployed, it would have been in keeping with standard Soviet practice.

When Philby had been first introduced to a professional Soviet recruiter in 1934, he had immediately agreed to devote his life to the Soviet cause. Then, having no job, he had been instructed to find a way of joining MI6, however long it might take. He was also expected to do that by his own efforts, being advised only that journalism was "a good way in."

Once in Paris, Hollis could have been given similar instructions and emolument by the GRU, as since 1935, on Stalin's order, the Comintern had been thoroughly integrated into the Soviet intelligence operations. As indicated in the CIA assessment of the Rote Kapelle, the GRU was prepared to pay for services at that time. Indeed, according to an MI5 document, Gouzenko was to state, "It is a rule that all agents must be paid even if prepared to work for ideological reasons. It is considered that payment ensures a direct hold on an agent." In his book *A Chapter of Accidents,* Goronwy Rees recorded how his friend the KGB spy Guy Burgess went to Paris in 1937 and had made other "mysterious visits" there associated with the "bundles of bank-notes" stuffed in his cupboards. The Comintern was well endowed with money by the Kremlin, and acceptance of a token sum was part of the formal GRU process known as "signing on."

If Hollis's trip to Paris resulted in his recruitment, it is relevant that it was also GRU practice to require prospective agents to pay their own expenses to such a meeting abroad, as an advance token of their good faith and commitment.

CHAPTER 7

Someone for Tennis

—

I N 2006, I WAS INFORMED IN WRITING BY THE DIRECTOR GEN-
eral of MI5, then Dame Eliza Manningham-Buller, that Hollis's "official
joining date was 8 June 1938." That conflicts with a previous statement
by Anthony Glees that after consulting Hollis family documents, he
was certain Roger had joined MI5 between December 31, 1937, and
March 13, 1938. Hollis was still at Wells on New Year's Eve and a document dated March 13 indicated that he was then in London and inside
MI5. "The March date came out clearly from Hollis's letters to his
mother or from her diary," Glees recalled when I consulted him again in
2007. The solution may be that Hollis was initially taken on for a trial
period, especially as there is no evidence that he secured any other employment in 1938.

As June 8 was a Wednesday, it was an unusual day for a newcomer to
begin work in any government department. So "the official joining
date" may have been that on which he became an established officer
after a probationary period. That this was standard practice then for
such "raw" recruits is shown by the details that Sir Dick White gave to
his biographer, Tom Bower. After accepting an unexpected invitation to
join MI5 in 1935, White was told that he was a "long-term probationer
under training" and only later realized that during that period he could
have been "disowned at a stroke." His training lasted about six months,
after which he was formally appointed on January 1, 1936. When Stella

Rimington joined MI5 in 1969, she was first assigned to "a section where all new joiners were put for a few months to be trained," as she recorded in her memoirs. As Hollis was an uninvited applicant with no police or military experience, such a probationary training period for him would seem to have been automatic. There was little evidence that he would be fitted for the work or would, necessarily, like it.

The first MI5 document bearing Hollis's initials, RHH, so far available to me was dated July 6, 1938, and showed that he was already involved in inquiries about dangerous Communists. It would seem to be extremely unlikely that a totally raw recruit would have been allowed to write on such secret documents for permanent record within a month of joining.

How had he managed to gain entry? Family records indicate that various relatives concerned about "poor Roger's" health and lack of income had urged Major Meldrum, his wife's relation, to try to find him a job. Asked how he had come to join MI5, when interrogated in 1969, Hollis replied that he had taken the initiative and had asked Meldrum, "Are there any jobs going in Intelligence?" That question was unusual when so little was known about MI5 and MI6 in those days and recalls Philby's evidence that new recruits to Soviet intelligence were required to achieve penetration of secret departments through their own initiative.

The only available witness evidence of the mode of Hollis's recruitment to MI5 is in a letter (dated March 10, 1982) sent to me by White, to whom I had been introduced by Lord (Victor) Rothschild several years previously. It briefly described a tennis match specially set up to enable White and a senior MI5 colleague, Jane Sissmore, to assess Hollis's capabilities. The chain of events leading up to this encounter—at the prestigious Ealing Lawn Tennis Club where Sissmore was a member—seems to have been as follows.

Meldrum was a friend of Sissmore's, possibly through tennis. He knew—probably through her—that in 1937, the head of MI5, Sir Vernon Kell, was convinced that war with Germany was inevitable and was expanding his small service in readiness. In those days, posts in MI5 were never advertised and volunteers were ignored; only candidates suggested by existing members or trusted outsiders were considered. In his letter, White stated that it was definitely Meldrum who first put forward Hollis as a candidate. Hollis was asked to submit his qualifications, and White recalled, "Hollis seemed a quite attractive candidate. He had plenty of Far Eastern experience and some knowledge of the Chinese language." White confirmed to me that Hollis did not volunteer any special knowledge of international communism at any stage of his recruitment, and one might wonder, as Sherlock Holmes had in a different situation, "Why didn't the dog bark?" Perhaps wishing to conceal his past association with notorious people like Ewert and Smedley, and possibly Sonia, he remained silent, as he certainly did about his connection with active British Communists such as Cockburn.

After some discussion inside MI5, it was decided that Hollis "should be informally interviewed at a social occasion to see whether he was worth more formal treatment." Jane Sissmore therefore asked Meldrum to invite Hollis to play tennis at the Ealing Club and White, then a junior colleague and a recent recruit to MI5 himself, was also asked to play and to give his opinion. Hollis agreed to attend, and it seems inevitable that Meldrum would have informed him of the purpose of the exercise.

White's recollection of the meeting continued: "At first sight, Jane and I were not very impressed. Hollis was shy and retiring and physically distinctly frail. We knew the reason for this was that he was suffering from TB, from which he had by no means fully recovered. Nor were his paper qualifications all that impressive. He had left Oxford without a degree and with a reputation of having wasted his time on wine, women and golf. And yet there was something gritty and hard headed about him which persuaded Jane and me to recommend his further consideration."

Hollis was then interviewed by an MI5 panel, according to Peter Wright, who consulted records when chairing the long official inquiry into Hollis's past. Wright told me that the panel rejected him and suggested that in view of his foreign experience, he might try the Secret Intelligence Service, MI6. Hollis duly sent in his application and was again rejected, having no real command of foreign languages and being medically unfit for overseas service, an essential requirement in MI6. Then, perhaps owing to Meldrum's persistence, Sissmore, who as a qualified barrister had persuasive power, induced the MI5 chief, Kell, to accept him.

According to Wright, Kell agreed to accept Hollis on condition that Jane Sissmore take responsibility for him, which she did. It also seems possible that because of serious doubts about the new recruit's health, with his tuberculosis still active, Kell had insisted on a lengthy trial period.

Positive vetting did not exist when Hollis was recruited, a "good background" being considered sufficient. So no substantive inquiries were made into his previous behavior. White and Sissmore—and perhaps Kell—had been impressed by the stress that Meldrum had put on Hollis's "highly honourable and stable family background" as the son of a minor bishop and a mother with ecclesiastical forebears and with an eldest brother in holy orders and another who was becoming a literary figure. White wrote, "When, later, I met his father and brothers I saw what he meant." Presumably, they would have been equally impressed by the family of Anthony Blunt.

As the date of the tennis match could be of significance, I checked with the Ealing Club on the unlikely chance that there was still a record of it. Astonishingly, after nearly seventy years there was! Mr. Eric Leach, the public relations officer there, provided information that assured me that the "look-see" at Hollis could have taken place only on Saturday, August 28, 1937, or Sunday, May 22, 1938. They were the only two days on which Miss Sissmore had signed in Dick White as a visitor.

The latter date would leave only sixteen days for all the ensuing events to happen before Hollis's official entry, according to MI5, on June 8. These included his "formal treatment," involving being interviewed by an MI5 panel that needed to be convened, notification of his rejection, further discussions with Meldrum, his application to MI6, consideration by MI6, notification of his rejection there, the further approach to MI5 with moves to induce the reluctant Kell to take him, and the eventual notification of his success. It would also have been normal practice for any new entrant to be given time to reinstall himself and his family in London—in Hollis's case, from Wells. Considering how slowly government departments operate, especially those dealing with secret affairs, it would seem to have been impossible for all that to have happened in sixteen days. The postal delays alone are likely to have accounted for about ten days, as the arrangements are unlikely to have been conducted by telephone.

The Hollis family documentary evidence that Roger was definitely inside MI5 before March 13, 1938, supports the contention that he was there in some probationary capacity before June 1938 and rules out May 22 as the date of the tennis match. The date is highly significant because if the tennis match occurred on August 28, 1937, it would mean that Hollis would have known that he stood a chance of entry to MI5 before his trip to Paris in November. Or, as seems more likely, he may even have been told, by then, that he had been successful. Had Hollis then mentioned his change of fortune to some Communist friend, like Cockburn, who was back in London by October 16, the GRU could have been informed and could then have issued an invitation for talks in Paris.

Hollis would have been warned by MI5 to remain silent about his prospects and, if appointed, only to say—ever—that he was "attached to the War Office." That description alone, however, would have been enough to excite GRU interest if it had been informed of it.

The earlier date for the tennis match would also explain why Hollis had quit his job with Ardath so cavalierly in October. Whatever the answer, it was a suspicious coincidence that, while in reduced circumstances, Hollis should have visited the foreign city that housed the main center for GRU recruitment before his entry to MI5. Significantly, Hollis had applied for three of the espionage targets considered by the GRU and KGB to be prime—*The Times*, MI5, and MI6.

KGB papers recently revealed in connection with the Philby case show the extent to which that agency had previously been trying, fruitlessly, to intrude a spy into MI6. So there can be little doubt that there were similar pressures inside the GRU to achieve the same with either or both British intelligence services.

Like the several young Englishmen of "good families" who were definitely recruited by Soviet intelligence in the late 1930s, Hollis may have been convinced that, with Hitler intent on war—a taste of which he had seen in Shanghai and detested—only the Soviet Union had the power and the will to counter him. In a letter home, he had described how he had disliked the strutting militarism and Hitlerism he had seen in Berlin, on his way back to China by railway after a vacation in Great Britain. Then, perhaps, the news from China, with the Japanese strutting in Peking and Shanghai, had pushed him over the edge.

Just as the Fascist assault in Spain had spurred many young Britons to action—in which some of the brightest sacrificed their lives—the Japanese invasion of China may have influenced Hollis into offering his services. After the horrors and injustice that he had witnessed in China, he may have been further conditioned by the appalling economic conditions in Britain that he had found on his return. Hollis not only was witnessing the heartache of mass unemployment, with Welsh coal miners begging on the London streets, but was part of it, and his repeated inability to find suitable employment could have edged him still closer to the brink.

So if Hollis had already been a Communist sympathizer, he would have been simply increasing his commitment by taking a more purposeful part, as happened with all the members of the Cambridge group. Such a feeling of taking an active and positive role in a power struggle by "helping the Comintern" was particularly attractive at that time when many people of all ages had a sense of impotence, particularly against the march of fascism and Nazism.

When investigating the Soviet penetration of MI5, Peter Wright suspected that while Hollis may have been recruited to the general Soviet cause while in China, his formal recruitment as an agent did not occur until 1937. "I believe that it was a combination of the disaster of his TB, the loss of his job with BAT, the difficulty of finding a job without a university degree when unemployment was so severe, and the rise of Nazism and the threat of war," he told me in 1980. Bitter disappointment at failure to find work has often been a factor in inducing young men to rebel against the system. In Hollis's case, because of the additional misfortune of his tuberculosis, the general advice to the KGB's recruiters given by General Pavel Sudoplatov may have applied: "Search for people who are hurt by fate or nature."

If Hollis was, in fact, recruited to the GRU service in Soviet eyes, that does not mean that he had consciously and coldly decided to become a traitor to his own country at that stage. As the Russian book *The GRU and the Atomic Bomb* repeatedly shows, the GRU approach was much more subtle. Sonia, for example, did not know that she was working for the GRU for almost two years after her agreement to help the Communist cause in China. The same applied to most other recruits. The GRU concentrated on ideologically motivated Communists who agreed first to work for the "peaceful" Communist and anti-Fascist cause through the Comintern.

The French lessons at Loches could have been Hollis's cover for the visit, for in his circumstances, he could hardly have justified a holiday in Paris while living with his parents. In that case, it would have been a GRU requirement that his wife know nothing about any clandestine meeting that could have occurred when her husband was briefly alone when they were in Paris. The couple were back in Wells for Christmas and attended the Wells Hunt Ball on New Year's Eve, perhaps celebrating his new career with MI5.

Wright, and those of his colleagues who eventually suspected Hollis, researched heavily into the background of his entry into MI5, but they never learned about the trip to France, so they could never ask him to explain it. Wright told me that when Hollis became suspect, he spoke of "his immense relief that the MI5 job had freed him from the chore of learning shorthand and typing." Was this statement a GRU-inspired cover in case his trip was ever discovered, so that it could be explained as part of a secretarial course?

All of the above may have been merely a concatenation of the coincidences with which the Hollis saga is littered. There was one further remarkable coincidence: Immediately after Hollis's appointment in MI5 had been confirmed, in early June 1938, Sonia again visited London, arriving by air from Rotterdam on June 10, and seeing her family, including her sister Brigitte and Jurgen. Sonia's route to London had taken her through Nazi Germany, which for a Jewess with a known Communist history was dangerous. That suggests that the visit, for which the GRU paid, was urgent. If Hollis had been recruited by the GRU, the odds are that the ultracautious Center would have forbidden any contact during any probationary period, though thought would have been given to the identity of possible couriers for such an important potential source. However, as soon as his entry to MI5 was due to be confirmed, arrangements for clandestine contact with a courier in London would have been urgently required.

According to evidence provided later by a GRU defector, Walter Krivitsky, the courier preferred by the Center is likely to have been an established, dedicated, female GRU operative with British nationality, who knew the Center's requirements and was already based, with impeccable cover, in London. Additionally, she should not have been of Russian origin but have ready contact with the Soviet embassy that was unlikely to arouse suspicion. Possession of a "safe house" for the depositing of information would have been a major advantage. It was a standard GRU precaution that once a spy had been recruited, there should be no further contact with any GRU officer. Contact was to be restricted to meetings with the courier to pick up documents, and even that should be done by *dubok* whenever practicable.

The only known candidate with all the required qualities was Sonia's younger sister, Brigitte, who was already on the GRU's books as a player in the Red Orchestra. She was known there as Brigitte Lewis, having secured British nationality in 1936 by marrying a young Englishman— precisely what Sonia would do later. So Sonia's visit to London in June 1938 may have been to instruct Brigitte personally regarding her new responsibility. Their other GRU activities, precisely at that time, show that they had the Center's permission and confidence to act jointly, as will be described.

Other events, on record, were soon to prove that Brigitte was an established GRU agent, and I have firsthand witness evidence that she did serve Roger Hollis in later years. While Brigitte had not been trained in radio operations, that would not have been a requirement as long as Hollis remained in London.

As Sonia already knew that she would not be going back to Poland, but was to be posted elsewhere, she took her children and their nanny with her to Britain on her 1938 visit and found a room for them in Felpham, near Bognor. They remained there for the summer while, on the pretext that she was returning to Poland, she visited Moscow for detailed instructions. (The reason Sonia was not allowed to take her children to Moscow was explained to me by her son Michael. It was essential that they should not learn to speak any Russian, which might one day betray the fact that their mother had spent time in the Soviet Union.)

The GRU Center decided that Sonia should move to Switzerland. From there, access to London would be easier or a courier could visit her—as Brigitte did—if problems arose. Both the KGB and the GRU were remarkably farsighted in their espionage planning, and fail-safe procedures were standard practice. So the possibility that a courier responsible for such a prime source as the first mole to be intruded into a British secret service might need assistance, or even replacement, would have been foreseen.

Whatever its precise date and purpose, Hollis's peculiar entry into MI5 would prove to have been a black day for both British and American security and defense. If he had, in fact, been recruited to the British section of the Red Orchestra, he was destined to become first violin.

CHAPTER 8

Inside MI5

—

H OLLIS WORKED IN LONDON ON HORSEFERRY ROAD, IN A
building to which MI5 had recently moved, as a desk officer assistant to
Jane Sissmore, who had taken responsibility for him following her part
in his recruitment. Sissmore—who became Mrs. John Archer through
an in-office marriage in 1939—was in a branch of B Division called Soviet Affairs. Released MI5 documents show that she was known as B4a
and signed her letters and memos with her initials, KMMS, her true first
name being Kathleen. B4a's main remit was "suspected cases of [Soviet]
espionage by individuals domiciled in the UK" and "review of espionage cases." As B4a (3), which Hollis soon became, he could hardly
have been in a better-informed position, with ready access to all the relevant information on file. A letter to Scotland Yard's Special Branch,
dated August 13, 1938, and initialed by Hollis, shows that he was already
concerned with the surveillance of a suspected Communist spy named
Ted Bramley. Another, dated September 5, 1938, shows him involved
with the case of William Rust, the Communist Party's "national organizer." A letter signed by him on November 1, 1938, shows him clearly
established as running the Rust case, as he would continue to do, with no
effective action being taken against any of the suspects.

Like all new members, Hollis was told that the prime function of the
security service was "the detection and prevention of espionage and
sabotage by the enemy in peace and in war." So from the start, he was

concerned with measures in opposition to subversive activities by agents of the Soviet Union and Communists in general. Among these was Bob Stewart, an affable Scot based at Communist Party headquarters near Covent Garden, who was the final link in a chain enabling Moscow to funnel regular supplies of money to finance the Communist Party and its loss-making paper, the *Daily Worker*. The money was delivered to him from the Soviet embassy, sometimes through cutouts, in wads of notes, usually in shoe boxes. A document dated August 24, 1939, shows that Hollis was involved with Scotland Yard's Special Branch in monitoring Stewart's movements. Further documents in Stewart's MI5 files show that by September 22 Hollis was established as his case officer, without any effective action.

The new recruit quickly encountered several seriously mistaken beliefs that had become firmly established in MI5 over the preceding years. The most damaging was the assumption that the Russians would not use people who were open Communists as intelligence agents or spies. They would be too obvious and, if exposed, would embarrass the local Communist Party. Yet it would transpire that Stewart was just such a person who was frequently used to service Soviet spies when their usual couriers were unavailable. Another was Oliver Green, known to Hollis as a dedicated Communist as early as July 6, 1938, when his initials, RHH, appeared on an MI5 document about him. Green would prove to be an important spymaster, running a ring of agents. That such a misbelief continued is extraordinary, because between February 1934 and January 1937, a radio-monitoring operation of radio traffic between Moscow and London, code-named Mask, had established the identities of several important Communists who were active agents. Stewart was among them but operated without hindrance throughout his long Communist career.

Another fallacy was the assumption that the Soviet Union operated only one espionage agency—referred to as the Russian Intelligence Service (RIS)—when the fact was that there were two, the KGB and the GRU, operating independently. As Stalin distrusted intelligence unless it was supplied by at least two independent sources, both the KGB and the GRU would be instructed to pursue the same line of inquiries through their spies in Great Britain or the United States in absolute mutual secrecy and reporting separately. The Molotov papers, for example, reveal many instances where this policy had paid rich dividends.

A further false belief, which was to cost MI5 and the nation heavily, was the assumption that no well-educated Briton from a good family could possibly be a traitor. Clearly, a spy inside MI5, such as Elli, could exploit such institutionalized fallacies to further his treacherous activities and to explain away failures that might come to light.

Because of its deviousness and deceptive practices, the intelligence world has been described as a "wilderness of mirrors," but Hollis was soon to find that MI5 was more like a wilderness of papers, in which he became entranced. A desk officer's work concentrated on consulting files lodged in the registry and routinely adding new information fed in from various sources. Hollis became fascinated by files and developed a lasting reputation for being more interested in pondering than in action, except when his own position was threatened. Throughout his career he was to pursue a minimalist policy—covertly to amass information about suspects, but to take as little overt action against them as possible. This fattened the files but would so often prove to be advantageous to the Kremlin that his consistent avoidance of action would become a staring anomaly.

That Hollis liked the work is indicated by a letter he sent to his mother-in-law on July 17, 1938, to mark the first anniversary of his wedding. Though White assured me that Hollis's starting pay was so poor that he had originally expressed doubt about being able to manage on it, the new recruit had written, "This job is really splendid and I'm enjoying it enormously." Perhaps he was also celebrating his official establishment as an MI5 officer after a long trial period. It also seems unlikely that if Hollis had first joined MI5 in June, without any police or military experience, he would have been actively involved in countering suspect Soviet agents as early as July 6.

Among the first files he encountered in his survey of suspect Communists were those on his old Oxford drinking companion Claud Cockburn. He would have been surprised—even shocked—to discover the degree of interest that MI5 had shown, and was still showing, in that ardent revolutionary, who was on its records as "a member of the Soviet Intelligence Service and of the Western European Bureau of the Comintern." (This was to be confirmed in the Comintern archives in Moscow, which state that in 1936–37, he was a "Communist Party official working for the Comintern" and describe him as "one of Fleet Street's cleverest journalists" whose contacts were "greatly admired."

At that time, the GRU was taking over the Comintern's intelligence assets.)

Hollis found that there were already four files on Cockburn, dating back to January 1933, showing that MI5 rated this "character," whom so many dismissed as a comical figure, not only as a dangerous revolutionary and effective propagandist, but as a major agent of the Russian Intelligence Service. A later file would describe what it called "the Cockburn Machine" as "controlling military, naval and industrial espionage and would be responsible for sabotage in the event of war or revolution." It would also state that in 1936–37 Cockburn received "considerable sums of money from the Moscow Narodny Bank," adding, "He enjoys the confidence of Moscow, so he can—and does—give orders to Pollitt," referring to Harry Pollitt, then general secretary of the Communist Party of Great Britain (CPGB). Cockburn was thus a glaring instance of a well-known, open Communist being used as an agent, though, as will be seen, it did not appear to affect the MI5 mind-set "rule."

The Cockburn documents, of which I have copies, completely dispose of the stance, taken by many of his friends, that his communism had been no more than an eccentric dalliance. They show that he was a totally committed Stalinist and dedicated Soviet agent intent on revolution, which he fervently believed could be accomplished in the United Kingdom. That was the true nature of the man who had been one of Hollis's closest friends at Oxford.

After Cockburn had founded *The Week* in 1933, the MI5 chief, Colonel Vernon Kell (soon to be Major General Sir Vernon), had taken a personal interest in his activities. His telephones were tapped and his letters intercepted over long periods, while he was assiduously followed and watch was kept on his accommodation addresses in Hampstead and elsewhere, to see who visited them. Several letters signed by Kell requesting information about Cockburn exist in the archives. Particular interest had been shown by White and Liddell in the trips that Cockburn made to Paris, with the regular involvement of MI6 trying to check on those he met there, though with little success. The heaviness of his whiskey drinking was a regular source of wonder to the Special Branch and MI5 watchers but did not seem to be construed as a symptom of the stress consequent of a conspiratorial life.

It was an invidious position for Hollis, but in such a circumstance, some newcomers to MI5 would have taken the chance to make an impression by offering their personal knowledge of the suspect for his file. Instead Hollis remained silent, in blatant breach of a strict MI5 rule that any officer who had any previous connection with any suspect must immediately declare it in writing on the relevant file.

Again, "Why didn't the dog bark?" Nobody could have blamed Hollis for having encountered Cockburn, who was a cousin of his other drinking pal at Oxford, Evelyn Waugh. The established fact that he knowingly risked serious censure by breaking an important rule, when so junior, implies that there had been more to the friendship about which he was anxious to avoid questioning. In view of Kell's personal interest in Cockburn, it was a particularly dangerous omission, suggesting that Hollis had strong reason for it. If Cockburn had been involved in Hollis's recruitment to Soviet service, however marginally, not only would the silence be explicable, but also the fact that in spite of the mass of incriminating material collected by MI5, Cockburn was *never* subjected to interrogation and survived unscathed. So, too, would Hollis's unusual act, when he eventually became director general, of removing the Cockburn files from the registry and storing them in his own safe, where nobody could browse through them. Of course, if he had been under GRU control, he could have been instructed to remain silent on Cockburn.

Doing so happened to involve particular risk because White had been a contemporary at Oxford and might have known of their association. Much more dangerously, as Hollis was soon to discover, one of MI5's sources about Cockburn's activities was Tom Driberg, their mutual Communist friend at Oxford. Working for MI5, inside the Communist Party, under the code name M8, Driberg, in typical fashion, was informing on his old comrade, with whom he remained in close touch. In 1935, for example, he had named, as assisting Cockburn, the leftwing journalist Philip Jordan, who was to figure peculiarly in the Hollis saga. An entry for November 2, 1938, reveals that Driberg had reported how the Soviet embassy was using Cockburn to check on the true political opinions of newspaper correspondents who wanted to visit Russia. Cockburn had been the link used to pass the Soviet requirements to Driberg, who had then made inquiries among journalists in Fleet Street, where he worked.

When Hollis had joined MI5, Driberg was being run by a highly effective officer, Maxwell Knight (B5b), from an autonomous outpost eventually based in an apartment in Dolphin Square. Knight visited MI5 headquarters rarely, so for some time, Hollis may not have known the identity of M8, as he was always referred to in the files. He may well have been shocked when he learned it.

Hollis committed an even graver offense in failing to admit his former friendship, in China, with the international Communist official Arthur Ewert. MI5 already had a file on Ewert and his many aliases, dating back to 1931. It recorded his Comintern activities in China, and as interest in him was resurrected in 1940, Hollis is likely to have been concerned with it.

On January 21, 1938, MI5 had boosted its reputation by the arrest of a small group of Woolwich Arsenal workers, led by the Moscow-trained Communist Percy Glading, who were passing copies of secret documents about new weapons to the KGB. After trial at the Old Bailey, Glading, Albert Williams, and George Whomack were sentenced to imprisonment on March 14. The success was due to patient work by Maxwell Knight and a female agent who had penetrated Communist Party headquarters, where Glading had been a member of the Central Committee. Within MI5 headquarters, Jane Sissmore was in charge of the Woolwich case, as many documents show, being particularly concerned with tracing the foreign Soviet agents controlling the British traitors. As an assistant to Sissmore, Hollis is likely to have seen the documents as part of his training and was to figure in the case later in ways that have since raised suspicion.

In addition to Sissmore's control, Hollis was working under White, who in early 1940, according to *The Security Service, 1908–1945: The Official History,* published in 1999 (though originally completed in 1946), "was supervising the work connected with the Communist Party and the Comintern." As his official biography would show, White understood little about communism at that time, being almost totally engaged in German counterespionage. The more senior Liddell was similarly involved, and Hollis became the driving force in his specialty, quickly being recognized as MI5's expert on communism and the prime understudy to Jane Sissmore in that respect. Continuing close collaboration with White was to be crucial to Hollis's entire career and the extent to which both men were to thrive on national—and international—intelligence disasters would be a subject of retrospective wonder.

At no time did Hollis express any past support for communism, as

White assured me, but that is of no significance, as the behavior of proven spies has shown. On KGB instructions, Harold ("Kim") Philby not only pretended to have abandoned his far left beliefs, but, before the outbreak of war, associated himself openly with anti-Communist and pro-Fascist organizations, as did the spy Guy Burgess.

Like other newcomers, Hollis may have found it difficult at first to conform to the culture of secrecy. In theory, officers were required to keep even close relatives ignorant of their true function, and if necessary, they were required to lie to maintain their cover. Being licensed to lie was a privilege of which Hollis would make increasing use.

According to contemporaries, Hollis was also soon giving the impression of being a well-informed student of Marxism and international communism, which, as White confirmed, he had never mentioned at his recruitment. Nor, apparently, did he ever mention to White the family connection with Peter the Great, which seems odd when both men were so close and jointly concerned with Russian affairs.

From being heartily outgoing and gregarious, as he had been at Oxford University and in China, Hollis had become quiet, withdrawn, and highly secretive, especially about his past, and he remained that way throughout his career. The MI5 officer Freddie Beith described him as "shy and self-effacing." Almost all his colleagues, including Dick White, regarded him as being "too reserved." The officer Derek Tangye recalled him to me as "austere, remote." According to Hollis's friend Sir Patrick Reilly, "His appearance was strange. There was always a vague impression of something odd. And he was very, very reserved." Women who had served in MI5 with him described him to me as "unimaginative and unutterably dull" and "withdrawn and to be avoided."

There was one odd exception to Hollis's reserve—he became known in the office for his fund of dirty stories. Former MI5 members consulted by Tom Bower for his biography of White recalled "his irksome nasal tone and his predilection for pinching women's bottoms, characteristics redeemed by his fund of good dirty jokes, which he told well." Peter Wright, who spent many hours with Hollis alone, says he was surprised by his store of the filthiest jokes he had ever heard. If Eve, who was a prude, knew about this, she may well have been shocked or even disgusted, which could not have helped the marriage, which would eventually become so unhappy that Colonel T. A. ("Tar") Robertson, a distinguished MI5 colleague, would tell me, "Roger had married the wrong woman." Nicholas Elliott of MI6, who had first worked in MI5, described Eve to me as "very boring—tough to be saddled with at a party." Hollis and his wife were then living at 18 Elsham Road, London, off Holland Road, and Eve was angry whenever Roger behaved stupidly in drink, for according to colleagues, he did not carry liquor well.

The psychological change in Hollis's character could have been partly a consequence of this progressive marital incompatibility, but an alternative reason presents itself—silent anxiety being an occupational consequence of espionage. If he was Elli, awareness of the constant danger of his position could have been responsible. If Elli was an active Soviet agent in late 1939, 1940, and the first half of 1941, he would have been spying when Stalin was effectively an ally of Hitler, which might have been construed as a capital offense during war.

A further factor could have been the GRU instruction, which Elli would have received, about the self-effacing requirements of "the conspiratorial life." The GRU ordered its penetration agents to be quietly efficient in their posts and to secure steady promotion to increase their access to secrets that way, rather than attracting attention by pushing for it. As the later MI5 chief Dame Stella Rimington was to remark in her memoirs, "The best and most successful spies are the quiet, apparently boring and dull people who go on doing the same thing in an unostentatious way year after year." In compensation for having to conceal their true nature, some penetration agents have reported enjoying a gratifying feeling of secret power, which might account for the recollection of a contemporary female secretary who told me, "Hollis looked at you as though he was laughing at you."

Whoever Elli was, he would quickly have experienced the complexity of a mole's position, which was to be vividly recalled by the proven spy Philby in a lecture he gave to KGB officers in Moscow in 1977 and that has now been published. He pointed out that "if he had consistently failed in his MI6 duties, he would have been sacked, while if he achieved too much, he would damage the KGB's interests, which were his prime concern." So some MI6 successes were essential, and when they had to be endured, it was wise to make the most of them in the interests of future promotion. It was a principle that Hollis would appear to practice in MI5.

In 1939, MI5, which was being rapidly expanded in anticipation of the forthcoming war, moved into the empty Wormwood Scrubs prison in London, where Hollis remained in B Branch, continuing to work closely with White because their fields overlapped. Their friendship was well-known inside MI5, and several former officers have told me that White was the dominant partner, to whom Hollis was likely to defer, though this soon changed as White recognized Hollis's superior expertise on Communist and Soviet affairs.

CHAPTER 9

The Krivitsky "Coincidence"

—

WHILE THREE OF THE TREACHEROUS GLADING GROUP AT Woolwich Arsenal had been jailed, an MI5 report on the case, signed by Jane Sissmore in February 1938, reveals that an infinitely more dangerous traitor was allowed to escape, with severe consequences to Western security. The report mentioned a young woman associate of the group, Melita (Letty) Sirnis. A file about her was started and her home in Finchley was put under surveillance, but the file was soon closed without any effective consequence. Sirnis, whose surname had actually changed to Norwood through marriage in 1935, was to become a significant Soviet spy, especially in the atomic field, and MI5's failure to follow up the discovery of her name in Glading's documents would be seen as a serious blunder leading to a parliamentary inquiry more than sixty years later. Her espionage career, which has been researched meticulously by the historian Dr. David Burke, will impact repeatedly on this narrative.

The MI5 files show that by May 1939, if not sooner, Hollis had become Cockburn's case officer, an extraordinary relationship that severely intensified the culpability of his silence. So it would seem inevitable that Hollis would soon have learned that M8 was his other old Communist acquaintance Driberg, with the realization that his failure to have registered his friendship with Cockburn might be exposed by such a vicious character at any time. Having inherited Cockburn as a long active case in which the director general had personal interest, Hollis had no alternative but to display apparent zeal, if only as insurance against the discovery of his former link with the suspect. A sensible precaution, whether he was Elli or not, would have been to demonstrate, in the files, that he was in assiduous pursuit of Cockburn, though without serious impact on his old friend's pro-Soviet endeavors. In a letter to the Foreign Office dated December 29, 1939, Hollis wrote with unconscious—or possibly conscious—humor, "Almost any contact of Claud Cockburn falls, almost automatically, under suspicion."

If he was Elli, it would also have been in his interest to learn all he could about Cockburn's activities and to subdue those that might be dangerous to either of them. As will be seen, this seems to be what he did.

There are many entries in the Cockburn files signed or initialed by Hollis. It was Hollis who wrote to the Home Office and the Post Office concerning the various warrants needed by MI5 to extend the surveillance, so he was perfectly placed to warn his old friend, had he so desired. It was to Hollis that Special Branch reported when they had searched a briefcase belonging to Cockburn's secretary at his digest, *The Week*, when she had returned from America. Released reports show that both Scotland Yard's Special Branch and MI5's own Watcher Service were involved in following Cockburn from pub to pub, into banks, post offices, or wherever, noting everything he did and everyone he met. The time spent on Cockburn underlines the importance MI5 attached to him. However, as would happen with so many of Hollis's cases, the suspect never did anything of significant consequence while the surveillance was in progress.

In September 1939, shortly after the outbreak of World War II, which British Communists did not support because Stalin had entered into a nonaggression pact with Hitler, there was widespread concern in MI5 about subversive statements being made by Cockburn, in both *The Week* and the *Daily Worker*. Cockburn had applied for an exit permit to visit Finland, which had been invaded by Soviet forces, but by the end of January 1940, the Home Office, in consultation with the Foreign Office, had decided to refuse it. That is recorded in the MI5 files in a letter from the Home Office dated February 2. Whether or not Hollis had already heard of the refusal, he wrote a spirited internal memo dated January 30, urging that Cockburn's application be rejected. He added, "May I be al-

lowed to suggest that for the dignity and security of this country the ultimate right to refuse leave to travel should rest in our hands." As will be
seen, Hollis would make a habit of putting forward suggestions for security improvements that already existed or could have no impact—a pattern of behavior that could never have any effect but made him appear
zealous.

Hollis specialized in compiling information on the activities of "the
Comintern and of Communist Refugees," and in the context of the case
against him, that requirement is particularly significant because Soviet
agents posing as Communist refugees were to play major roles in his career.

On November 13, 1939, Liddell noted in his diary, "Soviet espionage
seems to be on the increase." He made it clear that Jane Sissmore and
her assistants were very active in recording it. In fact, by June, Hollis
had become Sissmore's main assistant and was signing himself "B4a,"
perhaps in her absence, and also drafting letters for the MI5 director
general to governors of the prisons housing the convicted Woolwich
spies. His responsibility increased rapidly and was quickly to become
total, because Sissmore became involved almost full-time in a case of
great potential importance—the interrogation of a major GRU defector
calling himself General Walter Krivitsky.

Krivitsky, who had defected from his Paris base to the United States
with his wife and child during the latter part of 1938, had been using a
ghostwriter to reveal some of his exploits. In September 1939, the ghostwriter had warned the British Foreign Office that a cipher clerk in the
communications department of the Foreign Office, John King, was an
active Soviet agent. Among other acts of treachery, he had handed over
telegraphic messages giving Moscow insight into British negotiations
with Hitler, for which he was jailed for ten years in a secret trial. This
deplorable situation, in which a damaging British spy was to be exposed
only through chance information supplied by a defector to the United
States, was to be repeated many times throughout Hollis's twenty-seven
years in MI5.

On January 19, 1940, Krivitsky, who had been the GRU's chief in
Western Europe, arrived in London at MI5's request and was installed in
the Langham Hotel, near Regent's Park, as "Mr. Thomas." His visit was
rated so secret that even the FBI was never told about it.

Sissmore, by then Mrs. Jane Archer but posing as "Mrs. Moore," began questioning him on January 24. Krivitsky explained that he had defected because he had received a recall to Moscow and realized that he had been marked down for liquidation in Stalin's senseless purge of Red Army officers and agents. He had ceased to operate by September 1937. So, had Hollis been recruited to the GRU in Paris during his strange trip there in November, Krivitsky could not have known anything about it.

During his interrogation by MI5, spread over three weeks, he revealed information about several more British Soviet sources, though he was unable to identify them. It included substantial leads to both Kim Philby and Donald Maclean, about whom he had heard KGB gossip. Krivitsky also warned about the activities of a GRU controller who had been in the Soviet embassy in London since early 1937, Colonel Simon Kremer, whom he named and identified from an MI5 photograph, having met him on one of his trips to Moscow. The existence of the photograph shows that MI5 was already aware of Kremer, and as the Soviet Union was not then at war, MI5 could not excuse itself for failing to watch him by claiming that it had been given political orders to avoid putting Soviet "diplomats" under surveillance, as would happen after Germany attacked it in 1941.

Clearly, in view of the intense secrecy, it could be highly instructive to know whether or not the GRU and KGB Centers in Moscow were made aware of Krivitsky's visit and, if so, when and how they responded. Documents released unexpectedly from the KGB archives indicate that they were quickly informed by someone and responded dramatically. They show that within a month, in February, the activities of the KGB's station in the London embassy were suddenly closed down, on orders from Moscow, and its agents, including the highly productive Maclean and the rest of the Cambridge group, were put on ice. Its chief, Anatoli Gorski, was recalled to Moscow for urgent and prolonged discussions. This seemingly panicked move has hitherto been explained as part of Stalin's purge of KGB officers, Gorski allegedly being a candidate. However, the dates, circumstances, and consequences strongly suggest that it was the typical ruthless response to a quick warning from an MI5 source about Krivitsky's debriefing, together with some of its results.

This explanation is strongly supported by Gorski's return to his post in London, unharmed, at the end of 1940, when he revived all his agents, confident that it was safe to do so. In fact, he was held in such regard that later he would be switched to Washington, where he ran several groups of informers.

Earlier, in February, the director at the KGB Center had every reason to fear that MI5 would, in particular, take effective action to track down the two spies fingered by Krivitsky whom he knew to be Philby and Maclean. In fact, the defector's priceless information was used for little else than fattening the MI5 files. Even allowing for the advantages of hindsight, it is hard to believe that, given the facts supplied by Krivitsky and the facilities available to MI5, any good investigative journalist would have failed to put both Philby and Maclean on a short list.

The reluctance of MI5 to act effectively demands explanation. The director general and other superiors were remiss in not requiring resolute action, but their main and immediate concern was with the German threat. So responsibility for failure to follow up Krivitsky's leads to Soviet spies, quickly and forcefully, rested mainly with Jane Archer and Hollis. The blame attaching to Archer, however, is greatly reduced by the fact that shortly after completing her long report on Krivitsky, she was switched to totally different work and was fully replaced by Hollis, who assumed responsibility for Soviet affairs. So the mishandling of the Krivitsky case may be an early example of Hollis's stubborn determination to avoid effective action against Soviet agents whenever possible— a policy that, whatever its purposes, suited the Kremlin.

If Moscow had been alerted about Krivitsky's interrogation in London by an informant in MI5, who could it have been? It was held tightly secret from the media, and though several MI5 officers were aware of it, the only known Soviet spy then inside the agency was Elli. As Archer's chief assistant, who had taken over her normal work and would shortly replace her, Hollis knew the details and may have helped her to interpret the defector's data. Blunt is ruled out as the source because he did not join MI5 until June 1940. Philby, too, is a nonstarter, as he did not join MI6 until 1941. So Hollis is the sole known candidate. If he was Elli, it was certainly in his immediate interest to warn his GRU controller that a senior GRU defector was revealing dangerous information to MI5.

There is further evidence to suggest that the informant was a GRU source rather than a KGB agent—the fact that Kremer, the GRU controller in the Soviet embassy specifically named by Krivitsky, was not recalled to Moscow for consultation. If Elli was the source, his information would have reached Kremer through a courier. Kremer would then have known that none of his GRU agents, including Elli, was threatened by Krivitsky's disclosures and that MI5 was taking no action against him. His continued presence in London could also be explained by his necessity to remain in contact with Elli for further feedback. He would, however, have been routinely required to report to the GRU Center in Moscow all the information supplied by Elli, including the leads concerning two spies who, much later, proved to be Philby and Maclean. Realizing that the spies might be KGB assets, the GRU Center would have been required to warn the KGB Center in Moscow, which then urgently shut down its London operations. As with so many events involving Hollis, the timing of the resolute Moscow response seems too precise to be explained away as coincidence.

Krivitsky's information should also have alerted MI5 to the fact that the Soviet intelligence services were operating a "mole strategy"—the insertion of penetration agents into British government departments to discover secrets and influence policy. Further, they were making a two-pronged assault. While the Woolwich Arsenal group had been controlled by the KGB, King had been a GRU spy.

The debriefing of Krivitsky, as described in the MI5's *Official History* and in recently released MI5 files, reveals the extraordinary extent of the previous ignorance of the structure of the Soviet intelligence services. "For the first time," MI5 received insight into the separate natures of the KGB and the GRU and the rivalry between them. Even after the importance of this distinction between the two services had been exposed, it was not effectively appreciated, with the misleading Russian Intelligence Service mind-set continuing to dominate MI5 thinking. In fact, Krivitsky's information led to no useful action, which was astonishing considering that the forty-one-year-old defector was such a prime source. The FBI took note of his advice about the separateness of the GRU and the KGB, which it had learned from his earlier disclosures while in America, and appointed an officer, Emory Gregg, to become a GRU specialist, but MI5 continued to refer to "the RIS."

Had the many leads in Jane Archer's long report on Krivitsky's revelations, now on the Internet, been assiduously pursued, MI5 could have appreciated the extent of the Soviet assault. Appended to her report was a long list of Soviet agents' names and code names given by Krivitsky, but apart from King, whose prosecution could not be avoided, the MI5 policy seemed to be to know but not to act, a situation profoundly comforting to any agent.

Krivitsky had revealed the espionage "tradecraft" favored by the GRU, which differed from that used by the KGB. Once a new source had been recruited successfully, the GRU Center preferred to avoid further direct contact between him and any Soviet official, "source protection," especially of penetration agents, being paramount. To that end, a courier would be appointed to act as an intermediary in collecting information from the source and ensuring its quick delivery to the Soviet embassy. The GRU preferred couriers who were "illegals"—hidden agents operating under seemingly harmless cover—while the KGB made greater use of "legals"—agents who were career officers of the service working openly in the guise of diplomats stationed in an embassy or consulate.

The GRU also preferred women for the task of servicing its spies, while the KGB field officers were usually men. Whenever possible, the GRU chose women who were not of Russian origin, because if they were caught, they could be more easily disowned. The greatest care was taken in recruiting such women, who had to be proven, dedicated Communists. What Krivitsky was advising, in the case of any suspect GRU spy, was *cherchez la femme*, but regrettably, that sound advice was either forgotten or ignored by MI5, with savage consequences.

He told MI5 that the documents delivered to the London embassy by the couriers were usually dispatched to the Moscow Center by diplomatic pouch, but urgent material was sent by radio or telegram, in cipher, by the embassy. Sometimes, however, information could be transmitted by the courier if she was a trained radio operator. Senior officers in the embassy might learn the identity of the couriers but rarely learned the identity of the agents they were serving, knowing them only by code names. This increased the safety of the agents in the event of a Soviet defection.

Krivitsky left for Canada on February 16. Soon after Jane Archer had completed her report on his revelations, she was moved to a new section that coordinated the security liaison officers of the twelve regions into which the United Kingdom had been divided in anticipation of the expected German invasion. Hollis had already been promoted to her former post, B4a, which gave him responsibility for counterintelligence against Communists and especially against those abusing their refugee status. Documentary evidence of this promotion has recently been released.

Since MI5 regarded itself as "under obligation to preserve Krivitsky's anonymity," it did not inform the FBI of his disclosures or even of the fact that he had been interrogated. Released papers show that a year later, in the spring of 1941, Hollis was involved in preparing a twenty-eight-page "bowdlerized edition of Krivitsky's information prepared in MI5," from which "the necessary passages" had been deleted so that it could be sent to America for "the delectation of the FBI." Whether by accident or design, even that document failed to reach the FBI, and another Hollis memo, dated January 29, 1944, indicates that he was preparing another sanitized copy, "otherwise the FBI may think we are trying to hold back on them."

There was, however, one intelligence organization from which none of the details were withheld. In 1941, Anthony Blunt, the KGB spy then inside MI5, handed his controller a complete duplicate of Jane Archer's report on Krivitsky's debriefing, which resides in the Moscow archives. As could be said about so many situations concerning MI5's own security: "You could not make it up!"

Other B4a letters sent in November of that year referred to the Woolwich Arsenal spy George Whomack, indicating that Hollis had now become his case officer and was drafting letters about him for Kell. In April 1940, the Home Office was writing directly to Hollis, as B4a, about that traitor. When Whomack, an open Communist revolutionary who had pleaded guilty to providing the Russians with blueprints of naval weapons, was due for release from prison, the Admiralty sent MI5 a statement, dated March 30, 1940, warning, "This man is a traitor and should not be employed in any capacity in which he can do further harm to his country's interests." This instruction was placed in Whomack's MI5 file, and as his case officer, it was Hollis's duty to warn Special Branch to keep watch on the spy after his release to see where he tried to regain work. Whether through incompetence or by design, he failed to do so, and in February 1941, by which time Hollis had been promoted again to B4, MI5 received an indignant letter from D. Napier and Sons, a firm engaged in war work. They complained that they had been given no warning that Whomack, whom they had taken on in good faith, was a convicted spy. They had spotted him because within days he had become "firmly entrenched with the Communist element in the factory."

The message was seen by John Archer (D3), who passed it to Hollis. On February 26, in a written explanation, Hollis admitted that he had failed to ask Special Branch to keep watch on Whomack after his release. Next day, Archer, who was Jane Archer's husband, ensured that what he described as "a serious breach" was brought to the notice of Hollis's superiors. Later, an official summary of the MI5 file on the case, declassified in 2003, stated that "the case officer, Roger Hollis, overlooked the release of Whomack from prison, which ensured that no Special Branch watch was kept on him, allowing him to return to factory war work." This omission may have been the first time that Jane Archer came to regard Hollis as "untrustworthy," as she would later describe him when Peter Wright was inquiring into his character.

The MI5 files also show that Hollis had previously been responsible for ensuring that both Whomack and his co-conspirator Albert Williams had not been detained in a prison camp under the war emergency regulation 18b on their release from jail. In a letter to the Home Office dated November 2, 1940, Hollis had claimed that although the files showed that MI5 had recommended immediate detention for both traitors, "their file records were not available and consequently, I overlooked the fact that Whomack was already out on licence." He then argued, "In these circumstances it would be difficult to justify detention"—with which the Home Office lamely agreed.

Presumably, at that time, these derelictions of duty were ascribed to error, as it seems unlikely that even Archer would suspect that the son of a bishop could possibly be assisting the Russians. However, as will be seen, his wife, Jane, would eventually state that suspicion.

Omissions and commissions that allowed Soviet agents to operate without effective restraint were to occur repeatedly throughout Hollis's career. In February 1940, for instance, a Colonel Holt had written to Kell asking if MI5 was taking due note of *The Week*. On May 6, the letter was answered on Kell's behalf by Hollis, who wrote, "*The Week* is not, specifically, a Communist publication. From our point of view, there is no objection to the circulation of *The Week* and Claud Cockburn is in possession of an export permit for it." Yet, in the following month, after the disaster of Dunkirk, *The Week* was campaigning, in Moscow's—and Berlin's—interests, for Britain's withdrawal from the war, with Cockburn urging soldiers and factory workers to take no further part in it. In September 1940, he was also under surveillance because he was courting members of Charles de Gaulle's Free French forces in London in order to "pass information to the French Communist Party."

In his book *Spymaster,* W. J. West recorded evidence that Hollis had protected Cockburn during the Communist campaign of 1940 and early 1941 to end the war by making peace with Germany and to set up a People's Republic in Great Britain. Inevitably, this campaign ended in June 1941, when Germany attacked Russia and the Communist Party decided that the war was "just" after all.

By April 1940, Hollis was also involved in MI5's surveillance of his poetic Oxford contemporary Cecil Day-Lewis, who by that time had become such a dedicated Communist that he was known as Red Cecil. When asked for his opinion as to whether or not Day-Lewis was fit for a post in the Information Ministry, responsible for wartime propaganda, Hollis described him as "an intellectual, probably activated by his hatred of social inequality rather than by revolutionary desire," concluding, "I see no objection to his employment."

CHAPTER 10

Toxic Troika

PROMINENT AMONG THE GERMAN REFUGEE COMMUNISTS IN London was a Jewish family, the Kuczynskis, whose impact on the career of Roger Hollis was to be so profound that it is necessary to deal with them in detail. This is now possible because in March 2005, the MI5 management released a mass of files on the Kuczynskis, showing that they had been of interest to them, and to MI6, even before they had fled from the Nazis. The FBI was also to be deeply concerned, over many years, about the impact of their behavior on American security.

Most Jewish refugees repaid their debt to Great Britain by unswerving loyalty, but others, including at least five of the Kuczynski family, had prime loyalty to Stalin's Soviet Union and dedication to supplanting the Nazis by a pro-Soviet Communist regime. In the longer term, they also hoped to saddle Britain with that tyrannical and blood-soaked system.

The father, Professor Robert René Kuczynski, who had been a well-known demographer in Germany and America and had influential political and academic contacts in London, arrived in 1933 and became a lecturer and researcher at the London School of Economics (LSE). His English was fluent because he had spent six years at the Brookings Institution in Washington. He and his wife, Berthe, settled in Hampstead with their younger children because many other Jews were already there and they could find friendship and assistance.

In finding accommodations, they were helped by a young Communist, Gerty Sirnis, who was studying law at the LSE. Gerty was the elder sister of the future spy Melita Norwood, and both were daughters of a refugee from czarist Russia who by that time had died. (In 1935, Melita married the son of another czarist refugee, Nussbaum, who changed his name to Norwood.) Gerty lived with her mother in Lawn Road, close to Hampstead Heath, and Robert Kuczynski found accommodations there. The Kuczynskis and the Sirnises were treacherous families made for each other, and Hollis was repeatedly to avoid taking effective action against any of them.

Lawn Road contained a large block of apartments, already housing the highly successful KGB agent Arnold Deutsch, an Austrian who was to be heavily involved in the recruitment of Philby and other traitors. The area was not just a nest of spies, but a rookery, though "vulturery" would be more apt. So many proven Soviet agents and recruiters lived and operated in or near the Lawn Road apartments that MI5 could hardly have been unaware of it yet never interfered effectively with their activities.

On July 29, 1936, the Kuczynskis were joined by their thirty-two-year-old only son, Jurgen, who had been such a prominent Communist in Germany that the Home Office had a file about him extending back to June 1931. An MI5 entry dated March 25, 1937, even noted that he was a Soviet agent and that he "had been in touch with members of the Soviet Embassy in London." He, too, found accommodations in Lawn Road, with his staunchly Communist wife, Marguerite. Eventually, it transpired that he had been recruited to the GRU in Berlin by a Russian officer, had the code name Karo, and had visited Moscow at least twice. The Central Committee of the German Communist Party in exile (KPD) instructed him to become the political leader of the KPD's British branch, which was thoroughly subservient to the orders of the Soviet Communist Party. He soon did so. These Communist activities were known to MI5 at the time, as documents have now shown, one of them referring to him as a "rabid Bolshevik."

Early in 1937, the Lawn Road complex acquired another highly significant tenant—Colonel Simon Kremer, who, as the GRU defector Krivitsky was to inform MI5, had been posted to the Soviet Union's London embassy for intelligence purposes. A distinguished Red Army soldier aged thirty-seven, he had been selected by the GRU chief for the

London post. Why did Kremer, who had his wife and two children with him, choose to live in the Lawn Road complex? It would seem to be more than coincidence that Jurgen Kuczynski, with whom he was to be involved in major espionage activities, should already live there. It was not only convenient but carried a built-in excuse for their association—they were neighbors. They were also both Jewish. So the possibility that Kuczynski arranged the accommodations on GRU instructions presents itself, especially in view of the historic consequences. Whatever the details, MI5's failure to pay any effective attention to Krivitsky's warning about Kremer was to prove disastrous to Britain and America and hugely beneficial to the Soviet Union.

A file entry on October 5, 1939, referred to a report that Jurgen Kuczynski was also assisting another prominent German refugee, Hans Kahle, in "running an espionage system." Kahle, who had commanded a Communist brigade in the Spanish Civil War, had first moved to Paris, where as an MI5 document states, he managed the Comintern bureau to promote revolution, before seeking refuge in London.

Following further suspect activities, a Home Office warrant was imposed on Jurgen and Marguerite, so that their mail could be intercepted and read, as it was for years. The records state, however, that they were never subjected to surveillance or any telephone check.

Meanwhile, Melita Norwood had become friendly with Jurgen and other members of the Kuczynski family, a situation that would become of great significance to her future espionage. In 1934, when she was twenty-two, she had become a secretary working in the British Non-Ferrous Metals Research Association, which accumulated research reports on aluminum and other lightweight metals. She was based in the main office in London and, already an ardent Communist, was recruited to Soviet intelligence by another member of the British Communist Party. She was trained to photograph documents that might be useful to the Soviet aircraft industry and supplied them to a courier, usually through *duboks*.

A note in Robert Kuczynski's MI5 file, dated November 23, 1939, shortly after World War II began, described him as "dangerous" because he was "doing his best to spread defeatism by running down everything British and praising everything Russian," though Stalin was then an ally of Hitler, having joined him in the cynical pact that had triggered the war. Early in 1940, an MI5 entry described Jurgen as "a very dangerous person, violently hostile to Britain," for which reason he had been interned by the Home Office on January 20. He did not remain interned for long, however. Influential left-wingers masterminded by a Labour MP, D. N. Pritt—a prominent lawyer who, according to KGB archives, was a Soviet agent—bombarded the home secretary so persistently that he gave way.

On April 4, 1940, the MI5 officer Guy Liddell recorded a summary of evidence against Jurgen in his diary. Another entry described how he had brought the entire funds of the KPD out of Germany and was using the interest to finance Communist propaganda. Nevertheless, the deemed dangerous GRU agent was released from internment and enemy aliens restrictions two weeks later—in time for him to be instrumental in recruiting one of the most damaging spies of all time, a fellow German refugee named Klaus Fuchs.

On September 9—just one month after that recruitment—Dick White, quoting from a source code-named H, who was a friend of Jurgen's, gullibly accepted H's view that Kuczynski was just a "Communist intellectual and a fellow-traveller with Moscow," in spite of all the previous evidence on file. This was, presumably, Hollis's view, too, for he rarely disagreed with White and, as the expert on communism, influenced his judgment.

Though there are references to Hollis in the Kuczynski files so far released, showing that he was informed and involved, he left any suggestions to his assistant, Millicent Bagot (B4b2), and appears to have recorded few opinions on Jurgen. Among other MI5 officers, Bagot in particular, serious suspicion about Jurgen remained. Quoting information from a source, the file described him as "one of Moscow's most brilliant and dangerous propagandists," while another stated that "he is obsessed by a fanatical hatred of Britain and the British Empire." On November 23, 1940, Bagot therefore wrote to the Home Office, saying that Jurgen Kuczynski should be reinterned. Hollis (B4) initialed the file statement recording this but made no comment. Kuczynski remained free.

Recently, GRU archives cited in the Russian book *The GRU and the Atomic Bomb* have revealed that Jurgen was a much more significant agent than had been appreciated, and MI5's failure to monitor his activities is all the more reprehensible on that account.

Jurgen's wife, Marguerite, also served the GRU cause. Her MI5 file shows that she was "deeply involved in Comintern activity before and during the war" and provided money "for communist interests." Eventually, Jurgen was to admit to some of his nefarious espionage activities in his memoirs, when safely back in East Germany after the war, naming Claud Cockburn as "a comrade who knew thousands of diplomatic secrets." After securing a traveling scholarship at Oxford in 1927, Cockburn had studied in Berlin and Vienna, becoming fluent in German, and was a natural Communist comrade for Kuczynski. The relationship confirmed Cockburn's GRU connections.

Jurgen's younger sister, Brigitte, who had been born in 1910 in Berlin, had joined the German Communist Party and studied economics at the University of Heidelberg. She was arrested by the Nazis after the KPD was outlawed by Hitler when he became chancellor. After her release, she moved to Switzerland in 1933 and became a postgraduate student at the University of Basel in the Faculty of Philosophy, securing her PhD in 1934 cum laude. In Switzerland, she was in touch with other revolutionaries operating there, according to Jurgen's memoirs. Brigitte joined her parents in London in late 1935, perhaps having been posted there by the GRU, as, within a few months, on July 4, 1936, aged twenty-five, she secured British nationality by marrying Anthony Gordon Lewis, a research student only nineteen years old. As will be seen, the GRU was to require her elder sister Ursula to use the same device for espionage purposes.

Brigitte had quickly found separate accommodations in Hampstead, where she "first came to MI5 notice in November 1936 as a communist," and again in May 1938, by which time she had moved to one of the Lawn Road apartments, being noted as propaganda secretary of the St. Pancras branch of the British Communist Party. This was the branch to which Cockburn belonged, and it would have been her duty to liaise closely with him because of his access to the columns of the *Daily Worker, The Week,* and other journals to which he contributed. This further link of Cockburn with the Kuczynskis and with the GRU could have been of considerable significance concerning Hollis.

Brigitte is named as a member of the massive GRU series of spy rings operating in Western Europe—the *Rote Kapelle*—in the CIA handbook on that conspiracy. She eventually became a leading figure in the British Communist Party, in charge of the influential Adelaide ward of the Hampstead branch. Her MI5 file recorded "connections with undercover British communists," which may have been a gross understatement. Pursuing the misbelief that Russian intelligence would never employ such an open Communist as an agent, MI5 missed the fact that she recruited a young Briton to the GRU in 1938 and a more important one in April 1939, as will be described. When her brother, Jurgen, had arrived, it was she who had introduced him to the German Communist group. I have discovered witness evidence that she was to play a major role in the Hollis saga.

In December 1940, the U.S. embassy asked MI5 for a list of foreign Communists residing in Great Britain who were "considered dangerous" because some of them might try to enter the United States. Providing the list was now Hollis's responsibility, Jane Archer having left MI5 by that time. I have a copy of the list, sent to the Americans on December 26, and not one of the Kuczynskis was among the twenty Communists named, though both father and son had been specifically described in the MI5 files as "dangerous."

The omission of Jurgen was especially odd, in view of the existing MI5 description of him as "very dangerous" and his open friendship with prominent British Communists who were advocating revolution, such as Claud Cockburn and Cecil Day-Lewis, both of whom are named in Jurgen's memoirs as friends. The danger list had included Hans Kahle, who has recently been confirmed as an agent in GRU archives, and a woman named Hanna Klopstech, but as will be seen, both were able to continue to serve the GRU unhindered. Making all allowances for hindsight, the deliberate exclusion of Robert and Jurgen Kuczynski from the list supplied to the United States by MI5 constitutes a serious anomaly demanding explanation.

The eldest Kuczynski daughter, Ursula, was none other than the professional GRU agent and radio operator code-named Sonia. Jurgen, Sonia, and Brigitte were to operate as a pro-Russian team of three—a ruthless GRU troika that would inflict at least as much damage on Britain and America as the better-known KGB group commonly called the Cambridge Five. Sonia was to attribute the astonishing lack of action against her to the possible existence of a protective hand inside MI5. The same might be said of the lack of effective action against all the Kuczynskis.

The extraordinary extent to which this family was allowed to commit treachery of the most dangerous degree over so many years was to become one of the most inscrutable security scandals of the war and postwar periods. As documents show, MI5—and Hollis in particular— knew that the Kuczynski family was at the heart of the German Communist Party activity in Great Britain, and it was certainly his responsibility to keep an eye on them and counter them. Instead, they appeared to have been given protection. Five of them were active GRU agents, and none was arrested. As the official statement issued with the 2005 releases remarked concerning Jurgen, "It is clear that even at this early stage [1939] the possibility of Kuczynski being involved in espionage was acknowledged. Yet, except for a postal warrant, little effort seems to have been expended on the case."

CHAPTER 11

Traitors to Order

—

LIKE THE GERMAN COMMUNIST PARTY, THE AUSTRIAN COMmunist Party chose Great Britain as a safe base for its activities, treacherous if necessary, to assist the Soviet Union and to make preparations for a Communist Austria one day. At least three of its leaders were on the MI5 list entitled "Foreign Communists Considered Dangerous" supplied to the FBI in December 1940 but none of them was an active KGB or GRU agent. By contrast, one who was, a woman of lasting significance in the annals of espionage with massive impact on Hollis's career, was omitted from the list, though she had been subjected to close surveillance over many years.

She was Edith Tudor Hart, who in KGB documents was code-named Strela but was sometimes referred to, transparently, as Edith. She was a Jewess, born in Vienna in 1908 with the surname Suschitzky, her father being a radical left-winger who ran a bookshop, a common cover for Soviet agents. She trained as a teacher and traveled to England at age seventeen to work in a kindergarten and to learn the language. After two years, she returned to Vienna to study photography and joined the Austrian Communist Party, which, being banned, had to operate underground. She was quickly spotted and recruited by the Austrian KGB agent Arnold Deutsch and completed subversive missions of still unknown purpose in Paris and London in 1929.

The files on her show that because of her extreme Communist

stance, MI5 and Special Branch had been interested in Edith Suschitzky from early 1930, when she was living in London with a Welsh Communist medical student, Alexander Tudor Hart. Her mail was intercepted, and after taking part in a rally in Trafalgar Square in October 1930, she was expelled and returned to Vienna, where she was employed as a photographer by the Soviet TASS news agency. In August 1933, Tudor Hart, then fully qualified, went to Vienna, married Edith, and returned with her to London in June 1934, when she had to be admitted because she had become British. She set up a photography studio.

In the 1930s, both the KGB and the GRU had developed programs to recruit young Britons of the far left persuasion who were likely to achieve successful careers in various government services, where they would have access to information of value to the Soviet Union's objectives. The planners at the two Moscow Centers realized that such investments might not produce results for many years, but in terms of a worldwide Communist revolution with the Soviet Union in control, they knew that they were in for a long haul. The heaviest concentrations of young potential spies were at the universities, and Cambridge and Oxford were the prime targets because—as KGB documents record—the recruiters had realized that, in those days, it was easier to reach the higher echelons of government service with an "Oxbridge" degree and background. It is a tribute to the Soviet planners that so many of their most successful spies were recruited before they secured positions with access to secrets.

One of these was Harold "Kim" Philby, who had become an ardent Communist while at Cambridge University in 1933 and had then visited Vienna, where he was active in subversive operations organized by Austrian Communist extremists. In the process, he became involved with a Jewish Communist, Alice (Litzi) Friedman, whom he married in February 1934 to give her British nationality. They moved to London, where Litzi contacted Edith Tudor Hart, with whom she had been closely associated for years in Austria.

Edith was soon impressed by Philby's zeal for the Soviet cause, and after referring to the KGB authorities for permission, she organized a conspiratorial meeting with his first controller. This happened to be Arnold Deutsch, a fellow Austrian who had been posted to London in 1934 as an illegal and was living in the Lawn Road apartments in the Hampstead area. In the early summer of 1934, Edith escorted Philby to a bench in Regent's Park, where Deutsch was waiting, and handed him over. After two weeks, while Deutsch consulted the Center, they met again, and as Philby revealed in a lecture to KGB officers in Moscow in July 1977 (when he exulted in the damage he had inflicted on the United States), within a few minutes he had become a dedicated KGB agent for the rest of his life.

Though he had no access to information, no job, and no prospects apart from occasional journalism, he was told that he must try to gain entry into MI6. As he eventually would put this extraordinary requirement to his KGB audience, "from the very beginning, my first contact—and his two successors—impressed on me the importance of aiming at the British Secret Service."

Shortly after his own recruitment to KGB service, Philby was asked to make a list of Cambridge contemporaries who might be willing to serve and named seven possible recruits, the prime choice being Donald Maclean, a committed Marxist and open Communist already in line to enter the Foreign Office. On a trip to London, in December 1934, Maclean met Philby, who propositioned him. After only two days of consideration, Maclean accepted the offer unconditionally and was introduced to Deutsch. He did not know whether he was working for the Comintern or Soviet intelligence, but he did not care, being willing to become one of the vilest traitors to further his distorted ideals. Instructed to appear as if he had become disenchanted with communism, Maclean began to avoid old Marxist friends and any of the political discussions that had so absorbed him. In dispatches to and from the KGB Center, he was given the code name Orphan, and later Lyric, and gained entry to the Foreign Office in October 1935. He was destined to serve as a diplomat in Washington, where, as KGB records show, he inflicted incalculable damage.

The last name on Philby's recommended list had been Guy Burgess. He had been placed last because, though gifted intellectually and a committed Marxist, his behavior was so dominated by his flagrant homosexuality and addiction to alcohol that it was dangerously unpredictable. As I was to witness in various restaurants, Burgess could not resist drawing attention to himself, a habit hardly conducive to a spy's survival. Nevertheless, he was the second to be recruited. It seems that being a close friend of Maclean's, Burgess had seen through his sudden divorce from communism and had induced him to admit it was a sham. This was reported to his spymasters, who decided that he would be safer in the KGB fold.

Burgess met Deutsch early in 1935, just when he was leaving Cambridge to live in London, and was recruited primarily to bring him under some degree of Soviet control. In fact, the KGB had landed a major asset, who would produce a stream of valuable information from a succession of posts he was to occupy in the British Broadcasting Corporation (BBC), with secret services, and in various branches of the Foreign Office. His brash behavior turned out to be an advantage because nobody could believe that any professional organization would employ such a disreputable creature as a spy. He was given the code name Mädchen, meaning "Girl" (perhaps in view of his homosexuality), and set to work at talent spotting and developing "confidential contacts" among his many friends.

Like Philby, Burgess made an obvious pretense to have broken with communism and secured a job with the Conservative Party before joining the BBC and, later, a branch of MI6 prior to entering the Foreign Office. In reality, he remained so zealous that Deutsch reported that "the essence of Burgess's existence was his clandestine work for the cause." He, too, was to serve the Soviet interest in Washington.

The fourth Cambridge spy to be recruited was Anthony Blunt, who, after his exposure in 1979, said that his friend Burgess persuaded him to "join in his work for the Russians" in January 1937. Blunt was another promiscuous homosexual, but that does not seem to have been a factor affecting his decision. He had embraced Marxism but was not a committed Communist. Exactly how he had drifted into the psychological condition that induced him to become an ardent traitor is explained in an autobiographical sketch he wrote for the KGB in 1943 that was released in 1997. The situation in Germany and the impact of the Marxism already embraced by so many intellectual friends convinced him that communism was the way forward. Through Burgess, he was introduced to Deutsch, who operated unhindered by MI5, and he agreed to work to order for the Comintern in "the cause of peace." As Blunt was then a Cambridge don, aged twenty-nine, Deutsch saw him as a well-placed talent spotter for other agents and confidential contacts. He was given the code name Tony, then Johnson, and later Yan. As with Burgess and Philby, his subsequent behavior over many years was to demonstrate the power of the Communist ideal to induce a wellborn, intelligent man to betray family, friends, and his nation, unreservedly and in perpetuity, to benefit an alien country.

During his first two years, Blunt recruited two other Cambridge students, the American Michael Straight, code-named Nigel, and Leo Long, who was code-named Ralph. Straight agreed to assist "the cause" in the spring of 1937, but on returning to the United States, proved to be of small consequence. On the other hand, Long, a working-class student of modern languages committed to communism, was destined to supply a stream of valuable information.

Earlier in 1937, Blunt had made a much more significant contribution to espionage history by introducing John Cairncross, a Cambridge acquaintance, to Burgess. Cairncross was an outstanding student of languages and French history who secured top place in an examination for entry to the Foreign Office, where he had begun working in October 1936. Coming from a modest Scottish family, he was strongly left wing, and Blunt's KGB task was to lure him back to Cambridge on the pretext of meeting a prominent writer. He found that Blunt had another guest, Burgess, who sounded him out and, once back in London, arranged for Cairncross to be introduced to a KGB controller. Cairncross's contribution from the several highly secret posts he eventually occupied was to be immensely significant.

In September 1937, Blunt joined the Warburg Institute in London as editor for its publications on art history. He also lectured at the Courtauld Institute of Art there, both positions providing excellent cover for his political activities. In June 1940, he was to join MI5, where he betrayed every secret on which he could lay his hands. The whole Cambridge group had sprung from the original spotting of Philby by Edith Tudor Hart. She is credited to that effect in the KGB archives.

Edith had also been busy talent spotting among Oxford students. In 1936, she had noted an undergraduate who became an important spy under the code name Scott, whose identity has not yet been established. He developed into a successful recruiter himself and became the pivotal figure of the Oxford group, about which little has been disclosed. KGB documents have shown that he recommended concentration on students likely to go far in the Church because of the influence they could exert, especially if they became bishops. While Hollis had left Oxford in the previous decade, this ecclesiastical interest by Soviet intelligence strengthens the possibility that the GRU recruiters in Shanghai might have been keen to recruit a bishop's son. Scott remained active during Hollis's time in MI5 and is believed to have been still alive in 1990.

Throughout the 1930s, Edith had been subjected to intermittent surveillance but came to the special notice of Scotland Yard's Special Branch in March 1938, when inquiries into the Glading espionage case showed that "certain cameras and photographic equipment in Glading's possession had been purchased through Edith Tudor Hart's business." She had clearly been involved in the espionage, if only peripherally, but though MI5 was informed immediately, no effective action ensued.

Her name appears again in a letter to MI5 from Special Branch on July 23, 1938, about a group of Austrian Communist refugees, which she was serving as a link with the British Communist Party. The leader of the group was Engelbert Broda, a scientist who was highly suspect as a possible Soviet spy and recruiter. By October 1938, Hollis was Broda's case officer and was in regular contact with Special Branch about him. One letter from Hollis, dated October 31, revealed his own "liberal" tendency, which was soon to lead to catastrophic decisions about much more dangerous Soviet spies. In it, he suggested that the group of Austrians to which Broda and Tudor Hart belonged appeared to be "social democratic, rather than communist." He also assured Special Branch that he had been unable to trace any untoward activities on Broda's part. A letter from Hollis dated May 11, 1940, asked the MI5 surveillance team to keep watch on one of Broda's contacts at a special place. They did so for three days, but the man never appeared—a common feature of many cases handled by Hollis.

On KGB instructions, Philby joined the Royal Central Asian Society, reporting to Deutsch on people he met there and concentrated on pumping a bibulous old school friend, Tom Wylie, who was the resident clerk in the War Office, living in an apartment there. After a few other routine tasks, including spying on his own father, a famous Arabist, and visiting Germany, he was sent to Spain to cover the civil war as a freelance journalist, funded by the KGB after a brief course on codes and other tradecraft in Paris in January 1937. Upon his return to London in May, Philby induced *The Times* to employ him as a freelancer in Spain, which he reached via Paris in June. He covered the early part of World War II in France for *The Times* and was suddenly summoned to the War Office for an interview. In July 1940, he joined Section D of MI6, where Burgess, who may have recommended him, was already installed. It had taken him six years. Burgess had also cultivated Wylie, who was homo-sexual, and may have recommended him for work in Section D.

Edith's husband had moved to Spain to run a field hospital for the Communists in the civil war, and on his return, they were divorced, though she had given birth to a son in 1936. She claimed that she had been left penniless, but by specializing in child portraits, she became re-spected for her photographic work. She remained highly active on be-half of the KGB in 1939, as released Russian documents show. In late 1940, she seems to have helped to put Anthony Blunt, then in MI5, and possibly other KGB spies in touch with a new controller based in the So-viet embassy. In one of his reports to the KGB Center, Blunt mentioned that he knew who "Edith" was and that she knew his name but they had never met. By that time, Hollis was fully responsible for her case, and the surveillance teams were reporting to him through his assistant, Mil-licent Bagot.

By March 1941, Edith was elected a member of the Central Commit-tee of the Austrian Communist Party in exile and became the subject of continuing surveillance and mail interception since she was on such friendly terms with the leaders. Again, through 1942 and 1943, watchers saw and heard much, but nothing of significance. Edith's MI5 files record details of her shopping expeditions, lunches, taxi rides, whom she met, and what she was wearing, down to the color of her stockings, but, as with the surveillance of Cockburn, she met nobody of consequence while she was under surveillance.

Files record that on September 13, 1944, she telephoned the notori-ous Communist Party official, Comintern agent, and KGB courier Bob Stewart to arrange a meeting, but nothing of consequence was learned. It is now clear from KGB documents that he was a regular courier be-tween members of the Cambridge group and other spies and the Soviet embassy. Blunt, for example, reported in 1943 how he was working with Stewart in the absence of his usual controller. He was passing him his own MI5 information and that of Burgess and Long. Stewart may also have served the GRU as a courier, because, as will be seen, he was in regular contact with Sonia's sister Brigitte, who was a GRU agent. As he was officially responsible for liaison between the Communist Party and the Soviet embassy, he had legitimate reason for going to her home, as she was a prominent party official. Jurgen Kuczynski was also friendly with Stewart and in regular contact, as he records in his memoirs.

The MI5 *Official History* and Stewart's own file make it clear that Hollis knew about him in his early wartime capacity as a Comintern agent, especially after MI5 managed to bug Communist Party headquarters in London. The three volumes of Stewart's MI5 file open in 1920 with a statement that, then aged forty-three, he was a Communist and a secret agent of the "Third International." In 1932, he had been elected to the Central Committee of the Communist Party of Great Britain, and thereafter, his movements were monitored by Special Branch, while his office was bugged. Stewart was never approached by MI5 until after Blunt's confession to being a spy in 1963. Then being eighty-six, he simply refused any assistance.

Both Stewart and Edith Tudor Hart, who had also joined the CPGB, benefited from the degree to which Hollis—and the rest of MI5— continued to operate in the belief that both the GRU and the KGB always insisted that their agents should have no contact whatever with the Communist Party of the country in which they were working. As Wright later admitted, "We had missed the greatest CPGB secret of all." Both Philby and Blunt had advised the KGB of this self-delusive policy, so the Center was able to operate on pragmatic lines.

Edith had committed much of her mischief before Hollis joined MI5, but she had continued after he became responsible for overseeing subversive Communists, and she was never seriously investigated. Nor was Litzi Philby, yet another female traitor missed by Hollis. It has only recently been confirmed by KGB documents that Litzi was also an accredited KGB agent who was paid expenses. She, too, had been recruited by Edith and served under the code name Mary.

Litzi had separated from Philby in 1936 and returned to Vienna, but only to bring her parents to the safety of London, using her British citizenship. After a spell in Paris, she returned in 1938 and remained in contact with Edith throughout the war. A 1939 KGB document refers to payment for the pair of them. While cohabiting with a prominent German Communist in London, Litzi became friendly with Donald Maclean and in July 1939 sent a detailed report about him to the KGB.

Again, working in the false belief that open Communists were unlikely to be spies, Hollis's section failed to discover that Litzi also served as a courier between Burgess, Maclean, and Blunt and the Soviet embassy at times when other couriers were unavailable. In spite of Hollis's close working relationship with Philby through most of the war, he did not appear to know, at least officially, that Litzi had been Philby's wife—and still was legally—or if he did, he kept quiet about it. Officially divorced by Philby in 1946, Litzi married her German Communist living in East Berlin.

Edith and Litzi did all they could to betray the country that had given them safe refuge from the Nazis, and like the spies they helped to recruit and assisted, they did it with relish.

CHAPTER 12

In Charge of "Soviet Espionage"

THE RAPID EXPANSION OF MI5 HAD CAUSED A MANAGEMENT crisis that dismayed the prime minister, Winston Churchill. As a result, on May 28, 1940, MI5 was placed under overall control by a body called the Security Executive, headed by Lord Swinton, a politician. Its long-serving director general, Sir Vernon Kell, was dismissed on June 10, and a temporary replacement, Brigadier O. A. ("Jasper") Harker, a former head of B Division, was appointed in July, with Guy Liddell being placed in full control of B Division, responsible for all counterespionage.

Once the German bombing of London began, it soon became evident that the bulk of MI5 would have to move to the countryside, and the Blenheim estate, at Woodstock, near Oxford, had been requisitioned for the purpose. Most of MI5 was evacuated to Blenheim Palace during September–October 1940, but the staff had been aware of the projected move before that when parts of the registry—the accumulated files and dossiers vital to its work—had been photographed, the copies being sent there piecemeal in advance. That proved to have been a wise precaution, because MI5's offices in Wormwood Scrubs were bombed in September 1940, causing a fire. Credit for having suggested it was given to Hollis, as evidence of his innocence, by Anthony Glees, but the MI5 *Official History* shows that the idea had really been generated by Lord Rothschild, as Glees now accepts.

In its new location, the registry occupied part of the ground floor of Blenheim Palace, the home of the Duke of Marlborough, while the upper floors housed other departments. Some sections, including Hollis's, were in huts in the grounds. The small headquarters staff and those responsible for active counterespionage against the Germans remained in London, in St. James's Street. The MI5 staff had been expanded to 860 by mid-1941, 233 being officers. Most of them were at Blenheim, which was referred to in MI5 messages as "the Country," while its address was Box 500, Oxford.

Domestically, the Blenheim staff lived mainly in Oxford, billeted in various colleges or, as in Hollis's case, in rented houses. Most of them were ferried to and from Blenheim by red double-decker buses, which, according to a witness who worked there, became the subject of banter among the Oxford residents, who quickly learned the passengers' profession. Hollis and his wife lived at 29a Charlbury Road, from which he commuted by car to Blenheim, nine miles away.

Shortly before moving to Blenheim, Hollis had become the proud father of a son, Adrian, who was to be his only child. His wife had gone temporarily to the relative safety of the West Country with her parents and gave birth in a nursing home close to her husband's old school in Clifton, Bristol. On Adrian's birth certificate, Hollis described his occupation as "attached to War Office staff," as MI5 required.

Liddell's diaries show that in November 1940, Jane Archer, who was also then at Blenheim, had a major altercation with Harker over policy. The rough-tongued Jane thought Harker incompetent, said so, and was dismissed for insubordination. Liddell recorded that the office had lost "an extremely valuable officer." She had served for twenty-four years and "was far more efficient than most of the men." Jane's departure was hugely to Hollis's advantage, as it immediately elevated him to MI5's acknowledged expert on communism and Soviet affairs, for which he was to receive a crucial promotion that almost certainly would have gone to her.

At the same time, in November, Colonel Sir David Petrie, formerly of the Indian police, who was then with the Intelligence Corps, was instructed to carry out a survey of the situation in MI5. Following his report, in February 1941, he was appointed director general in April, and MI5 recovered most of its independence. Lord Swinton, who remained in charge of general policy, had already advised that B Division (counterespionage) should be divided into three parts, B, E, and F. Instructions to do that were issued on April 22, 1941, and in August, Hollis, who had held the position of B4 for more than a year, became part of the new F Division, which according to the MI5 *Official History* was responsible for keeping watch on "subversive activities" of all kinds. After more than two years of service, and with his health still in doubt, Hollis was promoted to the rank of assistant director, working under the much admired officer Jack Curry, who was eventually to write the *Official History*. The move greatly increased his access to sensitive information of potential interest to the Soviet Union.

F Division was divided into four sections, of which Hollis was in charge of F2. This was subdivided into three subsections, F2a, F2b, and F2c, each headed by a more junior officer. Of these, F2c was—or should have been—the most important, because the *Official History* confirms unequivocally that through it, Hollis became responsible for "Soviet espionage." It specifically states, "Mr. Hollis was in charge of F2c [Soviet espionage]," which meant countering the espionage effort being mounted by the KGB and the GRU. This is a prime admission by MI5, because some of Hollis's most ardent supporters have claimed that he could not be blamed for MI5's failure to detect Soviet spies such as Blunt, Philby, and the rest, as that was always the sole responsibility of B Division. They have argued that the simple fact that Hollis had never headed a Soviet counterespionage section is strong evidence in his favor, because a spy would have tried to insinuate himself into just such a position. Now, the certainty that, whether by chance or maneuver, Hollis did hold exactly that position could be construed as strong evidence against him, as it suited the GRU's requirements to perfection. As will be seen, whether through coincidence or not, the date of his takeover of Soviet counterespionage—August 1941—was one of extraordinary significance, for it marked the recruitment of one of the GRU's most damaging spies—Klaus Fuchs.

As the *Official History* explains, B Division had become overwhelmed with work, as it was rightly concentrating its wartime effort on the immediate threat posed by German, Italian, and Japanese spies. It was for that reason that the main effort against Soviet espionage and what the *Official History* describes as "Russian Intelligence" had been passed to Hollis's sections. This included responsibility for monitoring the activities of Russian GRU and KGB officers posing as diplomats, trade representatives, and other officials. A document from the KGB archives has confirmed that. It is a letter sent by Philby to the KGB Center after a long meeting with Hollis in which the latter had described his work, telling Philby that he dealt with "political movements and Soviet espionage."

If Hollis was Elli, his MI5 label "i/c Soviet espionage" was tragically grotesque, for the title could not then have been more literal.

A Soviet document has revealed that in 1941, the KGB spy Blunt, then installed inside MI5 since June 1940, reported to Moscow that MI5 was making no effort to watch the movements of intelligence officers attached to the Soviet embassy. This basic omission, which astonished the KGB Center, may have already been standard MI5 practice when Hollis took over Soviet counterespionage, as the Foreign Office was opposed to the surveillance of Soviet "diplomats," especially after Stalin became an ally. Hollis continued this negative stance, to the huge advantage of the KGB, the GRU, and the British traitors they were running.

Through F2a, Hollis was responsible for overseeing "the policy and activities of the British Communist Party," of which the potentially dangerous members included Claud Cockburn. The diaries of Guy Liddell show, repeatedly, the depth of the suspicion against Cockburn or anyone closely associated with him, while the new director general continued his predecessor's personal interest in the case. In that respect, Hollis's silence about his former friendship with Cockburn compounded his self-imposed risk.

During the early part of the war, the Security Executive had wanted to prosecute Cockburn for sedition, yet in a potted description of the British Communist Party and its activists prepared by Hollis in late 1940, Cockburn was described in rather flattering terms as "a journalist of outstanding ability," being "pre-eminent" among those on the *Daily Worker* (where Cockburn had helped to install his Spanish Civil War friend the GRU agent Hans Kahle as military correspondent).

The Security Executive had repeatedly asked MI5 for the necessary evidence for a prosecution, but Hollis had insisted that he could not provide any that would stand up in court. This may have been true, but it had also been against his interests that his past association with such a notorious Comintern activist might become known. Eventually, the war cabinet decided to suppress both *The Week* and the *Daily Worker*, with or without evidence, and the file on that event shows that Hollis was definitely the MI5 officer required to deal with the case. They were closed down on January 21, 1941, and remained that way until a few months after the invasion of Russia in June.

Through subsection F2b, Hollis continued his previous responsibilities for overseeing the activities of the Comintern and of Communist refugees, with released documents bearing his name or initials showing his personal interest. The *Official History* makes a point of stating that F2b was responsible for securing intelligence concerning the Comintern and its various ramifications, "including that about alien Communists resident in or visiting this country." This statement is of particular significance with respect to the Kuczynskis.

As part of the general expansion of MI5, Hollis secured the assistance of a former Oxford University drinking companion, Roger Fulford, with whom he had kept in touch. Fulford is cited by Anthony Glees as confirming that Hollis's policy was to know as much as possible about suspects and their activities but to take no overt action if it could be avoided.

The deference quickly paid to Hollis as the Soviet expert greatly increased his influence, especially over Dick White, who, on his own admission to me, had never encountered dedicated Communists, as Hollis had, at university and in China. Repeatedly, both Liddell and White were to defer to Hollis's recommendations concerning the Soviet threat, with deplorable consequences.

When Curry was moved to other work in October 1941, Hollis became assistant director in full charge of F Division (ADF), increasing his access and authority still further. The abrupt departure of Jane Archer from MI5 had certainly favored Hollis, for, being so much more senior, she would have been the obvious choice to head F Division.

Hollis also recruited a strong left-winger, Kemball Johnston, while others, such as Hugh Shillito, were allotted to him. His teams were small, but for surveillance work he could call on MI5's Watcher Service—a substantial group of men and women trained in the art of observing the activities of suspects without being noticed themselves—and on the detectives of Scotland Yard's Special Branch. At that stage, the surveillance task was supportable because the number of Russians known to be intelligence officers, or likely to be, was quite low. The KGB had only about five in London and the GRU about ten. Events and Russian archives would show that they were able to act with stunning success and without effective restraint or, usually, none at all. The services of a special department of the Post Office were also available to Hollis for the interception of letters and the tapping of telephones.

In 1983, White assured me in a letter that Hollis and F Division had "never been responsible for Russian counter-espionage, which had always been part of B Division." With the now officially confirmed transfer of responsibility of such an important function to F Division in 1941, it is difficult to accept White's statement as a lapse of memory. In his old age, and with a reputation beyond suspicion, he seemed prepared to accept responsibility for any incompetence himself in the general "establishment" drive to prove that his protégé had not been disloyal.

If Hollis was a spy, his ready access to information of prime interest to Moscow had increased with each promotion. Nevertheless, in 1983, the investigative author Nigel West claimed, in support of Hollis's innocence, that "at no time did he head a Soviet counter-espionage section which would have been a natural target for a Soviet agent. . . . The scenario does not fit Hollis," he declared. The *Official History* has now shown this belief to be completely false. Released MI5 documents prove that when the agency was reorganized after the war ended, Hollis continued to have a major role in the much expanded counterespionage effort against the Soviet threat—and it was a role he held until 1948. As B1, in the rejigged B Division, he worked directly under Dick White, then Director B. The scenario fitted Hollis exactly.

CHAPTER 13

Secrets by the Bagful

—

IN 1993, KGB DOCUMENTS BECAME AVAILABLE AS A RESULT OF a financial deal between American book publishers and the post-Soviet foreign intelligence service, the SVR (*Sluzhba Vneshni Razvedke*). The SVR saw little point in maintaining secrecy about cases that were already self-evident and well publicized, and it declassified archival documents about the Cambridge spies in particular, some of the money going to the KGB Veterans Association.

Such releases, especially where payment is required, need to be examined critically, because of the continuing danger of self-serving disinformation or concocted forgeries, but there can be no doubt about the authenticity of original documents that were supplied by the British spies themselves, often in their own handwriting, and which rest in their individual files in the KGB archives. They prove that from 1941 onward, when Hollis was in charge of Soviet counterespionage, the Cambridge University spies sent so much material to the KGB Center, mainly in the form of photographed secret documents, that a group of officers there suspected they were too good to be true. They argued that the British could not possibly be so lax. They could not see how security officials in MI5, MI6, and the Foreign Office could have failed to notice if traitorous Soviet agents were carrying out so many documents from highly secret departments. Many of the documents were top secret, and they were never missed—or if they were, nobody in authority cared. Small wonder that the KGB Center began to suspect that the Cambridge spies were plants deliberately supplying so much false information that it would saturate the Center's capability to deal with it all.

The exploits of Donald Maclean in particular were nothing short of astonishing, especially as they involved a woman whose complicity had been totally unknown to MI5 until 1993. Her name was Kitty Harris, and though millions of words had been written about Maclean's espionage career, nobody seemed to have been aware of her crucial role in it.

Kitty was born in London in 1900 of immigrant Jews who had fled Russia to avoid the czar's pogroms. The family moved to Canada and then to Chicago, where Kitty became not only an open Communist, but mistress of the most notorious American Communist, Earl Browder. After being recruited by the KGB, she went to China with Browder in 1928 and was posted to Great Britain for espionage duties in 1936 following intense training in Moscow. She began by running a London flat where the senior KGB officer who controlled Philby, Maclean, and Burgess could call to pick up the spoils and, on occasion, meet the spies safely. She also communicated with them through telephone signals such as ringing Philby's number and blowing twice into the mouthpiece. Then, after taking a course in photography, she was promoted to become Maclean's courier, meeting him first in Leicester Square on April 10, 1938. From then on, she received and photographed the stacks of reports, decoded diplomatic telegrams, and other secret documents that Maclean removed, almost daily, from the Foreign Office in Whitehall. Maclean took them to the flat so that they could be returned quickly.

Such a "safe house" served as a super*dubok*, being far safer than any open-air hiding place for messages or documents. The common use of safe houses by both GRU and KGB spy networks, which was completely missed by MI5, could have provided crucial clues to the behavior of other Soviet agents and their couriers, as will be seen. Obviously, it would have been a huge advantage to those running and using safe houses if the Center controlling them could be regularly assured through some insider source that the properties were not under MI5 surveillance.

Kitty's KGB dossier records that Maclean had utter contempt for Foreign Office and MI5 security. He assured her that, as the son of a former Cabinet minister, he could bamboozle any of the authorities if they ever questioned his removal of secret documents by claiming that he was working on them at home. If there were some that he had no right to remove, he would simply insist that he had put them in his briefcase by mistake and was certain that he would be believed. In fact, though he transmitted 4,593 documents to Moscow in his treacherous career—many of them involving prime American secrets—he was never questioned about any of them.

Dark-haired and petite, Kitty appealed to Maclean, who was then single, and she became his ardent lover, describing in her reports to the Moscow Center how Lyric required sex before and after every photographic session and sometimes in the middle of it! She was also suited to satisfy the psychological need for a confidante, which the traitor surely possessed because he was quick to inform her successor of his dangerous predicament.

Kitty was also marginally involved in Philby's crucial entry into MI6. Guy Burgess, who was working in the BBC, had been tasked to find a way of penetrating MI6 and had become friendly with an MI6 officer named David Footman. He suggested a radio program on a book written by Footman, who took the bait and, in return, later helped Burgess to join Section D of MI6, concerned with planning wartime sabotage operations abroad. Kitty was required to oversee and report on a meeting between Burgess and Footman in a London hotel. Once inside MI6, Burgess could help Philby join in 1940.

When Maclean was posted to the British embassy in Paris late in 1938, Kitty followed him, working with him there for eighteen months. In 1940, she was named as a Soviet agent by the senior GRU defector Walter Krivitsky, but the name rang no bells in MI5, and no effort seems to have been made to find her. This lack of action was especially curious because Kitty was also named in Jane Archer's list of "Soviet secret agents mentioned by Walter Krivitsky," along with the facts that she had been in London in 1936 and 1937 and, previously, had served as a courier for a major Soviet agent runner called Mally. Krivitsky had also insisted that there was a "Scotsman of good family" working as a Soviet mole in the Foreign Office, but the security authorities there considered the tip too vague to be pursued. Either MI5 decided against effective action on any of Krivitsky's leads or the information was deliberately stifled.

Kitty's sexual affair with Maclean ended in Paris early in 1940 when he met an American, Melinda Marling, whom he married, but she continued to work as his photographer and courier. With the German invasion of France in May, each had to escape separately, and their relationship ended completely.

The documents supplied by Maclean, which passed through Kitty's hands during the four years that she worked with him, filled forty-five boxes in the KGB archives, each containing more than three hundred pages. The hauls posed such a problem for the Soviet embassies in both London and Paris that he was eventually required to deliver his documents on Fridays to provide the whole weekend for copying.

While Maclean returned to London from Paris to be run by a different agent, Kitty moved to Moscow and in 1941 was assigned to America, where she became involved as a courier in the big Soviet spy ring that stole atomic bomb secrets in circumstances the KGB is not yet prepared to reveal. She also operated in Mexico, as deciphered KGB cables have confirmed.

There are further disclosures in the Kitty Harris files that could be relevant to the Hollis case. In 1927, when she had first been recruited to the GRU, she had been posted to Shanghai to begin her espionage career. The archives show that Kitty and Hollis shared friends there who are known to have been important Soviet spies. They may well have met in what an authorized book about her, by a former KGB officer, Igor Damaskin, describes as the "small goldfish bowl of the international community in Shanghai."

In 1946, when her health began to fail, Kitty was shipped to Russia, where she was dumped in Gorki, far out of Moscow, because she knew too much, "source protection" always being paramount. She was never allowed to meet Maclean after he had defected there in 1951, and she died in loneliness and penury in 1966.

With all such KGB releases, there is the need to appreciate that Soviet intelligence will always do what it can to burnish its own image by making MI5, and any other competing secret service, look incompetent, but the hard facts in Kitty's bulging files, some of which can be checked elsewhere, speak for themselves. The big question her case poses is, How many other Soviet agents completed their treachery without effective detection? And how many more may it suit the KGB and the GRU to reveal one day?

Like Maclean, the other Cambridge spies were self-drivers, achieving satisfaction as well as excitement from a sense of contribution. They were also free from interference. According to the KGB controller Yuri Modin in his book *My Five Cambridge Friends,* Burgess was bringing out so many Foreign Office documents for overnight photography that he and Modin began carrying identical suitcases, which they exchanged. On one occasion they were stopped by two policemen, but Burgess simply opened his suitcase and when the police realized that it contained nothing but papers, they saluted and departed!

Liddell's diaries confirm Burgess's close friendship with MI5 members, which enabled him to supply the KGB with MI5 secrets. They state, for example, that on April 11, 1941, Liddell, Hollis, and Valentine Vivian (from MI6) met "to discuss a project in which they agreed that Burgess might be used in the work." Entries in 1944 show that Burgess was visiting MI5 through his involvement in running a Swiss source code-named Orange. Burgess, who was also to operate in the United States, passed on every useful item that came his way, and the KGB archives show that during his espionage career, he handed over 1,600 documents.

Blunt's transfer from the army to MI5 in June 1940 was an unforeseeable bonanza for the KGB. Not only did he betray everything of significance in his own work, but, being entirely trusted, he was able to extract information from colleagues. Sir Dick White recalled to his biographer how Blunt would sit next to him at lunch in the MI5 canteen and talk about art but also discuss MI5's activities. He said that Blunt concentrated on those colleagues "preoccupied with sensitive issues connected with the communists and Russia." This interest led to Blunt's transfer to the counterespionage division, which was highly productive for the KGB. Internal security was so lax that Blunt was able to search the desks of colleagues during their lunch break and examine files to which he had no entitlement. White also remembered enjoying parties at private houses in the company of Blunt, Philby, and occasionally Burgess.

While serving in MI5 headquarters at 58 St. James's Street, Blunt met his controller, a Russian from the embassy, once a week, between nine and ten p.m. in different parts of London. He handed over his briefcase of documents to be photographed and received them back from the Russian early the following morning. On one occasion, when in the street with a Russian, he was questioned by a policeman, who examined his papers, which were ultrasecret German messages deciphered at Bletchley Park, the MI6 interception center in Buckinghamshire. On learning that he was from MI5, the policeman took no further action. Blunt's experience showed that wartime MI5 was the perfect internal environment for a spy—he did what he wished without raising a whiff of suspicion.

The number of secret documents, which were often thick files, attributed by the KGB to Blunt—referred to in the MI5 *Official History* as "Major Blunt"—is 1,771. They included American secrets of the greatest sensitivity, including plans for the D-Day landings.

Philby, who was to admit that he had achieved his greatest KGB success while working in Washington, delivered only 914 documents, though many of them were long and detailed, while he also supplied a great deal of secret information in letters and orally in his frequent meetings with his controllers.

The record number seems to have been held by John Cairncross, who smuggled out more than 5,800 documents from the various offices in which he worked. Cairncross, who deluded himself into believing that all he had done was to "fight fascism," though he continued his treachery after fascism had been eliminated, became private secretary to Lord Hankey late in 1940. As chairman of the wartime Scientific Advisory Committee, advising on which areas of research and development should be pursued, Hankey—and therefore Cairncross—had access to almost all documents concerning wartime scientific projects, including the names of the scientists involved. Cairncross gave the Russians copies of every sensitive document that came his way, including those about the atomic bomb project.

The total take from these five spies alone—17,526 classified documents—is a measure of the number of their meetings with Russians and emphasizes the enormousness of their treachery, which was far worse than ever suspected, and more may yet be revealed. The argument by some of Hollis's supporters that the traitors he missed did no great damage is blown away by these disclosures.

Hollis had inherited the Cambridge traitors, but they perpetrated their worst crimes during the war when he was "in charge of Soviet espionage." MI5 cannot be blamed for the incompetence of MI6 and the Foreign Office regarding their internal security, but it was responsible for the recruitment and continuing espionage of Blunt. The details of his treachery, as confirmed by his KGB files, show that internal security in MI5 was criminally negligent.

Possibly nothing would be known publicly about any of the Cambridge spies had not Maclean eventually been required to defect, following the American decipherment of a wartime KGB cable.

In deference to Cambridge University, readers should appreciate that it is now certain that spies were also recruited at Oxford University, by both the KGB and the GRU. The major culprit, code-named Scott, may have been the late Christopher Hill, the Communist historian who became master of Oxford's Balliol College. By failing to declare his membership in the British Communist Party, Hill worked in military intelligence and then in the Foreign Office during World War II. Because he was fluent in Russian, he was appointed head of the Russian desk in the Foreign Office in 1943 with the rank of major. His employment is a further testament of security incompetence by both the Foreign Office and MI5, because his membership of the Communist Party alone should have barred him. As will be seen, he would eventually confess to Anthony Glees that he had been "a Communist mole" during World War II.

Recruiters were also busy at other universities, such as London, where there were many open Communist students and recruitment to "the cause of peace" was rampant, as I witnessed myself as a student there. Officials of the KGB and the GRU rarely operated at the colleges, where they would have been too conspicuous and where, in fact, the vast majority of students wanted nothing to do with communism. They relied on talent spotters to name likely candidates among young Marxist-Leninists who were blindly convinced that the Communist Party, especially the Soviet Communist Party, could never be wrong. When these names, with brief descriptions, had been passed on to some KGB or GRU official, he or she would forward them to the relevant Center in Moscow, where they would be selected or rejected. Those selected would then be introduced to an experienced controller, in London or, if practicable, abroad. They were told that they would be working for peace and a better world. Only later would these political romantics realize that they were required to spy against their own country to further the political and strategic ambitions of the Soviet Union, though this discovery does not seem to have worried any of them. Some were even willing to be accessories to execution, knowing that when they betrayed a Soviet citizen working for the West, the penalty for treachery in the country they so admired was death.

CHAPTER 14

Enter Sonia

—

AMONG THE MANY SOVIET AGENTS OPERATING AGAINST GREAT Britain during World War II, none had a more charmed life than Sonia, which in Russian means "Dormouse." As we have seen, she had been recruited to the GRU in Shanghai by Richard Sorge, who, according to the officially approved book *The GRU and the Atomic Bomb,* passed on to her "the beautiful pseudonym Dormouse in 1932." However, Sonia's son Michael told me that she was never aware that Sorge had envisioned her as a dormouse, and she certainly never slept on the job.

She was regarded by the Soviet leadership as having given exceptional service, inflicting, perhaps, even more harm on the United States than on Great Britain. That view is fortified by details of her career revealed in officially sponsored books recently published in Russia, the title of one of them being *Superfrau in the GRU.*

Throughout her GRU career, Sonia served several purposes. She was a courier, receiving secret information given to her, directly or indirectly, by GRU spies who had access to it. She was a highly trained radio operator and cipher expert. She had also been trained and equipped for microphotography, so that on occasion she could send information in the form of microdots—messages so reduced that they could be disguised in letters as periods. Usually she delivered her information, which was almost always in documentary form, to a Soviet controller who was a member of the nearest embassy or consulate, where it was either sent to Moscow by diplomatic pouch or was encoded and transmitted by radio. Though more secure, pouch delivery was slow during wartime, sometimes taking weeks by ship. So in circumstances where speed was considered essential, Sonia encoded and transmitted the information directly to the Center herself. When necessary, she also passed to her spies requests and instructions given to her by her controller or transmitted to her by radio from the Center. She was also a talent spotter and, with agreement from the Center, recruited several other agents to the GRU cause. While in Moscow in 1938, Sonia had been called to the Kremlin to be presented with the prestigious Order of the Red Banner for her work in China and Poland, though more recent achievements during her visits to London may have been an important component. Deciphered GRU and KGB messages have shown that for ideologically motivated agents, Soviet decorations were a great psychological spur. The value of Sonia's past and potential achievements had been further recognized when she had been called to the Center for interview and praise by the GRU chief of intelligence himself—a rare accolade, perhaps giving him the opportunity to stress the particular importance of her future service.

In August 1938, she was posted to Switzerland, with the rank of major, to set up a station as an extension of the Rote Kapelle, operating against nearby Germany. On her way, Sonia had visited England yet again, covering her tracks by a roundabout route to pick up her children. While in London, she and her sister Brigitte made arrangements for the recruitment of some Englishmen to serve as spies under her control in Switzerland, such was the intimacy of their collaboration. One of these was Alexander Foote, a Liverpool man, who would also have an exciting undercover life destined to impact on Hollis's career. Foote's CV, released by MI5 in 2004, shows that he was born in 1905 and enlisted in the Royal Air Force in 1935 but deserted a year later to serve with the International Brigade in the Spanish Civil War, though he was not a member of the Communist Party. In 1938, he met the well-known Communist Douglas Springhall, who was later to be convicted of espionage, and was told there was a dangerous mission for him. Foote's telephone call to a Hampstead number was answered by Brigitte, who invited him to lunch at her apartment at 4 Lawn Road. She told him that he would be working in Germany for Ursula and gave him £10. His acceptance of the money completed his "signing on" to what he believed was the Comintern but was really Sonia's GRU Swiss spy ring.

In October, Sonia set up home and her clandestine radio station in a chalet near Montreux, being joined by her husband, Rudi. By conspiratorial arrangement, she met Foote in Geneva, gave him money, and dispatched him to Munich as a tourist, to learn German and make contacts in the BMW factory. She told him that he would be working "for the Comintern against Germany." Foote was required to inform Brigitte of any change of address, showing that she remained an active participant in the espionage ring.

Before leaving, Foote was asked by Sonia if he could recommend another recruit, and he suggested a friend, Leon ("Len") Beurton, a young motor mechanic born in London of a French father in 1914. He too had given up his work to fight for the Communists in the Spanish Civil War. His recruitment to the GRU in April 1939—a formative event for Sonia and, later, for Hollis—was also achieved in London by Brigitte. He joined Sonia, who sent him to Frankfurt to learn German and make friends in the IG Farben works. After nine months, having demonstrated their seriousness and ability to survive, the two recruits joined Sonia near Montreux. There, she instructed them in code work, the construction and operation of shortwave radio transmitters, and other espionage skills. At that stage, Sonia told them that they were working for "Red Army intelligence." So, of course, was her husband, Rudi, who was recalled in June to Shanghai for a new GRU assignment there.

Documents released in 2004 revealed that by August 1939, MI5 already had a file on Beurton because of his Communist connections and that with the outbreak of war shortly afterward, he was placed on the blacklist of suspected persons.

In December 1939, the GRU Center ordered Sonia to involve her recruits with a separate Swiss spy group called the Rote Drei (Red Trio), which was so successful against Germany that several books have been written about it. She visited its chief and told him the Center's plans for her team to take over the group's radio links with Moscow, which happened by early January 1940. This was a prelude to her transfer to a much more important role in England, though she was not then told of her precise destination.

In further preparation for her move, Sonia began to complain openly about Stalin's pact with Hitler, claiming to be disenchanted with him.

This was part of a complex legend that she was required to project to cover her new secret assignment. In fact, she never wavered from her total dedication to the Soviet cause, even after its collapse. Her true reaction to the Nazi-Soviet pact was probably like that of her brother, Jurgen, who handed out cigars to comrades in London "to celebrate the pact which will keep the USSR out of the war," as he recorded in his memoirs.

Sonia finally convinced Foote, Beurton, and other colleagues that she was so disappointed with Stalin that she was quitting all intelligence work forever. To strengthen the legend, after the outbreak of World War II in September 1939, she claimed that, being Jewish, she was desperately worried about her fate and that of her two children, should the Germans invade neutral Switzerland. That was most unlikely, because the Swiss watch industry was supplying mechanical fuses, aircraft instruments, and other war goods to Germany, and Hitler could not spare troops to occupy such a mountainous country when there was no military necessity. Sonia's destination, England, was a much more likely candidate for invasion and occupation. Indeed, when she moved there, the air Battle of Britain was still in progress, and after the defeat of France and the withdrawal from Dunkirk, an invasion seemed imminent. There was also the danger that if she was caught spying in Britain for the Soviet Union, which was then an ally of Germany, supplying the Nazis with oil and other war materials in the hope that Britain would be defeated and its empire dismembered, she could face a death sentence. That would never have been so in neutral Switzerland.

As Foote was later to admit, he was completely deluded by Sonia's claims, in spite of the obvious fact that many other GRU spies who were Jews were required to remain in Switzerland. Later, when Foote was in Moscow, he was assured by the GRU Center that Sonia had indeed ceased to work for them, showing that the legend (*ligenta biografia,* as the Center called it) had been inspired there. The truth was very different.

Graded as a Red Army major on active service, Sonia was under strict military discipline and in her memoirs was to stress how she had always regarded herself as a soldier. So when she had received an order from the Center to secure British nationality by divorcing her husband and marrying one of her English recruits, she did not demur. Her husband, Rudi, who was back serving the GRU in China, had already tamely agreed to the divorce.

On GRU instructions, Sonia divorced Rudi in a Swiss court in October 1939 as a step toward securing British nationality. As Foote was later to admit, he was the only witness and, at Sonia's requirement, had given false evidence claiming that Rudi had committed adultery with Sonia's sister Brigitte in a London hotel.

Sonia then married Beurton in Montreux on February 23, 1940, though she was to admit in her memoirs that she had not minded who helped her to become a British citizen. Beurton was seven years her junior, but it was to be a successful marriage lasting fifty-seven years. The fact that she married an Englishman on GRU instructions to enable her to enter Britain and stay there is further evidence that she did not leave Switzerland voluntarily but was posted by the GRU as part of a long-term plan. She wasted little time in applying for a British passport on March 11, 1940.

With a British passport given to her in May 1940, being fluent in English, and being able to pose as a refugee, she was ideally qualified for the tasks in Britain for which her superiors had been grooming her. With Beurton and Foote in tow, Sonia moved to Geneva, where she received her orders to switch to Oxford in November 1940, just a few weeks after most of MI5, including Hollis's section, had moved to Blenheim, nine miles away, which some explain as yet another coincidence. Sonia's admission, in her memoirs, that the GRU Center supplied her with instructions for her first meeting with her Soviet controller in London, along with recognition signs and passwords, is further evidence of a professional posting.

If Hollis was Elli, he would have been serviced in London by a courier who would simply have conveyed any information to the Soviet embassy, directly or indirectly, for onward passage to the Center in Moscow. Once Elli was at Blenheim, however, that would be much more difficult and sometimes impossible. With the regular German bombing of London making a rail journey to the capital uncertain, it was essential that the new courier in Oxford have an independent transmitting and receiving link with the Center. Sonia had that qualification. Brigitte, who may have been servicing Elli in London, did not.

Recently, I discovered another extraordinary coincidence. At precisely the time that Sonia was instructed by the GRU to leave Switzerland for Oxford, in December 1940, the GRU knew that Brigitte would no longer be available for service in London or anywhere near for an indefinite period. Her husband had been posted to Bristol by the organization for which he was working. A released MI5 document dated January 14, 1941, records that MI5 had just learned that "her address and that of her husband was Exeter Buildings, Redland, Bristol."

Surprisingly, released documents have revealed that certain MI5 officers realized at the time that Sonia's marriage had been a convenience to secure British nationality and that "as the daughter of Professor Kuczynski," there was cause for suspicion about her. The astute Millicent Bagot had alerted a colleague on May 10, 1940, warning that "Ursula Beurton's husband is on the Black List. Will you be taking up this case?" The colleague suggested that Sonia's passport should be refused because the marriage had been contrived. On December 4, 1940, the relevant MI5 file records, "It looks as if the family is on the move and we should make provision for their arrival. We cannot refuse to let them in. Have you any suggestions?" A further entry two days later stated, "It seems best to get her name on the Black List and arrange for us to be notified of her arrival so that a close eye may be kept on her activities." Another recommended that Mrs. Beurton be put under surveillance on the train.

All this reveals that even before she arrived in Great Britain, Sonia was under considerable suspicion as being a Soviet agent who had wheedled herself in for a nefarious purpose. The new facts are also evidence that exactly when Jurgen Kuczynski and his father were omitted from MI5's "Foreign Communists Considered Dangerous" list supplied to the FBI on December 26, 1940, Hollis knew that the suspect Sonia was on her way.

During the whole ten years when information about Sonia and her activities would seep into the MI5 records, Hollis never registered any personal knowledge of her. If he had encountered her, or her former husband, Rudi, in China, that was a far more serious omission than his deliberate failure to record his friendships with Cockburn and Ewert.

Sonia's new husband had been forbidden by the GRU to accompany her because he faced conscription into the British forces and was still needed by the Swiss spy ring. So she left Switzerland with just her two children in mid-December, traveling by bus to Barcelona, thence to Madrid and Lisbon, and, after many delays, reached Liverpool by the steamer *Avoceta,* in a convoy, on February 4, 1941.

Sonia was interrogated by a Security Control officer and told him that Beurton had been in Switzerland because he had needed treatment for tuberculosis, which was a lie, and that she was going to live with relatives, which was also untrue. On February 15, a letter from Security Control in Liverpool to the Home Office stated, "Mrs. Beurton (Case no. 186 in Central Security War Black List) is proceeding to her father, Prof RR Kuczynski, 78 Woodstock Rd, Oxford." Clearly, Sonia had given that address to her interrogator.

After one night in a Liverpool hotel, Sonia went by train directly to Oxford, a city with which she had no previous association, describing the train journey in some detail in one of her letters to her new husband, Len, which has recently been published in Eberhard Panitz's *Treffpunkt Banbury*. Her legend for choosing Oxford as a base was her claim that her parents had moved there from London because her father was attached to one of the colleges. Her father, who used the European title "Professor," was then reader in demography at the London School of Economics and was researching a populations project for which he visited Oxford libraries for brief periods. However, he and his family really remained based in London—at 12 Lawn Road, NW3—in spite of the bombing, having declined the opportunity to be evacuated to Cambridge with the rest of the LSE, possibly on GRU instructions. His presence in London would give Sonia a continuing excuse to visit there to contact her Soviet controller.

In October 1940, the very time when Sonia had first received her orders to move to Oxford but did not know her exact date of departure, her father had secured occasional lodgings there for himself in a small semidetached house in Headington Road. Then, in late January, when she was on her way, he registered himself, as an alien was required to do, as living at 78 Woodstock Road. That is recorded in a warning letter sent by Hollis's assistant, Millicent Bagot, to the Oxford chief constable, dated January 26, 1941, advising him that Kuczynski had just registered the new address and requesting information about any political activity. Clearly, he had moved only when he knew that Sonia was on her way to Oxford, to give her an accommodations address. Somehow Sonia received that information, before or on her arrival in Liverpool, enabling her to assure her security interrogator that she was going to Oxford because her father was living there.

His obituary notice in *The Times*, written by his daughter Brigitte and tracing his academic career, made no mention of any Oxford college. Neither did his son, Jurgen, in a detailed biography of his father published in 1957. Number 78 Woodstock Road is such a large Victorian house that it became student accommodations for St. Hugh's College, and records show that R. R. Kuczynski stayed there on occasion but was not a regular subtenant. In fact, there was no room there for Sonia and her children, and she went to a different temporary address. In her memoirs, she stated that while her parents were in Oxford "living with friends," when she arrived, they had no room for her and that they had to return to London soon afterward.

Some of Sonia's letters suggest that her relatives had made no proper living arrangements for their daughter and her two children when she arrived in Oxford. The circumstances of her arrival, described in a letter to Len dated "end of February 1941," are extraordinary. They indicate that she traveled from Liverpool to Oxford with two children and all her possessions on a winter's day, which would have been dark early, and when there would also have been a total wartime blackout. Somehow she found a temporary room at 8 Frenchay Road, which her father may have booked.

The story that her father lived in Oxford was part of Sonia's GRU legend for being there in case she was ever questioned. Her son Michael, who was with her throughout her espionage operations in Britain, when not at boarding school, has recently confirmed to me in writing that his grandfather Professor Robert Kuczynski knew about his daughter's activities on Russia's behalf and approved of them. Many years later, deciphering experts at GCHQ (the British version of the American National Security Agency) would find that he had done much more—he had provided her with doubled sets of trade statistics, which she used as the book codes she needed for enciphered radio contact with the GRU Center in Moscow. The whole operation of Sonia's move to Oxford, including her father's part in it, was smoothly professional and seems likely to have been organized and directed by the GRU Center.

Later, Sonia would claim that she chose Oxford to escape German bombs, though the city was a possible target with major military vehicle factories close by. She arrived only a few weeks after the devastating raid on Coventry had demonstrated the Germans' determination to target provincial cities. She records in her memoirs that she traveled to London twice a month to see her father and others, including Brigitte, "conspiratorially," as well as for family reasons. Further, she frequently slept in London during the bombing. Indeed, a letter to Len within three weeks of her arrival described how she had already "stayed nights in London, now and then" during the Blitz. She vividly described the scenes in the underground stations, into which thousands of Londoners had moved for safety, as I witnessed myself.

Serving officers in any army do not choose where they will go, particularly in wartime. Sonia's claim that she, a highly qualified GRU major with ten years of successful espionage behind her, was allowed to go where she wished is not credible. Her cover story—that with a pronounced German accent, no support, two children, and no personal transport, she went to unknown Oxfordshire, knowing nobody there, to discover and recruit a new group of agents—is laughable. In the English edition of her memoirs, Sonia was to admit the truth by commenting on the circumstances that eventually enabled her husband to join her in Oxford: "Len had received the same order from Center as I had—Go to England!"

Further evidence of the importance attached to Sonia's posting by the GRU Center surfaced in 1998, when details of the GRU's past radio operations were published for the first time by Major General Ivan Petrov, a former chief of the GRU Radio-Communications Service. Among the few early transmitters he chose to name was "Sonya's Station operated by Ursula Hamburger."

The Sonia case has been studied intensively for more than twenty years, but not until 2004 did MI5 reveal that she had been a known Communist under such suspicion that she was on the Security Control blacklist. Previously, Hollis's supporters have claimed that he could not be blamed for failing to detect her unremitting conspiratorial activities, virtually under his nose at Blenheim, because he did not know that she was there.

The GRU archives list Sonia as "part of the London *Residentura*'s apparatus in the 1940s." In her eventual safe retirement in East Germany, after nine years of unhampered espionage in Great Britain, she claimed that she came to suspect that someone in MI5 had been protecting her.

CHAPTER 15

Another Insidious Immigrant

O N THE OCCASIONS WHEN I VISITED THE ATOMIC ENERGY Research Establishment at Harwell in Berkshire, after its founding at the end of World War II, one of the least memorable figures was Dr. Klaus Fuchs, head of the Department of Theoretical Physics. "Fuchs looks an ascetic theoretic" was an insider joke but proved to be rather misleading. I was eventually to see him, in 1950, in the dock of the Old Bailey, being sentenced to the maximum prison term of fourteen years for espionage on a scale that would have merited execution in the country he cherished.

Like the Kuczynski troika, Fuchs was a German Communist refugee. Born in 1911, the son of a German Quaker preacher, Fuchs was on the run from the Gestapo for his underground work against the Nazis. He was ordered by the German Communist Party to seek refuge abroad and develop technical skills that would be of value in building a Communist Germany one day. On September 24, 1933, after a sojourn in Paris, he managed to secure asylum near Bristol with a family named Gunn who had pro-Soviet leanings, which they made no attempt to hide. Many books have described them as Quakers, which they never were.

Ronald Gunn introduced the twenty-two-year-old Fuchs to Professor Nevill Mott (later Sir) of Bristol University. Gunn and Mott were friends because they were both Old Cliftonians. Mott, who had entered

Clifton College at the same time as Hollis, was a far-left-winger and a member of the Society for Cultural Relations with the Soviet Union, a Communist front. He spoke German and employed German émigrés in his laboratory. Mott offered Fuchs, who was an outstanding mathematician, a research post to study for a PhD. Another colleague there was Herbert Skinner, an Englishman who would reappear in Fuchs's life story.

In 1934, Fuchs applied to the German consul in Bristol for renewal of his passport, whereupon the consul reported to the police there that Fuchs was "a notorious communist," supplying letters as evidence. To their eventual regret, MI5 officials regarded the information as "tainted" because it was believed to have originated from the Gestapo, especially when the Bristol police stated they had no evidence that Fuchs was taking part in Communist activities there. It should have been self-evident that Fuchs was likely to be a Communist because it was known that he was not a Jew and had fled Germany for political reasons. In fact, Fuchs was to confess that he had regarded himself as a member of the underground section of the KPD in Great Britain, working for a postwar Communist Germany, and had behaved accordingly. In Bristol, he had been openly active on a committee assisting Communists fighting in the Spanish Civil War.

In September 1937, Fuchs moved to Edinburgh University to work under Max Born, a distinguished German refugee scientist, later confessing that he had continued his Communist activity in that city. In his memoirs, Born attested that Fuchs was quite open about his Communist views when working with him and was "passionately" pro-Russian when the Soviet Union invaded Finland in November 1939. Before he had left Bristol, Fuchs made contact with another German refugee, Jurgen Kuczynski, who was to change his life. The GRU archives indicate that the two had known each other previously in Germany, and in his book *Freunde und gute Bekannte*, Jurgen wrote, "Klaus was a comrade and naturally came to me as I was the political leader in England." In a statement to the FBI, Fuchs eventually admitted that he knew Kuczynski to be "the leader of the underground German Communist Party in Britain."

Though based in London, Jurgen traveled around Britain on behalf of the Left Book Club and may have visited Bristol, or Fuchs may have first contacted him on a visit to London. In Edinburgh, Fuchs, together with another German physicist at the university, assisted Kuczynski in a scheme to send Communist leaflets to Germany.

In November 1939, shortly after the outbreak of war between Great Britain and Germany, Fuchs, by then a doctor of science, was summoned before the aliens tribunal in Edinburgh, where a testimonial from Born exempted him from restrictions. Fuchs is said to have affirmed before the tribunal that he should be granted asylum, as he feared for his life in Germany. Later (in April 1940), he was to tell the police that he had left Germany "to avoid arrest by the Gestapo for my political activity at the University."

In March 1940, two leading nuclear physicists, Professor Rudolf Peierls and Otto Frisch, who were Jewish refugee scientists working at Birmingham University, took a historic initiative. Fearful that the Nazis might be developing atomic weapons, they asked—and answered—a series of basic questions in a memorandum entitled *On the Construction of a "Super-bomb" Based on a Nuclear Chain Reaction in Uranium*. In easily understandable terms, they showed that an atomic bomb of devastating power might be much easier to build than previously believed. With astonishing foresight, they described how two small, harmless hemispheres of the metal uranium 235 could be rapidly brought together to form a critical mass, which would automatically create an enormous radioactive fireball. They even suggested a way of producing the rare uranium 235 in sufficient quantities. They submitted the now famed Frisch-Peierls memorandum to the government, which reacted by setting up a secret committee code-named Maud to explore the possibility.

Though the memorandum was regarded as secret, there has always been an academic camaraderie among scientists of all disciplines to discuss their ideas. From remarks made by Professor Born in his memoirs, there can be no doubt that Fuchs knew of the nuclear possibility, which had been widely discussed after the discovery of uranium fission in Germany had been made public in January 1939.

The GRU archives show that early in 1940, Fuchs had mentioned the atomic possibility to Jurgen Kuczynski, who had induced him to share his knowledge and ideas with a "representative of the Soviet Union." Fuchs had agreed to do so, but before any meeting could be arranged, the Germans overran northern Europe in May 1940, and invasion of

Great Britain seemed likely. Fuchs was therefore interned, along with many other Germans, and shipped to Canada, where he was held in an old army camp at Sherbrooke in Quebec.

There, Fuchs cemented relations with the hardened Communist Hans Kahle, a much older man. They may have discussed the nuclear possibility, because a Canadian Communist mathematician, Israel Halperin, who was also an explosives expert, supplied Fuchs with scientific journals, newspapers, and books. Halperin, who was Canadian born of Russian parents, was later recruited by the GRU and given the code name Bacon. The first steps in an important Anglo-Canadian atomic partnership had already been made in the autumn of 1940 with talks between the British atomic pioneer Professor John Cockcroft and the Canadian National Research Council. Halperin was involved with the council, so he could have informed Fuchs about the project.

Fuchs was released from internment, along with Kahle, on December 17, 1940, on the strong recommendation of the Royal Society, and of Born and Peierls in particular, and he returned by boat to Liverpool, which he reached on January 11, 1941. Exactly what happened then has only recently been revealed, following the release of GRU archives to Vladimir Lota. It is a disclosure that sheds entirely new light on Fuchs's treacherous behavior.

Fuchs quickly found his way to London to join German friends, who included Jurgen and possibly other members of the Kuczynski family. At a party to celebrate his return, Jurgen introduced him to Colonel Simon Kremer, a GRU officer from the Soviet embassy. This was the "representative of the Soviet Union" to whom Jurgen had hoped to introduce Fuchs earlier in the year, and Kremer seems to have been invited to the party for that purpose.

Kremer, who had operated without hindrance in London since February 1937 in spite of Walter Krivitsky's specific warning to MI5 about him, is described in *The GRU and the Atomic Bomb* as "one of the best operational officers of the London *rezidentura* who had recruited several valuable agents." He was also highly intelligent, with excellent English, and known for his courtesy. Jurgen introduced him to Fuchs as "Johnson." They talked about the military potential of atomic energy, and Fuchs, who was about to return to Edinburgh University, agreed to "prepare for Johnson a short account about the possibilities of atomic energy."

At that time, when Fuchs committed himself to Kremer, the Soviet Union was still an ally of Germany. This indicates that Fuchs's later statement that he decided to become a spy only after Russia was invaded was untrue. Like Philby and so many others, he spied because he was a totally committed Communist and never wavered from his dedication to the service of the Soviet Union. His eventual claim that he was a spontaneous volunteer to full-blooded espionage sounds more like a legend concocted for him to protect his recruiters should he ever be exposed. Like all the other Communist spies, he was worked over by an experienced recruiter, Jurgen Kuczynski, who convinced him that it was his duty to serve Russia, before being introduced to a professional controller, Kremer.

There is some evidence that the Soviet ambassador in London, Ivan Maisky, was involved. Kuczynski was friendly with him and may have approached him for advice. Maisky, who allegedly hated the embassy's KGB representative, Anatoli Gorski, may then have ensured that it was the embassy's GRU man who acquired the promising new source. In any event, MI5's failure—and Hollis's in particular—to pay proper attention to Kuczynski's and Kremer's activities had led directly to the recruitment of Fuchs.

Kremer reported about his meeting with Fuchs to his immediate chief, Ivan Sklyarov, a skilled GRU intelligence officer who had been sent to London as military attaché in October 1940. In turn, Sklyarov reported to the GRU Center in Moscow, so that inquiries about Fuchs could be made to ensure that he was not a British plant and could be relied upon as a source. The Center alone could order the recruitment of its individual spies, and it had controlled procedures concerning new sources. There were severe consequences for any officer who recruited a dud or dangerous source. The care with which each new agent was vetted before recruitment has been detailed by the GRU defector Vladimir Rezun. In his book *Inside Soviet Military Intelligence*, issued under his cover name, Viktor Suvorov, he described how the process of ensuring that the agent could be trusted, was not a plant, and was resolute enough to continue to deliver could last up to a year. The final stage of recruitment, which the Russians called "signing on"—which may have involved the signing of a small form—did not occur until the GRU Center was fully satisfied.

Although Kahle, who was also released, had been named in the "Foreign Communists Considered Dangerous" list supplied to the United States by MI5 in December 1940, he was permitted to carry out highly secret work for the Admiralty under Professor J. B. S. Haldane. That larger-than-life scientist, whose lectures on genetics I attended in the 1930s, was an open Communist in whom MI5 had taken an interest since 1928 because of his links with Soviet scientists. Haldane is now known to have been an active GRU spy, code-named Intelligentsia. By any standards, it was preposterous that Kahle should have been granted access to military secrets, which he systematically betrayed to the GRU, as Sonia has admitted in her autobiography. Presumably, he had been cleared by someone in MI5 after his return from internment.

The friendship between Fuchs and Kahle was to be dismissed repeatedly by MI5—and by Hollis in particular—as being of no consequence, as released MI5 papers show. Yet, a note about Kahle, prepared by the MI5 officer Michael Hanley on September 16, 1949, showed that in 1939, soon after Kahle had first arrived in England, he was "reported to be working for the OGPU [Soviet intelligence] with Jurgen Kuczynski, among refugees from Germany"!

Meanwhile, work had begun, in extreme secrecy, to design the world's first atomic bomb. The Maud committee did not complete its report on the weapon's feasibility until July 1941, but Peierls, who was professor of applied mathematics at Birmingham University, and his colleagues were already pursuing the theoretical aspects. As Peierls eventually described to the police and MI5, he urgently needed an assistant, and having met Fuchs casually and being aware of his ability, he wrote to him on May 10, inviting him to join his team to do work "of a special nature" that was also "urgent and secret." Fuchs was eventually to tell the FBI that he knew, before he joined the Birmingham team, that the work would be "in relation to atomic energy research." He also knew that it would be secret war work.

Expressing surprise, in view of his recent release from internment, he saw an opportunity and accepted. His alien registration form shows that he was given permission by the Edinburgh city police to reside in care of Birmingham University, from May 13, 1941.

It would have been standard academic practice for Peierls to have discussed the possibility of the job with Fuchs in advance, especially as his departure might incommode the revered Max Born. So his letter may have been the subsequent formal invitation, to which Birmingham University, the new employer, needed a formal response. The fact that Fuchs had time to consult the Alien Registrations Office in Edinburgh and secure permission to move by May 13 supports the contention that he had known about the opportunity for some days, at least. So does the evidence that he had time to discuss the move with Professor Born before accepting. These dates are crucial concerning the exact time he was given security clearance by MI5—a significant matter concerning the future veracity of MI5 on the issue, as will be seen.

On May 25, Fuchs wrote to Nevill Mott at Bristol, telling him that he was moving to Birmingham, and two days later, he took up residence there with Professor and Mrs. Peierls in Calthorpe Road. MI5 was to tell author Alan Moorehead that Fuchs "began to work on the atomic bomb in June 1941," while *Britain and Atomic Energy, 1939–1945* by the official historian Margaret Gowing states that Fuchs was "engaged on Maud work from 28 May."

Peierls had told the police that he was willing to accept Fuchs "subject to security clearance." As Fuchs was still a German citizen, he had needed security clearance anyway before he could be employed on secret work, and the person required to decide this either way had been Hollis, as several recently declassified MI5 papers have proved. Hollis, who had then succeeded Jane Archer as B4a, performed that function because Fuchs was a Communist refugee and was therefore his responsibility. It was to prove to be a minor event fraught with international consequences, especially for the United States.

In all his security work concerning the atomic project, Hollis was given technical assistance by Michael Perrin of Imperial Chemical Industries (ICI), the company already involved in it. As an industrial scientist, Perrin had been consulted from the earliest stages, especially concerning aspects of the research controlled by Peierls at Birmingham. He was therefore a natural choice to assist Hollis in the security examination of Fuchs and to plead for his clearance. Though Perrin may never have previously met Hollis, they had been brief contemporaries at Oxford. They were the same age, thirty-five, were both sons of bishops, and became friends. Their meeting to consider Fuchs was most probably held at Blenheim, where the records were kept in the MI5 registry. Perrin had a weekend country cottage near Henley-on-Thames, less than twenty miles from Oxford, so Blenheim could have been convenient, perhaps on a Saturday, which was a working day for wartime MI5.

An MI5 document dated March 2, 1950, reviewing the Fuchs case, stated, "In mid-1941 application was made for him to join a research team at Birmingham University on work connected with the Atomic Energy project." While Hollis later claimed that Fuchs was cleared in August, it is now certain that this happened in mid-May. In Peierls's memoirs, *Bird of Passage,* he stated that he had "asked for official clearance for Fuchs" and "in due course he got a full clearance and he started work in May 1941." The MI5 review of the Fuchs case continued, "After careful consideration of his security record, from which it appeared that he had taken no part in political activities whilst in the UK, Klaus Fuchs was allowed to join this team." The evidence clearly shows that his first clearance by MI5 took place *before* he joined the Birmingham team, as would have been normal practice.

So, sitting together in mid-May, Hollis and Perrin had reviewed Fuchs's meager MI5 file, which had been started in 1938, but they made no other inquiries. According to documents released by MI5 in 2003, the file contained his alien registration card, immigration papers, and the German consul's report, but there was no mention of his Communist activities either in Bristol or in Edinburgh. Fuchs was not seen or questioned. In particular, he was not asked if he had ever been a Communist, an omission that was to astonish the FBI chief, J. Edgar Hoover.

According to Perrin, Hollis stated that although MI5 had a routine objection to the employment of any aliens on secret work, it had no "positive adverse information on his [Fuchs's] activities in the UK." Further, MI5 doubted the validity of any other "adverse information known to them." When Perrin explained that it would be impracticable to deny Fuchs access to the most secret information if his services were to be of much use, Hollis cleared him with the standard proviso that Peierls should be told to limit his access, if possible. Fuchs signed the Official Secrets Act on June 18. There can therefore be no doubt that he had been cleared by MI5 in May, perhaps before he had left Edinburgh.

Hollis's own recorded statement and the MI5 archives leave no doubt that all the effective clearances of Fuchs were done by him. Perrin was "very anxious to get the services of Fuchs," but had Hollis firmly objected, he would not have been employed. Released MI5 documents show that, throughout Fuchs's career in Britain, Hollis was effectively his security case officer, and it was his advice that was decisive.

Whether or not Fuchs was the first scientist jointly cleared by Hollis and Perrin is so far not known. In any case, it would seem that because of this function, Hollis was one of the first people outside the atomic bomb project to be initiated into its existence. He and Perrin certainly cleared others, and in the course of time, their continuing and easy relationship seems to have made Hollis the natural liaison man with Tube Alloys, as the British bomb project was later called. It is significant that Perrin had overall responsibility inside Tube Alloys for security and intelligence, being cleared for access at all levels. The Hollis-Perrin partnership concerning vetting and other secret atomic affairs lasted at least until 1951. It was to make Hollis MI5's authority on the atomic project, with senior officers, who were kept in ignorance, deferring to his judgment, and would increase his influence, especially concerning relations with the United States on that subject.

CHAPTER 16

"Signing On"

F UCHS QUICKLY BEGAN HIS NEW WORK AT BIRMINGHAM UNIVER-
sity and soon gained exceptional access to secrets about nuclear
weapons. As Frisch had moved to Liverpool University, Fuchs replaced
him as the Peierlses' lodger, and he was looked after by Mrs. Peierls, a
former Russian scientist. Fuchs may well have been shown the Frisch-
Peierls memorandum with little delay, as after June 18, his work was to
develop a method of producing uranium 235 for use as a superexplosive
and to calculate the critical mass of that material required for a bomb.

Early in August, a German refugee informant told MI5 that Fuchs
"was well-known in Communist circles." Jurgen Kuczynski had organized a KPD branch in Birmingham, and Fuchs had quickly involved
himself with it. MI5 asked the Birmingham city police for any information it might have about Fuchs and received a negative reply, as there
was nothing on file. According to the official report *Britain and Atomic
Energy, 1945–1952*, MI5 passed this information to the government department employing Fuchs, blandly pointing out that "while it was impossible to assess the risk of leakage of information, any leakage would
be more likely to lead to Russia rather than to Germany." As will be
seen, statements in another MI5 document sent to Prime Minister
Clement Attlee in 1950 suggest that Hollis was responsible for this accurate prophecy, which indicated that, in his opinion, any leakage to Russia could be tolerated! He was also to express that opinion, quite firmly,

in a memo dated July 12, 1943, concerning another suspect atomic spy. Peierls was again routinely advised of the need for minimum disclosure to Fuchs, which Hollis already knew to be impracticable.

The leak to Russia was to become a flood, particularly after Germany invaded the Soviet Union on June 22, 1941. Fuchs then decided, according to his own eventual admissions, to pass all the information he could to Moscow. This date, however, may have been no more than coincidental with the fact that until then he did not have enough secret material to hand over. He had signed the Official Secrets Act only four days earlier. He was to claim that he went to London "to seek the advice of Jurgen Kuczynski," but the GRU archives state that he "remembered Johnson and decided to transmit what he knew about the atom bomb project to that representative of Russia."

Many years later, in an interview with the German film producer Joachim Helwig, quoted by KGB colonel Vladimir Tschikov in his book *Perseus: Espionage at Los Alamos,* Fuchs himself recalled how he had alerted Kuczynski in London about his new position in atomic research: "I informed him with the most general expressions about the type of my information, and returned to Birmingham." As the official statement on the release of the MI5 Jurgen Kuczynski papers in March 2005 put it, "His [Jurgen's] mail was watched throughout the war yet his role as the man who introduced Fuchs to Soviet Intelligence was completely missed."

Simon Kremer, whose GRU code name was Barch, sought advice from his London chief, Ivan Sklyarov, whose code name was Brion. After consultation with the GRU Center, Sklyarov was instructed to recruit Fuchs. A deciphered GRU message from London to the Center shows that on August 8, 1941, Kremer had a meeting with Fuchs in Birmingham. In the message, Fuchs was described as a "former acquaintance" of Kremer's, confirming that they had previously met socially. Either then or shortly afterward Fuchs was formally recruited as a GRU agent. It was probably at that stage that he was assigned his first GRU code name, Otto, which his controllers would use in their messages about him.

Another deciphered intercept, dated August 14, 1941, indicated that Sklyarov had also had a meeting with Fuchs in Birmingham on August 8. So both Sklyarov and Kremer seem to have been in Birmingham that day, and Fuchs's recruitment took place there. August 8, 1941, seems definitely to have been the date when Fuchs was "signed on" by the GRU.

For two senior Russian officers to have met Fuchs in Birmingham suggests a high degree of confidence that neither they nor their potential prize spy was under any degree of surveillance. Seven months earlier, Anthony Blunt had supplied Moscow with a complete copy of Walter Krivitsky's debriefing. So they would have been warned that MI5's attention had been drawn specifically to Kremer's espionage role, yet they were not deterred. It is also a remarkable coincidence that in August, Hollis assumed full responsibility for Soviet counterespionage, having been involved in the takeover process for several weeks, and knew or had access to all the relevant surveillance activities.

As readers will see, there would be a succession of occasions when Fuchs and other Soviet agents would do nothing suspicious while under surveillance, suggesting that they had been warned, especially as they resumed their conspiratorial activities shortly after the surveillance was lifted.

The GRU archives show that on his encounter with Kremer on August 8, 1941, Fuchs handed over six sheets of data. Kremer showed the six sheets to Sklyarov, who had some scientific training. Sklyarov then radioed the following coded message, which was not deciphered until years later, to the director at the GRU Center on August 10. "Barch conducted a meeting with the German physicist, Klaus Fuchs, who reported that he is in a special group in Birmingham University working on the theoretical aspects of creating a uranium bomb. The work is expected to take three months and then the results will be directed to Canada for production purposes. Assuming that at least one per cent of the atomic energy of uranium explosive is released, a 10 kilogram bomb will be equal to 1000 tons of dynamite. Brion." (In Vladimir Lota's later article, he claimed that Sklyarov's message told the Center that "the memorandum will follow shortly.")

This GRU archival document is of crucial historic interest, as is the reply sent the following day: "To Brion: Take all measures for obtaining information about the uranium bomb. Director."

Though the six pages supplied by Fuchs were dispatched to Moscow on August 10, 1941, by diplomatic pouch, they did not reach the GRU Center until early in September because of the exigencies of the war. They were studied there by the director, General Alexei Panfilov, who had technical training and rated them "very important," as they revealed that the British were researching a weapon that, as he put it, "would put humanity on the road to Hell." This suggests that the pages were not just Fuchs's own mathematical researches, as he was to claim, but something more general, such as the Frisch-Peierls memorandum, which had originally covered only three sheets. (In a recent article, Lota has stated that Fuchs supplied "a brief memorandum on the principles of the military use of uranium.")

Panfilov consulted a scientist and decided that because of the chaos being caused by the German invasion, there was little that the Soviet Union could do about it at that time. Nevertheless, the Center soon instructed Sklyarov to secure "reports about work on uranium in other British establishments such as Metropolitan-Vickers and Cambridge University," indicating that their active part in the project had been betrayed. He was also required to extract information about British uranium supplies and research in progress in France and Germany. As with all its sources, the GRU made no mention of the existence of Fuchs to the KGB.

After Fuchs's first meeting with Kremer, he was plagued by doubt or fear, and at his next London visit in December, he went to the embassy to be reassured. Kremer happened to be on duty and managed to calm him down. Colonel Tschikov recorded that Fuchs's "unconsidered step was a serious breach of the conspiracy rules. It bordered on a miracle that the British authorities did not identify him and did not put him under observation." Equally astonishing is the circumstance that Kremer was able to receive Fuchs safely when Krivitsky had blown his cover and his name and photograph were in files that had become Hollis's responsibility.

Russian records suggest that Kremer met Fuchs in a quiet London street in the blackout to receive information, but to have continued that practice would have been contrary to GRU tradecraft. Kremer was held in such high regard by the Center that his protection would have been a priority. So it seems more likely that Fuchs would have been provided with a courier who would collect his information and deliver it to the embassy. Kremer received technical questions from the Center to put to Fuchs—espionage to order—and again this could have been done more safely via a courier. As Krivitsky had revealed, such a courier is likely to have been a woman who was not Russian and had excellent cover. For such a potentially productive spy as Fuchs, she would also have been experienced and known to the Center as dedicated to Soviet and GRU service.

The Center would have preferred a German-speaking woman who could be passed off as a friend of Fuchs's, and having a safe house or apartment would have been an advantage. Fuchs is on record as having said, "This comrade [Jurgen Kuczynski] gave me a certain London address where I should go at a given time. For a period, the London address became my secret residence." In view of Fuchs's established habit of visiting Jurgen in Lawn Road, Brigitte Kuczynski (then Lewis) would seem a likely candidate as courier, with her residence there serving as the safe house. If spotted, Fuchs had the reasonable explanation that she was simply a German friend. As the case of Donald Maclean would show, MI5 was not clever at discovering safe houses run by female Soviet agents who were not Russians.

During his first six months as a spy, Fuchs delivered documents three times. The GRU archives show that during December 1941, he supplied a report covering forty sheets. He may also have given verbal information concerning what he had heard about the work of other scientists, as Fuchs had an exceptional memory.

On October 8, 1941, D. Griffiths, an MI5 officer in Hollis's F Division, recorded that a source, code-named Kaspar, had reported that Fuchs was "very well-known in communist circles." Griffiths declared, "If anything very serious against Fuchs should come to light later we should consider the cancellation of his permit. In the meantime, perhaps, it would be as well to warn the Ministry of Atomic Production of this man's communist connections." No action on this prophetic advice was taken by Hollis, whose inaction in such circumstances was to become his trademark—the "Hollis touch," reminiscent of Admiral Horatio Nelson's behavior when he put his telescope to his blind eye to read a signal he was determined to ignore.

After the German attack on Russia in June 1941, Kremer had begun to agitate for transfer to a combat post, but the Center had declined. With Elli so important to the GRU's London activities and with Stalin's personal interest in him, the Center would not have wished to disturb such a safe and productive arrangement. Yet in the summer of 1942, Kremer wangled a posting back to Moscow, after which he served in the field with distinction, becoming a major general. The evidence indicates that Fuchs then became inactive and out of touch, remaining so until the autumn, when he again sought out Jurgen Kuczynski, who smartly resolved his problem, as will be shown. It is another extraordinary coincidence that during that time, Hollis was out of action in a tuberculosis sanatorium in Cirencester. It is therefore difficult to avoid the suspicion that without the regular assurances of safety, which Hollis could have provided, the GRU applied its ruthless source protection rule and broke contact with Fuchs and his courier, and it was not resumed until the Center knew that Hollis was back in charge of "Soviet espionage" in MI5.

In that light, Kremer's transfer to Moscow may have been the result of the GRU Center's knowledge that Hollis would be out of action for several months. Perhaps, with Elli and therefore Fuchs both out of action, Kremer's request had been granted.

The GRU archives have recently yielded the existence of yet another major spy, described as a "superagent inside a British war agency in London," who leaked highly secret information to the Soviet embassy. On March 3, 1942, he supplied Sklyarov with "the first report on Hitler's plans for his Spring offensive in Russia." The information had been derived from secret German radio messages deciphered by "Station X," the MI6 interception center at Bletchley Park, in Buckinghamshire. This spy, code-named Dolly, continued to supply such intercepts throughout 1942 so voluminously that Sklyarov suggested sending some of it by diplomatic bag, but the Center rated it so important that he was ordered to continue to encode and cable it all.

The existence of Dolly and of two other productive British spies, code-named Ganow and Expert, has been revealed by the former GRU officer Vladimir Lota in a report entitled *The Secret Front: The General Staff's Eyes and Ears*, published only in Russian. Both Dolly and Ganow had rapid access to Station X–deciphered messages. Dolly also had access to details of meetings between Nazi foreign minister Joachim von Ribbentrop and the Japanese ambassador in Berlin concerning military plans. (The existence of "an excellent GRU agent in the War Office who handed over packages of German, Jap and Turkish cables deciphered by the British" has been confirmed by the grandson of the GRU chief Ivan Ilichev, writing in a Moscow newspaper.)

The contents of German intercepts of value to the Soviet military planners were being passed to them by British and American authorities, but in a disguised form to prevent any possible leak to the Nazis that their most secret messages were being decoded. Historians have judged these intercepts as having made a crucial contribution to the final Allied victory, especially to the air and U-boat aspects. Yet without any interference from the security authorities, Dolly, Ganow, and Expert knowingly and repeatedly over many months put that crucial asset at dangerous risk, had there been a well-placed German spy in Moscow.

In October 1942, Dolly reported within a few days on a meeting of British military intelligence officers to consider the situation on the Eastern Front. In the same month, Ganow provided precise information on German and Romanian troops in Russia. Expert also furnished details of negotiations between the American chief of staff, General George Marshall, and the British staff chiefs in London concerning the opening of a second front.

The facts that Lota was permitted to disclose about Dolly, Ganow, and Expert show that they are previously unknown GRU spies among the many entirely missed by MI5, and only now has it suited the GRU to reveal some of them. The dates of their activities and other circumstances eliminate all of the known spies and suspects. Though their treachery is now old history, the GRU still declines to reveal their identities. (It may have been in jest, but Lota hints that Dolly may have been close to Winston Churchill, even knowing "what he had for breakfast.")

Documents recently secured by the British researcher Nigel Bance show that the same information about German activities derived from deciphered messages had also been sent regularly by a clutch of British KGB spies passing stolen documents to the KGB controllers based in the Soviet embassy in London. The code names of the most productive were Scott, Elsa, and Zenchen. This double supply was a further example of the advantage of keeping the GRU and the KGB totally separate and independent.

CHAPTER 17

Calling Moscow

—

ONCE IN OXFORD, SONIA WASTED NO TIME. SHE PLACED HER children in boarding school, having money in three London bank accounts set up by GRU paymasters. Unable to find permanent lodgings in the city, she secured temporary accommodations at a rectory in Glympton, a village just three miles from Blenheim Palace, where Elli was almost certainly based at that time. The kindly vicar offered the self-styled refugee a room until she could find something better. Within days, she began constructing a radio transmitter for her espionage messages, as, incredibly, many years later, she was to demonstrate on British television. "Sonia's Station" had been established—close by MI5.

Before leaving Switzerland, she had received instructions on how to make contact with a Soviet GRU officer in London when she had documents that needed to be transported physically to Moscow, clearly showing that stolen items from some important source were expected from her. She visited London every fortnight, and a Soviet embassy official was soon to supply her with an advanced technology miniature transmitter that was more powerful and easier to conceal.

In April 1941, Sonia found a furnished bungalow in Kidlington, a village between Blenheim and Oxford and ideally placed for servicing an agent inside MI5, especially one who could call at a convenient *dubok* on the way home to Oxford by car. It is now certain, from the identification of some of her radio traffic, that she was transmitting substantial amounts of material long before she would have had time to find and re-cruit any new sources of her own. Her presence and activity so close to Blenheim have been dismissed by her and by MI5 as "pure coincidence." In a BBC broadcast in October 2002, Michael Hamburger said that his mother claimed never to have known that MI5 was at Blenheim. How-ever, it was almost impossible to live in the area and not know it, with such an influx of Londoners to such a famous estate, especially as the red double-decker buses that transported the MI5 staff to and from Oxford were so conspicuous. Many of the girls working there in the registry and as secretaries were housed in Keble College, and a friend who was studying at Oxford then told me how he and other undergraduates dated them and learned what they were doing. The GRU certainly knew about MI5's move, and it is inconceivable that they would not have alerted Sonia about its proximity for her own safety, had she not already been told about it before leaving Switzerland. One Oxford resident, Pamela Anderson, who knew Sonia, told me that she recalled her at-tending dances at Blenheim staged by the MI5 staff.

Hollis, who was then living in Oxford and reaching Blenheim by car, was the only officer there whom she may have known already through their mutual friends in Shanghai, such as Arthur Ewert, the senior GRU operator, and Agnes Smedley. If Hollis was Elli, the only known person who fits the requirements for the courier who serviced him while he was at Blenheim is unquestionably Sonia, as there is no evidence of any other professional Soviet courier operating in the Oxford area in the early 1940s. Insufficient attention has been paid to the coincidence that because of the uncertainty of quick access to London in wartime, such a courier would have needed on-the-spot transmitting facilities and ex-pertise in using them, as Sonia had.

Was it also coincidence that Elli was a major GRU spy who had to be serviced through *duboks* when possible and that Sonia was a GRU agent runner with wide experience of finding and servicing hiding places for messages? Archival GRU documents cited in *The GRU and the Atomic Bomb* confirm that Sonia made regular use of *duboks* in her work in Britain to reduce meetings with her agents, which might have been risky, though not one of them was ever spotted by MI5 or officially known to it. The Canadian defector Igor Gouzenko was later to stress the impor-tance of *duboks* in servicing Elli.

In view of the importance attached to Elli by the Kremlin, it is likely that most of his documents had to be passed by a courier to some GRU officer in the Soviet embassy, who would have had local responsibility for him. As has been proved by deciphered GRU cables, Sonia was in regular touch with GRU officers there, either directly on her occasional visits to London by train or through a cutout, who could conveniently have been her sister Brigitte, who visited her.

Sonia would have been aware of the danger that her illicit transmissions, when delivery in London was inconvenient, might be detected and tracked down. The fact that she and the GRU Center accepted this risk with some impunity suggests that she had been assured that it was slight or nonexistent. If she was servicing Elli, the GRU could have reassured her concerning a protective hand inside MI5, which would account for her confidence.

In 1939, a countrywide organization called the Radio Security Service (RSS) had been set up "to intercept illicit transmissions." It was run by the military Royal Corps of Signals assisted by hundreds of amateur radio enthusiasts. One of their functions was to listen for Morse signals—invariably in code—which might be emanating from German agents resident in Great Britain, dropped by parachute, or landed by submarine. The agents could be transmitting messages to Germany or, perhaps, guiding German bombers to their targets. Any intercepted messages were sent to the decoding center at Bletchley Park.

The RSS also had responsibility for locating any illicit transmitters. Detector vans with direction-finding equipment could be sent into an area to track down the precise position of a transmitter, with police on hand to arrest the culprit. As a former operator, James Johnston, told me, "Our direction-finding equipment was so refined that we were able to locate any wayward transmitter."

The RSS also picked up and recorded messages that, from their call signs, could be recognized as being sent by Soviet agents operating illicitly in Great Britain. The listeners could deduce the nationality of the traffic, its likely destination, and whether it was KGB or GRU, each service having its distinctive procedures. These messages were also sent to Bletchley, but the codes being used by the KGB and GRU were then extremely difficult to break. With Bletchley's efforts being concentrated on the more dangerous German radio traffic, which could be broken, priority was given to it.

In May 1941, it was ruled that the RSS should come under the direct control of MI6, to which its intercepts should be passed first for sifting. Those of German interest were passed to Bletchley automatically, as before, but because of the pressure on the decoders there, an MI6 officer consulted with an MI5 officer about those known to be Soviet. They then decided whether they should be sent to Bletchley or stored for possible decipherment later. I have impeccable witness evidence that for most of the war, these two officers were Kim Philby and Roger Hollis.

In a letter to me, Kenneth Morton Evans, a much respected senior RSS officer who later joined MI5, stated, "I well remember giving full details to Hollis in MI5 and Philby in MI6. I understood that the ciphers never yielded—at that time, anyway—and there was certainly no great deal of enthusiasm over them."

In June, Germany attacked the Soviet Union, and Churchill ruled that it should be treated as a full-blooded ally and that the deciphering of Soviet signals should cease. This order, however, was widely—and wisely—disobeyed. There is now witness and documentary evidence that while official Soviet embassy radio traffic was largely ignored, illicit traffic was still being recorded and British code breakers were soon reading some of it. The MI5 interest in intercepting illicit radio messages, including those to and from Moscow in the early 1940s, is referred to repeatedly in the diaries of Guy Liddell. The *Official History* of MI5 also records that in 1943, the RSS had intercepted "considerable bundles of Russian traffic." The chiefs of both MI6 and MI5 had agreed privately that Soviet espionage links should still be monitored. The *Official History*'s account of Hollis's interest in Soviet "wireless transmissions" is proof of that.

James Johnston recalled in letters to me that he and his colleagues had intercepted from an illegal transmitter in the Oxford area messages that he later believed to be Sonia's and had submitted them to MI6 or MI5. "Our logs recorded her traffic but they were returned with the reference NFA [no further action] or NFU [no further use]." According to Morton Evans, it was Hollis and Philby who decided that the logs should be returned to the RSS marked "NFA" or "NFU." This meant that the RSS was not required to send out its mobile detector vans. No such action was ever taken against Sonia during the whole duration of her illegal transmissions. "Her station continued to work, off and on," Johnston recalled. "It must be a mystery as to why she was not arrested."

Nevertheless, as late as 1986, Anthony Glees was assured by a former MI5 officer that Sonia could not possibly have transmitted so often without being apprehended. New, unquestionable evidence has proved this confidence to have been unfounded. A decoded message from the GRU chief in London to the director of the Moscow Center on July 31, 1941, records a meeting between Sonia and a Soviet embassy contact in London to discuss schedules and payment for her past radio communication work. It states how she had experienced difficulty in securing a response from Moscow on four successive nights when she had used her transmitter. She also mentioned her husband, Len, whose GRU code name was John, as archives have confirmed.

In her memoirs, Sonia claimed that she operated her station, sending out her call sign, twice a week for most of the time after the German attack on the Soviet Union right up to 1947, dealing with hundreds of coded messages in the process. In a BBC radio program in October 2002, her son Michael Hamburger revisited their postwar home, the Firs in Great Rollright, north of Oxford. He recalled that his mother had slept almost every afternoon and that he had never been able to understand why. He said that he had come to realize it was because she was up half the night working with her transmitter and receiver. Sonia received congratulations from the GRU Center for the quality of her transmissions. I have also spoken with a former GCHQ officer who was eventually involved in breaking some of her coded messages.

Intercepts of some wartime radio transmissions between Great Britain and the Soviet Union, recorded by Swedish intelligence during the war under the name Hasp, were handed to GCHQ in 1959, and some of them were decoded. One series of messages had been from Simon Kremer to the GRU Center in Moscow, describing meetings with Sonia. These messages showed that she was running agents allotted to her in 1941 and contained details of her payments to them and times and durations of her own broadcasts.

The Hasp intercepts also disposed of the claim that Sonia's transmissions would not have been powerful enough to reach Moscow. If her messages could reach Sweden, they could reach the Soviet Union, especially after she had received the advanced transmitter.

One deciphered GRU message reveals that Sonia was being paid the then reasonable sum of £700 a year plus her expenses. The latter included the costs of her work with microdots—the minutely reduced photographs of documents. Her son has told me that she had also been provided with a Minox spy camera for photographing documents. This suggests that she sometimes had access to papers that she needed to photograph and return quickly—perhaps to some *dubok* from which she had retrieved them. As with her transmitter, she kept the existence of the Minox secret from her children at that time, using her Leica for family photographs.

In 2003, the fact that Sonia had transmitted regularly over seven and perhaps eight years was proved beyond doubt by further documents in the GRU archives, such as the details of her coup with the Quebec Agreement. Unquestionably, Sonia had dealt directly with the GRU Center in Moscow and had received radioed instructions from them. Suggestions that Sonia was permitted to transmit because she was a double agent are disproved by the many MI5 papers about her. By the time MI5 had officially discovered anything treacherous to Britain about her, she had vanished. A claim that British intelligence was ingeniously using her transmissions to feed disinformation to Moscow is equally without foundation.

Sonia's first contact with a GRU officer after her arrival was long believed to have been with Colonel Kremer. However, deciphered messages and GRU archives have now revealed that her early contacts in London in 1941 were with a less conspicuous and more expendable officer, Captain Nikolai Aptekar, listed on the embassy staff as a chauffeur. Aptekar, whose GRU code name was Iris, was known to Sonia only as "Sergei," as were those who succeeded him. Sergei passed Sonia's information to Kremer.

Sonia had been forbidden to go to the Soviet embassy, so Aptekar met her conspiratorially on a London street. Her first contact should have been made in February, soon after her arrival, but according to her account, this was not accomplished until May 4. However, the MI5 officer Peter Wright, who was in charge of the eventual inquiries about her, told me that the May date was a GRU legend. He claimed that deciphered GRU messages had proved that she met one several weeks earlier, which would make more sense for such an important operator. A copy of a GRU document deciphered by GCHQ and in my possession indicates that she had been active very shortly after her arrival in February.

It now seems likely that soon after her arrival, Sonia made contact with Melita Norwood, the Soviet spy whom she had previously met and who was already established inside the British Non-Ferrous Metals Research Association in London. The historian Dr. David Burke, who has written a biography of Norwood and spoke with her many times, has assured me that Sonia serviced Norwood, who told him about her. Norwood was certainly being controlled then by the GRU, as she had been for several years. It seems likely that on occasion she was served by Sonia's sister Brigitte, who was far better placed in London, but the use of either of them was an important departure from GRU practice. Normally, the GRU preferred a situation in which spy and courier were ignorant of each other's true identities so that if one was caught, the other could not easily be betrayed. However, the use of a friend offered clear advantages. The pair always had a reason for meeting and could do so even at each other's homes.

With the establishment of Tube Alloys, the secret British project to develop the atomic bomb, the British Non-Ferrous Metals Research Association was quickly involved because it had facilities for supervising research on various metals to be used in uranium reactors—the devices that could produce the explosive element plutonium. As a result, Norwood, then secretary to a senior official of the association, saw not only the results of such research, but also the secret documents supplied by Tube Alloys explaining the background to it. According to Dr. Burke, she sat in, with her boss, on certain Tube Alloys meetings, taking notes for him and ensuring that when she typed them out, she made an extra carbon copy for herself. Much that she gleaned was of great value to Soviet atomic scientists, as various GRU and KGB documents confirm. Whether she had been officially cleared for access to such secrets is unknown. The only relevant information so far disclosed by MI5 states that she was vetted in 1945. If so, the vetting was probably done by Hollis, assisted by Michael Perrin.

It would seem likely that it was when Norwood became an atomic source that she passed under the control of Sonia. Norwood, who had first been given the code name Tina, confessed to Dr. Burke that she usually left her material in *duboks* in parts of London, where a courier picked them up and, when necessary, left instructions. What is certain is that Sonia was not posted to Oxford specifically to serve Norwood, who was not an atomic source when the transit from Switzerland was ordered by the GRU.

CHAPTER 18

An Enlightening Book

—

IN MARCH 1942, WHILE HOLLIS WAS AWAY IN A SANATORIUM
near Cirencester with a recurrence of his tuberculosis, he was temporarily replaced by Roger Fulford, who occasionally went to see him to tell
him what was happening, to discuss important issues, and generally to
keep him in touch. During this time, Hollis submitted a memorandum
on Soviet communism to the MI5 director general, Sir David Petrie,
dated June 25, 1942, soon after the signing of the Anglo-Soviet Treaty
making the two countries formal allies. Much has been made of this by
Hollis's supporters since it was found in the National Archives, because
it warned that while Great Britain should cooperate with the Russians in
the war effort, care should be taken to watch what the Comintern was
still doing and would do later. It stated: "In the past, the Communists
have made a regular practice of ganging up with the lesser enemy until
the major enemy is defeated. Germany is the major enemy at present but
I see no reason to think that we and the United States are not lesser enemies, to be dealt with later as occasion offers. If Russian Communism
has become merely a domestic matter, Stalin ought to call off his bloodhounds."

This memorandum, which continued in the same vein, has been
put forward as conclusive evidence that Hollis was a hard-line anti-
Communist, but as head of the MI5 branch for overseeing the Communist threat, what other kind of memo could he have written? And why

did he write it at all? Sanatorium treatment consisted of enforced bed rest and exposure to fresh air, and to alleviate the boredom, Hollis had basic books about communism with him. When he submitted the document, he had been away from work for three months and would have been concerned about his future.

His covering letter to Petrie and his memorandum, entitled "The Revolutionary Programme of the Communists," were based on his study of Stalin's book on Lenin and other Communist publications. Quoting from the books, he reminded his chief that he was still on the ball, if absent. His letter also promoted the case for having an MI5 section to counter revolutionary communism after the war.

On July 6, Petrie passed the document to the Home Office and the Foreign Office, where its warnings were effectively ignored and did no harm to Soviet interests, as Hollis had anticipated because he had carefully avoided suggesting that the government needed to revise its attitude toward Russia. The whole document was just the kind of initiative that Kim Philby would have taken, as his 1977 lecture to the KGB would indicate. As will be seen, when Philby was extending his penetration of MI6, he was most vociferous about the dangers of Communist subversion. As a result, on his return to duty, Hollis became the accepted MI5 authority on international communism, which later enhanced his situation with the emergence of the cold war.

In assessing such an initiative, it must always be remembered that the first duty of any Soviet spy intruded into a secret department was to remain there without raising suspicions. The essential art of mole espionage was, and remains, securing access to valuable information while appearing to be efficiently engaged in normal operations. This meant doing the department's work effectively, which in his case required operating against Soviet interests. That was the way not only to remaining in post, but to securing promotion to a position even more productive to Moscow. It was the method adopted by Philby, who developed such a reputation as an assiduous worker that none of his MI6 colleagues could believe he was a spy. It also offered a reason for the habit of staying late in the office, which Hollis was also to adopt.

In 1942, probably just before leaving the sanatorium, Hollis became much enamored of a book called *Russian Glory* by Philip Jordan, who had been the first Fleet Street journalist to report from Soviet soil after the German invasion of June 1941. The German attack, which broke the cynically calculated nonaggression pact between Stalin and Hitler signed in 1939, had forced the Soviet Union into becoming an ally of Great Britain and the United States. The sudden assault had appalled all ardent Communists and Russophiles who had approved the pact in the belief that it would keep the Soviet Union out of the war, regardless of the indisputable fact that it had enabled Hitler to unleash total war against Poland, immediately involving Britain and France.

Jordan, then aged forty, had been a war correspondent reporting on the Republican side during the Spanish Civil War. He may not have been a Communist Party member, but the Liddell diaries show the strength of security concern about him at the outbreak of World War II. He was barred from any post in the Ministry of Information, and on October 3, 1939, when he had applied to go to Paris as a war correspondent for the *News Chronicle,* a liberal newspaper, Liddell suspected that he would also be working there for his close Communist friend Claud Cockburn.

Later, on the opening page of his slim volume, Jordan stated his political position: "Ever since the Spanish Civil War my life had been in some way mixed up with Communism and the men of the extreme left." He stressed his support for the system, which he had "preached for five years," and referred to the Soviet Union as "the Promised Land." He also referred to "those of us who wish to see Socialism born into the world at large" and, elsewhere in the book, used "Socialism" as a synonym for pro-Soviet revolutionary communism, a misleading device introduced by Lenin.

As there is impeccable witness evidence that Hollis enjoyed this book and sometimes reread it, it is reasonable to assume that, by and large, he agreed with its sentiments. As such, *Russian Glory* can be read as a rare source of evidence concerning Hollis's political attitude, not only in 1942 but in subsequent years. The witness, according to Anthony Glees, was a close relative of Hollis. Glees told me that after he had published his rebuttal of the charges against Hollis, *The Secrets of the Service,* in 1987, this relative gave him Hollis's original copy of the book, in gratitude.

The book, which is still available in some libraries, was essentially a panegyric of Stalin and the Russian people. In the 1940s, the Russians were rightly admired for their sacrificial, scorched-earth resistance to the savage German assault, though those of us who were in the forces then were surprised at the ease with which the Soviet defenses were overwhelmed in the first months. Jordan's claims, however, betrayed the self-deluded attitude to Stalin and his system, which was standard for committed Communists at the time. The Russians were projected throughout as superior—"a new race of men" forged by Lenin and Stalin out of a basically indolent people, "proving that human nature can be forcibly changed." They were "constitutionally tougher and could work longer hours than the British without any fall in output or accuracy."

Every aspect of the Red Army was eulogized. The Russians were doughtier fighters. Their weapons were far better maintained than those of the British Army or Royal Air Force. The Soviet industry was superior. The Russians did not make planning mistakes. They had a natural "genius for improvisation." All the workers were "happy" and anxious to please.

There was little mention of the harsh penalties for failure or the forced labor in the prison camps, while every oppressive aspect of the Soviet system was excused. The appalling living conditions of the Russian people were due to "the envy and hatred of the capitalistic world, which had forced the State to prepare for war." Stalin's "abhorrent" prewar restraints on his people had been necessary because Russia had not really been at peace, being constantly at war with capitalism. The great leader's prewar execution of Red Army generals, after staged show trials, was referred to approvingly as "the purging of its incompetents and traitors."

Readers were assured that Stalin had been "forced" into his pact with Hitler by his distrust of Neville Chamberlain. He had invaded Poland to get rid of the "fascist crooks, who preferred to sacrifice their people rather than accept Russian aid," meaning communization and Red Army occupation. Stalin's treatment of Polish Jews helped to solve Poland's problem of having too many! Jordan excused the surreptitious mass removal of populations as "quiet and sensible." In short, all Stalin's atrocities were legitimized on the grounds of long-term necessity and goals.

This astonishing naïveté was interspersed with a tirade of abuse against British politicians. Jordan demanded the removal of "all those tarred with the dishonourable brush of Munich" when Stalin's pact with Hitler had been more responsible for the German invasion of Poland, which had started World War II. He expressed his hatred of all Tories, whom he blamed for deliberately helping Hitler to arm in the hope that he would destroy the Soviet Union. While Lenin and Stalin were depicted as unerring geniuses—always "wise, with foresight"—the British government and the War Office were filled with bumbling idiots who had made a second front impossible.

Just as Philby would have done in such a propaganda exercise, Jordan leavened it with a few saving criticisms of the Communist system, which of course would be dealt with once capitalism had been defeated. In sum, the book's message was that the Soviet Union deserved to be helped in every possible way, which was encouraging for any Soviet agent already in place.

It is difficult to believe that Hollis could have chosen this book for special praise without being in considerable sympathy with its contents. Maybe the many tributes to the special Russian spirit gave pleasure to someone with pretensions to being descended from Peter the Great. After his experience with the Japanese in China, Hollis shared Jordan's strong antifascism and was known to be anti-American. If Hollis had been recruited to the GRU, Jordan's firsthand account of the wartime conditions inside the Soviet Union would help to explain why he would have wanted to continue his personal contribution with added enthusiasm, just as Philby, Blunt, and other Soviet spies did after the German attack.

It would be instructive to know whether or not Hollis ever expressed his views about *Russian Glory* inside MI5. Those of us who lived to see the Soviet system collapse in utter failure are best able to measure the political judgment of those, like Jordan, Philby, and possibly Hollis, who were so determined to shackle us all within its obscene orbit. It would also be of interest to know whether, at that time, Hollis knew Jordan, who was one of Cockburn's closest friends. As will be seen, they were to share delicate security problems when Jordan became chief press officer and public relations adviser to the prime minister, Clement Attlee, in December 1947. Jordan was to die, aged forty-nine, in peculiar circumstances connected with his friendship with one of the most notorious Soviet spies.

On October 7, 1942, Guy Liddell dined with Hollis shortly after the latter's return to work. Hollis took the initiative to promote the memorandum he had sent in June to the director general, David Petrie, warning that the Russians would be even more actively engaged in espionage and subversion once the war was over. He also took the opportunity to convince Liddell that Roger Fulford's views on the threat were "unsound," indicating that it was just as well that he was back in charge. Hollis sought out Liddell on October 27 to "talk about the Communists" and convinced him that MI5 was "extremely well informed about their activities," though no action of consequence against them was being taken.

Privately, five days later, Liddell confided to his diary his view about Hollis's efforts to counter Soviet espionage: "The Russians are far better in the matter of espionage than any other country. I am certain that they are bedded down here and that we should be making more active investigations." He was right on all three points.

Around that time, the Hollis family moved to better accommodations in nearby Oxford, at 2 Garford Road. Apart from a few foreign trips, after the war, Hollis was to remain essentially a desk officer, compiling thousands of files on possible suspects. Other officers were responsible for any fieldwork or action resulting from his information. Among the most productive field officers was Maxwell Knight, who operated under the code name M because he had taken over M Section, which was in charge of placing and running agents inside the British Communist Party.

One of Knight's assistants, Joan Miller, told me of his relationship with Hollis both before and during the war. Knight's considerable successes in uncovering suspicious activities by Communists eventually ended on Hollis's desk, but they rarely produced any action. Knight repeatedly voiced his belief that MI5 itself had been penetrated by Soviet spies, as it certainly had by Anthony Blunt in June 1940.

Entries in Liddell's diaries in 1943 and 1944 show that Hollis was determined to end Knight's relative independence and bring his work firmly under his own control in F Division. As usual, he pursued this objective with determination, with papers to Liddell recommending that Knight be forbidden to run agents on his own, with his remit restricted to talent spotting and advising.

Hollis, Liddell, and others had become concerned about their discovery that Knight was sexually involved with his secretary. After a long talk with Hollis in March 1944, Liddell wrote, "When the head of a section who is married is known to be living with his secretary, the general atmosphere within the section is likely to deteriorate." In view of Hollis's future relationship with his secretary, which was to continue openly for eighteen years, this was hypocritical on his part but provided a further lever for denigrating Knight with the MI5 directors. As Knight had been so successful, especially in exposing the Woolwich Arsenal ring, any limitation of his activities was in the Soviet interest.

Later, in 1986, Joan Miller put her experience on record in a little memoir, *One Girl's War*, which MI5 tried to ban. She stated that in 1941, one of Maxwell Knight's papers, entitled "The Comintern Is Not Dead," predicted with great accuracy the development in Russia's policy with regard to Great Britain after the war. Hollis, to whom the paper was first submitted, sent it back with the comment that it was overtheoretical, yet it seems to have been very similar to the memorandum he submitted to Petrie in the following year, when it suited his personal purpose.

Miller also recalled an incident in 1942 when an old lady insisted that a man working in the BBC was a Communist spy. Her report, which she said would have been passed to Hollis, was ignored. The man was Guy Burgess, who was known to Hollis through Fulford and was doing MI5 work for Blunt—a long-term friend. Burgess and Fulford had become acquainted through joint work for the BBC before the war, as W. J. West recorded in *Truth Betrayed*.

In 1943, Joan Miller moved to a department where she had to read incoming telegrams and noticed that an army major was copying some of them. An inquiry showed that the contents had been leaking to Communists, but when Hollis was told, he simply had the major transferred without any interrogation. This preference to resolve any internal security problem with the minimum of penalty and the maximum suppression of publicity—to become known in MI5 as "amicable elimination"—was to typify his whole career.

In that context, another entry in Liddell's diary, following a meeting with Hollis in October 1943, is enlightening. After discussing possible action against a suspect suggested by Liddell, but to which Hollis objected on human rights' grounds, Liddell deplored his colleague's "liberal mind," writing, "Roger's view is that the country is full of evilly-intentioned persons but there is no necessity to drag them out of their holes. They had much better be left to rot in obscurity and will be swamped by the common sense of the community as a whole." As Liddell clearly thought, such a working philosophy was excessively restrictive to MI5 when opposing a ruthless adversary, for whom the end justified any means. On the other hand, it suited the GRU and the KGB perfectly, for it meant that while the files on suspects were fattened by reports on hundreds of man-hours of surveillance, no action was taken against what has turned out to be a horde of highly successful Soviet spies and operatives. What might be called Hollis's law, because he obeyed it throughout his career, might be stated, "The need for action against any suspect is inversely proportional to the fatness of the relevant file."

Joan Miller told me that she became convinced, on her own initiative, that Hollis had been a Soviet agent.

CHAPTER 19

In the City

—

A N MI5 FILE STATES THAT SONIA'S HUSBAND, LEN BEURTON, returned to England on July 30, 1942, "on Moscow's instructions." As he was on the Security Control's blacklist, he was interviewed by that wartime agency. To cover his income from the GRU, he claimed that he had been able to live for two years in Switzerland because he had inherited $20,000 from a French relative. He said that he had collected it in cash, had never banked it, and had none left. He made no mention about being in Switzerland for medical treatment, as Sonia had stated. He said that he had gone to Germany in January 1939 to try to sell some property belonging to Professor Kuczynski. He also claimed that he had already been friendly with Ursula, which was how he had come to marry her. Like his wife, whom he joined in Kidlington, Beurton was a professional liar. He was interrogated again by MI5 in London on October 20, and because he repeated the same lies convincingly, the MI5 officer, who signed himself D. Vesey, reported that Beurton had "made a good impression." The MI5 documents also reveal that Beurton had the nerve to try to "gain employment with British intelligence"! Once reunited with Sonia, he was able to assist her, perhaps by emptying *duboks* on occasion or ensuring that she was not being followed—which she never was. There is also new information that he serviced an atomic scientist, previously unknown as a Soviet source, working in Oxford.

In the autumn of 1942, Sonia moved into Oxford itself. This was only a few months after the start of the "Baedeker raids" following Hitler's order that the Luftwaffe should destroy every city in the well-known guidebook *Baedeker's Great Britain,* which made Oxford a prime target. Nevertheless, Sonia and Len moved to Avenue Cottage, 50a George Street (now Middle Way), which had been the coachman's dwelling attached to an elegant Regency house, called the Avenue, in Woodstock Road. The consequences of Sonia's move proved to be so extraordinary, and with such impact on British and American interests, that I have devoted much effort to examining the circumstances and visiting the area.

The big house was occupied by Neville Laski, a distinguished lawyer who was very active in the Jewish community along with his wife, Sissie. Laski, then aged fifty-three, had been president of the Board of Deputies of British Jews, the legal body for protecting the civil and political rights of Jews. Occupying that position for six years, he had been deeply involved with the Home Office concerning the immigration of refugees from Germany from 1933 onward.

Sissie was regarded as an outstanding worker for the refugees at the Temporary Shelter in London, and she may have alerted Sonia about the vacant cottage, treating her simply as another German Jew in need of help. She was the daughter of a senior rabbi named Gaster, and one of her brothers, Jack, was a prominent Communist. Described as "ultra-patriotic," Laski may have been innocently involved in the arrival of Robert and Jurgen Kuczysnki, who gained entry as political refugees, though Jurgen had probably been posted to Great Britain by the GRU. As Jurgen's memoirs state, he was scheduled to meet his GRU controller in Copenhagen "to receive further instructions" in July 1936.

The Laskis' daughter, Pamela Anderson, has recently described to me how Sonia insinuated herself into the company of Sissie, who spoke fluent German and was "queen of the people looking after Jewish refugees." She said that Sonia visited the big house whenever she could and occasionally invited Mrs. Laski to the cottage for coffee. She was "all over my mother, who was a sucker for a hard-luck story." Pamela disliked Sonia and became suspicious when she strung up an aerial from the cottage to a shed in the Laskis' garden.

Sonia's son Michael Hamburger recalled playing with the young Laski boys, Philip, who was about the same age, and John, indicating that the relationship with the Laskis was regular. He told me that his mother was "on particularly good terms with Mrs. Laski. They liked and respected each other and had chats in the garden." As will shortly be seen, an excuse to be on the grounds could have been of great conspiratorial value to Sonia.

There is no evidence that Neville and Sissie Laski were ever aware of the Kuczynskis' nefarious activities. On the contrary, their politics were Conservative to the point where Neville openly disapproved of those of his famous Marxist brother, being convinced that Harold Laski's far left notoriety had damaged his career.

Meanwhile, Sonia had acquired a bicycle, which she used for some of her clandestine meetings with her sources and for emptying *duboks*. This means that such spies were being serviced locally, in or not far from Oxford. When not in use, her transmitter, which she was soon using at least twice a week, was hidden in a cavity of the old stone wall surrounding the Laski property. To keep her nocturnal transmissions secret from her children, who might mention them to others, she lodged both back in boarding school.

By coincidence, the Laski and Beurton households were not far from where Hollis was living, having just returned from his sojourn in the Cirencester sanatorium. Laski, who was well-known in Oxford, is likely to have been friendly with Hollis because both had been at Clifton College and were keen members of the Old Cliftonian Society, with Laski making it his business to contact "old boys" living in his area. Pamela Anderson has confirmed that her father was a particularly keen Old Cliftonian, sending his two boys there, and had an extensive social life, "meeting as many Old Cliftonians as he could in the Oxford area, as well as in London." Like Hollis, Laski was a heavy drinker, and they both had unhappy marriages, inducing them to seek outside company.

Documents now in the National Archives show that Laski had also been a major prewar source of information about British Fascists for Special Branch and MI5. As a prominent Jew who had fought in World War I and been badly wounded at Gallipoli, he had bravely attended prewar Fascist meetings, and copies of his reports to Special Branch or the Home Office would have ended up in Hollis's department, which had a section responsible for overseeing Fascists. So it would also have been in MI5's interest for Hollis to have cultivated Laski socially, as a source of information about Fascists as well as about Communist Jewish immigrants. The Liddell diaries for September 25, 1939, record a meeting with White, Hollis, and others about the British Union of Fascists and Oswald Mosley, showing that Hollis was involved. The two Old Cliftonians, therefore, had good reasons to meet in Oxford when living so conveniently close. Documents held by the Old Cliftonian Society in Bristol—at present unavailable—might prove that they were friends.

Having lived in the International Settlement in Shanghai at the same time, Sonia and Hollis found themselves within a mile of each other in Oxford in 1942. As MI5 documents have recently revealed, Hollis knew exactly where she was and, being effectively her case officer, also knew that she was an espionage suspect.

In the early autumn of 1942, Jurgen Kuczynski, acting on GRU instructions, told Sonia that he had met a scientist friend who was working in Birmingham. Effectively, he told her that the scientist was a Soviet spy and suggested that she should act as his courier because his previous contact was no longer available. Sonia immediately agreed, and Jurgen gave her details for a meeting in Birmingham. The scientist was Klaus Fuchs, and to have handed over control of such a crucially important spy—as he was by then—to Sonia, the GRU clearly must have had great confidence in her continuing safety, even when transmitting.

According to Sonia's memoirs, Jurgen had told her that Fuchs had lost touch with the Center "for quite some time" and had come to him to ask to be put back in contact. It is a remarkable coincidence that during that time, Hollis had been away from his office in the sanatorium and was due to return. There would be other occasions when Fuchs would be out of action when Hollis was temporarily away from the office, out of control of counterespionage operations. The facts suggest that Fuchs, being so valuable as a source of atomic secrets, was regularly instructed to avoid contact with his controller at times when the GRU could not be certain—from an informant inside MI5—that he was not under surveillance. It is a further coincidence that on September 28, 1942, almost immediately after Hollis's return to duty in MI5 and with Fuchs's new controller in position, Stalin decreed full speed ahead on the Soviet atomic bomb program.

The GRU Center was pleased with Sonia's takeover. She had the standard GRU requirements for a courier, being a dedicated Communist, a woman, and not Russian and maintaining excellent illegal cover. She was also an established operator with transmitting facilities— Sonia's Station. Had Hollis paid proper attention to her after her arrival, instead of assuring his colleagues that she was a harmless housewife (as according to her MI5 file he did), this mutation moment in British, American, and Russian atomic history should not have happened. The same applies to his lack of action against Jurgen Kuczynski, whose role in the Fuchs saga was only part of the damage inflicted by that dangerous and open Communist.

Evidence suggests that Jurgen told his sister Fuchs's real name. This breach of standard tradecraft may have been inescapable, as she may already have met him socially with Jurgen on one of her many visits to London. She had already shown, through her handling of Melita Norwood, that former friendships could even be advantageous. In television interviews late in her life, Sonia was to make conflicting statements about her knowledge of Fuchs while she had been his courier. According to the first, she did not know what Fuchs did or what the documents he gave her were about. She then claimed that she had passed on the material because she did not want America to have a monopoly on the atomic bomb, implying that she had known what Fuchs was doing.

Because of the mutual dedication of Jurgen and Sonia to the GRU cause, it would also seem unlikely that brother had resisted telling sister about the bomb project, if only to stress the importance of her new assignment. In any case, this recent revelation by the GRU of how Sonia came to service Fuchs is proof that she had been posted to Oxford from Switzerland not for that purpose, but to serve someone else. That someone is most unlikely to have been Norwood, because when the GRU decided to post Sonia to England, the atomic bomb had not been envisaged and there were no atomic documents passing through Norwood's hands. When the flow of information about uranium began to cross Norwood's desk, she became much more important. When Sonia had been originally posted to Oxford, the only known GRU spy likely to have been based in that area was Elli.

Sonia's willingness to serve as Fuchs's courier so readily might have been conditioned by a lack of such work during several previous months. She hated being inactive, as her memoirs and letters show, and during those months, Hollis had been out of action in the sanatorium, with no certainty for much of the time when, or if, he would return to duty. It may be significant that while Igor Gouzenko began working as a cipher clerk in the GRU Center in Moscow in May 1942, he did not hear about Elli from his deskmate until "late in 1942," as he told me. Hollis was out of action in the Cirencester sanatorium during the spring and summer but was back on full duty by October.

In her memoirs, compiled under firm and continuing GRU control, as her son has confirmed to me, Sonia was to explain that she moved into Oxford because the owners of her Kidlington bungalow wished to return there, but that may have been another part of her legend. When she became the courier for Fuchs, she needed easier access to a railway station, not only to meet him but to get his documents to London with minimum delay. Shortly after her move to Avenue Cottage, Hollis returned to duty. Residence in Oxford would have substantially eased her task of servicing two major suppliers in the area.

During October 1942, shortly after Hollis had returned to his office at Blenheim, where all Soviet suspects under surveillance were listed, Sonia traveled by train to Birmingham, where she met Fuchs. They went to a café opposite the railway station, where they spoke in German. They agreed upon mutual arrangements for further meetings at locations near Banbury, between Oxford and Birmingham, and Fuchs then handed over eighty-five pages of secret documents constituting "several reports by different scientists about their work on the Tube Alloys Project."

Fuchs's documents were in Moscow within a month. The tightest degree of secrecy and security was demanded from everybody involved with atomic weapons information, yet Stalin and his scientists knew it all on a regular basis from Fuchs and other Soviet spies via reliable couriers like Sonia.

After the Home Office had received an assurance from MI5 in June 1942 that it had no security objection, Fuchs had been granted British citizenship on July 30 so that he could go to "prohibited places." Until then, he had needed police permission to stray from Birmingham.

As Sonia was eventually permitted by the GRU to describe, in an English edition of her memoirs, she met Fuchs at regular intervals, at weekends, in countryside places near Banbury. She would arrive by train in the morning, and Fuchs would join her in the afternoon, also traveling by train. They would walk arm in arm and never stay together longer than an hour. Nor would they meet in the same place twice. With her wide and intimate experience of conspiratorial dealings, Sonia was well qualified to serve Fuchs's need for a reassuring confidante to share his stress.

He supplied her with uranium 235 production data and details of the physics of the atomic bomb. Later, she recalled with relish how on one occasion, Fuchs gave her more than one hundred pages of drawings and formulas for onward passage to the Soviet embassy.

Fuchs had taken the oath of allegiance to the sovereign on August 7, 1942, so his continuing treachery made him legally a traitor, as he surely realized. It was a year almost to the day since Fuchs had been signed on by the GRU. His naturalization greatly facilitated his meetings with his courier and with sources of information.

Sonia has revealed that she occasionally used *duboks* for fixing meetings with Fuchs but usually dealt with him by personal contact. They would pose as lovers as they discussed the merits of communism and the details for the next tryst. It would seem likely that the GRU agreed to this procedure and may even have ordered it, possibly because the Center knew that neither was under suspicion or surveillance. If Sonia was also servicing Elli again by that time, she may have relied on *duboks* more in his case, as Gouzenko's evidence stated, but meetings may sometimes have been necessary, and again, the GRU Center could have known from Elli that she was not being watched.

Late in 1942, MI5 learned that while Fuchs had been in Canada, he had become a close friend of Hans Kahle's, but though the association was noted in his file, it was rated by Hollis as "not significant"—the "Hollis touch" again. In fact, while in London, Sonia had been put in touch with Kahle, who, after fighting in the Spanish Civil War as a lieutenant, had returned to Great Britain, where he promoted himself to lieutenant colonel and wrote as a military authority for the *Daily Worker*, which gave him a legitimate excuse to secure military information. He was well-known to MI5, which had reported to MI6 as early as October 14, 1939, that he was "said to be running the OGPU espionage system in this country, assisted by Professor RR Kuczynski and his son Jurgen." Nevertheless, Sonia was still able to service Kahle occasionally as his courier, delivering his reports to Moscow, possibly through her sister Brigitte, who was in regular touch with other Soviet agents. In her memoirs, Sonia recalled that she sometimes stayed with Brigitte.

An informer "inside German refugee circles" warned MI5 that Fuchs was taking part in Communist propaganda activities in Birmingham, but as the police there had already reported negatively, nothing was done. From late 1941, then, Hollis had evidence that Fuchs was a

Communist, yet he behaved as though he had no knowledge of his closeness to Jurgen, though he was responsible for overseeing German Communist refugees.

While Sonia was so busy, on November 29, 1942, the terrierlike Hugh Shillito informed MI5's deputy director general, through his immediate superior, Hollis, about his "suspicions concerning Ursula Beurton." He was particularly concerned that her claim that her husband had originally gone to Switzerland for medical treatment seemed to have been false. Shillito had suggested that, as Len Beurton had probably spied for the Soviets in Switzerland, he might do the same in the United Kingdom and should be put under some kind of surveillance. He repeated his concern on December 19 in a letter asking for the police to make "discreet inquiries," while the Beurtons' telephone should also be tapped. Then, in a letter to his old chief, Jack Curry, who was on loan to MI6—and perhaps in response to a lack of interest in MI5—he had reported that several features about Beurton "point to him as a likely candidate for Soviet espionage."

In the following month, a detective from the Oxford city police called on Mrs. Laski, who claimed to know little about the Beurtons' background while admitting to being on friendly terms with them. She said that they were paying three and a half guineas a week rent—a substantial sum in those days—and appeared to be living comfortably, with a son at an expensive prep school. How they were able to afford this when it was on Beurton's record that he had returned from Switzerland penniless raised no interest in MI5.

The police duly reported to MI5 that the Beurtons had a large wireless set and "had recently had a special pole erected for the aerial." They suggested that "you may think this worthy of further inquiry," and someone in MI5 has heavily marked the paragraph as specially relevant, as indeed it was, being an essential part of Sonia's Station. However, that blatant clue to her traitorous activities failed to provoke any known response from Hollis, who, fully installed back on duty, was responsible for any action—or inaction.

CHAPTER 20

Flagrant "Divergence"

I N FEBRUARY 1943, WITH THE WORST OF THE LUFTWAFFE'S
Blitz over, Hollis was moved back to the London headquarters, where
the director general, Sir David Petrie, wanted all his divisional heads on
tap. Hollis's team, however, remained at Blenheim, which he visited
regularly, his external letters bearing the address Box 500, Oxford, and
the telegraph code name Snuffbox. To reach Blenheim by car or rail in
those days, Hollis would have needed to go via Oxford.

Within a few weeks, he was faced with the chance discovery by others that the national organizer of the Communist Party, Douglas
("Dave") Springhall, one of his prime targets, had been a GRU agent
for several years, having recruited spies among the clerical staff of secret
establishments and elsewhere. As MI5's *Official History* and released
MI5 documents record, Springhall's treachery had come to light purely
through the patriotism of an astute member of the public. A clerk in the
Air Ministry, Olive Sheehan, who had given him details about advances
in jet propulsion to pass to the GRU Center, shared an apartment with a
woman friend who overheard the two traitors conspiring. The friend reported it to an RAF officer she knew. Shortly afterward, Springhall
called again to pick up another letter containing secret information.
Sheehan, who was unwell, had left it with her companion to hand to
Springhall, but the RAF officer, who was on hand, steamed open the en-

velope and found that it contained details of "Window"—an ingenious system for jamming radar.

Next day, Springhall was arrested, and on July 28, he was sentenced to seven years' imprisonment, while Sheehan received only three months when she agreed to testify for the prosecution. During the trial, which was held in camera, it transpired that Springhall not only had come to the notice of MI5 after being expelled from the navy for sedition, but had also been sent to prison for two months during the 1926 general strike, when he had been a Young Communist League agitator. Recently released MI5 records show that he had been under surveillance by Scotland Yard and MI5 at intervals since 1928. He had been suspected of running "a courier service for Soviet espionage" and took professional precautions against being followed. His letters had been opened, and his telephone had been tapped. His file showed that he was actively causing dissension within the navy and the army. He had been in Moscow several times, spending more than a year at the Lenin School for Comintern agents. A report by Special Branch detectives dated June 1934 stated that he had been "very closely in touch with Claud Cockburn." He had visited Moscow again in 1935 and had then gone to Spain with a political position in the International Brigade. In 1939, Springhall had arrived back from Moscow, where he had been British representative at Comintern headquarters involved in GRU business, and it has since become known that he and his agents had become part of the British section of the Red Orchestra and recruited other spies for service in Germany and Switzerland. He also became responsible for the secret coded communications between the Communist Party and Moscow— an area of special interest to Hollis.

All this had been in the MI5 files, but Springhall had managed to be an active spy until exposed by a fluke circumstance that could not be ignored. Following the established MI5 practice, Hollis had preferred to assume that in spite of all the information and surveillance, such an open Communist would never have been permitted to indulge in serious espionage. Incredibly, the Springhall case has been advanced by Hollis's supporters as an example of his "first-rate record" and "proof that the work against Communists was kept alive by Hollis." In fact, his lack of action until forced to take it by circumstances outside his control constituted an anomaly that went entirely unnoticed. Later inquiries would reveal that Springhall had many contacts with Communist intellectuals, including Cambridge dons, and had probably served as a cutout between dons who had been talent-spotting promising students and Soviet agents who then tried to recruit them. Checks revealed one Communist inside MI5, who was removed, but not Anthony Blunt, who had been excluded from a military intelligence course in 1939 because of his past Communist associations. Another was found in MI6, but not Kim Philby, who had been married to a proven Soviet agent. Hollis, who knew that Philby had a Communist past, claimed to believe that "he had mended his ways," as he put it. Nor was the trail sufficiently explored to reveal any of the other members of the Cambridge group, who continued to remove secret documents by the score.

True to his training, Springhall refused to give any help whatever, but scrutiny of his diary by the police identified a twenty-three-year-old Special Operations Executive (SOE) officer, Captain Ormond Uren, who was also sentenced to seven years' imprisonment on September 22 for divulging the complete layout of the SOE's organization. The diary also contained the name of an MI6 female secretary, Ray Milne, who handled highly secret intercepts and was a Communist and "peace movement" sympathizer. She was questioned by Hollis and by the head of her MI6 section, who decided that she should be removed from her access but not prosecuted.

As Philby was to reveal, his own practice, approved by the KGB, had been to smother evidence against Soviet interests whenever he could but to exploit it, in the interests of his professional reputation, when he could not. Hollis did exactly that with the Springhall case. A letter from him to the resident MI5 officer in Ottawa, dated November 5, 1943, shows that he and his staff were claiming credit for MI5's much belated part in the conviction. Hollis then prepared a detailed summary of the case and sent copies to the RCMP in Ottawa (with an extra copy to pass to the FBI). He followed up with copies to security and intelligence contacts in Australia, the Indian police, the Middle East, and the American embassy in London. Clearly, he wanted them to appreciate what he considered to have been a successful case, though as with every other espionage incident with which he would be associated, success had been the result of chance information that he could not ignore and not of any MI5 initiative. Save for the observation of the patriotic woman and the alert action of the RAF officer, Springhall and Uren could have continued their treachery.

Springhall's conviction should have finally convinced Hollis and his colleagues that Russian intelligence was prepared to use flagrantly open Communists as agents. However, the MI5 *Official History* describes the Springhall case as "an important divergence from previous experience," and it was treated as a one-off aberration. Meanwhile, the blatantly open Communist James Klugman, who had been recruited by the KGB at Cambridge, had insinuated himself into a position in the army, where his treacherous activities would help to ensure that postwar Yugoslavia became a Communist dictatorship. The oversight of Klugman, who had been known to MI5 since 1937, had been Hollis's responsibility prior to his call-up for war service, as MI5 documents have shown. In 1952, MI5 was *still* assuring author Alan Moorehead that the Russian Intelligence Service had forbidden open connection with the Communist Party!

The obtuse continuation of this fallacy as MI5 policy enabled several other highly dangerous spies to pursue their treachery without interference—so much so that it is fair to ask to what extent the known former communism of Philby, Maclean, Blunt, Klugman, Fuchs, the Kuczynskis, Norwood, Kahle, Haldane, and others was used deliberately to ridicule the concept that they could possibly be Soviet spies. It is also fair to wonder who was mainly culpable for the continuation of this disastrous mind-set. As the person in charge of Soviet counterespionage, and later of protective security against the much greater cold war Soviet threat, Hollis would seem to have been a major influence.

On March 16, 1943, Liddell had met Hollis to discuss the need for more resolute action against Communist infiltration, and Hollis prepared a list of fifty-seven members of the Communist Party known to be in the British Armed Forces or involved in secret government work. A memo from Hollis to the Home Office dated November 10, 1943, urged that all cases where it was intended to transfer Communist scientists out of top-secret work should first be referred to him. He would then advise the heads of the government departments concerned about the need for any or no action. At that time, Fuchs was working on the atomic bomb and receiving instructions from Sonia on how to continue his treachery in America!

Meanwhile, in April 1943, the Foreign Office had become anxious about the activities of left-wing German refugees who hoped to influence postwar German politics and asked MI5 to investigate. As members of the former KPD were involved, Hollis's department was mainly concerned, and during the summer, it became clear that the Communists were dominating the refugee scene with the intention of helping to create a postwar Germany subservient to the Kremlin. MI5 was also made aware that the leading German Communists involved were taking their orders from Moscow, where a Free German National Committee, including captured German generals, had been established.

A Free German Committee was set up in Great Britain at an inaugural conference attended by about five hundred refugees in London in September 1943. It was chaired by Professor Robert Kuczynski. A contemporary account of the proceedings in the National Archives refers to "Communists, all of the old gang, including Robert Kuczynski." One of the speakers was Hans Kahle, who described himself as a representative of the Moscow committee and was elected to the British puppet counterpart, along with another Communist who had been listed by MI5 as dangerous three years previously. They appealed for the creation of a Free German Movement to be recognized by "the British authorities." As early as 1938, Jurgen Kuczynski had founded the Free Germany Cultural Union in Britain, a KPD front that claimed one thousand members and had branches in Manchester, Glasgow, Birmingham, and Oxford. In 1939, he had toured twenty British towns speaking for the Left Book Club and collecting money for the KPD.

Though a report by the Postal and Telegraph Censorship, dated December 20, 1943, drew MI5's attention to the activities of these obvious Moscow-controlled Communist fronts, they caused little concern in MI5. In particular, MI5 continued to pay no effective attention to Professor Kuczynski or his menacing brood.

Meanwhile, toward the end of 1942, as national journalism had ceased to be a reserved occupation, there had been concern in government departments about the inevitable call-up of Cockburn for military service. In the War Office, there was appalled objection to such an anti-British Communist being allowed to wear a uniform and fear that, "being clever," Cockburn would soon be commissioned and would spread dissension in the Soviet interest. Cockburn eventually received his call-up for medical examination, which he passed, but he was then ignored and continued with the *Daily Worker*. In June 1943, Cockburn had created a further problem for Hollis by trying to become an accredited war correspondent for the *Daily Worker* so that he could operate in Algiers, possibly to assist in the establishment of a revolutionary government there. The War Office, which had its own file on Cockburn, rejected him, and its action was approved by the Cabinet, indicating the importance attached to him and the continuing anathema at the prospect that he would be wearing a British uniform. Nevertheless, Cockburn managed to reach Algiers, causing angry concern there among the American authorities, who eventually forced him to depart. Hollis had left the granting of an exit permit for Cockburn to the Foreign Office and may have been relieved to see him back in London, frustrated but unscathed.

Hollis's move to London brought him into contact with Kim Philby when Section 5 of MI6 was switched to the capital in late 1943. It was to be an encounter of massive benefit to the KGB and possibly to the GRU. Section 5 was responsible for collecting counterespionage information from foreign countries by illegal means—Philby specializing in Spain and Portugal—and, as its main "customer" was MI5, there was legitimate reason for regular liaison, especially with Hollis. Their offices were within two minutes' walk, Philby's being in Ryder Street, and they both served on a Joint Intelligence subcommittee, where they learned much that was secret outside their own remits.

Dick White was a great admirer of Philby at that time, as his biography has revealed, and could have stimulated Hollis's interest in him. Philby has described how he "cultivated MI5 assiduously" and, to curry friendship, would slip its officers information supposed to be "for MI6 eyes only." Hollis and Philby sometimes lunched and socialized together at their Pall Mall clubs.

Hollis continued to encounter other dedicated Communists, if unwittingly, in the shape of Anthony Blunt and Guy Burgess, who, as the Liddell diaries prove, was often in the MI5 office, visiting Blunt or Liddell himself. Hollis also consorted with them convivially in the Reform Club. They were all dedicated drinkers. What went on in the minds of these proven traitors when they were drinking with the man they knew to be responsible for detecting Soviet spies—especially when two or more of them were in his company—can only be imagined.

CHAPTER 21

Two-Headed Colossus

—

THE MASSIVE KGB FILES ON KIM PHILBY, RELEASED IN MOS-
cow, showed that his espionage inside MI6 had inflicted far greater damage on British and American security than anyone had imagined.
Exactly how he had managed to insinuate himself into such a commanding position became known only in 1999 with the surprise publication of
The Security Service, 1908–1945: The Official History. He owed his reputation as "the Spy of the Century" to the initiative of Roger Hollis.

Soon after his arrival in London in February–March 1943, when he
had become friendly with Philby, Hollis suggested that MI6 should try
to intercept, and possibly decipher, radio transmissions between Moscow and the British Communist Party headquarters and with certain
London members of that party known to be operating illicit transmitters
and receivers from their homes. It may be another coincidence, but a
small American team based in Washington had begun to do exactly that
regarding KGB transmissions between New York and Moscow a few
weeks earlier.

As the project was beyond the remit or resources of MI5, Hollis
urged the setting up of a new section in MI6 to do it, with relevant results being passed to MI5. Understandably, this has been interpreted as
evidence that he could not have been a Soviet agent because such a move
was so obviously opposed to Soviet interests. However, as the *Official
History* states, the London end of the communication system with

Moscow had been mainly in the hands of Bob Stewart, the well-known Comintern worker and Communist Party official. Surveillance of Stewart and others who were involved had revealed that both the London and Moscow transmitting and receiving stations, which had been part of the Comintern's network, had been out of commission weeks before Hollis made his suggestion. Hollis knew that because one of his sections had organized the surveillance.

Hollis put forward his idea to his chief, David Petrie, pointing out that MI5 would benefit because any intercepted messages to and from illicit radio operators in London would automatically be passed to MI5 and to himself in particular. Petrie discussed the idea with his opposite number in MI6, Stewart Menzies, who liked it and decided to set up a new section, 9, to specialize in all aspects of international communism and its links with Moscow, including the interception of messages between Moscow and other countries, and to concentrate on anti-Soviet counterespionage in general. The *Official History* specifically gives Hollis the credit for first advancing the idea, but the outcome was to be a massive disaster for British and American intelligence and a major triumph for the KGB. Hollis's unusual intervention was the first of several that he made during his long career. They are all consistent with the supposition that he was an agent of the GRU.

To help establish the new Section 9, in May 1943, MI5 loaned Jack Curry to MI6, and as he set about organizing the necessary changes, Philby informed his controller what was happening, as KGB documents have proved. The KGB Center then urged Philby to do all he could to secure control of Section 9 when Curry returned to MI5 because it would also run all the work of the British secret services against the Soviet Union and its friends. A released letter reveals that Hollis was in direct communication with Curry in April 1944, so he may have been kept informed of the progress in MI6 concerning his suggestion. Curry returned to MI5 in November 1944, and by that time, Philby had cleverly exploited an internal MI6 squabble that led to the sacking of the loyal, strongly anti-Communist officer Felix Cowgill, who had also been bidding for control of the new section.

A Foreign Office official, Robert Cecil, who observed Philby's activities at the time, noted that he had become vociferous in warning against the dangers of Soviet and Communist subversion. Coincidentally, this was what Hollis had done in writing from his sickbed in the sanatorium in the previous year and appeared to have done again with his new suggestion.

Neither Dick White nor Hollis liked Cowgill, who brusquely resented any intrusions into his MI6 work by MI5. So they both expressed pleasure when, in October 1944, Philby was promoted to be head of Section 9 by Menzies. The MI6 chief had been completely fooled by Philby, whom he had begun to regard as his "best man," and gave him a major role in drafting the charter for the new section.

Philby duly awarded himself responsibility "for the collection and interpretation of information concerning Soviet and Communist espionage and subversion in all parts of the world outside British territory." This involved the setting up of what Cecil described (in *The Missing Dimension*, edited by Christopher Andrew and David Dilks) as "a substantial number of overseas stations" for MI6 officers working under diplomatic cover and directly responsible to Philby. The charter also required him "to maintain the closest liaison for the reciprocal exchange of intelligence on these subjects with MI5."

Because of Hollis's already established working association with Philby, the latter's promotion was to MI5's advantage in securing as much future information as possible from MI6. However, if Hollis was a GRU agent, the requirement for reciprocal exchange between Philby and himself became almost tantamount to having a spy inside MI6, which, so far as is known, the GRU did not have. As Hollis already had responsibility for the collection and interpretation of information concerning Soviet and Communist espionage and subversion *inside* all British territory, the two of them bestrode the relevant intelligence world like a two-headed colossus. The situation also fulfilled Stalin's requirement that any major field of interest, such as British counterespionage, should be covered by both a KGB and a GRU agent, providing a continuing double check.

A particularly significant aspect of this remarkable situation, which was to last throughout the war, ensured that any intercepted messages to or from illicit radio operators in Britain would automatically be passed from Philby's section to Hollis for possible action. The messages would be in code, and it was Hollis who would decide whether to try to have them deciphered or not. If Hollis was Elli, the situation gave him the power to stifle any investigation into the transmitting activities of the Soviet agent serving as courier for any information he supplied. The

GRU Center could also be regularly assured that its transmissions were safe. While this may sound conspiratorial, a string of subsequent events that otherwise seem inexplicable all support it.

The revelation by the *Official History* that Hollis not only had been in charge of Soviet counterespionage during the war, but had been initially responsible for placing Philby in precisely the same position in MI6 was an entirely unexpected windfall. It states, "The formation of Section 9 was the result of Mr Hollis' action in urging the importance of the question of the use of wireless for the transmission of messages between London and Moscow." Of course, it makes no mention of the fact that it put a KGB spy in prime espionage position. The *Official History* was written in 1946, years before Philby's treachery became known or the MI5 suspicions against Hollis arose, and was published in its original form in 1999, though carefully edited.

Philby quickly expanded his department into a staff of more than thirty. They included the redoubtable Jane Archer, who had been fired by MI5, a recruitment that he would proudly describe in his memoirs, *My Silent War,* rating her as one of the "ablest professional intelligence officers ever employed by MI5." He capitalized on her knowledge of communism by putting her in charge of interpreting the wireless traffic of the anti-Nazi, pro-Soviet National Liberation movements in Eastern Europe. Her appointment suited Hollis by keeping Jane too busy to contemplate returning to MI5, as she would do eventually, while he entrenched himself there as the acknowledged authority on international communism.

The flow of information to Philby from his large staff eventually enabled him to inform the KGB Center in advance about any British attempts to infiltrate agents into Communist-controlled countries, as he eventually did with savage consequences for the agents. He betrayed British and American efforts to infiltrate anti-Communist Balkan refugees back into their own countries so that they were ambushed and executed. The same applied to agents infiltrated into Poland and east Ukraine, some by parachute. There may have been up to one thousand deaths, with Philby being responsible for many of them. The Foreign Office, and Robert Cecil in particular, had tried to induce Philby to scale down his demands for further expansion but had failed. In retrospect, some have imagined that it would have been in Russia's interests for him to have settled for a smaller, less effective department. In fact, the bigger the department, with him in full control, the bigger the waste of British intelligence resources. And the more important he became, the greater the chance that he might become chief of the whole of MI6. There appears to have been a genuine possibility that Philby was in line to become the chief, "C," which makes the concept that a Soviet spy might have risen to become chief of the smaller MI5 more plausible.

Philby's promotion also meant that he moved from the MI6 outstation in Ryder Street to the headquarters at 55 Broadway in Victoria, where all the secret records were housed. He stifled or denigrated information supplied by several Soviet defectors. He was often able to angle MI6 reports used by the government to help formulate foreign policy so that they reflected the Soviet Union's interests. Through his close association with Hollis, he could report on all MI5's anti-Soviet activities and perhaps much more, because Freddie Beith remembered Hollis as being "nosey about things that were not his business."

Philby's exalted position also gave him influence in the wartime equivalent of GCHQ, which intercepted and deciphered radioed messages and was run by MI6. According to the MI5 officer Peter Wright, the postwar GCHQ possessed some ninety thousand intercepted Russian messages, and on Philby's advice, their decipherment was terminated on the grounds that the effort would not be worthwhile. Later, when his written advice was discovered after his defection, a start was made, but by then many of the messages had been destroyed.

Meanwhile, as is shown by an entry in Guy Liddell's diary on July 10, 1944, Hollis knew about the latest American attempts to intercept and, hopefully, decipher clandestine Russian messages being sent between Moscow and New York, which was the KGB's main U.S. espionage center, particularly regarding the Kremlin's efforts to secure atomic bomb secrets. The first deciphering breakthrough by the American team that had been working on Russian codes since February 1943 had occurred in November of that year, becoming the early stage of an operation code-named Bride and, in 1961, Venona. When Hollis had first heard of Bride is uncertain, but he probably knew about it by May 1944, because early in July, the FBI sent him a report on the subject that was so secret, MI5 had first been required to agree that not even MI6 would be told anything about it. To have been trusted with such a document, Hollis is likely to have had previous communication with the FBI on that subject. Coincidentally, the KGB changed its code system in May

1944 to make it more difficult to break, and soon afterward, both the KGB and the GRU also changed the code names of most of their agents. Pure chance? Or the Moscow response to information, treacherously received, that code breakers in both the United States and United Kingdom were mounting a determined effort to decipher Soviet intelligence messages?

Whether Hollis resisted briefing Philby about the FBI work on Soviet codes is so far unknown, but Bride/Venona, which has been called "the greatest secret of the cold war," was certainly leaked to the Russians. Blame for the leakage has been attributed to an American, William Weisband, who had been born in the Soviet Union of Russian parents and had joined the U.S. Army in 1942. As a fluent Russian speaker, he became involved in the Bride operation, but according to his Soviet controller in America, Alexander Feklisov, he was not activated until early 1945. When the KGB and the GRU took action to strengthen their codes, Weisband was serving in North Africa, where he had been posted in mid-1943. The FBI officer Robert Lamphere, who was centrally involved with Bride/Venona, was to become so sure that Hollis had been responsible for the "initial tip-off" to Moscow about the project that he would state that belief in his memoirs, *The FBI-KGB War*: "The prime culprit in this affair was Hollis." The recently released FBI report to Hollis about the successful breakages explains Lamphere's belief.

On all counts, Philby was in the perfect position to nullify British efforts to counter Soviet espionage, as he did consistently, without raising suspicion, because while doing Moscow's bidding, he remained vociferous in railing against Communist subversion. As KGB general Oleg Kalugin was to put it in his autobiography, Philby became "the fox guarding the hen-house." At the same time, Hollis was the guard dog that rarely barked or bit. Like MI5, MI6 was then a law unto itself, with no external oversight whatever, which was a huge advantage and consolation to any spy inside either agency.

Philby's new appointment also involved him with the Joint Intelligence Committee (JIC), where, as the Kremlin's ear, he learned many of the nation's most significant secrets. By working late in the office, he acquired not only a reputation for devotion to duty, but access to documents he was not entitled to see. Only after his guilt was proved did his colleagues realize why he had been so obliging in offering to lock their desks and filing cabinets for them when "working late." KGB documents in Philby's own hand chillingly reveal how he sat in his MI6 office or in his home after a hard day, writing details about all his MI6 colleagues and their secret operations and plans, along with their character strengths and, especially, weaknesses that might be exploited. He revealed everything he knew about the operations of MI6 and MI5, leading to the deaths of many of their agents. Like his co-conspirators, he did his worst against Great Britain and the United States, and they all deserve to be vilified forever, especially now that we have a clearer view of the tyrannical, discredited system they were hoping to impose on us.

KGB documents show that whenever Philby was faced with required action damaging to the Kremlin's interests, he took advice from the Center. Often he was urged to stifle the action, but sometimes he was told not to interfere, as he needed to score occasional MI6 successes to maintain his cover. As for any intercepted Soviet wireless messages—the basis of Hollis's original suggestion—it transpired that few could be deciphered then, and those that were proved to be of little consequence, especially as Philby could warn Moscow about them.

Philby's acquisition of responsibility for all MI6's counterespionage work against Russia has been described as "a masterstroke in the history of espionage." The extent of Hollis's contribution to this stunning success seems never to have been appreciated before, least of all by White and other officers of MI5, unless they chose to remain silent about it. Nobody appears to have recognized the significance of this major disclosure in MI5's own *Official History* about Hollis's crucial role in Philby's espionage. It was a gross anomaly in Hollis's career that was never spotted by those who eventually suspected and interrogated him, though the facts were lying in the registry in Jack Curry's book.

It was most unusual for an MI5 officer, especially one as junior as Hollis, to suggest changes in MI6, which resented any invasions of its "turf." Indeed, according to Sir Percy Cradock, a former chairman of the JIC, it was common practice in MI6 to refer to MI5 as "the enemy." For that reason, Hollis, who was known for his caution, may well have consulted Philby for friendly advice about the possible reaction in MI6 before pressing for its adoption. In that case, he would have received encouragement. It could have been counterproductive for Philby to put forward such an idea himself and then press for control of it, and it is not impossible that it originated in conversations between the two men. Hollis may also have taken advice from Dick White, who made it clear in his biography that he was delighted with Philby's appointment, as he had always felt that he should be promoted. It would have been natural for Hollis to have asked White how his suggestion might be received in both MI5 and MI6.

Outrageously, the release of the *Official History*, which had been compiled exclusively for internal use, was entirely the consequence of another security blunder by MI5. In 1997, MI5 learned that its proven Soviet spy Anthony Blunt had supplied the KGB with an entire draft of the *Official History* before he had left in 1945! As the officially approved introduction to *The Guy Liddell Diaries* reveals, it was only when the KGB decided to declassify some of its stolen documents that the MI5 management felt driven to follow suit—a disgraceful situation for any security agency. Until its appearance in 1999, the extraordinary part that Hollis had played in making Philby's triumph possible was unknown outside the secret services, and even there it does not seem to have been appreciated.

Though it is hard to believe that Philby was unaware of Hollis's crucial role in making him a master spy he made no mention of it in his memoirs, *My Silent War*. Nor did his biographer, Genrikh Borovik, who received Philby's full cooperation, record it. In that large book, *The Philby Files*, Philby makes no mention of Hollis at all. As Sherlock Holmes might, again, have asked himself, "Why didn't the dog bark?"

Until his death, Philby was to insist, when questioned, that he did not know whether Hollis was a Soviet agent or not. Whether Hollis knew that Philby was a spy until shortly before his defection also remains unknown. Nor is there any evidence that the GRU Center knew it, such was the secrecy regarding sources. However, if Hollis was a secret Communist sympathizer, it would have been unusual for Philby, as another, not to have recognized him as such during their many conversations.

When MI5's *Official History* was being compiled, the section heads wrote their own accounts of their activities and passed them to the editor. Hollis submitted his part in creating MI6's Section 9 as his best, personal, wartime shot, never thinking that it would be published. He did that, of course, when Philby was regarded by the MI6 chief as his best officer and long before the traitor was exposed.

Philby's promotion meant that he became Hollis's opposite number, "investigating Soviet and Communist affairs," as he related in *My Silent*

War. Philby described Hollis there as "likeable, of cautious bent," noting that they were soon "exchanging information without reserve on either side" and that in their statements to the Foreign Office and service departments, "they never failed to work out an agreed approach." In other words, as Philby and Hollis each became the accepted authority on communism and Soviet counterespionage in their respective services and their colleagues deferred to them, they had cornered the market.

Written in Moscow in 1966–67, *My Silent War* contained some KGB disinformation, but there is no doubt that after Philby's new appointment, the two men were required to meet regularly and exchange views in the line of duty. Those who knew them both agree that Philby had the superior intellect and was probably able to dominate his MI5 partner on most issues. However, Hollis's part in it was probably greater than generally appreciated because he was the more experienced in counterespionage work by several years. If he was Elli, he was also a more experienced mole.

Under the interchange arrangement, Hollis could have told Philby what he knew of MI5 moves concerning any Soviet spies and agents. These seem to have been few, but negative evidence—that the Soviet spies were not being pursued—was of enormous value to Moscow. In short, Hollis became Philby's main source of what was happening in MI5—or not happening—about countering Soviet espionage, and the relevant details were channeled to the KGB as a regular service. They even included information about the surveillance of Cockburn, as letters between MI5 and Philby concerning his contacts reveal.

For the KGB, Hollis's close liaison with Philby was like having an extra spy inside MI5, where they already had Blunt. It is now certain from declassified KGB documents that Philby reported to Moscow in detail on his meetings with Hollis. As they confided in each other, Philby was able to tell Moscow that MI5 had bugged the headquarters of the British Communist Party, confirming the tip also supplied by Blunt. Officials there were warned, with the result that MI5 heard only disinformation suggesting that the party was solidly and loyally behind the war effort.

If Hollis was Elli—and somebody was—there can be no doubt that he would have funneled to the GRU all the information about MI6's work that he received from Philby. If the GRU's records ever become available, it would be fascinating to see how much it knew about the activities of MI6, where it had no known spy.

It seems likely that between 1944 and 1946, when Philby and Hollis worked together in London, little that MI5 was doing was unknown to the KGB. One of the documents Philby passed to his controller described, in detail, Hollis's F Division at Blenheim, including the fact that Hollis had invited him there to see it. Blunt also reported on his MI5 colleagues. So there can be little doubt that there was a KGB file on Hollis. The fact that several KGB defectors have insisted there was no such file in the KGB archives could be a measure of the intense security in which it was kept.

CHAPTER 22

Red Light from Green

WHILE HOLLIS HAD BEEN IN THE SANATORIUM, ONE OF HIS assistants, Hugh Shillito, had interrogated a veteran Communist named Oliver Green, who had been arrested for forging coupons necessary to obtain gas, which was severely rationed during the war. A routine police search of his house had revealed photographs of War Office secret documents about German weapons, the organization of German forces, and other matters, which MI5 traced to weekly intelligence summaries.

On February 4, 1942, Green had been sentenced to fifteen months' imprisonment for forging the coupons, which as a printer he had been able to do. The MI5 files showed that he had been known as a Communist Party member since 1935, and in April 1938, Maxwell Knight had reported that he was employed in Great Britain on a "secret mission for the Party," though no action had been taken. A further report on July 4, 1938, had stated that Green was taking a printing course in preparation for a special job. It had been initialed by Hollis on July 6, showing that he was already active regarding Communist subversion and had known that Green was suspect.

Shillito (F2b/c) was detailed to visit Green in Brixton Prison on August 11, 1942, to question him, and the full details of the consequences of this and later interrogations became public only in 2006 with the release of the relevant MI5 files. To induce Green to talk, Shillito immediately offered him incentives to confess to espionage for the Soviet Union. He was assured that anything he said would not be used in evidence against him. He was warned that if he failed to cooperate, there would be investigation into his Communist friends. Further, when threatened with possible prosecution under the Official Secrets Acts, he was told that his cooperation would be rewarded by a recommendation for a reduction in any sentence.

Green confessed not only to being a Soviet agent, but to running a sizable spy ring of informants. His sources—all Communists—included a fitter in an aircraft factory, a merchant sailor, a member of the RAF, and someone in a secret government department. They were widespread, and he needed to travel far to service them. He once saw fifteen in one month but normally contacted each one once a fortnight. Green and his agents were paid expenses doled out by the GRU in cash. The standard precautions had to be used at each meeting, hiding places for messages being used occasionally. Green confirmed that his sources never met a Russian GRU officer. The GRU tradecraft required him to be the sole intermediary for their information.

Born in 1904, Green had been apprenticed in the printing trade and had gone to Spain early in 1937 to fight in the International Brigade. After being wounded, he was asked if he would "undertake espionage against Franco," the Fascist Spanish general, and he agreed, but when he was introduced to a GRU recruiter, he was urged to return to England and spy for the USSR there. He was willing and was given a token sum of £40 in dollars—part of the signing-on process—and then received details about a rendezvous with a Soviet controller in London. He was required to find his own way back and returned early in 1938, beginning operations a year later, during which time he was given £500, found a safe house, acquired photographic equipment, and had been allotted some agents. He had been forging gas coupons so that he could visit them.

Green was questioned several times by Shillito in August and November 1942. On November 21, by which time Hollis was back at work from his sojourn in the sanatorium and in overall control of the case, as the documents prove, Green was interrogated more thoroughly. While refusing to give any names, which he claimed he did not know, he provided details of the Soviet methods used to avoid detection. He indicated that his Russian contacts were posing as members of the Soviet Trade Delegation based in London. He then disclosed that several agents in Britain were transmitting directly to Moscow by radio and gave details of their methods used to contact the Center late at night, the messages being encoded and sent by high-speed Morse. He said that the operators had made their own radio sets, which were usually kept outside in a hollow in a post or wall in case their house was searched.

As his evidence confirmed much that Walter Krivitsky had recently revealed, Shillito was quickly in no doubt that Green and his associates had been working for the "Fourth Department of Russian Intelligence," which was another name for the GRU. In the method preferred by the GRU, he had been recruited abroad. He said that all his agents had been handed to him by his Russian controller and that he had never been allowed to recruit any himself. He was required to photograph all the documents secured by his agents so that they could be quickly returned.

Green then revealed that he had been told the Moscow Center had a spy inside MI5. There can be no doubt that he gave that warning loud and clear, because in 2007, the MI5 website, which was featuring the Green case, highlighted his claim "that there was a Soviet spy in the Security Service." Green said that he had been assured that should he or any other agent become suspect by MI5, the Center would be told immediately so that action there could be taken to warn the agent and those servicing him. This was the first witness evidence of a traitorous protective hand for GRU agents inside MI5. To be effective, the MI5 spy, described by Shillito in his report as an "agent in the Security Service," would need to have been involved in Communist or Soviet counterespionage, as Hollis had been while Green had been active. Green could not have been referring to Blunt, who was solely KGB.

By December 2, 1942, Shillito had given Hollis a full note of his findings. This was around the time that Igor Gouzenko had heard of such a spy, code-named Elli, while working in the code room of the GRU Center in Moscow. What Hollis—or anybody else—thought about Green's claim is unknown, but he passed a copy to the director general, David Petrie, on that day, praising his assistant in a covering letter for his "perseverance and imagination."

In the copy of this report in the National Archives, someone in MI5 had specially marked Green's claim about the "agent in the Security Service," but there is no evidence that action of any kind was taken as a result. With most counterespionage officers concentrated on the German threat, it was Hollis's responsibility to initiate any action, but like Gouzenko's confirmation of such an agent three years later, Green's warning was stifled somehow. Petrie and the rest of the management may have dismissed it as a GRU invention to give its agents reassurance, or perhaps the claim was considered "unthinkable."

Hollis also sent Shillito's report to Guy Liddell (director of counterespionage), who in a long reply on December 8 praised it and recommended an inquiry into the illicit wireless activities and made some suggestions for doing so. He made no comment on the existence of an agent inside MI5, however. Hollis suggested that "a slightly expurgated copy" should be made for circulation outside the office, and when that was eventually done, with many cuts, the original subheading "Agent" in the British Security Service was downgraded to "Informant."

Green left Brixton Prison on December 3, 1942, and was followed by MI5 watchers to his address with great difficulty, as, being professional, he took all manner of evasive actions. On December 5, Hollis initialed a memo from Shillito requesting a letter check on Green. His telephone was also tapped, with one call showing that when he had left prison, he had joined the St. Pancras branch of the Communist Party. This was the branch to which Cockburn belonged and where Brigitte Kuczynski— one of the toxic troika—had been propaganda secretary and still belonged, being an important member of the Rote Kapelle, as the CIA handbook records.

On December 3, 1942, Roger Fulford reported on an interview with a woman Communist in whom Green had foolishly confided. She confirmed that Green had been regularly funded through surreptitious meetings with Soviet controllers whom he believed to be Russians. He had received extra money to pay his agents, who had to sign receipts. His chief controller had given him a radio transmitter, which he had passed to a trained agent while practicing in Morse to make himself proficient. It was all standard GRU tradecraft, as the Sonia case would eventually confirm, and there could be little doubt that Green had admitted the truth. Nevertheless, he was never prosecuted for his extensive espionage. At some stage, MI5 decided that his prosecution on security grounds "would not help the war effort." A trial, even in camera, when he might have testified about a Soviet spy inside MI5, would not have been welcome to the management. The case became one of many that would be resolved by "amicable elimination"—a cover-up in what MI5 regarded as its best interests. Later, the practice would be extended, by Hollis in particular, to include major villains, with MI5 not so much dispensing justice as dispensing with it.

The Green case was a further example of a homegrown Communist being used by the GRU as an active spy.

On September 30, 1944, information about the GRU's use of photography by its agents was reported by Hollis in a letter to M. J. Lynch of the U.S. embassy, for onward passage to the FBI. MI5 interest in Green continued until September 1946, fattening his files but achieving nothing else. Such items show that Hollis had remained regularly informed about Green and could hardly have failed to recollect his warning about a mole inside MI5 when Gouzenko made the same allegation in 1945.

A study of the Green files shows that he was a competent and dedicated agent runner in charge of a ring considered sufficiently productive by the exacting standards of the GRU Center. His evidence was a series of revelations from someone inside the Rote Kapelle conspiracy against Great Britain. His details of illicit GRU transmitters were all in the MI5 records available to Hollis on his return from the sanatorium. Yet nothing effective was done, or ever would be done, to track them down.

MI5's much sanitized *Official History* lamely records that "Green's statements regarding the use of wireless transmitters have never been satisfactorily cleared up." Yet down the road from Blenheim, where the files were compiled, Sonia was transmitting the most sensitive information. (Coincidentally, two days after Shillito had written to Hollis about Green's possible call-up for military service on December 17, 1942, he had repeated his fears to Hollis about Sonia and her treacherous husband, but without effective response.)

Green's other important disclosure, demanding action, was his statement that the GRU had an agent on the staff of MI5. The possibility that there were two GRU spies in MI5 at same time would seem to have been very unlikely, so although Green would not have known the code name, he may have been referring to Elli. The *Official History* avoided mentioning that Green had fingered a GRU spy inside MI5. Instead, it inadvertently belittled Hollis by stating that "the only important success obtained during the war" by F2c, the Soviet espionage section, which he ran, was "Shillito's painstaking disclosure of Green's organization."

Nor did MI5 appear to appreciate the significance of Green's statement that the GRU had provided him with a safe house. The use of such abodes by other much more dangerous operators, like couriers running Maclean, Philby, Fuchs, and possibly Elli himself, was completely missed or deliberately ignored.

CHAPTER 23

A High-Level Culprit

—

THE KGB RECORDS HAVE REVEALED THAT, EARLY IN 1943, THE chief KGB officer in the Soviet embassy in London received a list from one of his agents naming all the people known to be working on the atomic bomb project in Great Britain. He noted that one of them, Klaus Fuchs, seemed to be doing particularly important research at Birmingham University, and after inquiries in Moscow had shown that he was an ardent Communist, it was eventually agreed that an attempt should be made to recruit him. It was not until the end of November that the KGB Center discovered that Fuchs had been working for the GRU for more than two years—further evidence that the two agencies kept the identities of their own sources and couriers, such as Elli and Sonia, tightly secret from each other.

In the spring of 1943, Sonia asked Fuchs to prepare a list of all the atomic information available to him. The GRU Center then passed his response to the State Defense Committee, which selected the top-priority items and passed them to the KGB for follow-up action by its foreign agents. The GRU chief, Lieutenant General Ilichev, sent Sonia a list of twelve urgent requirements, which she passed to Fuchs on June 28—espionage to order, again. These recorded events show that Fuchs was under continuing direction and control from the military intelligence Center itself, as presumably was Elli.

In the beginning of August, the Center urged Sonia to concentrate on securing the maximum amount of information from Fuchs and delivering it to London. In the following month, never happier than when actively servicing the Soviet cause, she brought off the prime single achievement of her career—the receipt and transit of the Anglo-American Quebec Agreement just sixteen days after it had been signed in utmost secrecy in Canada. In light of what is now known from various archives, what clues are there to the identity of the spy who provided Sonia with that supersecret in such damaging detail?

The culprit could not have been Klaus Fuchs. He knew about the British determination to send scientists, including himself, to America if concord could be reached, but he would not have had access to such a particularly secret political document at Birmingham University. Fuchs was eventually to insist that all his contacts with Sonia had been on country roads outside Banbury except for the first, and only, occasion when she had visited him in Birmingham. He did not visit Oxford for that purpose. In her memoirs, Sonia specifically stated that Fuchs did not know her address—a routine GRU requirement. She also made it clear that, unusually for GRU agents, they did not use hiding places for the transfer of his documents, but always met posing as German refugee friends so that he could put them into her hand. *Duboks* were reserved for the transfer of messages concerning future meetings. Further, the GRU archives show that after seeing Fuchs in mid-August, Sonia did not meet him again until November.

The fact that the GRU chiefs allowed the authors of *Superfrau in the GRU* to reveal the coup but kept its source secret from them indicates that it was someone else whom they are not yet prepared to name, perhaps because close relatives are still alive.

Nor could the traitor have been any of the minor agents Sonia claimed to have recruited. He had to be a spy with exceptional, high-level, and rapid access to top-secret political information and who could safely visit Oxford and deposit a document near Sonia's house.

Letters dated March 1945 from the diplomat Sir Ronald Campbell to the Privy Council requesting copies of the Quebec Agreement to show to the foreign secretary confirm that the Foreign Office had been excluded in 1943. Sonia's document could therefore not have leaked from there. That deficiency eliminates Donald Maclean or any other Foreign

Office diplomat or official. The GRU had no known spy in the Foreign Office at that time anyway, and as Sonia did not serve any KGB agent, Philby, Blunt, Burgess, and Cairncross are also eliminated.

The only GRU spy known to have been operating in the Oxford area with potential need of a courier with independent transmitting capability was Elli. Further, the date was not long after the time when, according to Igor Gouzenko, information from Elli was so highly prized that it went straight to Stalin, as the Quebec information certainly did.

Elli was in MI5, where the director general, David Petrie, would have received a copy of the Quebec Agreement because of his responsibility for its security. It was standard practice that information on extremely secret issues requiring MI5 protection from foreign intelligence agents was imparted to the director general, who then decided which divisional heads needed to receive it.

It seems most unlikely that such a supersecret document as the Quebec Agreement would ever have been sent to Blenheim, to reside in the registry there where so many might see it. So if the culprit was Elli, he had to be based then in MI5 headquarters in London.

Hollis seems to fit all the requirements. He was then based at MI5 headquarters and needed to visit the Oxford area regularly because his staff was still at Blenheim, living in and around the city. Documentary evidence indicates that Hollis was the only MI5 section chief who had already been informed officially that the atomic bomb project existed. Because of his close connection with Michael Perrin when clearing scientists, like Fuchs, to work on it, he had known about the project for more than two years. He was also one of the few people who knew the names of all the scientists chosen to move to America, because he had been involved in clearing them for work on the bomb there. That was necessary because, as Margaret Gowing states in her officially sponsored book, *Independence and Deterrence,* Britain had given General Leslie Groves, chief of the American atomic project, a specific undertaking to make security checks on them. By 1943, Hollis was regarded as MI5's atomic expert. So the Quebec Agreement may have been circulated to him on that account as well. He could then have written a summary rather than remove the document itself.

There is further documentary evidence that Hollis was one of the few who knew exactly what was going on before, during, and after the Quebec talks. This occurred mainly because of his continuing working relationship with Perrin, who had overall responsibility for intelligence and security in Tube Alloys. The volumes of the official history of the atomic bomb by Gowing make it clear that Perrin was a most important figure in the talks leading to the Quebec Agreement. Documents now in the National Archives also reveal the extent to which Perrin was involved in the preliminary negotiations. He had talks with Vannevar Bush, then the chief American scientist on the embryo project, who visited London with Henry Stimson, the U.S. war secretary. Gowing's book *Britain and Atomic Energy, 1939–1945,* specifically states, "The draft agreement was one result of the London talks with Stimson and Bush."

Clearly, Perrin knew the nature of the Quebec Agreement in advance. He also knew that the agreement had been signed because he had been given the all-clear to dispatch the first batch of scientists. He is also likely to have confided in Hollis to explain the reason for the haste. They had already become mutually trusting colleagues, and with MI5 then being regarded as utterly secure, Perrin may have felt no reason to withhold any details during their meetings in their London offices or at Blenheim. Hollis may therefore have been told all that the Sonia Station eventually provided, whether he had seen the text of the agreement itself or not. The text of *Superfrau* states, "On 4 September, Sonia reported data on the results of the conference," suggesting that she sent all that she had learned from her source. As she dealt with her information so expeditiously, the odds are that she received it on that day and knew that the dispatch was urgent, though in view of the time needed for encoding, it might have reached her on the preceding day.

On September 4, Sonia also transmitted a list of the atomic scientists chosen to work in America. Where did she get it? The fact that the first batch of scientists had all been cleared in advance is shown by the haste with which they arrived in America. Hollis was involved in their clearance.

Information about Hollis's attitude, precisely at that time, to any leakage of information to Moscow could be significant, and by chance, it exists for all to see in an MI5 file entry now in the National Archives. In the file on Otto Frisch, coauthor of the historic atomic bomb memorandum, there is an item dated July 12, 1943, concerning one of his friends, the atomic scientist Engelbert Broda, who not only was suspected of being a Soviet agent, but, as late as 2006, was named (wrongly) by MI5 as having probably recruited the traitor Alan May. It states that Hollis "has decided that it would be quite useless to take any measure to discover if Broda is passing the information he possesses to the Russians, although he thinks it quite possible that he would do so." Such a defeatist attitude not only was in the interests of Broda and Soviet intelligence, but could have conditioned Hollis into regarding any leakage of the Quebec Agreement to Russia as inevitable anyway.

Hollis had particular reasons for being in the Oxford area at the relevant time. On Thursday, September 2, he had written a "Most Secret" letter to Special Branch about the possibility of interviewing Olive Sheehan, the female accomplice of the Soviet agent David Springhall, who was still serving her short prison sentence. As his letter went into precise details of the case, with a list of many other names, which could have been obtained only from documents held in the registry in Blenheim, he needed to be there on that day. Under Hollis's direction, his assistants were also engaged, at that very time, in preparing a list of Communist Party members working in secret government departments or in the British Armed Forces. All the records being consulted were, again, stored at Blenheim, and as the information was to be supplied to the prime minister's office, Hollis had a pressing reason to be there on that score, too.

Early September was also the very time when Hollis and Perrin were actively engaged together as a matter of urgency in going through the motions of vetting more of the scientists for dispatch to America. This had to be done at Blenheim, where their records were held, so Hollis had that further reason to be in the Oxford area. September 4 was a Saturday, but MI5 was working a six-day week, and there is documentary proof that its Blenheim outstation was in business that day. A letter from Box 500, Oxford, dated September 4, 1943, was dictated and signed that day by Hugh Shillito, one of Hollis's assistants.

Among possible suspects, Hollis was unique in having a reason to visit the house where Sonia lived on the edge of its grounds. Neville Laski, the owner of the big house, who was usually there at the weekend, was a source of information for Hollis, and they also had the common interest of being ardent Old Cliftonians. So Hollis would have had a ready excuse for being in that area.

As the leak was of such massive proportions, the supplier of the information is also likely to have been someone who could be confident that neither Sonia nor her transmissions were under surveillance. That factor reduces the candidates to a small number, of whom Hollis was certainly one, as the evidence of the reliable MI5 officer Kenneth Morton Evans has confirmed. Not only did Hollis know which suspected Soviet agents were under surveillance, but he had full control of the circumstances.

Another factor worthy of note is Sonia's confidence that her message would not be intercepted, because at that time, she had additional reason to fear that her activities might have been betrayed by her former husband, Rudi Hamburger, with whom she had managed to remain in occasional touch. Rudi, who had continued his full-time dedication to GRU espionage, had been arrested "for espionage and sabotage" in April 1943 by U.S. security authorities, while operating in Iran. As documents released in 2006 show, he had confessed that "he had been a professional agent for the Russians and would remain one." He admitted that he had been spying on British and American activities in Iran on behalf of the Red Army. The Americans handed him to British security for further interrogation, and reports to MI5 induced Shillito to renew his interest in Sonia with an MI5 memo dated October 29, 1943, seeking information about Mrs. Len Beurton, "now living in Oxford."

In the previous month, both the FBI and MI6 were requesting information from MI5 about Rudi and his former wife. This was known to Hollis, and if he had been the supplier of the Quebec information, he would have also known that no action whatever to trace Sonia's transmitter was in train. He also knew that Rudi had not incriminated Sonia during his interrogation.

Sonia's receipt of supersecret information of such consequence supports the contention that the GRU had posted her to Oxford specifically to service a source who had high-level access and operated in that area. The speed with which she dealt with it shows that the source sometimes produced information so urgent that it needed to reach Moscow without delay rather than being transferred to the Soviet embassy in London. Hollis is the only known candidate who fulfills those requirements. In her modest circumstances, it is most unlikely that Sonia could have found and recruited such a high-level source. All the details support the supposition that the source had already been on the GRU books and that Sonia had been sent specifically from Switzerland to service it.

While "smoking gun" evidence is unlikely to be found so long after the event, the documentary evidence that Hollis had been in Blenheim on September 2, 1943, is close to it. If it could also be shown that he had visited the Laski home that day or on either of the two subsequent days, it would be closer still.

As late as March 1951, Winston Churchill was urging President Harry Truman to agree to the publication of the full terms of the Quebec Agreement, of which he was particularly proud, but for congressional reasons, Truman still wanted to preserve the secrecy. Had Stalin known, he could have obliged Churchill by publishing it himself—a comical situation had it not been so pathetic.

CHAPTER 24

Calamitous Clearance

—

KLAUS FUCHS RECEIVED HIS VISA FOR TRANSFER TO AMER-
ica on November 22, 1943. He met Sonia that day to tell her that he and
several other scientists were going there, which confirms that he had not
been the source of the list of such scientists that she had already received
and transmitted on September 4. He also gave her precise details of his
departure, which was eventually scheduled for December. She needed
the American address of his sister and was also required to tell him the
arrangements for contacting his new courier once he was on American
soil. Sonia passed on the Center's commendation for his work and gave
him £50.

Fuchs's transfer to the United States, as a temporary British government official to work alongside American nuclear scientists, had
required a further examination of his security credentials. So on November 17, MI5 had been asked if there was any objection to the grant of
an exit permit. As records released in 2003 prove, Hollis was in charge
of the examination and responsible for the ill-fated result. By that time,
he was head of the whole of F Division and had a junior officer who was
responsible for his old task of overseeing Communist refugees, but he
chose to do the clearance himself. In reply to a specific American questionnaire about Fuchs's security, Hollis had reported that he was politically inactive and there were no security objections to him—a clearance
on which the Americans believed they could depend.

The thinking behind this clearance, which was to have such devastating consequences, is revealed in a recently released MI5 document about the Fuchs case, signed by J. C. Robertson in 1949. It states, "In 1943, this case was dealt with on the basis that he would be of less danger to security on the other side of the Atlantic." Whoever had been originally responsible for that cynical assessment could not have made a more politically damaging blunder—unless it had been deliberate. Driving any wedge between Great Britain and the United States had long been a high Soviet priority.

According to the official history of Britain's atomic project, *Independence and Deterrence,* the Americans were never told that Fuchs's clearance had been "qualified." That had been so to the extent that there had always been some official reservation about him because of reports about his communism and connections with active Communists, such as Hans Kahle. At that point in time, Hollis was especially alert to the connection between communism and Soviet espionage. Earlier in November, he had sent a memo to his chief, David Petrie, about the danger of scientists known to be Communists engaged in secret work and had also written to the Home Office about it, thereby indicating that he was "on the ball."

Margaret Gowing describes the omission of alerting the Americans to the reservation about Fuchs as a "major error of judgment." If that is what it was, it could hardly have been more major, for Hollis's assurance would quickly prove to have been catastrophically misleading.

On January 10, 1944, Hollis compounded the deception by recommending that the deliberate dishonesty should be continued, though this was not to become fully known until 2004, when an MI5 report sent to Prime Minister Clement Attlee on February 7, 1950, was declassified. Fuchs had arrived in the United States on December 3, 1943, with fourteen other British scientists, including Rudolf Peierls and Otto Frisch, who were all quickly set to work on various aspects of the bomb project, being based mainly in New York City. On January 10, 1944, the Supply Ministry, the London government department employing and paying Fuchs, told MI5 that he might be required to stay on in the United States longer than previously expected. As this was deemed such a "very important matter vis à vis the Americans," the cautious Michael Perrin suggested to Hollis, in writing, that "the case should be reviewed." Hollis immediately replied that "there was no objection to Fuchs remaining in the US," having made no further checks. He then added cynically that "it might not be desirable to make any mention to the US authorities of the earlier allegations of Communist affiliations."

Another MI5 document in Fuchs's file released in 2004 confirmed that on January 10, 1944, "Fuchs' record was examined again by the Security Service in view of his membership of the British Mission to the US and of the extremely secret nature of that mission." The conclusion reached was that "it was unlikely that he would attempt to make political contacts in the US"—an assessment that proved to be correct, as Fuchs was to concentrate on espionage there, taking care to remain silent about his political views.

As was customary, the Supply Ministry followed MI5's advice, and this opportunity to warn American security authorities of Fuchs's previous Communist connections was ignored. Had they known of them, it is unlikely that Fuchs would have been allowed to work in the Los Alamos atomic bomb laboratory. Indeed, the supercautious chief of the U.S. atom bomb project, General Leslie Groves, might well have demanded his recall to Great Britain.

Details of the American aspects of the situation, which had led to the disastrous entry of Fuchs into the United States, have been revealed by the FBI's release of a letter to General Groves from Dr. W. L. Webster of the British Central Scientific Office in Washington. When Groves had been presented with a list of the British scientists joining the project, he had insisted on carrying out a security check on all of them. British officials had been so offended that he had been talked out of it, but he still refused entry for the scientists until given a clear statement concerning their security status. Webster's letter then told him, "I have been instructed by the Director of Tube Alloys that I am to give you an assurance that each person has been subjected to a special clearance by the Security Organization in Great Britain." (After Fuchs's exposure, Groves was bitter when none of the British who had resented his suspicions sent him any apology. Had he then known how superficial the clearance of Fuchs had been, he might have been more vociferous.)

The U.S. government was to sever its atomic collaboration with Great Britain for a different security failure in 1946, but the eventual exposure of Fuchs in 1950, coupled with Hollis's actions and omissions, ruined any chance of restoring it for many years. This was to prove extremely expensive to British taxpayers, because research already secretly accomplished by the Americans had to be repeated. A later report to Attlee (almost certainly prepared by Hollis) attempted to excuse the deception of the U.S. authorities by explaining that the negative advice had been given because no reliable evidence that Fuchs had Communist affiliations had existed.

So if Hollis was Elli, he had brought off a double coup for Soviet intelligence. He had kept Fuchs in prime espionage position, and he had ensured that if the U.S. government eventually realized what the British had done, it would compromise atomic collaboration with Britain, as it eventually did. Had the U.S. authorities been warned that Fuchs had Communist links—as they should have been—Hollis's decision to avoid warning them ensured that Fuchs would give maximum service to the Soviet Union.

A GRU archival document prepared in 1945 recorded that during January 1944, Fuchs was transferred to the KGB while in America, and the GRU had no further dealings with him. This implies that Sonia did not service him after he returned to Britain, where he remained under KGB control. The same document also recorded, "During the time that he operated for the GRU, Fuchs communicated many valuable documents about the theoretical calculations of uranium atomic fission and the creation of the atomic bomb. These materials were forwarded to the Chief for Scientific Affairs of the State Committee for Defense. In all, during 1941–1943 Fuchs provided more than 570 sheets of valuable materials."

Sonia's part in expediting Fuchs's espionage was crucial, but it had lasted little more than one year of the eight during which he systematically stole atomic secrets for Russia, his major crimes being committed in the United States. Also, it was only one of the twenty years that she devoted to the GRU. These facts must always be remembered when assessing her overall career as a GRU agent, in which she serviced other spies and for which she was so highly honored in Moscow.

The fact that Fuchs had been able to betray so many secrets because Hollis had repeatedly ensured his security clearance is regarded by MI5 as pure coincidence. So is the fact that the Radio Security Service was never encouraged to locate the transmitter used by Fuchs's courier, Sonia. Whatever the reason, the United States is owed a particular apology for the damage inflicted by Sonia, as well as by Fuchs, which it never seems to have received from any British authority.

Melita Norwood was also transferred to the KGB at the same time as Fuchs, and thus Sonia was no longer required to serve her. The circumstances in which Norwood, who had already been named in 1938 in MI5 documents as a treacherous Communist, secured official access to atomic secrets three years later are unknown. What is certain is that this, too, happened on Hollis's Communist watch.

The Communist menace was reanimated early in 1944 when MI5 suggested a better vetting system for people with access to secrets. Grimly unimpressed by MI5's performance, Churchill reacted by giving the vetting responsibility to a secret panel of Whitehall officials. Churchill's panel was deeply resented by MI5, with Hollis trying to insist that all such cases should first be referred to him. In a memo to Petrie on February 24, 1944, he recommended his minimalist policy, arguing that the aim was "to deter possible leakers" rather than transfer suspects out of secret work to less sensitive jobs: "Such transfers might reveal to the person concerned that he was viewed with suspicion," and "for this reason we would be unlikely to bring many cases before the Panel." This excuse for inaction allowed suspects to continue to have access to secrets. Meanwhile, Communists like Maclean and Burgess in the Foreign Office, Philby in MI6, and Blunt in MI5 itself continued to leak like ruptured drains without interference from Hollis or anyone else, to the delight—and amazement—of the Russians.

The dire situation did not go unnoticed by Hollis's assistants, such as J. H. Marriott, who in a memo dated July 12, 1945, drew his attention to "the unsatisfactory state of affairs which, by reason of the presence there of members of the Communist Party, prevails at many establishments on secret work where they should not be employed, even though the war is over." Hollis agreed, expressing his particular concern about the Royal Aircraft Establishment at Farnborough, but no effective action ensued.

Eventually, largely through lack of initiative by Hollis in informing Churchill's panel about suspect cases, it slowly died from disuse, to the relief of MI5.

CHAPTER 25

An Enlightening Letter

—

WHEN SONIA'S HUSBAND, LEN, HAD REGISTERED THE BIRTH of his son, Peter, shortly after his wife's Quebec coup, he had described his occupation on the birth certificate as "of independent means"—meaning "paid by the GRU." Sonia made no attempt to hide her membership of the conspiratorial Kuczynski clan, by giving her correct maiden name on the certificate, of which I have a copy. (Contrary to statements in several books, at no time in Great Britain did Sonia or Len ever take the unnecessary risk of using the name Brewer or any other pseudonym.) The Beurton file also shows that MI5 soon knew about the birth.

In July 1943, Len had been bold enough to ask MI5 for help in joining the RAF in return for "having rendered valuable assistance in Switzerland." Soon afterward, he joined the RAF as a radio operator, and Sonia quickly had a stream of male visitors, noticed by the Laskis. On November 3, 1943, the persistent Hugh Shillito continued to pursue Len, urging the RAF security authorities that if he had access to anything that the Russians did not know, "we should consider turning him out of it." He requested a report from Beurton's commanding officer, and the traitor was eventually transferred to the army, where, it was felt, he could do less damage.

There was, however, no further interest in Sonia herself, and the reason for that is revealed in a letter signed and sent by Hollis to the Amer-

ican embassy in London on August 10, 1944. It clearly represented the
view he already held within MI5 and had imposed on his colleagues because it was entered into the registry file on the Beurtons and is now in
the National Archives.

The letter was in response to one sent to MI5 on behalf of the FBI by
the U.S. embassy official M. J. Lynch. Dated July 24, 1944, and referring
to the arrest of Rudi Hamburger in Iran, Lynch's letter asked for details
about his former wife (Sonia) and her children. Though addressed to
another officer, Hollis insisted on answering it. He first explained that
while Ursula Beurton's father was not definitely known to be a member
of the Communist Party, her brother, Jurgen, was "a Communist of
some importance and has been the subject of correspondence between
us." (That statement would prove to be highly significant in the context
of the eventual trial of Fuchs.) Hollis then stated that Ursula's four sisters had all come to MI5's notice "in a Communist connection." He
recorded that Ursula had come to Britain, as Mrs. Beurton, in 1942,
though she had arrived in February 1941, as was stated repeatedly in the
Beurton file, which presumably he had consulted. He stated that her first
son, Michael, had been born in Shanghai in February 1931 and that a
third child, Peter, had been born on September 8, 1943, in Oxford,
where she was living at Avenue Cottage.

These statements are evidence that Hollis was aware that Sonia had
been in Shanghai the same time he was. The file also shows that he had
known she had been domiciled in Oxford, very close to the Laskis, for
about two years. He also knew, from the Beurton file, that she had been
a Soviet agent in Switzerland and, from the information of his assistant
Shillito and the police, that both she and her husband, Len, had been on
the Security Control blacklist of suspected persons and had remained
under considerable suspicion in Oxford. He was also aware from the
Rudi Hamburger file that she had been previously married to a full-
blooded GRU spy who was still active and "had been handed back to the
Russians at dead of night on a lonely road," as an MI5 memo records.

Nevertheless, he assured the FBI, through Lynch, in the following
terms: "Mrs. Beurton appears to devote her time to her children and domestic affairs. She has not come to notice in any political connection,
nor is there anything to show that she has maintained contact with her
first husband. There is no doubt that she, herself, has Communist sympathies and her present husband has been the subject of investigation on

account of possible Communist activities. He is, however, now serving in the RAF and our investigations have, so far, failed to substantiate the suspicions against him."

In that letter, Hollis could hardly have given Sonia a fuller security clearance, both to the FBI and within MI5 itself, because the text was copied to the Beurton file in the MI5 registry as the official view of its expert on Soviet espionage and Communist affairs. He had effectively cleared Sonia, both with the U.S. authorities and within MI5, as he had previously cleared Fuchs, and he had done his best to clear Len. Yet Sonia had not only been servicing Fuchs, but had transmitted the Quebec Agreement in the service of a major GRU spy!

There is also new evidence that she and Len may have recruited and serviced a further fellow German Communist—an atomic scientist working at the Clarendon Laboratory in Oxford, whose wife Sonia had met socially. If so, that would be yet another Soviet spy missed by Hollis.

The text of Hollis's letter could hardly have suited the GRU chiefs better had they written it themselves. It confirmed the safety of Sonia's cover, almost certainly placing her beyond further interference by MI5, of which there is, in fact, no trace until 1947, when it was forced on them by events. Hollis's overriding opinion, which was fraught with damaging consequence, effectively gave Sonia free rein to continue to service her remaining agents, who may still have included Elli.

As the officer in charge of Soviet espionage, Hollis prevailed in this issue over his more cautious colleagues—as he would do repeatedly in other situations—to the Soviet Union's general benefit. Naïvely, Dick White and other superiors had deferred to his expert opinion. Hollis could, of course, have argued that he was simply stating the facts as they were because MI5 had acquired no hard evidence of espionage in Britain against either of the Beurtons. Under Hollis's guidance, there had been little field effort to do so.

A further intriguing question poses itself: Why did Hollis insert such a false date about Sonia's arrival in the Oxford area, reducing it by at least a year, when the MI5 records repeatedly stated that she had arrived in February 1941? Sheer sloppiness seems a most unlikely answer when he was aware that the irascible FBI chief, J. Edgar Hoover, might see the document and possibly raise questions directly with the MI5 director general, as he sometimes did.

What particular purpose could this falsification—taken at some risk to his reputation inside MI5—have served? If Hollis was Elli and Sonia had been sent to service him, he would have been scared that someone might spot the coincidence that she had arrived in the Oxford area shortly after MI5 had been evacuated there. So stating in writing that she had not arrived until 1942 greatly reduced the danger that some astute FBI officer might do just that.

Hollis's feeble comment on Sonia's brother, Jurgen, was to have an astonishing consequence—the GRU agent's appointment to a U.S. Bombing Research Mission to assess the effects of Allied bombing on German war production and morale. Using her radio set in Oxford, Sonia secured the GRU Center's delighted agreement to the venture, and Jurgen was to serve as a German-speaking statistician. Around the same time, Jurgen was even more incredibly involved in an American venture to parachute "anti-Nazi" German refugees sheltering in Britain into Germany to report on conditions there. When searching for volunteers, the young American in charge was urged to seek the help of Dr. Jurgen Kuczynski, who, after an interval in which Sonia again consulted the GRU to clear his involvement, recommended a list of dedicated Communists who were all first approved by the Moscow Center!

Further letters from the U.S. embassy in 1945 show that the FBI had been unimpressed by Hollis's reply. They told Hollis that Sonia had certainly been maintaining contact with her previous husband, Rudi, "as late as December 1942." In faraway Washington, they knew more about Sonia than Hollis admitted. In response, Hollis wrote unapologetically, "I was interested to see that Hamburger was still in contact with his former wife, two years after her remarriage to Beurton," but he offered no assistance, suggesting that the FBI should try MI6, where any requests would have been handled by Kim Philby.

On August 25, 1946, John Cimperman, then the intelligence officer at the U.S. embassy, wrote to Hollis asking him to "make arrangements to interview Ursula Beurton" to ascertain Rudi's whereabouts. MI5 declined any action, a file note about the reply stating, "There seems to be no good reason for supposing that the lady can answer the question. I am doubtful whether we can properly ask her." Sonia was not to be disturbed for the FBI! The various implications of Hollis's letters to the U.S. embassy seem indicative of an MI5 protective hand for GRU agents—and perhaps a self-protective hand. Had these been Hollis's only errors of such consequence, the charitable might dismiss them as due to sluggish incompetence, but as further MI5 documents will show, his protective blind-eye practice continued blatantly, especially with relation to Fuchs and later, again, with Sonia.

In my view, these letters, unknown until 2004, may be as near to "smoking gun" evidence against Hollis as any that still exists.

CHAPTER 26

First Atomic Spy?

IT HAS BEEN WIDELY ACCEPTED BY STUDENTS OF ESPIONAGE
that the first warning signal to the Soviet Union about the existence of
the atomic bomb project was provided late in September 1941 by the
Scottish traitor John Cairncross. Recruited at Cambridge University
and under KGB guidance, he had cleverly intruded himself into secretarial work with the uranium committee (Maud), which by July 1941 had
agreed that an atomic bomb was possible. The government proposed to
pursue its development with urgency, and on September 20, the armed
forces chiefs decided to initiate work on a plant to make a uranium
weapon. Cairncross saw a detailed report of the outline plans and gave
a summary to his KGB controller, Anatoli Gorski, code-named Vadim.
There is no doubt from KGB documents reproduced in the *Daily Telegraph* on January 12, 1998, that Cairncross was the source of that information.

Colonel Vladimir Barkovsky, a KGB officer code-named Dan who
was in the Soviet embassy in London when Cairncross's atomic information arrived there, has described it, with pride, as "the first in the history of the Russian Intelligence Service." In a lecture to American
military intelligence officers and atomic weapons officials in 1994, he described how he had made a summary of "a bunch of documents," which
was radioed in code to the KGB Center in Moscow. Photographs of the
documents were then dispatched there "by diplomats' pouch." Later,

Cairncross passed Gorski a complete copy of the Maud report, which revealed a method for producing uranium explosive and estimates of the critical amount required for a bomb. In Barkovsky's retirement, when he talked freely to researchers in Moscow, he recalled how he had to rush the photography because the copy had to be returned to Cairncross with all speed.

Details of the Center's reaction to this coup are given in a KGB archival document secured by Nigel Bance and reproduced and translated in his book *Ultimate Deception*, which he published under the pseudonym Jerry Dan in 2003. The document is a letter sent by General Victor Kravchenko to Lavrenti Beria, the KGB chief, to alert him about Great Britain's atomic plans. It confirms that the information reached the KGB Center in Moscow in late September 1941, to be followed by more early in October. It urged Beria to "task the foreign agent network to collect specific authentic materials relating to the building of apparatus and experimental plant to manufacture uranium bombs."

Other documents, however, have now shown that the rival organization, the GRU, had been informed of the project at least five weeks earlier by its own atomic spy, Klaus Fuchs. As already described, a deciphered message sent from London to the GRU Center in Moscow revealed that the GRU officer Simon Kremer had a meeting with Fuchs on August 8, 1941. Either then or very shortly after, Fuchs was formally recruited as a GRU agent. For that to have been permitted, the GRU Center would have been told the nature of Fuchs's work in advance of that date. So the date of August 8 proves that the GRU knew the simple but crucial fact that an embryo British atom bomb project existed more than five weeks before the KGB did, including possibly details of the Frisch-Peierls memorandum. It would even seem likely that in making the arrangements for Fuchs to meet Kremer ("Johnson") again, Jurgen Kuczynski would have told the Russian the nature of the information that the scientist wanted to impart. So the GRU could have known of the existence of a possible bomb project as early as July 1941.

The GRU Center is now known, from officially published material, to have instructed its officers in London, and perhaps elsewhere, to discover all they could about the uranium bomb on August 11, 1941. So the Center appears to have waited for Fuchs to supply some details before acting on the news. However, that instruction proves beyond doubt that the GRU knew about the project several weeks before the KGB got wind of it. It is significant that the KGB's Barkovsky had been told nothing of the recruitment of Fuchs by the GRU's Kremer, who was working in the same building.

Though the true date of Fuchs's recruitment is in the KGB's own archives, KGB officers who even cite it in their writings still stubbornly insist that their agency was first with the atom bomb news, being unwilling to give the GRU the credit. It was in part to redress this that the GRU decided to declassify some of its archival papers and publish extracts from them in *The GRU and the Atomic Bomb*. The book states specifically that the GRU was first with the information, and the KGB has not challenged it since.

It is possible that neither Kuczynski nor Fuchs was first with the bare news of the existence of the bomb project. Another source may have alerted the GRU as early as May 1941. For Hollis to have conducted his first review of Fuchs as a security risk, he is likely of necessity to have been informed about the existence of the bomb project. Michael Perrin, who assisted Hollis, wanted Fuchs to work in the project and, when discussing the case, would have stressed its importance to the war effort and its urgency in view of the possible atomic threat from Germany, which was then the driving force. Perrin would have had no qualms about briefing the responsible MI5 officer about its general purpose, as MI5 was regarded as being inviolably secure in those days. So Hollis was almost certainly among the first British officials outside the war's most secret project to know about its existence, small though it was at that stage. He may have been the first MI5 officer to be inducted into the project, and it may be significant that there is no mention of any aspect of it in the MI5 *Official History*, from which particularly sensitive material was excluded before its publication. Throughout the war, nobody was better informed on the whole atomic project than Michael Perrin, and as Hollis was notoriously nosy—to an extent that was to cause concern in GCHQ—he could have kept himself abreast of the program as it unfolded. Released MI5 documents, particularly those dealing with the Quebec Agreement, show the closeness and continuity of Hollis's relationship with Perrin, who was an unwitting supplier of atomic information to his friend.

This atomic aspect of Hollis's access to secrets of special interest to the Soviet Union does not seem to have been appreciated before, least of all by those in MI5 who came to suspect him. Even at this late date, it is worthy of examination, especially as Hollis was to become recognized as MI5's atomic expert and would be a consultant and adviser to the influential Official Committee on Atomic Energy (code-named GEN 75) set up in August 1945 to report directly to the prime minister.

Hollis probably knew of the project three or four months earlier than Cairncross because he had cleared Fuchs to work in it in May 1941. He could not have told Philby about it, because in the spring of 1941, that traitor was still teaching in an SOE school in Hampshire. Hollis could therefore have been the Kremlin's first source of what was then the West's greatest military secret—the simple fact that an atomic bomb was sufficiently feasible for teams of scientists to be working on it.

Intriguing evidence from a KGB source supports the contention that Soviet intelligence had been alerted to the bomb project by May 1941 or soon afterward. At that time, the section of the KGB responsible for collecting scientific information was headed by Leonid Kvasnikov, who in May or June decided to ask KGB officers serving in Great Britain to collect any information about the military application of atomic energy. Later, he was to claim that he had done so on his own scientific initiative, but he may have been advised that there was something worth collecting—the usual Moscow response to information from an intelligence source. If Hollis had alerted the GRU Center about the atomic project in May, it would have been required to inform the State Defense Committee of such an important development. The committee would then have informed the KGB without revealing the source.

The May date for a tip from Hollis about the involvement of Fuchs in the project would mean that the GRU took about two months to secure him on August 8. That would be consistent with the usual practices of ultracareful consultations, checking, and agreement within the Center to ensure that Fuchs could be trusted. It would have been essential, first, to be certain that he was not a plant working for British intelligence and to make the meeting arrangements that had to be set up in England, with agreed recognition signs and passwords. The previously accepted version of events—that Fuchs approached Jurgen Kuczynski and was fully recruited within a couple of weeks or so—does not conform with the now well-known tradecraft of the Soviet intelligence services. A substantially earlier date for the GRU's knowledge of Fuchs as a potential spy does so, and the documented events already described show that to have been the case.

We have only Fuchs's word for the story that he volunteered his services, and when he made his confession, he did all he could to protect the Kuczynskis and his other conspiratorial friends. In his technical confession to Michael Perrin, for instance, he stated quite falsely that his first contact with the Russians had been early in 1942, six months later than the true date, and told other lies. He also referred to his courier only as "he," concealing Sonia's major role until she was safely in Communist Germany. Hollis's potential in the atomic capacity was to be intensified through his contact with the Official Committee on Atomic Energy, eventually becoming inestimable when he became MI5's director general. The possibility that Hollis was an atomic source and effectively talent-spotted Fuchs gives a new conceivable dimension to the Elli case. As Fuchs and Alan May both claimed for themselves, he may have convinced himself, as others would, that by helping to prevent the United States from having an atomic bomb monopoly, he was doing the world a service for the future.

Clearly, the GRU would have continued to treasure such a priceless asset and ensure its continuity by all possible means, especially by keeping knowledge of Elli's identity limited to as few people as possible. If his information suddenly dried up, Stalin would have asked why, and if it had been owing to any incompetence on the part of the GRU, heads would have rolled. A further reason for keeping his existence as secret as possible was the KGB's propensity for seizing the GRU's prime assets, if it could, as it did with Fuchs.

CHAPTER 27

Enormoz

—

AS WE HAVE SEEN, PURLOINED ATOMIC INFORMATION REACHED the Kremlin at such a pace that the Soviet leadership began to suspect that the American-British project was a hoax to induce them into wasting resources on work that could not be completed in time to affect the war. Both Stalin and Lavrenti Beria, the KGB chief, doubted that British security could be so lax that crucial details about such a secret weapon could be pilfered by amateur spies like Klaus Fuchs. Nor could the KGB Center understand how people like Philby, Maclean, and Blunt with known Communist affiliations had been accepted for secret work.

The fact that Philby repeatedly assured them that MI6 did not have a single agent operating inside the Soviet Union—as was true—strengthened their suspicions, especially when they had so many operating in Great Britain. As a result, the purloined information, including atomic secrets, had been treated as provocations to be filed but ignored.

The GRU's archives, however, show that its chief had been more impressed and had consulted senior members of the Academy of Sciences to stimulate high-level interest in the atomic bomb. He was eventually instructed, in mid-February 1942, to send all his intelligence material directly to Beria. This material helped to convince the KGB chief that the project was genuine, and in March he prepared a memo for Stalin on the U.S.-U.K. atomic project, urging him to take action. The long letter in which he summarized all the evidence is reproduced in *The GRU and the Atomic Bomb*.

Stalin reacted slowly, because of higher priorities for other weapons demanded by the German advances, with whole industries being transferred far eastward, but when the State Defense Committee followed up with a further letter in June, Stalin "meditated in his office," then announced, "It is necessary to make it!" On September 28, 1942, he issued a detailed full-speed-ahead decree to various scientific academies, institutes, and commissariats that is reproduced and translated in Nigel Bance's book *Ultimate Deception*. Nevertheless, a funded nuclear program could not be set up until 1943. The instruction to do that, signed by Vyacheslav Molotov, deputy chief of the State Defense Committee, on February 11, named Professor Igor Kurchatov as leader of the atomic laboratories and required him to report by July 1 on the possibility of producing a uranium bomb. In 1939, Kurchatov had written a memo about the military potential of nuclear fission; he had then been switched to other work, but on November 27, 1942, Molotov showed him the papers supplied by Fuchs and others. Because of the extreme Soviet attachment to secrecy, especially concerning spies, Molotov had stored all the reports from both the KGB and the GRU in his safe.

Kurchatov, who proved to be an outstanding and charismatic leader, was astonished and delighted, declaring that the data had "huge, inestimable significance for our State and science." In particular, he realized that Fuchs's information shortened the time required to build plants to produce atomic explosive and that the quickest way to a bomb was to use plutonium rather than uranium alone. He said that the stolen information filled in just what he and his colleagues were lacking. In March 1943, as Russian records reveal, he stated that the whole material, which then included documents supplied by Melita Norwood, showed that it was "technically possible to solve the uranium problem in a much shorter period than our scientists believed."

Molotov introduced Kurchatov to Stalin, and new laboratories were founded. Beria also set up a massive intelligence program to secure more information about American, British, and Canadian atomic research by every possible means. He assigned the code name Enormoz to the foreign research, because it was concerned with an explosive of enormous power. The name also became synonymous with the Soviet intelligence effort to secure it, which became enormous itself. The Soviet atom bomb project and Enormoz were both directed and controlled by Beria, who continued as head of the KGB, being an exceptionally capable, if ruthless, manager and administrator.

So in August 1943, the GRU was pressured into a special agreement to share its atomic sources with the KGB, but with each case being considered separately and depending on the operational requirements. The GRU was in no hurry to comply but, according to its archives, agreed to transfer some of its precious atomic assets at a conference of GRU and KGB leaders, presided over by the much feared Beria, at the beginning of 1944. The KGB's tough general Pavel Sudoplatov was named as chief coordinator of future GRU and KGB atomic activities, the work being centered in the Lubyanka building in Moscow.

Without his knowledge, Fuchs was formally handed over to the KGB on January 21, 1944, as was Norwood, around the same time, but as the Gouzenko case was to reveal, the GRU remained in command of its substantial atomic assets in Canada, including the atomic spy Alan May. The GRU also managed to maintain exclusive contact with some other atomic agents, as Bance's research has confirmed.

If Hollis was a GRU spy, he would have been considered not an atomic asset, being completely nontechnical, but an intelligence asset, and so would not have been automatically transferred to KGB control. (Peter Wright and other MI5 colleagues who suspected Hollis assumed that he, too, had been permanently transferred to the KGB at the end of 1943, which may have been a major blunder in assessing the case.)

In September 1943, Sonia's exposure of the Quebec Agreement had eliminated any remaining doubts about the Soviet need for an atomic project, and though she had produced her third child only a few weeks previously, it was she who had given Fuchs his final instructions, in November 1943, for his first clandestine meeting with his new KGB courier in New York City, where he remained for nine months. There, he was controlled by an exceptionally able KGB officer, Anatoli Yatskov, posing under the name of Yakovlev.

In September 1944, a letter from Kurchatov to Beria referred to three thousand new pages of purloined atomic information, mainly from America. The final total, from various sources, exceeded ten thousand. In the following month, Sonia received special greetings from the director at the GRU Center. This praise was perhaps, belatedly, for her outstanding work with Fuchs, but in view of the year's delay in that respect, it may have been for her more recent dealings. She was also transmitting information about Jurgen's espionage activities at the time, but as these had not yielded much by then, the praise may have been earned for her assistance to some other spy, perhaps the individual who had supplied the details of the Quebec Agreement.

Meanwhile, the U.S. authorities had accepted Hollis's assurances that Fuchs was secure because they had been given no indication that his security clearances had originally been qualified. So he was never checked in America—as he otherwise would have been—while given access to the most secret facilities.

In New York, Fuchs, who was given the KGB code name Rest (later Charles), worked on calculations for the production of uranium 235 and was allowed to visit secret establishments. In short order, he made contact with a new American courier working for Yatskov in February 1944, passing on all he learned.

Early in 1944, according to Margaret Gowing's official history of Great Britain's continuing part in the bomb project, when it was clear that Fuchs would be remaining in America, Michael Perrin went out of his way to ask MI5 for the latest and most detailed views on him. He wanted to be sure that, regarding American sensitivity about security, "we do not slip up in any way." MI5 replied that there was no objection to Fuchs remaining in the United States, as he had never been very active politically—which was incorrect. This had been a specific opportunity for Hollis to alert American security officials to the fact that Fuchs was a dedicated Communist, as MI5 then knew, and that his original clearance had been qualified. He did not do so.

When Rudolf Peierls, who had also been sent to America, was invited to join the ultrasecret bomb design team at Los Alamos in New Mexico, he agreed as long as he could take Fuchs with him. In that way, Fuchs arrived at Los Alamos on August 14, 1944. According to the Los Alamos scientist Joseph Hirschfelder, Fuchs was eventually involved in the editing of a twenty-five-volume secret Los Alamos encyclopedia, summarizing all the research carried out there. Throughout his time at Los Alamos, Fuchs remained silent about his Communist beliefs and aloof from political discussion, especially about the moral rights and wrongs of producing an atomic bomb. Even his closest colleagues did not think that he was pro-Russian. He also acquired a reputation as a sporadic heavy drinker who could hold his liquor.

In spite of the exceptional security imposed at Los Alamos, he contrived to give his new courier a long written report on all that he learned about the original uranium "gun" bomb and the more efficient plutonium "implosion" bomb. The gun bomb, code-named Little Boy, consisted essentially of a three-inch-caliber, smooth-bore gun through which a bullet of uranium 235, at the breech end, could be fired through a hollow cylinder of uranium 235 fitted near the muzzle. The two together would constitute a critical mass, which would instantly create an atomic explosion. (Amazingly, this gun principle had been put forward in the original Frisch-Peierls memorandum.)

In the implosion design, code-named Fat Man, a sphere of plutonium could be instantaneously squeezed into a dense, solid, critical mass by being surrounded by specially shaped packs of high explosive, which directed their power inward. Though the first weapon to be used, against Hiroshima, would be a gun bomb, the implosion type, which was eventually dropped on Nagasaki, was to be the preferred design because it was far more efficient in its use of scarce nuclear explosive. While Little Boy used about 135 pounds of uranium 235, Fat Man needed only about 14 pounds of plutonium and produced a greater blast.

The overall size of the bomb had to be governed by the fact that it had to fit into the bomb bay of an existing airplane. Little Boy was twelve feet six inches long and twenty-eight inches in diameter, its all-up weight being 8,900 pounds, much of this owing to a six-inch-thick steel casing that served as a tamper to delay its disintegration. Fat Man was a couple of feet shorter but was five feet in diameter and weighed 10,300 pounds.

Such information was of inestimable value to Russia's scientists and weapons designers, and Fuchs supplied a flood of it, including a sketch of the complex detonating mechanism of Fat Man. He also told them the critical mass of nuclear explosive required. In Little Boy, the two uranium 235 pieces formed a cylinder about seven inches long and six and a quarter inches in diameter. In Fat Man, the plutonium was compressed into a solid core about the size of a tennis ball. Fuchs also provided the invaluable information that the plutonium bomb had been originally planned as a gun assembly, but scientists had discovered that it would predetonate.

Fuchs's courier passed all that information to Yatskov, and it was quickly transferred to the Enormoz analysts in Moscow. In a succession of meetings, Fuchs was also to give the Russians documents about the production of fissionable materials and about the huge plants being built in America for that purpose. As KGB records show, in February 1945, Fuchs handed over a summary he had written of "the whole problem of making an atomic bomb." Then, early in July, Kurchatov received a KGB report giving precise details of the structure of the plutonium bomb, which was about to be tested in America. The information probably derived mainly from Fuchs, who later provided the technical results of the test. American atomic spies provided additional information.

Three months later, in London, Michael Serpell, an M15 counterespionage officer, decided to review the Fuchs file. In addition to the Gestapo information, he noted that Fuchs's name had appeared in a diary seized from a GRU agent, Israel Halperin, in Canada after the defection of Igor Gouzenko. He recommended that Fuchs be more thoroughly investigated, marking the file to that effect, but the advice was ignored by someone more senior.

Though well versed in the complexities of weapons, as a graduate of the Royal Military College of Science who later attended three atomic bomb tests, I could not fully appreciate the scale of Fuchs's treachery and his value to the Russians until I was able to examine the internal intricacies of nuclear bombs and warheads in 2002. When visiting the Atomic Weapons Research Establishment at Aldermaston in Berkshire, I was privileged to study the secret display of bombs and missile warheads, which are cut away to show their precise construction. Fuchs had revealed far more than the principles underlying Little Boy and Fat Man. He had provided nuts-and-bolts details of their complex construction and wiring, which saved the Russian designers months of effort.

No wonder the official U.S. report *Soviet Atomic Espionage*, issued in 1951, stated, "It is hardly an exaggeration to say that Fuchs, alone, has influenced the safety of more people and accomplished greater damage than any other spy, not only in the history of the United States but in the history of nations." The authors of the report were still unaware that the person responsible for keeping Fuchs in place, both in Great Britain and in the United States, had been Roger Hollis.

CHAPTER 28

The Strange Behavior of Roger Hollis

—

NOT LONG AFTER HOLLIS HAD CLEARED FUCHS FOR THE THIRD time, MI5 was faced with the first exposure of an atomic spy in the form of Alan May, another British scientist, when Igor Gouzenko shocked the free world with his revelations early in September 1945. After Gouzenko had also made the Elli allegation, the nearest available British intelligence officer flew to Ottawa on September 8 to learn all that he could. He was the MI6 representative in Washington, Peter Dwyer, who had already alerted London headquarters of the defection by secret telegram. Dwyer was joined by another officer who has been named as "Hollis from Britain" but was, in fact, Jean-Paul Evans from British Security Coordination, the intelligence-gathering outfit based in New York City and run by the Canadian William Stephenson. Neither of them was permitted to speak to Gouzenko directly because he had been spirited out of Ottawa to escape the KGB hard men who were looking for him.

After a briefing by the Canadian authorities, Dwyer quickly sent a fuller telegram giving all the details about Elli that Gouzenko had revealed to the Royal Canadian Mounted Police. Unless it has been destroyed, that telegram, which in our conversations the MI5 officer Peter Wright and I would refer to as the "Elligram," still exists in the MI6 archives. Wright, who examined it, assured me that it contained all the details about Elli, including the statement that he had "something Russian in his background." Dwyer was also representing MI5 at that stage, because the resident MI5 officer in Ottawa was being replaced, so the El-ligram, which was sent to MI6 headquarters in London, was also passed to MI5. Documents on the Gouzenko case, released in 2004, have con-firmed that MI5 first heard the details of the defection from MI6.

Though the MI6 chief, Stewart Menzies, was quickly convinced that Elli was not in his agency but was in MI5, he called in the head of his So-viet counterespionage section and suggested that he fly to Canada to bring back more detailed information. Thanks to Hollis, that man was Philby, who realized that Gouzenko was a low-level GRU official and would therefore have no knowledge of his own KGB activities. Appre-ciating that he would learn all about the case anyway by remaining at his London headquarters, Philby had no wish to move from that source of other information valuable to his KGB masters. It was a luck-of-the-devil decision for him because he was almost immediately embroiled in an extremely dangerous situation that required his icy control.

On September 4, the KGB officer Konstantin Volkov, stationed in Is-tanbul, had offered to defect to Great Britain with the promise of expos-ing seven British KGB spies operating in London. He had made this offer to a British consulate official, John Reed, who spoke Russian and later gave me a firsthand account of the incident and its consequences. As bait to secure the £27,000 he was requiring, Volkov had stated in writing that judging from the code names he had seen, there were two KGB agents in the Foreign Office and five in intelligence. When Reed's report was eventually passed to MI6, after bureaucratic delay, Philby read that one of the agents was "Head of a Department of British Intel-ligence" and immediately realized that it was himself.

On September 19, Philby alerted his Soviet controller, Kreshin, who warned the KGB Center and then ordered him to stay in London and delay any MI6 action about Volkov until the KGB had captured him in Istanbul. This duly happened, through incredible incompetence and disregard by the Foreign Office and by MI6 officials, with Volkov being spirited back by air to Moscow on September 24—sedated, heavily ban-daged, and on a stretcher. Philby, on the other hand, behaved with re-markable calm, and Volkov, with his priceless disclosures, which could have exposed Maclean, Burgess, Blunt, Cairncross, and others serving the KGB, disappeared to his death.

After successfully delaying any MI6 action for a fortnight, during which Volkov had been removed, Philby went through the motions of visiting Istanbul on September 26 on what he knew was a useless mission, returning to London to deal with any repercussions of the case that might be raised by MI5 or the Foreign Office, though neither did anything.

The reaction inside MI5, which was responsible for investigating Volkov's allegations, was appalling. There, it was eventually left to Hollis to examine them, and he did nothing of consequence, which some of his fellow officers would later see as being consistent with the possibility that he had feared that one of the alleged spies might be himself. After the defection of Maclean and Burgess, with suspicion finally falling on Philby in 1951, the awful truth of Volkov's information was to become apparent. White then asked Hollis why he had done so little, and according to White's official biography, Hollis replied, "It didn't seem important," and that ludicrous response was accepted as adequate. Hollis's record contains several such instances where he was convincing at appearing innocently naïve.

KGB documents cited in *The Mitrokhin Archive*—a stash of notes about KGB documents written by the defector Vasili Mitrokhin and smuggled out of Russia in 1992—have shown that before his execution, Volkov confessed that he had intended to reveal not only Philby's treachery, but clues to more than three hundred other Soviet agents operating worldwide.

Philby's known behavior throughout the Volkov episode is a prime example of the advantages enjoyed by a traitor infiltrated into any intelligence service. He is likely to be among the first to spot any clues to his danger and is often well placed to deflect or eliminate them. And the higher he is in the agency, the greater his chance of taking effective action to protect himself. The gross inadequacy of the MI6 inquest into the Volkov case and the lack of reaction in MI5 must have strengthened Philby's belief that his chance of being caught by such incompetent outfits was small. If Hollis was Elli, the same applied to him.

Significantly, when the Elligram was examined by Peter Wright, it was seen to be creased, with grimy edges, as it would have been had it been folded into four, taken out of the office in somebody's pocket, and then returned. It had also been initialed by Philby. There is no doubt, from a KGB report cited by Philby's Russian biographer, Genrikh Borovik, and from other documents now available, that Philby showed the telegram to his KGB controller in London, who immediately alerted the Moscow Center. Both the KGB and GRU centers had already learned of Gouzenko's disappearance from the Ottawa Soviet embassy, and Philby's action confirmed that he had defected successfully. When Philby told Menzies that it would be difficult for him to spare the time to visit Canada, he proposed that since Elli appeared to be in MI5, someone from that agency should be sent. In particular, Philby suggested that his MI5 counterpart and friend, Hollis, should go.

There was good reason why Philby, who could not be sure that all the information from Canada would continue to be sent to Menzies, chose Hollis. He was confident that his friend would tell him everything on his return, and he would then be able to report to his controller and influence Hollis's further actions, which he might not be able to do if any other MI5 officer was sent. He may also have taken advice from his controller about the choice, with which Menzies agreed.

Exactly when and how Philby communicated with Hollis about the proposed task of dealing with Gouzenko is now known from a document found in Philby's effects after his death and published in 1999 in the book by his widow, Rufina. It stated that it was his duty to telephone the information directly to his MI5 counterpart, Roger Hollis, especially as a suspect atomic scientist, Alan May, was involved, Hollis being by that time MI5's established expert on atomic issues. They then met in Hollis's office when they agreed that Gouzenko was telling the truth. On that same day, they met with a Special Branch officer from Scotland Yard to discuss the surveillance of May. As Philby recorded, he quickly warned the KGB.

Eventually, Philby wrote a formal note to Hollis stating that the Gouzenko case seemed to be more in his province, and the letter is said to exist in the MI5 files. Supporters of Hollis have argued that if he had been a Soviet agent, he would have destroyed the letter, because after Philby's exposure as a spy, it incriminated him. The fact that he did not do so was therefore evidence of Hollis's innocence. As it is now established that Hollis was in charge of Soviet counterespionage in MI5 at the time, the letter was of no consequence, as it had been officially quite proper for Philby to approach him, and Philby's document proves that he did so.

Hollis accepted the task and, probably supported by Dick White, put the suggestion to his superiors, who quickly concurred. At that time,

MI5 was responsible for "dealing with counter-espionage in the Empire" (as Hollis was quick to point out later in a letter he sent to Philby on February 19, 1946). So the case really should have been handled by MI5 anyway. The fact that Hollis was the resident authority on both Soviet espionage and atomic matters may also have swung the decision in his favor. He spoke no Russian, but neither did anyone else in MI5.

Hollis was detailed to interrogate Gouzenko, an assignment for which he had no experience, though the GRU defector could hardly have been more important to the whole free world. According to his MI5 colleague Freddie Beith, he was seen as a bad choice. "His withdrawn, diffident, and buttoned-up manner was unsuitable for interrogation work," Beith told me. Until that time, he had probably never operated officially outside his office.

Meanwhile, Gouzenko was still in the hands of the RCMP, who were moving him and his family to a succession of cottages. As the RCMP secured information from the defector, they sent copies of it to William Stephenson, the coordinator of Anglo-American intelligence in New York. Stephenson, who was a Canadian, had been involved in the Gouzenko case from the beginning and had set up a separate secure communications channel to link London, New York, and Ottawa for secret discussions about it. The British high commissioner in Ottawa, Malcolm MacDonald, insisted that only that channel should be used, and as Stephenson regarded himself as more connected with MI6 than with MI5, he sent all the information directly to Menzies, whom he named only as "C." (His own code name in the messages was 48,000, not Intrepid, as is commonly believed.) Furthermore, he sent it "For C's eyes only" in a code that only Menzies himself could decipher. In spite of such precautions, Menzies passed news of all the developments to his Soviet counterespionage expert Philby, who informed his KGB controller on a regular basis. The complete extent of Philby's day-to-day knowledge of the Gouzenko case was revealed by the release of MI5's massive archive in May 2007. Not only did MI5 have to send all its telegrams to the RCMP via Philby in MI6, but he was also first to see all the replies, including photostats of Gouzenko's original statements in Russian, which no doubt his KGB controller translated for him!

By September 10, Hollis had known most of Gouzenko's revelations, which were the talk of the London office, where the defector, referred to by the code name Corby, was accepted as "exceptionally accurate." Hollis's action on that day was intriguing, especially when reviewed in the context of Elli's and Moscow's reaction to the exposure of his existence. Within twenty-four hours of Gouzenko's disappearance from his GRU post in Ottawa, the GRU Center knew that he had intended to defect because it had been informed about the loss of the incriminating documents, which he had removed. So by September 6, the GRU Center was fully alert to its immense problems, and a damage limitation operation was quickly put in train. Soviet telegrams, which have since been deciphered along with published KGB documents, reveal the depth of this concern, including that about Elli. The director of the KGB Center (code-named Viktor) repeatedly instructed the Soviet controllers in the London embassy to reduce their meetings with Philby and other members of the Cambridge group and to watch for increased surveillance. The GRU Center urged similar precautions.

Examination of Gouzenko's record would have quickly reminded the GRU investigators that he had worked in the decoding center in Moscow, where messages from and about Elli were deciphered. So the protection of this highly valued penetration agent would have been among their first considerations. There would also have been special concern for any GRU agents, such as controllers and couriers, involved with Elli. If Elli was still based at, or visiting, Blenheim, as Hollis was, these would have been stationed nearby. Sonia is on record as stating that following the Gouzenko defection, the Center cut contact with her for many months to reduce the risk of not only her detection, but that of any agents she was serving. Fuchs was no longer one of them by that time. Neither was Norwood.

It is clear from decoded messages and published KGB documents that the two Centers—GRU and KGB—understandably feared that MI5 would make a major and sustained effort to identify Elli. This was expected to involve the continued surveillance of possible suspects, and in that process, other spies such as Philby and Burgess might be at risk. In view of the advice known to have been passed to Philby through his controller in this connection, it would seem highly probable that Elli would also have been warned to take special care and that GRU contact with him, in particular, would then have been suspended. In fact, the fears of both the GRU and the KGB chiefs had been unwarranted. MI5 did nothing beyond watching May, who had been allowed to return to London to take up an academic appointment at King's College, fixed weeks before Gouzenko's defection.

Gouzenko had revealed that May was scheduled to meet a new GRU controller on October 7 outside the British Museum, and MI5 needed to know his identity and, hopefully, arrest the traitor in the act of handing over secret information. May had therefore been allowed to fly to Great Britain on September 15, being watched by an RCMP officer and then by an MI5 watcher on the train to London.

Meanwhile, the response of Elli himself to his predicament may easily be imagined, especially if he recalled the original warning from Oliver Green about a GRU agent inside MI5 and feared that others might do so. The defection of any GRU coding officer was dangerous news for Elli, and the fact that Gouzenko had claimed there was a GRU spy in MI5 would have been terrifying. When the first news of Gouzenko's defection reached MI5, Elli would have realized that it was possible the GRU cipher clerk might know of his existence and might report it. The incident had not stopped the KGB from contacting Philby through his controller. If Hollis was Elli, then any action he might have taken at that time could be of exceptional interest. One declassified letter, which he dictated and signed in his tiny handwriting on September 10, 1945, when he may have been beset by fear and the need for evasive action, has surfaced in the National Archives. Stamped "Secret," it was addressed to the Foreign Office, from Box 500 in Oxford, showing that, while based in London, he still operated out of Blenheim.

On that day, whether Hollis was a spy or just in line of his MI5 duty, his first priority should have been to assess the significance of Gouzenko's revelations, especially about May, and what action they were likely to require by MI5. Yet he chose to make time to send another gratuitous letter and a facile report to the Foreign Office about the views of German Communists in Great Britain regarding Russia's postwar policy for Europe. Addressed to T. E. Bromley, who was the Foreign Office liaison man with MI5 and MI6, the report appeared to make two main points. It warned that the German Communists would set up a Soviet-style state in the Russian zone of Germany, which was obvious to all observers at the time. It also stated that Russia intended to withdraw its troops from the zone once the East German government was fully established, which turned out to be false, never had been likely, and was contrary to defense intelligence reports, to which I had access then.

As the report was unlikely to affect Foreign Office policy, which was far more realistic, being based on data from its own intelligence agency, MI6, one wonders why Hollis sent it, especially at that time. If he was Elli and felt under threat, as assuredly he would have, it was sensible to remind MI5 and other authorities that he was strongly anti-Soviet, just as he had done from his sickbed three years earlier.

A casual statement in the covering letter offers a further motive. Hollis stated that his information had reached MI5 from "a source in this country which has proved reliable on other occasions." Elli's couriers, both near Blenheim and in London, may have been German Communists sheltering as refugees in Britain. So if Hollis came to be questioned about his connection with either of them, having perhaps been spotted consulting one of them in an emergency, as the Gouzenko situation certainly was, he could claim that they were simply valuable intelligence sources, serving MI5's purposes. He could then point to his letter of September 10 as documentary proof of that. The letter would have provided a convincing fallback position. Otherwise, the timing of the letter at the height of the Gouzenko furor makes little sense. Sending such a letter was just what Philby would have done or what advice from the GRU Center might have suggested. In view of Philby's statement that they usually agreed on reports sent to the Foreign Office, and are now known to have been in close touch at that time, Hollis may have consulted him before submitting it, a contention supported by the nature of some recently released correspondence between the two.

Oddly, Anthony Glees presents the letter as evidence of his innocence, for it showed that he was "keeping tabs" on German Communists. In view of the threat posed by Gouzenko, the date of the letter is a truly extraordinary coincidence, but Hollis was the all-time king of coincidences.

Hollis left for New York by air on September 17, and on that same day, shortly after eight p.m., a top-priority KGB message of the greatest significance was transmitted from Viktor (Lieutenant General P. M. Fitin) in Moscow to Philby's London controller in a code that was broken many years later by GCHQ. It stated, "The Chiefs have given their consent to the confirmation of the accuracy of your telegram concerning Stanley's data about the events in Canada in the Neighbours' sphere of activity. Stanley's information does correspond to the facts."

Stanley was, then, Philby's code name, so this was clearly an answer to the information about Elli contained in the Elligram—which Philby had shown to his controller, who had sent its contents to the KGB Center. It meant that the State Defense Committee (the Chiefs) had given the KGB Center permission to ask the GRU Center (the Neighbours) whether they had such a spy called Elli in MI5 and whether the other details given by Gouzenko were correct. The GRU had told the KGB that they had such a spy and that the details were correct.

This decoded telegram is documentary *proof* of four issues crucial to an examination of the Hollis case. It is confirmation *from Moscow* that there was a GRU spy called Elli in MI5. It confirms that the details about him provided by Gouzenko—including the Russian connection—were accurate. As the KGB had clearly known nothing about Elli's existence, it proves that Elli could not have been any KGB spy such as Philby, Blunt, or Leo Long, who had all been recruited by the KGB and remained with that agency. It also showed that, apart from atomic affairs, the GRU and the KGB were still operating so independently in 1945 that they needed to secure permission even to confer about a serious intelligence event. They shared intelligence via the State Defense Committee but not the sources of it, and it is most unlikely that the GRU ever revealed Elli's identity to the KGB. With Stalin's personal interest in Elli, the GRU would have wanted to hang on to him exclusively.

Because of the deep concern about Elli, by both the GRU and the KGB, the evidence also suggests that Elli was still in place in September 1945. No officer who has retired from MI5 since, apart from Hollis, fits the facts about Elli described by Gouzenko.

No radio traffic showing the precise results of any further consultations between the KGB and the GRU concerning the Elli revelations has ever been decoded, but some instructions have been. The KGB specifically told Philby that he would have to warn another British Soviet spy (unnamed in the telegram) about Gouzenko's revelations when the spy returned from abroad. That spy was almost certainly Blunt, a proven traitor who was in Italy at the time, but Hollis was also abroad—on the way to Canada.

Other deciphered radio traffic showed that GRU controllers were required to report all details of their agents to the Center, which was why Gouzenko's friend in the Moscow cipher room had learned such details about Elli as the "something Russian in his background." (Later, Gouzenko was in no doubt that this former friend would have been shot for having broken the rules in talking to him about Elli.)

Understandably, MI5's counterespionage chief, Guy Liddell, objected to receiving the information from Hollis in Ottawa secondhand through MI6, and a message from him dated September 19 urged Hollis to arrange direct communication with MI5 headquarters in London. Hollis was not permitted to do so, and information about Gouzenko continued to be sent via MI6 through 1946 and probably beyond. There were two reasons for Hollis's failure. The high commissioner, Malcolm MacDonald, had complete faith in William Stephenson and continued to insist on using his channel exclusively, as Hollis reported to Liddell on September 22. Further, Stephenson, with whom I corresponded later, told me that he did not trust Hollis, having been warned by Liddell that he was "violently anti-American." The MI6 chief, Stewart Menzies, of course, was more than happy with the arrangement.

CHAPTER 29

In a New World

—

HOLLIS WAS IN NEW YORK BY SEPTEMBER 19, 1945, AND AFTER learning all he could from William Stephenson (who told me that he had received him coldly), he flew on to Ottawa, where he was briefed by the RCMP. This took some time, as he needed to know the whole Gouzenko story and especially the information about Alan May, the British scientist who was the first exposed atomic spy. He was told that in February 1945, Colonel Nickolai Zabotin, the GRU chief in Ottawa, had been ordered by the Moscow Center to contact May and had been given a password that the scientist already knew. Zabotin had instructed Lieutenant Pavel Angelov to telephone May (code-named Alek by the GRU) in Montreal, saying that he had a gift for him. During several meetings, May had handed over documents for photography, had provided minute samples of uranium 235 and uranium 233, and had confirmed the operating principles of the bomb.

Inquiries regarding the MI5 spy Elli had been poorly handled by the RCMP, which had little experience in counterespionage. The Canadian government was concentrating on the Canadian aspects, which were overwhelming its limited resources. One of the Canadian lists of spies fingered by Gouzenko included "Elli—an unidentified agent in England in 1943," but the RCMP regarded that as none of their business and left it to MI5, and Hollis in particular, for action.

Hollis was unable to see Gouzenko, because to protect the defector and his family from the KGB, which was prepared to seize them by force, they remained in secret places under armed guard. As Gouzenko's wife, Svetlana, told me in writing, they were moved among various cottages for about three weeks before being taken to the distant Camp X by the RCMP.

Meanwhile, in London, as documents show, MI5 was planning to plant incriminating secret documents on May, hoping that he would have them on his person when he met a Russian contact, the intention being to threaten him with possessing them during interrogation or even to use as false evidence in a trial. Later, MI5 was to induce the Tube Alloys chief, Sir Wallace Akers, to offer May two secret documents, in a feigned show of trust, but he declined them.

On September 24, there was a meeting in Ottawa between Canadian prime minister Mackenzie King, his chief civil servant, Norman Robertson, and Malcolm MacDonald, the British high commissioner, with Hollis in attendance, to discuss the Gouzenko case. The effect on such an inexperienced officer of finding himself representing the United Kingdom's interest in such exalted company is unrecorded. The only contribution by Hollis recorded by Mackenzie King was, "The Russians have got a lot of information on the atomic bomb." An MI5 telegram from Liddell on that date, however, shows that Hollis had been briefed to insist that no action should be taken against any of the spies in Canada before October 7, the day on which May was due to meet his controller in London. The suspect was to be watched that day, but Liddell realized that he would almost surely have been warned of his danger. (He had, if only through Philby.) Liddell expressed great concern about the political damage if May defected to Russia—"the thing we most fear"—adding that "he must be behind bars," indicating that he wanted him prosecuted.

In his report to London about the September 24 meeting, Hollis stated that it had been agreed that "the diplomatic aspects of the Gouzenko case had over-riding importance" because of fears of disrupting relations with the Soviet Union. He stated that MacDonald was drafting a recommendation to the Foreign Office against any publicity whatever. In spite of the horrific extent of the espionage, action should be limited to a secret diplomatic protest to the Kremlin, coupled with unpublicized interrogation of the known Canadian spies and of May. Hollis clearly agreed with this astonishing suggestion that the entire case, including the defection, should be completely covered up, advising MI5, "We are strongly opposed to the arrest of May unless necessitated by an attempt to escape to Russia. In this contingency, could he not be charged with attempting to leave the country illegally, thus avoiding the notoriety of Official Secrets Act charges?" Such feeble action would, of course, have been most welcome in Moscow.

Ensuing MI5 documents show that Hollis had quickly become regarded as being in charge of the whole Gouzenko case by other departments, such as the Foreign Office, and was the main recipient for any questions or information. He was to favor and perpetrate cover-ups throughout his professional career, and if he was Elli, stifling the whole Gouzenko affair was deeply in his interest. The last thing that Elli would have wanted was any publicity about his existence, which might generate questions in Parliament or the media.

The stifling of the Elli allegation was also encouraged by the MI5 leadership on three counts. A Labour government headed by Clement Attlee had been unexpectedly elected in July 1945. At that time, MI5 was directly responsible to the prime minister, and confirmation of a Soviet spy within its ranks would have meant a disastrous start with the new regime. It could disrupt the interchange of intelligence information with the FBI and, on the political front, could also end the atomic weapons partnership with the United States forged at Quebec in 1943. Continuing Winston Churchill's policy, Attlee was hoping to prolong the partnership, which he knew was being opposed by powerful American scientists, generals, and politicians.

Both Churchill and Attlee had quickly realized that without independent nuclear weapons, Britain would not merit a seat at the political "top table." Their scientific advisers, who knew the colossal cost and effort of the Manhattan Project in producing the atomic bomb, had told them that without continuing American cooperation, war-torn Britain would probably be unable to become and remain a credible nuclear power. So on September 25, Attlee sent a letter to President Harry Truman, who had succeeded Franklin Roosevelt following his death the previous April. In it, he stressed the "joint achievement" while suggesting that the two should meet, urgently, to discuss future control of military atomic power. Truman delayed replying for three weeks because he was anxious not to upset Stalin, while being urged by his own advisers to withhold atomic secrets from the Soviet Union. The whole issue had, of course, been bedeviled by Gouzenko's disclosures of Soviet espionage in the United States as well as Canada, about which Truman had been informed by the FBI, which had sent agents to Ottawa as early as September 10. Attlee therefore telegraphed Washington asking for urgent talks, and a meeting was fixed for November 9.

Hollis left Canada by air for New York and then London on September 27, arriving on the following day and imparting all the information he had gleaned to his superiors on September 29. Dick White confirmed to me in writing that Hollis's discussions at that stage had been solely with the RCMP, the Canadian Department of External Affairs, and Malcolm MacDonald. Hollis had concentrated on the May case, which was also of deep interest to his friend Philby, who was giving the KGB a running commentary.

In Ottawa, there was still hope that the Russians were not yet certain Gouzenko was in Canadian hands, but Philby had informed them of that long before. Any chance that Great Britain would agree to a course of action avoiding publicity was eliminated by a communication from the chief Foreign Office official, Sir Alexander Cadogan, who had consulted Foreign Secretary Ernest Bevin. While confirming that there would be no British action before the hoped-for meeting of May with a Russian on October 7, the robust Bevin was insisting that the agents should all be arrested and prosecuted, regardless of the consequences of any publicity. Rightly, as time showed, Bevin did not think that publicity would have any effect on Soviet policy, and he wanted the traitors brought to justice.

Still in deep shock at the Soviet duplicity exposed by Gouzenko, Mackenzie King and his advisers flew to Washington on September 29 for discussions with Truman about the implications of the international crisis caused by the revelations. Truman agreed with them that any arrests should be deferred until more could be discovered about the Soviet agents, especially about May and any spy ring involved with him, since he had visited American atomic research laboratories.

Hollis and Liddell inspected the British Museum rendezvous site, where it was hoped May would meet a Russian, and saw that it was overlooked by a pub, where arrangements were made for watchers to be installed. On October 7, Hollis was sent to meet the *Queen Mary* when she docked at Southampton, bringing the Canadian prime minister and Robertson for discussions about the Gouzenko affair with Premier Attlee. His mission was to inform Mackenzie King that the Foreign Office wanted his approval for May to be arrested if caught that evening meeting a GRU contact. King agreed, but neither May nor any contact appeared. The stakeout was repeated on October 17 and 27 with the same result. (Shortly before May died in 2003, he made a tape-recorded statement in which he admitted having been warned to avoid any meetings.)

Meanwhile, as Mackenzie King's diaries show, Hollis—and presumably his MI5 superiors—had quickly changed their attitude to conform with Bevin's and began to press for rapid action. So Hollis sent a message via "C" to the RCMP warning that delay in arresting the spies might imperil the whole operation. With Liddell's backing, he stated that the Russians might "get in first with some trumped-up charge while the suspects destroyed evidence and perfected their cover stories"—which they never did. However, on the same day, he attended a meeting at the Foreign Office, where it was realized that nothing could be done without first securing the joint agreement of Attlee, Mackenzie King, and Truman, which would take time. That suited the RCMP chiefs, who were sensibly recommending delay so that any of the unknown co-conspirators of the spies could be detected. Attlee agreed to the delay counseled by both Truman and Mackenzie King so that the spies' associates might be identified. It was to last nearly four months.

Documents from the KGB archives and released MI5 papers have now shown that on his return, Hollis personally briefed Philby in full detail about what was happening in MI5 about May and every other aspect of the Gouzenko affair. The papers stressed the difficulties and divides being faced by the British, U.S., and Canadian governments in trying to arrange the simultaneous arrest of all the suspects without previous publicity. The contents of another KGB document, revealed in the Russian biography of Philby by Borovik, show how that traitor continued to send details of the information about Gouzenko's debriefing to the KGB Center.

One of Philby's reports detailed MI5's reasons for believing (wrongly, as it turned out) that May would never easily admit guilt. This may be the explanation of May's failure to attempt to defect with Russian assistance—the GRU assumed that he would simply obey their standard advice and admit nothing while denying everything. Alternatively, the Russians may have written him off, having decided to dismiss all the espionage charges as a crude, trumped-up provocation, as they eventually did.

On November 3, the Foreign Office had asked MI5 to ensure that Hollis would be in Washington for the meeting, scheduled for that month, between Attlee and Truman, with Mackenzie King present, to discuss atomic energy policy. The problems of the Gouzenko case were also to be discussed, and Hollis was to be on hand to give advice. He duly returned to North America and probably paid a courtesy call to the FBI headquarters to discuss the May affair, but the FBI was not informed of the alleged spy inside MI5 code-named Elli.

Hollis was in Ottawa on November 7 when he was told that the Foreign Office was pressing for the prosecution of May to prevent his defection. He then moved to Washington, where Attlee and Mackenzie King arrived on November 9. By that time, there was increasing mistrust of Russia's motives in the minds of all three leaders, fueled largely by the alarming information being gleaned by the RCMP from Gouzenko. To what extent Hollis was called in for advice to the leaders is unknown.

The three leaders issued a declaration on November 15 urging the setting up of a commission, under the United Nations, to promote the control of atomic energy to ensure its use for purely peaceful purposes. Though nothing binding had been secured from Truman, Attlee returned to London with some hope of a new era of atomic collaboration with America—what was to become known in Downing Street as "the Great Prize."

At last, on November 21, 1945, according to an MI5 document (dated May 23, 1946), Hollis came face-to-face with Gouzenko during a further visit to Ottawa. Gouzenko had been brought back to the capital on another quick, protected visit, and Hollis was taken to interview him in the Justice Department in the presence of an RCMP officer who spoke Russian. Gouzenko told me, "He [Hollis] was introduced as a 'gentleman from England.' He was only about forty, but he was so stooped that he approached me in a crouching way as though anxious that his face should not be seen. I was surprised that this man, who seemed almost afraid to talk to me, asked me very little when I told him that the GRU had a spy inside MI5 in England, known by the code name Elli. We talked in English, but for such a short time that we did not even sit down.

He took very few notes, if any, and behaved as though he wanted to get away from me as quickly as possible."

Much later, Gouzenko repeated that account in an interview with Professor Peter Hennessy, then with *The Times*. He recalled the meeting as having lasted only a few minutes, when the object should have been to extract as much information from the defector as possible. He confirmed that the two had remained standing while he told Hollis about Elli and that "maybe, he asked me one or two questions." This account is supported by an MI5 document, dated May 23, 1946, which requested the RCMP to ask Gouzenko for more details about the GRU's messages to its Ottawa outpost about controlling the activities of Canadian Communists. Hollis had not questioned him sufficiently about the subject. (The document bears a written comment: "Presumably this refers to the meeting on 21/11/45.")

Proof that Gouzenko was not speaking with lengthy hindsight has been supplied by the Canadian reporter John Picton. He has put on record (in John Sawatsky's *Gouzenko: The Untold Story*) what Gouzenko had told him only a few months after his defection. The Russian had said that the meeting with Hollis had been extremely brief—"about three minutes"—with few questions asked. He said that the MI5 man, whose name was not revealed, approached him "with caution." Gouzenko also told William McMurtry, a Toronto lawyer, that the man, now known to be Hollis, was "almost trying to shield his face" and "spent a very short time" with him.

For Hollis to have treated Gouzenko so cavalierly after waiting so long to interview him and putting the RCMP to considerable trouble to arrange it demands explanation. Here was an ambitious officer with his first opportunity to question a Russian defector face-to-face. He knew that Gouzenko had exposed May as a traitor who had betrayed major secrets about the atomic bomb project, causing consternation in Downing Street and the White House and threatening postwar relations with the Kremlin. The situation could hardly have been more propitious for impressing his superiors in London, but he ended it with all speed. He even failed to put obvious questions about May to Gouzenko and—as MI5 documents show—was driven to ask the RCMP to pose them piecemeal weeks later.

Though MI5 has released many of its papers relating to the Gouzenko case, it has pointedly withheld Hollis's report on his interview and any other statements he made about Elli. It also released a mass of papers about the May case in 2007, and there was no mention of Elli there, either. Later, a request to MI5 from Peter Hennessy seeking information about the Hollis reports on Gouzenko met blank refusal.

A thorough search of the RCMP records made in July 2005 for Dr. David Levy, a Canadian academic, produced the statement "We were unable to locate any information about Hollis's visits to Ottawa in September and November." A former RCMP counterintelligence officer who has been making long inquiries in Canada has also found that no documents about Hollis's activities in Ottawa seem to exist there any longer. He has confirmed to Dr. Levy that Hollis had only one brief meeting with Gouzenko. As a Russian-speaking RCMP representative had accompanied Hollis during his interview with Gouzenko, it would have been standard practice for him to have reported on the event. The RCMP officer believes that this report and others involving Hollis have been "weeded out" and destroyed. Why, after so many years? It may be that the original reports in MI5 no longer exist, either, and in that case, it may be that the Canadians were requested to destroy theirs. If so, by whom?

According to the MI5 officer Peter Wright, Hollis said that he was "unimpressed" by Gouzenko and doubted that Elli existed and that if he did, he was not in MI5. For no legitimate reason, Hollis then suggested that Elli might be a member of the Double-Cross System, the extremely successful wartime group that had "turned" captured German spies and used them to deceive the enemy. Hollis had not been associated with it in any way, so his suggestion could have been an attempt to deflect suspicion from himself.

Hollis was to tell Dick White that he had found his encounter with Gouzenko "distasteful," which was conveniently supposed to account for his discomfort at the interview and for his dismissive report. White told me in writing that he appreciated his friend's feelings because he, too, disliked dealing with defectors—a sensitivity that no efficient counterintelligence officer could afford.

Later, Hollis submitted a longer statement, which according to Peter Wright, who read it, disparaged Gouzenko and undermined his credibility, though he would prove to be the most productive defector of all time. That statement has also been withheld or destroyed.

In the previous year, Philby had debriefed a GRU defector, Major Ismail Akhmedov, in Turkey, where both had then been based. Although Akhmedov had provided a mass of information, Philby had submitted only a fraction of it to MI6 headquarters and had derided him as a source. Whether by coincidence or not, Hollis did exactly the same with Gouzenko. Hollis's supporters have stressed his honesty, but he seems to have been far from honest in his report on his meeting with Gouzenko.

Though it was clear that Elli was a GRU spy, neither Hollis nor anyone else recalled Walter Krivitsky's advice and looked for a woman courier servicing him in Great Britain. Nor is there any evidence that Oliver Green's 1942 allegation about a GRU spy inside MI5 was recalled. The final result of Hollis's various activities was the burial of the Elli case for more than thirty years.

On February 6, 1946, Hollis, Liddell, and MI5 legal advisers decided that "it would be desirable" to charge and deal with May in Canada, where he had committed his offenses. His trial and imprisonment there would reduce the publicity and take the spotlight off MI5 and the British government. So Hollis dispatched a telegram (via Philby) urging the RCMP "to consult their legal authorities" about a Canadian trial and to obtain a warrant so that the British police could quietly arrest May and escort him to Canada under the Fugitive Offenders Act.

The Canadians were to have none of it. The failed gambit to limit the traitor's offenses to Canada, when in fact he had been recruited in Britain and had first operated as a spy there, would not deter MI5 from eventually claiming that the arrest and conviction of May had been a triumph for the service.

CHAPTER 30

A Mystery Resolved

O N FEBRUARY 14, 1946, THE CANADIAN AUTHORITIES AD-vised MI5 that on the following day they would be making a public statement about setting up a royal commission to "investigate leakages of information to a Foreign Power" and that all the Canadian suspects would be arrested in predawn raids by the RCMP. MI5 officers therefore interviewed Alan May in London on the afternoon of February 15, when he denied having any contact with Russians.

May was questioned again on February 20, and when asked why he had failed to keep the appointment outside the British Museum, he answered, "I had decided to wash my hands of the whole business." Then, in a turnabout, he admitted all that Igor Gouzenko had alleged against him, signing a statement to that effect and even confessing that he had "taken a few dollars." He claimed that as science was international, the Russians were entitled to his information.

On the same day, Hollis saw the director of public prosecutions, who, along with the attorney general, agreed that May's admissions could be used in either a Canadian or a British court. The RCMP was immediately informed by Hollis. Both Hollis and Philby then attended a meeting in the Foreign Office on March 1, 1946, with May still at liberty, to consider a formal request from Canada that his prosecution should be delayed until nearer the time when the Canadian Royal Commission report on the whole affair would be published.

By then, MI6 had been reorganized to deal with the postwar Soviet threat, its departments being renamed Requirement Sections. The previous Section 9, headed by Philby, became Requirement Section 5 (R5), with the traitor still in control and with a much expanded remit. Whether Hollis was a spy or not, documents show that much of what was going on in MI5 was leaked straight to Moscow through the continuing Philby-Hollis axis. Replying to a query from Philby about GRU operations revealed by Gouzenko, Hollis stated, "The close cooperation which we have had over this case has given you just as much information as we have about it and, as you know, we have welcomed this."

After surveillance of May had failed to produce any result, he was arrested outside King's College, London, on March 4. His academic colleagues were so astonished that I had difficulty in dissuading his chief, Dr. Flint, my old physics mentor at King's, from publicly declaring May's innocence.

On the following day, Philby wrote to Hollis, stating that MI6's "atomic expert would be interested to know (in the greatest possible detail) whether May disclosed to the Russians anything having a specific bearing on the manufacture and assembly of the actual weapon." Whether or not this impudent effort produced any result for the KGB is not recorded.

During March, Hollis asked the RCMP for a formal statement from Gouzenko explaining in detail how he learned that "Alek" was May, thereby admitting that he had failed to ask him that prime question during his brief interview. The telegram was sent via Philby.

On May Day 1946, May was tried at the Old Bailey. Hollis and Philby both attended. Though May was described by his lawyer as simply an international scientist following his conscience, he had signed the Official Secrets Act on May 29, 1942, on formally joining Tube Alloys and had accepted a token sum of money from the Russians. As he pleaded guilty, no details of the information he had imparted were given.

The May case could not have happened at a worse time for Anglo-American relations and the Great Prize in particular. Early in October 1945, Truman had asked his government to consider legislation for the postwar control of atomic energy. This eventually resulted in a bill masterminded by Senator Brien McMahon, who was in favor of international control and a reasonable exchange of scientific information among allies. However, in March 1946, General Leslie Groves, who had commanded the U.S. atomic bomb project, had written a letter, which was read in the Senate, about the seriousness of May's treachery. May had visited certain American laboratories because Groves had been assured he had been cleared for access by "British Intelligence." Consequently, the May case emphatically reinforced the demand by many senators and congressmen for much stricter limitations. Eventually the McMahon Act, passed in August 1946, ruled out any exchange of nuclear weapons information with any other country. I discussed the situation with McMahon when he visited London, and although he genuinely regretted terminating the collaboration, he explained that the betrayal of American atomic secrets by a British scientist had made its continuation impossible.

The British government and its atomic officials and scientists were horrified at this abrupt ending of the Quebec Agreement and were to do all they could to reestablish some sharing arrangement, but far worse espionage cases would demolish their hopes. It would take twelve years and cost the U.K. taxpayers billions, in current pounds, before the political damage could be totally repaired.

Gouzenko's evidence showed that May had been recruited before moving to Canada early in 1943, and that could have happened only in Great Britain. So efforts were made to discover any of his acquaintances who might have been implicated in his recruitment, with particular suspicion being directed at the Austrian Communist Engelbert Broda. The two had been friends when May had been working for Tube Alloys at the Cavendish Laboratory in 1942. May was interviewed in prison by two MI5 officers in the hope that he would reveal his recruiter and other contacts. Instead, they found him unhelpful and "deeply resentful against the Intelligence services." Nevertheless, they remained optimistic about future interviews as shown by an artful, sympathetic letter from Philby. They tried again on November 23, 1946, lecturing May on the damage that Communists like himself could do, but he declined any assistance. His only reaction to the Canadian Royal Commission report, which MI5 had hopefully supplied to stimulate him, was anger at the misspelling of his first name as Allan, an error that has been repeated in many books. MI5's ace interviewer William Skardon tried yet again on March 21, 1949, but May had not mellowed.

Though Hollis was MI5's specialist on Communists and subversive activities, he gave the impression of having failed to understand that May's dedication to the Soviet creed and so-called internationalism had been sufficient to make him into a spy. Nor did he apply the obvious connection to other British atomic scientists known to have Communist leanings, of which there were several, including Fuchs. In view of the clear similarity, which had been proved in the cases of the Canadian culprits exposed by Gouzenko, this omission is hard to explain unless it was deliberate. It had not been missed in the Foreign Office, where an internal note to the chief official on the Gouzenko case, dated August 10, 1946, stated, "The Soviet Government worked almost exclusively through the Communist Party and Communist cells."

The case was the first clear evidence that the Soviets had penetrated the nuclear project, and Soviet archives show that the KGB Center expected a major check on all other atomic scientists. That did not happen because Hollis, who had been May's case officer with his on-the-spot inquiries in Canada and later in London, played down his treachery as a one-off aberration. Had MI5, and Hollis in particular, made a more sustained effort to investigate May's past, they would have discovered that while at Trinity Hall, Cambridge, in the 1930s, he had been a prominent Communist who had made no secret of his beliefs. He had been a leading activist of the pro-Soviet Association of Scientific Workers, which was a GRU and KGB talent-spotting agency. Inquiries in Cambridge might have led to May's openly Communist friend Donald Maclean, then established in the Foreign Office.

Whether or not May had been cleared for security before joining the bomb project is uncertain. A released MI5 document states that "presumably he was vetted at an earlier date," but nothing could be found in the records. Though he had not formally joined Tube Alloys until 1942, May had already been involved in research for the Maud committee while working at Bristol in 1941. Possibly no British-born scientists were subjected to security clearance during the war, though the American authorities were to be assured that all those working in the United States had been.

As early as August 1952, government officials were wondering how, on May's release with remission for good conduct, which was due in December, they might help him find a job to deter him from defecting to Russia. Though his value as a source was regarded as small, being so outdated, his possible defection was foreseen as a public relations disaster, especially in America. Hollis was almost alone in declaring that the impact would be slight.

Prior to May's release on December 29, after he had served six and a half years, MI5 applied for a warrant to tap his telephone and open his letters, while ports and airports were warned to "deter his departure" should he attempt to leave Great Britain. At a cabinet meeting, the prime minister, the reelected Winston Churchill, declared that May "should certainly be kept under close observation by the police because his departure to an Iron Curtain country would cause public outcry and end the chances of US/UK collaboration in atomic matters."

May celebrated his first day of freedom by declaring that he "had acted rightly and that many others thought so, too!" As Hollis remarked, his stance did not improve his chances of employment. When visited at his home in January 1953 by Skardon, he declared himself unrepentant and loath to change his identity, also pointing out that he had never used his middle name, Nunn.

Many research laboratories and institutes were approached on May's behalf, and after seven months, a Cambridge radio company offered him a post researching color television. This was aborted, however, because of Supply Ministry fears that the U.S. Navy would end sharing guided weapons data, as the company also worked in that field. May then compounded the problem on August 1, 1953, by marrying a Cambridge schools' medical officer, Hildegarde Broda, the divorced wife of his former colleague Engelbert, an immigrant Austrian Communist who had long been on MI5's books as a suspect spy. Immediately, MI5 officers asked: Had the Brodas been involved in May's espionage, perhaps having recruited him to the GRU?

After divorcing in 1946, Engelbert had returned to Austria, but MI5 inquiries and surveillance showed that Hildegarde also had Communist sympathies, leading Hollis to declare that the marriage had made May's "resettlement" even more difficult, "especially with the Americans." He thought it more likely that the Mays might move abroad and warned the Home Office. While May was still unemployed in November, ports were reminded to watch for him.

At last, in January 1954, May began research work at the Cambridge laboratory of Dr. W. A. Wooster, a distinguished crystallographer who had a small company, Crystal Structures Ltd. This produced relief all around, but the ultrasecret machinations behind this appointment, which would have caused a furor had they leaked, were not revealed until 2007.

May had been a friend of Wooster, whom I recall as a prominent, open Communist, but that did not deter MI5 after May had warned them that unless he found suitable employment within a year of his release, he would look abroad. With Home Office agreement, Dick White, then director general, and Hollis, then his deputy, organized and administered a secret deal in which £1,400 a year was paid to Wooster out of MI5 funds to employ May. The media, both in Great Britain and in the United States, would have regarded this as a bribe on behalf of a criminal who had inflicted great damage on both countries, secretly paid with taxpayers' money mainly to prevent embarrassment to the government and to MI5. The deal would also have been attacked as sending the wrong message to traitors. As it was never exposed, it could only have encouraged Hollis to use bribery in more audacious forms to benefit far worse Soviet spies, as he would repeatedly do.

Whether May was aware of the deal is unknown because the details remain concealed in several documents listed in the May archives as having been withheld indefinitely. Indeed, the short memos revealing it may have inadvertently "slipped into sight," as MI5 might have put it. One memo by Hollis to White, in June 1954, recorded, "When the employment for Nunn May became acute it was decided that there should be some form of subsidy—£2000 over a period of two years was mentioned as a likely expenditure by the Security Service. With the payments due next month we shall have expended £1,400 over the first year." In November, White is recorded as being keen to be rid of the subsidy but recommending payment for another year. How long it was continued remains secret, as the May archives end in 1955 with details of action—approved by the cabinet—to prevent either May or his wife from securing a passport, as their defection could still prejudice Anglo-American relations. Their letters were still being intercepted, and MI5 suggested that "the Mays' daily woman cleaner should be recruited as an informant." The heavy concentration of MI5's interest and resources on the May case, so long after he had been convicted, certainly diminished the chances of any attention being paid to the Elli case.

Until the appearance of the Russian book *The GRU and the Atomic Bomb* in 2002, nobody in the West had any idea where and how May had really been recruited. Nor, apparently, had anyone in authority heard of the GRU agent who pulled off the coup, though he had been active in various parts of Europe and Great Britain for thirty years. His name was Jan Chernyak, and he was one of the GRU's most successful "illegal" operators. Born of Hungarian-Czech parents, he had become a GRU agent in 1933, when he was twenty-four, and after an advanced training course in Moscow, he was posted to Germany, where he recruited well-placed, anti-Nazi spies who provided a stream of valuable information about weaponry and radar. Because he operated independently, he survived when other members of the Red Orchestra were rounded up by the Gestapo.

In the late spring of 1942, the GRU Center instructed him to go to Britain and recruit May, then working at the Cavendish Laboratory of Cambridge University. Documents supplied by Fuchs had revealed that a group of scientists there, under Professor Hans von Halban, was conducting important investigations connected with uranium fission and the creation of an atom bomb. The Center knew that in his youth, May, who was then thirty-one, had held left-wing views and had condemned Nazism. The GRU archives recorded that in 1936 he had visited the Soviet Union with a group of British scientific workers. In Leningrad, he had established friendly relations with a physicist there, and they had exchanged technical information. The GRU induced the physicist to write May a letter, which was passed to Chernyak to use as a means of making contact and to recruit him, ostensibly, for "the struggle against fascism." So Chernyak left for London and then went to Cambridge to study the situation at closer range and gather supplementary data. How, as a foreigner, he did this so easily during wartime has not been explained.

Chernyak found May's address—16 Jesus Lane—and phone number; he called and explained to May that he had brought a letter from an old friend. May agreed to see the stranger, who had little difficulty convincing him that he should assist Soviet physicists by giving them information. The GRU archives indicate that the scientist agreed, partly because he knew about Churchill's promise to render aid to Russia during the war with Germany.

At the second meeting, the agent obtained documentary information about the basic directions of the scientific research on the uranium problem in Cambridge. Later, May gave him data about devices for separating uranium 235 and a description of a process for making plutonium, together with drawings of a uranium reactor and details of the principles of its operation. Since he was one of the earliest scientists to have been recruited by the Maud committee, his knowledge was considerable, including details of possible bomb designs.

The conspiratorial collaboration lasted about eight months and ended only because Halban's team, including May, was transferred to the Montreal laboratory of the Canadian National Research Council in January 1943. At their last meeting, they discussed conditions for the restoration of communication in Montreal. Chernyak did not know if there were any GRU operatives in Canada, but he assumed that when it was necessary, the Center would find some way of restoring contact with the valuable source, as it eventually did in February 1945.

All the documents supplied by May had reached the chief Soviet atomic scientist, Igor Kurchatov. Either Chernyak had managed to deliver them to some GRU controller at the Soviet embassy in London or had smuggled them out when he returned to Europe.

In February 1995, Chernyak, who was then in a Moscow hospital, aged eighty-six, was awarded the high rank of Hero of Russia, the gold star being presented by the chief of the General Staff of the Armed Forces and with the GRU's commander in chief also present. Several days later, he died. His achievement remained secret until 2002, when it was deemed safe to reveal it in the officially sponsored *The GRU and the Atomic Bomb* (published only in Russia), which stated that the records of his many other successes must remain closed until further order. As a military organization, the GRU remains highly disciplined concerning information about former officers and agents who served it well, with particular concern about surviving relatives. It is also aware that a reputation for such ironclad integrity remains a major asset in recruiting further agents today. This would seem to dispose of the MI5 belief that if Hollis had been an agent, the Russians would have made political capital out of such a coup by now.

As the Gestapo, with its vast resources, failed to detect any of Chernyak's activities, it is not surprising that MI5, with its limited counter-Soviet manpower during the war, should have missed him, though for all that British counterintelligence knew, the intruder might have been a German spy. An MI5 "Summary of the Canadian Case" in 1949 admitted that it did not know "by whom or when" May had been recruited.

In 1962, May was appointed professor of physics at the University of Ghana and went there with his wife and adopted son without incident. He returned to Cambridge in 1978 and remained silent about his past until shortly before he died in January 2003, aged ninety-one. He then signed a four-page statement that did little more than repeat his self-justification and expressed no remorse. He claimed that he had first passed technical secrets to the Russians in 1941, after the Germans had invaded the Soviet Union, probably at that stage through the Communist Party. He may even have preceded Fuchs as an atomic spy, though only by a few days. He also stated that he had been warned not to attend the proposed meeting with a Soviet controller after he had returned to London from Canada.

Deservedly, May lived long enough to see the total collapse of the corrupt and cruel dictatorship that he had so steadfastly admired and assisted.

CHAPTER 31

Blind Eye to Elli

—

As Igor Gouzenko had proved to be correct in every detail about Alan May's treachery, his allegations about Elli, a spy inside MI5 itself, clearly merited most thorough investigation. Gouzenko's general evidence and the consequent conviction of so many Soviet penetration agents in Canada should also have alerted MI5, and Hollis in particular, to the extent to which the GRU—and presumably the KGB—was pursuing a mole strategy. It did not. All the moles in British establishments continued their treachery unmolested—a further strange anomaly.

Though the FBI had quickly sent officers to Ottawa after Gouzenko's defection, both the Canadians and MI5 failed to tell them about Gouzenko's warning concerning Elli. The FBI officer Robert Lamphere believed that the Canadians had been asked by MI5 to withhold it. He was astonished when he discovered that the warning had been almost totally ignored and still more puzzled when he learned how Hollis had dealt with it. Lamphere assured me that had such an allegation been made about the FBI, there would have been a major investigation to prove it or refute it. He regarded Hollis's behavior over the Elli revelation as suspicious in the extreme. The diaries of the Canadian prime minister, Mackenzie King, showed that both he and his foreign affairs chief, Norman Robertson, thought the British officials had not really grasped the full significance of the Gouzenko disclosures.

The grim humor of the whole situation created by Gouzenko's revelations was exemplified in May 1946 by an exchange of letters between Hollis and Sir Harold Caccia of the Foreign Office. Caccia observed, "The Russians are likely to penetrate our governmental organizations, particularly the Foreign Office. It looks as if the Foreign Service ought to be particularly on their guard against any members or ex-members of the Party and against 'drawing-room' communists." Hollis replied, "To judge from the Canadian case, the Russians do make use of the ideological pull to recruit agents, and there are undoubtedly people in Government service who have been." He then suggested that Caccia should give him the names of any suspects. Caccia did not oblige, but both Maclean and Burgess, who were still stuffing their briefcases with Foreign Office documents, qualified as "drawing-room communists," while Fuchs had already been offered a senior post at the ultrasecret Harwell atomic station, which he would join in two months' time with Hollis's fervent blessing.

Hollis seems to have been in Washington again on July 20, 1946, because information was sent to him there from the RCMP. If he visited Ottawa, then he seems to have made no effort to see Gouzenko. He was certainly back in London on August 19, and still in command of the case when he received a letter from the Home Office about the Canadian Royal Commission report, which had been published on June 27.

A brief MI5 paper about Elli sent to MI6 by Michael Hanley and dated December 6, 1949, is documentary proof not only that Gouzenko's Elli allegation was recorded in the MI5 files, but that interest in his identity was still alive then, if only marginally. As a result, the lack of interest displayed by Hollis ensured that nothing effective about Elli was ever put in train.

The official reaction inside MI5 to the Elli case was remarkably similar to that inside MI6 and in the Foreign Office to the Konstantin Volkov case. The information supplied by Volkov baldly stated the existence of several KGB spies, of whom Philby eventually proved to be one and Maclean and Burgess two others, but the MI6 and Foreign Office managements simply declined to entertain the possibility of such treachery within their departments. The MI5 management took precisely the same view about Gouzenko's evidence regarding Elli. The exposure of a Soviet spy inside MI5 not only would have shattered the agency's reputation, but coming so soon after the May case, it would have been catastrophic for relations with America in every branch of intelligence.

If Elli had been sent out to resolve the Elli problem in the GRU's— and Elli's—interest, he had succeeded. The similarity between the behavior of Philby and Hollis in the two critical circumstances, which were of incalculable potential to British counterintelligence, is suggestive, to say the least. There is no escaping the fact that both the Volkov threat and the Elli threat to the Soviet spy machine were disposed of by Philby and Hollis—working in tandem.

Shortly after May's conviction, in August 1946, Hollis was involved in an incident that was to intensify suspicion about him later in his career. A GRU naval officer, Lieutenant Skripkin, serving in the Far East, had approached British naval intelligence authorities there with the intention of defecting. His offer had been accepted, and copies of two reports about the plans for his defection were sent to Hollis's department in MI5. As Peter Wright later detailed, the reports, dated May and July 1946, arrived in August, when Hollis instructed a junior officer to create a file and place it in the registry to await further developments. The reports had been stapled together in the Far East and remained that way in the MI5 registry.

Meanwhile, Skripkin had returned to Moscow to make secret arrangements to take his wife with him and was apprehended by KGB officers pretending to be MI6 men. He was eventually executed. Officially, the British authorities were unaware of the disaster, so it was generally assumed either that Skripkin had changed his mind or that his offer had been a time-wasting provocation. When the truth emerged seven years later, it would seem to support the suspicion that MI5 was harboring a GRU spy who had revealed Skripkin's planned defection.

Further interest in Gouzenko and his allegations seems to have lapsed until May 1952, when, during inquiries into the Cambridge spy group, and while there was still no suspicion against Hollis, MI5 asked the RCMP to ask Gouzenko, among other things, for a more detailed statement about Elli. Gouzenko's lengthy written response, dated May 6, of which I have secured a copy, began, "Regarding your request for information about the person in British MI5 . . ." He then repeated his previous information, adding a few detail such as his recollection that one of the *duboks* where documents to and from Elli were hidden was "a split between stones of a certain tomb." He confirmed that he had seen the main Elli telegram himself and had not just been told about it by his companion decoder. He also confirmed that his colleague had said, "This man has something Russian in his background."

Gouzenko also expressed his disgust at the British failure to identify Elli, stating that "the mistake was that the task of finding the agent was given to MI5 itself." He suggested that it was not too late to get some other agency to detect him. By that time, Gouzenko was convinced that the person sent to interview him—whose name he still did not know at that stage—had been Elli himself, and he told me later, "If I had defected to England, I would not have survived."

In spite of his reiteration of the information about Elli, interest collapsed for twenty years, possibly because Hollis became deputy director general in 1953 and overall chief three years later, when "the Hollis touch" became pervasive.

In 1972, an MI5 officer calling himself Stewart flew from Washington to Toronto to interview Gouzenko again as part of the ongoing investigations into the Soviet penetration of MI5, which were code-named Fluency. Still in fear of his safety, Gouzenko was reluctant to be interviewed alone, and it was eventually agreed that his wife could be present. In a room at the Royal York Hotel, he was shown a substantial typewritten report that was allegedly Hollis's account of his original interview. Immediately afterward, Gouzenko—who still had never heard Hollis's name—told several friends, including prominent journalists, what had happened (recorded in John Sawatsky's book *Gouzenko: The Untold Story*). Gouzenko had exclaimed that the document was all lies, including a statement that he had told his MI5 interrogator that he knew the British had a high-ranking mole in the Kremlin. Gouzenko said that the document attributed other false statements to him guaranteed to discredit him as a witness and create the impression that he was unreliable. He told Peter Worthington, then editor in chief of the *Toronto Sun*, "Whoever wrote that report about a fake interview had to be working for the Soviets." Worthington put his account on record in a letter to *The Spectator* on May 2, 1987.

Gouzenko also told Robert Reguly, another Canadian journalist, that the report had been doctored to conceal references to the spy inside MI5. This may be one reason for MI5's continuing failure to release Hollis's account of his interview—even sixty years after the event.

Later, Gouzenko, who had then learned the identity of his original interrogator, told me, "I could not understand how Hollis had written so much when he had asked me so little. I soon discovered why, because the report was full of nonsense and lies. As Stewart read the report to me, it became clear that it had been faked to destroy my credibility so that my information about the spy in MI5 called Elli could be ignored. I suspect that Hollis himself was Elli. Every time I said, 'That's nonsense!' about some paragraph in the report, Stewart commented, 'I'm glad to hear you say so.' "

Gouzenko vehemently denied having told Hollis that he knew Britain had a high-ranking mole in the Kremlin, stressing that he could not have known such a thing and that it was impossible anyway. Later, in 1973, Stewart visited him again to show him six pictures, but he could not pick out the one that was Hollis after so long, as his eyesight was failing owing to diabetes. By the time my disclosures about Hollis broke, in 1981, and pictures of him were published, Gouzenko was blind. He was most anxious that nobody should know of that because of his continuing fear of assassination by SMERSH, the avenging arm of the KGB, responsible for dealing with all traitors.

According to Peter Wright, when Stewart returned to London and submitted his report, the MI5 chief, then Martin Furnival Jones, said he was "unimpressed." He argued that Hollis's attempts to discredit Gouzenko were due simply to his disbelief that there could possibly be such a spy inside MI5. Yet in 1945, Anthony Blunt had been there for four years, as Furnival Jones well knew.

CHAPTER 32

The Denigration of Igor Gouzenko

—

I N FEBRUARY 1946, GOUZENKO APPEARED BEFORE A ROYAL COM-mission set up in Canada to investigate his documents and allegations in depth. As demonstrated by its weighty report, published the following June, he proved to be such an impressive and reliable informant with excellent recall that the commissioners had no reservations in accepting him as a truthful witness who did not try to embroider his stories. They thanked him for "a great public service."

The FBI counterintelligence officer Robert Lamphere confirmed to me that all of Gouzenko's information supplied by the Canadian authorities to the FBI about GRU agents operating in America proved to be correct, including his lead to a spy calling himself Witczak (real name Litvin), who managed to escape. The FBI's specialist on the GRU, Emory Gregg, was especially impressed by Gouzenko's statements, which had revealed that the GRU was using Canada to control some spies operating in the United States.

No defector had ever yielded such a haul of spies and agents. Gouzenko's documents and his information enabled the Canadian authorities to expose several GRU networks, send five GRU agents to prison, and remove other suspects from access to secrets. The Soviet intelligence chief, Lavrenti Beria, circulated a stiff rebuke to the Ottawa GRU, stating that the defection had done great damage to the Soviet Union. That the blackest day in the GRU's history was September 5,

1945, the day of Gouzenko's defection, is made clear in the officially sponsored Russian book *The GRU and the Atomic Bomb*. He is referred to there as "the Scorpion." To this day, his name is reviled by the GRU, which is reluctant to answer any questions about him.

When Mackenzie King first met Gouzenko in July 1946, he told him that he was very pleased with the way he had conducted himself throughout the period of great anxiety. In an interview, he told him, "The people of Canada and the world are your debtors." Later, he wrote, "I thought that he had done a great service and wanted him to know that I appreciated his manliness, his courage and his standing for the right."

Yet this young man who had done so much to alert the West to the dangers of Soviet subversion gradually became an object of derision, not only in Canada, but in the inner intelligence circles of Great Britain and the United States and among many journalists and authors. Some writers even denigrated his physical appearance, describing him as "squat and ugly," while Mackenzie King, in his diary, remembered him as "clean cut, steady eyes, keen intellect," a description confirmed by photographs taken at the time but withheld because of the assassination danger and not published until 2006, one of them being on the cover of *The Gouzenko Affair*.

Like most defectors who had been reared in Communist regimes, Gouzenko and his wife found it difficult to adjust to capitalism and democratic freedom. Contrary to his expectation, once he had come to realize the full extent and value of his action, the Canadian government failed to award him any regular allowance on which to subsist. In 1947, an appreciative Ottawa businessman gave him an annuity worth $100 (Canadian) a month, but for the first sixteen years of their freedom, Gouzenko and his family lived mainly on what he could earn by charging fees for interviews and for his various writings. These included an autobiography and a best-selling novel about Stalin, *The Fall of a Titan*. Unlike so many other defectors, he never made false new claims about his inside knowledge to generate publicity or improve his prestige. He pleaded for a better deal for defectors so that more Russians would follow his example. With poor money sense, he spent lavishly when in funds. He bought an overlarge car and made bad investments, which included a farm. People who tried to advise him failed.

In 1962, Gouzenko, who could not take an ordinary job for personal security reasons, was belatedly awarded an index-linked state pension of $500 (Canadian) a month, increased at intervals until it eventually rose to $1,667. He continued to bleat in public, however, mainly to stress that Canada was doing little to encourage more Soviet defectors. He felt a particular sense of frustration over the lack of action to dismantle the KGB networks he knew existed in Canada and over Britain's failure to resolve the Elli case.

When Gouzenko had been in the act of defecting, trying to find someone in authority who would listen to his story, strong-arm KGB men from the Soviet embassy had broken into his apartment in the hope of taking him by force. Once he had defected and caused such a furor, he remained in fear of capture or assassination by SMERSH. Gouzenko knew that the previous GRU defector, Walter Krivitsky, who had warned of the Soviet penetration of Western institutions, had been found shot dead in a Washington hotel room. He knew that his offense was much greater, because of its far-reaching political results, and assumed that he had been sentenced to death by a military court in Moscow. He was right. In the late 1960s, a Soviet agent calling himself Anton Sabotka, who had been living under deep cover in Canada for four years, was ordered to kill Gouzenko. Instead, he confessed all to the RCMP. Gouzenko's justifiable fear, which ordinary Canadians regarded as exaggerated, undermined his relations with two sectors of society—journalists and the RCMP.

The Canadian authorities had fully appreciated the continuing danger surrounding the Gouzenkos early in 1947 by giving them a false name and a carefully concocted identity legend, indicating that they were Czech immigrants. When Svetlana Gouzenko, who had also been condemned to death, sent me a photograph of herself, it had to be taken from behind, showing only part of her face. Their eldest daughter, Evy, told me that she did not learn of her true identity until she was sixteen.

Gouzenko was in some demand to appear on television but declined to do so unless completely hooded. Though this added some aura of conspiracy, it exasperated many interviewers and reduced his authority by making him a figure of fun. Yet new information exposed in *The Mitrokhin Archive* has proved that Gouzenko's fears were not exaggerated. For the rest of his life, the KGB intermittently tried to track him down. When the KGB drew up a death list of "particularly dangerous traitors" in 1962, Gouzenko's name was on it. It stated that they had all been sentenced to death and that the sentences would be "carried out abroad." Had Gouzenko revealed his features on television, the whole effort by the Canadian authorities to hide him and his family would have been nullified.

In spite of what appeared to be eccentric behavior, Gouzenko retained many staunch friends among leading Canadian journalists, but among the liberal and Far Left, he was greatly disliked. He had brought them a message about Russia that they did not want to hear, and they missed no opportunity to shoot the messenger by undermining his credibility. Like many Russians, Gouzenko was used to drinking as a normal part of social life, but he was not the habitual drunkard that many authors, journalists, and MI5 officers made him out to be.

The originator of the eventual belief in MI5 that Gouzenko had become "an irretrievable alcoholic," as Peter Wright described him to me in 1980 and later in his book, is unknown, but Gouzenko was not reinterviewed by any MI5 officer until after Hollis had retired and had himself been interrogated. The fact that Gouzenko was completely rational and with good recall when interviewed by the MI5 officer Robert Stewart in 1972 is evidence that the previous conviction in MI5 that he was a hopeless drunk was an internal deception. Gouzenko's daughter Evy insists, "My father was never an alcoholic and opposed heavy drinking." Whenever I spoke with him, he was coherent and rational in all respects.

In defense of his reputation, Gouzenko was quick not only to take offense, but to sue for libel, which also did not endear him to his critics. Unpleasant stories about him were regularly retold by the Mounties who were detailed to protect him because of his assassination fear, which some of them regarded as ridiculous. He had also brought the wrong message to the RCMP because he had revealed, at a stroke, the extent of the treachery going on under their noses and made their small intelligence branch look incompetent. His Mountie bodyguards came to hate him, believing that he was wasting their time. He was suspicious of some of them and demanded their replacement, sometimes late at night. A special report, *Commission of Enquiry Concerning Certain Activities of the RCMP*, published in 1981, stated that the inquiries had shown that Gouzenko was ridiculed so often in the RCMP files that anyone reading them would regard him as a "constant trouble-maker."

Over the years, his general reputation in Canada degenerated into that of a nuisance. That also became the view in Great Britain, but for more sinister and disgraceful reasons. From my contacts with intelligence officers over many years, I soon learned that most of them actively disliked defectors, because whatever their value, they were traitors to their own countries, at least in legal terms. Considering that the first clues to almost every case claimed as a success by MI5 and MI6 came from defectors to the United States, this seems uncharitable, but the gut feeling that they were not to be trusted was widespread and certainly affected the attitude of both services to Gouzenko.

Unquestionably, the foundation of the particular dislike of Gouzenko in MI5 derived from the report on him submitted by Hollis, even though his information had led to the successful conviction of Alan May. Hollis let it be known that, in his view, a spy inside MI5 was unthinkable and any suggestion that there was one was outrageous, as was the person who made it. It was, of course, in the Soviet interest for Gouzenko to be denigrated and to suffer, if only to discourage other defectors.

It is clear from Dick White's letters to me that he agreed with Hollis, having a particular dislike of defectors himself. There was therefore little chance that any "time-wasting" attention would be paid to Gouzenko's allegations about the MI5 spy code-named Elli, especially when any proof of his existence would be catastrophic for relations with the United States. The allegations about Elli therefore lay fallow, even when Venona decrypts proved his existence, and Gouzenko was dismissed as overimaginative, if not deluded. The GRU and the KGB had assumed that the Elli material would touch off a major mole hunt inside MI5 and took precautions, but to their pleased astonishment, nothing was done. Instead, the policy of marginalizing Gouzenko as a witness was to continue in MI5 and still persists.

In the early 1960s, the MI5 officers Peter Wright and Arthur Martin, who were deeply concerned about the number of counterespionage cases that were running into the sand, began a close study of the possibility that Elli or some other Soviet spy was still in MI5, operating at a high level. Pursuing this fear, Wright discovered that Martin's research assistant had acquired a book of private notes about possible penetration cases made by a former female officer, who had retired to marry around 1951. It contained the suspicions of Maxwell Knight and Gouzenko's Elli allegations. According to Wright, the officer had surmised, "If MI5 is penetrated, I think it is most likely to be Roger Hollis or Graham

Mitchell." (Mitchell, a close colleague of Hollis's, eventually became his deputy director general.)

Wright therefore wanted to question Gouzenko but allowed himself to be fobbed off by the RCMP, who did not want the case reopened. They claimed that their notes of Gouzenko's original debriefing could not be found. Later, Wright explained his failure to consult Gouzenko, which he could easily have done by letter, by trotting out the MI5 myth that by the mid-1960s, Gouzenko was an alcoholic with an unreliable memory. Clearly he had fallen for the false rumors, because Gouzenko could not have been more approachable or his memory for past events more consistent when I spoke to him several times on the telephone and corresponded with him as late as 1982.

The hearsay description of Gouzenko as an embroiderer has appeared in so many books and newspaper articles that it seems to be established as fact. Dick White typified the attitude when he wrote to me, in response to some information that Gouzenko had just given me, saying that he was "not impressed by his after-thoughts in extreme old age." Gouzenko was then sixty-one, and even those in Canada who disliked him agreed that his recall of details remained remarkable.

Igor Gouzenko died near Toronto from the long-term results of diabetes on June 25, 1982, aged sixty-three, and was buried in an unmarked grave to protect his widow. She brilliantly described to me the treatment meted out to them by writing, "Legend says that when Rome was in peril, clamorous geese awakened the sleeping Roman soldiers, thus saving the city. I feel that is what we did in 1945, when we awakened democracy. I suspect that, to celebrate their victory, the Roman soldiers served roast goose! That is the state in which we have been living since 1945—roasted." I continued to correspond with Svetlana, who consulted her late husband's notes for me. She died in September 2001 and is buried alongside Igor, a marked gravestone then being erected.

On April 15, 2004, the chairman of the Historic Sites and Monuments Board of Canada, representing the Canadian government, presented two of Gouzenko's daughters with a federal plaque, which was later placed in Dundonald Park in Ottawa. It was mounted on a pedestal alongside another bearing a commemorative plaque, placed there by the city of Ottawa in the previous year. That municipal plaque states that it was "in recognition of the courage of Igor Gouzenko and his wife, Svetlana, for their historic flight to freedom in Canada." It goes on to describe their vicissitudes and accomplishments. The chosen site was directly across from the apartment building where the Gouzenkos had lived before their defection and where they had nearly been captured by the KGB. With the Canadian coat of arms in the top left-hand corner, and in gold lettering on a garnet background, the federal plaque briefly describes how Igor Gouzenko "exposed the existence of a Soviet spy ring in Canada with links to others in the United States and Great Britain." It also states, "The Gouzenko Affair brought the realities of the emerging Cold War to the attention of the Canadian public."

At the unveiling ceremony, at the end of a two-day conference on the Gouzenko affair, an address was made by the senator for the area on behalf of the Canadian government. The event was a formal vindication and official rehabilitation of Gouzenko, recognizing him as an important figure in Canadian history. As a personal tribute to the family, a smaller bronze replica of the plaque was presented to Gouzenko's daughter Evy Wilson, to whom I am indebted for information. These events owed much to the patient prodding of bureaucratic authority by Andrew Kavchak, who was determined to see Gouzenko's role in Canadian history more openly acknowledged. He has recorded the story in a booklet, *Remembering Gouzenko,* published in 2004.

The entirely unexpected rehabilitation of Igor Gouzenko's integrity reestablished the honesty and accuracy of the information he had provided. That included his statement that the British spy Elli had been inside MI5, not in MI6 or in any other MI. It is fair to ask where this vindication leaves the reputations of Hollis, White, and all the other critics, academic and journalistic, who went out of their way to denigrate him.

CHAPTER 33

Long Shot Shot Down

—

WHEN, IN 1981, I PUBLISHED THE THEN EXISTING EVIDENCE linking Elli with Hollis in *Their Trade Is Treachery,* though without proof of the Russian connection (which came later), immediate opposition was mounted from two quarters. It came from those establishment figures for whom proof of Hollis's guilt would have been a personal disaster, such as Dick White, who had consistently promoted him, government ministers, and senior Whitehall officials who had worked with him. They have been supported by most academics. The other quarter consisted of journalists and "spy writers," who had no particular regard for Hollis, who had died in 1973, but sprang to defend his reputation to undermine mine. They had been severely scooped, and the standard journalistic practice of dealing with that situation, if it has not been officially confirmed, is to argue that the scoop is simply not true.

The critics had some initial success in convincing their readers that Elli was none other than Kim Philby, who happened to have served in Section 5 of MI6. (In Gouzenko's original statement on his defection, when his command of English was modest, he had said that Elli was in "5 of MI." Though Gouzenko later assured me, and others, that it had been his Russian way of saying "MI5," the statement was seized on by various critics, who either did not know or ignored the fact that his written statement to MI5 via the RCMP, in May 1952, had begun, "Regarding your request for information about the person in British MI5 . . ." He had then stated, "There is not the slightest doubt in my mind that there was a GRU agent inside MI5 during 1942–43 and, possibly, later on.") Documents since obtained for publication by Oleg Tsarev, the former KGB officer granted access to the KGB archives, and published in his chillingly revealing book, *Crown Jewels* (jointly authored by espionage historian Nigel West), have now disposed of this canard. They prove that although Philby had a succession of code names, Elli was never one of them. Further, to have had regular access to the files on Soviet intelligence officers serving in Great Britain, Elli had to be in MI5, not MI6.

Later, it was argued that Elli must have been Anthony Blunt, whose treachery had been publicly exposed in 1979, because he had admitted bringing out hundreds of MI5 files to be photographed by his Soviet controllers. Again, KGB documents have since shown that although he, too, had been given several code names over the years, he had never been called Elli. Further, in his confession in 1964, he admitted that he had never been asked for information about Hollis's F Division, which dealt with Soviet intelligence officers based in Great Britain. He said that his controller had warned him, for safety's sake, not to ask for files to which he did not need access for his MI5 work and, specifically, not to bother with personal files on Soviet intelligence officers—suggesting that they already had access to them. Those files were kept at Blenheim, while Blunt was always based in London, and as Wright told me, a check was made to determine if Blunt had ever drawn such files. It had happened only about five times.

When Major Ismail Akhmedov, who had defected from the GRU in 1942, was interviewed by Wright, he said that the GRU would never have told the KGB about Elli or revealed his real name. He had never been in a position to know about Elli himself, because at that time such British spies were run by the tough GRU female officer code-named Vera (who was later purged because she knew too much). During his many long interrogations, mainly by Wright, Blunt himself became convinced that he could not possibly have been Elli.

In 1990, the Cambridge don Christopher Andrew—working in collaboration with the KGB defector Oleg Gordievsky, who had escaped from Moscow in September 1985, having spied for Britain for eleven years—published a book, *KGB: The Inside Story*. Dealing with Gouzenko's allegation about the British GRU spy called Elli, they stated, "Gouzenko's alcoholism and increasingly confused memory made it difficult to clarify the incomplete and confused version of the Elli story given at his first debriefing." The only authority for these personal deficiencies given by Andrew and Gordievsky in their book was Peter Wright. I discussed the issue with him at length in Tasmania, and his views on Gouzenko's character, which he had used to avoid visiting him, were based entirely on what other officers, including Hollis, had told him.

In their book, Andrew and Gordievsky also announced, with some flourish, that Elli was none other than Leo Long, the self-confessed, minor KGB agent recruited by Blunt at Cambridge. "That code-name appears in large letters on the cover of Long's KGB operational file," the book stated. Allegedly, Gordievsky had handled the file in 1981 during the normal course of his duties when stationed in Moscow. I have been unable to find any evidence that Gordievsky had ever mentioned this seemingly important fact during any of his many official debriefings. He had not mentioned it when questioned in 1981, when the Thatcher government was desperate to disprove the evidence against Hollis revealed in *Their Trade Is Treachery*. When Gordon Brook-Shepherd interviewed Gordievsky for his book on Soviet defectors, *The Storm Birds*, published in 1988, he made no mention of Elli being Long. That is significant because the book was in part an MI5-inspired exercise in which the author did all he could to ridicule the concept that Hollis could have been a Soviet agent. The omission indicates that MI5 had not then heard of the claim that Elli was Long. Otherwise, Brook-Shepherd would have been encouraged to make the most of it.

Apparently, Gordievsky recalled it only while the joint book with Andrew was being prepared. The circumstances have been convincingly analyzed by John Cairncross in his autobiography published in 1997, where he effectively disposed of the myth that Elli was Leo Long.

Since Gordievsky's sudden recollection, examination of the KGB archives by researchers, which unexpectedly became possible after the collapse of the Soviet Union, has revealed that Long's code name was *not* Elli. It was Ralph, as Oleg Tsarev stated in 1993 in *Deadly Illusions*, authored jointly with the late John Costello and later confirmed in *Crown Jewels*.

As a photograph taken at the time proves, Costello also saw the Long files, sitting with Tsarev in the Lubyanka headquarters of the KGB, to which the files had been delivered. In September 2007, Tsarev reconfirmed the code name to me, stating, "Files carry the names given at the time when they were first registered, so Ralph stays. As for Elli, I do not remember coming across the code name." Clearly, the name Elli had *not* been on the cover of Long's file or anywhere else in it. The file bore the original name Ralph and, presumably, still does. As Long had ceased spying more than twenty years before Gordievsky claimed to have seen the file, it is inconceivable that his code name had been changed subsequently.

In an on-the-record interview with General Vitaly Pavlov of the KGB in 2002, about the established system of recording the code names and real names of KGB agents, the Russian historian Dr. Svetlana Chervonnaya was told that even if a code name was changed, the file would still be known by the original one. (The real name would appear only once—at the start of page one of the first volume.) In 1991 (see *Daily Telegraph*, June 16), Tsarev had already pointed out that if Gordievsky had ever handled the Long file he would have been required to sign it under standing KGB rules, which it was dangerous to disobey. Tsarev stated, "His signature is not there."

The huge mass of evidence from the KGB files presented by Tsarev in the books he coauthored has been accepted as true by intelligence specialists. So there are no grounds for suspecting that his statements about the Long file are KGB disinformation, especially as the file was also seen by Costello, whom I met regularly. I have recently been in touch with Tsarev, and he remains certain that Long was never called Elli. In an interview in November 2008, Tsarev, aged sixty-two, also assured Dr. Chervonnaya that Long's code name was Ralph, not Elli.

The existence of the KGB file on Long and other available documents proves that he was a KGB agent and always had been. The brief, handwritten autobiography that Blunt sent to KGB headquarters in 1943, which has become available for examination, states that he recruited Long for the KGB, and Long himself has confirmed that he was recruited by Blunt.

As Guy Liddell's diaries confirm, Long worked not in MI5, but in MI 14(b), where he collated and analyzed strategic information about the German armed forces. Nor did he make use of hiding places for his messages—instead he passed them directly to Blunt, whom he met openly. Blunt then handed them on to his KGB controller, as Blunt and KGB records have separately confirmed. In *KGB: The Inside Story,* the authors agree that during the war, Long was "run personally by Blunt as a Soviet sub-agent." After the war, when Long worked as a civilian for the Control Commission in Germany in 1946, he again gave information only to Blunt. So, unlike the Elli described by Gouzenko, Long did not have a Soviet courier or controller and had no need for *duboks*. Long had nothing whatever "Russian in his background," never had access to MI5 files, and never worked at Blenheim.

Andrew has since observed that, in Russian, Elli can mean two capital L's—Leo Long's initials—but two Russians, Oleg Tsarev and Dr. Chervonnaya, have separately stated to me that "El" is the Russian pronunciation of the letter L, whether lower- or uppercase, just as it is in English, and that two L's would be written Elel, not Elli. The second half of Elli, "li," has no meaning in Russian. Yet Andrew goes even further in his recent contribution to *The Gouzenko Affair*, where he not only claims that "the real Elli was identified in 1985," but castigates Wright for failing to spot "the clue" that "Elli can be translated as the plural of the Roman letter L"!

This is a convenient point to state that it is now generally agreed that the content of Guy Liddell's diaries eliminates the possibility that he himself was a Russian agent of any kind, in spite of the last three letters of his name. So he too could not have been Elli. In fact, the only remaining credible candidate is Hollis, a name that also contains three relevant letters.

So far, the GRU has made no comment about Elli, close relatives of whom may still be alive.

CHAPTER 34

Protective Perfidy

———

HAVING LOST KLAUS FUCHS AS A SUPPLIER WHEN HE MOVED to the United States at the end of 1943, and Melita Norwood, who was also transferred to the KGB, Sonia had continued to transmit items of information received from sources that included her father, brother, and Hans Kahle on her visits to London. She may also have gleaned material from minor agents, whom she claims to have found and recruited, though these may have been GRU legendary cover for a much more important supplier.

Hollis had moved to London in February 1943 but still visited Blenheim about twice a week. So if he was Elli, Sonia could have continued to service him there until the end of the war and experienced no interference from MI5 with any of her sources. As her transmission of the Quebec Agreement document proved, she was certainly servicing one spy with exceptional high-level access. Unlike Fuchs, Sonia was never handed over to the KGB but remained a GRU spy until her retirement, as her son Michael Hamburger recently confirmed to me.

After the final defeat of Germany in May 1945, Mrs. Laski organized a street celebration party in Oxford, which Sonia attended and enjoyed, for she was to include a photograph of it in her memoirs. Shortly afterward, the previous tenant of her cottage required its return, so Sonia needed to find new accommodations. In any case, if she had been servicing Elli, she no longer needed to reside in Oxford, because the whole of

MI5 was soon transferred back to London, and nobody in it had professional reasons to visit the area. She found an empty house, called the Firs, about twenty miles north, in the Cotswold village of Great Rollright, near Chipping Norton. The fact that she was prepared to move to such a remote area with a poor bus service when MI5 was moving back to London is another odd coincidence.

Once installed, Sonia lost little time in stringing up her aerial across the courtyard. That she continued to transmit to the Center from her new home is beyond dispute. Some of her contacts, like Kahle and her brother, Jurgen, quickly returned to Germany, but her transmissions showed that she retained at least one productive source who visited her or was contacted during her trips to London. It has been suggested that this was Norwood, but a deciphered KGB document dated September 16, 1945, shows that Norwood, then code-named Tina (later Hola), was being run by KGB officers in the embassy, with whom Sonia had no contact. It seems more likely, from recent evidence, that one of Sonia's continuing sources was a man—an atomic scientist based in the Clarendon Laboratory in Oxford and whose wife may have visited the Firs.

James Johnston, formerly of the Radio Security Service, told me that in 1946, he and his colleagues at the Arkley station, near London, continued to monitor and log regular transmissions from an illegal source in the Oxford area, which they now recognize as being Sonia's home in Great Rollright. These logs were returned from MI6 marked "NFU"—meaning "no further use"—and eventually they were all destroyed. Johnston regards this destruction as an intelligence disaster—"a mad decision"—because some of them could probably have been deciphered. He greatly doubted that Sonia could have continued to escape detection and interrogation without some protection, either in MI6, MI5, or both. If Sonia had been servicing Elli, it remained greatly in his interest that she not be identified and questioned.

Sonia stated in her memoirs that during 1946 and without explanation, the GRU remained out of contact with her for many months, as they had with others following the Gouzenko defection—the ruthless "source protection" reaction. The Center would have regarded both Fuchs and Elli as seriously threatened by Gouzenko's revelations and by the general alert that they should have caused in MI5. Incredibly, MI5 continued to take no effective action, and again, it is fair to ask why.

At first, Sonia lived alone in the Firs with her children. Her son

Michael remembered several Communists visiting the house on secret business when he and his siblings would be sent out and doors would be locked. Then, in January 1947, Sonia's husband, Len, who was still in the army in Germany, was demobilized, and he returned to Great Britain and found a job, first in London and then in an aluminum factory in Banbury, which he reached from the Firs by motorcycle. Nigel Bance has discovered evidence that Len also helped to service the atomic source in the Clarendon Laboratory. Sonia was friendly with the scientist's wife, and Len had taken food parcels to her relatives in Germany when returning there from leave after the end of the war.

Meanwhile, after the successful explosion of the two nuclear bombs that forced the Japanese surrender in 1945, Fuchs knew that he would soon be posted back to Britain because the Americans were anxious to end the atomic partnership and to proceed alone with building a nuclear arsenal under sole U.S. control. The British government—then headed by Clement Attlee, who had defeated Churchill in an election—had decided to pursue atomic research only three weeks after the Japanese surrender, to have any pretense at remaining a major political power. So Fuchs was suddenly extremely valuable to it, and toward the end of November 1945, he was offered a senior post at the new Atomic Energy Research Establishment, to be built on a disused airfield at Harwell in Berkshire.

In the previous month, the KGB had received precise details of the structure and size of the more advanced American plutonium bomb and its components, including an ingenious initiating device called the Urchin. In April 1946, Fuchs attended a most secret "Conference on the Super"—to consider ways of building a much more powerful weapon, which later became known as the hydrogen bomb, or H-bomb. Before leaving Los Alamos on June 14, Fuchs reviewed every paper on thermonuclear (H-bomb) weapons in the archives and reached England via Montreal, flying back from there in an RAF plane at the beginning of July. It may have been more than coincidence that a few months later, Russian scientists began a study on the same subject.

Following the imprisonment of Alan May for what was a moderate degree of espionage, Fuchs would have been less than human had he not been relieved to quit the United States. He knew that he had been guilty of espionage on such a shattering scale that he might face the death penalty there. He took up his new post at Harwell on August 1, 1946, the very day President Truman signed the Atomic Energy Act, nationalizing all aspects of atomic development. When the U.S. Senate made it clear that the United States should pursue both atomic weapons and power research without any foreign ties, Attlee reinforced his decision that Britain needed to develop an independent deterrent. On October 25, some government ministers argued that, being so impoverished by the war, the United Kingdom could not afford to build an atomic bomb, but Foreign Secretary Ernest Bevin famously declared, "We've got to have the bloody Union Jack on top of it!" and prevailed. Fuchs would therefore become deeply involved in research aimed at producing independent British nuclear weapons and aspects of nuclear power, utilizing all he had learned in the United States and serving on many secret committees.

According to KGB archives, the Russians had been unsure of Fuchs's precise whereabouts in Great Britain until the autumn of 1946, because, like the GRU, the KGB had suspended contact with him following the defection of Gouzenko. Before leaving America, Fuchs had been given routine instructions by the KGB on how to resume contact but was to claim that he did not do so. However, it has recently been established by Dr. Chervonnaya that for safety's sake, the KGB had intended to locate its further meetings with Fuchs in Paris. The KGB intelligence officer who had controlled him in the United States, Anatoli Yatskov (posing as Yakovlev), was switched to Paris to set up a safe house there, leaving New York City on December 27, 1946. He remained in Paris until the spring of 1948, and it would seem likely that Fuchs made some visits to him, which would account for the puzzling apparent gap in his supply of atomic information at a time when Soviet scientists were desperately in need of it. The reason for Yatskov's sudden recall from Paris to Moscow is also revealing.

In an interview in Moscow, the former KGB agent runner Alexander Feklisov told Dr. Chervonnaya that early in 1948, the KGB Center received a tip from "a very reliable and important source" that MI5 had sent a message to its French counterpart warning that Yatskov was a senior Soviet intelligence officer. Shortly afterward, Yatskov was recalled to Moscow—another rapid KGB response to information from an established source about secret action taken by MI5.

Perhaps to cover the Paris contact, Fuchs was eventually to claim that he had been so severely frightened by the ten years' sentence given to May that he had suspended his supply of information. He may also have been warned that soon after his arrival at Harwell, he would be subjected to a routine security check. This was duly done, because the newly appointed security officer there, Wing Commander Henry Arnold, had drawn attention to the fact that Fuchs was a German who had become naturalized, though this had been common knowledge in MI5 for years. Arnold quickly became sufficiently suspicious of Fuchs to write to MI5 on October 1, 1946, suggesting that he was "too good to be true."

In that same month, the MI5 officer Michael Serpell discovered a highly significant fact about Fuchs: As a young man, he had served as a "communist penetration agent in the Nazi Party," which implied that he was a skilled simulator. Serpell expressed deep concern and suggested that Fuchs be reexamined, but Hollis, then his immediate superior, rejected this advice, decreeing, "Present action should be limited to warning Arnold about the background of Fuchs." That instruction is further evidence that Hollis was established as MI5's link with Harwell, being considered its atomic expert.

By that time, he had been switched from F Division, where he had specialized in Soviet counterespionage, to B Division, which was responsible for counterespionage in general, and had been concentrating on the Germans and their allies. Gouzenko's revelations and subsequent developments had clearly indicated that after the German defeat, the counterespionage effort needed to be focused on the newly exposed Soviet threat. Dick White (director of counterespionage) was senior, but Hollis (B1) was by far the more experienced regarding Soviet and Communist affairs. So contact between the two became more intimate than ever, with Hollis's actions and advice being highly influential.

This move by Hollis to such a key post in Soviet counterespionage has only recently come to light with the release of MI5's papers concerning Fuchs. It is the final—and total—disproof of the claim by Hollis's supporters that he was never involved in counterespionage.

With the retirement of the director general, Sir David Petrie, early in 1946, Sir Percy Sillitoe, a former chief constable, took over on April 30. Though it may have been coincidence that Sillitoe had been offered the post shortly after the exposure of the atomic spy May, the appointment of "an honest copper" had been something of a vote of no confidence in the existing MI5 management. Attlee had been impressed by Sillitoe, then aged fifty-eight, because of his administrative ability and integrity and his tough treatment of criminals in Sheffield and Glasgow. The new director general was expected to new-broom MI5, and the arrival of an outsider was resented by many of the staff. Most of the talented wartime recruits had quickly left to pursue their peacetime careers. So on several counts, a major reorganization of the scaled-down, peacetime service had become necessary.

In the course of his duties, Hollis's attention was again drawn to Fuchs's relationship with Kahle, but he explained that away as due entirely to their chance companionship in the Canadian detention camp. Yet a report on Kahle by Michael Hanley dated September 16, 1949, would show that the MI5 files already recorded that "from 1941–1946 Kahle worked very hard as a communist organizer and propagandist in the UK. He was a member of the Executive of the German Communist Party in Great Britain." Hanley was to conclude, "The whole tenor of Kahle's career suggests that, in addition to many other political activities, he was working for the Soviet Security Police." He was, in fact, working for the GRU and, like Fuchs, seemed to have enjoyed a protective hand inside MI5, where Elli was a GRU agent.

Released MI5 archives show that on October 15, 1946, James Robertson (B4) told a colleague that he thought it possible "that Fuchs had been passing vitally important information to the Russians." On November 27, Jane Archer, who had been coaxed back to MI5, being in C Division, urged that the Atomic Energy Directorate should be warned that "Fuchs is a possible (I would prefer to say probable) Russian agent." She recommended that he "should be divorced from all contact with atomic energy." She added that to allow him to continue "may compromise the future of atomic energy secrecy." Hollis ignored this profoundly prophetic statement and threw his weight against her. On December 4, 1946, he wrote a message to White saying, "I, myself, can see nothing on this file which persuades me that Fuchs is in any way likely to be engaged in espionage or that he is anything more than anti-Nazi."

As usual, White agreed with that disastrous opinion, saying that "there was nothing of a positive nature against Fuchs." Pursuing the blind-eye policy, neither made any attempt to find anything. Yet by that time, Fuchs was one of the few Harwell scientists involved in weapons work because he regularly visited Fort Halstead in Kent, where a team headed by William Penney was trying to design a British atom bomb. So the more cautious and more senior Liddell decided that "as there were such important issues at stake" there should be an inquiry, which should also apply to Fuchs's friend Rudolf Peierls, who had also returned to Britain. On December 20, 1946, he sent a note to White and Hollis "for action." It stated that "we cannot possibly afford to leave matters as they are. There is a prima facie case for investigation of both Fuchs and Peierls. I think it would be unwise to make any approach to the Ministry of Supply [Fuchs's employer then] until we know more about both these people."

Reluctantly, on January 14, 1947, Hollis instructed Serpell to secure Home Office warrants (HOWs) to tap the telephones and open the mail of both men, requiring a report "at the end of two months or sooner if anything of significance arose." The HOWs were granted on January 18, though they took a while to be put into effect. During February, March, and part of April 1947, Fuchs was kept under surveillance by MI5 watchers, both at Harwell and in London, which he visited for discussions at the Supply Ministry. No suspicious behavior of any kind by him, or by Peierls, was observed.

On April 2, Hollis's assistant Graham Mitchell reported to Hollis that after two months, the complete lack of any behavior of security interest "went far to dispose of any case against Peierls" and suggested that the warrant on that suspect should be canceled. Though Mitchell had referred only to Peierls, Hollis responded on April 10, by writing to White that as the findings were completely negative, he wanted approval to cancel the surveillance warrant on Fuchs as well. White agreed. By May 7, the watch had been discontinued, and by May 22, the telephone taps and all other aspects of the surveillance were abandoned. Hollis and Michael Perrin then went through the motions of clearing Fuchs again, though without questioning him. Clearly Hollis, who had been opposed to the surveillance, was responsible for ending it, seemingly as quickly as he could. He had systematically contrived to give Fuchs the benefit of all doubt, as he had already done with Sonia.

During the whole of the ten weeks or so that Fuchs was watched, he did nothing suspicious. He met no known Communists or Russian agents. Yet as will shortly be seen, in June 1947, only two or three weeks after all surveillance had ended, he took steps to meet two well-known German Communists in London in order to restore his connection with the KGB and to resume spying. That was surely one of the most extraordinary anomalies of the entire Hollis saga. Fuchs's inactivity after the surveillance ceased would just have covered the time needed for Moscow to be advised of its ending by a well-placed source in London and for Fuchs to be informed that it was safe to operate again, as events would prove that it was.

So who could have been the prime informant leading to that rapid Moscow response? It could not have been Blunt, the only known spy inside MI5 apart from Elli. Blunt had quit MI5 in 1945, after being appointed surveyor of the king's pictures, to return to the Courtauld Institute, which he headed. Though he continued to carry out conspiratorial services for Burgess, acting as a go-between with a KGB courier, photographing Foreign Office documents for him in the safety of his apartment in the institute, and even picking up KGB money hidden in *duboks,* he had no further access to MI5 documents.

Eventually, on November 25, 1947, in connection with the formal establishment of Fuchs as a scientific civil servant, Martin Furnival Jones (C2 Protective Security) informed Hollis that in his view, Fuchs's employers, the Supply Ministry, should be given "a full statement" about him. He added, "I do not think they have ever been given the story." Hollis immediately wrote to White, "In my opinion, there is really nothing we can usefully give the Supply Ministry and I should be inclined to answer that we have no objection to the establishment of Fuchs." By that time—on September 27—Fuchs had made contact with his new KGB controller, met him in a London pub, handed over secret documents, and answered urgent questions posed by Russian scientists!

White's response to Hollis's letter was to write Liddell on December 2, saying that he was inclined to agree with Hollis, but in view of Liddell's previous interest in the case, he would like him to see the papers before action was taken. Having studied the papers, Liddell called a meeting with White, Hollis, and Furnival Jones on December 10. It was agreed that if the Supply Ministry approached MI5 about Fuchs, it should be told, "We consider that the records indicate only that Fuchs held anti-Nazi views and associated with Germans of similar views and we think the security risk is very slight." Those were Hollis's words in a letter sent to Jane Archer's C Division, recording, seemingly with some relish, that his view had not only prevailed, but been supported by White and others. Clearly, as a result of Hollis's determination, MI5 was to take no initiative to inform Fuchs's employers concerning any doubts about him. Fuchs's charmed life was to continue—with savage consequences for Britain and America and rich reward for the Soviet Union.

With all this newly available documentary evidence, nobody can now deny that from start to finish, the prime responsibility for employing Fuchs on atomic bomb research and keeping him there was Hollis's. His successive blind-eye clearances enabled Fuchs to supply the Soviet Union with information of incalculable value while he was in Britain, in America, and then in Britain again. In short, Hollis repeatedly expedited what would become known as "the greatest crime in history"—the virtual theft of the atomic bomb and the H-bomb.

It is also an inescapable fact that the questioning of Fuchs, which was never done until it was forced on MI5 late in 1949, might have led to the exposure of Sonia and that thorough interrogation of her might have spelled disaster for Elli.

The MI5 documents reveal that for whatever reason, Hollis's behavior throughout the Fuchs case was an exhibition of stubborn determination to keep him in place and to prevent any questioning of him, which is precisely what happened until 1949, when the FBI provided evidence that could not be ignored.

CHAPTER 35

Back in Full Flood

—

AFTER THE QUICK SURRENDER OF JAPAN, STALIN HAD AP-preciated the political as well as military value of atomic weapons in the coming struggle with the West. The successful explosion of the atomic bombs over Hiroshima and Nagasaki had presented him and his generals with a stark situation: Russia could no longer rely on the military strategy that had saved it from Napoleon and then from Hitler. That was the scorched-earth policy of drawing invading forces deeper and deeper into Russia's vast land over terrain made inhospitable, while maintaining the strategic reserves that would eventually counterattack when the invaders were overstretched and winter-bound. With a monopoly of nuclear weapons, the Western allies could dispense with a mass invasion by eliminating cities, making large-scale withdrawal impossible, and destroying the strategic reserves. So the arrival of the atomic bomb on the military-political scene had suddenly darkened the dream of pushing Moscow-controlled communism throughout Western Europe by conventional forces, assisted by conspired revolution.

At a meeting in mid-August 1945, Stalin expressed his fury that the atomic bomb had destroyed his military advantages and demanded the provision of atomic weapons in the shortest possible time. On August 20, the State Defense Committee formally set up a special Committee on the Atomic Bomb headed by Lavrenti Beria. Stalin personally ordered his atomic chief, Igor Kurchatov, to speed the development of the atomic project, giving it top priority for resources in spite of all the shortages and industrial damage. He was greatly influenced by the fact that the Americans had used the weapons and wondered to what extent that might have been a warning to him if he pushed too far.

Just two months later, in Great Britain, the Joint Intelligence Committee concluded that "atomic developments are the paramount potentiality of the future" and that an accurate awareness of the progress of any Soviet atomic bomb program was essential to strategic planning. Automatically, atomic intelligence was an MI6 responsibility and an officer by the name of Eric Welsh was placed in charge of a small team to pursue it. On November 20, 1945, all details of the project were reported to Moscow by Kim Philby. Subsequently, the intelligence was essentially restricted to long-distance chemical analysis of the air blowing from Soviet testing grounds. By monitoring the traces of the gas krypton in the atmosphere, it was also possible to deduce the levels of plutonium production, as recorded by Dr. Michael Goodman in his comprehensive book *Spying on the Nuclear Bear*. Attempts were made to use Russian deserters by parachuting them into the Soviet Union in a CIA operation code-named Red Socks, but the deserters were quickly caught and executed.

Soviet archival records show that by the time the MI5 surveillance of Fuchs ended in May 1947, Stalin and Beria were exerting threatening pressure on the Soviet scientists to stage an atomic bomb test with all speed. Stalin was desperate to show the world that the Soviet Union was a nuclear power. Fuchs had been a major source of the technical information that was enabling them to speed the project, and there were still many abstruse questions he could answer. As a consequence, Kurchatov urged both the KGB and the GRU to induce their spies to provide as many Western atomic secrets as possible. The KGB was therefore under increasing pressure to reestablish regular contact with Fuchs, if it could be done with reasonable safety.

Is it just another coincidence that precisely when the Soviet Union needed to contact Fuchs most urgently, Hollis was ensuring that active surveillance of the spy by MI5 would cease? As Alan May revealed on his deathbed, he himself had been specifically warned, in a way he declined to specify, that any meeting with a controller would be too dangerous, and Fuchs may have received similar service.

Whatever the reason, Fuchs did nothing further to contact his Soviet masters until June, soon after the surveillance had ended. According to his own story, he contacted his Russian friends then entirely on his own initiative. He had lost touch with Sonia since leaving Britain for America in 1943 and knew that Jurgen Kuczynski had already returned alone to Germany. So he claimed that he contacted Jurgen's wife, Marguerite, whom he knew. As a minor Soviet agent herself, Marguerite knew about Fuchs's original recruitment to the GRU, but as she was about to rejoin Jurgen, she wanted no problems. So she put him in touch with other German Communist refugees. One of these, who is said to have put the spy in direct contact with his new KGB controller, was Hanna Klopstech, who had been on the "Foreign Communists Considered Dangerous" list that MI5 had prepared for the U.S. embassy in late 1940.

Fuchs was to tell the FBI that he had already known "Big Hanna" during his previous time in Great Britain and contacted her at her home. As in the past, she was able to operate without hindrance, and on July 19, 1947, according to Fuchs's statement to the FBI, she met him by the gate at Hampton Court. She had been in touch with the Soviet embassy and gave him details and recognition signals for an eventual meeting with a new case officer in a London pub called the Nagshead. This was to be Alexander Feklisov, who posed as an official attached to the Association for Cultural Relations with the USSR, calling himself Alexander Fomin. He had honed his intelligence skills in Washington, running several Soviet agents there.

Feklisov, who published his memoirs, *The Man Behind the Rosenbergs,* in 2001, revealed that while he had been back in Moscow in 1947, working in the British counterintelligence section, the KGB had selected him to run Fuchs in Great Britain once the spy had been reactivated after his surveillance. Clearly, with the flow of Fuchs's information being increasingly important, a further arrangement depending solely on trips to Paris would have been ineffective. So Feklisov left for London on August 30 and had less than a month to familiarize himself with the capital before his first meeting with Fuchs, which was scheduled for Saturday, September 27, 1947, at eight p.m.

After his agent-running experience in the United States, Feklisov was not surprised to find that, of the current embassy staff, only the resident KGB chief knew of the existence of Fuchs. Under the same strict ruling, he knew nothing about the Cambridge spies being run by his embassy colleague and friend Yuri Modin. Neither of them knew anything about any of the British spies, such as Elli, being run by the GRU from a different office in the same building.

Fuchs, whose code name had been changed from Otto to Rest and then, in October 1944, to Charles, always met Feklisov in pubs on the outskirts of London on Saturday evenings. A seasoned spy, Fuchs performed the standard KGB protective ritual, driving from Harwell in his sports car, checking that he was not being followed, parking at a railway station, and boarding a train for London at the last moment. The two conspirators would spot each other in the bar, then leave separately and meet outside, talking mainly in the street. KGB archives have shown that at each meeting, Fuchs handed over new information in documentary form, including the answers to previous questions, and that Feklisov then gave the material to a waiting colleague and returned to continue the discussion. At one meeting, Feklisov offered Fuchs £200, of which the traitor took £100, claiming that taking it was a symbol of his loyalty to the Soviet cause—a further "signing on."

Feklisov also went through the counterespionage motions immediately prior to his meetings with Fuchs but never saw any trace that he was being followed. During the early part of the war, with resources being concentrated on the German threat, Soviet "diplomats" had not been subjected to routine surveillance. With the war long over, however, and with the Soviet Union as MI5's main counterespionage target, Feklisov's freedom of action is a cause for wonder.

The Russian claimed that he and his KGB colleagues in the Soviet embassy believed that when Fuchs eventually became suspect, the MI5 management had wrongly assumed that he was being controlled by a completely unknown illegal. That would explain why MI5 seemed to be paying no special attention to any KGB or GRU officers from the Soviet embassy or trade delegations. If that was true, it was another major error of judgment—or worse. The KGB knew from Anthony Blunt that this had been MI5's wartime policy, but he had left in 1945. So how could Feklisov still be confident that the policy had not changed after the Germans had ceased to be a threat? Was there still an informant in MI5? In his memoirs, referring to Fuchs's eventual confession, Feklisov specifically stated, "We had enough sources within British intelligence at the time to find out all these details." Philby was not the only one.

Meanwhile, eventually reacting to the Gouzenko revelations and the May case, Prime Minister Clement Attlee had set up the highly secret

Cabinet Committee on Subversive Activities, which began its work in May 1947. All it did was to extend the system of negative vetting to more civil servants with access to secret information. This meant that before allowing them regular access to important secrets, what was known about them from existing records would be checked, but they were not to be questioned or subjected to inquiries. If there was nothing relevant in the files, they were nodded through.

In October, the known Communist Klaus Fuchs flew to Washington as the British delegate to the first tripartite conference at which American, Canadian, and British scientists would decide which secret atomic documents could be declassified and published. It was a perfect opportunity to collect still more atomic information for transmission to Moscow via his new friend Feklisov.

The released FBI documents "Philby, Burgess, Maclean" have recently shown that Donald Maclean, then in Washington as the British member of a secretariat serving the Joint Congressional Committee on Atomic Energy, also attended the conference, as a "visitor." In 1947, Maclean had been made joint secretary of the combined policy committee on atomic bomb collaboration, which had been established in 1943 at the Quebec conference. This gave him access to atomic policy secrets of the greatest interest to the Kremlin because he had a pass giving him unescorted access to U.S. Atomic Energy Commission headquarters. He knew all about the supposedly secret Anglo-American plans for obtaining supplies of uranium, along with details of early intelligence operations to check on Soviet atomic research.

So Stalin had *two* of his most productive spies sitting in at the most secret tripartite conference. Both were British and had been vouched for as secure by MI5 and the Foreign Office.

When Maclean left the United States in September 1948 for a post in Cairo, the U.S. Atomic Energy Commission gave him a farewell lunch, such had been the trust misplaced in him by Great Britain's essential ally.

CHAPTER 36

Another GRU Defector

BY THE TIME FEKLISOV AND FUCHS FIRST MET, ON SEPTEMber 27, 1947, an event had occurred that should have led to the arrest of Sonia and then possibly of Fuchs, and to which far too little critical attention has been paid. Alexander Foote, who had served Sonia during her espionage in Switzerland and remained in service there after she had left, had defected back to Great Britain from the GRU while in Berlin. The MI5 papers on the Foote case, released in 2004, showed that the many accounts of it published previously had been seriously inaccurate, mainly because MI5 had staged an operation to deceive Parliament and the British and American public about it.

Foote had moved from Switzerland to Moscow in January 1945 and, after tough interrogations and instruction, had been sent to the Russian sector of Berlin for further GRU work in June 1947. He gave himself up to British authorities in Berlin on July 2, 1947, and was quickly in the hands of an MI6 representative, who took a statement. This included the fact that Sonia and Len Beurton were in Britain, as MI5 was aware, along with some details of their wartime activities in Switzerland. A copy of his statement was brought back to MI5 headquarters on July 5.

Meanwhile, on July 3, in London, an unnamed MI6 officer went to see Hollis, who as B1 was in charge of the case, with Dick White in overall command. As Foote had worked only against the Germans and was returning to his homeland, he could not be prosecuted for treachery. Hollis was in favor of leaving Foote with MI6, which was considering using him as a double agent in South America, where he would have been out of the way. After that possibility had been discarded, there was discussion as to which agency should debrief him fully.

MI6 considered retaining control of Foote, with Philby in charge of the case, but it was soon decided that he should be dealt with by MI5, where, according to a memo dated July 25, "Hollis ruled" that the interrogation of Foote should be carried out by two of his own officers, with another acting as administration officer and all reporting to him daily.

Foote was flown to Hanover, safe in the British-controlled part of Germany, and was interrogated there over three days. Anxious to return to Great Britain, he spoke freely, revealing that Ursula Beurton's GRU code name had been Sonia and that while living in Britain, she had "continued connections with Russia." He gave details of her radio sets and said that she had worked for Red Army intelligence (GRU) in Shanghai, as had her first husband, Rudi. Foote admitted that "on indications supplied to me by a certain Brigitte Lewis, I kept a conspiratorial rendezvous with 'Sonia' in Geneva." So Hollis had been quickly informed that the former Brigitte Kuczynski, who had long been on file, had been involved and that her sister Ursula Beurton, whom he had dismissed as harmless, had been a long-term Soviet agent, using radio to transmit espionage information to the GRU Center, with which she had remained in touch.

As early as July 15, 1947, a report to Hollis by J. H. Marriott (B1b) had reminded him that Sonia had proceeded to Britain at the end of 1940 "with at least Russian concurrence and the possibility cannot be excluded that she came here with a mission." Marriott noted that she had "made her home in and around Oxford," though he seemed to have made no connection with the presence of MI5 in the area. He concluded, "It is, I think, desirable that we should investigate contacts of the Beurton family," asking for a letter and phone check. Nothing of significance resulted.

In a summary about the Kuczynski clan prepared for Hollis on July 17, 1947, from the many files on that malevolent family, Michael Serpell stated, "Ursula Beurton is a Soviet agent of long standing, like her first husband, Rudi Hamburger." Another document recorded, "In December 1940 she left Switzerland on instructions from Moscow." It ended, "This woman is well known and Foote's account tallies with existing records." On July 20, Foote told his interrogator, "It was Ursula who had brought Rudi into the racket," and that she had needed to make "a quick getaway from China and had forced herself on to the Master of a Soviet ship in a Chinese port." The GRU had quickly known of Foote's defection, and it would have been standard practice for Sonia to have been informed of her danger by the GRU Center.

So Hollis had firm evidence that she was a full-blooded Soviet agent, professionally skilled in radio transmission, and that she had come to Oxford early in 1941 on GRU instructions. Serpell therefore recommended to Hollis, "We should consider extending the investigation of Ursula Beurton and her husband to cover other members of the Kuczynski family, such as Brigitte." A document dated July 19 recorded Sonia's address as the Firs, Great Rollright.

On agreeing to be held incommunicado for several weeks, Foote was airlifted to London under escort on August 7 for a prolonged debriefing by Hollis's MI5 team. This would have been a frightening situation for Elli, as it was known that Foote had spent time at the GRU Center, where he might have heard gossip. He had, for example, learned that the Gouzenko defection had "disrupted the whole Red Army network in the Americas," with all agents who were using forged passports being withdrawn.

He was installed in an apartment at 19 Rugby Mansions, West London. As is clearly stated in a letter signed on August 7, Hollis insisted that the RAF, from which Foote had deserted to join Sonia in Switzerland, should be kept in complete ignorance about him. The RAF might want to prosecute him, and Hollis was determined to keep full control, especially over any eventual publicity, which might include information about Sonia, who was then completely unknown to the public. The threat of informing the RAF also gave MI5 a hold over Foote's future behavior.

The interrogations were held mainly in MI5's accommodation address, room 055 in the War Office. On August 9, Hollis received a long note about Foote from Serpell and the interviews continued until September 18. Foote provided a mass of further information about GRU operations and conspiratorial practice, giving details of Sonia's professional skill at constructing and operating radio transmitters. At first, he insisted that Sonia had been a GRU agent only up to the time of the Hitler-Stalin pact, when she had become disenchanted, and that the couple had been dormant in Britain since 1941, indicating that Sonia had been skilled at imposing her legend. Later, however, he confirmed that while he had been at the GRU Center in Moscow, he had heard of Sonia's "continuing connections with Russia." He said that Sonia had worked as a GRU officer in Poland and China. He also revealed that he knew that Sonia's brother, Jurgen Kuczynski, had taken reports to the Soviet embassy in London and had commented that somehow the GRU Center knew that "he was not followed by the British authorities." He then gave details of his meeting with Brigitte and how she had recruited him and Len Beurton. Foote told his interrogators that he felt bad about "ratting on the Beurtons," but in fact the records show that Sonia's past was already known in MI5.

It was Hollis who made the decisions, positive or negative, and no effective action against Brigitte, who was still living in London, was ever taken. She was never questioned, and it is reasonable to wonder why. Surprise witness information presented in chapter 82 may provide the answer. Hollis was also told (as he knew already) that "Jurgen Kuczynski's file reveals a wide range of communist contacts in France, Switzerland, the USA and Mexico," but he was to maintain his minimalist policy toward all the Kuczynskis and anyone connected with them.

Details of the last interview with Foote, on September 18, show that MI5 felt it had some future hold over him because of his confessed perjury as a witness at Sonia's divorce case. He had raised the possibility of employment in intelligence but had been turned down. Meanwhile, the Hollis team had decided that the MI5 officer Courtney Young should "take up the project of producing Foote's autobiography" for publication. Foote had received help from Serpell, who had introduced him to a friend, Desmond Vesey, who was by then a member of a publishing firm, the Museum Press. (This would seem to be the D. Vesey who had been a wartime member of MI5.) MI5 insisted that Foote's story had to end at the time of his defection back to Great Britain. He was forbidden to mention anything about his "dealings with British intelligence."

After six weeks of cooperation, Foote was given a false cover story to enable him to secure an identity card and a ration book. He left on September 20 to stay with his sister. A final general account of the Foote case was submitted to Hollis on October 16. On December 11, Foote, who had by then moved back to London, was interviewed again by William Skardon. He was warned not to indulge in any intrigue or meet any of his former acquaintances.

What quickly ensued beggars belief. The "White-Hollis axis" was to behave in a most extraordinary way.

CHAPTER 37

The Firs Fiasco

—

Documents released by MI5 in 2004 show that all further inquiries about Sonia resulting from Foote's revelations were controlled by the White-Hollis axis. As director of counterespionage (DB), Dick White had overall command, but the work was done mainly by Hollis (B1) and his assistants. It has been stated in authoritative books that Hollis could not have been involved in the tragicomedy that unfolded in September 1947 because he was in Australia. However, the truth, recently established from Australian and British archives, is that Hollis did not visit Australia until 1948, and documents initialed by him prove that he was deeply involved in the Sonia case as late as December 1947 and was still B1 at the London headquarters.

On March 25, 1946, John Cimperman, the FBI representative in the U.S. embassy, had written to Hollis asking him to make arrangements to "interview Ursula Beurton for the purpose of ascertaining Rudolf's present whereabouts." The only result had been an unproductive letter to Kim Philby asking if MI6 knew where Rudi was. Hollis was resolutely opposed to any questioning of Sonia, even to assist the FBI at a time when Prime Minister Attlee was hoping to convince the U.S. authorities that British security could be trusted so that atomic cooperation could be resumed. In 1947, however, following the unexpected information about Sonia provided by Foote, it suddenly became impossible to avoid intervening.

MI5 records show that as early as July 24, 1947, immediately after Foote's initial revelations in Berlin, a Home Office warrant had been obtained to intercept and read Sonia's letters, cables, and bank accounts. The warrant extended to Brigitte and other members of the Kuczynski family. Oddly, no attempt was made to tap Sonia's own telephone, though Brigitte's was still being tapped in October. The White-Hollis axis also decreed that any human surveillance of Sonia's home, the Firs in Great Rollright, was impracticable, though there is no evidence that anyone from MI5 had visited the area. Nor was Sonia ever put under surveillance on her visits to London, though she went there regularly, ostensibly to visit various relatives, as the Kuczynski files recorded. There is no evidence either that any checks were ever made to discover if she was transmitting at the Firs, though MI5 knew from Foote that illicit radio operation was her specialty. Whatever their purpose, these omissions benefited Sonia and the GRU. Significantly, perhaps, the intercepted information about "the entire Kuczynski clan" passed to Hollis's assistants—and which I have read—yielded nothing whatever of intelligence value.

Foote's evidence about Sonia put the Hollis-White axis in an awkward predicament following Hollis's assurance to his colleagues four years previously, and then to the FBI in 1944, that Sonia seemed to be just a harmless housewife. Any evidence that she had really been active in Britain threatened the reputation of both.

By September 6, 1947, the chief constable of Oxfordshire had been asked by MI5 to make inquiries about Sonia and Len, and the FBI was routinely informed of developments through the Washington embassy. With what seems like unusual haste, if not panic, White, with Hollis's agreement, ordered an immediate interrogation of Sonia, once the police had confirmed her continuing residence at the Firs. According to White's official biography, the reason he had ruled out any prior surveillance to see whom she might be meeting or any telephone tap was that she would probably detect them, which seems unprofessionally defeatist and unconvincing. As a result, two MI5 officers, the patient interrogator William Skardon and Michael Serpell, who had previously expressed suspicions about Fuchs and Sonia, were detailed to visit the Firs on Saturday, September 13.

It is clear from Skardon's report on the episode that the interrogators were instructed to confine their questioning to the Beurtons' activities in

Switzerland before 1940, as revealed by Foote. There is no evidence of any intention of asking Sonia about pro-Soviet activities in Great Britain, though Hollis knew that she had "continued connections with Russia." Hollis's opinion that, while residing in and around Oxford, Sonia had been a harmless housewife was not to be sullied by any awkward admissions. That, too, benefited the Soviet cause.

According to Skardon's own report, now in the National Archives, he and Serpell picked up Detective Herbert of the Oxfordshire police and arrived at the Firs at one-twenty p.m., apparently without giving notice. The fact that the Beurtons were not having lunch does not seem to have surprised them. Through a window, they could see Sonia's father, who had recently lost his wife, reading in the living room as she, "unimpressive with frowsy, unkempt hair," opened the door. The father bowed his way out of the living room as Herbert introduced Skardon as "Mr. Sneddon" and Serpell as "Mr. Saville," who wished to talk to her. She immediately produced Len, who was "completely overshadowed by his wife." Herbert then left, but only after Sonia had insisted on seeing his police card. She did not ask to see the MI5 officers' identity cards, which suggests that she knew they were not detectives.

In her memoirs, Sonia recalled that, "rapidly and without pausing for breath," the officers told her they knew she had been a Soviet spy against the Germans in Switzerland. However, they were sure she had done nothing illegal since her arrival in Britain and was completely loyal, because they also knew she had become disillusioned when the Soviet Union had attacked Finland! Her memory is supported by Skardon's report on the visit, which stated, "I made it clear that we possessed information which made it necessary to interrogate her in connection with her past," later adding, "There was reason to suppose that she had given up working for the Russians on ideological grounds when they behaved so badly, from an anti-Fascist point of view, at the beginning of the war." Skardon, who had not been previously involved in the case, had clearly been given that spurious information by Hollis or one of his staff. Sonia also recorded that "they kept stressing, again and again, that they knew of my disillusionment with communism after the invasion of Finland by the Soviet Union" and "they knew that I was a loyal British subject." This strange practice of putting a manufactured explanation into a suspect's mouth, which seems to have originated in

MI5 during the Hollis-White association, was to be used again, more than once, in a traitor's interest in similarly suspicious circumstances, as will be seen.

Sonia immediately insisted that she would not cooperate or answer any questions about her past activities, which were none of their business. She appeared to be confident that MI5 had no recent evidence against her, because for more than a year and without explanation, the GRU Center had cut off radio contact with her. There were three reasons for the Center's ruthless behavior. Any local service for Elli had ceased after the departure of MI5 from Blenheim. At the same time, the GRU Center would have feared that Elli's safety could be seriously threatened by the inquiries, which should have followed the defection of Igor Gouzenko. Also, the defection of Foote in July 1946 had required that Sonia should be inactive, as had the surveillance of Fuchs a few months earlier.

Skardon eventually reported, "We could not force an entry into the past, that is pre-1940, with Mrs. Beurton." When Serpell made menacing references about the legality of her divorce from Hamburger, she became more resistant than ever. It would seem she had been made aware that MI5 officers had no powers of arrest and that once the detective had left, there was nothing they could do. In that respect, it had been a mistake to send the detective away unless that had been part of Skardon's instructions from the White-Hollis axis. Skardon reported, "We used every possible piece of cajolery and artificial guile without any success whatever."

When Len was interviewed alone, he admitted that he had first met his wife through Brigitte in 1936 but claimed that he had met her again in Switzerland "quite by chance" in 1939 and insisted that he had then gone to Germany on "family business," which he declined to discuss.

The MI5 men left at four p.m., saying they would call again the next day in the hope that Sonia might change her mind. In a further one and a half hours at the Firs on September 14, Skardon warned her that her refusal to talk might make life difficult for her relatives, but she told them nothing. "Towards the end, Mrs. Beurton was psychologically at her lowest ebb but she suddenly became possessed of an excess of resistance," he reported. "Our hopes were not realized." Having been professionally trained in Moscow, Sonia was a convincing actress. Skardon then concluded, "As a result of this interrogation, we regard ourselves as confirmed in our beliefs and take Foote's story to be substantially true." He declared himself "reasonably satisfied that the Beurtons had nothing more to do with Intelligence and were not at present involved in espionage." It was a major blunder by a man who was rather gullible, in spite of his later reputation. Like Foote, he had swallowed Sonia's legend, taking some comfort in her promise to contact Detective Herbert if she ever changed her mind. The report can only have been welcome to Hollis, who could inform his colleagues and the FBI that his catastrophic clearance of the most successful woman espionage agent of all time had been fully justified. Any admissions of current treachery by Sonia could have been disastrous for Hollis, and clearly his assistants had been briefed not to try to extract any.

Sonia had never been asked why she had moved from Switzerland to the Oxford area, which was the major question. Indeed, I have found no evidence that any MI5 officer seriously wondered why she had chosen to live there throughout her residence in Great Britain.

The officers had learned from Foote that Sonia was an expert illicit radio operator, and they could hardly have missed her aerial in the courtyard, unless she had removed it, knowing they were coming. Yet she was not questioned about her transmissions, though those who had instructed the interrogators knew that clandestine radio operations had been her specialty, as the MI5 papers prove. It is fair to ask why not. Nor did anyone ever make a search of the house, which could have revealed transmitting equipment and even her Minox camera. According to an informant, the equipment for Sonia's Station was kept in the cellar, reached from the sitting room through a little door, as I saw when I visited the Firs—not without a frisson—years later. Backed by MI5, the Oxfordshire chief constable could have secured a search warrant and Detective Herbert could have executed it.

The whole perfunctory exercise appeared to be nothing more than going through unavoidable motions to confirm Foote's statements for the written records and was guaranteed to produce nothing of much consequence. No effort whatever had been made to find out if Sonia had been active in Britain, and Skardon seems to have been instructed to avoid making any. To what extent had the interrogation been conditioned by Hollis's 1944 letter, which was in both the MI5 and FBI files, dismissing Sonia as a threat? All that the visits had achieved, apart from showing that Sonia had never been a double agent, as has been suggested, was to warn her that MI5 was aware of her existence in the area.

The behavior of the father, Len, and Sonia, coupled with the odd fact that they were not at lunch at one-twenty p.m. on a Saturday, suggests that they had been forewarned of the visit that day and had rehearsed the situation. In her memoirs, Sonia stated that she had been warned about a month previously of Foote's defection because he was supposed to have visited "an Austrian comrade," muttering, "Sonia and Len! Great danger! Don't work! Destroy everything!" and then to have run away. That unlikely story sounds like GRU-inspired disinformation to cover the true source of her subsequent composure. In any case, Sonia and Len would have had their legend fully prepared for such a contingency, having practiced it under GRU instruction: Admit nothing and try to find out what the interrogators know. On September 18, Percy Sillitoe had the unwelcome task of informing the Oxfordshire chief constable that the interview of the Beurtons had been "disappointing," accepting the opinion of Skardon, endorsed by White and Hollis, that "there is no reason to suspect them of present or even recent espionage activities. It is not anticipated that any further steps will be taken."

In fact, Sonia, on her own account, was due to attend an important secret rendezvous the very next day, as Foote later learned from her sister Brigitte, whom he had met in London before she knew that he had defected. Brigitte, who had first recruited him and Len to the GRU, told him that Sonia and Len had just had a narrow escape. That conspiratorial rendezvous suggests that even though the GRU ignored her radio signals, Sonia was still serving somebody other than Fuchs, by delivering documents in London.

According to Dr. David Burke, there is some evidence that Melita Norwood was returned to GRU control after the war and that Sonia may have been involved in servicing her again, though London would not have been convenient. There is no doubt that Norwood continued to be active after the war, delivering copies of documents about metallic problems being dealt with at Harwell until she retired in 1977. As will be seen, her contact may have been Sonia's sister Brigitte. The MI5 management decided not to interrogate Brigitte on any count, partly for lack of evidence but also because "as an active Communist she was not likely to be helpful."

On September 15, the day after the second visit to the Firs, MI5 suspended the postal check on the Firs and on the whole Kuczynski family. The Beurton file was then marked "File Closed." As had happened with Fuchs, the rapid suspension of surveillance on suspect Soviet spies was a Hollis trademark.

On September 20, a further and seemingly final report on the failed interrogation at the Firs was submitted to Hollis by Marriott. Hollis initialed it on September 21, showing that he was definitely in the office and involved. Pathetically, it confirmed that the letter and cable checks on Sonia had been discontinued on September 15 so that "nothing could harm the possibility that, on reflection, she might become more cooperative."

Hollis and White could hardly have been unaware of the possibility that the sudden appearance of two security officers and a policeman on Sonia's doorstep might panic her into joining her brother, Jurgen, in Berlin. Indeed, that might have been the prime purpose of the interview, for as will be seen, a myth that she had done exactly that within a few days of the Firs fiasco was to be propagated, by White in particular. The disappearance of Sonia behind the iron curtain, where she could not be questioned by prying investigators, would have been welcome to Hollis, especially if he was Elli. If she failed to oblige, a common belief that she had fled the country might serve to prevent inquiries, as indeed it did.

To Sonia's surprise, the GRU was content for her and Len to continue to live in Great Britain, and they remained at the Firs, fully composed, for almost three more years—a fact unknown to the public until discovered by my son, Michael, when researching for me in 1983. The Center seems to have been assured that they were entirely safe in doing so, despite the obvious fact that Sonia was a hostage to fortune regarding the precious Fuchs and Norwood, apart from others she had serviced.

The truth that Sonia and Len were so sure of their safety that they continued living exactly as before was well-known within MI5. In a letter dated December 1, 1947, sent by Marriott to the Special Branch to update Scotland Yard's information about the Kuczynski family, Sonia was described as living at the Firs, Great Rollright, with Len, who was working in Banbury. It also stated that "both were active in the affairs of the local Communist Party." The letter also told Scotland Yard that

Sonia's sister Brigitte was living at 62a Belsize Park Gardens and was "secretary to the Adelaide Ward of the Hampstead Branch of the Communist Party." Brigitte had been quickly informed of the Firs fiasco because her father, who was to die two months later, had arranged to see her on the morning after the first MI5 visit. The chance that the seasoned Brigitte would then make any move likely to be detectable by MI5 was zero.

A credible scenario to account for MI5's unseemly haste in staging the Firs "interview" and then closing down the issue with all speed presents itself. The attempted interrogation of Sonia and the closure of her MI5 file in mid-September occurred shortly before Fuchs was reactivated by meeting with his new KGB controller, Alexander Feklisov. The KGB Center had been under great pressure from Stalin and Beria to restore contact with Fuchs in London, but that could not be done safely until Sonia's potentially dangerous situation had been resolved. While it had been in MI5's genuine interest that Sonia be interrogated, it was essential for the Soviet interest that Sonia be eliminated from the equation without damage as speedily as possible. The events that had so rapidly removed the Sonia danger appear to have achieved everything the KGB required. Fuchs and Feklisov met on September 27 and on later occasions without hindrance of any kind. Was this truly remarkable conjunction of dates just another coincidence?

Russian records (mentioned in *The Haunted Wood* by Allen Weinstein and Alexander Vassiliev) show that Feklisov was warned about the MI5 visit to the Firs by the KGB Center, either before he met Fuchs for the first time or soon afterward. This appears to have been yet another rapid Moscow response to a tip-off from a source in London, as Sonia, in Great Rollright, was out of touch with Moscow. Who could the source have been? The indication that the information passed to Feklisov originated from Moscow and not from the London embassy itself suggests that the KGB Center had been informed by the GRU Center, which had quickly learned of the MI5 visit from one of its own London sources. That could have been Brigitte or an even better-informed agent, Elli.

On several occasions, when eventually safe in East Berlin, Sonia was to say that both she and her husband suspected that someone in MI5 must have been protecting them. In her last interview, aged ninety-three, she again raised the possibility that she and Len had survived because they were being protected by another Soviet agent inside MI5, but she claimed to have no idea of his identity.

Whatever the background facts, the whole Sonia episode had indeed been a disgraceful performance by Hollis, White, and others who regarded themselves as polished professionals who had accepted responsibility for protecting the nation—and its chief ally—from espionage and subversion.

CHAPTER 38

Australian Assignment

—

EARLY IN 1948, FOLLOWING THE DECISION BY WINSTON CHUR-
chill, and later by Clement Attlee, to bar Communists from access to
any defense secrets, Percy Sillitoe needed to expand C Division, which
was responsible for protective security. According to the MI5 officer
Freddie Beith, the management decided that because of the fast-
developing cold war, C Division was to become the most important
peacetime section. In addition to regulating the selection and supervision of all public servants with access to classified information, it was responsible for devising precautions and physical measures for protecting
secrets—matters of profound interest to any opposing intelligence service.

Since its main targets were Communists and potential Soviet spies,
Hollis was promoted to be its new chief with the rank of director. This
meant that at the regular directors' meetings, he learned much about
what other departments were doing and planning.

In making his choice, Sillitoe had been greatly influenced by White,
who suggested Hollis as the best-qualified candidate, though he had, in
fact, dealt disastrously with the Gouzenko case and had turned deaf ears
to the ticking time bombs of Fuchs and Sonia. By that time, MI5 had re-
united in a single London headquarters in Curzon Street, and it was at
an office party there that the announcement of Hollis's promotion was
made. It was widely resented because it was known that Hollis had

played no part in MI5's brilliant successes against the German intelligence services. Beith, who was present at the party, recalled to me in writing, "Hollis had come from nowhere under the aegis of White, who had previously insisted that nobody without a university degree should reach Director rank. There were officers senior to him and better qualified. It was widely believed that White had him promoted as part of a trend to surround himself with less able men whom he could dominate. White would always do the thinking and Hollis the deferring."

In fact, who was the more successful in manipulating the other is a matter worthy of research, as MI5 documents show that Hollis, who was persuasive as well as determined, was usually able to impose his will. Careerwise, both benefited from their mutual support, especially in explaining away their failures, which, when they admitted them, they minimized as "slips."

In support of counterespionage, Hollis remained very much concerned with it. So though he had left Communist and Russian affairs, he remained involved with them as the acknowledged expert in those fields, especially as the Soviet Union had clearly become the main adversary. As director C, Hollis had also inherited responsibility for MI5's public relations and occasional contacts with the media. He was to make peculiar use of it.

There was also resentment because the forty-two-year-old Hollis had started an affair with his twenty-seven-year-old secretary, Val Hammond, that they did not attempt to hide and which soon became the talk of the office. Affairs in the office were not uncommon in the secret services, but Hollis's rankled because once he became director of security, he was forever stressing the danger of illicit sexual involvements, which might expose an officer or agent to blackmail. His position was particularly piquant because of the holier-than-thou attitude he had taken concerning Maxwell Knight's relationship with his secretary.

His decision to have an open sexual relationship with his own secretary was another display of brass nerve and showed that he was prepared to take risks, because in those days, being seen to be cheating on one's wife with the risk of a divorce case was a career disadvantage. Roger Hollis was no orthodox figure.

Unlike her boss, Val Hammond was a university graduate who was to remain with Hollis throughout his career, long after she could easily have achieved officer status. Hollis's wife condoned the affair and they decided to stay together, but her doctor told me that she was deeply upset when Roger and Val went off on walking tours.

By that time, Hollis, who celebrated his promotion by adopting the Whitehall garb of senior office—pin-striped trousers, black jacket, and black homburg hat—was living at 6 Campden Hill Square, a fashionable part of London, leasing the house and later buying the leasehold. He was to remain there until he retired in 1965. Wright described the home as "tatty," the breakfast room as "dingy," and the corridors as "strewn with piles of old clothes," which Eve collected for charity. Beith described dining there as a grim experience: "The house was dark and cheerless. There were trunks full of old clothes. Hollis would switch on the TV and watch as we ate." Other visitors assumed that the couple was not overly concerned about creature comforts.

At the time of his promotion, the extent of Hollis's ineffectiveness against the Communist threat had not become apparent. In particular, the penetration of MI5 itself by Blunt, and to some extent by Burgess, was still unknown. Nevertheless, Beith told me that as early as 1948, he had become convinced that Hollis was a Soviet sympathizer and warned others that he should not be trusted with their information.

In January 1948, Anglo-American decrypts of KGB traffic had shown that a major espionage effort was being mounted in Australia, which had been singled out for political penetration. An unknown spy had given Soviet diplomats in Canberra a secret report on security in the western Mediterranean entitled *British Post-Hostilities Planning Paper,* which had been supplied to the Australian Foreign Office. President Truman was told by his security advisers that there was "a leak in high government circles in Australia to Russia," and the British were asked for an explanation. MI5 assured the United States that investigations were under way, but on February 17, a British request for the release to Australia of American guided missile data was refused.

Australia was then being envisaged as the "Arsenal of the Empire," where British missiles and nuclear weapons could be tested in the vast outbacks, as I was to witness at the Woomera firing range. So in February 1948, Sillitoe went to Canberra to alert Prime Minister Ben Chifley that British investigations had revealed some possible traitors and urged him to extend the undercover inquiries in Australia. Before leaving Canberra, Sillitoe agreed to send out MI5 officers to work on the case, the first to arrive being Hollis's former assistant Robert Hemblys-Scales.

In May 1948, the United States brought the security issue to a head by breaking off the whole defense-sharing agreement with Australia. This threatened the British-Australian rocket development project, which was essential to Britain and was providing Australia with new technology. In July 1948, Attlee wrote to the prime ministers of Australia, New Zealand, Canada, and South Africa, stressing the danger from Communist subversion and inviting them to visit London to discuss security issues. Chifley went that month and met British ministers and Sillitoe at Chequers, the prime minister's country home, where it seems to have been agreed that Hollis, MI5's authority on protective security, would be sent to Australia. He was also MI5's expert on communism, which was seen as the fount of the security problem in Australia, as it had been in Canada.

Chifley left Great Britain convinced that Australia needed to set up a security service along the lines of MI5, which had not then been exposed as gravely ineffective against the Soviet assault. Hollis arrived in Canberra in August at a time when, if he was Elli, he could have taken some comfort in knowing that the suspicions against both Fuchs and Sonia had been allayed. For two months, he and Hemblys-Scales tried to identify the Australian owners of the code names mentioned in the KGB traffic. They were not allowed to reveal the fact that the clues had come from code breaks.

It was a pantomime situation. There was Hollis advising on security following the leak of a few documents in Australia when MI5's own security had been so appalling that one of his own colleagues, Anthony Blunt, had abstracted more than seventeen hundred from the MI5 office!

As more clues came from London, Hollis named twelve Australians he believed to have been responsible for leaks, but none was ever prosecuted, with one defecting to Moscow. He returned to London in September 1948 but was back in Australia in February 1949, when there is a record of his presence at a meeting with Chifley and others, including his MI5 colleague Courtney Young, who remained as a resident security liaison officer. Hollis had previously visited Washington to brief officials there on the proposals for the Australian Security Intelligence Organization (ASIO). These were presented to the Australian government on February 7, 1949, and the setting up of ASIO was formally agreed upon at that meeting. Its purpose was to defend Australia against espionage and sabotage.

Like MI5, on which it was modeled, ASIO put power in the hands of its director general and his staff, with no mechanisms for accountability, making it, as MI5 had always been, a law unto itself. Hollis recommended a directive to ensure that ministers would not concern themselves with detailed information that the security service might obtain. As a result, the entire document issued by Chifley on March 16, 1949, had been drafted by MI5. (As Dr. Philip Murphy of Reading University has pointed out, "When, in September 1952, the British Home Secretary, Sir David Maxwell-Fyfe, sought for the first time formally to define the constitutional position of MI5, his directive to the MI5 Director General followed the Australian document virtually clause for clause." So by an unforeseeable fluke, Hollis had effectively drafted MI5's first charter three and a half years before the British government imposed it!)

Hollis's supporters have credited him with inducing the Australian government to set up ASIO, which was clearly against Soviet interests, but the Australian archives have since shown that the driving force was Sillitoe. Hollis had no option but to carry out his chief's requirements. It is a genuine coincidence that the sister organization, the Australian Security Intelligence Service, had been set up with the assistance of former MI6 officer Charles ("Dick") Ellis, who later confessed to having spied for Germany for money and is suspected of having been a Soviet agent, too.

ASIO's greatest coup was in securing the defection of two KGB officers serving in Canberra, Vladimir Petrov and his wife, in 1954. Unfortunately for Hollis, who had returned permanently from Canberra, probably in late March 1949, the Petrovs' information was to expose further serious incompetence in MI5's control of espionage in Great Britain.

In 1959, ASIO wished to bug the new Soviet embassy in Canberra, and Hollis, by then the MI5 chief, sent his technical officer, Peter Wright, to assist in what was known as Operation Mole. A listening device was planted illicitly in a window frame of an important room. Eventually, as Wright told me, it transmitted all the noises made in the room, even the shuffling of papers, but nothing of interest was ever heard because no Russian ever spoke a word there! Since a similar failure had resulted from an attempt to bug the Soviet embassy in Ottawa, called Operation Dew-worm, when it was being rebuilt after a fire,

Wright believed that both high-tech attempts had been betrayed in advance by a source inside MI5. He told me that Hollis was one of the very few people who knew about both operations.

The KGB traffic with Australia had used a code system that had proved easy to decipher, but shortly after Hollis had returned to Britain in 1948, it was changed and decipherment was never possible again. Because of the timing, both Wright and FBI officer Robert Lamphere suspected that Hollis had informed Moscow of the code weakness. Both recalled the circumstances in which the Soviet coding system and agents' code names had been changed in October 1944, after Hollis had learned of the American achievement in breaking some of the Russian messages.

While Hollis was concentrating on Australian affairs, in 1948, a long-term GRU spy, Ernest Weiss, masquerading as Walter Lock, a bachelor concert pianist living in Paddington, was confronted by Skardon after his cover had been blown by the captured papers of the Paris-based Rote Kapelle spymaster Henri Robinson. These had been available since 1946, but by accident or design, they had "slipped out of sight" for two years inside MI5, allegedly lost in the wilderness of papers. With the GRU code name Jean, Weiss had run a network of informants, including spies inside the Royal Aircraft Establishment at Farnborough, and, according to the CIA handbook on the Rote Kapelle, probably ran a particularly important agent in Britain (wrongly thought, at one time, to have been Philby) during 1939 and 1940 before the arrival of Sonia in the country.

Weiss was legally a traitor, because on orders from Moscow, he had become a naturalized Briton. Nevertheless, in return for a confession, which enabled MI5 to update its files, he was promised immunity from prosecution or publicity—the face-saving "amicable elimination" that the MI5 management would use repeatedly.

CHAPTER 39

Betraying the Superbomb

AFTER THE FIRST MEETING BETWEEN KLAUS FUCHS AND HIS new KGB controller, Alexander Feklisov, in a London pub on Saturday, September 27, 1947, which was to be followed by eight more, the Russian filed a report that has recently become available in Moscow. It showed that Fuchs had betrayed all he knew about the American H-bomb research, handing over a sketch of a possible mechanism. This and subsequent prime betrayals were confirmed in September 2006 by MI5's release of a statement that Fuchs had made to Henry Arnold, the Harwell security chief, on January 26, 1950. Fuchs confessed that he had disclosed to the Russians "information regarding initiators and the broad principles of the Super Bomb." A back check by the FBI on the "Super" meetings Fuchs had attended indicated that he had betrayed crucial data.

Before leaving, Feklisov gave Fuchs a list of ten technical questions posed by Igor Kurchatov, the scientific head of the Soviet nuclear project, so that he could answer them in time for the next meeting. They included questions about the H-bomb—a further example of espionage on specific demand.

Eventually, Soviet scientists found their own way to devising a thermonuclear weapon and may have been the first to develop a usable H-bomb small enough to be carried by an airplane and, later, by a rocket. For the next forty years, international politics would be dominated by the struggle of the two superpowers to achieve thermonuclear superiority, or at least parity.

After Fuchs had returned from the tripartite atomic conference in Washington, he again met Feklisov, whom he knew only by the cover name Eugene, on March 13, 1948, and handed over sixty-seven pages of secret information, also answering many questions. According to the Soviet atomic scientist German Goncharov, they contained details of a scheme for a superbomb patented by Fuchs, in partnership with the American mathematician John von Neumann, when he had still been at Los Alamos. A modification of the idea, called "radiation implosion," eventually produced the American H-bomb, but by the time that was conceived, Fuchs was in jail. The documents supplied by Fuchs were regarded as so crucial that the KGB sent them to Stalin on April 20. On June 10, Stalin ordered Kurchatov and his colleagues to develop thermonuclear weapons.

Meanwhile, on January 1, 1948, MI5 had assured the Ministry of Supply, regarding its employment of Fuchs, "We think that the security risk is very slight."

As the Harwell scientist most knowledgeable about atomic weapons, Fuchs continued his regular visits to Fort Halstead, where he learned about William Penney's progress on developing a British bomb. So Fuchs was a more important contributor to all three bomb projects— American, British, and Russian—than has previously been publicly appreciated. Feklisov rated him as the most important wartime spy, and Fuchs's photograph is on display in the Russian museum at the original atomic research station called Arzamas 16. In all, there can be little doubt that he was the most productive single atomic source for the Russians, increasing the culpability of those who had repeatedly cleared him as secure for secret work.

The KGB records and Feklisov's memoirs show that in March 1948, Fuchs and the Center were badly scared when I published a report in the *Daily Express* stating that MI5 had discovered that three atomic scientists at Harwell were Communists and might have to leave, as they eventually did. Unfortunately, Fuchs was not one of them and continued to lead a charmed life, as he might have done until his retirement but for the patience of an exceptionally gifted American code breaker, Meredith

Gardner, who was struggling with some enciphered KGB telegrams that had seemed to be unbreakable.

In May 1948, Fuchs failed to appear for a scheduled meeting with Feklisov following a further newspaper report by me that the three scientists had been removed from Harwell. The purge of known Communists from government departments concerned with secret work was intensifying—mainly to impress the American security authorities, hopes then being high that the interchange of atomic weapons secrets might be restored, as Lorna Arnold has recorded in her excellent *Britain and the H-Bomb*. As a result, as KGB records have revealed, the Center was discussing the possibility of inducing Fuchs to defect to secure his safety and his expertise for the Soviet bomb program. That contingency was abandoned as unnecessary, however, after Fuchs attended a meeting with Feklisov on July 10, 1948. Presumably, the Center's fear had been allayed. Whether coincidentally or not, Hollis was in London at that time, prior to his visit to Australia.

In *The Man Behind the Rosenbergs*, Feklisov disclosed that during the summer of 1948, the KGB Center sent an urgent message to the London embassy warning that Fuchs could be placed back under close surveillance by MI5 at any moment. Exactly at that time, Fuchs's employers in the Supply Ministry were reconsidering his security risk prior to his establishment as a civil servant, and some of the officials there were expressing doubts. A released document has shown that it was not until August 1948 that the Supply Ministry officials were finally convinced, by MI5's advice, that the security risk concerning Fuchs was slight and then proceeded with his establishment. Somehow, the KGB Center had been informed about these doubts. The fact that Feklisov, in London, had to be told about the danger by Moscow suggests that the warning had not come from a KGB source in Britain. A GRU source in London, such as Elli, would have reported through a courier to the GRU Center in Moscow, which would then have alerted the KGB Center there, without revealing the identity of the asset.

As a precaution, the KGB suspended contact with Fuchs for a while—an interval in his espionage that, in his eventual confession, he was to attribute to a crisis of conscience. This suspension coincided with Hollis's absence in Canberra—from August to mid-September—and

Feklisov did not meet Fuchs again until October 23, 1948—the month after Hollis's return from Australia.

By that time, the Russian atomic scientists were under such pressure from Stalin to produce a workable atomic bomb without further delay that they decided to copy the American Fat Man weapon, because even though they had a more efficient design, they could not be sure that it would work the first time. Lavrenti Beria had warned them that if the first test failed, they would be harshly treated. So Fuchs was asked more specific questions, through Feklisov, about the construction of the plutonium bomb used over Nagasaki, and he answered them, saving the Russians further time.

I was pleased to learn from KGB documents that in the meantime, Fuchs had been disturbed again by further newspaper articles of mine about more Communist atomic scientists at Harwell. Feklisov has recorded that the Center was so perturbed, it set up an emergency evacuation procedure for the traitor.

At the October meeting, Fuchs reported that it was planned for the RAF to have two hundred atom bombs at its disposal, a figure that eventually proved to be accurate. According to MI5 archives and his own account, he continued to hand over "parcels" of documents until February 1949, when he ceased to see Feklisov. That was exactly the time—February 7—that Hollis left Great Britain to return to Canberra. It may be a further coincidence, but the dates of the various intervals when contact between Fuchs and Feklisov was suspended would all support the contention that the conspirators were instructed not to meet until they had been reassured, through a source in MI5, that it was still safe to do so.

In total, the two had met nine times, the number of contacts clearly being limited to reduce the chance of detection, though in retrospect, the risk appears to have been minuscule. Though the end of the war with Germany had released pressure on the Watcher Service and Russia had been recognized as the new opponent, Soviet intelligence officers were still not being routinely tailed—an anomaly that continued. The extent to which Fuchs was able to transfer masses of stolen information to a Russian embassy officer in public places so soon after being officially suspect—he gave Feklisov ninety documents—suggests rather more than sheer incompetence by MI5.

Russian archives indicate that only Kurchatov, the Soviet project chief, and very few others knew about the stolen data—almost entirely American secrets—that were cleverly fed to other scientists who could make use of them as though they had been discoveries and developments accomplished in Russia. This would account for the vehement claim by those scientists, years later, that spies had contributed little to the success of their endeavors.

CHAPTER 40

A Brilliant Break

—

AROUND AUGUST 22, 1949, AN INTERCEPTED SOVIET WARTIME message between New York and the KGB Center, sent in 1944, had been deciphered in Washington. When studied by the FBI officer Robert Lamphere, who later briefed me on the details, it was found to summarize a scientific paper about a method of making uranium explosive. The author, who had clearly been one of the British scientists working in New York, was referred to in the KGB message by the code name Rest. Lamphere and a colleague quickly deduced that the paper had probably been written by Klaus Fuchs. The FBI immediately opened a file with the code name Foocase, which has now been released.

The deciphering of Soviet wartime messages, which had been recorded and filed, had been secretly continued as an Anglo-American project over several years under the code name Bride, then Drug, and later Venona, and was to yield more details. A partially deciphered telegram was passed to GCHQ in Cheltenham, which managed to complete it. The message revealed that Rest had a sister, Kristel, living in Cambridge, Massachusetts, who had been visited by a Soviet agent with the cover name Goose. MI5 then called a meeting attended by Henry Arnold, the Harwell security officer, who was asked if he knew of any person at Harwell who had a background in the United States and whom he had reason to suspect. He said that only one person stood out, and it was Fuchs. On September 5, White called in Michael Perrin, who examined the evidence and said that Fuchs had almost certainly been working for the Russians. Hollis was informed, his reaction being so far unknown.

A released document shows that on the following day, a meeting was held in MI5 headquarters to discuss the surveillance of Fuchs, for which a Home Office warrant would be required. Another, dated September 7 from J. C. Robertson (B2a), who would be in charge of the surveillance, warned that Arnold, the Harwell security officer who would be involved, should not be told about the code breaks, which were supposed to be ultrasecret.

These dates dispose of the belief that Fuchs was identified only after protracted detective work by MI5. Conclusive evidence was eventually produced that way, but he had been named as the likeliest suspect by the deciphering of KGB cables by the FBI.

A note from Guy Liddell to Dick White dated September 13, 1949, refers to "our present renewed interest in Fuchs." It also confirms that Rudolf Peierls, too, was being subjected to surveillance and phone and letter checks. Meanwhile, FBI checks on the movements of Fuchs's sister, Kristel, in America showed that they had matched those mentioned in deciphered cables. So the priority was firmly on Fuchs, with a "twenty-four-hour watch."

Meanwhile, on August 29, the Russians had tested their first atomic bomb—quickly named "Joe 1"—five years ahead of the time that had been forecast by U.S. and British intelligence. This had immediately enabled Stalin to take a tougher stance against the West in cementing his hold over Eastern Europe, because Fuchs had assured the KGB that the American stockpile of bombs was far too small to permit any preemptive nuclear attack. (In June 1946, when the U.S. Joint Chiefs of Staff had begun to draw up a contingency plan for use in the event of a war against the Soviet Union [code-named Pincher], they possessed only nine atomic bombs.)

The seismic evidence of a massive explosion in Russia was immediately available, but because it took time for American and British scientists to collect and analyze the radioactive atmospheric dust, there was no certainty that a successful Soviet test had occurred until September 13. The moment when White and Hollis heard the news is unknown, but when they did so, the severe political implications for the Fuchs case could not have escaped them. What Hollis then felt about his consistent role in ensuring that Fuchs had been able to transfer secrets to Moscow over eight years would be instructive. The devastating role of MI5's expert on Soviet counterintelligence was fully on record in the registry files, yet if anyone in MI5 noticed the anomalies, he did not speak out.

In the United States, the shock of losing the nuclear monopoly so soon induced the intelligence authorities there to suspect that the Soviet scientists had been assisted by one or more atomic spies. An FBI memo dated September 13 shows that Fuchs was their prime suspect, while another dated September 26 shows that the agency had positively identified him. Had J. Edgar Hoover been able to see the MI5 files showing how Hollis had serially enabled Fuchs to continue his treachery, the shock inside the FBI would have been seismic.

Fuchs was to be watched in London, in and around Harwell, and, if necessary, in Oxford, indicating that he was already suspected of having had meetings in the Oxford area, where, since joining Harwell, he had frequently visited the university's Clarendon Laboratory to meet other refugee scientists. His telephone was to be tapped and his mail opened. His contacts were to be investigated. His bank account would also be examined. Extra security policemen were drafted into Harwell.

The assistance of Henry Arnold—a delightful man with whom I later discussed the case at length—was formally enlisted, and on September 9, 1949, he had supplied a note on Fuchs's character and habits. He disclosed that Fuchs slept more often at the home of his Harwell friends the Skinners than at his own address, which was then in Abingdon. Arnold described him as "mentally tough, extremely shrewd," and "fond of both whisky and women." Arnold undertook to visit MI5 weekly for discussions.

The surveillance revealed that Fuchs and Mrs. Erna Skinner, who was of Austrian origin, sometimes both slept at the houses of friends, suggesting that they might be involved sexually. She may have been the essential woman in whom the heavily stressed spy needed to confide. Otherwise, as with Fuchs's previous period of surveillance, nothing whatever untoward was noted.

On September 19, the MI5 officer Michael Hanley recorded that Arnold suspected that Fuchs was running "an espionage organisation" in Harwell. On October 24, Arnold informed MI5 that Fuchs had revealed that his father had been offered a professorship at Leipzig University in Soviet-occupied territory. Arnold had told Fuchs that it would create a serious problem because the security authorities abhorred a situation where a relative might be arrested and pressured.

The KGB had been quickly warned about Fuchs's danger by its MI6 spy Kim Philby, who had been posted to Washington to serve as MI6 liaison officer with the FBI and CIA, arriving there on October 10. While in London, being briefed about his new duties, he had been told about the first American code break indicating that there had been a Soviet spy in Los Alamos. He had passed that information to his KGB controller in London, who had alerted the Moscow Center, which may also have warned Fuchs because he made no conspiratorial errors.

During October 1949, the continuing American investigations confirmed that the suspect British scientist had made visits to certain places and people that had also been made by Fuchs. Further decipherment of cables by GCHQ (after Fuchs's arrest) would expose Simon Kremer's meeting with Fuchs on August 8, 1941, when he had been signed on by the GRU. Fuchs's proper name had been used in a cable along with facts relating to the atomic project.

On November 16, 1949, a top-level meeting to discuss "the case of Dr. Fuchs" was held in the room of Lord Portal, the wartime RAF chief who had been given command of the atomic project. As a recently released memorandum shows, it was attended by Perrin and three senior MI5 officers—Percy Sillitoe, Martin Furnival Jones, and Arthur Martin. As director of protective security, Hollis was not required. However, in view of their close association with the Fuchs case over so many years, Perrin is likely to have consulted him before the meeting.

The meeting had special significance regarding relations with America, because on September 29, the government's Official Committee on Atomic Energy, of which Perrin was a member, had sent a particularly upbeat memo to the prime minister. It had assured Attlee that, following technical talks in Washington, there was a good chance of "complete cooperation on the design, storage and methods of delivery of atomic weapons," including "the use of American facilities for testing them" along with "complete exchange of intelligence information." This would have been a major political achievement for Attlee and his Labour government but was obviously gravely jeopardized by the Fuchs situation. For that reason and because of the adverse implications for MI5 and Fuchs's scientific value to the British atomic project, the meeting decided that the case should be buried, if possible, with Fuchs continuing to assist.

The consensus appears to have been that Fuchs should be told that if he admitted his crimes, he would not be charged. Further, he could remain at Harwell unless the Americans objected, at which point a university professorship would be found for him. His value as an outside consultant would be limited, especially if the university was in Australia, as was suggested, so it seems clear that it was the cover-up that was all-important.

The MI5 men pointed out that, as surveillance had once again proved negative, the only way of securing evidence of Fuchs's "current and future reliability" was to interrogate him, though this was "the step most likely to precipitate his defection to the Russians." Later, a memorandum addressed to Attlee clearly stated that while Perrin and Sir John Cockcroft, the Harwell chief, wanted to retain Fuchs's services if possible, there was already sufficient evidence of his treachery to make it "essential to remove him from Harwell." It was agreed that this should be done in such a way that he "should not defect to the Russians."

The FBI's Foocase files show that Hoover was kept informed of the developments, mainly through Geoffrey Patterson, the MI5 representative in Washington. In a message dated October 29, Patterson stressed that Fuchs had been exposed only through information supplied by the FBI. He took the opportunity to state that MI5 had no evidence that Fuchs was still active. The FBI was also assured that because of extreme secrecy attached to "the source"—the Venona breaks—Fuchs would not be interrogated without Hoover's permission, which was sought on November 7. A week later, Hoover agreed.

Sillitoe therefore undertook to arrange for Fuchs's interrogation, hopefully in such a way that he would not abscond. A memo makes it clear that the interrogation should "provide incentives which would make his defection less likely" as well as removing him from further access to secret information.

As additional evidence has since corroborated, the hope was that even if Fuchs admitted that he had given atomic bomb secrets to Russia, he might agree to leave Harwell voluntarily if offered an incentive so attractive that he would not wish to defect. This was the convenient process of "eliminating him amicably." With such a damage limitation deal, a security and political scandal might be avoided, with the British and American public being told nothing about the case and the reputations of MI5, and of Hollis and White in particular, being unsullied.

The heavy surveillance of Fuchs was continued. His letters were tested for secret ink and the telephones of friends, such as Herbert Skinner, were also tapped. Once again, nothing of any significance was discovered. Like Alan May, Fuchs met no Russian agent, no suspect Communists, no one else of intelligence interest.

Exactly what occurred next first came to public light only because in March 1950, after Fuchs's conviction, MI5 prepared a top-secret, ten-page memorandum for its French counterpart. A copy of it was in Moscow within a few days, leaked either from France or by a source in MI5 itself. As a result, it recently became available to researchers through the opening of the KGB archives, and was subsequently reproduced in *The Haunted Wood*. Perhaps the original remains classified in the MI5 records. It would seem likely that Hollis had a hand in drafting it, as he had been the case officer responsible for overseeing Soviet espionage during Fuchs's early treachery and because of his repeated involvement in his clearances.

The memorandum confirmed that the MI5 management decided Fuchs had to be removed from Harwell, but there was no intention at that stage of prosecuting him. Their priority was "preventive security." It also meant damage limitation, especially to reputations. Confirmation of these MI5 machinations appeared in Fuchs case documents released in 2003 and 2006.

Conveniently, the MI5 managers agreed that there was no evidence to suggest that Fuchs was "currently engaged in espionage," the pious hope being that his treachery had ended when he had left America. So the possibility of hushing up the case with an offer of an academic inducement to leave Harwell was further considered. MI5 papers show that Fuchs was deliberately led to believe that he would be treated leniently if he confessed. Though as a former policeman Sillitoe was uncomfortable with such a solution, colleagues pointed out that it would limit damage to U.S. relations, avoid any leakage of the crucial decipherment of Soviet telegrams, and reduce the risk of his defection. The fact that avoiding a trial would also save MI5's skin could have been regarded as incidental. In its memorandum, MI5 made no mention of the code breaks, which were to remain completely secret from the British and American publics for a further thirty years until the renegade MI5 officer Peter Wright revealed details of them to me. I then published details of Operation Bride (later Venona) in *Their Trade Is Treachery* in 1981, explaining how Fuchs had been identified.

Coincidentally, unless Fuchs had received a warning of his predicament, he resolved Harwell's dilemma by volunteering to resign. In the middle of October, he asked Henry Arnold for advice, explaining that his position might be untenable because his father was definitely accepting a professorship in theology in the Soviet zone of Germany. He was told officially that scientists with relatives behind the iron curtain who could be threatened were regarded as insupportable security risks. Shortly afterward, in agreement with MI5, John Cockcroft, the Harwell chief, told Fuchs that he must definitely leave Harwell because of his father's situation. Fuchs agreed.

CHAPTER 41

Confessions—of a Kind

SURPRISINGLY, ON DECEMBER 21, 1949, KLAUS FUCHS SUB-
mitted himself to questioning by the MI5 interrogator William Skardon
(posing as Sneddon), assisted by Henry Arnold, who told me that he
had first suspected Fuchs in 1947 because he was so demonstrably zealous about security. After being warned to avoid frightening Fuchs into
defecting, Skardon interviewed him in his disarmingly friendly manner.
Fuchs admitted to having been a youthful Communist and confirmed
that he had joined Rudolf Peierls in Birmingham in May 1941, beginning work on the atomic bomb "a little later." When Skardon told him
there was evidence that he had passed atomic secrets to the Russians, he
denied any espionage.

Skardon had been authorized to encourage Fuchs to assume that if he
made a frank admission, he might be allowed to remain at Harwell, and
on December 30 he assured him that otherwise, he would be helped to
find another scientific post in England. MI5 papers show that by then,
Fuchs had revealed his treachery to his friend Erna Skinner, who had remained silent (as was to be publicly confirmed by her husband in 1952).

MI5 received information that Fuchs might take a holiday in
Switzerland and decided that although he might defect from there, no
action could be taken to restrain him from leaving the country.

On January 10, John Cockcroft saw Fuchs and told him that he must
leave Harwell because of his father's move to the Russian zone of Ger-

many but confirmed that there was still a possibility of a university post. He then told him that "if he could give the Security Service more assistance there might be some chance of the position being reversed," clearly implying that he might even be allowed to remain at Harwell.

After deep thought, Fuchs asked to see Skardon again on January 23, 1950. The earlier interviews had been recorded by a perceptive MI5 officer named Evelyn Grist. She felt that Fuchs had been lying on four specific points and urged Skardon to concentrate on them. He did so on January 24 and persuaded Fuchs to confess that he had been passing top-secret information to the Russians for several years. It is possible that Fuchs decided to confess partly to shield his mentally ill sister, Kristel, who had assisted his espionage in America, appearing in KGB documents with the code name Ant. Fuchs may have wanted to spare her from tough interrogation by the FBI and subsequent prosecution.

The possibility of "turning" Fuchs and using him as a double agent was considered and would have avoided embarrassing publicity, but the FBI had to be told of the confession and was expecting prosecution because of the enormous damage he had done to American interests. The evidence in the deciphered cables could not be used in court because it would have told the KGB chiefs that their messages were being broken, though they already knew it. So as the surveillance had been totally unproductive, the only way to convict Fuchs under British law was to secure a signed confession.

In a statement to Skardon, which Fuchs signed on January 27, 1950, in an MI5 room in the War Office, he admitted that he had decided early in life that the Soviet Communist Party could never be wrong. So he had wanted to do all he could to ensure that Germany would be a pro-Soviet Communist state after the war. Fuchs claimed that when he learned that his work at Birmingham was to help in producing an atomic bomb, which was soon after he had begun it in the spring of 1941, he decided "to inform Russia." He stated that he had volunteered to spy entirely on his own initiative and contacted "another member of the Communist Party" (meaning the German Communist Party in London), who had put him in touch with a Russian whom he declined to name.

Fuchs admitted that since beginning to spy, he had maintained "continuous" contact with Russian agents. While claiming moral doubts and mental agonies about his treachery, he insisted that he did not know the names of any of the intermediaries who had passed his offerings to the

Soviet embassy. At that stage, he needed to protect Sonia, as he appears to have known that she was still in Great Britain. Fortunately for her, MI5 failed to pursue Walter Krivitsky's advice—with a GRU spy, *cherchez la femme*—and appears to have avoided making any serious effort to track down Fuchs's courier then or at any other time. The agency had, of course, long been lulled by its Soviet expert into the belief that Sonia was simply a harmless housewife, especially after the Firs fiasco.

Three days later, January 30, Fuchs made a secret technical confession, giving scientific details of his treachery to Michael Perrin in the War Office. In view of Perrin's knowledge of the upbeat memo to the prime minister about the resumption of atomic interchange with America, his feelings may be imagined. Without Perrin's knowledge, MI5 tape-recorded the proceedings, but as Perrin later told Professor Robert Williams, the recording proved to be unintelligible! Fuchs told Perrin that his first contact with the Russians had been in "early 1942." That was a lie, as the date is now known to have been in August 1941. The discrepancy of several months seems to have been part of his effort to hide the identities of his contacts.

The whole technical confession proved Fuchs's treachery to have been even worse than imagined, though nowhere near as detailed as the Russian archives would eventually reveal. Fuchs admitted that he had given the Russians the principles of how to make the plutonium bomb and almost everything else he knew. However, he claimed that he had given only limited information on the H-bomb when, as Soviet documents have since shown, he had told them all he could recall. He also lied about his relationship with the "father of the American H-bomb," Edward Teller, and the number of times they had met, probably to protect Teller, who may have unwittingly told him too much in their several scientific discussions after Fuchs had left Los Alamos.

He had also done all he could to protect his Russian and other Communist contacts, refusing to name them and even avoiding mention of Alexander Feklisov's cover name, Eugene. In that connection, a statement by Feklisov in his memoirs may be highly significant. He claimed that Soviet intelligence had been able to secure precise details of the interrogations of Fuchs because "we had enough sources within British intelligence at the time to find out all these details later on." He reproduced details of Skardon's questions and Fuchs's replies, implying that the KGB had enjoyed access to written MI5 records. Kim Philby was then based in Washington and had no access to such records or to his friend Hollis, who might otherwise have told him about them. At that time, there was no known spy in MI5 apart from Elli.

It is now known that Fuchs had also lied about the details of his recruitment to the GRU. Evidence from close friends, both at Los Alamos and at Harwell, has shown that even when drunk, as he often was at parties, Fuchs never dropped his guard. Yet MI5 accepted his two confessions as the full truth—perhaps wanting to believe that the damage had not been worse. Russian archives and interviews with his former KGB controllers have since shown that the MI5 management and Perrin had not been of this world. As later events would confirm, Fuchs had been a fundamental Communist, whose faith in the Soviet system and its destiny in controlling the world never really wavered. Feklisov was to pay tribute to his "unbreakability and strong will."

On February 1, FBI chief J. Edgar Hoover passed the grim news to President Harry Truman's office that the British scientist who had worked in Los Alamos had been "in the employ of the Russian government doing espionage work since 1941." On February 2, Fuchs was arrested and charged.

Not until documents about the Kuczynski family were released in March 2005 did MI5 reveal that after Fuchs had been arrested, Skardon saw him again on February 28 and asked him to name those who had introduced him to Soviet intelligence. Fuchs offered to do so if Skardon would give him an assurance not to harm them if that was the only act of which they were guilty. He also required a promise that their names would not be given to any foreign intelligence organization. When Skardon agreed, Fuchs named Jurgen Kuczynski as the person who had first introduced him to Soviet intelligence in 1941 and Hanna Klopstech as the woman who had put him back in touch in 1947. Fuchs was aware that Jurgen had left Great Britain (in November 1945), because Jurgen's wife, Marguerite, had told him so, and he knew that she, too, was then safely in Berlin. He also knew that Klopstech had left for Germany (on August 20, 1947).

Presumably, Skardon had taken advice from senior colleagues before agreeing so readily, because the promise implied that neither miscreant would ever be prosecuted for those treacherous services. The reason this crucial interview was kept secret for fifty-five years will become apparent in the next chapter. Fuchs was to admit that the courier who serviced him in the Banbury area was a woman and "an alien" but avoided naming her or saying that she was German.

The credit for inducing Fuchs to confess anything is usually given to Skardon, but long after his release, when living in East Germany, Fuchs attributed it to his closest Harwell colleague, the scientist Herbert Skinner. He told Markus Wolf, former chief of the Stasi, the East German intelligence agency, that when he realized he was under suspicion, he was confident he could weather it. However, when Skinner openly discussed with him the Harwell suspicions that he was a spy, he asked Fuchs if they were well-founded or not. Fuchs claimed that, unable to lie to such a close friend, he did not reply, and Skinner reported the fact to Henry Arnold, who alerted MI5. However, the evidence that Fuchs had probably been treacherous to Skinner by seducing his wife throws doubt on the story.

The full details of Fuchs's espionage have recently emerged largely as a result of acrimonious disagreement between Russian atomic scientists and the KGB concerning the practical value of the technical secrets that the various spies supplied. Documents published by both the Russian and the British authorities show that, without doubt, Fuchs was easily the most productive spy concerning the precise structure of atomic weapons. This view has been reinforced by GRU archival material and by the research of Dr. Svetlana Chervonnaya, who was told that in later years, when Soviet scientists were referring to the first atomic weapon they had constructed and tested, they would call it "the Fuchs bomb."

In their well-documented book *Bombshell*, the American authors Joseph Albright and Marcia Kunstell showed that a young American spy in Los Alamos, Theodore ("Ted") Hall, also gave the KGB details about the mechanism of atomic bombs. Fuchs had been supplying documents for more than three years before Hall began to give the Russians information in October 1944, but the American provided valuable confirmation, along with new data.

Born in New York in 1925, his father a Jewish furrier who had fled czarist Russia to escape the pogroms, Hall became a scientific and mathematical prodigy, entering Harvard University when only sixteen. There, he was quickly converted to communism by a roommate, also of Russian origin. Because of his brilliance in quantum mechanics, he was recruited into the Manhattan Project and found himself at Los Alamos, where at only nineteen he became the first, and perhaps the only, teenage spy. Once in contact with a KGB courier, he was given the Russian code name Mlad, meaning "Youngster," and supplied all he knew, including details of the implosion principle, which the Soviet scientists were to use in copying the Nagasaki bomb.

Hall spied consistently until he left atomic work and, though he did not know it, was unmasked by a KGB message, deciphered in 1951, which mentioned his real name. When interrogated by FBI officers, he denied everything and escaped arrest because the evidence of deciphered cables could not be used in court without revealing the Bride/Venona secret, wrongly believed by the U.S. and British authorities to be still secure.

In 1962, after working in American universities, Hall switched to the Cavendish Laboratory in Cambridge, posing as a patriot in the scientific community until he retired. He was publicly exposed—by an enterprising American journalist—in 1995 when details of the Bride/Venona decoding operations were finally released. He expressed no shame but blamed his treachery on his youth, though, like Fuchs, he had been a lifelong traitor to the country that had offered his family freedom. He died at age seventy-four.

GRU archives have also recently revealed the existence of a further highly productive Soviet spy inside the Manhattan Project. Because he was still alive, only his operational pseudonym, Delmar, was disclosed. Delmar was unique in that, after being posted to the United States as an illegal agent to run other spies, he managed to penetrate the atomic target himself. This arose from the fluke circumstance that he had been born in America of Russian Jewish immigrant parents, who had returned to Russia in 1933, taking their son with them. He was recruited to the GRU and in 1939 was sent back, under his own name, to the United States, where in 1943 he was drafted into the army. After training, he was posted, seemingly by chance, to the major atomic center at Oak Ridge, Tennessee, in August 1944. Oak Ridge was the heart of the project, where the pilot plants for making uranium 235 and plutonium were located, along with the uranium 235 production plant. After providing the Center with a stream of information, he was discharged from the army in September 1945 and recalled to Moscow four years later. There is no evidence that the KGB ever knew the identity of Delmar, who had continued to supply his information to a GRU controller in the United States. The controller transmitted it to the GRU Center, which passed it to the collating agency run by General Pavel Sudoplatov of the KGB. From there, it was funneled to the Soviet scientists. The archival information on Delmar is proof that the GRU could run an important agent like Elli without revealing his identity to the KGB or anyone else.

Delmar died in Moscow, aged ninety-three, in January 2006 and in the following year was named by President Vladimir Putin as George Koval and appointed a Hero of Russia, the highest state honor. Any close relatives he had were living in Russia. Had they been living in the United States or the United Kingdom, his identity would not have been revealed by the GRU in their lifetime.

CHAPTER 42

Misleading the Attorney General

WHEN KLAUS FUCHS WAS ARRESTED AND CHARGED, ON FEBruary 2, 1950, the general shock at Harwell was tempered with gallows humor, such as the quip about his fondness for small children: "The children called him Uncle Klaus; the Russians called him Santa Klaus." Presumably, Hollis appeared shocked, if only because he knew that he was responsible for having cleared him six times, though that never emerged at the trial. The views of the MI5 colleagues, like Jane Archer, who had warned about Fuchs may be imagined.

The news of the arrest provoked surprise at KGB headquarters, where they were hoping that he might just be moved from Harwell, and Stalin was informed on February 5 in a report listing the spy's tremendous contributions to the Soviet bomb program and the KGB's success in securing them.

A document released in May 2003 revealed the almost pantomime nature of MI5's reaction. Though the arrest of Fuchs had been given worldwide publicity by the media, MI5 watchers were instructed to "keep observation on two public houses (which had been named by Fuchs) on Saturday evenings for at least one month beginning with Saturday February 4." It is hard to believe that the watchers really expected any Soviet agent to turn up.

Another MI5 document, dated February 8, 1950, contained a list of Russians known to be in the United Kingdom between 1946 and March

1949. It did not include Alexander Feklisov, who, to avoid attracting attention by a quick departure, was not recalled to Moscow until April 1950.

Fuchs's confessions had already caused consternation in Whitehall. The government had previously decided to send the impressive General Sir Gerald Templer, vice chief of the General Staff, to Washington to improve the chance of restoring the exchange of atomic information, and the Fuchs case became public a few days before his arrival. The situation was eloquently expressed by a senior American atomic energy official: "We were getting very close to going into bed with the British with a new agreement. Then the Fuchs affair hit the fan and that was the end of it."

The repeated clearances of Fuchs, on Hollis's insistence, had not only assisted the Russians to produce their first atomic bomb, but had ruined all hope of a resumption of the Anglo-American nuclear weapons partnership. This was to cost Great Britain enormous sums in research and development. Creating any kind of rift between Britain and America had always been a high-priority project for Soviet intelligence and would continue to be.

Whatever his motives may have been, Hollis's actions and inactions throughout Fuchs's atomic career had been disastrous, yet he escaped official censure or, so far as is known, personal admonishment of any kind. Instead, he was promoted! As his superiors—Guy Liddell and Dick White in particular—had eventually supported his consistent view that Fuchs had posed no danger, they decided to hang together rather than separately. Presumably, somewhere still inside MI5, Elli was feeling not only safe but quietly triumphant.

A report from MI5's legal adviser to the director of public prosecutions pointed out that the only evidence that could be produced in court consisted entirely of statements volunteered by Fuchs. It then drew his attention to the inducements that had been offered to him to confess, as they might render his responses inadmissible as evidence. Fortunately, Fuchs resolved the problem by pleading guilty on March 1 at his Old Bailey trial, which I attended. This plea meant that little of the evidence was mentioned, and some of that had been falsified. Before the trial, MI5 had launched a damage limitation exercise, and certain information given to the attorney general, Sir Hartley Shawcross, and stated by him at the trial, was monstrously fallacious.

Shawcross assured the court that the intermediary who had intro-duced Fuchs to the Soviets was "a foreign communist who was then in this country and not recognized by the authorities to be a communist." Yet on the previous day, Fuchs had told William Skardon that the inter-mediary had been Jurgen Kuczynski. With Skardon himself due to ap-pear in the witness box, it is inconceivable that he had failed to give that crucial breakthrough to his MI5 superiors before the trial began. In fact, Kuczynski had been easily the best-known foreign Communist in Great Britain before he had returned to Germany in November 1945. An entry on his MI5 file by Guy Liddell, dated April 4, 1940, had stated, "Jurgen Kuczynski has been known to us as a Communist since June 1931, when he was employed by the Communist Central Organization in Berlin. He is believed to have been in touch with the Soviet Embassy in 1937." An-other, dated May 8, 1940, stated, "He had brought the whole funds of the German Communist Party out of Germany." There were many other references in a similar vein. The official statement issued with the Kuczynski family files, released in March 2005, revealed that, from No-vember 1939, Jurgen's mail had been intercepted because "both Dr. Jur-gen and Marguerite [his wife] were believed to be closely connected with Communist espionage." Later, Hollis, in his letter to the FBI via the American embassy in August 1944, had described Jurgen Kuczynski as "a Communist of some importance."

So why was such a palpably false statement made to the court? Two obvious answers present themselves. The first is that the truth would have raised the question in the media and in Parliament as to why such an open foreign Communist had been allowed to operate as a Soviet agent. The second is that admission of the truth in open court might have put investigative journalists on the trail of Jurgen's relatives. This could have led to the discovery that Sonia had spied under the noses of MI5 at Blenheim and had been posted to Oxford to service someone else who had never been pursued.

What Skardon thought as he heard the attorney general unwittingly tell such a lie can only be imagined, but it suited him. In view of his own disastrous performance in the Firs fiasco, it was not in his personal inter-est to have any of the Kuczynskis named in the document. Even less so was it in the interests of Hollis or White after their own calamitous ac-tivities in that respect.

The prosecution also stated that Fuchs appeared to have taken no interest in communism in Britain or "had any association at all with British members of the Communist Party," claiming that was still the case following investigations made about him. Nothing was said about his regular association with members of the German Communist Party in Britain.

The court was told that Fuchs had "remained in Canada [that is, in the internment camp] until the beginning of 1942." In fact, the home secretary had authorized his release on October 17, 1940, and according to an MI5 document, Fuchs had landed in Liverpool on January 11, 1941. The false date was calculated to reduce the apparent time during which Fuchs had spied in England, which again was to MI5's advantage. It was also stated that he then went to Glasgow University instead of back to Edinburgh, a false lead that muddied the waters for any investigators.

Shawcross alleged that Fuchs had signed the Official Secrets Act on June 18, 1942, pointing out that the document was Exhibit 4 in the evidence against him. In fact, he had signed it on June 18, 1941. MI5 knew that because Hollis had given him a conditional clearance in the previous month, and the correct date appears in several MI5 documents now in the National Archives. The false date appears in the full transcript of the trial sent to the FBI chief, J. Edgar Hoover, which had been prepared by Scotland Yard's Special Branch and has since been declassified. Once again, the FBI had been seriously misled. The false date also appears in the report of the trial in *The Times* of March 2, 1950. If Exhibit 4, lying there in the court, did bear the later date, it was a forgery.

The indictment on which the case was brought was restricted to four chosen occasions on which Fuchs had met a Soviet agent, two of them being in America. Four occasions sufficed to secure conviction, but dating the first to 1943 appeared to reduce by two years the time during which Fuchs had spied before leaving for the United States. That suited MI5's public image, as it inferred that almost all his serious espionage had been committed on American soil, with the U.S. security authorities being at fault.

Any statement regarding the date when Fuchs had begun to spy for Russia was avoided, though he had confessed that he had wasted no time in contacting a Soviet agent in 1941 once he had learned he was working on an atomic bomb.

The American researcher Professor Robert Williams discovered that the indictment had originally stated that Fuchs had committed an offense in 1943 in Banbury, but that had been changed to Birmingham in the indictment read in court. This was also false, because Sonia, who alone controlled Fuchs in 1943, did not meet him in Birmingham again after their first encounter there in 1942.

There was no mention whatever of Banbury during the trial, though it had been the center for most of the meetings. Any outside curiosity about Banbury might have led to the discovery of Sonia's involvement and curiosity about reasons for her presence in Oxford. This distortion was a further step in a concerted and ongoing effort to make Sonia into a nonperson of minimal security interest to MI5. It may also have been to eliminate Oxford from the evidence, along with any speculation about the proximity of MI5 at Blenheim.

Years later, I discussed these manipulations of the legal system with Shawcross at his home. He told me that all such details in his statement would have been arranged by the Treasury solicitor, acting on the advice of MI5. It would be instructive to know which MI5 officer briefed the Treasury solicitor, because the false statements amounted to a serious deception of the judge, the court, Parliament, and the public, both British and American. It would almost certainly have been MI5's legal adviser, but there can be little doubt that Hollis had been involved, not only because of his uniquely long association with the case when in charge of Soviet espionage, but because of his current post as director of protective security and his experience of atomic affairs. As has been officially stated, "In support of counter-espionage the Director of the Protective Security Branch is very much concerned with it." Hollis also attended the weekly directors' meetings, where he learned about the activities of other departments. His friendship with Michael Perrin, who had been a witness at the pretrial hearing, was a further reason for involvement.

No doubt MI5 could have argued that its prime purpose in promoting the false statements had been to deceive Soviet intelligence, though according to Alexander Feklisov, its chance of doing that would appear to have been remote.

It has also been claimed that the Fuchs case was complicated by the political secret that the government was building its own atomic bomb and did not want the world—and particularly the Americans—to know. This was completely false, as I can testify from personal involvement.

The project to build an independent British bomb had been planned as early as 1945, with a target date of 1952. Journalists, myself included, had written about it, and Parliament was told by Clement Attlee that atomic weapons were being developed on May 12, 1948. According to Margaret Gowing, the U.S. government learned that Great Britain intended to make atomic bombs in 1948, and the Joint Congressional Committee on Atomic Energy was shocked to hear it.

Fuchs had misled his barrister and made him look a fool by putting forward a theory that he had suffered from "controlled schizophrenia," in which his mind had acted like a sieve, allowing it to leak secrets for a period and then closing for a while before opening again. As the GRU records have shown, Fuchs ceased to spy only when out of touch with a controller or advised to do so. His explanation was scorned by the judge, Lord Chief Justice Goddard.

As Fuchs had begun his spying when Russia was an ally, he escaped the death sentence (which, I sensed, the tough Goddard, known throughout the legal profession as "Doggie," would have imposed with satisfaction) and was sentenced for the maximum time permissible—fourteen years, of which he was to serve nine. As Henry Arnold was to state later, "The trial was rushed through so that as little as possible came out in court." Whatever the secret purposes, the deliberate deception of the attorney general, the lord chief justice, and the British and American publics on such a scale was inexcusable in a democracy.

Apparently, at one stage after his arrest, Fuchs had thought he might face a death sentence. In Moscow, full transcripts of the trial were immediately supplied to Stalin, Beria, and eighteen other top officials, as File 1146 of Vyacheslav Molotov's private papers reveals. Jointly, they decided that the Soviet TASS news agency should announce that Fuchs was "unknown to the Soviet government" and that the confession was a "crude provocation."

My report on the trial, which covered most of the front page of the *Daily Express* on the following day, was headlined FUCHS GAVE BOMB TO RUSSIA. Declassified documents have confirmed its accuracy.

CHAPTER 43

Misleading the Prime Minister

—

THE MI5 CHIEF, PERCY SILLITOE, THE FORMER POLICE OFFI-
cer brought in by Prime Minister Clement Attlee in 1946 to sharpen up
the agency, was furious about its failure to discover Fuchs's treachery,
especially as he was fully aware of the huge political importance of Attlee's personal drive to renew the partnership on atomic weapons with
the United States. He would have been even angrier had he known that
details of Fuchs's Communist activities in prewar Germany had been
available in Gestapo records, which had been confiscated at the end of
the war but had not been consulted. Dr. Svetlana Chervonnaya has recently confirmed that a prewar Gestapo list titled "Communist Party
Members in Germany" contained "Klaus Fuchs, student." Such was the
continuing complacency in MI5 that there is no evidence of any internal
inquiry to discover who had been at fault.

As the prime minister was then responsible for MI5, his office realized that he would be required to respond in person to severe parliamentary and media criticism of the agency, so it asked Sillitoe to submit a
summary of the Fuchs case. It would seem axiomatic that Attlee's chief
adviser on public relations in Number 10 Downing Street would have
been involved. This was none other than Philip Jordan, author of the
flagrantly pro-Soviet book *Russian Glory* that Hollis had so admired.
The former journalist, who had been on MI5's list as a suspect Commu-

nist, had been appointed to the post in 1947 and presumably had been cleared for security.

Sillitoe ordered his staff to prepare summarized statements about the background to the Fuchs disaster; these were forwarded to Downing Street under his name but could have been prepared only by those who had been involved in the case. The documents became available in the National Archives in October 2003 and September 2006. The true authors are not named, but there can be little doubt that Hollis, as a prime source, was involved, along with Dick White.

The first document—of three pages—had been sent to the prime minister by Sillitoe on January 31, before Fuchs's arrest, as MI5 wanted his approval to send the papers to the director of public prosecutions. It sought to diminish the damage done by Fuchs by stating that in his confession, he had said that the worst he had done was to reveal "how the plutonium bomb was made." It then stated that two days later, Fuchs had admitted to Henry Arnold that he had disclosed to the Russians "certain details dealing with atomic development and research." It deliberately avoided informing the prime minister that these details were about the ultrasecret H-bomb. MI5 also seemed to be hoping that if there was to be a trial, it might be heard in camera.

A second document was sent by Sillitoe to Attlee on February 7, 1950, five days after Fuchs's arrest and three weeks before his trial. It stated that MI5 was first asked to inquire about Fuchs in August 1941 and cleared him after that date. The statement was false. More reliable documentary evidence shows that Hollis and Michael Perrin had cleared Fuchs in May 1941 and that he started secret work at Birmingham University on May 28. Fuchs had even signed the Official Secrets Act in June 1941, giving him access to secrets that would not have been available to him had he not been already cleared.

The prime minister was also told that MI5 had received a report from a refugee source stating that Fuchs was well-known in "communist circles." It went on to say that this information was passed to the requisite government department with a statement that any leakages would be more likely to reach the Russians than the Germans. Such a prophetic statement had indeed been made, almost certainly by Hollis. Sillitoe's submission to Number 10 clearly gave Attlee the impression that from the very first day of Fuchs's involvement in secret work, MI5 had warned that leakage to the Russians was possible and had been proved right. It passed the buck to the government department employing him for failing to heed the brilliant warning.

The report told Attlee that in November 1947, when the ministry then responsible for atomic research wished to make Fuchs a fully established civil servant—by which time he had been spying for six years—MI5 had responded by declaring the security risk to be slight. The final paragraph stated that MI5 did not have grounds to investigate Fuchs "from an espionage point of view" until August 1949 and that, "with the collaboration of the FBI," MI5 had pursued its inquiries "to their present conclusion"—that is, the arrest of Fuchs following his confessions. The prime minister was not told that the FBI had been entirely responsible for supplying the original lead and the early indication that Fuchs was a spy.

No doubt Sillitoe felt it was his duty to protect the reputation of his service, and he appreciated the damage the case would do to public confidence in MI5. Whether he was aware of the sheer dishonesty of the information fed to Attlee through him is unknown, but there can be no doubt that those officers who induced him to mislead his prime minister knew the truth, which was damaging to MI5's reputation and, particularly, to their own.

Sillitoe has been blamed for misleading the prime minister, but the real culprits were those who prepared the briefs. They did what they could to prevent Attlee from knowing the full facts and assured him that the conviction of Fuchs was an MI5 triumph, when the whole episode had been a security, political, and strategic disaster.

The privately fuming Attlee had to remain silent until after Fuchs's conviction, by which time MI5 was under a barrage of press criticism for clearing Fuchs in the first place and for allowing him to spy for so long. I pitched in with several features in the *Daily Express* that were deeply resented by MI5. Under the D-Notice system, a form of peacetime censorship, journalists were forbidden to name members of MI5, save for the chief, Percy Sillitoe, so all the ignominy descended on him.

After the trial, continuing to whine about its built-in inability to defend itself publicly, MI5 quickly submitted a further three-page damage limitation document to the prime minister to bolster Sillitoe's original statement. It urged Attlee to counter the "ill-informed criticism of the security authorities" by making a statement in Parliament "putting the facts in their proper perspective." It suggested exactly how he should proceed. The document stated that Fuchs had taken "no active part in political activities throughout the whole of his eight years residence in Britain." The truth was that MI5 had made no real effort to discover his substantial activities before he had been recruited by the GRU, which had then told him to desist.

No mention was made of Fuchs's admission that he had been introduced to the GRU by Jurgen Kuczynski, which was also in MI5's records, following William Skardon's interview. The document continued, "The public has been left with the impression that a notorious communist was negligently cleared by the Security Service for work in one of the most secret branches of defense research and that he would be there to this day had it not been for the perspicacity of the FBI." Apart from the fact that Fuchs's communism had not been "notorious," in the sense that it was widely known, the impression was accurate. Attlee was then invited to mislead the nation by declaring that Fuchs's record "only became available from the investigations which the Security Service conducted, in the latter part of 1949." The author of the report clearly realized that if Attlee baldly denied that the FBI had virtually caught Fuchs, Hoover might respond. So the prime minister was advised to avoid saying that, because it was necessary to "retain a proper cover for the true source of the original intelligence." Whether Attlee had been told verbally that the information had derived from deciphered Soviet telegrams is unknown. Finally, Attlee was advised to point out the limitations imposed on MI5's counterespionage activities by our democratic way of life.

As the public criticism of MI5 continued, the management considered it necessary to send the prime minister yet another two-page apologia, also marked "top secret." It blamed the police for failing to discover any Communist activities by Fuchs in Birmingham, Edinburgh, or elsewhere, without mentioning the several tips it had received directly from sources. The statement stressed that MI5's responsibility was limited to tendering advice and that final decisions were taken by the government departments concerned. In reality, the government departments relied on the nature and tone of the advice given by MI5, which in those days wielded an overriding influence not only in Whitehall, but among politicians, who tended to hold the secret services in excessive awe.

The statement claimed credit for exposing the spy by stating that the

FBI "did not pinpoint Fuchs." In fact, the information supplied by the FBI effectively did that, as testified by Perrin's response only a few days after receiving the first FBI alert. The MI5 information supplied to Hoover through Geoffrey Patterson had clearly admitted that the credit for unmasking Fuchs belonged to the FBI. Yet in stating that "Fuchs has been caught and speedily prosecuted," the document gave the impression of brilliant detective work by MI5. (In a memo dated February 28 concerning a statement MI5 planned to distribute, Hoover noted, "The sly British are gradually getting round to having unearthed Fuchs themselves.")

Finally, MI5 told Attlee that any "false step" might have alerted Fuchs to escape to Russia. He was not told of the planned deal to allow Fuchs to retire from Harwell and quietly move, unscathed and full of academic honor, to a university, abroad if necessary. On March 6, 1950, acting on MI5's briefings, Attlee assured Parliament that there were no grounds for casting "the slightest slur on the security services." He deplored the "loose talk in the Press suggesting inefficiency," adding, "I entirely deny that." He said that the evidence from America had not pointed to any individual when it had clearly indicated Fuchs. He assured MPs that "a proper watch was kept at intervals" when, in fact, prior to the FBI information, Fuchs had been under surveillance only in the restricted period after his return from America. He praised MI5, which "had got to work with great energy" after receiving information from the United States.

It would by no means be the last time that a prime minister would be induced to mislead Parliament and the public to preserve the reputation of MI5 and those in it.

To MI5's dismay, Attlee ordered an independent inquiry into how the spy had been able to secure a prime position in secret atomic work and to keep it when he was a known Communist, indicating that he was really far from satisfied by the security service's performance. The move immediately descended into comedy, damaging to Anglo-U.S. relations, when it was announced that the war minister would be one of those "called on to carry out the purge in the overhauling of the Secret Service of Great Britain [MI5] as a result of the breakdown in security screening in the Fuchs case." His name was John Strachey, and as Hoover was quick to point out, he was a former Communist Party personality who had been denied entry to the United States in 1938 on that score!

If the inquiry was ever carried out, its results seem to have remained secret. It may have been no more than window dressing to placate the American authorities. One thing is certain: Any "purge" had no impact on the continuing meteoric promotion of the master of the disaster, Roger Hollis.

Conscious-stricken by having been pressured into lying to the prime minister, Sillitoe called a meeting of the whole of B Division and angrily warned them that he would never cover up for their blunders again.

CHAPTER 44

Alienating the Americans

T HE EXPOSURE OF FUCHS'S TREACHERY SO SOON AFTER THE successful Soviet atomic bomb test, years earlier than expected, caused consternation at every political and military level in the United States. The extent of the resentment in Washington and elsewhere at Fuchs's betrayal of America's most treasured secrets, followed by its exacerbation by British official stupidity—or worse—is exposed by the FBI Foocase files.

It was obvious to the FBI that while he was in America, Fuchs had couriers and controllers whose identities must be discovered with all speed, especially as they may have been servicing other spies who might be American citizens. Any delay would increase their chances of escaping from the United States. So, expecting maximum cooperation from MI5, especially after providing the original clues, Hoover dispatched a senior agent, Lish Whitson, to London with the remit of securing permission for Fuchs to be interrogated by FBI specialists. He quickly learned that under British law, this could not be allowed before the trial, though MI5 officers were still being permitted to question him. A message from Whitson dated February 11 informed Hoover that after conversations "with all the MI5 representatives having an interest in the Fuchs case, MI5 had absolutely no clues as to the identities of Fuchs' three contacts in Britain." Hoover had already noted, "At no time have the British furnished any information about the fact that Fuchs had been interned as an enemy alien."

Whitson sent an immediate account of the trial to Hoover, including the false statements made by the attorney general. Meanwhile, the Home Office had decided that no interrogation of Fuchs by any foreigners could be allowed, even after the trial, as it would establish a precedent. In retaliation, Hoover angrily ordered Robert Lamphere and other officers to give no further information about their operations to MI5. Until then, the FBI had kept MI5 fully informed about their efforts to identify KGB agents who had been involved with Fuchs in America. Later, they discovered that these agents were being regularly warned from Moscow, in detailed ways, that they were in danger.

The recent research of Dr. Svetlana Chervonnaya has revealed that in early October 1949, a KGB officer, Ivan Kamanev, had been ordered by Moscow to leave his base in New York to warn Fuchs's former courier with the cover name Goose that he might have to quit the United States in a hurry and that money would be provided. Kamanev was then ordered to leave the United States himself with all speed—which he did. There is also evidence that Julius Rosenberg, who was to be executed for his treachery, knew that Fuchs was under suspicion even before the scientist had confessed. During the 1949 Christmas holidays, Rosenberg had warned the American atomic spy David Greenglass that he might have to flee the United States because "something was happening" that might force him to do so.

Detailed evidence from KGB documents (cited by West and Tsarev in *Crown Jewels*) show that while Philby had been told of the code-break evidence incriminating Fuchs in late September, his information did not reach the KGB until after Fuchs's arrest. So he is unlikely to have been responsible for Moscow's advance knowledge of Fuchs's danger. Satisfied that there had been no leaks from the FBI, Lamphere and others suspected MI5 as their source. This suspicion was strengthened when Hoover lifted his ban after the FBI was eventually allowed to interrogate Fuchs. Lamphere learned that throughout the time of the ban, which had lasted from early February 1950 until late May, the suspect American KGB agents had received no further warnings from Moscow. Yet as soon as the ban was lifted and MI5 was told again what the FBI was doing, the warnings from Moscow resumed and some of the suspects were urged to make arrangements to escape, several of which were successful. Lamphere suspected that Soviet intelligence was being given a running commentary on the FBI operations by someone in MI5.

Even when Fuchs had decided not to appeal his conviction, the British ban on the FBI was continued, though Sillitoe let Hoover know that he was trying to have it lifted. On March 23, Hoover recorded his curt reaction to an offer that William Skardon or some other MI5 officer should interrogate Fuchs on the FBI's behalf: "The MI5 interrogators are not really of an investigative type as they do not seem to grasp the purport of any question."

On April 5, Hoover warned the U.K. government, through Geoffrey Patterson, that the American public would react badly to the continued refusal, pointing out that he would have to expose it in evidence that he would be required to give to the Joint Congressional Committee on Atomic Energy. On April 21, Hoover was told that the ban imposed by the Home Office was final, so he turned up the heat by describing the infuriating situation to the committee's chairman, Senator Brien McMahon, who reacted angrily. Meanwhile in London, Sillitoe was stressing the danger the ban was causing to his relations with Hoover, and on April 28, he was able to inform Hoover that he had been successful in having it lifted. The news was passed to the FBI by none other than the MI6 man in Washington, Mr. Kim Philby!

However, Hoover's frustration was just beginning, because on May 9, he learned that the FBI interrogation of Fuchs was to be permitted only under five conditions. He was prepared to accept the first three: Fuchs must consent to be questioned; a prison officer must be present; an MI5 officer must also be present. The other two conditions incensed him: The interrogation must be confined to counterintelligence and security matters and should not concern itself with the technical aspects of atomic energy; after the interrogation, nothing could be said publicly except that "the US authorities have received every possible facility from the British Security authorities," and under no circumstances should a member of the FBI or any other U.S. spokesman mention that an FBI representative had interrogated Fuchs.

It should surely have been clear to the meanest minds among the British "authorities" that the last two conditions would enrage Hoover, because in the American democratic system he could not possibly fulfill them. First, to carry out the urgent task of discovering Fuchs's American contacts, his interrogators needed to know exactly what technical data had gone to the Russians. Second, as Hoover put it, "the FBI needed to furnish the results to the Atomic Energy Commission and the Joint Congressional Committee on Atomic Energy." If any of the American contacts were exposed, they would have to be tried in open court, and Fuchs's answers to questions could be part of the evidence. Nevertheless, the Foreign Office had even pressured the American ambassador to "ensure that there was no disclosure of this concession in the US."

Hoover's immediate response was, "We will not interview Fuchs unless it is without unreasonable restraints!" On May 12, he raised the stakes by informing Gordon Dean, chairman of the U.S. Atomic Energy Commission, about the restrictions. Dean was appalled. Then he alerted the U.S. attorney general and State Department officials, who were equally dismayed. He also informed the president's office. So on top of the damage done by a British spy's treachery, Great Britain's reputation as a reliable and helpful ally was being besmirched at the highest levels.

Any restrictions of the inquiries were in the Kremlin's interest, as was the damage being inflicted on the Anglo-American alliance. So it could be informative to know exactly who had been responsible for the restraints that had been bound to offend the U.S. government. Recently released British documents identify the culprit as Roger Hollis— without any doubt.

The documents are declassified reports of meetings of the Official Committee on Atomic Energy, set up by Attlee as the main forum for interdepartmental discussions on atomic policy and reporting directly to him. As its prime concern was the restoration of access to American atomic secrets—the Great Prize—its chairman was the Foreign Office mandarin Sir Roger Makins. As early as February 8, it met to consider Fuchs's arrest, noting that "it was particularly unfortunate that the case should have become public when there was so much discussion in the US about the H-bomb project." At a March meeting, after Fuchs's conviction, it was agreed that as "it was so important to reach an agreement with the Americans about atomic weapons . . . we should invite them to inspect our whole security system in the atomic energy field but the time is not yet ripe for this."

The reports reveal that there were fears that if granted access to Fuchs, the FBI might probe him about details of the British nuclear weapons program, which the government was anxious to keep secret as a bargaining counter in its continuing bid to restore atomic interchange. One document, dated May 8, 1950, shows that Hollis was the MI5 officer called in by the committee for advice on the matter. He advised that MI5 should first secure the FBI's agreement to limit its interrogation of Fuchs to questions about counterespionage and security. MI5 was also to stipulate that its representative, Skardon, must always be present during the interrogation to object if the FBI men strayed beyond their remit and also to learn what they knew. The committee's acceptance of Hollis's unwise advice was a further instance of the influential power of MI5 in those days.

As a result of warnings to the U.K. Foreign Office from the U.S. State Department, and horrific publicity in the U.S. press, wiser counsel eventually prevailed and the MI5 advice was overruled on both counts. However, Britain's behavior was not quickly forgotten. Hollis's recommendations had achieved nothing apart from souring relations with Washington and, in particular, between MI5 and the FBI, which realized that some Soviet agents might have escaped during the delay. So whether by accident or design, Hollis had benefited the Soviet cause. Whether those concerned in the Kremlin were able to gloat over the bad blood as it was being created is unknown, but Philby was on hand to brief them if nobody else did.

Hoover selected Special Agents Robert Lamphere and Hugh Clegg to interrogate Fuchs, and they first met Skardon and Dick White, whom they quickly regarded as rather ingenuous. They reported that White considered Fuchs's memory to be "amazingly short for details" and "not trained and adjusted to retaining small details of his transactions." Apparently, it had not occurred to White that a poor memory, when it suited, was an essential part of a spy's armory, especially when protecting contacts. Fuchs's excellent memory had been respected in Los Alamos and Harwell.

On May 20, the two FBI men and Skardon were taken to Wormwood Scrubs prison in a blacked-out police van to begin several days of questioning but were permitted to speak to Fuchs for only one hour at a time. With some difficulty, they induced him to identify the man who had been his regular courier in the United States, code-named Goose in KGB telegrams. He was Harry Gold, an American born of Russian parents and known to Fuchs only by the cover name Raymond. As the

Foocase records show, Gold had been tracked down by laborious FBI detective work and had already confessed. His arrest led to the exposure of other spies, including David Greenglass, an American soldier who had been stationed at Los Alamos; Julius and Ethel Rosenberg (Greenglass's sister); and Morris and Lona Cohen. The eventual execution of the Rosenbergs caused international outrage, but further secret decipherment of KGB messages, which could not be revealed at the time, had proved that Julius had been a persistent traitor. The Cohens were warned in time to escape to Moscow, from which they would eventually move to Great Britain to continue their treachery. As the research of Svetlana Chervonnaya has shown, Alexander Feklisov and the other KGB officers who had run the American spy ring experienced agonies of remorse for the deaths of the Rosenbergs, blaming the Center for having recruited such a weak reed as Gold.

Fuchs had given such an accurate description of Eugene that the FBI had quickly identified the man calling himself Fomin in London as Feklisov, who had operated for several years in Washington. Nevertheless, MI5 declined to agree, especially after Fuchs failed to select Fomin's photograph when shown a batch containing it.

Hoover kept Truman informed of the proceedings, stating that Fuchs himself had estimated that he had speeded production of the Soviet atomic bomb "by several years." In prison, he had even made a copy of a sketch of an atom bomb, which he had given to Gold in June 1945!

Lamphere told me later that during one of their fifteen meetings, Fuchs mentioned that his Banbury courier was female but claimed that he did not know her name. As early as May 8, the FBI already had Ursula Beurton on a list of probables, describing her "as a known Soviet agent, as is, or was, her sister, her present husband and her former husband."

Reading the FBI files, one cannot fail to be impressed by the meticulous and patient professionalism of that organization. It was, of course, much larger than MI5 and with greater resources, but its British counterpart was far too desk-bound, poorly led, amateurish by comparison, and perhaps still deeply penetrated, as it certainly had been during the war.

CHAPTER 45

Unhampered Escape

—

MI5's INTEREST IN SONIA HAD BEEN REIGNITED AFTER FUCHS revealed that it had been her brother, Jurgen, who had put him in touch with the Russians. A backtrack of her file showed that MI5 had known she had visited Prague in January 1949 "for a fortnight's holiday," though in fact she had gone there to meet Jurgen by arrangement. While there, she had visited the Soviet embassy, which she dared not do in London, and left a message for the GRU Center, which had not been answering her signals from the Firs, her house in Great Rollright.

An MI5 paper dated October 26, 1949, about Sonia's passport record showed that MI5 had been fully aware that she was back from Prague and resident in the United Kingdom. FBI documents have also shown that as late as November 1949, Sonia was visited at the Firs by close relatives of her former husband, Rudi Hamburger, also a Soviet spy. They reveal that when Rudi had been handed back to the Russians after being arrested in Iran in 1943, he had been sentenced to five years in a forced labor camp, in spite of all his efforts for the GRU. He eventually left an account of his dreadful experience, and his son Michael recently told me that, after having worked as an engineer in the labor camp, his father had been sentenced to a further five years but had managed to secure his release after two. The FBI documents also show that Sonia had somehow managed to remain in touch with Rudi, and though she knew how appallingly he had been treated, she remained totally committed to the Soviet cause.

Meanwhile, in October 1949 unnamed MI5 officers had completed, for internal use only, a three-volume report entitled *The Case of the Rote Kapelle*, which has recently been released into the National Archives. The report shows that in spite of the suspicions of Sonia recorded by other officers, the authors had adopted the Hollis view that during her eight years in Britain, she had simply been a harmless housewife. "There is no evidence that Ursula did any intelligence work in the British Isles between 1941 and 1949," the report states.

Though they knew about her activities in Poland as well as those of her sister Brigitte, who visited her there in 1937, they had accepted her GRU legend, given to them by the defector Alexander Foote, that she had become disillusioned with Stalin after his nonaggression pact with Hitler in August 1939. They also assumed that she had divorced Rudi Hamburger because she was passionately in love with Beurton. Her consequent acquisition of right of entry into Great Britain was interpreted as a fortuitous bonus for her when, in fact, the GRU had ordered her to marry either of her two British assistants. Considering that Sonia had been so blatantly treacherous for so long, especially with her transmissions, it is extraordinary that mature MI5 officers could have been so gullible, unless pressured by higher authority.

By December 6, MI5 had officially discovered her espionage exploits in Shanghai, but only from a publication, *Sorge's Own Story*, and had simply noted it in her file. During that month, just when MI5 became certain that Fuchs was guilty, Sonia felt (as she was to state in her memoirs) that her position was "critical"—so much so that she dared not visit her old Shanghai friend Agnes Smedley, who was at death's door in an Oxford hospital. This suggests that she had received a warning about Fuchs's dangerous predicament.

In the autumn of 1949, Sonia's husband, Len, who had still been working in Banbury, had suffered a motorcycle accident, breaking a leg. By that time, Sonia had applied for a visa to visit the so-called German Democratic Republic (GDR), a separate Communist state founded on October 7, 1949, and her request to live there permanently had been secretly approved by the GRU. A letter written by her to Jurgen in January 1950 shows that she was desperate to join him in Germany, saying that she was "like a fish out of water" in Great Britain, which may have been a coded way of informing him of her danger.

Unable to secure a visa from the British or American occupation authorities, she thought of trying the Russians. As late as January 28, she wrote a relaxed letter from the Firs about Len's injuries. According to her memoirs, Sonia cycled to a railway underpass to inspect a *dubok*, hidden under a tree, and found a message from the GRU, approving her departure to Germany.

In an interview with William Skardon in a room at the War Office on January 31, 1950, Fuchs had been shown a large spread of photographs of suspected Soviet officers and agents whom the spy might have encountered. These had included an easily recognizable picture of Sonia, indicating that MI5 suspected some connection. Fuchs had selected a few possibles but completely ignored that of Sonia.

Late in February, Sonia announced to her neighbors that she was going to fly to Germany for a holiday and would be taking her two younger children with her. Having buried her transmitter, which she had retained after the Firs fiasco—a measure of her confidence in her continuing safety—she left on February 28, the day before Fuchs's trial, with no intention of returning. She was to claim that she fled only after reading of Fuchs's arrest in the newspapers. So, having remained at the Firs a further twenty-four days, she cannot have felt in immediate danger, and one wonders why.

As documents show, MI5 appeared to have had no idea that she had fled, though Peter Wright told me that he suspected she was permitted to escape because any interrogation of her could have revealed that she had serviced Elli. In his autobiography, Markus Wolf stated that as an intelligence officer, he was amazed that Sonia had managed to flee Britain after Fuchs's arrest.

Len could not accompany Sonia, partly because his leg was still in plaster, but mainly because he had to clear up the house and avoid the suspicion, and possible publicity, that would be created if they bolted together. He remained there, with Sonia's eighteen-year-old-son, Michael, for four months, keeping up the pretense with the neighbors that his wife would be returning. He was not questioned by MI5 or anybody else. Michael has recently described to me how he watched Len destroy all the remaining incriminating equipment, including the Minox camera.

This dismayed him, as he had never seen the tiny camera before, but Len felt that it would be too dangerous to take with him or leave behind with Michael.

The fact that Len and Sonia had not thought it necessary to destroy such technical evidence during the five-month interval between Fuchs's arrest and Len's departure supports the suspicion that they knew they would not be investigated. Looking at the broader picture, the fact that the GRU Center had considered it safe for the Beurtons to remain for *more than two years* in Great Britain after the Firs fiasco when they knew so much and still kept their incriminating equipment strongly suggests that there was a rock solid reason for their confidence that they would not be disturbed.

Len defected on June 27 and joined Sonia in East Berlin. Michael decided to remain in Britain to complete his education—at Aberdeen University. He was never questioned. Later, he was to become a distinguished German authority on Shakespeare and retranslated *Romeo and Juliet* in Berlin in 2004.

The Beurtons were British traitors who had defected behind the iron curtain, yet either MI5 knew nothing about their departure or someone there was glad to see them go. Both would be dependent on the GRU to find them jobs, so there was never any danger, once they were in East Germany, that either would ever release any information about any spy in MI5 without GRU permission.

In MI5, the pantomime of apparent ignorance continued when, in March 1950, some MI5 officers, believing that Sonia was still in Britain, were discussing her reinterrogation. Kenneth Morton Evans was strongly in favor of interrogating both her and Brigitte "repeatedly until it is established beyond doubt that nothing more can be extracted from them."

Foote was interviewed again on May 18, 1950, to secure information that might be used in a "renewed attempt to question Ursula Beurton on her espionage activities." He then revealed that he had met Brigitte by accident and she had told him that Sonia had been so upset by the MI5 visit in 1947 that she had canceled an important rendezvous scheduled for the following day. He also said that Jurgen had been "embarrassed by his sister's arrival in the U.K. in 1941 since he had feared that her activities as a spy might prejudice his political activities," thus confirming that Sonia had been posted to Britain for specific espionage activities that her brother knew about. All this finally alerted MI5 to the possibility that Sonia had been active in Britain after all!

A now hilarious memo from J. C. Robertson dated May 20, 1950, about the value of interviewing Sonia again—in Britain, where he thought she was still residing—commented, "This would seem to be worthwhile doing. She may have been impressed and possibly alarmed by the arrest of Fuchs. If so, she may be still more alarmed by learning of our knowledge that she was still active at the end of 1947 and may, therefore, be induced to talk." Two days later, J. H. Marriott commented, "The fact that we had not interviewed Brigitte could, I think, in some ways be more disconcerting to Ursula, who would think that we have been keeping a close watch on her." He then added, "If we do interrogate Brigitte, we are, I think, bound to disclose that we really know very little about what is going on."

While such officers were poring over their papers at their desks and sending one another secret memos from different rooms of the same building in Curzon Street, Sonia had been safe in the Soviet sector of Berlin for nearly three months. There was worse to come.

On July 25, 1950, at Dick White's request, Percy Sillitoe asked the Oxfordshire chief constable "to establish the whereabouts" of the Beurtons. This followed an MI5 suggestion that the letter check on the Firs should be renewed. On August 8, Sillitoe received an answer: Sonia had gone to Berlin (in February) and had been joined by Len, who had flown from Northolt on June 27. Further, on July 13, all their household effects at the Firs had been sold by public auction, with Sonia's sister Renate overseeing the sale.

The chief constable intensified Sillitoe's discomfort by adding, "Information has been received from a reliable source that Mrs. Beurton had obtained employment and intended staying in Berlin." Was this the moment Sillitoe decided, as he would state in his memoirs, that the MI in MI5 stood for Muttonhead Institute? It seems possible, especially when a check then revealed that on January 11, Sonia had applied for a military permit to visit Germany and nobody had spotted it. Neither Sillitoe nor anyone else in MI5 seems to have investigated the possibility that before that date, Sonia had been warned of Fuchs's—and her own—predicament.

On August 14, Marriott had the ignominy of informing MI6, "We have now received a police report that all the Beurtons' household goods were sold by public auction on 13 July." The MI6 response is not available. (Only later—on December 7—was it realized that Sonia could not have arrived in Germany before February 28 because her travel permit was not valid until that date.)

MI5 reestablished a telephone check on Brigitte and her new husband, the Communist John Nicolson (whose name in the MI5 documents was misspelled), but it produced nothing, and neither Brigitte nor her husband was ever questioned.

On August 22, the hapless White, who may have just returned from vacation, was informed in writing that Sonia had left for Berlin in February and had been joined by Len—a double defection under MI5's nose. White's informant Marriott suggested that Brigitte should now be investigated. She never was. That document is proof that White—and Hollis—knew that Sonia had remained in Britain for more than two years after the Firs fiasco, but as will be seen, that did not stop them from persevering, for public consumption, with the myth that she had vanished within days of that futile visit.

The redoubtable Evelyn McBarnet then suggested that Skardon revisit Fuchs in Stafford Prison and show him the photograph of Sonia again. He did so on November 30, 1950, and—according to his own report—showed him photographs of several women, including members of the Kuczynski family. Fuchs failed to identify any except Ursula Beurton, whom he immediately described as "my contact in Banbury." Skardon added, "He has no doubt at all that she is the contact but is unable to say why he failed to identify her previously." The likely answer would seem to be that Fuchs had been told by one of the friends who visited him in prison that, like Jurgen, Sonia was then unassailably safe in Berlin.

Later, Peter Wright confirmed to me that MI5 had been desperate to avoid admitting the Firs fiasco to the FBI, coupled with the growing realization that Sonia had serviced Fuchs under the noses of all those MI5 officers stationed at Blenheim. Hoover's eventual reaction, if he recalled Hollis's 1944 assurance that Sonia was a harmless housewife, is unavailable. Several MI5 documents indicate that, fearful of Hoover's response, MI5 did not reveal Fuchs's recognition of Sonia to the United States until December 18, when a letter was sent by Michael Hanley to Geoffrey Patterson in Washington, asking him to pass on the news to the FBI. It stated that "at last, Fuchs has identified Ursula Beurton as his contact."

In July 1953, MI5 was still looking at Sonia's relatives, intercepting her letters to them (which I have read) without any useful result beyond swelling the files. Meanwhile, the charade had been extended with plans being laid for the interrogation of Jurgen Kuczynski in Berlin, where he had become a professor at the university. On December 18, 1950, Michael Hanley had told Geoffrey Patterson that, as Kuczynski might be living in the American sector of Berlin, he should suggest that the CIA interrogate him. For good measure, he added, "In this connection, MI6 will probably write to Kim Philby" (who was in Washington). A month later, on January 19, 1951, Hanley had the ignominy of informing Patterson, "Unfortunately, it has now transpired that Kuczynski sublet his house in the American sector in June 1950 and moved to the Russian sector." Jurgen had deemed it safe to remain in the American sector for more than two months after Fuchs's conviction but had then been advised to move. Later, he revealed that he had been warned to do so by the East German leader Walter Ulbricht, who, like him, had been an agent of the GRU, with which he was still in touch.

In 1947, Foote had also identified Sonia's sister Brigitte as a seasoned GRU agent, yet she was never interrogated, though she was living as a well-known, open Communist in London. As will be seen, this omission may have been the greatest error of all, unless, as with Sonia, the failure was due to someone's deliberate policy. The charmed lives of the Kuczynski troika constitute a major anomaly supporting the suspicion of the continuing existence of a supermole inside MI5, someone skilled at protecting others as well as himself.

The complacent, desk-oriented mind-set of postwar MI5 was put on record for all time by the counterespionage officer R. T. Reed (B2b) on September 16, 1952. In a filed note, he wrote, "I take an optimistic view of the extent to which we have uncovered Russian espionage over the last fifteen years. We seem to have in our records pretty well everyone who is ever mentioned by spies that we uncover and interrogate. Fuchs' statement, including his contact with Ursula Beurton, is confirmed by everything we have in our records. Jurgen Kuczynski was well-known and we were aware of Hanna Klopstech." Concerning Ursula, he continued, "Of course, her own activities were well recorded."

The fact that Ursula, Jurgen, and Klopstech had inflicted so much damage over so many years and then had all managed to move to East Germany without penalty, never having being effectively interrogated, seems to have been inconsequential as long as it was all in the records.

CHAPTER 46

Volume of Deception

—

ARLIAMENT AND THE PUBLIC HEARD NOTHING ABOUT SONIA'S spying relationship with Fuchs for thirty years, save for a brief and misleading reference in 1952 to "a woman" in an MI5-inspired book called *The Traitors*, which will be dealt with in chapter 49. Meanwhile, in October 1949, Alexander Foote's autobiography had been published under the title *Handbook for Spies* and became something of a classic in espionage literature, in both Great Britain and the United States. It appeared to be a firsthand account of Soviet espionage by an honest man who had been converted to communism when young and gullible, had been cleverly induced to become a successful GRU agent, and had eventually realized his folly. In reality, it was rather different.

After his return to Britain in August 1947, Foote had needed money, and MI5 could not prevent him from writing his memoirs, as he had never operated against Britain, only against the Germans. He could not tell the story of his recruitment and work for the GRU without mentioning Sonia, her sister Brigitte, and Len, who were all still in England. Dick White and Roger Hollis in particular were opposed to any publicity that might induce investigators to try to track down any of them. So a compromise was reached in which Foote agreed to various amendments and falsehoods. These were inserted by MI5, using the argument that Foote might face serious libel actions if he used real names, though none of them would have dared to sue.

The MI5 counterespionage officer Courtney Young was detailed by White to "ghost" the book to his requirements. Nevertheless, when it was published—by Museum Press—it was at pains to stress that the story was "entirely factual," with "every incident and every character true and genuine," and "wherever possible, actual names being given." As a result, it has been widely used as a reliable work of reference.

Foote knew that Sonia's first married name had been Hamburger and that when she had married Len it became Beurton, but these names were changed, creating difficulties for any investigator wishing to find any of the GRU spies. Sonia was called Maria Schultz, previously married to Alfred Schultz, while Len was Bill Phillips. Even Sonia's nanny was given a fabricated name, all of which confused many people for a long time, with the pseudonyms appearing in other books by writers who had accepted what they believed to be Foote's honest statements.

The fabrications had been agreed to several months before the book appeared, which was just as well for MI5, because in October 1949, the secret inquiries into Fuchs's treachery were under way. Presumably, Hollis and White congratulated themselves on their foresight, as the use of Sonia's true name might have led to her discovery by the media.

Making the most of MI5's license to lie, the book faked even the date of Foote's defection in Berlin, which was given as August 2 instead of July 2. The apartment where Brigitte had recruited Foote was described as being in St. John's Wood when it had really been in Lawn Road, Hampstead. Any suggestion that the falsehoods were inserted to fool the Russians would have been fatuous, as the GRU knew all the facts, which were in the Center's records, as MI5 was aware.

According to Peter Wright, MI5 regarded the book as "a successful exercise in anti-Soviet propaganda." Whatever MI5's alleged purpose, the false statements helped to cover its appalling incompetence, or worse, in handling the Sonia case, as they made it difficult for any investigator to track down Sonia or Brigitte, though in 1949 Sonia was still at the Firs and Brigitte was in London.

The book stressed Foote's original belief that from the time Sonia had arrived in England, she had no connection with any Russian spy net, having ended her allegiance to the GRU.

In October 1949, MI5's serial failure to record Sonia's treachery was also recorded in a three-volume secret survey of the Rote Kapelle, prepared for internal use and recently released into the National Archives.

While it listed her "RIS espionage missions" in China, Poland, and Switzerland, it stated, "She is not known to have engaged in any subversive activity in the UK." It also accepted Sonia's GRU legend that in 1939, "she had been disillusioned by the Russo-German Pact."

Sometime later, the disgraceful myth that Sonia had fled to Germany in panic in 1947, only two days after the Firs fiasco, when she had realized that MI5 was on her trail, was promoted by leading figures in MI5 such as Dick White. The bald statement that Sonia had fled in 1947 appeared in various books, even the CIA's later two-volume history of the Rote Kapelle. White was to assure me in writing, "When we did learn about her she bolted back to Germany in 1947." In reply, I told White that inquiries in Great Rollright had proved beyond question that the two traitors had remained there until 1950 and that I had published the evidence of witnesses to that effect in my book *Too Secret Too Long* in 1984. Nevertheless, when briefing Tom Bower for his official biography not long afterward, White repeated that they had disappeared in 1947, "two days after the interview," a totally false claim that appeared in the book.

This MI5 myth was generally accepted until 1983, when my son, Michael, was assisting me with research. He found—as Sonia was to confirm in her memoirs—that she had remained at the Firs with the children until February 1950. In May 1949, Mr. and Mrs. Tom Greathead had moved into the house, assisting Sonia there in return for board and lodging. They recalled that Sonia was constantly typing in foreign languages. Sonia had explained that she did translation work for the government, but without stating which government. They noted that nothing was ever left in a wastepaper basket—every scrap of paper was burned daily in the garden, indicating that she was still active. Former local members of the Home Guard wondered why Sonia was in the habit of stringing up radio aerials. No official watched the Firs to check on her activities, and she and Len were never bothered again by MI5. Several other witnesses, who were neighbors, confirmed her continuing tenure of the Firs, which her son Michael Hamburger reconfirmed in 2002.

What was the purpose of this deception, which, as White's false assertion showed, was MI5 inspired? Once Foote was a free agent, the true identity and whereabouts of Sonia might leak. In that event, after MI5's failure in dealing with her, it was in the service's interest for investigators to believe that it was pointless for anyone to look for her or her transmissions, as she had been safely behind the iron curtain since 1947! While this may sound excessively conspiratorial, I find it impossible to explain the facts as a "cock-up," even given the astounding incompetence of MI5 at that time. The fact that the CIA had received the same false information, presumably from MI5, supports the contention of deliberate deception.

Who else but Sonia gained any benefit from the Firs fiasco and the later faking of her flight? The answer, of course, could be Elli and the GRU, which he served. The purpose of the deception was certainly not to fool the GRU, which knew that Sonia was still in Great Rollright.

The lie about Sonia's flight was the beginning of the systematic denigration of her as an agent, mirroring that of Igor Gouzenko as a source. In a letter written in 1983, Dick White assured me that she had been no more than "a magpie sending back everything she could pick up from relatives and friends, which could not have been important when Russia was an ally." This was in spite of her brilliant handling of Fuchs, then fully known to White. Some magpie, especially in view of her coup with the Quebec Agreement under the noses of White, Hollis, and their colleagues!

White was an exceptionally pleasant man who charmed his successive political masters to such an extent that he developed a reputation as the "White Knight" whose judgment could always be trusted to be well-founded and honest. On the other hand, he was regarded by some of his colleagues as weak and prone to taking the easy way out. Bower does his best for White in his biography, but the facts, which he presented with White's agreement, show that against the Russian threat, he was a failure in MI5 and that he knew it.

Looking at all the facts, as now disclosed by MI5's own records, it is difficult to avoid suspecting that when Foote revealed his knowledge of Sonia's existence in Great Britain in 1947, there was some degree of panic somewhere in MI5. This may have required steps to be taken to provoke her into quitting the country. When that ploy—her feeble interrogation—failed, MI5 made the pretense that she had indeed fled to Soviet-controlled territory and was therefore permanently unavailable for questioning. The mythical flight was part of her hoped-for "amicable elimination" from the espionage scene.

The holding of Foote by MI5 for ten weeks conforms with the suspicion that the prevention of any questioning of Sonia by anybody was a prime objective. Foote needed money and had a story to tell, but any investigation of Sonia by the media might have been devastating for Elli and for the reputation of MI5. Perhaps, before Foote was released, he had been assured by MI5 that Sonia was in Soviet territory and beyond questioning. He appears never to have made any attempt to contact her, even when he became disenchanted by MI5.

Sonia's eventual view of *Handbook for Spies* was that it was "infamous" and written by a "traitor." Brigitte's opinion of her exposure as a GRU recruiter is unknown. However, because of MI5's insistence on hiding their true identities—and perhaps for other reasons—the traitorous pair do not seem to have been much concerned.

A more pressing reason for MI5's pretense that Sonia had disappeared in 1947 was given to me by a former officer of GCHQ. Because of Foote's wide knowledge of illicit GRU communication methods and codes, he was interviewed comprehensively by Ray Frawley, a GCHQ officer described to me by a close colleague as "an intellectual tiger." Frawley found the talks highly productive. He also learned about Sonia, and it would have been automatic for him to have tried to interview her, as she knew so much more. He did not do this, almost certainly— according to the colleague—because GCHQ had been assured by Foote that she was unavailable, as she had fled to Germany. There was the additional risk to MI5—and especially, perhaps, to Elli—that Frawley might learn about Sonia's illicit transmissions in Britain and wonder why they had been ignored.

When White knew that he was terminally ill, it was in his interest to shoulder the blame for the farcical interview with Sonia at the Firs. By that time, the official suspicion that Hollis, who was then dead, may have been a spy was common knowledge, and any further evidence against him could damage White's reputation as the person who had helped to recruit him and had promoted him serially.

Significantly, the deception was reiterated and fortified when *Handbook for Spies* was reprinted, surprisingly and for no apparent reason, in a slightly revised version in 1964, after Foote's death. By that time, Sonia's crucial role in the Fuchs case was fully known to MI5, but no mention was made of it. The lies about her were retained, including the myth that she had lost the will to spy after being disgusted by Stalin's pact with Hitler and simply wished to "sink back into respectable obscurity," when, by the 1964 edition, MI5 knew that she had serviced Fuchs and others.

The text, again published by Museum Press, mused on the Kremlin's generosity in allowing its foreign agents to retire from service if circumstances permitted. It also claimed that Sonia had left Switzerland in 1940 because she wished to return to England, where, in fact, she had never previously lived. It stated that Sonia had left Switzerland "for London" when it should have been "for Oxford," as MI5 well knew. There can be no doubt that the second edition of this book was another MI5 deception operation, because it contained an appendix about codes written specially by Peter Wright, as he confirmed to me.

I have compared the two editions. The second opened with an inserted introduction, missing from the first, containing two new, blatant lies. It stated that "Sonia is living quietly in England" and "Foote's original recruiter is now living equally quietly behind the Iron Curtain." As MI5 then knew, it was Sonia who was behind the iron curtain, having fled there in 1950 after the arrest of Fuchs. Brigitte, the original recruiter, was still rooted in Hampstead, where she would stay until she died.

This double falsehood could have originated only in MI5, where Hollis, by then director general, always took a personal interest in anything to be published about his organization, especially a book originally ghosted by it, as Wright also confirmed to me. So it would seem certain that Hollis would have insisted on seeing the text of the newly inserted introduction in the second edition of *Handbook for Spies* before its publication and that someone in MI5 wrote it.

What could be the purpose of putting this double falsehood on public record? One clear result was to make it almost impossible for any investigator to find Maria Schultz (or Maria Phillips) living in England or her unnamed sister (Brigitte) behind the iron curtain. This may have been partly to cover the shame of the Firs fiasco, or it may have been in some officer's particular interest. Who stood to benefit from this further move to muddy the waters about Sonia, especially about her connection with Oxford? The person with most to fear from any interview with Sonia may have been Elli, and as will be seen, he may have had even more to fear, should any investigative writer ever have tracked down

Brigitte. Though Brigitte was living in London under a different married name, nobody was likely to start looking for her when it had been stated authoritatively that she was behind the iron curtain.

It is another extraordinary coincidence that this double dose of false information should have been put on record at just the time—1963–64—when Hollis had agreed to a mole hunt inside MI5 and had learned that he was under suspicion himself by some of his colleagues. As chapter 80 will indicate, it could have been a panic measure to deter anyone from seeking Brigitte, in particular as her exposure at that time might have spelled disaster for Hollis and the whole of MI5. Museum Press may have wished to reissue the book in 1964 because the spate of spy cases made it topical, and someone in MI5 had then taken the opportunity to insert the further falsehoods. The two editions constituted what Wright called a "deniable operation"—MI5-speak for an operation that, if exposed, could be denied by plausible lies already manufactured in advance.

The 1964 edition also contained an additional chapter entitled "Orpheus in the Underworld" about the recent Gordon Lonsdale spy case, which appeared to be to MI5's credit. The chapter was presented as though written by Alexander Foote, who ended by telling the reader, "Now go back to the normal world, forget espionage, and leave the underworld. I shall of course remain there." Yet Foote had already been dead for eight years!

He had died in August 1956, having been put out to grass with a dull job in the Ministry of Agriculture, where he had become progressively disillusioned with MI5's failure to follow up his leads or secure any other benefit from his defection. He had found it increasingly difficult to understand why the Beurtons had not been placed under surveillance when he had first alerted MI5 about their presence. Then, following the fiasco at the Firs, and for other reasons, he became convinced that there were Soviet spies operating at high levels in both MI5 and MI6. He also believed that someone in MI5 had effectively blocked his efforts to convince the authorities of the seriousness and scope of the threat from the GRU.

Handbook for Spies went out of its way to marginalize Sonia, an exceptionally effective GRU officer. As with Gouzenko, the truth appeared to threaten the MI5 spy called Elli. All in all, MI5's proven abuse of Foote in this deception operation casts doubt on the veracity of any book published with its connivance. MI5's main counterespionage function was to deceive Soviet intelligence, but it was more successful at deceiving the British public, which funded its operations and salaries.

Meanwhile, in jail, Fuchs gave lectures on atomic physics, including the basis of bomb construction. (The copious notes taken by one fellow prisoner, the murderer Donald Hume, came into my possession.) When interviewed in prison by a reporter, Fuchs said, "British security is symbolized by a very fine veneer on top and utter departmental confusion beneath."

Alexander Feklisov was to tell Dr. Svetlana Chervonnaya that "reliable people" visited Fuchs in jail on the KGB's behalf, "to let him feel that we still valued him," though in time he would be heavily censured for having pleaded guilty. These visitors included some of his former scientific friends, one of whom now seems to have been yet another Soviet agent.

In December 1950, the government had deprived Fuchs of his British citizenship. This had angered him because he felt that he had cooperated with the British and American authorities. Subsequently, he deduced that he would be unable to work anywhere behind the iron curtain because he would be held responsible for the arrest of some of his American conspirators and, especially, for the execution of the Rosenbergs. He thought that he might go to India but somehow learned that he would be accepted by the German Democratic Republic, which needed scientists.

The British authorities could not get Fuchs behind the iron curtain quickly enough. On the day of his release, June 23, 1959, he was escorted to London Airport by police so that he could not be interviewed by the media. As will be seen, it was a crucial time for the Great Prize— the restoration of access to American atomic secrets—and the government was anxious to limit publicity about the traitorous British scientist who had betrayed America's most secret weapon.

Once in East Germany, Fuchs showed that he was an uncompromising Communist fundamentalist, as he always had been. He quickly applied for citizenship and was granted membership in the East German Communist Party, eventually becoming a member of the Central Committee. He followed the party line on every issue, always supporting the Soviet Union, which had done nothing for him in spite of his priceless services. So much for the moral qualms he had raised in his confession!

He was given a senior post in an atomic research institute near Dresden, married, and lived quietly. In his autobiography, Markus Wolf relates how for many years he was forbidden by the KGB even to approach Fuchs, whom he admired. He states that on Soviet orders, Fuchs remained silent for more than twenty years after his arrest, being forbidden to give interviews of any kind. Even when Wolf, who eventually came to know Fuchs well, was allowed to see him in the 1970s, he was forbidden to discuss his espionage. Efforts by KGB officers to secure some recognition for Fuchs's crucial espionage were rejected.

Honored for his services to the GDR, Fuchs died in 1988, aged seventy-eight. The *Times* obituary, which named Roger Hollis as the main culprit in the failure to detect him, was entitled "Traitor by Courtesy of Incompetence"—a diagnosis with which I disagree unless the incompetence was contrived. Wolf wrote that Fuchs had "made the greatest single contribution to Moscow's ability to build an atom bomb," adding that his information had "changed the world's balance of power by breaking America's nuclear monopoly earlier than otherwise."

CHAPTER 47

Hollis at Bay

———

On JUNE 19–21, 1950, A TOP-SECRET TRIPARTITE CONFERENCE of British, American, and Canadian officials to discuss security standards was held in Washington. It was particularly important because in the interest of restoring the atomic partnership, the British government was desperate to allay American doubts about British security, exacerbated by the recently proven espionage of Klaus Fuchs. The official account of it, which I secured from an American source, along with relevant MI5 files released in 2003 and 2004 are highly revealing.

Again assisted by Michael Perrin, Roger Hollis was there as the delegate from MI5, being director of protective security and its acknowledged atomic expert, as well as a consultant to the British Official Committee on Atomic Energy, of which Perrin was a member. The opportunity was also seized to explain why Fuchs had managed to escape detection while in Great Britain. Though Hollis knew that the Fuchs case was going to be raised, he claimed to have neglected to brief himself on the details and told the conference that because of that omission, he would be speaking off the record, which was an odd thing to say at a top-secret meeting. In fact, the document shows that Hollis gave a substantial amount of details, including many dates, indicating that he had consulted records.

An MI5 report released in 2004 and entitled *Summary of Security Ac-*

tion in Fuchs's Case looks suspiciously like a brief prepared for Hollis for the conference. It is undated but contains, word for word, the alleged facts about Fuchs stated by Hollis in Washington and then recorded in the official British account of what happened. It would seem that Hollis had it with him. In that event, his preliminary statement was a deception that, of course, he could have explained as fence mending "in the national interest."

The official account recorded that Hollis admitted that, throughout, he "had been concerned with all the security clearance aspects of the case," which disposes of any doubt about his responsibility for the Fuchs disaster. He then listed the various clearances of Fuchs, making misstatements of fact and omitting the recommendations for thorough investigation that had been made by several MI5 colleagues. He stated that Fuchs's potential for the atomic project had been recognized "at the end of 1941," when the true date was May 1941.

He admitted that although "a serious mistake had undoubtedly been made," the treachery had been difficult to detect because the espionage involved had required only brief and occasional meetings with Soviet couriers or controllers. However, that problem applied to most spies, and as would later be revealed, Hollis had also failed to detect any of the scores of frequent meetings between the Cambridge spies—like Philby, Blunt, and Burgess—and their Soviet contacts.

Hollis did not mention that since Fuchs had been a German refugee, he had also been the MI5 officer responsible for overseeing his activities. He did say that Fuchs had been friendly with a "well-known communist" in the Canadian prison camp but avoided saying that this was the notorious Hans Kahle, who had been listed as a "dangerous communist" in an MI5 document supplied to the FBI via the U.S. embassy in London in 1940, as some of the Americans present might have recalled. He also avoided mentioning Jurgen Kuczynski, though Fuchs had already admitted that the German Communist had been instrumental in his recruitment to the GRU.

Hollis stated that when Fuchs had joined Harwell in 1946, his case for establishment as a civil servant had been specially considered because Fuchs was not British born of British parents, but that was false because that requirement was not introduced until 1950, *after* Fuchs's conviction and because of it. Summing up, Hollis stressed that the "covert investigation" of Fuchs by MI5 had been "thorough." Since then, some more honest MI5 officer has written on the *Summary of Security Action in Fuchs's Case* in the MI5 file, "It was NOT thorough."

In view of the seriousness of Hollis's position when trying to explain his repeated failures to the Americans, his statement that he had not briefed himself on the details of the Fuchs case sounds highly implausible for such a cautious man. It was Perrin who suggested to the conference that the U.K. delegates should review the Fuchs case, and he would not have done that without first discussing the whole matter with Hollis, who was to be required to do most of the explaining. So Hollis's claim that he had not been briefed seems to be more like a built-in excuse for his misstatements of fact and omissions, should he ever be challenged about them.

The relevant MI5 documents concerning Hollis's role in the whole Fuchs scandal suggest that he would not have escaped American censure had he exposed the facts honestly, including his previous advice that the U.S. atomic authorities be misled about them. It was a virtuoso display of brass nerve, cool dissimulation, and power of persuasion without a whisper of apology. If he was Elli, the situation was supercharged with tension and surely unique in the annals of espionage. However, the fact that both Fuchs and Donald Maclean had attended a previous tripartite conference while both were actively spying makes the concept credible.

His American counterparts appeared so sympathetic that Hollis's colleagues were told later that he had "run rings round them," which meant that he had evaded telling them the truth. They were, however, well aware that whatever his excuses, he was responsible for enabling Fuchs to continue his spying in the United States and so provide the Russians with a blueprint of the atomic bomb. Nor could the Americans present at the conference understand why, before his arrest and confession, Fuchs had *never* been asked if he had been a Communist.

At a meeting of the Official Committee on Atomic Energy in London on July 5, Perrin, with Hollis present, presented a rosy review of the proceedings in Washington. He said that the Americans had been impressed by the British purge procedure, while admitting that they were "a good deal more thoroughgoing than we are" and suggesting that "it behooves us to put our house in order." Prophetically, he feared that since the FBI had not been invited to the conference, the agency would claim that "the British had pulled wool over the eyes of the Americans."

A letter to Perrin from the British embassy in Washington confirmed that the FBI had not been convinced by the case presented by him and by Hollis and that Congress endorsed the U.S. government's decision to maintain the ban on exchanging atomic secrets.

Later, Perrin was to make it clear to the American author Robert Williams, who informed me immediately after his meeting with him, that while he had been present at the discussions to give technical advice on the security clearances of Fuchs, the decision had always been taken by Hollis. In that way, Fuchs had been cleared six times. The Washington conference had offered a unique opportunity to confront Hollis about his serial responsibility for the Fuchs debacle. It had been missed.

KGB documents have also revealed that Fuchs was not the only atomic scientist spy active in Great Britain. A still officially unknown traitor, then a young Communist physicist with the code name Moor, recruited early in 1943, was passing over a mass of material, including official British and American reports. As he also rifled the secret files of the laboratory library, with access to its safe, he would seem to have been in some large establishment, probably at one of the universities involved. There is evidence that this was Oxford and that he worked in the Clarendon Laboratory, under MI5's nose, before being seconded to ICI, where he worked on the production of uranium 235 by the gaseous diffusion process. The KGB officer who controlled him, Colonel Vladimir Barkovsky, revealed many details about him to Nigel Bance. Moor was an open member of the Communist Party of Great Britain and might have been caught had MI5 not still been blinded by the belief that the Russians avoided using such people as spies. If he had been through the clearance process, Hollis would also have been responsible, as he certainly was in failing to detect his treachery.

Without hindrance, Moor met Barkovsky in Oxford and then in Birmingham, where he worked at the university along with Fuchs, before moving to the ICI facility near Mold in Wales. Barkovsky testified to Bance that Moor had handed over "an enormous quantity of documents" between 1943 and 1945. These covered both British and American atomic work. Barkovsky claimed that Moor induced him to study a book on atomic physics so that he could explain some of the material in greater detail. KGB documents confirm that until the end of 1944, the Russians received the preponderance of their atomic secrets from British sources under the averted eyes of MI5.

It has been asserted that Moor was the late Sir Eric Rideal, professor of colloidal science at Cambridge at the time, but the staid Sir Eric, whom I knew, was in his fifties then, and the evidence suggests that the spy was much younger and more of an extrovert. Barkovsky named Rideal to Bance as an occasional source but gave his code name as Alkit, after the name of a clothing company shop in London where they used to meet. Further, Rideal had been only marginally involved in the bomb project. Though most of the British scientists who had worked on it were named in the official statement issued by the government on August 12, 1945, there was no mention of Rideal. Moor fits the description of a Cambridge graduate of Russian origin, though he was born in Great Britain. Whoever he was, he was another damaging Soviet spy missed by MI5.

There was a further British atomic spy with the code name Kelly whose identity remains unresolved. KGB records show that Kelly also supplied many documents. He may have been another German refugee atomic scientist at the Clarendon Laboratory who has been deeply investigated by Bance.

It all amounted to a staggering failure by the security authorities, not only to detect the spies and their controllers, but to prevent their regular abstraction of top-secret documents to channel to Moscow. President Truman wondered why Stalin expressed no surprise when told about the existence of an enormously powerful bomb at the Potsdam conference in 1945. He had been informed of its development, stage by stage, since 1941.

CHAPTER 48

Italian Fiasco

—

IN 2003, RUSSIAN SOURCES ADMITTED THAT ANOTHER FOREIGN-born British atomic scientist, Bruno Pontecorvo, had been a long-term Soviet spy who had managed to escape to Moscow. An interval of only eight weeks had spared Hollis from further ignominy at the Washington conference.

Pontecorvo, who had worked in the British atomic project in Canada since early 1943, arrived in the United Kingdom to take up a research post at Harwell in February 1949. According to the senior KGB officer General Pavel Sudoplatov, he had been a source of atomic secrets leaking from Canada for several years. His treachery has now been described in *The Atom Bomb and the KGB*, published in Moscow in 2003. Its author, F. D. Popov, claimed that as an ideological Communist, Pontecorvo volunteered his services to the KGB once he had access to secrets in Canada and continued to spy until the summer of 1950.

He had been born into a Jewish family in Pisa in 1913 and in 1934 achieved a doctorate in physics at Rome University under the tutelage of Enrico Fermi, who was already distinguished as an atomic scientist. In 1936, he went to Paris and worked under the Communist scientist Frédéric Joliot-Curie until the Germans attacked France in May 1940. Pontecorvo then fled to the United States, arriving in New York in August. He secured a job with an oil company and renewed his friendship with Fermi, who was working on the atomic bomb project in Chicago.

Early in 1943, he was invited to join the Anglo-Canadian atomic research team based in Montreal and went there to work on the heavy water uranium reactor being developed at Chalk River.

Popov claims that Pontecorvo quickly contacted the Soviet embassy in Ottawa by means of a letter. The senior KGB officer there expressed interest but waited for the potential spy to produce some offering to ensure that he was not a plant or provocation. Pontecorvo delivered it in the form of "secret documents and calculations," for which he was paid. Only then, Popov states, "was operational communication established." He appears to have been given the code name Quantum, which is mentioned in several deciphered Venona messages, though it was probably changed over time.

Pontecorvo is said to have provided valuable information about Fermi's pioneer atomic-reactor work at Chicago and to have reported regularly to a Soviet contact about the Anglo-Canadian project. In some way he had been controlled, while in Canada, by Lieutenant Colonel Yuri Vasilevsky, the KGB resident in Mexico City from 1943 to 1945. Vasilevsky had an exceptionally reliable courier there in the shape of Kitty Harris, who had previously serviced Donald Maclean in London and Paris. During that time, and later, Pontecorvo made regular trips to the United States, ostensibly to sustain his residence permit there in case he eventually decided to take American citizenship. On these occasions, he could have met Vasilevsky or his courier.

So Pontecorvo was yet another refugee who repaid his host nations—the United States, Canada, and Great Britain—with treachery. In the process, he made trips to Europe, including one to England in early December 1947, when he was told that a post would be created for him at Harwell if he wanted it. He then visited Milan and Paris—more opportunities for Soviet contact. Popov claims that Pontecorvo continued to spy on nuclear reactor work when he was at Harwell and that Vasilevsky was in touch with him while he was there, meetings being arranged in Switzerland and Italy when Pontecorvo went there for conferences or holiday. Pontecorvo was a keen tennis player, and Popov claims that he received KGB instructions and delivered information on microfilms concealed in tennis balls!

While he had been spying in Canada, Pontecorvo was unknown to the GRU defector Igor Gouzenko, because the KGB operated quite separately from the GRU. Nevertheless, Gouzenko knew that a KGB spy ring existed and, after his defection, had repeatedly warned the RCMP about it. No effective notice was taken, and it is fair to wonder why, especially as Hollis had been in charge of the British aspects of the inquiries there. Otherwise, Pontecorvo might have been exposed before he left Canada.

Aged thirty-six when he reached Harwell, "Ponte," as he became known, was popular and regarded as above suspicion. Nevertheless, to cover himself after Fuchs's arrest, he thought it wise to inform the security chief, Henry Arnold, that he had a brother, Gilberto, who was a well-known Communist. Arnold reported this to MI5 on March 1, 1950, stating that Bruno had assured him that he was not a Communist himself. On the following day, however, information reached MI5 from Sweden that both Pontecorvo and his wife, who was Swedish, were "avowed Communists."

On April 6, Pontecorvo reassured Arnold that neither he nor his wife was a Communist. By that time, Pontecorvo had been offered a professorship at Liverpool University to pursue nonsecret research. So his Harwell superiors, who had helped to secure the post, urged him to take it, for after the conviction of Fuchs, neither they nor MI5 had any wish to be landed with another possible spy case. This was a further example of "eliminating him amicably," as had been the original plan with Fuchs.

Pontecorvo's interest in communism had been known to the FBI since February 1943, when he had been suspect enough for officers to carry out a "discreet search" of the home he had retained in Oklahoma. They had found documents and books suggesting that he was a Communist sympathizer, at least. So when Pontecorvo had moved to Canada, the FBI had quickly passed their findings to the nearest British authority. That was the intelligence organization British Security Coordination, based in New York under William Stephenson, whose links with the Canadian government were close, as the Gouzenko case would show. Whatever had happened to the papers there, they had never reached MI5, as was recently revealed by a released Foreign Office file containing an MI5 report on Pontecorvo, compiled in 1950.

Only one inquiry about Pontecorvo had been made by any British authority during the war. In a letter sent to Tube Alloys in London in 1943, the Canadian authorities had asked for any information about him, including security objections. After consulting MI5, Tube Alloys had endorsed Pontecorvo's value as a scientist but left his clearance to the

Canadians. Both the Canadian National Research Council and the Royal Canadian Mounted Police later informed me that, at the time, they had "accepted the security check made by the British." By "the British," the Canadians meant not MI5 in London, but British Security Coordination in New York.

Nevertheless, in telephone inquiries in 1950, Canadian officials assured me that Pontecorvo had been cleared in Britain before he had reached Canada as a member of the British atomic team. British officials, however, declared correctly that he had never worked in Britain before joining the Canadian project. He had been living in France and then in America, as a refugee.

Pontecorvo had become a British subject in 1948 entirely on the basis that he had lived five years in Canada, a dispensation that was then legally permissible. In the naturalization process, MI5 had been asked by the Home Office to vet him, but all they had done was to report, "Nothing recorded against." Before he had joined Harwell in 1949, MI5 was asked to vet him again and relied on the views of a few fellow scientists who declared him "not politically minded." No special inquiries were made about him, as positive vetting had not then been started, though a "purge procedure" to root out any Communists engaged on secret work had been introduced by Clement Attlee in the previous year. There is some evidence that at least one of his so-called screenings did not really take place and that Pontecorvo was simply nodded through by the MI5 officer Graham Mitchell, who allegedly recorded that certain inquires had been made when they had not. MI5 was involved in screening him then, as documents released to the National Archives in May 2003 have fully confirmed.

On July 25, 1950, Pontecorvo set off by car with his wife and three sons for a holiday in Italy. They never returned. Early in September, they were spirited away to Russia by the KGB, probably by ship, after they had flown to Helsinki. Had the KGB been warned to remove him because he had been exposed as a secret Communist? If so, by whom?

Because Pontecorvo, a flamboyant figure, was somewhat unpredictable and had sent misleading messages to Harwell, the security officer there did not begin to make inquiries about his absence until September 21. What was clearly going to be another devastating security scandal did not become public until October 20, when news of his disappearance broke in Italian newspapers. Nobody could find proof that the Pontecorvos were in Russia, but few doubted it, least of all the Americans, who saw their vanishing act as yet another British security fiasco, especially in view of the warning about him, which the FBI had passed over in 1943. A letter to the Cabinet Office from the British embassy in Washington, dated October 21, shows the extent of the alarm there concerning American public reaction to yet another British disaster.

The case was regarded as potentially so damaging, especially in view of the serial shambles of Pontecorvo's clearances, that Guy Liddell, the MI5 deputy chief, was sent to brief Prime Minister Attlee, probably in the absence of Percy Sillitoe. His two-page top-secret report on the meeting, dated October 23, 1950, and released only in 2003, shows that he grossly understated Pontecorvo's access to secrets. When the prime minister asked Liddell "how far Pontecorvo had access to vital information," he was told that his employers believed that "for several years, he seemed to have had hardly any contact with secret work." This was entirely contrary to the warning that MI5 itself had passed to Pontecorvo's employers six months previously, stating emphatically that the scientist had access to top-secret information and was a potential security risk. Whether deliberately, through sheer incompetence, or through accepting someone else's advice, Liddell seriously misinformed the prime minister in a way that was to the advantage of those MI5 officers with reputations at risk from the defection.

There is now documentary evidence that MI5's action was intentional. A long report of the case by MI5 to the Foreign Office reveals that some official crossed out "As Bruno Pontecorvo has access to top secret information" so that the sentence read simply, "From the security standpoint a potential security risk existed." This would seem to have been done in preparing a misleading brief to send to the Washington embassy to minimize MI5's incompetence in American eyes. The prime minister was given the same treatment, and whoever was responsible was being dishonest. The whole incident recalled that of a few months previously, when the prime minister had been deliberately misinformed by MI5 about the Fuchs case.

As the repercussions rumbled on, MI5 submitted a further report to the prime minister on October 25, 1950, entitled *Action Taken by the Security Service in Connection with the Pontecorvo Case*. Released in 2003, the document admitted that MI5 did not know whether or not it had vetted the scientist prior to his joining the British atomic team in Canada in 1943. Had MI5 been consulted, it would simply have replied, "Nothing recorded against," because there was nothing about him in the files. The British Security Coordination (New York) records could not be checked because they had been destroyed.

The document sent to the prime minister stated that on November 27, 1947, MI5 had "vetted Pontecorvo for the Home Office in connection with his naturalisation proceedings," but all it had done was to reply, "Nothing recorded against." Immediately afterward, he had been vetted again because Harwell might eventually want to employ him. In that process, MI5 had written to the Harwell security officer Henry Arnold, asking him to make inquiries about Pontecorvo's "reliability and loyalty." As Arnold had never met him, all he could do was question the few scientists there who had. He reported that Pontecorvo seemed to be "a straightforward fellow with no political leanings." On that evidence, MI5 told the Supply Ministry, his future employer, that it "did not wish to advise against Pontecorvo being granted permanent status in Government service."

Almost incredibly, in view of what Liddell had told the prime minister *only two days earlier,* the MI5 document included a paragraph revealing that on April 25, 1950, MI5 had informed the Supply Ministry, "As Bruno Pontecorvo has access to top secret information, from the security standpoint it is considered that a potential security risk exists." Whether this gross anomaly was ever brought to the prime minister's attention is unknown.

On November 6, Hollis met Michael Perrin and George Strauss, the supply minister, to give them the MI5 report on the case. The MI5 document recording this meeting is further proof that Hollis (then director of protective security) was the officer responsible for advising Harwell and the other atomic establishments on security matters. By that time, he had been made aware of the FBI evidence and was anxious that the government should know that the "slip," as he called it, had not been MI5's fault. It was less than five months since he had managed to explain away his successive clearances of Fuchs as a series of slips at the Washington conference.

Hollis urged that "the utmost care should be taken to avoid the release of this information" and was particularly concerned that the FBI should not learn the details. He warned that it could stir up animosity in the FBI and imperil the secret deal whereby neither agency would say anything about the other without prior consultation and agreement. Clearly, he feared that Hoover might publicly express his concern about British security precautions.

Hollis, who was held in some contempt by the FBI, was also sensitive to the fact that MI5 was under attack again in the media for its general incompetence. News about the "slip" would certainly have exacerbated it, for clearly the MI5 management had taken no initiative to consult the FBI about Pontecorvo, though it knew that he had spent several years in America. There can be no doubt that MI5 told the truth about Pontecorvo's access to the supply minister but then deliberately misled the prime minister. In briefing Liddell, and through his own statements, Hollis, MI5's atomic expert, had been at the heart of this deception. The greatest care should have been taken in preparing a brief for the prime minister, who might have decided to make a statement to the nation through Parliament, as he had with the Fuchs case. As a result, the barrage of questions was fielded by Supply Minister Strauss, who declined to be informative. Through the mystique attached to MI5, Strauss may have been convinced that it was genuinely in the national interest to reveal the minimum, but in view of his former support for the release of Jurgen Kuczynski from internment—in time to recruit Fuchs, as he knew by then—he had personal reasons to avoid any parliamentary discussion about spies.

Meanwhile, the British ambassador in Washington, Sir Oliver Franks, joined in the deception by advising that the "story should be played down" in the United States, with emphasis on the nonsecret nature of Pontecorvo's work. A Foreign Office document on the subject in the form of a letter from Perrin to Sir Roger Makins, deputy undersecretary of state, dated November 9, 1950, shows that with the collusion of other senior diplomats, lies were eventually told to the Americans. Specifically, the letter, which was advice on how the Foreign Office should respond to queries raised by the ambassador, stated that since 1945, Pontecorvo had been involved only on nonsecret work on cosmic rays and "had been given no access to specialised knowledge."

Again, this was contrary to the statement made in MI5's own report, prepared six months previously, that Pontecorvo had had access to top-secret information. It was also stated that he had been only an adviser on the physics of nuclear reactors in Canada when he had been deeply involved in it. Pontecorvo had also been working on new methods of detecting uranium ores, which was of the greatest interest to the Soviet Union at that time. It was also inevitable that through scientific and social gossip, and just by keeping his eyes and ears open, the convivial Pontecorvo would have learned a great deal about the secret work of other Harwell scientists.

Perrin's letter to Makins had been based on information supplied by MI5, and most likely by Hollis, because it shows that a copy of it was passed to him. The letter reiterated Hollis's warning that the release of security information about the Pontecorvo case should be avoided. There is no evidence that MI5 ever made any attempt to investigate Pontecorvo's possible treachery, either in Canada or in Great Britain, or to discover his possible Soviet contacts. Whether incidentally or by design, this was to the Soviet advantage. Inaction would also have been in the interests of Elli, who would not have relished any resurrection of interest in the Canadian spy rings, which may have caused the possible reexamination of Gouzenko.

Finally, Perrin, who had been asked to assess the case in ways to "minimise its impact," told the Foreign Office that while "some slip" had been made, it had been the fault of British Security Coordination in New York and not of MI5. He ended his letter, "I think it is going to be a very tricky business to evade the American question and suggest that it would be worth while for you and me to have a discussion on this matter with Roger Hollis of MI5."

After being spirited (along with his family) to the Soviet Union by the KGB, Pontecorvo spent some time in Moscow, where, according to Popov, he was regarded as so important that he was interviewed by Lavrenti Beria, the KGB chief. Allegedly, they discussed the plutonium bomb and "the hydrogen problem." Pontecorvo then began nuclear research at a newly built institute at Dubna, about eighty miles from Moscow, and in 1952, he became a Soviet citizen. Three years later at a press conference held at Dubna, he claimed that he had left Britain because of the "witch hunts," but he could not have chosen a more damaging way of doing it. When he was eventually permitted to attend conferences in Italy and elsewhere, he declined to offer any explanation to former friends, giving the impression that he had immigrated because Russia was where he had decided to work. That may have been true, but it is possible that the KGB had scared him into defecting by warning him that he was in danger of following Fuchs to jail. The known details of his defection indicate that he was certainly contacted by the KGB while he was on vacation in Italy and under Soviet control during the defection. At that time, Soviet scientists were under great pressure from Stalin to develop an H-bomb, which would be based on derivatives of heavy water, on which Pontecorvo was a specialist.

Further, he would have been of little value as a spy once he had left Harwell for Liverpool. On the other hand, the KGB may have been warned that Pontecorvo was in some danger. Clearly, the decision to spirit him to Moscow had been made at a high level. However the defection was accomplished, the whole case was another security and political disaster during White's and Hollis's watch. For his various services, the traitor received two Orders of Lenin.

Of all the known spies who lived to experience the Soviet collapse, only Pontecorvo was honest enough to admit his folly. In 1992, a year before he died, when asked why he had defected from Great Britain to the Soviet Union and dedicated his life to the Communist cause, he replied, "The simple explanation is that I was a cretin. Communism was like a religion, a revealed religion—with myths and rites to explain it. It was the absolute absence of logic. I was naïve. After a few years I understood what an idiot I was."

The Pontecorvo story, which will not be fully resolved until the KGB archives on the subject are opened, was another tale of deception, and not only by the defector. It was a further demonstration, after the false information given to the prime minister and to the criminal court about the Fuchs case, that the secret services had no qualms about putting their parochial interests before their public duty.

CHAPTER 49

Another Volume of Deception

FOLLOWING THE PUBLIC CENSURE OF MI5 FOR ITS BLUNDERS over the Fuchs case, my former Fleet Street colleague Alan Moorehead, who had made a fine reputation as a war correspondent, became involved in a project that proved to be a further MI5 deception operation. Moorehead was to be secretly assisted by the MI5 management to write a book that would present their sanitized version of the Fuchs case and some other security disasters in another attempt to offset the severe public criticism of British security, in both Great Britain and the United States.

Released MI5 documents show that Dick White and Roger Hollis were the sponsors of the project, with William Skardon acting as chief contact. The director general, Percy Sillitoe, was induced to approve it, as several letters to and from the home secretary under his name clearly show.

More than thirty years later, when briefing Tom Bower for his official biography, Sir Dick White took responsibility for suggesting the book, eventually titled *The Traitors*, and for choosing Moorehead, whom he may have met during the war. He claimed that he had first put forward the idea in a meeting with Prime Minister Clement Attlee in defense of "the hammering we are getting in the press." White had allegedly argued that the book would help MI5's morale, which was low, and show how difficult it was to detect spies. What he also meant was that through the book, MI5 and the government would be able to distort the truth under an authoritative name.

As the director of C Branch, in charge of protective security, Hollis was responsible for any project involving publicity concerning MI5, and as he had also been the officer mainly concerned with both the May and the Fuchs cases, he was consulted regularly by White concerning Moorehead's briefings. Hollis never lost an opportunity to stress the difficulties of spotting a clever traitor to excuse the incompetence of his checks, as he had done at the tripartite conference in Washington. As the book repeated the themes of the apologia made there by Hollis, it may have been a concomitant originally suggested by him. There would have been the prospect of American sales to influence opinion there, in the hope of speeding resumption of the interchange of atomic information, though those Americans who mattered knew the truth.

Unwilling to settle into general reporting when the war ended, Moorehead had become a temporary civil servant in the public relations department of the Defense Ministry and so had signed the Official Secrets Act requirements, which could facilitate his access to classified information. A letter from Hollis to the chief official at the Home Office referred to "discussions, which led up to the decision to publish this book with Government assistance."

Moorehead was approached and offered the project, which was likely to make him enough money through sales and serialization to enable him to quit his government job, as MI5 wanted him to do, so that the author would appear to be unbiased. Documents make it clear that MI5 hoped Moorehead would have left government service by the time the book appeared, as indeed he had by the summer of 1952 when it was launched, with serialization in *The Sunday Times*. It was also understood that the book would appear to have been written entirely on Moorehead's own journalistic initiative, as it certainly did.

Moorehead accepted on condition that he could secure a succession of interviews with Fuchs, which would have been an international scoop. It was understood that when he wrote to various departments, such as the Prison Commission or Supply Ministry, for help to secure the interviews, he would make it appear that the book was his proposition. MI5 supported this pretense, as shown by a letter from its legal chief, Bernard Hill, dated March 22, 1951, to Michael Perrin (then at the Supply Ministry).

On March 6, 1951, Moorehead visited the deputy chairman of the Prison Commission, Philip Allen, and said that "for some time, he had the idea of writing a serious study of Fuchs." Without telling him that MI5 was already sponsoring the book, he said that he hoped to get factual information from MI5. Allen then wrote to Sillitoe on March 7, telling him about the project and asking him what he thought about the idea. On March 15, Sillitoe, who already knew about it, saw Allen and said that the book would have "great and outstanding propaganda value." Another pantomime was being staged with a distinguished cast.

A series of interviews with Fuchs in prison would have been a dream for any writer at that time, for it was clear that little of the true story of his historic treachery had been told at his trial. Both White and Hollis were keen for Fuchs to be interviewed as long as they were able to censor and modify Moorehead's script, which was an essential feature of the deal. A formal request to interview Fuchs was passed to the Prison Commission with a covering memo from Dick White. On April 27, 1951, however, both Moorehead and MI5 received brief replies stating that the home secretary had ruled against any interviews of the convicted spy, which would have created a precedent. In any case, Fuchs himself was not prepared to collaborate.

Moorehead was deeply disappointed at losing such a prestigious scoop but agreed to complete the book with information supplied by MI5 and other official sources.

Acting on White's instructions, Skardon visited Fuchs in Stafford Prison on November 29, 1951, to tell him of the book project and that Moorehead was being given "a certain amount of official encouragement to put the case into the correct perspective from the British point of view." He invited Fuchs to vet the chapters about himself—the next best thing to an interview—but the wily spy said only that he would consider it. Eventually, he declined to cooperate in any way.

One of the book's prime purposes, which Moorehead was required to accomplish, was to counter the growing public belief that MI5 had known that Fuchs had told an aliens tribunal in November 1939 that he had fled from the Nazis because they knew he was a Communist. MI5, and Hollis in particular, instigated a thorough search of the records in April 1951 and decided that Fuchs had not confessed his communism at the tribunal, though the official shorthand notes had been destroyed. As Fuchs was not Jewish, he seemed to have had no other reason for being a refugee, but his records showed that he had lied when originally applying for refugee status, claiming to have been persecuted by the Nazis because he was a Socialist, though this was a euphemism regularly used by Communists, the USSR being the Union of Soviet Socialist Republics.

Moorehead did what he could in the book to absolve MI5 of any blame for being unaware that Fuchs was a dedicated Communist. The truth was that MI5 had relied on old, secondhand records and had never asked Fuchs about his politics, a crucial fact withheld from the book. The author had also been encouraged to promote the myth—which the Kuczynskis, Norwood, and others had so obviously disproved—that it was "a settled rule of the Russian Intelligence Service" not to use open Communists as spies.

As *The Traitors* was virtually an official document intended for a mass audience, in America as well as Britain, and has since been widely quoted as a reliable source, and, like *Handbook for Spies,* has misled investigators, it is worthy of critical examination.

The book maintained the false belief that Fuchs, whose father was a Quaker preacher, had been invited to Britain by a Quaker, Ronald Gunn, when in fact his host was an open Soviet-oriented, atheistic Communist, as MI5 knew by that time. Gunn had written to Fuchs in prison on September 30, 1951, and MI5 had the letter in its files, but Moorehead does not seem to have been told about it or to have interviewed Gunn.

Moorehead was not informed about Sonia, though Fuchs had already positively identified her as his courier in November 1950. He was told (and wrote) that Fuchs had established contact with a Russian agent "soon after he arrived in Birmingham in 1941" and had begun passing "carbon copies" in October 1941. He was informed only that when "the woman" who became Fuchs's courier in 1942 left Banbury, after servicing the spy, she traveled by train, "no doubt for London." Long before the book was finally vetted, Sonia's former whereabouts and habits were in MI5's records, and that false information given to Moorehead was a further attempt to hide her past residence in or near Oxford. The consistent effort to conceal her true whereabouts, starting with Alexander Foote's *Handbook for Spies* in 1949, the false evidence at the Fuchs trial in 1950, followed by Moorehead's *Traitors* in 1952 and, in 1964, by the second edition of *Handbook for Spies,* indicates a degree of desperation to conceal the Oxford connection. While it was in the MI5 managers' general interest to avoid letting Parliament and the British and American people know that Sonia had spied under their noses, it was of far greater significance to Elli. Hollis was the only officer involved in all four mendacious projects. (Though Moorehead was briefed about Gouzenko, he was told nothing about Elli.)

Moorehead was also induced to state that "the woman had never been arrested" in such a way as to suggest to the reader that MI5 did not know who or where she was, when by late 1951, they knew all about her relations with Fuchs. The misinformation was given to Moorehead by Skardon, who may have been keen to hide his part in the Firs fiasco, which was never mentioned in the book. To that end, there was no mention of her brother, Jurgen Kuczynski. It was merely stated that Fuchs had been introduced to his Soviet controller by a "German refugee."

The 222-page book concentrated on Fuchs's espionage in the United States and contained little about his recruitment and basic treachery in England before he left for America. The author was assured that the agency originally responsible for hiring Fuchs had been the wartime Ministry of Aircraft Production, MI5's role having been purely advisory. He was also told that MI5 had advised the ministry that if Fuchs did give away any secret information, it was more likely to go to the Russians than to the Germans.

As an additional bonus, Moorehead was given what little MI5 then knew about the Alan May case. Since nobody had heard from Pontecorvo for two years, MI5 also took the opportunity to make use of that mystery by briefing Moorehead about it, risking a possible libel action by bracketing the missing scientist with May and Fuchs and branding him a traitor.

In his description of "the true events," Moorehead was briefed to state that Pontecorvo had been "examined a third time"—implying that this was by MI5—early in 1948, when he had applied for and been granted British nationality. In fact, he had never been properly examined at all. There had been a gross security misunderstanding between the British and Canadian authorities, with each assuming that the other had screened him when neither had! This "cock-up" was certainly known to MI5 at the time of Moorehead's briefings, because I had reported it in detail on the front page of the *Daily Express* on November 27, 1950, when it had caused some commotion in Whitehall. The entire Pontecorvo security muddle was unwittingly covered up by Moorehead.

The FBI information about Pontecorvo was known to MI5 when Moorehead was briefed on the case in 1951, but that, too, was withheld from him. Moorehead's book suggested that Pontecorvo might even be dead, when in fact he was working in the new nuclear research establishment at Dubna.

Moorehead was induced to state that all three traitors were "exceptional cases" as an excuse for MI5's failure to spot any of them. The difficulty of detecting a spy who meets a controller only occasionally was stressed as an excuse for incompetence when that was a feature of most Russian spies. *The Traitors* was also at pains to explain that the failures were due to bad luck and lack of resources.

Moorehead also pointed out that "a man who was once a communist is not, necessarily, always a communist"—a rather lame attempt to explain why the communism of Fuchs and May had not barred them from top-secret employment. In fact, all the Communists who were committed enough to betray their country remained dedicated to the cause.

The author also appeared to have accepted Fuchs's story that he had simply obeyed his conscience and sincerely regretted the damage he had done. In fact, Fuchs had always been and remained a committed Communist, doing what the party—really the GRU and KGB—not his conscience, demanded. All he ever regretted was being exposed.

Every page of Moorehead's script was vetted by MI5, and as the declassified documents show, many changes were made. At the end of his first chapter, Moorehead acknowledged help given to him by the Supply Ministry and by "scientists and officials" who had known the traitors, but naming none of them. He made no mention of MI5. Nor did he disclose that while he had been writing the book, he had been a salaried government servant. He was also at pains to state, "This is in no way an official book." He could not have been more obliging in making the MI5 operation "deniable."

An FBI document dated June 2, 1952, shows that shortly before the book was published, and without MI5's or the publisher's knowledge, the resident FBI officer in London received a full set of the galley proofs and passed them to his chief, J. Edgar Hoover. This produced an astute response describing the book as "an attempt to whitewash the previous Labour Government and the British Security Services." It ended, "The high degree of factual accuracy and the defence of British security would seem to suggest an influence of MI5 in the preparation of this book."

The Traitors was published in June 1952—and later in America— and was widely reviewed, its contents being generally accepted as fact because of Moorehead's reputation. It appeared to be no more than the results of research by a scrupulous journalist. The most interesting review was by Fuchs's closest friend and former Harwell colleague, Herbert Skinner, who had quickly spotted what he called "the whitewashing of security." He believed that to some extent, Fuchs had been driven by a power complex, enjoying "the sense of power which spying gave him." Fuchs had stated to Henry Arnold, "I *am* Harwell," though this comment seems to have been made somewhat in jest.

Letters to Moorehead from Dick White, Henry Arnold, Michael Perrin, Lord Portal, and others expressed their appreciation of the signed copies of the book that he had presented to them. Like Arnold, they all agreed that it was "to the good from the security point of view."

Fuchs's own response to *The Traitors* was relayed to me by Donald Hume, the murderer who was in prison with the spy and became friendly with him. He told me, in a long statement that I still possess, that Fuchs had confirmed that the book was "accurate only in places" and was "filled with glaring mistakes."

Moorehead, who retired to his native Australia, lodged his papers with the University of Canberra. These were consulted by Tom Bower for his biography of Dick White, and they show that the "White Knight" had briefed Moorehead on many details, some of which can be shown to have been manifestly false. For example, the MI5 warning to Fuchs's employers in August 1941 that he was more likely to betray secrets to the Russians than to the Germans was attributed by White to Jane Archer, yet Guy Liddell's diaries reveal that she had been dismissed from MI5 in November 1940. The officer who had really made that judgment was almost certainly Hollis, who had taken over responsibility for Soviet affairs in April 1941. There are other examples of White's determination to absolve Hollis of any suspicious action or inaction.

The Traitors, which is still quoted as an authoritative account of the events, is further evidence that the veracity of any book published with the connivance of MI5 is in doubt, and that applies to its own brochures. Moorehead would not be the last writer, journalistic or academic, to be deliberately misled by the MI5 management in the defense of the reputation of their service and its failures.

CHAPTER 50

Betrayal Beyond Belief

SHATTERING NEW EVIDENCE OF THE VICIOUS EXTENT OF THE treachery perpetrated by British traitors on Russia's behalf has come to light with the release of remarkable documents from Soviet archives. In 1999, at an intelligence conference at Oxford University, Oleg Tsarev, who had served in the First Chief Directorate of the KGB, presented a paper revealing that copies of the most sensitive documents concerning Britain's postwar grand strategy and defense planning had regularly arrived on Stalin's desk.

In the following year, Tsarev gave further details of this previously unknown intelligence disaster at another conference, held at the Norwegian Institute for Defense Studies in Oslo, in a paper entitled "Soviet Intelligence on British Defense Plans." The documents had been part of what had become known as Operation Unthinkable—the concept that Great Britain and the United States might need to fight the Soviet Union using nuclear weapons. Their betrayal constitutes one of the greatest espionage achievements of the Soviet intelligence service and marks yet another abject defeat of the British security system.

As Tsarev stressed, Stalin did not trust intelligence analysts and demanded to see "raw intelligence"—straight translations of the stolen reports themselves—which he read voraciously. In that way, he received five fundamental strategic documents leaked between June 1945—immediately after the Allied defeat of Germany—and July 1950. For his study, Tsarev was restricted to the period 1945–1950 and has told me that he is still not permitted to comment regarding any later documents. So the leaks may have continued into the 1960s and even beyond.

The first document reported by Tsarev was dated June 29, 1945. Under the title *The Security of the British Empire,* its sixty-seven pages laid the foundations for British military policy for many years ahead and originated from the planning staff of the chief of the Imperial General Staff (CIGS) in the War Office. The Russian records show that Stalin saw it in September—a lapse of nine weeks. The document contained the British thinking about a European defense alliance, which eventually materialized as the North Atlantic Treaty Organization (NATO). It also revealed that the Soviet Union had been fully recognized as the next aggressive opponent by the defense chiefs and that two hostile international camps were being created.

The second document, dated July 11, 1945, was called *Summary of War Results.* It was a thirty-page report that had originated in the Foreign Office but would have had a wide, but secret, distribution. It was on Stalin's desk on September 10, 1945, an interval of two months.

The third document, written in 1946 and titled *Strategic Position of the British Empire,* was prepared by Sir Alan Brooke, the former CIGS, and other staff chiefs. It originated in the War Office and reached Stalin on October 17, 1946.

Tsarev stated that there was then "a spell of nearly two years" before "yet another fundamental document landed on Stalin's desk." As Dr. Julian Lewis's excellent study *Changing Direction* records, another major document, *The Overall Strategic Plan,* had been completed in May 1947 and apparently did not leak to Moscow. This may have been due to the fact that operations by both GRU and KGB agents in Great Britain had been suspended until further orders following the Gouzenko affair. The Soviet spymasters had assumed—wrongly, as it transpired—that after the conviction of the spy Alan May, the British security authorities would make a sustained effort to detect the activities of any others.

The hemorrhage restarted with *The Strength and Structure of the British Armed Forces,* a 186-page report of intense Russian interest dated February 28, 1949. It was written by a working group from the three services and reached Stalin on August 6, a lapse of five months. A document released in 2005 showed that such studies were far from being academic exercises. In 1948, the fear of conflict with the Soviet Union was so real that the Home Office began emergency planning to intern Communists in the event of war, and the director general of MI5 was asked for assistance. The project was, in fact, still being discussed in 1954. Early in 1950, a report to President Truman by the U.S. National Security Council—NSC-68—indicated that war was inevitable unless the Soviet Union could be deterred by massive American rearmament coupled with a campaign of political, economic, and psychological warfare.

The fifth major leak was a seventy-page document, *Defense Policy and Global Strategy*, dated May 1, 1950, and approved by the Cabinet Defense Committee on May 25. It dealt with the role of nuclear weapons in both cold war and real war and reached Stalin on August 15, 1950—after about three months.

A sixth document concerning the Korean War, which was then in progress, also happened to contain an extra bonus for the Red Army. Important talks with American officials about that conflict were to take place toward the end of July 1950, and in advance, the Foreign Office provided the British participants with a fifty-page document entitled *The Foreign Office Instructions*. This reached Stalin on August 6—in about a week, probably having been specially flown to Moscow—and was of prime strategic importance because it contained an appendix referring to a Joint Intelligence Committee memorandum called "Probability of a War with the Soviet Union." As with some of the other documents, it was revealing about America's defense plans. As Tsarev put it, "Britain's special relations with the USA would, from time to time, give Soviet intelligence unique access to what the Americans thought about the contemporary situation."

In that connection, the researcher Nigel Bance, who has gained access to some archives in Moscow, has recorded two further leakages of potentially catastrophic proportions, alleged to have occurred in London on June 26 and July 26, 1948. They were documents about an American contingency plan, code-named Chevalier, for a preemptive nuclear strike on the USSR. According to Bance, the spy who supplied them was a British officer in a secret service, believed to have been MI5 because he was a close colleague of Guy Liddell's.

With all this information, Stalin had almost complete insight into Great Britain's capabilities and intentions and into some of America's. Later Russian studies of the archives may show that he and his successors—and the Red Army planners—continued to enjoy that extraordinary privilege, which was probably unprecedented in military history, offering huge advantages in the event of war.

The perpetrators of this massive treachery remain unknown because Tsarev did not have access to the original copies of the pilfered reports, which might have revealed the identities of the British spies who had provided them. He saw only the Russian translations and, as he could not find the originals in the KGB archives, assumed that they had been lost. From what he called "the circumstantial facts," he deduced that the reports could have been supplied by various members of the Cambridge group—Maclean, Philby, Burgess, and Cairncross—who happened to have encountered them. There is, however, a simpler explanation: All the documents were supplied by the same agent who operated for the GRU, where the originals may still be stored in the archives, having never left them.

Support for that possibility may be contained in Tsarev's statement that one of the reports was "sent to Stalin, Molotov and Beria on 17 October 1946." At that time, Lavrenti Beria was head of the KGB, and had it arrived at the KGB Center, he would have been shown such a prestigious coup immediately after translation to give him the option of taking it to Stalin in person, as he liked to do. Further, in both papers that Tsarev delivered in Oxford and Oslo, he was careful to give the credit not to the KGB, but only to "the Soviet Intelligence Service"—the joint name for the KGB and the GRU.

Tsarev also revealed that the copy of the report entitled *The Strength and Structure of the British Armed Forces* had another document attached to it—an analysis of that report made by the Soviet Committee on Information. This was a department of the State Defense Committee (SDC, code-named the Chiefs) to which both the KGB and the GRU submitted their prime findings for processing. Intelligence specialists working for the Committee on Information analyzed and summarized the stolen reports and passed their findings to their SDC superiors. It was the SDC that would then have recommended whether or not a report was important enough to be sent to Stalin. The fact that *all* the reports mentioned by Tsarev had been sent to the dictator looks like further evidence that they had passed through the State Defense Committee. If so, the evidence would suggest that the original source of the documents was the only other intelligence agency supplying the SDC, namely the GRU, which had received them from one or more GRU agents.

That is supported by the fact that the documents were Russian translations of the originals—just what the GRU would have supplied to the SDC. All the reports embodied the kind of military information of particular interest to the GRU and in which its agents specialized. So the originals could still be in the archives of the GRU. The Russian translations of the stolen documents would not have disclosed their British source because both the KGB and the GRU kept their sources secret from outsiders—even from the State Defense Committee—unless required to reveal them under pressure. Significantly, the private papers of Stalin and Molotov, now available for examination, do not contain the names of any intelligence sources.

In view of the Quebec conference report supplied by Sonia, she should be considered as a possible courier for some of the strategic documents. Her son has confirmed that she was still busy in 1945 before the Gouzenko disaster and later, when her contact with the Center was resumed. She made regular trips to London, where she had an efficient assistant, as chapter 80 will show.

In that case, one source could have been Elli, the GRU spy inside MI5, whose reports are known to have been passed to Stalin after translation on a regular basis. As all the reports were on the same basic subject, they may well have been supplied by the same treacherous hand, especially in view of Nigel Bance's evidence that the Chevalier documents had been supplied by an officer in a British secret service who was friendly with the senior MI5 officer Guy Liddell. There is also the confirmed knowledge that the complete plans for the D-Day landings (Overlord) had reached Moscow from a GRU source.

Evidence that copies of such strategic defense papers were sent to MI5 is given by a Joint Intelligence Committee report for April 5, 1957, released in 2006. It shows that the JIC was essentially an adviser to the Chiefs of Staff and received their reports to enable it to function in that respect. The director general of MI5 was a permanent member of the JIC and could have given sensible advice only if he had been able to study the reports issued by the Chiefs of Staff before the meetings.

The time of the pilfering of the first two reports was before the defection of Igor Gouzenko, when Elli was still active, so far as is known. Further, during part of the interval when Stalin received no reports, as

Tsarev described, Hollis was abroad in Australia, helping to set up the security agency there. The chronology shows that Hollis was in MI5's headquarters in London at all the relevant times when the documents were pilfered and, presumably, photographed by the Russians before being returned. Again, all this may have been coincidence, but no other known or suspected GRU agent fits the requirements, including the fact that he was a close colleague of Liddell's.

Whoever was responsible for these gross acts of treachery deserves eternal censure. Historians in both Russia and the West have claimed that by providing Stalin with so much secret information about his opponents' plans and capabilities, Britain's traitors happened to do the world a major service by helping to prevent war. That might be true, but it was not their prime intention, which was to subject their country and all its people to a tyrannical regime based on a bogus philosophy.

CHAPTER 51

Rigorous Scrutiny—for Some

—

IN JUNE 1947, A MIXED COMMITTEE OF U.K. MINISTERS AND officials had agreed that Communists should not be employed on any secret work because of their likely prime loyalty to the Soviet Union. On receipt of "adverse advice" from MI5, which was to be the arbiter, they should be quietly switched to posts where they would have no access to secrets. MI5 documents show that Hollis had been opposed to the process, arguing that such moves could alert such Communists to the fact that they were suspect.

This "purge procedure," as it eventually became known, was announced by Prime Minister Clement Attlee on March 15, 1948, and MI5 continued to rely on its files to provide the necessary information, as Peter Hennessy records in *The Secret State*. As a result, several scoops came my way because the general secretary of the Institution of Professional Civil Servants, Stanley Mayne, gave me the details whenever one of his members was purged. Unknown to MI5—and to me at that stage—Mayne was an ardent Communist himself and wasted no opportunity to present his comrades as victims of intolerance.

On April 5, 1950, after Fuchs had been convicted, Attlee initiated action that resulted in the establishment of the Committee on Positive Vetting under the able chairmanship of a senior Treasury official. Until then, any vetting of candidates for access to highly secret information had been negative, meaning that only files containing known information were consulted. Under positive vetting (PV), candidates would be required to provide information about any Communist connections, along with those of any close relations. The committee balked at including "brothers and sisters" but agreed that to do otherwise "would be to deviate from American practice." Those subjected to PV would also be required to name character referees, who would be questioned, and inquiries could be made about their private lives, contacts, and behavior, including illicit sexual activity, which might indicate character defect or lay them open to blackmail.

The chief MI5 representative on the committee was Roger Hollis, as director of protective security and MI5's acknowledged atomic expert. He was accompanied by his assistant Graham Mitchell—an invidious circumstance considering that both men were to come under intense MI5 suspicion of being Soviet spies.

The relevant cabinet papers, which have recently been released, clearly show that the prime purpose of the whole action was to resecure access to the American atomic weapons information totally denied since 1946, when the McMahon Act had been severely toughened by Congress, following the case of the British spy Alan May. They also reveal that it resulted from a recommendation by the tripartite conference, which Hollis had attended in 1950, urging that "in future, no-one should be given access to classified atomic energy information unless he has passed an open enquiry into his loyalty, character and background."

In that context, some of the wording in the PV Committee's secret reports was crudely honest: "We want the Americans' atomic secrets and we won't get them unless they modify the McMahon Act," followed by, "For Atomic Energy we need American help."

The fact that Hollis had been almost entirely responsible for the Fuchs debacle, which had destroyed any hope of changing Congress's mind, enhanced the peculiarity of the situation. The committee admitted that, previously, most secret government departments had relied "completely on the check provided by the Security Service [MI5] procedure," which usually had been no more than a look at the relevant file, if any. That admission, with which Hollis agreed, officially repudiated the excuse, which MI5 had made to the prime minister, that the main fault had lain with the government department employing Fuchs, as MI5 was purely advisory. The truth was that all secret departments had relied on

MI5's information and advice about security matters and that MI5 was fully aware of that.

During the committee's meetings, it was noted that the FBI's procedures for examining applicants for sensitive government posts were "extremely elaborate," with the involvement of "intensive police inquiries." In line with Hollis's liberal approach, the committee agreed that these would be "repugnant to British thinking." They also feared that the public might think the action was being taken "merely to placate the Americans." For such reasons, the possibility of keeping the introduction of PV secret from the public was seriously considered but was ruled out as impractical.

The committee's deliberations were suddenly accelerated by a firm decision by the prime minister to bypass it and introduce PV for those with access to atomic secrets, whatever its advice might be. When announcing it in October 1951, by which time the Anglo-American security issue had been seriously exacerbated by the defection of Maclean and Burgess, who had both operated in Washington, he publicly admitted that its main purpose was to restore atomic interchange with the United States. The American authorities were assured that greater precautions would be taken in future and that "any secrets they might choose to share would be more securely held."

Again, there was to be heavy reliance on advice from MI5, with "deep inquiries being passed to MI5, which would use their discretion about involving the police." Realizing that the new protective system would put a strain on his resources, Hollis pleaded for the numbers of people requiring PV to be kept as small as possible. At first, when the thinking was to restrict the system to those involved with atomic work at high levels, the number was estimated at about one thousand, but it was soon agreed that it would also have to apply to those working on guided missiles and other secret projects, with the total backlog soon exceeding ten thousand.

It was argued that the armed forces should be exempt because the background and behavior of regular officers was well-known, but in view of the hoped-for supply of atomic weapons for the RAF, and later the army and navy, it was decided that many posts in all three services would require PV, especially inside the Admiralty, War Office, and Air Ministry.

As MI5 was to be so dominantly involved in the process, committee members raised the obvious point that those officers involved in checking the security status of others should first be subjected to positive vetting themselves. Whenever that issue was mentioned, Hollis and Mitchell opposed it rigorously, arguing that both MI5 and MI6 were above suspicion, when in fact both agencies had already been penetrated by Soviet spies who had inflicted severe damage on British and American interests. The committee was not told that new recruits were taken on purely on the say-so of those recommending them and on their family and educational backgrounds.

Again, the mystique attached to MI5 and MI6 overbore the other members, and it was agreed that both agencies could make their own arrangements for vetting their staff at all levels. In the result, Hollis was to take no action whatever until shortly before his retirement in 1965, when Peter Wright urged him to PV the whole service. Friendly colleagues then went through the motions of vetting one another in the office, as several of them have described to me with some amusement. Neither Hollis nor Mitchell was ever positively vetted, and there was little on written record about either of them when they came under deep internal suspicion of being Soviet penetration agents themselves. Neither had ever been asked about any past Communist connections, which Hollis might have found awkward, especially if quizzed about his association with Claud Cockburn or Arthur Ewert. He could also have been embarrassed by questions about his illicit relationship with his secretary, which exposed him to possible Soviet pressure.

MI6 also avoided positively vetting its staff until 1963. Neither the FBI nor the CIA was informed of these exemptions and, presumably, continued to assume that their British counterparts were as meticulous as they were in vetting their staffs. Had the American authorities known that MI5 staff were not vetted, it is unlikely that General Leslie Groves would have accepted the British assurances about Fuchs. Again, whatever his motives had been, Hollis's behavior had suited the Soviet purpose.

As for those departments not so exempted, PV was restricted to people with access to information of top-secret category, but that included so many civil servants, including new recruits, that the list remained irreducible in the Foreign Office and some other heavily staffed departments owing to the steady influx of recruits as others left.

CHAPTER 52

Escape at the Double

—

HOLLIS'S FIRST OVERT SECURITY SHOCK IN HIS NEW PO-
sition came in May 1951 with the joint defection to the Soviet Union of
the Foreign Office "diplomats" Donald Maclean and Guy Burgess, who
had both worked, treacherously, in the United States. Both had widely
known character defects and Communist backgrounds, which should
have barred them from any access to classified information. Both had
become drunkards, with Maclean being subject to bouts of mindless violence, often in public, while Burgess, an aggressive homosexual, had
been reported to his superiors for wild, insulting, and indiscreet behavior. Both were well-known to Fleet Street journalists as being unstable, mainly because of their noisy and often aggressive behavior in
clubs, bars, and restaurants. By the time they fled, they were no longer
young, starry-eyed idealists but hardened traitors aged thirty-eight and
forty. They had committed most of their serious treachery during the
war, when Hollis had been responsible for monitoring and countering
all aspects of Soviet espionage. Their voluminous KGB records, made
available in the 1990s, reveal that MI5, and Hollis in particular, had
failed calamitously on all counts, though the Foreign Office was heavily
to blame for incredibly lax internal security.

Maclean's treachery had continued, catastrophically for Anglo-
American relations, in the British embassy in Washington, where he had
served from May 1944 to September 1948. While there, as fully de-

scribed in Michael Goodman's book *Spying on the Nuclear Bear*, Maclean had been "indoctrinated into the inner circle of atomic policy making." In February 1947, he had become secretary to the Anglo-American Combined Policy Committee and also knew some of its assessments of the Soviet nuclear weapons program—a matter of enormous interest to the Kremlin. His treachery was discovered only by the American decoding of KGB messages referring to a spy code-named Homer. They showed that Homer had been providing details of high-level cable traffic between the United States and Great Britain. Again, as with Fuchs, the first indication had originated in the United States. Later messages revealed that Homer had access to secret reports of conversations between Winston Churchill and the U.S. president, indicating that the spy might have then been in the British embassy.

MI5 first received news of the break in January 1949 from the FBI officer Robert Lamphere, who told me the facts as he recalled them and, later, recorded in his book *The FBI-KGB War*. As further code breaks were made, Lamphere passed them to MI5 and GCHQ, where the possible suspects were slowly narrowed down until, in March 1951, one break revealed that Homer had a pregnant wife who was staying in New York. That evidence enabled MI5 to identify Maclean, but the consequences were so horrific for Anglo-American relations that the FBI was not notified. Indeed, Lamphere told me that whenever he had asked what progress was being made, he had been assured there was nothing new to report. He stated, "MI5 double-crossed me in this matter."

The Foreign Office was also insisting that nobody be told anything in case its precious Maclean proved to be innocent. Meanwhile, the KGB was being kept fully informed of events by the ubiquitous Kim Philby. In September 1949, Philby had been given the most important field post in MI6—liaison officer with the CIA in Washington. Before he had left London, MI6 had briefed him about the Homer code breaks, and he learned more when he reached the U.S. capital. He quickly realized that Homer must be Maclean and warned the KGB Center.

With reluctance, the Foreign Office agreed that Maclean, by then posted back to Whitehall headquarters after calamitous service in Cairo and psychiatric treatment for his drunken violence, should be put under surveillance to discover any Soviet contacts before being interrogated. Though Percy Sillitoe involved himself, Dick White was effectively in command of the operation, as is now known from his statements to his biographer. The appointment of a policeman as director general had been deeply resented by White and Hollis, who isolated him whenever they could, as Sillitoe's son confirmed to me.

To assist him with the Maclean case, White chose Hollis, a few other MI5 officers, and a police officer from Scotland Yard's Special Branch. Though accepting the truth revealed by the code breaks, White seemed baffled, being unable to appreciate that a senior diplomat, then head of the American department and son of a former cabinet minister, could possibly be a traitor. It was a view even more strongly held by some of the Foreign Office mandarins.

Routine checks were quickly put in place. Maclean's office telephone was tapped and his access to top-secret papers was reduced and finally ended. His mail was intercepted and examined. The surveillance was a combined MI5 and Special Branch police responsibility and, ridiculously in retrospect, it was decided that the watchers would restrict their operations to central London. It was hoped that Maclean might be seen contacting a Soviet controller in his lunch break or on his way to the railway station. He lived at Tatsfield in Surrey, returning there by train each evening, and surveillance ceased when he boarded the train home at London's Charing Cross station. It was not resumed until he arrived back at that station next morning. The possibility that he might contact his controller outside London, even on the train, was set aside on the grounds that further surveillance was beyond the available watcher resources and that outside the capital, Maclean would spot it. That was an extraordinary decision because Soviet diplomats were entitled to travel within a radius of thirty miles of their embassy, and Tatsfield was within that distance. Telephone conversations at the Tatsfield house were monitored by the Post Office on behalf of MI5, but the likelihood that such an experienced spy would reveal anything that way was negligible. Maclean was on his guard because he had been warned of his danger— intensified by the recent impact of the Fuchs conviction—soon after Philby's tip-off to the KGB about the Homer code break. Being alerted, he had already noticed the MI5 watchers.

The KGB chiefs, who were greatly perturbed, had broken off any direct contact with him, because not only had they assumed that Maclean would be under MI5 surveillance, but their London agents had actually detected the watchers following him, noting that it ceased at the railway station. They were, however, still in regular touch with Philby in the

United States. When he told them that Maclean had finally been identified as Homer, they decided that their chief Foreign Office spy would almost certainly have to escape to the safety of Russia. They were aware that Maclean would break easily under pressure and endanger Philby, the KGB's prime secret service asset. He might also expose Anthony Blunt and other members of the Cambridge group.

On August 4, 1950, Philby's fellow spy Guy Burgess had started duty in a Foreign Office post in Washington and was lodging in Philby's house in Nebraska Avenue. Because of the interchange of intelligence information, Philby gleaned so many American secrets that he was later to state in Moscow, "I regard the position which I held in Washington as even more advantageous than my earlier post as head of the counterespionage section in London." To offload those secrets, he needed a courier, and KGB records have shown that Burgess sometimes served that purpose. Evidence indicates that it was he who took news of the Homer identification to Philby's main Soviet controller, who was based in New York, for transmission to Moscow. Later in the spring of 1951, Philby ordered Burgess to return to Britain to warn Maclean of his fate when he reported back to the Foreign Office.

To engineer his recall to London, Burgess deliberately disgraced himself by perpetrating a string of driving offenses in and around Washington, which culminated in his return to the Foreign Office in May, when he quickly visited Maclean in his office. He warned Maclean to be ready to flee to the Soviet Union under instructions that would be relayed to him, probably at short notice. The office was bugged, but having been warned of that, Burgess slipped the information to his co-conspirator in writing. In short order, Burgess was required to resign from the Foreign Service, but he had achieved his KGB objective.

Surveillance of Maclean in London was intensified in the second week of May, and the watchers reported meetings with Burgess. White—and presumably Hollis—regarded them as of no consequence, another gross misjudgment unless it was deliberate. Burgess was also liaising with Blunt, who was meeting the Soviet controller in charge of the situation and was actively involved in the escape plan. This KGB controller was Yuri Modin, who was posing as a diplomat in the Soviet embassy. There was no effective surveillance of Modin, which meant that he could meet both Blunt and Burgess in safety. In his memoirs, *My Five Cambridge Friends,* Modin confirms that Blunt was deeply involved in organizing the escape. He has also confirmed that he and his colleagues had checked on the MI5 watch on Maclean and had satisfied themselves that it ended in London.

Maclean, who had been expressing his increasing anxiety in bouts of drunkenness, was more than ready to flee rather than face the risk of imprisonment and was awaiting final KGB instructions. His condition was not improved when White ordered the watchers to make their surveillance obvious in the hope that it might panic their prey into some rash action. That ploy failed even after an MI5 car pursued a taxi containing Maclean so closely that it bumped the rear of it.

Reluctantly, the Foreign Office chiefs agreed with MI5 that, as surveillance had failed, Maclean should be interrogated, probably by William Skardon, to secure a confession or, more hopefully, a convincing denial. For that purpose, more evidence would be helpful, so White and Hollis insisted on a further period of watching and waiting. If a confession could be obtained, Maclean might be amicably disposed of by retiring on the grounds of ill health with no publicity, "in the national interest." As with Fuchs, there was no firm intention to prosecute at that stage. However, again as with Fuchs, there was a strong probability that if Maclean confessed, the U.S. authorities would insist on a trial because of the damage he had done to American interests, especially on atomic policy. The FBI could achieve that through leaked publicity, as it had done with the Gouzenko case, and congressmen could then demand retribution in the form of prosecution. In that case, a confession would be essential to avoid disclosure of the evidence of the highly secret code breaks, though, unknown to MI5, these had already been betrayed to the Russians. This likely demand for the public prosecution of a senior Foreign Office figure was a further reason for the suspension of liaison with the American security authorities about the case.

White and the Foreign Office chiefs were mainly interested in finding out how much damage Maclean might have caused, who his controllers were, and what he might know about any other spies. So interrogation would have to be lengthy and undisturbed by the pressure of publicity.

At a meeting in the Foreign Office on Monday, May 21, the MI5 chief, Percy Sillitoe, who was anxious to maintain relations with the FBI, especially after the damage inflicted by the Fuchs case, insisted that J. Edgar Hoover be fully informed of the situation, with a complete ac count of MI5's results and further intentions. Dick White, however, delayed action and continued the limited surveillance in the belief that there was still no need for haste, though warned by a Foreign Office diplomat on May 23 that he should not delay the interrogation because Maclean appeared to be "cracking up." On the afternoon of Friday, May 25, the MI5 team considered the possibility of waiting a few more weeks until Mrs. Maclean had entered the hospital to give birth so that the Tatsfield house could be searched in the hope of finding clues. However, on that day, Foreign Secretary Herbert Morrison signed his formal approval for an interrogation of Maclean by MI5. Maclean was to be confronted on the morning of Monday, May 28, probably in a friendly way, seeking his assistance in resolving certain issues, with hostile questioning to come later.

At that stage, White, Hollis, and the Foreign Office chiefs had all realized that Maclean had spotted the London watchers. Nevertheless, he was allowed to go home for the weekend as usual. Whether through leakage of the Monday confrontation from one of the several who knew about the plans for it or yet another coincidence, the KGB Center had already decided that Maclean must defect on the evening of that very Friday, May 25. Maclean was supposed to be on duty in London on the Saturday morning, but realizing that his absence would be noted too soon for safety, he arranged to be excused on a domestic pretext. His request was granted by the Foreign Office as soon as asked without MI5 being informed. (The high-level official who granted it, Roger Makins, who liked Maclean, decided there was no risk because he believed the suspect was under MI5 surveillance around his country home as well as in London!)

The KGB was insisting that Burgess should also defect with Maclean, because the Center had decided that both were "burnt out" for any further use. It was clear to them that Burgess could also crack under interrogation and expose Philby, Blunt, and the rest. It now seems possible, from KGB sources, that Burgess was cynically tricked into accompanying Maclean by a promise that he could return one day, but in fact, both were to be held in Russia until they died. However, as will be seen, Burgess was aware that he might be away for a long time.

Yuri Modin has claimed that the decision to spring the pair on the Friday had nothing to do with any knowledge of the interrogation date and was just a fluke circumstance, a weekend being the obvious time to stage it. He has also claimed that while walking along Oxford Street on the evening of Wednesday, May 23, he happened to see an advertisement for weekend boat trip tours to the Brittany coast in a travel agent's window. He allegedly passed the information to Burgess, who bought the tickets on the following day. Burgess then hired a car. In another version, however, Modin said that it was Blunt who suggested the cross-Channel cruise ship. Blunt, who was always anxious to save his own skin, was so close to Modin that he may have known Burgess would never return. Safe behind the iron curtain, Burgess could never be interrogated and betray anybody.

As Friday, May 25, happened to be Maclean's thirty-eighth birthday, some friends joined him for lunch in Soho. The shrewdly observant Cyril Connolly, who met him and some of his guests in the street, told me of the encounter shortly after the defection and, later, described it in *The Missing Diplomats.* He stated that Maclean had seemed "mellow" and had talked confidently about his future and his expected child.

There is witness evidence that Burgess was aware he might not be making a quick return. Early on the Friday, he had telephoned the country home of his close friend Goronwy Rees, who was staying in Oxford for a few days. When Mrs. Rees answered the call, Burgess told her he was about to do something that would "shock many people" and that they would not be meeting again, perhaps for a long time. Maclean was also aware by that time that they would be defecting very shortly, as he later admitted.

In the early evening, Burgess drove to the Macleans' home at Tatsfield. The two men had dinner with Maclean's wife, who had always known her husband was a Soviet agent and had accepted that he must defect, though she was due to give birth within three weeks. The traitors then drove to Southampton, eighty miles away, allegedly leaving Tatsfield so late that they arrived at the dockside with only minutes to spare. They abandoned the car, boarded the boat, and left it at Saint-Malo, apparently being entirely sure that they were not being followed. The source of this assurance has never been established, but the KGB was clearly confident that Maclean would not be under surveillance of any kind. The MI5 officer Peter Wright told me later that when he and his colleagues reexamined the facts of the defection, they regarded it as "incredible" that Maclean had not been under surveillance over the weekend before he defected, suspecting that the situation might have been contrived by White and Hollis.

Investigations later showed that after the boat docked at Saint-Malo at eleven forty-five on the following day, the defectors disembarked, ostensibly to explore the town, while leaving their luggage aboard. It has generally been believed that they went to Rennes by taxi and then to Paris by train, took another train to Switzerland, and then flew to Prague, meeting KGB officers who organized the rest of the journey to Soviet territory.

Allegedly, the Foreign Office did not learn of Maclean's flight until the late morning of Monday, May 28, when his wife was telephoned because he had not arrived for work. She announced that her husband was missing. In a series of prearranged lies that were completely believed, Mrs. Maclean said that her husband had disappeared with a man she did not know who had called himself Styles. By that time, the traitors were beyond recovery.

A call from the Foreign Office to White was officially the first that MI5 knew that the bird had flown. The defection, then officially thought to involve only Maclean, caused alarm and consternation. The first reaction in all departments, including Downing Street, was to cover up the disaster from the public and from everyone else not in the know for as long as possible. Even the foreign secretary was not told of the defection of two officials from his department for four days! Later, he was to express his indignation about how little he had been told and say, "It was a remarkable coincidence that I should have given that order on 25th May and they went missing on the night of 25th May."

Clinging to straws, White and his colleagues suggested that their quarry had simply gone on a drunken spree. Later on the Monday, Special Branch reported that a car abandoned at Southampton dock had been hired by Guy Burgess, allegedly adding to White's bewilderment. Slowly, they realized—or affected to—that they were probably dealing with not one traitor, but two.

White decided that he would follow the trail to France and seek the help of the French police. In continuing slapstick style, he arrived at London Airport with an out-of-date passport, a professional blunder of which any Fleet Street foreign correspondent would have been ashamed. After a delay for a new passport to be issued, he went to Paris for a few futile days, and the French police were to complain that they had been alerted far too late.

Meanwhile, Sillitoe's deputy Guy Liddell, who had been over-friendly with Burgess, had asked Blunt, who was also a friend, to obtain the keys to Burgess's apartment, as this would avoid obtaining a search warrant from the Home Office—a process that would alert more people about the defection. Blunt used the opportunity to search the apartment and remove a revealing telegram from Philby and letters that compromised himself and could have led to his immediate interrogation. This sending of one Soviet spy to assist in the investigation into the disappearance of two others was MI5 farce at its most farcical.

On his return from France, White set up a small team to carry out a "postmortem." It included Hollis and his deputy in C Branch, Graham Mitchell. When eventually, with Foreign Office agreement, MI5 questioned Mrs. Maclean on May 30—five days after the defection—it was done by the famed William Skardon. As he had with Sonia, he assured White that she was innocent. The Maclean house was never searched—presumably to avoid distress to Mrs. Maclean.

Maclean's brother, Alan, who also worked for the Foreign Office, was next to be interviewed by Skardon, posing as "Jim Sneddon." He was questioned about Burgess and told about his sister-in-law's account of the flight, which Skardon appeared to have swallowed, as Alan Maclean recorded in his memoirs.

Though information incriminating Burgess flowed in from his friends, including Blunt, who lied convincingly, as usual, White said that he could not bring himself to believe that such a loudmouthed, dirty, promiscuous homosexual as Burgess could ever have been a spy. Nor could he accept Maclean as an ideological spy, as Fuchs had been. As his immediate chief, Guy Liddell, had been Burgess's friend, White is said to have suspected that he had tipped him off in time for the two to defect!

That scenario is the authorized version of "the Great Escape," as told by British authorities, by White in his biography, and by some academics. There are, however, so many discrepancies and peculiarities that it is difficult to believe, even with the acceptance that MI5 was prone to monumental "cock-ups." A different scenario, which would explain them all, is demanded by recently discovered information.

CHAPTER 53

A More Credible Scenario?

W HEN WHITE, HOLLIS, AND THE FOREIGN OFFICE CHIEFS finally accepted that Maclean must be a long-term Soviet spy, their reactions were the same. Their first priority was to decide what would be best for the good name of the Foreign Office throughout the world and the reputation of MI5 with the public, within Whitehall, and with Washington. The last was crucial in view of the need to reestablish trust after the all too recent security disasters of the Fuchs and Pontecorvo cases. Among the few in the Foreign Office who were aware of the appalling problem, there was disbelief, set in concrete, that anyone so senior, so clever, and from such an impeccable background could possibly be a traitor. In any case, the immediate requirement was to contain the situation and take no irreversible action for as long as possible. In this, the Foreign Office was fully supported by White and Hollis, who throughout their careers put high priority on preserving the best possible relations with all Whitehall mandarins and senior politicians. In this endeavor, White's natural charm and "coolness under fire" earned him a splendid reputation where it mattered most.

In assuring the Foreign Office chiefs that there appeared to be no reason for haste in interrogating Maclean, White had preferred to please them at the risk of offending the FBI, and Hoover in particular. Had the Americans not been involved, through having supplied the original code breaks, the whole affair could have been hushed up. That such a move was feasible within the closed confines of Whitehall was to be proved in 1963 when the traitor Anthony Blunt would be offered immunity from prosecution and publicity—a deal for "eliminating him amicably," which remained secret for sixteen years and through several governments. In that same year, even Kim Philby was offered immunity, and my conversations with Peter Wright showed that for many years, within MI5, there had been a climate of opinion that any home-bred spies should be offered secret-for-all-time immunity in return for a confession, however minimal.

Knowing White and others who knew him better, I have no doubt that he would have agreed to such a course for Maclean—in the national interest and to please his political masters. The future prime minister Harold Macmillan sincerely believed that whatever the information passed to the Russians by Maclean and Burgess, it was less damaging than what he called the "demoralization" caused by public knowledge of their treachery. To have risked offending the Americans, as White did, the stakes had to be great, and they were. The prospect of the trial and imprisonment of a senior diplomat, with the attendant worldwide publicity and speculation, was unprecedented and terrifying, especially in view of what he might reveal. If some way could be found of avoiding such horrors, it would have the approval of senior government ministers, who would be spared their share of the ignominy of another spy case, which is never good for votes or political image.

In fiction, and possibly in fact in former times, the ideal solution would have been to give Maclean a revolver and expect him to do the decent thing, but they all had to be realistic and appreciate that the American involvement required some more conventional action. The MI5 chief, Percy Sillitoe, the "honest cop," favored the due process of law, but White continued to ask, What action would do the least damage to the nation and to all those more intimately concerned, including himself and his close colleagues?

A possible scenario presents itself: If Maclean could not be eliminated, that other age-old penalty—banishment—might be the next best solution. With the fortuitous existence of the iron curtain, he might be banished forever, far out of sight of lawyers, the public, and especially the probing media.

Ideally, Maclean should decide to banish himself—to defect to save himself from ignominy and the misery of a long prison sentence. It might even be possible for this to happen in such a way that his treachery could be kept secret, or at least be not provable, for many months, maybe years, should that also suit the KGB, as it well might. It could be officially stated that he had simply disappeared and that nobody knew where he had gone, as had happened with Pontecorvo, about whom the Russians had said nothing. In that context, much could be made of the recent breakdown of Maclean's health, for which there was evidence in the shape of drunken and violent behavior. There would be speculation, but that could be contained by bland official statements and, as long as there was no certainty, by the laws of libel, especially if it could be hinted that for all anyone knew, Maclean might one day return. His disappearance would deprive MI5 of discovering any accomplices, but that would be a small price compared with the horrors of a trial.

The damage that had already been assessed—and it was realized that there was probably much more—had revealed the extent of his widespread access to secrets of supreme interest to the Kremlin. Declassified American documents have since shown that during his stint in the Washington embassy, he had given the KGB such a vast amount of political atomic intelligence that, as an American source put it, "practically everything was compromised." He had also betrayed British and American codes and ciphers. Nevertheless, sending him to prison would not repair the damage. Instead, the publicity would inflict more in all directions, especially on Anglo-American relations. So a disappearance, which would prevent a trial, would be preferable on all counts. The FBI would complain that MI5 had been incompetent in allowing Maclean to escape, but that would be a worthwhile trade-off, especially as it could be pointed out (as it eventually was) that without the evidence to arrest him, he could travel wherever he liked under British law.

To expedite such a desirable solution, MI5 and the Foreign Office would need to take actions that would appear to show the U.S. authorities that Maclean had been subjected to the expected measures. The first secret step would be to make their quarry aware that he was under deep suspicion and in danger of arrest. This could be done by instructing the watchers, who were keeping Maclean under surveillance, to make sure he spotted them—as indeed both they and he did. (Shortly after Burgess's return from Washington, Maclean lunched with him at the RAC Club in Pall Mall, where he confided that he knew he was being tailed.) The watchers might wonder about such an odd requirement, but that could be justified—as indeed it was—by explaining that Maclean was so near breakdown that the purpose was to panic him into some rash act that would betray him.

Of course, if Maclean was to defect successfully, he could not be under surveillance at his home, for that would require telling the watchers to let him escape, which would have been impossible to justify to them. That problem, however, could be resolved at a stroke—as indeed it was—simply by instructing the watchers to cease their operations as soon as Maclean caught the train home. The watchers could be told that surveillance around Tatsfield would be too difficult. As a further stimulus, which Maclean was unlikely to miss, the circulation of top-secret papers to him could be ended—as it was.

A serious problem would have remained, however: Maclean needed to be absolutely sure that nobody would be tailing him when he fled his home at Tatsfield and that he would have at least forty-eight hours to reach safety. Once he knew that he was suspect, such an experienced spy would have expected to be under surveillance anywhere, but both he and Burgess behaved as though they had been assured that outside London, they were in no danger and could plan accordingly.

White could not easily have put the crucial information that Maclean was entirely free from supervision in his direction, but Hollis could have done so. The watchers had reported meetings between Burgess and Maclean. Hollis was aware that Burgess, whom he knew from his MI5 connections and their joint membership of the Reform Club, was such a close friend of Blunt's that they seemed almost inseparable. As will be seen, he probably knew that Blunt had journeyed to Southampton on May 7 to meet Burgess on his return from Washington and that Burgess had spent that night in Blunt's apartment.

Hollis had been friendly with Blunt during the war, when they were both in MI5, and they had kept in touch at their clubs. Hollis also attended some of Blunt's art lectures at the Courtauld Institute and had a professional reason for seeking contact at any time. MI5 had even arranged with Blunt to use a room at the Courtauld for interviewing agents.

When interrogated in 1969, Hollis was to admit meeting Blunt "now and again" at Pall Mall clubs. As Blunt would later confess, he was adept at keeping himself informed about MI5's operations through gossip with old colleagues who were still in the British Security Service, trusted him, and valued his advice. Indeed, as will be seen, this source of leakages would be cited by a prime minister (Margaret Thatcher) in an attempt to account for serious security breaches.

So well-chosen gossip between Hollis and Blunt, over a drink, could have done the trick, for it could have included the news that Maclean was to be interrogated and exactly when. All that was then needed was for Blunt to tell Burgess, on which Hollis could have banked, knowing, too, that Burgess was seeing Maclean.

In 2001, significant witness evidence that Hollis was in direct contact with Blunt at the relevant time was discovered by Miranda Carter during research for her thorough biography *Anthony Blunt: His Lives*. Shortly after the double defection, one of Blunt's friends, an art student who had been one of his lovers in the late 1940s, joined him for dinner at the Reform Club and found Hollis sitting there with him. The witness had met Hollis once before, at a Courtauld Institute lecture. Later, he remarked to Miranda Carter that seeing them together in the Reform Club at that time had made him suspect that Hollis might have been involved in the spies' escape. From the questions that Blunt and Hollis asked him, he came to think they were trying to find out how much he suspected.

Whether Hollis and White had ever suspected that Burgess might also defect is unknown, but when he did so and it seemed likely that he, too, had been a long-term Soviet spy, his departure could have been seen as a bonus and a reason for mutual congratulation. What is certain is that over the ensuing years, Hollis was to be extremely sensitive to the possibility that Maclean or Burgess might claim to reveal something derogatory about him, Dick White, or high-level Foreign Office men— so much so that he called me in to help nullify any damaging statements, as will be seen. He was also to be extremely lenient toward Blunt when he was exposed as a most dangerous traitor in 1963 and remained concerned that one day Blunt might volunteer some revelations out of spite.

During the weeks of fruitless surveillance of Maclean, White would have been concerned about the growing delay in informing the FBI about the progress—or lack of it—being made. On May 21, Percy Sillitoe had insisted that a full account of MI5's action on the Maclean case should be passed to Hoover, but the voluminous FBI records of the Maclean and Burgess defection show that it never reached anyone in the FBI. Those records, now on the Internet, were meticulously researched by John Costello, and they showed that Hoover and the FBI officer most deeply concerned, Robert Lamphere, did not even know that Maclean had been pinpointed by MI5 as Homer until told of his defection. It has been assumed that Philby, who was still in Washington, intercepted the information before it reached the FBI, but that would not have been possible. Lamphere assured me (in a letter) that the link between MI5 and the FBI was not Philby, but MI5's own man in Washington, Geoffrey Patterson. On someone's instructions in London, the information had never been sent. Later, an MI5 officer, Arthur Martin, apologized to Lamphere for this breach of faith, claiming that the pressure had come from the Foreign Office.

As a cover, within the Foreign Office a false rumor was being circulated indicating that the holdup in the whole operation had been due to Hoover's delay in approving Maclean's interrogation. According to his biography, White had a reason for keeping Hoover in the dark. He claimed to have been worried that Hoover might, in fact, interfere by taking some precipitate action of his own, though according to Lamphere, this would have been most unlikely.

On all counts, then, there was need to stimulate Maclean into defecting without delay. What better way than to let him know, through some intermediary, that he was to be handed over to MI5 in the immediate future, probably when he returned to the office on Monday, May 28? By whatever means this may have been achieved, Maclean seems to have been made aware of it in good time. The researcher Anthony Cave Brown, who interviewed Modin in connection with his book *Treason in the Blood*, recorded in 1994 that Modin admitted knowing that Maclean's interrogation was imminent and that he had "acted from information received."

The easy explanation is to invoke yet another tip-off from Philby, who was still in Washington, but a study of the time scales makes this most unlikely. Those of us, like John Costello, who have made a detailed examination of the circumstances have been driven to the view that if Maclean did receive a final warning, it had originated from someone inside MI5. It could easily have reached Maclean through further gossip between Hollis and Blunt.

The generally accepted scenario of the escape has been undermined by crucial new information discovered in the KGB archives in 1993. As Tsarev and Costello record in *Deadly Illusions*, instructions detailing exactly how Maclean should make his escape, along with Burgess, were sent by the KGB Center to the London embassy on May 17, 1951—eight days before the double defection. Such action was altogether more in keeping with the KGB's professionalism. The concept that two such emotionally fragile and alcohol-dependent figures as Maclean and Burgess would be required to make their way unescorted across Europe—with so much to lose if the defection failed—makes little sense. In his autobiography, the KGB defector Oleg Gordievsky recalls some of his KGB colleagues being involved in planning the escape.

In 2003, further information from another KGB source was reported by Nigel Bance in his book *Ultimate Deception*. The source claimed that the two defectors were met almost immediately by KGB officers in Saint-Malo and driven to Bordeaux, where a Soviet freighter was berthed. The claim is in keeping with the firm control required by the KGB Center and the use of such a freighter to spirit Philby, another drunk, out of Beirut twelve years later. Convincing, independent witness evidence of this is recorded in *The Great Spy Scandal*, published in 1955.

The last-minute arrival of the defectors was observed by another passenger, William Lyons, a Londoner who was on a business trip. He noted that the two, whom he later recognized as Maclean and Burgess, were greeted by another man, already on board. He recalled that it was raining so heavily when the ship docked at Saint-Malo that the three men were the only passengers who immediately ventured ashore. There was a car waiting, and it quickly whisked the three away.

Once the defection instructions had been received by the KGB chief in London, a few days would have been needed to involve Modin, Blunt, and any others who may have been concerned. Time would also have been required to get the freighter in place. With British habits concerning the weekend in mind, a Friday night would have been the ideal time to set the escape in motion. So May 25 might have been the date set by the KGB Center, or the planned date, possibly for the following weekend, may have been brought forward following a leak about the intended interrogation of Maclean on May 28.

Precisely what happened at Tatsfield on that Friday evening may never be known, because the only evidence came from Mrs. Maclean, who was part of the plot and has since remained silent about it. In Robert Cecil's biography of Donald Maclean, *A Divided Life*, he recorded that after Mrs. Maclean eventually joined her husband in Russia she met the

Moscow-based correspondent of the London *Daily Worker*, Sam Russell, there and told him "she knew what Donald had been doing and had co-operated." Later Russell confirmed that to Cecil, who discovered she had made similar statements to others once safely behind the iron curtain. Yuri Modin has revealed that Maclean had been reluctant to leave his wife so near to childbirth until she had agreed that he must escape without delay. Her part would have been rehearsed, and she played her role faultlessly, having been assured that she would be able to join her husband. It seems likely that Maclean did go home on the Friday evening, but other aspects of Mrs. Maclean's evidence are suspect. Here were two seasoned spies on a carefully planned mission crucial to themselves as well as to their fellow spies. The journey to Southampton in premotorway days could be long in time, and if they missed the boat, their freedom could be at stake. So the story that the two fugitives had a leisurely meal at Maclean's house and then left so late that they nearly missed the boat is hard to believe. It would seem much more likely that they arrived in good time and holed up close by the dock in the car, boarding the ship as late as possible. The story that Modin, under great pressure to arrange the escape at short notice, happened to see the advertisement for the Saint-Malo trip while strolling down Oxford Street also overstretches belief. The planning seems to have been much more deliberate, and the KGB archival information that the Center sent details of the escape plan to London on May 17 is evidence that Modin's account was disinformation.

White's unlikely theory that Maclean was just on a drunken spree provided the excuse for a further forty-eight-hour delay, which gave the defectors time to get to the safety of Soviet custody aboard ship. His belated trip to Paris to consult with the French police looked like resolute action but served only to build in yet more delay, as did his passport farce.

There is some evidence that an immigration officer at Southampton recognized Maclean and reported his presence to MI5 headquarters around midnight. If that is ever confirmed, it would infer that the immigration officer had been warned to look out for the runaway. Since no action was then taken by MI5, it would support the contention that the defection was "managed." This was the view that quickly prevailed inside the FBI.

CHAPTER 54

A List of Nine

—

WHETHER WHITE OR HOLLIS KNEW THAT BURGESS WOULD flee with Maclean is uncertain, but I have evidence from two prime witnesses that the MI5 story that nobody suspected Burgess and that he was never under surveillance is untrue. According to Pamela Synge, a member of MI5 who was involved in the saga, one of the first actions after receiving news that Homer was probably British was an examination of the document that had been submitted by the would-be KGB defector Konstantin Volkov. It was seen that Volkov had offered to give leads to seven Soviet agents, five in British intelligence and two in the Foreign Office. Under the guidance of Guy Liddell, nine possible suspects were selected, and they were all put under some degree of physical and telephone surveillance for several weeks. Of those who were on this "List of Nine," as the operation became known, the only three who matter for this discussion are Donald Maclean, Guy Burgess, and Anthony Blunt.

Independent confirmation that Burgess had been under some degree of surveillance for months came my way in 1982, when a former army officer, Richard Birch-Reynardson (whom I met grouse shooting), told me how he had been posted to Washington, solely to keep a secret watch on Burgess. Before going there, in the summer of 1950, he had been summoned by the War Office to a meeting with a security officer (probably from MI5) in a building near Berkeley Square. He was told that social opportunities would be created so that he would meet Burgess frequently at embassy parties and other occasions and was required to curry friendship with him. He was instructed to report on his activities and conversations, with the names of his friends and contacts.

Birch-Reynardson demurred when warned that Burgess was a lecherous homosexual but was assured that his military duty did not require him to oblige in that capacity. For several months, he functioned as an aide to General Neil Ritchie, head of the British military mission at the Pentagon, as cover for his real mission. This device enabled Burgess to be watched without informing either the Foreign Office or the FBI. However, apart from occasions when Burgess was drunk or rowdy, the officer saw nothing detrimental and was later convinced that the spy had been warned of his situation in advance. As soon as Burgess was ordered home in the spring of 1951, Birch-Reynardson was recalled and his post with General Ritchie was abolished.

Dick White is not supposed to have had any indication that Burgess was a Soviet spy until June 6, twelve days after the defection, but that conflicts with the events put on record by Goronwy Rees himself in his book *Chapter of Accidents*. On Saturday, May 26, the day after the flight, Burgess's live-in boyfriend had telephoned Mrs. Rees at her home in Sonning in some distress to say that Burgess was missing. Rees learned this from his wife when he returned home from Oxford on the evening of May 27, along with details of a call from Burgess on the previous Friday, warning that he was about to shock his friends and might not be seeing them for a long time. Rees immediately feared that his friend, who had once told him he was a Comintern agent, had defected to Moscow.

He therefore telephoned the MI6 officer David Footman, who was a friend of Burgess's, and told him the facts, also asking him to inform MI5. Footman did so by speaking to Guy Liddell at his home. Next day—Monday—Footman informed Rees that Liddell would be contacting him. Late on the Sunday evening, Rees had also telephoned his friend Blunt to tell him that he believed Burgess had defected to Russia. Blunt claimed to be "greatly distressed" by the news and raced down to Rees's home next day, when he tried hard and long to talk him out of reporting anything to MI5 and especially of revealing that Burgess had once admitted his Comintern connection. Blunt knew that as barely forty-eight hours had elapsed since the escape, the two traitors might not yet be safe. Neither he nor any of his co-conspirators wanted any intrusion by anyone who might alert the media about the defection if MI5 confirmed it to him. On the following day—Tuesday—Blunt also informed Liddell of Rees's suspicion regarding Burgess.

The subsequent behavior of the MI5 officials was peculiar, to say the least. Supposedly, White, Hollis, and company were desperate for information about Maclean's disappearance, and by Monday afternoon, they knew from Special Branch that Burgess had gone with him. Rees clearly had information about Burgess that was highly relevant, and though Footman had already passed that on to them, efficient investigators would have lost no time in interrogating Rees firsthand. Instead, they delayed any formal meeting with him at MI5 headquarters until June 6—eight days later.

A few days before that encounter, Rees had been softened up at an informal lunch meeting with Liddell. To his surprise, Rees also found Blunt there. The situation in which Liddell was grilling Rees about the escape of two Soviet spies in the company of another who had just helped to organize it—and would probably report the conversation to the KGB that night—was grotesque even for MI5. It surely makes the concept that Hollis was consulting Blunt before the defection easier to accept.

On June 6, Rees visited MI5 headquarters in Curzon Street by formal invitation and was confronted by White, who according to his biographer disliked him on sight. He was told that Burgess had indeed disappeared and was officially told that Maclean had gone, too. In fact, Rees's information, which MI5 had chosen to ignore, had been deadly accurate on all counts. Rees then stated that Burgess was a Communist and Soviet agent, adding that he had assumed MI5 had been aware of it. White and Liddell still doubted that the Russians would employ such an indiscreet and reckless man, though the Foreign Office had chosen to do just that.

Rees had been frightened out of initiating any publicity, but that proved to be of no consequence. On that same day, June 6, the news that a hunt was on in Europe for two missing Foreign Office diplomats had been secured by the resident *Daily Express* correspondent in Paris, and when his dispatch arrived I was immediately involved in following up the lead. Inquiries in Paris had produced the names of the fugitives along with the belief that they had reached Soviet territory.

MI5 had a secret informant in every Fleet Street office and was quickly tipped off that a front-page scoop to be headlined YARD HUNTS TWO BRITONS and indicating that they had gone to Russia would be appearing the following morning, but without the names because of legal concerns about libel. (An MI5 file released in March 2007 states that the distinguished *Daily Express* journalist Sefton Delmer volunteered "covert co-operation on the case.") News of the break was quickly flashed by MI5 to Washington, where the FBI chief, J. Edgar Hoover, realized what had happened and concluded, with justification, that he had been deliberately kept in the dark. The CIA chiefs, who had been told nothing, immediately suspected that the defection had been assisted by the British security authorities, the subsequent newspaper accounts being part of a calculated deception.

Late in the evening of June 6, news of the imminent *Daily Express* scoop also reached Prime Minister Clement Attlee's chief press adviser, who was dining at his London home with his wife and a guest. He was the pro-Soviet former journalist Philip Jordan, whose book *Russian Glory* had so impressed Hollis. After a year's stint in Washington as the British embassy press officer, where he had become very friendly with Maclean, Jordan had been promoted to the Downing Street post in 1947, having been cleared for both positions probably by Hollis himself. In his exalted and influential position, Jordan would have needed some continuing link with MI5.

On receiving the news on the telephone probably from MI5—Jordan returned to his dinner table "ashen-faced," according to Kitty Muggeridge, who was the guest. "Philip looked so tragically ill that it seemed the bottom had dropped right out of his world," Kitty told Andrew Boyle, who recorded it in his book *The Climate of Treason*. That same night, Jordan cried out from his bed, and his wife found him dead. He was forty-eight. His death certificate indicated natural causes. Later, when the writer Malcolm Muggeridge, Kitty's husband, invited Attlee to attend a memorial service for Jordan and to provide a discretionary pension for his widow, the prime minister responded with a peremptory "No!" on both counts.

Jordan had been in regular contact with Maclean in London, as evidence given in *The Climate of Treason* revealed. As Attlee's media adviser, had Jordan been told, or learned, of the home secretary's agreement of May 25 that Maclean should be interrogated? Had he also been a guest at Maclean's birthday lunch? The future release of cabinet and MI5 documents may answer these questions.

On June 7, after the appearance of the *Daily Express* disclosure, the Foreign Office named the runaways but tried to limit the damage by issuing a misleading statement. It claimed that Maclean had suffered a breakdown "owing to overstrain," when by that time it was clear to White and others that a consoling telegram from Paris to Mrs. Maclean had been sent by Soviet intelligence. It seemed immediately obvious that to have deserted his pregnant wife, Maclean, whose Communist sympathy was quickly discovered by the newspapers, must have fled under extreme pressure. It was also obvious that Maclean had fled as a result of something he had learned when Burgess had returned from America. Burgess's association with Blunt was also quickly discovered by the media.

The publicity was massive and continued literally for years, as I was visually reminded in 2005 by the FBI's release of all its cuttings from British and American newspapers, labeled "Philby, Burgess, Maclean." As released Foreign Office and cabinet papers have confirmed, the effect on Anglo-American intelligence relations so soon after the Fuchs and Pontecorvo disasters was catastrophic. U.S. press criticism was very severe, with calls for pressure on the British Foreign Office to "clean house." Maclean's involvement in "atomic affairs" was soon made public, with leading American politicians stressing its seriousness for Anglo-U.S. relations. The consternation was quickly compounded in the media by the search for a "third Man," who had allegedly warned Maclean that he was about to be interrogated.

On June 11, Parliament was given a noncommittal cover-up statement by the foreign secretary. The government also claimed, with monstrous falsehood, that neither Maclean nor Burgess had been given access to top-secret information. Meanwhile, Hoover was furious that Maclean had escaped, having discovered that during his stint in Washington, the traitor had been allowed unescorted access to the U.S. Atomic Energy Commission's headquarters. He had been the Kremlin's man at important meetings about the Korean War and was aware of targets that General Douglas MacArthur had or had not permission to destroy—information that Maclean was eventually to regard as perhaps his greatest coup.

In an attempt to pacify Hoover, Percy Sillitoe flew to Washington. His son Tony told me that when his father had called for the relevant files before leaving, Hollis had said they were unavailable. The documents that the MI5 chief took with him had been deliberately doctored to reduce the time when MI5 had first targeted Maclean and in other ways. The gambit did not fool Hoover. Fortunately for Sillitoe, he had previously agreed on a deal with Hoover that the FBI and MI5 would each make no public statements about the activities of the other without consultation and agreement. Privately, however, Hoover accused MI5 of stupidity in allowing Maclean to escape, in failing to spot the link with Burgess, and for its laxity over the positive vetting of officials. Sillitoe took the chastisement with little response, reporting that Hoover had been "co-operative." Meanwhile, MI5 and the Foreign Office took another sustained hammering from the media in both Great Britain and the United States.

The early suspicion of Blunt (whose code name on the List of Nine was Blunden) is also contrary to the official story, which claimed that he had never been suspect until after his friend Burgess had defected. Pam Synge, who took part in the telephone tapping, told me that all that resulted from the surveillance of Blunt was disclosure of his unsavory private life with "rough trade," so he was struck from the list. However, the fact that he had been suspect as a possible spy before the dual escape enhances the concept that Hollis used him as a means of warning Burgess and Maclean that it was safe for them to defect. It is now known from Blunt's own evidence and KGB material that he, too, was urged by the Center to defect, because he knew about Philby and other spies, but he was so confident of surviving any MI5 interrogation that he declined.

A recently released MI5 file has disclosed that in September 1951, White's counterespionage branch received information that Blunt was a committed Communist. The information had derived from Moura Budberg, a London socialite who was an acquaintance of Blunt's and had Soviet connections, having once been the mistress of the writer Maxim Gorky. She had also been friendly with both Maclean and Burgess, so her tip—stated at a social gathering—should have been taken seriously. Instead, some unnamed officer in MI5 decided that as the information was "insufficiently reliable," no mention of it should be attached to Blunt's file. This blunder—if that is what it was—was reminiscent of MI5's fatal decision to disregard as "tainted" the early tip that Fuchs was a Communist. It meant that when Blunt was first interrogated in late 1951, there was no mention of Moura Budberg, who could have been interviewed. The MI5 file also revealed a further reason why she should have been questioned about Blunt. In a letter addressed to White in January 1951, MI5 had been told that Moura Budberg had been a Soviet agent herself, and the management had spent a lot of money and time keeping her under surveillance. That should have increased the likelihood that she knew significant details about all three traitors, but the opportunity to question her had been lost.

White frequently observed, "One of the things to be learnt about spying is that the least likely is the most probable." What would seem to be least likely to the ordinary citizen is the extraordinary fact that while every major traitor in the Cambridge group was exposed in his lifetime, not one of them was arrested and put on trial. Coincidence? I hardly think so. Nor would it seem to be a coincidence that the MI5 papers on the double defection have not yet been released after more than fifty years.

In America, where Hoover immediately ordered a full-scale investigation into the activities of Maclean and Burgess during their stay in the United States, the double defection intensified the distrust of Great Britain's reputation in security, intelligence, and political circles, which persisted for years. A U.S. security memorandum concerning the case dated October 26, 1955, was to state that both spies seemed to have been "protected from exposure and dismissal for a long time by other highly placed officials in the British Government."

An assisted defection for Maclean—an extreme form of "amicable elimination"—may be interpreted as having been purely in the interests of MI5, the Foreign Office, the government, and those officials and politicians whose reputations would have been damaged to a greater degree by an open trial. Nevertheless, Soviet intelligence benefited hugely by the international demonstration to its other spies and agents that in the event of exposure, they could be rescued even at the last minute, with the added bonus of total concealment of the details of their treachery.

In spite of their seemingly incompetent performances against the Soviet opposition, both White and Hollis received one promotion after another. Being senior, White was able repeatedly to secure promotion for his friend. If both had been involved in a deception operation to facilitate Maclean's flight, White may have had no alternative. What is certain is that after the double defection, the two remained inextricably linked.

Sometime in 1951, Hollis visited Germany on vacation with Anthony Courtney, a former naval officer who had become a Tory MP. Courtney told me in writing that he was startled when Hollis remarked, "My experience is that every man, without exception, has his price—but mine is a very high one." As Courtney agreed, it was an extraordinary statement to be volunteered by a man who would become head of MI5.

CHAPTER 55

Reluctant Riddance

T HE BEHAVIOR OF THE KGB CHIEFS FOLLOWING THEIR AP-
parent drubbing of MI5 in the double defection was surprising. The
Center knew, from Kim Philby if from nobody else, that the British authorities were aware the fugitives had defected to Russia. So they could
have capitalized on the British discomfiture by producing them at a press
conference—a move dreaded by both MI5 and the Foreign Office. By
stressing the ease with which the two spies had operated for so long and
then escaped—all under the eyes of MI5—the Soviets could have exacerbated the British rift with the American intelligence authorities. Instead, they preferred to acknowledge nothing and kept quiet about the
two runaways for several years, reducing inquiries that might incriminate not only Philby but Blunt and other assets, source protection being
the prime priority.

The reaction in Washington was very different. The departure of
Burgess, with Maclean, so soon after his return to Great Britain, immediately generated suspicion about Philby's possible role in the flight. His
close relationship with Burgess in Washington was investigated, and on
examining Philby's career, the American security authorities realized
that there were too many anomalies to be explained by coincidence. If
he, too, had been a Soviet spy, the damage he could have done would
have been immense. So early in June 1951, the CIA chief, General Walter Bedell Smith, supported by the FBI's J. Edgar Hoover, insisted on

Philby's recall to London. Clearly, they expected swift action against the suspect by the British authorities. Both the American and the British media had already raised the likelihood that a third man had been involved in the escape by warning Maclean of his danger, and Philby's name had quickly surfaced as a candidate. Within MI6, however, the view that Philby, one of its senior members, who had even been in line for the position of chief, could have been so treacherous was hardly considered. Within MI5, the naïve Dick White, according to his biographer, did not seriously suspect the man he had so admired of being a spy at that stage.

To have been a fly on the wall when White and Hollis were discussing this possibility would have been intriguing. How did they react to the eventuality that, as collaborators and admirers of Philby, they had both been deceived for so many years by a traitor totally committed to the Soviet cause? In that case, how did Hollis come to terms with the reality that he had been initially responsible for putting Philby in a prime position to promote his espionage? How did he feel about all the secret information of MI5's counterespionage activities that he had given to Philby in many letters and verbally, in the line of duty? Were they both aware that if Philby proved to be a spy, they and many of their colleagues had wasted much of their professional lives? There was small danger of public censure, as little leaked from MI5 or MI6 in those days, though mandarins and ministers might hear of their crass misjudgment. Clearly, there was even greater need, "in the national interest," to conceal the truth about Philby than about the two defectors, because he was part of the intelligence establishment.

In view of the American pressure, and especially after the row with Hoover over the double defection, MI5 had to set an inquiry in motion. Philby had already been given the code name Peach in the previous List of Nine investigations, when he was one of the suspects, and what was known to MI5 of his record was examined. Allegedly, it was only then that White discovered that Philby's first wife, Litzi, had been a Communist. However, there is evidence that in 1946, White had been told that by his reliable informant Klop Ustinov (father of the famous actor Peter). White had taken the view that Philby's decision to marry her so that she could enter the safety of Great Britain as a Jewish refugee had been laudable! Further, Philby's file should have shown that by the time he had needed to divorce Litzi, in 1946, she was known to have been not only a Communist, but a Soviet agent. In some respects White was a simple soul, but as his letters to me showed, he was capable of supplying false information when it suited him or his service.

After breaking with Litzi, Philby had cohabited with a nonpolitical partner, Aileen Furse, who had borne him three children and was about to produce a fourth. Keen to secure promotion, he had needed the badge of respectability generally considered essential for a senior Whitehall position in those days. So in 1946, he had faced the divorce that he had delayed because his marriage to an active KGB agent might have been exposed in the process. After consulting the KGB Center, he had made a frank confession to his MI6 chiefs, claiming that his marriage to Litzi had just been youthful folly. Though MI6 knew that Litzi, then safe in Berlin, had been a KGB agent, Philby's story had been accepted and, amazingly, he was not questioned further about her. He had secured his decree in September 1946 and had married Aileen. Because of his close working relationship with Hollis, it would have been reasonable for Philby to have first sounded him out concerning MI5's likely reaction to his proposed admission. In view of his own marital position with an openly flaunted mistress, Hollis could have assured him that admission was the best policy.

Though MI5's official information about Philby was limited, because MI6 declined to provide his records, the number of his counterespionage cases that had collapsed seemed ominous. White gave special consideration to the circumstances in which the would-be KGB defector Konstantin Volkov, who claimed knowledge of Soviet agents inside British intelligence in 1945, had been captured by the KGB and executed. When he asked Hollis why he had not pursued that case at the time, he claimed lamely that "it had not seemed important." In truth, for most of the relevant time, in September 1945, Hollis may have been more concerned with his own involvement in the Gouzenko affair following the Elli revelation.

White also considered the case of Ismail Akhmedov, a GRU defector in Istanbul who had given Philby so much information that it had filled forty-two pages, of which he had sent only four to London, with a comment deriding the defector as a source. Whether White saw any comparison with Hollis's behavior regarding Gouzenko is unknown. Then there was Philby's record in connection with Anglo-American attempts to infiltrate anti-Communist Albanian refugees back into their homeland, many of whom were ambushed and executed after Philby had regularly tipped off the KGB. (Lord Bethell, who researched the incidents, suspected that up to one thousand were betrayed. The same had happened to teams of parachutists dropped into Ukraine and Poland.)

Aware of his danger and wishing to appear helpful, Philby had volunteered some information about Maclean to MI5, but it was so out of character that it served only to increase suspicion about him. Little progress was made, however, until the autumn of 1951, when, according to further code breaks, it seemed likely that a KGB agent appearing in the deciphered traffic as "Stanley" was Philby. To satisfy growing American demands, it was necessary to subject Philby to a formal interrogation, and White, with no experience as an interrogator and overestimating his abilities, decided to do it himself.

Philby had returned from America by air on June 12, 1951, unescorted, rejecting the opportunity to defect and confident that he was capable of withstanding any interrogation that either MI6 or MI5 could mount. The May and Fuchs cases had convinced him that whatever the evidence, it would be almost impossible for a British court to convict a suspect spy without a confession. So all he had to do was continue to protest his innocence.

With the reluctant permission of MI6, he was called in for a friendly talk with White, who told him that he was seeking clarification of the Maclean and Burgess defections. White's biographer, Tom Bower, described the confrontation as "a clash of intellects" in which "White's was inferior." He failed to pursue leads with which a more hostile interrogator might have trapped the cunning traitor into admitting a lie. Philby dismissed the Albanian deaths as due to "the clumsy Americans."

Though eventually convinced that he was dealing with a spy, White had achieved nothing of value at the end of two days of questioning. He agreed with Philby's assertion that Soviet intelligence would never have employed an indiscreet, drunken, homosexual reprobate like Burgess as any kind of spy. His biography states that he blamed himself forever for the errors in his performance, but how hard he really tried may never be known. Later, Philby was to attribute his escape to White's ineffectiveness.

Philby was asked about a striking photograph of himself, which had been taken by Edith Tudor Hart, his original recruiter who was strongly suspected by MI5 of being a Soviet agent. He simply denied knowing her, and if further inquiries were made, they produced nothing. In the process, Edith received an anonymous telephone call and destroyed her copy of the portrait. The call could have been made by Philby or by some mole in MI5.

On examining Philby's career more thoroughly, the American security authorities had concluded that the number of anomalies in it was totally beyond belief for an innocent man and was insupportable for anyone involved in intelligence. Meanwhile, the most that White could do was to submit a report to the MI6 chief, Stewart Menzies, stating that Philby was definitely suspect. Few, if any, of Philby's colleagues in MI6 believed that, but under continuing American pressure, even though all the evidence was circumstantial, Philby agreed with Menzies that he should quietly resign. In lieu of a pension, he was given £4,000, a substantial sum in those days, though part of it was paid in installments. It was a classic use of "amicable elimination" with no publicity damaging to the reputation of the secret services or its officers, including Philby.

The foreign secretary was never told anything about Philby's financial settlement or even that he was suspected of having tipped off Maclean. When he eventually learned the truth in 1955, he complained bitterly.

Entirely as a result of the American pressure, Philby was out by July 1951, the managements of both MI5 and MI6 being relieved to be rid of the problem with no further public damage to their reputations.

The loss of Philby was a major disaster for the KGB. However, like Blunt, Philby continued to have access to old colleagues who believed he had been treated unfairly and probably continued to trust him, even when he was named as a probable spy in a New York newspaper. As Lord Bethell recorded, Philby came to London several times a week and was often seen in clubs with former colleagues, "drinking deeply and complaining loudly." To what extent, if any, Philby continued to meet Hollis socially is not known. Hollis certainly had access to the records of the inquiries into the case and knew how Philby had managed to escape, simply by asserting that whatever the apparent evidence, he was not a spy and had never been one. It was a stance that he would use himself in similar circumstances.

Four months later, in November, Philby was summoned back to MI6 headquarters, where he was told that a judicial inquiry had been opened into the Maclean-Burgess escape and that he would be required to give evidence. Philby was subjected to a more hostile interrogation by Helenus Milmo, a wartime MI5 officer with legal qualifications, who conducted the inquiry. Though Milmo ended the exercise convinced that Philby had been a spy, he failed to secure any admission. The MI6 officer Nicholas Elliott, who saw the record of the encounter, told me that Philby simply took the laconic line that while the circumstances might look bad, he was not a spy and had never been. When Hollis was asked his opinion of the process, he took the legalistic view that without proof, the suspect should be given the benefit of the doubt. Inquiries were suspended pending further evidence. No assessment of the possible damage Philby might have inflicted was attempted because it would have been so extensive.

Over ensuing months, Philby was also questioned several times by William Skardon, who failed to break him. Though temporarily of little further use to the KGB, apart from the gossip he could acquire from ex-colleagues, Philby felt relieved to have survived. He found modestly paid work in the City and then in freelance journalism. At the end of the war, the KGB had offered him an annual pension of £1,500, but along with the other Cambridge spies, who had been offered £1,200, he had refused it because of the difficulty of explaining the regular money if it were ever exposed during an inquiry, though they had all accepted smaller sums for expenses.

CHAPTER 56

Suspicious Aftermaths

—

THE ALLEGED FAILURE OF FOREIGN OFFICE SECURITY TO BE aware of the Communist backgrounds of Maclean and Burgess indicated, glaringly, that positive vetting had not been applied in their cases. The system was therefore spruced up so that any former membership of the Communist Party or links with it, even through relatives, would be a bar to employment in posts requiring access to top-secret information. Later, homosexuality, then a criminal offense, was added to the scope of the inquiries because of the blackmail danger, though it had not been a significant factor in the treachery of either traitor.

At intervals, relatives of both Maclean and Burgess received letters showing that the defectors were alive, though these were usually posted in England, and never in Russia. Then, in 1952, "the great spy scandal," as the double defection had become known in Fleet Street, was resurrected when Mrs. Maclean left Great Britain with her three children to live abroad, first in Paris and then in Switzerland. She pretended that she was going to divorce her husband, but on September 11, 1953, less than a year after declaring Geneva to be her permanent home, she was spirited out to Moscow by the KGB in an orchestrated operation of which she had always been part. The Kremlin kept the mystery going by issuing statements declaring that the disappearance of the diplomats and of Mrs. Maclean had nothing whatever to do with the Soviet Union.

Meanwhile, in April 1952, an MI5 watcher leaving a bus on his way home near London spotted a Russian, Pavel Kuznetsov, whom he knew to be a Soviet intelligence officer. The Russian was talking to another man who turned out to be William Marshall, a young employee of the Diplomatic Wireless Service who had previously served as a cipher clerk in the British embassy in Moscow. Later, Marshall was caught carrying secret information in the company of Kuznetsov and was jailed for five years. It was MI5's only real success during the whole of Percy Sillitoe's tenure and was due to a fluke circumstance that had demanded action.

With the reelection of Winston Churchill as prime minister and his determination to use his reputation in the United States to achieve restoration of the interchange of atomic weapons information, the government set hopeful store by the successful test of Britain's first atomic bomb in Australia in 1952. However, the United States spurned the approach, with one congressman expressing the general Washington opinion, "We would be trading a horse for a rabbit."

In September 1953, Sillitoe retired, utterly disillusioned. He had frequently returned home disenchanted by the incompetence and odd behavior of his staff and on one occasion had remarked to his wife, "I sometimes think I am working in a madhouse." He was replaced as director general by Dick White, who immediately appointed Roger Hollis as his deputy, a promotion that White's biographer described as "a poor reflection on MI5 and on White himself," as it "betokened his propensity to retain weak men," though which of the two really was weaker remains a matter for conjecture. Their joint responsibility for the Maclean and Burgess debacle, so soon after the Fuchs disaster, and their common knowledge of the true facts of both cases may have bound them together indissolubly.

Hollis's promotion, which was widely resented among the rank and file, gave him far greater influence and much wider access to information. His duties included responsibility for overseas security problems in colonial countries and for liaison with the security organizations of Canada, Australia, and the United States. It also brought him even closer to White.

Not until January 1954, in answer to a parliamentary question, did the Foreign Office admit that Maclean and Burgess were "behind the Iron Curtain." Then, to the great dismay of Whitehall and MI5, public interest in the traitors was rekindled the following April by the defection of a senior KGB officer, Vladimir Petrov, who had been directing a spy ring from the Soviet embassy in Canberra. Petrov's wife was also an intelligence officer, and a ham-fisted attempt by armed KGB thugs, flown from Moscow to force her to return there, was thwarted at Darwin Airport, intensifying the publicity. Both were granted asylum in Australia and eventually gave evidence against disloyal citizens there. Petrov, who proved to be a reliable witness, confirmed privately to the Australian authorities that Maclean and Burgess had both been longtime Soviet agents who had been recruited while at Cambridge. The Foreign Office was informed of this, but the foreign secretary and other ministers were advised by the secret services to avoid making this known for as long as possible.

As a liaison man with the Australian security authority, and because of his previous involvement in the Burgess and Maclean defection, Hollis had a professional interest in the Petrov affair, but according to a GCHQ officer, Teddy Poulden, it was suspiciously greater than it should have been. Petrov's defection came as no surprise to Poulden and others in GCHQ because they had heard of it in advance through intercepted radio messages. GCHQ informed Hollis that the defection was expected within a few days, confirming what he had already been told by the Australian security officials who were arranging it. After Petrov had defected, Hollis asked Poulden for details of how GCHQ had obtained its advance knowledge. Poulden declined to tell him on security grounds, as he had no need to know. Hollis pressed repeatedly for details, then took his demands to Poulden's superior, who upheld the decision and congratulated Poulden. From then on, Poulden was suspicious of Hollis, as he told me. Because of that and other episodes, Sir Leonard ("Joe") Hooper, who headed GCHQ until 1973 and then was coordinator of intelligence in the Cabinet Office until 1978, seemed convinced that there had been a high-level spy in MI5 and that it had been either Hollis or Graham Mitchell.

It soon became apparent, from Petrov's information, that the KGB Center in Moscow had been forewarned of his defection when it became imminent, as the Australian prime minister, Sir William McMahon, eventually stated publicly. Later, the Australian security officer in charge of the Petrov defection, Michael Thwaites, told me that in view of the precautions taken in Australia, it was extremely unlikely that the Russians became aware of the defection plans from a leakage there. If

the leak reached Moscow from London, Hollis could have been responsible, and that could explain the concern he had shown about GCHQ's
advance knowledge. If GCHQ had discovered the information through
an intercepted and deciphered Soviet signal, he may have feared that it
might have given clues to the source. Several MI5 officers have told me
that, like Philby, Hollis was unduly curious about security and intelligence matters outside his province.

Meanwhile, in 1954, Dick White, MI5's new director general, had
decided that further inquiries into the Cambridge group, including Kim
Philby, should be ended because he doubted there would be any more
revelations. He was to tell his biographer that he was to regret this decision for the rest of his life, as it protected not only Philby, but Blunt and
several others.

In the autumn of 1953, the director of a KGB espionage ring in
Tokyo, Yuri Rastvorov, had made contact with British intelligence authorities there in order to defect to the West. He had declined to go to
Great Britain or to any British-controlled territory because he believed
that British intelligence was penetrated by the Soviets and that he might
be assassinated. Having agreed to go to Australia, he had learned that
his flight from Tokyo to Sydney would touch down at Singapore, which
was then a British colony. Such was his fear that he had fled from the airport to the American embassy and defected to the CIA. When debriefed, he had said that he knew British intelligence was penetrated
because a few years previously, a GRU officer named Vladimir Skripkin, who had been in the process of defecting, had been betrayed by a
British source and been caught and executed. That was the case dealt
with in 1946 by Hollis, as previously described.

When Rastvorov's allegation was passed to MI5, where Hollis had
become deputy director general, it was glibly assumed that Philby had
been to blame, as he had been concerning the would-be defector Konstantin Volkov. This explanation was accepted until further information
accrued from another KGB defector to the CIA, Anatoli Golitsin, who
fled via Helsinki in 1961 and claimed to have been involved in countering the attempted defection of Skripkin. He said that the KGB had received photographic copies of both reports about Skripkin originally
sent from Japan to MI5 and that the details in them concerning the contact arrangements had led to his capture. He recalled that the reports had
reached Moscow from London, and his description of their contents was

remarkably accurate. Later, Golitsin was shown the two documents in the MI5 file and declared them to be identical with those he had seen in Moscow, including marks indicating that the originals had been stapled together, as those in MI5 still were.

The most disturbing aspect of this startling information is that when Rastvorov's disclosure reached MI5 in 1954, nothing of consequence was done about it. Again, the comparison with Philby's activities presents itself—someone was able to stifle it, perhaps in the interest of his own safety as well as that of the other intelligence agency he was serving.

Coupled with the suspicious defector situation was the regular breakdown of efforts by MI5's agent runners to recruit double agents to operate against Soviet intelligence officers based in Great Britain. Sometimes, when the KGB or the GRU attempted to recruit a businessman or university student, the target would report the attempt to MI5 and then accept the Soviet offer while working under MI5 control. Almost invariably, when that happened, the Russians detected the truth so quickly that it seemed they must have been informed by some source, most likely to have been inside MI5. The same appeared to apply to occasions when MI5 received advance information of a conspiratorial meeting between a suspected agent and his Soviet controller. The watchers would be stationed with extreme care, but the meeting would not take place.

Later, MI5 investigators were to reexamine more than fifty attempts by its officers and agents to penetrate Soviet intelligence and failed to find one that had not collapsed within a few weeks, while Soviet penetrations often endured for years. The distinguished MI5 officer Colonel "Tar" Robertson told me that after he had retired, an insider still working in the agency informed him that the case deaths and other disappointing failures were so persistent that only a spy could be responsible for them. The dearth of Soviet defectors to Britain during the whole of Hollis's MI5 career may have had a similar explanation.

CHAPTER 57

Pamphlet of Deception

IT WAS NOT UNTIL SEPTEMBER 1955 THAT NEWSPAPER PUBLICITY about the defection of the KGB officer Vladimir Petrov in Australia forced the Foreign Office to admit—more than four years after the double defection—that the missing diplomats had indeed been long-term Soviet agents. This was followed on September 23 by the publication of a government white paper entitled *Report Concerning the Disappearance of Two Former Foreign Office Officials*. It was assumed that the report had been compiled by the Foreign Office, but the brief for it was drafted in MI5 by Graham Mitchell, then in charge of counterespionage. Mitchell had been in the team assembled by Dick White to perform the postmortem on the Maclean and Burgess defections and was instructed by him and by Hollis to "take into account outside interests," meaning, especially, American interests. Mitchell's brief was then passed to the law officers and the Foreign Office to be developed into the four-thousand-word white paper. As this was supposed to be the official record of what had occurred, which ministers would have to defend in Parliament, there can be no doubt that White, by then director general, and Hollis, his deputy, paid close attention to the wording of the entire document. It was White who "sold" the completed white paper to the prime minister, then Anthony Eden.

As a result, though it had been pored over by many eyes and pawed over by many hands, it was strewn with statements now proven to be false—as they were known to be inside MI5 at the time. It understated the traitors' access to important secrets, with no reference to Maclean's special access to shared Anglo-American atomic affairs while in Washington. Its purpose was to limit the damage to the reputations of MI5, the Foreign Office, and the government and was nothing less than yet another deniable deception operation on Parliament and the public, both British and American. It suggested that proper action had been taken concerning the drunken and violent behavior of both Maclean and Burgess, which was manifestly untrue. While admitting that the "security authorities" had failed in allowing the traitors to escape, it stated that serious suspicion against Maclean was aroused "only shortly" before he disappeared, when in fact he had been on a short list of suspects for many weeks. It claimed that action to find the diplomats had been put into effect "immediately," when in fact MI5 had delayed it for two crucial days. It alleged that before the suspicion, there had been no grounds for doubting Maclean's loyalty, but there was easily available evidence that Maclean had been an active Communist at Cambridge.

The document was so worded as to support the belief that Maclean had not been warned by anybody but had detected the surveillance, which had been enough to trigger the flight. It stressed that there was no evidence admissible in a British court to hold Maclean, when in fact the authorities did have legal power to prevent, or at least delay, Maclean from leaving the country while under such serious suspicion. Otherwise, why were the French authorities asked to intercept the two men? Much was made of the importance of not telling "the other side"—the Kremlin—how much the British authorities knew. There were also elementary errors of fact that none of the perpetrators had checked. Even the name of the Cambridge college attended by Maclean was wrong.

The document was ridiculed by the media and by many MPs as a transparent ploy, which earned it the name "Whitewash Paper," which eventually generated the term *Whitehall whitewash machinery*. If it was a self-serving MI5 fake—as it was—and if Sillitoe could have taken doctored files to Hoover—as he did—then the possibility that MI5 deliberately encouraged the defection seems more credible. As the FBI files "Philby, Burgess, Maclean" testify, the publicity generated by the Whitewash Paper in the United States was appalling.

In the following month, Marcus Lipton, a Labour backbencher, used the parliamentary privilege protecting him from a possible slander suit to table a question to Foreign Secretary Harold Macmillan, asking if he had "made up his mind to cover up at all costs the dubious Third Man activities of Harold Philby." This induced Hollis to make another personal intervention.

In a letter, Hollis asked Lipton to visit him. When the MP declined, "Hands-on" Hollis, who could have sent someone more junior, went alone to meet Lipton in the House of Commons lobby to discover how much he really knew. Hollis wanted to know Lipton's source, but the MP was unhelpful. (According to Robert Lamphere of the FBI, Lipton had been tipped off about Philby by a CIA officer and covered his true source.)

For two years—from 1952 to 1954—William Skardon had continued to visit Philby on occasion with various queries, still in the hope of trapping him, but he had no success. In the meantime, the KGB had contacted Philby again, through Blunt and the KGB controller Yuri Modin, and given him money.

Macmillan was determined to prevent any "muckraking" public inquiry into the Maclean-Burgess-Philby affair, as he told the cabinet on October 20, 1955. Instead, he set up a secret committee of inquiry, under a young Foreign Office official, that recommended that Philby should be questioned again, but only by his old service, MI6, which was under Foreign Office control. As a result, he was cross-examined by three old MI6 colleagues who were anxious to prove his innocence. The results could then be used to brief Macmillan for his answer to Lipton's allegation.

Philby readily agreed, and tape recordings of the event show that he was encouraged to parry questions until acceptable answers were put into his mouth. The law officers then prepared a brief for Macmillan, based on the MI6 interviews. When I discussed this brief with Macmillan in his study at his home, Birch Grove, in 1981, he said that the law officers had been certain Philby was guilty but there was no evidence that would have carried weight in a court of law.

A parliamentary debate on the white paper, which I attended, was held on November 7, 1955, and Macmillan spoke for an hour, making several false statements in the process. He said that there had been no starting point for an interview with Maclean. To allay the suspicions about a third man, he suggested that Maclean had become frightened into defecting by the arrest of Fuchs in the previous year. To explain the delay in telling Parliament about Petrov's prime disclosure, he claimed that Petrov had objected to any of his information being passed to Britain, which he described as "a most important point." It was a point that had been invented because the Australian officer in charge of the defection, Michael Thwaites, assured me that Petrov had made no such threat and was in no position to do so. The invention could have originated only in MI5, which was the agency in touch with the Australian authorities.

Exceeding his brief, Macmillan answered Lipton's third man gibe by telling Parliament that no evidence had been found that Philby had been responsible for warning Burgess and Maclean. He said he had no reason to conclude that Philby had betrayed the interests of his country or to identify him with the so-called third man. Later, Macmillan assured me that in spite of Philby's eventual defection, he was unrepentant and regarded his clearance of the traitor as "in defense of public liberties." What the statement showed was that no ministerial comment concerning a suspect spy, or any important security issue, is necessarily to be believed. Significantly, no MI5 papers on the double defection and its consequences have been released.

Greatly relieved, and almost unable to believe his luck, Philby, who had been given advance notice of Macmillan's effective exoneration, gave a press conference to declare that he was not the third man and had no Communist connections. He hid behind the Official Secrets Acts to avoid answering questions. He even had the effrontery to declare that any publicity would damage MI6 and MI5!

The public clearance of Philby, which events would prove to have been an appalling blunder greatly to the KGB's advantage, was badly received by both the FBI and the CIA. It reinforced suspicions there that the British had no intention of prosecuting traitors who had been members of the "establishment," and of the secret services in particular, no matter how much damage they had inflicted on British and American interests or how many agents they might have betrayed to their deaths.

The Soviet authorities publicly ignored both the Petrov disclosures and the white paper. Then, on February 11, 1956, after all had seemed quiet again, British journalists in Moscow were summoned to a press conference, where they found Burgess and Maclean on display.

Burgess handed out a statement claiming that they had never been spies but were simply Communists who had left Great Britain because they believed that the Foreign Office policy would lead to war and they could best work for world peace in the Soviet Union. The statement included a disclosure that caused great alarm to Hollis—that Burgess had been closely associated with MI5. At that stage, while MI6 was under deep suspicion for having employed Philby, no hint of treachery had been ascribed to MI5. In fact, as the Guy Liddell diaries have confirmed, Burgess had been employed by his friend Blunt in a long-running wartime operation to penetrate the embassies of neutral countries and involving the examination of their diplomatic pouches when this was possible. Of course, the two traitors had passed all the relevant results to the KGB.

After deep thought and discussion inside MI5, Hollis decided to make a preemptive strike. On the morning of February 26, Rear Admiral George Thomson, who as secretary of the D Notice Committee was the liaison man between journalists and the secret services, asked me to attend his office. There I met Bernard Hill, the head of MI5's legal department, who said that he urgently needed my help. He said that in the fortnight since the emergence of Maclean and Burgess, analysis had convinced MI5 that it was the prelude to further statements calculated to sow distrust between the United States and Great Britain. He said it was certain that Burgess and Maclean had been produced so that they could be used to make damaging allegations about the Foreign Office and MI5 itself when it suited the Kremlin to do so.

As I was the chief writer on intelligence affairs for the *Daily Express*, which then had a huge circulation, Hill wanted me to publish a prominent article warning the public that whatever the defectors might say in future would be lies constructed by the KGB. He admitted that MI5 had acquired evidence of Maclean's treachery over many years, and though there was nothing legal to prevent the return of Burgess to Great Britain, MI5 knew that "he had been a bloody spy." Nevertheless, he advised me not to say so just in case Burgess ever did manage to return and sued for libel! I detected almost a sense of panic in the urgency with which Hill required the publicity—without, of course, any mention of MI5 as the source. After he had left, Thomson, a regular lunch companion, told me that he and Hill were acting on the instructions of Roger Hollis, against whom at that time there was no public suspicion.

The *Daily Express* duly obliged on the following morning with a front-page splash, headlined BEWARE THE DIPLOMATS!, and the admiral telephoned me to say that MI5 was delighted. Though Hollis must have felt that he could trust me not to mention the origin of the story at that time, he was taking a risk, because with Admiral Thomson present, he could not have denied MI5's involvement had I named it as the source. So Hollis's immediate need must have been great, possibly being focused on MI5's role in the double defection. Perhaps what he feared most was a statement by the defectors that MI5, and he in particular, had colluded in their escape.

Surprisingly, the defectors were never used to make derogatory statements of any kind—or for much other public purpose. So why didn't the Soviet dogs bark? The KGB always put the safety of its agents first, and Philby, Blunt, Cairncross, and others were still free and of possible future use. Silence, the hallmark of most secret services, was preferable to any short-term propaganda gain.

The defectors' experience on arrival in Russia had been disappointing in the extreme, in view of the astounding service they had given to the Soviet cause. Instead of being welcomed as heroes, Maclean and Burgess were summarily exiled to Kuibishev, a boring industrial city, for several months, ostensibly to undergo "drying out" treatment in a rest home. Meanwhile, a thorough check on their credentials was made to ensure that they had not been turned—a possibility occasioned by the ease with which they had escaped.

In light of what is now known about Stalin's behavior, they were perhaps fortunate not to have been eliminated in one of his insane purges of foreign agents. Instead, they were eventually allowed to live in Moscow, but under restricted conditions. Maclean was given an advisory post and was eventually held in high regard, but Burgess had no function, living a dull, circumscribed life with a male electrician partner in a run-down flat, where he had to remain each day until informed by telephone that he could venture out.

Maclean's life improved when his wife arrived with their children in Moscow, but she eventually left her husband to cohabit with Philby. Later, after thirty years in exile, she returned to the United States and remained silent about her experiences. Both Maclean and Burgess, who continued as habitual drunkards, paid a heavy price for their treachery. Though they put on brave faces, the workers' paradise for which they had sacrificed their lives turned out to be a defectors' hell. Understandably, Burgess let it be known to visiting friends that he would like to return to Great Britain, if only to see his mother, and Hollis did all he could to ensure that this would never happen, as I know from another occasion for which he needed my services.

After Burgess had surfaced in 1956, his friend Tom Driberg, who was temporarily out of Parliament, wrote to him about the possibility of writing a book about him and, with KGB agreement, visited him in Moscow, arriving on August 10. As the recent KGB defector Vasili Mitrokhin has confirmed, Driberg picked up homosexual partners from the urinal behind the Metropole Hotel. One of them was a planted KGB agent who lured him into a compromising situation with photographic evidence of his exploits. Though Driberg claimed that he was immune to such a threat, he wanted to return to Parliament and agreed to be recruited, the money on offer also being an irresistible inducement for him. He was given the KGB code name Lepage.

On his return to London at the end of August, he reported to MI5, for which he had been an informant since he had entered Parliament in 1942, when he had begun to report on the political activities and private lives of other members. His MI5 controllers told him that they had no objection to the book, which was to be called *Guy Burgess: A Portrait with a Background,* as long as they could see it in advance and vet it in what was to be another deniable deception operation.

As Labour was in opposition and likely to remain there, MI5 condoned Driberg's KGB roles as a Soviet agent of influence and as a source of inside information and personal scandals about the Labour Party—as long as it continued to receive the same service. He was to function that way for the next twelve years, being of particular value to the KGB when he was chairman of the party in 1957 and 1958. His information was so highly rated that it was passed to the Politburo. He was also used, in the Soviet interest, to support the campaign for British nuclear disarmament inside the Labour Party.

Driberg's first active measure for the KGB was publication of his book about Burgess, promoting the blatant lie that the defector had never been a Soviet spy, which suited MI5. He had even returned to Moscow to enable the KGB to check the proofs! The KGB was delighted when Driberg said that he was convinced of Burgess's innocence, but the operation was to prove to be an MI5 sting.

In November 1956, by which time Hollis was MI5's director general, I was approached again by Admiral Thomson on behalf of MI5. He told me that I—and the *Daily Express*—might be interested to know that Burgess had now committed an offense under the Official Secrets Act for which he could be charged if ever he returned to Great Britain. On his first visit to Moscow, Driberg had unwittingly induced Burgess to re-call some incidents and names concerning the brief time he had spent in the Special Operations Executive during the war. These had been included in the proofs, which Burgess—and the KGB—vetted on Driberg's second visit to Moscow. Driberg then advised his British publisher to submit the script to MI5 for formal vetting, without revealing that Hollis and others had already seen it. The publisher was then warned by MI5 that unless some of the details about the SOE were deleted, they risked prosecution. The publisher obliged, and the book duly appeared. It was at that point that Thomson was asked to inform me that I should warn Burgess that simply by giving the SOE information to Driberg, he had breached the Official Secrets Act and would defi-nitely be arrested if he ever returned to Britain. The story appeared in the *Daily Express* as a news item under the title "Burgess Burns His Boats," and I received a furious call from Driberg, whom I referred to Admiral Thomson, who confirmed the situation to him.

I then took Thomson out to lunch to discover why MI5 had gone to such trouble, obviously involving deep discussion, to devise such a thin technical charge. He told me that Hollis was determined to prevent Burgess from returning to Britain. Apparently, the home secretary had been prepared to allow Burgess to return on compassionate grounds, and Hollis wanted to ensure that he never did so. I felt then, as I do now, that Hollis had a special reason to fear what Burgess might say if put on trial or when interviewed, for it was not his last device to prevent the de-fector's return. Could it have been the truth about MI5's part in the 1951 escape? Or did Burgess know or suspect something else?

Driberg's book was a tissue of KGB lies, which were dutifully regur-gitated in a review by the author's fellow agent Claud Cockburn, who assured his readers that Burgess had been caught speeding in America only because he was still suffering from the effects of concussion after a fall weeks before. Further, he had been prosecuted only because the governor of Maryland was anti-British!

In 1959, as released cabinet documents have shown, Burgess, then desperate to visit his ailing mother in England, approached members of a British mission to Moscow, led by Harold Macmillan, for permission to do so. When the attorney general ruled that there were no grounds on which he could be prosecuted, it was decided that Burgess's plea should be ignored in the hope that he would conclude it was not safe for him ever to return.

Though Hollis's next seemingly panicked attempt to prevent the return of either traitor did not occur until April 1962, it is convenient to deal with it now. Through official channels—mine was a Defense Ministry contact, Lieutenant Colonel L. G. ("Sammy") Lohan, who had close links with MI5 (being on its payroll)—a few journalists were told that a tip had been received from Dutch intelligence that both Burgess and Maclean might be attending a Communist conference in Cuba. It was hinted that on the way, their airliner would be touching down at Prestwick Airport in Scotland. Some MI5 officers would have been delighted to intercept and interrogate them, but Hollis ensured that they would be unable to do so. On the morning of April 17, Scotland Yard announced that the police had applied for warrants for the arrest of the two men, which they did at the request of MI5. In fact, the traitors never moved out of Moscow and had never intended to do so, Burgess then being severely ill with diabetes. Journalists, who had run the false story, including me, were eventually told that the tip-off from Dutch intelligence must have been wrong.

Clearly, the whole episode had been a deception operation, which had the full connivance of MI5 and the Metropolitan Police, to warn off the traitors yet again. In September 1963, it was announced that Burgess had died, aged fifty-two, and MI5's worries in his respect subsided. Maclean was to last a further twenty years.

CHAPTER 58

A Ruthless Defamation

—

WHILE THE SECURITY-INTELLIGENCE ESTABLISHMENT WAS still mired in the mess created by the Maclean-Burgess-Philby affair, it generated another major disaster with international implications and extraordinary impact on Hollis's career. In April 1956, the joint Soviet leaders Nikita Khrushchev and Nikolai Bulganin were due to visit Great Britain on a goodwill mission, at the invitation of Prime Minister Anthony Eden, who attached great importance to the occasion in reducing East-West tensions, which was also in America's interest. They were scheduled to arrive at Portsmouth harbor in the new cruiser *Ordzhonikidze*, escorted by two destroyers. Political discussions would then be held in Downing Street and Chequers, the prime minister's weekend retreat.

Two years previously, the Admiralty (which controls the Royal Navy) had asked MI6, as well as its own intelligence service, to secure any information about the "underwater noise characteristics of Russian warships," which would be helpful for operations by submarines. In particular, naval intelligence was keen to discover whether the warships were fitted with an antisonar device that decreased the cavitation effects produced by the screws, reducing underwater noise. MI6, MI5, and the Admiralty had then separately compiled a series of intelligence operations, code-named Claret, some of which would involve the use of frogmen for surreptitious underwater inspection.

Following letters to the prime minister suggesting that the opportunity to inspect the visiting warships should not be missed, Eden had responded on September 29, 1955, with, "These ships are our guests and, however we think others would behave, we should take no action which involves the slightest risk of detection." He sent a copy to the foreign secretary, who was responsible for warning MI6 of the veto.

On April 6, the Admiralty asked Eden for authority to collect electronic intelligence while the Russian ships were still in the North Sea. He even forbade that, replying in writing, "I am sorry but we cannot do anything of this kind on this occasion." The total ban could not have been clearer and applied to all departments, but displaying arrogant contempt for the prime minister and his office and supreme confidence in its ability to conceal its activities, the MI5 management, headed by White and Hollis, decided to eavesdrop on all the conversations in the Soviet leaders' rooms in Claridge's hotel in London, where they were staying after their ship had berthed on April 18. Peter Wright, the MI5 officer in charge of the bugging operation, has described it in detail. It involved the first trial of an advanced eavesdropping system and the use of an office in a nearby private building. No edict from a "wet" prime minister was going to halt the MI5 operation, which worked well but yielded nothing of value. The Russian leaders had either assumed or been warned that their rooms would be bugged. According to Wright, MI5 was also involved in an operation whereby a radar image of the cruiser was obtained by equipment concealed in a cave in the cliffs near Dover.

Meanwhile, before Eden's edict, MI6, which had a separate naval section in a London outstation headed by Nicholas Elliott, had contacted a forty-six-year-old retired naval frogman, Commander Lionel Crabb, to carry out its part of Claret. His employment ensured that the Admiralty could deny any connection with it should problems arise. Further, should the operation be successful, MI6 could claim the credit. MI5, which was required to give some support, was approached by the MI6 technical liaison officer, John Henry, and a meeting was held in Dick White's room with Hollis, his deputy, present. They agreed to assist in any way they could, though it was noted that Foreign Office approval had not been obtained and they knew of the prime ministerial ban. Documents indicate that Elliott had not been informed of the ban owing to a failure of communication inside MI6.

Keen to oblige, Crabb arrived in Portsmouth on the evening of April 17—the day before the warships arrived—along with an MI6 officer, and they checked into a convenient hotel, registering their names and addresses. The MI6 man, Ted Davies, called himself "Bernard Smith." Crabb then telephoned an old diving companion, a lieutenant commander still operating at the nearby Underwater Weapons and Countermeasures Establishment, known as HMS *Vernon*. According to a statement by this officer, released only in 2006, they met in a pub, where Crabb asked his friend to assist him in a secret dive by helping him to don his equipment. While stressing that the operation was entirely unofficial and should not be mentioned at HMS *Vernon*, Crabb declined to explain its purpose. Nevertheless, the officer, who probably guessed it, agreed, and in the afternoon of April 18, they staged a rehearsal in Portsmouth dockyard, where a small boat was moored. In the boat, Crabb, helped by the officer, slid into the water and soon returned, having decided that he needed some extra weights.

Shortly before seven a.m. on the morning of April 19, with the Russian ships docked, Crabb, the naval officer, and the MI6 man arrived at the dockyard. The frogman then began the dive with enough oxygen to last two hours, his task being to examine the cruiser's rudder and propellers. When he had not returned by nine-fifteen, the officer reported Crabb's disappearance to HMS *Vernon*, which informed the Admiralty, where the horrific potential consequences were quickly realized. The naval officer was ordered to keep his mouth shut and "to take no further part in the affair." It was also decided to make no effort to find Crabb or his body because that might alert the Russians and would involve the Portsmouth naval authorities, who knew nothing about the operation.

Management of the crisis was taken over by the director of naval intelligence, Rear Admiral J. G. T. Inglis, who ordered the production of a "convincing cover story," as there was immediate fear that the media would discover that the gallant Crabb, who was a wartime George Medalist ("for undaunted devotion to duty") and holder of the Order of the British Empire, had lost his life in an illicit operation that had been specifically banned by the prime minister. The deception needed to explain why there had been no rescue or recovery operation.

The panic was intensified on the evening of April 21 when the admiral in charge of the Russian ships told the British admiral who was entertaining him that three of his sailors had seen a frogman at about seven-thirty a.m. on April 19 on the surface for one or two minutes between the two destroyers, though he was not proposing to lodge any complaint.

At meetings involving the chief of MI6 (John Sinclair), the director general of MI5 (Dick White), and the director of naval intelligence, it was agreed that the episode had to be suppressed until the Russian visit was over and for longer if possible. To protect MI6, it was also decided that it would be acknowledged as a naval operation, if publicity ensued. Without mentioning MI5's own infringement of Eden's edict, White decided that he would do all he could to avert a public scandal "in the national interest." Though he was not required to lie to the public, because MI5's involvement was not then known, he was prepared to abet a series of deliberate lies.

By agreement, the cover-up operation was controlled by the Admiralty, with all concerned, including Crabb's grieving mother, being urged to remain silent. False statements were drafted to deal with any media inquiries. It was also decided that MI5 should arrange the removal of the telltale pages from the hotel registry because Crabb was well-known as a freelance diver and "Smith" had described himself as "attached Foreign Office"—the standard cover for MI6 operatives. In a ham-fisted operation in which the hotel manager was threatened with the Official Secrets Act, local police tore out offending pages.

On April 29, the Admiralty issued the false statement that Crabb had failed to return from trials of underwater equipment in Stokes Bay, three miles from Portsmouth. Inevitably, reporters learned about the missing pages, and after the issue of more lies by government departments, the truth was partially published in newspapers, including the likely Russian connection.

The Admiralty then prepared a statement proving how ruthless secret government departments can be when desperate to protect their own interests. It was not only false but, callously, put the entire blame on the dead frogman, whom it disowned. It stated, "To put an end to the speculation which the presumed death of Commander Crabb has aroused, the Admiralty have now decided to give the known facts in full. Commander Crabb was engaged to conduct, on 19 April, experiments with a secret underwater apparatus. The location of the trials was in the Stokes Bay area but Crabb and his assistant were instructed to go in a boat from Portsmouth Dockyard. As soon as Crabb was dressed for diving and shortly after the boat had left its mooring, he slipped over the side and was last seen swimming towards the Russian ships close by. He paid no attention when recalled by his assistant and it can only be presumed that, in a spirit of adventure, he was determined, on his own initiative, to inspect the Russian ships. It can only be presumed that he died while diving on his unauthorized expedition."

This succession of lies, concocted for both Parliament and the public, not only blamed Crabb for the disaster, but accused him of wantonly disobeying orders, when in fact he had been carrying out the Admiralty's requirements given to him by MI6. Government spokesmen delight in accusing the media of indulging in "conspiracy theories," but here was a conspiracy so foul that few journalists would have entertained it as possible. The statement is evidence—for all time—of the lengths to which intelligence departments will go to save their professional skins, allegedly "in the interests of national security."

The statement was modified before release, but the Admiralty persisted, as long as it could, in alleging that Crabb's approach to the Russian warships was entirely unauthorized, implying that he had disobeyed orders—a dreadful slur on a loyal and distinguished officer who had died in the line of duty. The lieutenant commander who had assisted Crabb, and whose name is obliterated from the released documents, was ordered to remain silent.

By May 3—after the Russian ships had left—it became obvious to the conspirators that the matter could no longer be kept quiet. Only then was Eden told what had really happened—a delay of more than two weeks. Meanwhile, on April 28, Eden had sent a message to Khrushchev saying, "I am sure that your visit and our talks have helped to remove suspicion." Until then, like the public, he had assumed that the Admiralty's statements had been true and that Crabb's death had been a tragic accident in Stokes Bay, unconnected with the Russians.

Understandably, Eden was incandescent, knowing that intense publicity and parliamentary questions were inevitable. With tough disciplinary action in mind, he instructed Sir Edward Bridges, then head of the Civil Service and an archetypal Whitehall mandarin, to launch a searching inquiry into why the Crabb mission had been undertaken and why its failure had not been reported to ministers.

Late on May 3, the Soviet government sent a note of protest to the British government, which responded six days later with a note expressing regret and an assurance that Crabb had been in the vicinity of the Russian ships "without any permission whatever." The Kremlin released the text of both notes.

Eden was required to answer parliamentary questions, which he declined to do, and a debate was forced on May 14, with Eden declaring that what had been done (which he refused to explain) had been without the authority or knowledge of ministers and that disciplinary action was being taken against those responsible for the "misconceived and inept operation."

On the same day, the chief constable of the crime office in Chichester wrote to all the local police authorities in the Portsmouth area, warning them that should Crabb's body surface, "it is absolutely essential that the finding of the body is not disclosed to the Press." Even the police were involved in the cover-up.

The report by Bridges, which was submitted to Eden on May 18 but kept secret until 2006, did all it could to explain away the calamity so that no serious censure should attach to any senior official. It stated that the prime minister had not been informed because the Admiralty regarded the Foreign Office, which controlled MI6, as being responsible for the operation, while the Foreign Office thought that the Admiralty was responsible. So neither was to blame, as each thought the other had informed their ministers! However, Bridges could not avoid reporting that the MI6 chief, John Sinclair, had failed to consult his parent ministry, the Foreign Office, sufficiently about the venture and that had he done so, the operation would not have been allowed.

Eden's written comments on the various paragraphs of the twenty-three-page report—"Ridiculous!" "This proves nothing," "Against orders"—showed his contempt for it.

In late July, Eden fired Sinclair, with the released documents indicating that he would have liked more high-level dismissals. However, under pressure from the establishment, the director of naval intelligence, top civil servants in the Admiralty and Foreign Office, and lesser fry escaped with severe admonishments. They would not have done so had Eden been informed of a much bigger operation that had been staged in total secrecy shortly after the Crabb disaster. The Admiralty had proposed to deploy a small team of its own divers from HMS *Vernon*, but this was officially canceled. Incredibly, however, as cabinet papers released in 2005 disclosed, the operation went ahead unofficially, with the divers successfully examining the sonar equipment under the Russian ships. The information they gleaned was of immediate value to Britain's submarines and was also something exceptional, which the navy could "trade" with its American ally.

The cabinet papers revealed that there was such determination by the Admiralty to conceal this illicit operation that sixteen years later, in April 1972, when the BBC got wind of it, Sir Burke Trend, then cabinet secretary, took near panic steps to block a television documentary that threatened to expose it. The then prime minister, foreign secretary, defense minister, and D-Notice secretary were all brought into the Whitehall cover-up process. A memo from the D-Notice secretary dated April 11, 1972, confirmed that "a naval team from Vernon did, separately, dive under the Russian ships."

The Defense Ministry and MI5 were ordered to discover and silence a naval officer who had been involved in the operation and apparently had been willing to tell his story to the BBC. The D-Notice secretary was then instructed to lean on the BBC "at a high level to cancel the program," which it did in 1973 when, under pressure, the officer eventually declined to take part and others in retirement were threatened with prosecution under the Official Secrets Act. Once again, "national interest" had been invoked by those at the highest levels, including Prime Minister Edward Heath, on the grounds that Anglo-Soviet relations would be jeopardized, to conceal officials' illicit activities and blunders.

Further details of the panic and the extent of the cover-up emerged in 2008 with the release of Defense Ministry documents following a demand under the Freedom of Information Act. They confirmed the Admiralty's disgraceful lies and revealed that in March 1981, one of the HMS Vernon frogmen (identity withheld) who had inspected the Russian ship had written to the office of the prime minister, then Margaret Thatcher, urging that she should be told the truth, as she then was. In July 1985, the Granada TV company regenerated the project, but once again, the authorities joined forces and suppressed the truth under threat of prosecution "in the national interest."

The sacking of John Sinclair in 1956 created a vacancy for a new chief of MI6. Unaware of MI5's illicit bugging operation, or its part in the Crabb affair and its cover-up, Prime Minister Eden replaced him with Dick White. This meant that a new director general was needed for MI5, and White had no hesitation in recommending his friend Roger

Hollis, though he was better informed than anyone else about his deputy's blunders over the Whomack, Fuchs, Sonia, and Kuczynski cases. He was also aware that in those more censorious times, Hollis's long extramarital affair with his secretary was a potential scandal if the Russians ever decided to exploit it. What internal pressures, based on the previous joint ventures that bound them, induced White to suggest Hollis may never be known.

Sick of the whole business, as he eventually told me, Eden agreed to the appointment. Nobody could have been more pleasantly surprised than Hollis, who had expected to remain deputy director general until retirement because he was a year older than White. Though both had been party to the failed illicit operation and the failed deceptive cover-up, each benefited personally from what had been a tragedy with severe international consequences. The White-Hollis axis became more influential than either of them could have imagined, especially after their many joint catastrophes, particularly their expediting of "the greatest crime in history"—the betrayal of the secrets of the atomic bomb.

Following previous reviews of the nation's security arrangements, it had long been recognized that the director general of MI5 should have "unusual experience and a rare combination of qualities." Instead, a university dropout with no foreign languages, little field experience, an appalling counterespionage record, a negative personality, mediocre qualities of leadership, doubtful health, and a mistress installed in his office found himself in charge of the nation's first line of defense against spies and saboteurs. It was to be a unique position of uncontrolled power because successive home secretaries, to whom Hollis would be responsible, took little interest in MI5. Consultation was rare then, and MI5 was effectively its own judge and jury.

Further publicity about the Crabb affair had become unavoidable when, on June 9, 1957, three fishermen in a boat encountered the badly decomposed body of a frogman in the sea off Chichester harbor. This required an inquest, and the released documents provide a further demonstration of the power of the intelligence authorities in promoting deception of the public, even the judiciary being susceptible to pressure. The director of naval intelligence, J. G. T. Inglis, was quick to inform both the coroner and the chief constable concerned of the embarrassing problems. A letter dated June 17, 1957, stated that both the coroner and chief constable were being "most co-operative." Crabb's friend, the anonymous lieutenant commander, would be required to give evidence, but he was to be smuggled into the court, which would be sitting without a jury, with his evidence being held in camera. The coroner had also agreed that there would be no adjournment during which "delicate matters might be probed." He duly returned an open verdict, saying that he was satisfied the remains were those of Crabb. That opinion is fully supported by the official papers about the inquest, which have recently become available in the Chichester archives.

It has been stated repeatedly in books and elsewhere that when the frogman's body was eventually found, the head and hands were missing. As this suggested that *only* the head and hands were missing, it supported the conspiracy theory that the Russians had captured Crabb, put a different body in his rubber suit, and cut off the head and hands to make precise identification impossible. However, the evidence of the pathologist, with the photographs now available, reveal that except for the left upper forearm bone, the entire arms were missing, indicating that the hands had rotted away with the rest. Further, the documents show that Crabb did not like wet suits with a hood but stipulated a neck seal, which made it easier for the head to rot and become disconnected. In fact, the photographs show that the neck and much of the upper chest had disappeared.

Without seeing the remains, one of Crabb's former diving colleagues, Sydney Knowles, described a small scar on the left leg previously inflicted by barbed wire. The pictures of the body's leg show such a scar in exactly the right place. The size of the body, its muscular legs, and ginger pubic hairs confirmed the identity beyond reasonable doubt. A still secret report of an Admiralty Board of Inquiry into the cause of Crabb's death had concluded that because of strong tides and being weighted, he had become trapped in the underwater timbers of a jetty, where he had run out of oxygen. There were indeed ingrained rust marks on both legs of the wet suit, suggesting that the diver had been trapped by some submerged metal structure and held there for a long time. The successful surreptitious examination of the cruiser by the naval diving team also seemed to dispose of the theory that the Russians had deployed their own frogmen as underwater sentries who had killed or captured Crabb. The HMS *Vernon* frogmen had found no evidence of underwater stays to support such sentries or any other devices. However, Eden's papers, as reported in his official biography, indicated that his belief—and perhaps that of some other officials—was that Crabb had been discovered and killed by the Russians. Eden, of course, knew nothing of the HMS *Vernon* team's negative findings.

The possibility that Crabb's mission had been betrayed in advance was strengthened in the early 1960s when the KGB defector Anatoli Golitsin volunteered information that Soviet naval intelligence had been warned of Crabb's mission. He even cited the affair as evidence that MI5 or MI6 was penetrated. The researcher Nigel Bance, who has been regularly in touch with senior KGB officers who were active at the time, has claimed that Soviet intelligence had a month's advance warning of Crabb's operation.

The notorious KGB chief, Ivan Serov, had visited the Soviet embassy in London in March 1956 to finalize arrangements for the leaders' visit. When in Moscow, Bance visited Serov's daughter, and she showed him a holdall containing her father's papers. One document was a summary of the Crabb affair. It stated that during Serov's visit, he had been contacted by a Soviet agent inside MI5 who warned him of the project to inspect the cruiser, stating that it would be conducted by Crabb, on whom the KGB already had a file. Serov had accompanied Bulganin and Khrushchev on the *Ordzhonikidze* but had remained aboard the ship in Portsmouth, possibly to oversee any security operation.

Both White and Hollis had been fully aware of the operation. Wright told me that as MI5's technical expert, he, too, had been informed of it in advance by John Henry and had passed the information to his senior colleague, Colonel Malcolm Cumming. An MI5 member, Pam Synge, was later to describe to me how Cumming had told her, with almost schoolboy excitement, "Crabb is going under that Russian warship in the morning!"

Though Crabb's tragic death occurred more than half a century ago, the Russians have remained officially silent about it—possibly because of its extraordinary unforeseen consequence, for which, if Hollis had been Elli, both he and the Soviet government had reason to be ecstatic.

CHAPTER 59

Master of Minimalism

—

IN ADDITION TO THE VIRTUALLY UNCONTROLLED POWER WIELDED by the MI5 chief, Roger Hollis inherited the mystique then attached to the post. This enabled the holder to indicate, by no more than a knowing smile, that some details were too secret even for a prime minister to be enlightened about them—a situation described to me by a former intelligence officer as almost suggesting, "If I told you that, I'd have to shoot you!"

Hollis's first prime minister, Anthony Eden, told me that he had hated any contact with the security or intelligence agencies, as they caused nothing but trouble for politicians, the whole secrets world being a place of dirty games from which a wise leader remained aloof. His second prime minister, Harold Macmillan, thought the same until forced to take interest by a series of security calamities. There was nobody else to check on the action—or inaction—of the director general because the concept of any parliamentary oversight of MI5 was then unthinkable and would remain so for a further thirty years.

Dick White always justified his recommendation of Hollis as his successor by claiming that he had been the best man available, which was a poor reflection on MI5. By securing the appointment, White ensured that he would wield some personal advantage in any differences of opinion that might arise among other members of the two agencies. He would be more likely to secure agreement in controversial circumstances from a man so indebted to him than from a director general of greater independence, as those of the Philby defection were to show. If the two colleagues had previously been involved in dubious operations, such as the Maclean and Burgess defection, then it was in their joint interest that nobody from outside the service, who might make inquiries, should be appointed.

While the issue was not perhaps in Eden's mind, his decision to put an MI5 man in charge of MI6 seemed likely to reduce the built-in rivalry between the two agencies, as it did, with White and Hollis working almost in tandem.

Even with his exalted rank, Hollis remained so unimpressive that Harold Macmillan was to describe him as "an insignificant man." Within MI5 there was little doubt that White had deliberately left behind a person who was beholden to him in the event of future conflicts between MI5 and MI6. One female MI5 officer, who did not believe that Hollis was disloyal, told me, "We were somewhat astonished when told that he had been made DG, as we realized that he had been promoted above his capabilities, and this always leads to trouble." Another described him as "an appalling DG. He moved like a wraith; looked through you. It was a standing joke that everything would go wrong, and it did." Nor did he show any signs of growing into the job. Surveying Hollis's whole record, as he eventually had to, Sir Michael (later Lord) Havers, then attorney general, described him to me as "a blundering buffoon." Macmillan's biographer, Sir Alistair Horne, concluded that MI5 during Hollis's reign as director general was inept and in disarray and that he had "a great deal to be reticent and retiring about."

In 1952, the home secretary, then Sir David Maxwell Fyfe, had issued a new directive to the MI5 director general pointing out that the task of the British Security Service was the defense of the realm from dangers arising from espionage and sabotage. It stressed that it must limit its work to that task and avoid inquiries outside it. Hollis was to misinterpret this in pursuing his minimalist policy of simply monitoring and attempting to control suspicious circumstances and the people involved in them. Action, such as the arrest of suspects, was to be taken only when unavoidable. The directive was a ready-made excuse for lack of action, a policy that Hollis was able to impose throughout the service. Whether by default or design, it happened to benefit the Soviet intelligence services.

Though newspaper editors were told of the appointments of both White and Hollis in confidence, the identities of both chiefs remained secret from the public until after they had retired, when I revealed them to an American journalist, who published them, making it possible for the British media to do the same. By then, both MI5 and MI6 had been responsible for so many blunders, I felt that those nominally responsible should be identified. In those days, the two chiefs were under no threat of terrorist attack, their names were well-known to the Russians, and the secrecy was essentially to maintain their personal privacy, which was particularly necessary in Hollis's case. Such appointments are now officially announced.

If Hollis was Elli, fortune had favored the villain, who had achieved the ultimate with scant effort on his part in the interests of MI5. He had right of access to any documents he wished and, having his own safe, could retain them—as he did with some of Claud Cockburn's files. He had his own private cipher for sending and receiving messages. He could demand information from subordinates without having to give reasons. The aura attached to his new position gave him almost complete immunity to tough investigation.

As a permanent member of the Joint Intelligence Committee, he was privy to all the nation's major intelligence secrets, with access to the intelligence gleaned by MI6, GCHQ, and every other source. The extent of such up-to-the-minute knowledge is described in detail in Sir Percy Cradock's authoritative book *Know Your Enemy*. Hollis's personal association with the chiefs of other Western agencies broadened this access.

For the GRU in particular, if Hollis was Elli, the appointment carried one crucial advantage. Throughout the cold war, each side dearly wished to secure a spy capable of discovering whether the opposition was ever seriously being driven to consider staging a surprise nuclear attack. As chapter 50 has shown, Stalin and his generals had been regularly supplied with details of Britain's war plans by a spy, or spies, between 1945 and 1950 and perhaps beyond. At the very time that Hollis was promoted, a secret report, of which I was given details, was circulating in Whitehall stating that the Soviet Union was believed to be flexing its muscles for possible armed conflict. JIC reports, recently declassified, show that defense plans were being based on possible war with the Soviet bloc in 1957. This was the generally agreed date, then, when the Soviet Union would have reached a military position strong enough to make its leaders believe they could launch an effective war against the West.

The detailed extent of Hollis's access to defense plans is shown by a JIC document, dated November 18, 1957, concerning a new "War Book" on the transition states from peace to nuclear war, which would have to be achieved in seven days. It reveals that it was the JIC that would declare an intelligence alert, with MI5, MI6, and GCHQ looking for indicators of Soviet preparations for war. The emergency operations that would then ensue are described in great detail, and Hollis is named as being present during the JIC discussions. The authoritative presence of a man with such a proven record of catastrophic judgment was potentially disastrous for both Britain and America, whether he was a spy or not.

Hollis would have been one of the first people to learn of any Western decision to stage a preemptive nuclear strike. Though this was extremely unlikely, the Soviet leaders believed it possible, and with sound reason from their standpoint. Their purpose in securing advance warning was not necessarily to make a preemptive strike themselves, but to take possible political action to defuse the situation. As chapter 63 will record, the top-priority function of the GRU in particular, from the mid-1950s onward, was to secure advanced warning of any imminent atomic attack by Britain and America.

Because of the close collaboration of the U.S. and U.K. atomic forces, with the first wave of bombers having to be launched from Britain for geographic reasons, the United States could not then stage a preemptive strike alone. Through the meetings of the JIC, Hollis would also have known the RAF's prime Soviet targets and the main British targets considered likely for Soviet attack. He would have known the warning times, which the British defenses were capable of providing, and the number of H-bombs required to render Britain useless for further military operations. (The figure given to Macmillan by Sir William Penney was "five! Or shall we say eight, to be on the safe side"—a remark that the former prime minister delighted in retailing at shoot lunches.)

As Russian disclosures, such as Alexander Feklisov's book, *The Man Behind the Rosenbergs,* have revealed, Soviet agents had also secured Pentagon reports of detailed plans for preemptive nuclear strikes against major Soviet cities before the Kremlin was in a position to reply with adequate strength. With code names like Charioteer and Dropshot, they were only contingency plans devised in the usual defense process of dealing with all possible military scenarios, but any news about them was crucial for the Kremlin's counterplanners.

According to Tom Bower, "White was aware that if, during a nuclear alert, a key British official was compromised by the Soviets or was actually a Soviet spy, Britain's capability or response could be fatally crippled." Whether the Kremlin also knew the details of British first-strike contingency plans may be revealed by further research in the Soviet state archives.

Senior British military attachés with experience of the GRU while working in Moscow have advised me that Hollis's final appointment would have carried one consequent disadvantage. If Elli had become director general, his use as a general source would have been much reduced on GRU instructions. His value as a source of nuclear political information would have been so great that he would have been advised to restrict contacts with his controller or cutout to serious situations and to ignore other issues, in the interests of his continuing security. In that situation, his GRU status would soon have been changed from "agent," under some degree of control by the Center, to "confidential contact." The term *confidential contact*, which was used by both MI5 and the Soviet intelligence services, is defined in *KGB Lexicon*, secured by the defector Vasili Mitrokhin, as "individuals of foreign nationality, who, without being agents, communicate to intelligence officers information of interest to them and carry out confidential requests, which in substance are of an intelligence nature, on the basis of ideological and political affinity, material interest, friendly or other relations which they have established with the intelligence officers." Nigel Bance has secured tape-recorded statements made in Moscow in December 2002, alleging that Hollis did have that prime function. In one tape, which I have heard, a former senior KGB officer states that by the time the KGB learned that Hollis had any illicit connection with Moscow, he was listed in KGB archives as "a confidential contact in touch with Soviet Intelligence."

The tape was a discussion of a document prepared by Colonel Georgi Goncharov, identified as a former head of the British counterintelligence service at KGB headquarters in Moscow. The document was described as having been compiled in the late 1970s for Colonel General Grigori Grigorenko, head of the Counterintelligence Directorate, before anything about Hollis had been published, and concentrated on what the KGB knew about him then. It was allegedly for an in-house history of the KGB being prepared for Grigorenko. That such a history existed is confirmed in *KGB: The Inside Story* by Christopher Andrew and Oleg Gordievsky, according to whom it was completed in 1978— three years before there was any publicity about the official suspicion inside MI5 that Hollis had been a Soviet agent.

Indicating that the Soviet intelligence service with which Hollis had maintained relations was the GRU, the statement mentioned Hollis's connection with Sonia and claimed that when she had visited Moscow from Shanghai in the 1930s, his name had appeared in her debriefings and there was some reference to "Hollis having been compromised." This would not necessarily be proof of their personal association in China, which is one of the crucial missing links, but it could indicate that some other GRU agent, possibly Arthur Ewert, had named him to her.

There was also a brief statement alleging that on one of her visits to London, Sonia had reported about Hollis to her brother, Jurgen. If true, and if Hollis eventually knew that, it would help to explain why he had always been so soft on the Kuczynskis and on Jurgen in particular.

There was also mention of Hollis's association with Cockburn and his involvement in the Gouzenko affair, including the "investigation into a Soviet agent in British counterintelligence." The KGB informant claimed to have read all these details while serving in the KGB so they could at least disprove statements that no KGB file on Hollis ever existed.

There were other statements supporting the contention that Hollis had, at one time, been an agent under some degree of control but had later become a confidential contact, which would accord with his prime function then being to warn of any imminent increase in the nuclear threat. As will be seen, there is British witness evidence supporting that contention.

CHAPTER 60

A Warning from Hoover

—

WHEN ROGER HOLLIS BECAME DIRECTOR GENERAL IN 1956, Martin Furnival Jones was appointed head of counterespionage. As Peter Wright was to report, Furnival Jones was shocked to learn the extent to which the number of Soviet intelligence officers posing as diplomats, trade officials, chauffeurs, press officers, and journalists had been allowed to swell over the preceding years—to about three hundred. This had been determined by MI5's established counterespionage methods such as telephone tapping, radio monitoring, and surveillance. Then, a new system of checking the identity and purpose of suspects, called "movements analysis," was introduced and showed that the number was steadily increasing, indicating that both the KGB and the GRU were finding more agents and sources. With the Foreign Office and MI6 reluctant to offend the Russians for fear of retaliation in Moscow, Hollis made little effort to back Furnival Jones's demands for a reduction. Instead, he turned the usual blind eye, and the rise in Russian intelligence numbers increased steadily throughout his reign.

Hollis was already a member of the Reform Club in Pall Mall, where he drank with Blunt, White, Liddell, and, in the past, Burgess. On becoming director general, he joined the Travelers Club, also frequented by White and other "spooks." He continued his affair with his secretary, which was widely assumed to be his reason for remaining in the office until eight p.m. or later, though he was often there alone, as Philby had been in his MI6 lair. Evidence of this habit has been supplied to me by several former MI5 contemporaries, such as Tony Henley, who told me that he often did night duty to get an extra thirty shillings and was surprised to find how regularly Hollis worked late. One of Hollis's personal friends told Anthony Glees that this habit caused continual friction with his wife, who presumed that his secretary was also working overtime.

In spite of his own illicit relationship, Hollis continued to take a puritanical attitude toward others. Freddie Beith told me that he was present when Hollis addressed senior members of the staff and told them that, as in the case of Caesar's wife, their lifestyle must be above reproach. Peter Wright told me that when Hollis heard that an MI5 agent runner was having an affair with one of his female agents, he insisted that he should be fired, as he was, in spite of pleading by the head of personnel and other officers incensed by his decision.

Hollis was also remembered for his parsimony with the money allotted to MI5. Beith told me that, seemingly to ingratiate himself with the Treasury, Hollis liked to return a substantial sum at the end of the year, a habit that infuriated agent runners, who were limited in what they could offer people to become agents. The practice made it difficult for him ever to seek an increase. Several former officers recalled his preoccupation with avoiding being the cause of embarrassment to any Whitehall department, even when this came at the expense of MI5's effectiveness.

Because of a succession of spy scandals, Hollis was not destined to enjoy the roller-coaster ride of his nine years as director general. The first case during his reign had begun the previous March and resulted in another embarrassing defection. A twenty-two-year-old RAF fighter pilot, Flying Officer Anthony Wraight, had been spotted visiting the Soviet embassy, where he had contacted a GRU officer. In October 1956, he was interviewed by MI5 and cautioned. He then disappeared and in December flew to Berlin and defected behind the iron curtain. This was a poor start to Hollis's leadership, especially as East Berlin radio made propaganda out of it.

Three years later, Wraight walked into the American embassy in Moscow and asked to be repatriated to Great Britain. He was and, after interrogation, was sentenced to three years' imprisonment. Though Wraight had managed to defect and returned entirely of his own volition, the case was to be listed among MI5's "triumphs." In reality, MI5's operations continued to fall apart in ways suggesting that Soviet intelligence had advance warning about them, the most dramatic example being the so-called Arago affair, which was to impress Wright and others and was most responsible for triggering what became known as "the great mole hunt."

In the autumn of 1957, Frantisek Tisler, a cipher clerk in the Czech embassy in Washington who had been recruited by the FBI under the code name Arago, had provided information that was passed directly to Hollis in a letter by J. Edgar Hoover. It suggested that Soviet intelligence must have a spy inside MI5 who could be tapped at short notice. Tisler had also revealed the betrayal of a new MI5 system for detecting and following Soviet-bloc cars in London by keeping watch near some of the Thames bridges instead of, more obviously, near the relevant embassies. The ruse, approved by Hollis and code-named Coverpoint, seemed to have been betrayed almost immediately, because the suspect cars all used other bridges, and the project had to be abandoned within a fortnight. The Soviet intelligence officer who had provided this information to the Czechs belonged to the GRU, suggesting it was that organization that had penetrated MI5. Elli, of course, was an MI5 spy recruited by the GRU, but Hoover had never been told any of the evidence about him. Otherwise he might have been more pressing.

Through the FBI, Tisler also supplied the name of a British spy working for the Czechs: Brian Linney, an electronics engineer who was providing information about a new airborne missile. Linney was put under surveillance in the hope of catching him with his controller, who was known to be the Czech military attaché in London, Colonel Oldrich Pribyl, but the Czech never attended the projected meeting, suggesting that he had been warned. Later, Linney confessed and was jailed—another British spy detected only after a tip from the United States that could not be ignored.

Meanwhile, Hollis realized that Hoover's letter about Tisler, which had proved to be accurate concerning Linney, required action of some kind regarding the possibility that MI5 was harboring a spy. Otherwise he could have dismissed it as unthinkable, as most of his MI5 colleagues would have agreed. His situation was not helped by the fact that he was already in long-running difficulties with Hoover concerning atomic security. In connection with lingering American doubts about the interchange of atomic secrets with Great Britain, an FBI officer, Charles

Bates, had been sent to Britain to oversee the security being exerted by MI5. After visits to the Aldermaston and Windscale atomic stations in January 1955, Bates had reported to Hoover that MI5 was exerting inadequate security. He had also been astonished to find that MI5 did not positively vet its own members and had reported that to Hoover.

Lewis Strauss, the tough chairman of the U.S. Atomic Energy Commission, had then told the British ambassador in Washington that unless security was improved, no more atomic information would ever be forthcoming. That was unwelcome news, because in July 1954, the British government had secretly decided to produce and stockpile H-bombs in a bid to remain a credible atomic power and also to secure "the Great Prize" of atomic interchange. Bates had returned to Britain to recheck in April 1956 when improvements had been made, but they were still considered insufficient. After a further visit, Bates reported a better situation.

To placate Hoover over Tisler, Hollis asked Peter Wright to carry out a discreet investigation and wrote to the FBI chief, assuring him that action was in progress following his tip. That was the true beginning of the long inquiries that would end in Hollis himself becoming the prime suspect.

Protected by his diplomatic immunity, the Czech Pribyl continued his treachery through his involvement in an operation that resulted in the loss of more than one hundred agents working overseas for MI6. This had been perpetrated by another Czech, Karel Zbytek, who had defected to Britain in the early 1950s and had acquired British citizenship. He had secured a post as a filing clerk with the Czech Intelligence Office, which was recruiting Czech exiles to counter the Communist regime in Prague. The office had been successful until the spring of 1956, when Zbytek had offered his services to Pribyl for money, identifying eight Czech agents operating for MI6 at high level in Czechoslovakia, two of whom were executed. From then on, Zbytek, later known as "the Czech Philby," met regularly with controllers in London, gradually revealing the entire British operation in return for £40,000. MI5 knew nothing about this treachery until 1969, when it was revealed by Czech defectors to the CIA, which alerted MI5.

Fears of a traitor inside MI5 gradually intensified because there were so many instances where surveillance by the watchers came to nothing. Whenever the watchers were staked out for a surveillance operation, the

Russians appeared to know of the location in advance and avoided it. Advance warning also seemed to have been given about technical operations, such as the bugging of Soviet buildings. Former MI5 officers confirmed to me that inquiries into the reasons why cases had collapsed were discouraged by the top management as a waste of time—"water over the dam."

Charles Bates was posted to London as the FBI's station chief in 1958, and when he made his courtesy call at MI5 headquarters, Hollis said, "Well, Mr. Bates, it was you, wasn't it, who said that security here was inadequate? Life is full of strange twists." Unabashed, Bates replied, "Well, one has to treat facts as they fall."

Bates remembered Hollis as "mousy, with a crooked smile, hunched, courteous, but withdrawn." He told me over a long lunch that his research showed that since the end of World War II, MI5 had never discovered a spy of any consequence from its own resources. It had reacted solely to discoveries by others forced upon it and that it could hardly avoid. Bates put that situation to the MI5 officer Arthur Martin, who said he would examine the record. After a few days, he admitted that Bates was absolutely correct. According to Tom Bower, Bates had made the same criticism to Dick White while he was still head of MI5, and he, too, had conceded that MI5 had failed to recruit a single Soviet source. All their apparent successes of any consequence had originated from tips from the CIA or FBI via Soviet defectors. Bates attributed the failure partly to the principle, established by Hollis since his earliest days in charge of countering Soviet espionage, that when MI5 had suspicions, its job was to build up files and review them instead of doing legwork to detect security incidents and bringing cases to court.

In October 1957, Hollis's requirement to prevent or hush up any further spy scandals suddenly intensified with the surprise resumption of an exchange of secret atomic information with the United States. On a visit to Washington by Prime Minister Macmillan for talks with President Dwight Eisenhower, who was keen to improve the relationship in the cold war with Russia, the president delighted the whole British team by producing the draft of a directive setting up an Anglo-American committee on atomic cooperation. When converted to the bilateral Agreement for Cooperation on the Uses of Atomic Energy for Mutual Defense Purposes in 1958, this effectively ended the totally restrictive 1946 McMahon Act, which had followed the May spy case and had cost the British so much in duplicating research. (By 1958, British scientists had successfully exploded atomic weapons of megaton yield—with American observers present—on the Pacific's Christmas Island, as I witnessed.)

Suddenly, through the American president's generosity, the Great Prize, ensuring "a seat at the top table" through a continuing nuclear capability, had been secured in spite of all the past disasters. Clearly, any further espionage or intelligence scandal could threaten the new accord, which was treasured by Macmillan as a major political achievement, and what quickly happened in security circles as a consequence can be described only as panic. In the interim, the scientific papers written by Klaus Fuchs after his employment at Harwell in 1946 had been collected in an archive of one hundred folders stored in a safe at the Atomic Weapons Research Establishment at Aldermaston, as was recently described to me by Dr. Lorna Arnold, a former official historian there. Shortly after ratification of the new agreement, all the Fuchs papers disappeared and were destroyed along with many others. This was followed by an orgy of burning and shredding at various establishments by visiting officials, said to be from the Ministry of Defense.

Who took the panicked decision to eliminate part of the nation's history is uncertain. Dr. Arnold concluded that some individual or committee had decided to reduce the risk that any more secret atomic documents might be abstracted by spies and find their way to Moscow, with violent reaction from Congress if the treachery was exposed. There also seems to have been some fear that American officials would ask for copies of some of the papers, with consequent resurrection of their censure of British security when they fully realized how much Fuchs had betrayed, especially concerning the H-bomb.

Some committee seems likely to have been responsible, along with some input from MI5 regarding protective security and, possibly, agreement from the prime minister. Macmillan would almost certainly have approved, as his reaction to another fraught incident suggests. His official biography records that immediately prior to a visit to Washington, a major fire in an atomic plant at Windscale in Cumbria had released a cloud of radioactive dust, contaminating large areas of England and Wales. A scathing report by Sir William Penney, showing that the accident had been caused by faulty instruments and faulty judgment by technical staff, awaited Macmillan on his return, when—as he recorded in his diary—he feared that publication of it might induce Congress to reject Eisenhower's proposed bilateral agreement. He quickly ordered the destruction of copies of Penney's report.

Future releases of official papers may reveal exactly what had happened to the Fuchs documents, unless they, too, have been destroyed. Ironically, all was not irrevocably lost to history by their destruction. Thanks to Fuchs himself, many of them still reside in the archives of the old Soviet Union.

With Fuchs, Pontecorvo, Sonia, the other Kuczynskis, Maclean, Burgess, and Philby, the fifties had been eventful for Hollis. The sixties were to be calamitous.

CHAPTER 61

Master of Disaster

OFFICIAL DOCUMENTS HAVE PROVED THAT IN FEBRUARY 1960, the Czech Intelligence Service, which operated as an arm of the KGB, recruited an ambitious member of the British Parliament, John Stonehouse, who was prepared to provide political information in return for money to fund his social life. For the next ten years, this traitor, who achieved important positions in Labour governments and was a prime contact of mine, met his controllers in London and elsewhere without hindrance from MI5.

Throughout Hollis's command, the buildup of KGB and GRU officers in the Soviet embassy and trade and press departments and their counterparts in Soviet-bloc embassies continued apace, without effective restraint. I witnessed it firsthand and missed no opportunity to expose it in my newspaper. The lack of remedial action has been confirmed by the recent MI5 chief, Dame Stella Rimington, in her memoirs, *Open Secret,* and by an only recently released report of a secret Whitehall discussion entitled *Soviet Intelligence Activities in the UK,* dated May 25, 1971. In Anthony Glees's book *The Stasi Files,* he has written that in the 1960s, not only the Soviet Union but also their Eastern European allies such as the Czechs had been allowed to build up their so-called diplomatic and commercial representation practically unchecked.

To give a firsthand example of their industrious activities, I was approached in 1960 by Anatoli Strelnikov, a tall, rather imposing Russian who claimed to be in the press department of the Soviet embassy. As I was trying to secure permission to visit a Soviet space research station, I cultivated him and we met for lunch on several occasions. From the nature of his questions, which were obviously to discover my insider sources of military information, it was quickly apparent that he was a trained intelligence officer, and to clear my position, I asked Admiral George Thomson, the D-Notice secretary, to find out what MI5 knew about him. He did so and told me that Strelnikov was a KGB officer and gave me a telephone number to ring a senior MI5 man who called himself Macaulay but whose real name was Michael McCaul. Whenever I met Strelnikov, I took McCaul out to lunch and told him all that had happened.

In the spring of 1961, McCaul asked me to publish a series of MI5 case records showing the methods used by the KGB to suborn visitors to Moscow. The British electronics industry was about to stage a big exhibition there to boost exports, and McCaul was in no doubt that unless warned of the dangers, some of those who might be of future use would be targeted by the KGB for possible recruitment. I agreed, and a large feature appeared in the *Daily Express* on April 5, 1961.

Immediately afterward, I was invited to lunch by Strelnikov, who complained bitterly about the article, saying that it was "terrible for peace." When I explained that writing such articles was what I was paid to do, he seized the opportunity and said, "We will pay you more to write for us . . . work for us." When it came time to pay the bill, he flashed a wad of banknotes and repeated, "Don't forget! Work for us!"

When I reported to McCaul, he was delighted and, after taking advice, asked me to induce my editor to send a letter of complaint to the foreign secretary so that Strelnikov could be expelled. The editor declined to do so, because after a long struggle, he had managed to secure permission to open a *Daily Express* office in Moscow and felt sure that the KGB would have it closed. As the aggrieved party, I offered to write the letter myself, but after taking advice within MI5, McCaul insisted that without the editor's letter nothing could be done. As a result, not only did Strelnikov complete his tour of duty, but he returned to London for a second and was still there in 1968. As he had first arrived in 1958, he completed ten years in London, and the fact that the KGB sent him back indicated that he was successful in recruiting others. During his second term, he controlled a KGB operation involving the release of incriminating sexual photographs, previously taken in Moscow, that ruined the career of Commander Anthony Courtney, the Tory MP, who recorded his misfortune in his book, *Sailor in a Russian Frame*. Later, Courtney was to express his wonderment to me that his friend Roger Hollis had escaped exposure, as he was sure that Philby would have reported his illicit sexual situation to the KGB. He regarded the Russians' behavior as evidence that they had reason to avoid besmirching Hollis.

It has since transpired that one of Strelnikov's targets was none other than the lady who became Parliament's first female Speaker—Baroness Boothroyd. She has told me what happened—and did not happen—after she first met the handsome Russian in 1964.

When young, Betty Boothroyd was secretary to a Labour peer, Lord Walston, and became friendly with Strelnikov, who took her to her favorite restaurants. In return, he wanted information about Labour policy and politicians, especially those with antinuclear views. He had also spotted a likely political "highflier" because Betty was intent on a parliamentary career. She eventually warned MI5 about him, but all that happened was that MI5 asked her to spy on certain far left Labour MPs for them. She declined and believes that because of her friendship with Strelnikov (and perhaps her refusal to spy on colleagues), Hollis ensured that she was banned as a security risk from the Foreign Office, where Walston was a junior minister. She believed that in 1965, while Hollis did nothing about Strelnikov, he vindictively tried to wreck her chances of becoming a Labour MP. Hollis told Prime Minister Harold Wilson that MI5 had secured letters indicating that she had been having an affair with Strelnikov. He did not tell the prime minister that he had asked her to monitor Labour MPs. Baroness Boothroyd denied any romance with Strelnikov to me.

Hollis received the routine knighthood for his appointment as director general in 1960, a year that marked the exposure of a series of major security disasters that were to last until his retirement. The first of these, which became known as "the Navy Secrets Case," had begun when a Polish intelligence officer named Michal Goleniewski, who was volunteering information to the CIA, fingered a civilian employed by the British Admiralty. This man, who had been recruited by Polish intelligence for money while serving in the British embassy in Warsaw, was quickly identified as Harry Houghton, a clerk in the Underwater Detection Establishment at Portland, Dorset, where he had regular access to secret information about nuclear submarines and antisubmarine warfare. Full details of the treachery of this evil man have recently become available in the form of KGB documents released to Oleg Tsarev and the English researcher Nigel West and published in *Crown Jewels*.

While working in Warsaw as a clerk for the naval attaché, he had volunteered to supply naval secrets for money. He was recruited by Polish intelligence early in 1952 but later was handed over to the KGB, supplying more than one thousand documents, including codebooks. By October 1952, he was back in Great Britain, transferred to the post at the Underwater Detection Establishment, and immediately made contact in London with a new KGB controller who was posing as a diplomat in the Soviet embassy. At Portland, security was so lax that Houghton gained access to the safe room where classified documents were stored and was given a miniature camera to photograph them. During a series of monthly meetings with KGB officers, he supplied more than five thousand secret pages. Their examination has shown that in the event of war, he could have been an extremely damaging spy.

For the last three years of his treachery, he was assisted by his mistress, Ethel Gee, a filing clerk, who also had access to secrets and revealed them for money. Their joint espionage continued unnoticed until May 1960, when, following Goleniewski's tip to the CIA, they were put under long surveillance. They were arrested in London on January 7, 1961, along with their courier, Gordon Lonsdale, a Russian posing as a Canadian dealer in vending machines. MI5 owed the discovery of Lonsdale's true identity to the FBI officer Charles Bates. Hollis and his team were confident that Lonsdale was a Canadian, for they had seen his passport and birth certificate, heard his accent, and accepted his legend. Bates, however, soon discovered that the Gordon Lonsdale on the birth certificate and passport was dead and that his identity had been usurped by the KGB. The FBI even traced the fake Lonsdale to his old school in San Francisco, where his mother had then been living. He was identified as a Russian by the name of Konon Molody.

Houghton, whose code name had been Shah, had operated for almost nine years without hindrance. While security officials in the Warsaw embassy and the Portland research station were responsible for the ease with which he extracted documents, MI5 had failed totally to prevent the activities of his Soviet controllers, who had met him regularly.

But for the chance tip-off from Goleniewski courtesy of the CIA, Houghton could well have continued indefinitely. Instead he was jailed, along with Gee and Molody.

The surveillance had also exposed two highly professional Soviet agents, calling themselves Peter and Helen Kroger, who were identified from FBI fingerprints as none other than Morris and Lona Cohen—wanted American traitors who had fled their homeland in 1950 after being implicated in atomic espionage. They were among those who had been warned in the United States of their danger, by someone suspected by the FBI of being in MI5. They had escaped to Moscow via Poland and, in 1955, had been posted by the KGB to Great Britain, where they had been servicing an unknown number of spies from a house in Ruislip while posing as dealers in antiquarian books. After their arrest, a powerful radio transmitter was found hidden in the house, but none of their messages had ever been detected. Bates believed, as Peter Wright did, that the whole operation was wound up too early and that several other important spies escaped, because the Krogers were dealing with more than Lonsdale. "The big fish got away," Bates told me, as did the Labour politician Lord Wigg after he had become closely involved with MI5.

Recently, information released in Russia has shown that the Krogers had been more important as couriers for American atomic spies such as Theodore Hall than previously realized, and they may have been functioning in Britain in that capacity with other KGB agents as yet unknown. Small wonder that in 1996, President Boris Yeltsin honored them posthumously as Heroes of Russia!

It may be asked why, if Hollis was Elli, he did not warn Moscow as soon as he knew that Houghton was suspect. Had he done so, the leakage could quickly have become apparent, and he would hardly have risked that for the sake of a naval clerk, being completely ignorant at that stage of the existence of Molody and the Krogers, about whom he would have been told nothing. It was also essential for Elli to notch up the occasional success for MI5, and unlike a defector, Houghton posed no personal threat because he could not possibly have known anything about Elli. As for the GRU, if he had alerted them, it is most unlikely that they would have requested any action by their prime source to protect spies who were all run by their rivals, the KGB.

All five Soviet agents—Houghton, Gee, Molody (Lonsdale), and the Cohens (Krogers)—were given long jail sentences, the convictions being regarded as a triumph for Hollis and his team in spite of the years of unnoticed and unhindered treachery. No mention was made at the trials that they had all been detected only as a result of information supplied by the CIA. Instead, a legend was leaked to the media suggesting that MI5 had brilliantly been alerted to Houghton's treachery by discovering that he was spending more than he earned. By coincidence—or otherwise—Houghton's Russian controller, Nikolai Korovin, left London for Moscow shortly *before* the spy was arrested.

In anticipation of the inevitable onslaught by political opponents about the inadequacy of the security precautions that had enabled all five to operate for so long, Prime Minister Macmillan set up an inquiry headed by Sir Charles Romer, a former appeals judge. The inquiry discovered that Houghton had broken almost every rule in the spy's self-preservation code—being loudmouthed, flashing wads of banknotes in pubs, and living blatantly above his means. His wife had become so suspicious that she had reported him to his superiors on several occasions, but they had ignored her. In spite of such obvious symptoms, Houghton had operated for seven years under the noses of the various security authorities. The slackness had been so appalling that Macmillan declined to publish Romer's findings while fobbing Parliament off by giving a brief summary, which put the main blame on the Admiralty. Not until 2007 did the full report become available, after the Cabinet Office yielded to a freedom of information request from Dr. Michael Goodman.

The Romer report revealed that the security situation, particularly at Portland, had been such a shambles that publication of the details could have serious political consequences. The U.S. government had an agreement with the British on the exchange of information on underwater detection, and the inevitable rage in Washington and the American media at more British spies revealing their secrets had to be minimized. That seems to have been the main reason for Macmillan's decision to keep the Romer report secret, though the details were so disgraceful that they would have also blackened his own reputation and that of his government.

The report reveals that "Hands-on" Hollis decided to represent MI5 himself throughout the seven-week inquiry, with none of the MI5 officers involved in the case giving evidence, though some documents were supplied. He claimed that MI5 had already begun investigating

Houghton a few weeks before the CIA warning, following a police report that he was behaving suspiciously.

The report gave Hollis and his team all the credit for following up the CIA lead so successfully. Yet as I recall the case, almost all the surveillance had been carried out by Special Branch detectives, if only because MI5 officers have no powers of arrest, but they were never mentioned in the report and none were called to give evidence.

Nevertheless, MI5 was severely censured for failing to take any action after it had received a copy of an Admiralty report four years earlier, in 1956, stating that Houghton's wife had warned in writing that Houghton was "divulging secret information to people who ought not to get it." Pursuing Hollis's minimalist policy, MI5 had failed to interview Mrs. Houghton and simply reported back that it had no adverse information about Houghton in its files. The inquiry concluded that "it is startling and reprehensible that nothing whatever was done." Romer was unaware that glancing at the files was the standard response, as the Fuchs and Sonia cases had shown so calamitously.

Hollis took the opportunity to stress the difficulties of watching so many Soviet officials when his resources were small, but he was to make little subsequent effort to have their numbers reduced. Along with the Admiralty, he played down the damage that Houghton had inflicted, and though Macmillan passed on that view to Parliament, feeling that he had to protect the security services (as all prime ministers do), his papers show that he did not believe it. He wrote in his diary, "Although I was assured by experts that no serious leakage had taken place . . . I had an uneasy feeling that either the Underwater Establishment served no very useful purpose or there were secrets of the highest possible importance." The KGB files on Houghton have now proved that Macmillan had been deliberately misled, a fact made known to me at the time by Admiral Sir Ray Lygo, then vice chief of the naval staff, who told me that the leakages had been "very severe and took years to rectify."

CHAPTER 62

Another Spy in MI6

—

BEFORE THE POLISH AGENT MICHAL GOLENIEWSKI HAD DE-
fected to America at Christmas 1959, he had also told the CIA that there
was an active KGB spy operating inside MI6 and supplied some details
about his work. He told of copies of MI6 documents that he had seen
and how the spy had betrayed details of British agents in Poland and
elsewhere who had then been eliminated. Some of the documents
showed that, at some time, the spy had worked in MI6 headquarters in
London.

In spite of their experience with Kim Philby, Dick White and his MI6
colleagues could not bring themselves to believe there was such a spy in
their ranks and did nothing effective. Instead, they conveniently concluded that the documents must have been stolen from a safe in Brussels
that they knew had been entered. When MI5 finally interviewed Goleniewski in America, he also revealed that the spy had operated for
MI6 in Berlin. That evidence then pointed to George Blake, an officer
of Dutch-Egyptian origin who had joined MI6 in 1947, had taken a
Russian-language course, and in 1948 had been posted to Korea, where
he had been captured during the war there in 1950 and interned until
April 1953. On his release, after recovery leave, he had worked in the
London headquarters and then in the MI6 station in Berlin from 1955 to
1959. He had then returned to London to spend a further eighteen
months in MI6 headquarters. At the time of his exposure, he was attend-

ing an Arabic-languages course at a Foreign Office school at Shemlah in Lebanon.

At first, White and his colleagues countered the circumstantial evidence by believing that Blake had notched up too many apparent successes, ignoring the principle that both the KGB and the GRU allowed their penetration agents some minor triumphs to maintain their credibility with their employers. Then, in 1961, another KGB defector to the CIA, Anatoli Golitsin, also fingered the MI6 spy, giving his KGB code name of Diomid, meaning "Diamond," which, as it transpired, had been well chosen. There was also the inescapable fact that the leakage of secrets had suddenly ceased when Blake had been posted to Lebanon.

In March 1961, Nicholas Elliott, an MI6 officer then based in Beirut, induced Blake to return briefly to London for a discussion about promotion. After consulting his KGB controller, Blake did so, and after a long interrogation in which he denied any treachery, he suddenly broke and made a detailed confession. He confessed to major acts of treachery, including the betrayal of more than forty agents and subagents. Later, he was to claim that the number was more than four hundred, a figure since admitted by the KGB. While a few were "turned," most of them were executed, as the former KGB chief Major General Oleg Kalugin confirmed on British television. Blake had also enabled the KGB to kidnap prominent East Germans who had defected to the West and admitted to photographing hundreds of top-secret documents by hiding behind his desk when the security guard locked his office during the lunch break. He also confessed to having ruined a major American intelligence project, as will be detailed in chapter 64.

In his autobiography, *No Other Choice,* published in 1990, Blake explained why he had confessed. He had been incensed by a suggestion that he had been forced into spying by the KGB! He explained that after being transferred from the navy to MI6 because of his fluency in Dutch and German, he had been given an MI6 booklet, *The Theory and Practice of Communism.* It was that which had first induced him to become a Marxist after he had originally intended to enter the Church. During his internment in North Korea, he had become "increasingly sure that the creation of a communist society was both feasible and desirable" and had convinced himself that he was on the wrong side. In the autumn of 1951, he had decided to "render assistance to a great cause" and volunteered his services to a KGB officer.

On his return to Great Britain, though treated most sympathetically by MI6, he quickly contacted a KGB officer, who turned out to be Nick-olai Korovin, the Soviet embassy official who was running Harry Houghton. Korovin insisted that the first contact be held abroad for se-curity's sake, the venue being The Hague, as Blake was visiting relatives in Holland. After that, they met in north London at least once a month. The MI6 security had been so lax that Blake had been able to take out bulky documents or photograph them in his office with minimal risk.

When Blake had been posted to Berlin at the beginning of 1955, Ko-rovin had gone there to introduce him to his new controller. Then, after Blake had returned to London four years later, they had resumed their regular contact. In Lebanon, where he had been posted in September 1960, he had again established contact with the KGB.

Blake claimed that he had always realized he might be caught but sto-ically accepted the risk for the Soviet cause. His behavior was a further example of how an intellectually able man could ponder privately about the Soviet system and, with no pressure from anyone else or any bribe, decide irretrievably to dedicate his life to it through dangerous treach-ery. While he had lost his belief in Jesus, he retained belief in an Almighty God, though brought up to believe that communism was the enemy of God. As with so many other traitors, maybe including Elli, the religious factor was involved.

When informed of the case, Harold Macmillan realized that because the original tip had come from the CIA, prosecution could not be avoided. Also, because Blake was not an establishment figure like Blunt or Philby, there was no intention of offering him immunity in return for a confession. He was an outsider, disliked by his colleagues.

The attorney general, then Sir Reginald Manningham-Buller (whose daughter recently headed MI5), told me there was great concern that Blake might withdraw his confession, but he did not. On May 23, 1961, after a short trial, mostly in camera, where he pleaded guilty and in which the fact that only a chance tip from the CIA had led to his expo-sure was withheld, he was given a record sentence of forty-two years' imprisonment. The judge remarked that he had "undone most of the work of British Intelligence since the end of the war."

Macmillan was most anxious to ensure that the public not be told that Blake had belonged to MI6. This was partly because the agency did not then theoretically exist, but also because the details would have demonstrated its gross incompetence in allowing treachery on such a scale to continue for so long. Macmillan also believed it vital to avoid letting the public know that MI6 was run by the Foreign Office. He therefore induced the D-Notice chief, Admiral George Thomson, to issue a blanket notice preventing the media from revealing that Blake had belonged to MI6 and any other details of the case and seemed unable to understand why they could not be completely silenced.

The huge sentence implied that Blake had done terrible things, and the Labour opposition demanded an explanation of the blanket ban. To offset this, Macmillan offered to tell the full truth to three selected Labour Privy Councillors, who could then assure their colleagues that secrecy was essential but would be bound by their special oath to remain silent about the details. One of them was the maverick George Brown (later to become foreign secretary), who quickly told me everything over lunch at the Écu de France restaurant in Jermyn Street, with his permission to publish, so that it all appeared in the *Daily Express* the following day. (I was to discover years later that the whole conversation had been overheard by MI5, which regularly bugged certain seats in the restaurant, including mine.) Like Macmillan, Hollis was appalled by the publicity, which exposed MI5's incompetence as well as that of MI6.

Blake's extreme sentence, which MI5 officers deplored because they felt it would deter others from confessing in the future, proved to be academic, because after only six years, he escaped to Russia in October 1966. This was not due to any effort by the KGB, which had written him off, but had been organized by ignorant do-gooders who believed his sentence to be excessive, though he would have been executed in Russia for such offenses. A released fellow prisoner arranged his escape by rope ladder and hid him in a London apartment until the hue and cry had subsided, when the do-gooders smuggled him in a caravan to East Berlin.

A recently released paper showed that Dick White, then the MI6 chief, briefed Prime Minister Harold Wilson on the escape on October 31. He played down Blake's importance as a spy by saying that he had "done little harm to the security of the State before he was caught," which hardly accorded with the forty-two-year sentence. He said that as he had been interrogated by MI6 a coincidental forty-two times, he had probably confessed all that he had done. White then assured Wilson that it was unlikely Blake would end up in the Soviet Union because he had let the KGB down by admitting his guilt. Events quickly showed that this was another gross misjudgment. In Moscow, Blake was treated like a hero.

Nevertheless, as the escape had been so easy, he was investigated for several months in the Soviet Union as a possible plant, but in 1970, he received the Order of Lenin, which he had certainly earned, and has since lived quite well. He was eventually to realize that the whole Russian effort to build a Communist society had been a miserable failure but still claims to have no regrets. In July 2000, ten years after the collapse of Soviet communism and its exposure as an inhuman tyranny, Blake appeared on Russian television to explain how he had found God again!

It might be asked why, if Elli still existed inside MI5, the KGB had not been forewarned in 1961, before Blake was tricked into returning to London from Lebanon, from which he could have been spirited away. Peter Wright assured me that as a security precaution, the MI5 management was not told anything about the Blake case until very shortly before his arrival in London. Hollis had to be informed then, because MI5 would be providing surveillance. In any case, the GRU would have been unlikely to involve a prime spy like Elli in a risky operation to save any KGB agent.

The security weakness that had allowed Houghton, Gee, Lonsdale, the Krogers, and Blake to spy so damagingly for so long until, in all cases, their existence became known only through defectors to the CIA generated severe criticism in Parliament and the press. The government was forced to take further action, and on May 11, 1961, it announced the appointment of an independent committee, headed by Lord Radcliffe, to review security procedures with the object of improving them. The need for such a step was a savage indictment of those in charge and of Hollis and White in particular.

The new KGB defector, Golitsin, who in his early debriefings in America and then in Britain was to supply some startling leads, gave immediate impetus to the suspicion that there was a Soviet spy in MI5. As already described, he confirmed the information supplied by Yuri Rastvorov, the previous KGB defector to the CIA, about another Russian, Vladimir Skripkin, who had tried to defect but had been betrayed by a source believed to have been inside MI5. In addition, he supplied what seemed to be near proof of the existence of a spy in MI5 during the late 1950s, long after Blunt and Philby had left secret service.

In 1957, Peter Wright had been involved in writing a program of technical research to improve MI5's capabilities to eavesdrop on foreign embassy telephone traffic, to intercept radio messages, to develop new secret inks, and other assets. It also contained recommendations for improving the technical facilities of MI6. The paper, intended to induce the government to provide money for the projects, became known as "the Technics Document" and was, of course, highly secret. Golitsin claimed that he had not only seen a copy of this report in the KGB files, but had helped to translate it and said that it had been kept in a safe reserved for "material from the British Security Service." Without prompting, he was able to describe one particular page of it in such detail that his MI5 debriefers had no doubt that he had seen it. Inquiries showed that Hollis was among the few officers who had seen the report. Had the document first been secured by the GRU, a copy would have been sent to the State Defense Committee, which would have passed it to the KGB, whose own spy, Philby, had long been out of access.

Hollis's supporters have made sustained attempts to allege that it was Golitsin's evidence in 1961 that initiated the mole hunt in MI5. In that way, they hoped to ridicule it, because after his first flush of revelations, Golitsin began to make preposterous claims. In fact, the serious suspicion of the existence of a spy in MI5 had originated with Igor Gouzenko's Elli allegation in 1945 and had been strengthened by Hoover's 1957 warning letter to Hollis about Frantisek Tisler and by many otherwise inexplicable anomalies and events. Being KGB, Golitsin would have had no knowledge of Elli, the GRU spy, least of all his identity.

CHAPTER 63

The Penkovsky Problem

—

IF DICK WHITE FELT ANY SHAME FOR THE RAVAGES INFLICTED by George Blake—and he had been MI6 chief for four years when the case exploded—it was probably offset by what he was to rate as his greatest success. A historic episode, which some regard as proving the case against Hollis to be false, began in December 1960, when Greville Wynne, a British businessman with MI6 contacts who was visiting Moscow for commercial reasons, was approached by Soviet intelligence officer Colonel Oleg Penkovsky. The Russian claimed to be so disenchanted with the Soviet system that he wished to reveal all the military secrets he knew to the West. This was his third attempt to do so; his earlier efforts, which had begun four months previously, had been rejected by CIA and Canadian intelligence officers.

Such a senior "walk-in," as volunteer spies are called, had seemed too good to be genuine, and they had dismissed him as an attempted plant or provocation. This belief had been intensified when they learned that Penkovsky, then forty-two, was a senior officer of the Intelligence Directorate of the General Staff in Moscow—the GRU—and came from a distinguished and privileged military family.

When Wynne reported the approach to MI6, along with a letter from Penkovsky, on his return to London, it was taken seriously, and by late January 1961, MI6 and the CIA had agreed to run the Russian as a joint operation. So early in April, Wynne, who behaved with great bravery knowing the risks he faced, was given instructions. He contacted the Russian on another business visit to Moscow and received the first wad of GRU documents.

Penkovsky was due to visit London under cover of being a technical member of the Soviet Trade Delegation, but really to consult with GRU agents in the embassy searching for British technological secrets. So MI6, in conjunction with the CIA, decided to debrief him there to see what more he had to offer. By then code-named Hero by the CIA and Alex by MI6, he arrived in London on April 20. A team of two CIA men and two from MI6 was selected for the debriefing task. Both Americans and one of the Britons could speak Russian, but as one of the CIA men was the most fluent, he posed most of the questions and did most of the translation.

What happened from the U.S. standpoint was first made public in 1993 after the American writer Jerrold Schecter had been given access to CIA archives and published his findings in *The Spy Who Saved the World*. At seventeen meetings in London, Leeds, and Birmingham, which Penkovsky also visited for "trade reasons," he provided a mass of secret information. It included Soviet plans for fighting a localized war in Germany, missile training manuals, and copies of training lectures. Examination of his documents showed that they were genuine and revealed that the West had been overestimating the true strength of the Soviet capability to mount long-range missile attacks. Contrary to American intelligence estimates, the Soviets were behind in the development of intercontinental missiles and not ahead in numbers, as previously feared. Spy satellites had already indicated that the estimates had been wrong, but this was confirmation, which eventually helped to convince President John Kennedy that Soviet leader Nikita Khrushchev was in no position to fight a nuclear war.

Hero's stock soared as he named scores of GRU Red Army officers operating under diplomatic cover, though many of them were already known. MI5 was involved in organizing security for the Russian and providing photographs of GRU and KGB officers from its files for him to identify.

Penkovsky was asked if he knew the names or code names of any British or American traitors working for the GRU. He did not, because in his various appointments, he had never had access to them, having worked in the directorate covering Pakistan, India, and Ceylon. His total ignorance of the Anglo-American directorate was prime evidence of the extent to which the GRU guarded the identities of its major agents, such as Elli.

The defector stated that the GRU had been told by the Soviet leadership that its top-priority mission was to secure early warning of any planned attack by the West, atomic or otherwise. He signed a recruitment contract, declaring that he was determined to provide the same service to the West. He also testified that the GRU competed with the KGB in espionage and hated its rival because the KGB had the task of checking him and all his colleagues for security. "They rejoice over each other's failures," he said.

The interrogators quickly realized that they were dealing with a strange character of enormous ego, who said that he wanted to be "the best spy in history." Later, he was to insist on being photographed in the uniforms of a British and an American colonel. It soon became clear that he was embittered because he had never been made a general, and the CIA men suspected that had he been promoted, he would never have defected. Penkovsky required money, not only as payment for his services, but to enable him to take back expensive presents for the GRU chief, Ivan Serov, and other superiors and their wives.

It was decided to run him as an agent in place in Moscow, reporting to MI6 and the CIA whenever arrangements could be made. Before returning home on May 6, he was given a Minox camera for photographing more documents. He also received instructions for passing information to MI6 and CIA agents working under diplomatic cover in Moscow, through quick, "brush" contact in the street, through dead-letter boxes, or at meetings elsewhere. One of these contacts was Janet Chisholm, the Russian-speaking wife of an MI6 officer, Ruari Chisholm, who was posing as a diplomat in Moscow. She had worked in MI6 and, courageously, agreed to serve as a courier. Penkovsky eventually provided film of about five thousand more documents.

Wynne, who agreed to service Penkovsky when he could, returned to Moscow on May 27, 1961, and gave him 3,000 rubles provided by MI6. Later, on July 18, Penkovsky visited London again for a Soviet trade exhibition and continued his flood of information to MI6 and the CIA. He behaved increasingly with what seemed to be dangerously overconfident carelessness for a trained intelligence officer. Nicholas Elliott told me that he demanded £1,000 to spend in London shops, claiming that the information he had given was worth far more. When it was suggested that his Russian companions would be suspicious if they saw him spending so much English money, his response was, "Whose neck will get it, yours or mine?" He was given the money, which he spent mainly on more presents to take back for senior Moscow officials and their wives.

He demanded to meet the Queen to declare his undying loyalty. Eventually he was fobbed off with a knight—Sir Dick White, who professed to be representing Lord Mountbatten. Increasingly, to White and the others, Penkovsky seemed to be unstable and motivated by a personal hatred of Khrushchev rather than of the regime. Before returning home on August 7, he was introduced to Janet Chisholm and eventually met her in Moscow, usually when she was with her children in a park, though they also communicated in other places.

Penkovsky visited Paris on GRU business on September 20 and was interrogated many more times. He handed over rolls of film and returned to Moscow on October 14. By then, his debriefing had totaled 140 hours.

While Penkovsky was being run, several events of the greatest political significance for East-West relations had been initiated by President Kennedy and by Khrushchev. The failed American-backed Bay of Pigs invasion of Marxist Cuba by Cuban exiles occurred in mid-April 1961, just when Penkovsky was being recruited. Khrushchev was demanding a settlement of the Berlin situation and initiated a political crisis by ordering the building of the Berlin Wall, mainly to stem the flood of emigration from East to West. President Kennedy and his brother Robert, his attorney general, had instructed the CIA to organize a highly secret project, code-named Operation Mongoose, in a further attempt to overthrow Cuban dictator Fidel Castro and his regime by inspiring an internal revolt. It was planned to culminate in a triumphal march into Havana in October 1962. With so many people involved, news of it leaked to the KGB.

From recent publications, and in particular the remarkable book *One Hell of a Gamble* by the Russian historian Aleksandr Fursenko and the American Timothy Naftali, it is clear that Khrushchev deliberately created what became known as "the Cuban missile crisis" by proposing to use Cuba as a permanent base to counter America's nuclear missile supremacy.

According to the KGB defector Vasili Mitrokhin, Khrushchev had previously accepted some falsely based KGB intelligence indicating that the Pentagon was convinced of the necessity of initiating a war with the Soviet Union as soon as possible. Lacking missiles with a long enough range to reach American cities, Khrushchev decided in May 1962 to install intermediate-range nuclear missiles in Cuba, which is just ninety miles from the United States. There, they could serve as a deterrent both to the invasion plans for Cuba and to a Western nuclear strike on the Soviet Union by putting the American cities of the eastern seaboard and even Washington under constant threat.

A Soviet delegation was sent to see Castro, who avidly wanted the weapons, along with guided antiaircraft missiles. So Soviet workers quickly began to build sixteen launching sites in Cuba for the nuclear rockets, and the Red Army regiments that would man them were selected.

From the beginning, Penkovsky's information was valuable to the Western political leaders, and to President Kennedy in particular, especially with respect to the evaluation and resolution of the crisis Khrushchev was causing over Berlin. However, contrary to common belief, the defector did not specifically warn that the Russians were in the process of installing medium-range nuclear missiles on Cuban soil. The CIA chief, John McCone, was the first to do that, as aerial and ground intelligence showed that thousands of technicians and large quantities of supplies were pouring in there. McCone was disbelieved, but on August 10, 1962, reconnaissance photographs and further intelligence reports convinced him that he was right. Kennedy, however, believed the Soviet ambassador, who assured him that there were none there. Penkovsky's training manuals confirmed that the weapons were SS-4's, so McCone reiterated his warning on September 6.

In preparing *One Hell of a Gamble*, the authors had unprecedented access not only to all the American records, but to some Russian archives. The 404-page blow-by-blow account, which names several important GRU players in the drama, makes no mention of Penkovsky.

On October 14, 1962, a high-level reconnaissance flight over Cuba confirmed the existence of fourteen intermediate-range missiles and some launching sites under construction. Kennedy was given the news two days later. He brooded on the evidence for several days before becoming fully convinced by it. On October 22, he broadcast to the world his intention that the U.S. Navy would blockade Cuba and turn back any Soviet ships involved in the missile buildup. On the following day, I saw the aerial photographs at the U.S. embassy in London. They left no room for doubt.

When the United States, Great Britain, and NATO all went on red alert—Macmillan authorized the RAF's V-bomber force to be ready for fifteen minutes' takeoff—Khrushchev backed down. He agreed to withdraw the missiles provided Kennedy promised not to invade Cuba and eventually to remove American medium-range missiles based in Turkey, a deal that was accepted.

The situation had been far more dangerous than anyone outside Russia had imagined. A shipload of megaton warheads for the missiles was already in a Cuban port waiting to be unloaded. Four Russian submarines with nuclear torpedoes were on station nearby. The Red Army commander in Cuba had battlefield nuclear weapons and permission to use them if Cuba was attacked—which could have precipitated a full-scale nuclear war. Cabinet papers released in 2006 revealed the extent to which American plans had progressed for a preemptive strike by missiles and bombers on the Soviet Union. They showed that Prime Minister Macmillan had been deeply shocked by the American determination to wage nuclear war, alone if necessary.

Afterward, Khrushchev complimented the GRU for providing him with information, which, he was told, came from agents and from intercepted telephone conversations in Washington. As will be seen, GRU agents in London were also involved, and these may have included Elli. Detailed analysis of the crisis has confirmed that each side seemed to know precisely what the other was doing, the Russians from human sources, the Americans from aerial and satellite reconnaissance as well as their GRU contacts.

While Khrushchev's withdrawal, which he announced on October 28, seemed to have been a political defeat for him, especially among his own people, the deal meant that for nearly thirty more years, Cuba remained a client Communist state of the Soviet Union, while Castro retained total power until 2008.

On October 22, 1962, shortly after a KGB search of Penkovsky's apartment had revealed the Minox camera, he was arrested by the KGB outside GRU headquarters in Moscow, a fact unknown to MI6 or the CIA until November 2. Wynne, who had been allowed to return behind the iron curtain, not knowing that Penkovsky was already in prison, was arrested while visiting Budapest. He had been under KGB surveillance for months. The Chisholms escaped trial under diplomatic privilege, the husband dying not long afterward from natural causes while Janet lived until 2004.

After a show trial to provide maximum exposure of British and American perfidy, Penkovsky, who admitted his guilt, was sentenced to death and was executed on May 16, 1963. Wynne was sentenced to eight years in a Soviet prison, where he was harshly treated. In Parliament, the Foreign Office denied any involvement of Wynne in intelligence operations.

How the two had been caught was uncertain until October 8, 1990, when Jerrold Schechter was officially briefed on the case in Moscow by two KGB officers who had been involved in it. They claimed that a leakage of military information to the United States had become apparent in 1961 and that laborious investigation had produced a list of suspects including Penkovsky. Wynne had come under suspicion in December 1961, when he had been observed with Mrs. Chisholm.

The KGB claimed that it had become suspicious of Mrs. Chisholm's husband when he had first arrived in Moscow in June 1960 in the guise of a second secretary at the British embassy. Previously, Chisholm had been a very active MI6 field officer in Berlin, and it seems certain that his traitorous colleague George Blake had blown him, an eventuality that had not occurred to the MI6 management. The KGB had also known that Mrs. Chisholm had been assisting her husband. So they had begun following her, routinely. At the end of 1961, and again in 1962, they had observed her brush contacts and meetings with Penkovsky.

The KGB showed Schechter a video of a meeting between Penkovsky and Mrs. Chisholm at a safe house on December 30, 1961, which has since been screened on television. So according to the KGB account at that time, only eight months after he had become a spy, Penkovsky had appeared to the KGB to be a dangerous traitor. Nevertheless, he had been allowed to continue to operate in Moscow for a further ten months and had even been jollied along with commendations.

On January 5, 1962, when Penkovsky had passed some film rolls to Mrs. Chisholm, he had become aware that he was being watched by the KGB. He had also spotted a car following him. He had noticed the same car again a week later, and the surveillance had become increasingly heavy. In the following month, a KGB officer had spotted an encounter in a Moscow store between Penkovsky and a British diplomat known to them as an MI6 officer. On July 5, when he had met Wynne in the Peking Restaurant in Moscow, they had both realized they were being watched by several KGB agents, and they never met again conspiratorially. Wynne had managed to catch a flight back to London.

In spite of all the obvious signs of suspicion, Penkovsky had continued to collect information and attempted to pass it, until his arrest. Because of his increasingly odd behavior and wildly cavalier attitude to his safety, some MI5 officers, including Wright, became convinced that he had been a GRU plant. This view seemed to be demolished when he was executed, but in view of the long time that he was permitted to consort with Mrs. Chisholm, it seemed that he might originally have been intruded as a double and then, through greed for money or egotistical satisfaction, had betrayed far more than had been permitted.

The KGB repeatedly denied to Schechter that they had delayed the arrest to protect any mole in British or U.S. intelligence who had alerted them, attributing their eventual success to patient inquiries. They said that such a delay was standard practice to learn all they could and insisted that the arrests had been entirely due to good and patient tradecraft. That explanation was in the interest of the KGB's reputation, and had there been a mole, even one serving the GRU, the KGB would have been required to protect his identity.

While MI5 had not been involved in the debriefing of Penkovsky, the agency had been required to organize security for him, including surveillance to ensure, as far as possible, that he was not under Soviet suspicion. Peter Wright had arranged continuous watcher coverage and set up microphones to record the defector's words and gave me details when I visited him in Tasmania in 1980, when his memory was still good. As director general, Hollis was informed of the operation immediately before it began, and though he did not need to know Penkovsky's true name, he demanded to be told it and eventually was. This has led Hollis's supporters to claim that all the evidence against him, however suggestive, can safely be dismissed, because if he had been a spy, he would immediately have warned Moscow and Penkovsky would never have been allowed out of Russia a second time. Penkovsky's return to London on schedule in July 1961 was complete proof of Hollis's innocence, they believe. "It's as simple as that!" one TV pundit proclaimed—a statement in which MI5 has also taken comfort.

Whatever the truth, it is rarely, if ever, simplistic in the espionage world, especially where the safety of a particularly valuable source is concerned, as the findings of former CIA counterintelligence chief Tennent ("Pete") Bagley convincingly demonstrate. In his book *Spy Wars*, published in 2007, Bagley, who was deeply involved in the Penkovsky case, quotes evidence from the official memoir of a former deputy chief of KGB foreign intelligence, General Vitaly Pavlov, stating that the KGB had quickly learned "from a foreign source" that Penkovsky was briefing the MI6-CIA team. His research has convinced him that this happened within weeks of the spy's first meetings in London, for the KGB had bugged a table in a Moscow restaurant where Penkovsky and Wynne were dining only a fortnight after the first series of meetings in London. The KGB had been aware of Penkovsky's treason sixteen months before they arrested him.

As standard routine, the Russians' first priority had been to protect the source, which Bagley believes to have been "presumably a mole in American or British intelligence close to the operation." Because such penetration agents were valued so highly, it was essential to avoid giving any indication that Penkovsky had been detected. For that reason, he was allowed to visit London and Paris, since otherwise the CIA and MI6 would have been alerted that a leak had occurred and would have immediately launched an inquiry to discover the culprit. Eventually, Penkovsky would have to be arrested, but before then, the KGB decided that it was essential to build up convincing evidence, visible to the CIA and MI6, that he had been detected through long, routine surveillance. The gambit worked. After Penkovsky's arrest, there was an inquiry within MI6 and the CIA to check for any leak there. It produced nothing, but even among the most conspiratorial minds, nobody really suspected that Penkovsky had been blown, simply because sufficient time had elapsed for him to have betrayed himself by his insecure behavior or through routine KGB counterespionage.

It is clear that the KGB avoided alerting the GRU about their discovery. To what extent has only recently been revealed by extracts from the diary of the GRU chief Ivan Serov, secured in Moscow by Nigel Bance. Not until April 1962 did Serov know about Penkovsky's treachery, when the KGB chief, then Vladimir Semichastny, told him about the long surveillance because an arrest was imminent. Serov was furious that the GRU had been kept in ignorance but had to agree to the continuation of the surveillance. In his diary entry, Serov refers to "the traitor," so Penkovsky was not a GRU plant.

During the time that the KGB was building up hard evidence from surveillance for trial proceedings, Penkovsky made five further applications for official trips abroad, after his return to Moscow following the Paris visit. All had been backed by the GRU, but the KGB had turned them down on the pretext that they were making inquiries about his father, who had been killed in 1919 fighting the Bolsheviks—as the KGB had long known.

Preventing Penkovsky's further trips abroad forced his Western handlers to meet him in Moscow, where he could be routinely surveyed. Eventually, the KGB tailed him in ways he could not fail to notice in the hope of panicking him into actions that would provide unsuspicious reasons to arrest him—as they eventually did. Because the Russian intelligence agencies continue to protect the identity of highly valued agents, even after their demise, partly for the sake of close relatives, the KGB and its successor has maintained the official line that Penkovsky was unmasked through routine surveillance. However, according to Bagley, in 1996, after the collapse of the Soviet Union, KGB insiders admitted that the surveillance story had been a ruse. Whoever the still unidentified informer was, the fact that the KGB knew about Penkovsky's collaboration with the West before his trip to Paris and made no effort to prevent it disposes of the facile assertion that if Hollis had alerted Moscow, the defector would never have been allowed out of the Soviet Union.

CHAPTER 64

Another Enlightening Case

THROUGH THEIR WEEKLY MEETINGS ON THE JOINT INTELLI-
gence Committee and in other ways, Hollis had ready access to White,
who was so excited about his Penkovsky windfall, as his biography has
shown, that he was personally supervising the case for MI6 and chatting
about it enthusiastically to close colleagues. So Hollis would have
learned that while Penkovsky knew the names of Soviet GRU officers
placed in various locations abroad, he had no knowledge of any of their
British or American agents.

Had he been a spy, Hollis would therefore have known that he was in
no danger of exposure and with no urgent need to take the risk of consulting his controller—if indeed he had one at that time, when because
of his position he is likely to have been elevated to confidential contact,
a Communist sympathizer who can be approached for assistance but is
not expected to be in regular contact.

The Soviet leadership would have regarded his capability to give
warning of any nuclear strike decision as so crucial that he would have
been advised to avoid courting any unnecessary danger. Further, being
so near retirement, and with no wish to live in Russia following the experiences of Burgess, Maclean, and Philby there, he is likely to have
been particularly averse to putting himself at any avoidable risk.

Nevertheless, Penkovsky's appearance in London on April 20, 1961,
could have been an anxious time for any Soviet source, especially as

only two days later, George Blake, the confessed MI6 spy, would be committed for trial. While it was extremely unlikely that Blake would have known anything dangerous to Hollis, the interrogation of any Soviet agent is always a trying period for another spy. On May 3, perhaps while he may still have been pondering what to do or not to do, Hollis sat with White in the well of the Old Bailey's Central Criminal Court to hear Blake being sentenced to forty-two years' imprisonment.

Weighing all the factors, had Hollis been a spy, he would have realized that if he alerted the GRU Center about Penkovsky, he would lose control of events. Penkovsky was due to return to London in July, just two months later. If he was prevented from doing so, or even arrested, there would be immediate suspicion, in both MI6 and the CIA, that someone had "blown him," followed by a major inquiry to trace the culprit. Following the letter Hollis had received from the American FBI chief, J. Edgar Hoover, in 1958, there was already deepening suspicion among some MI5 officers that their service was penetrated by a high-level Soviet agent, and the blowing of Penkovsky would intensify the effort to identify him. By genuine coincidence, if Hollis was Elli, he quickly had further reason to avoid interfering. Peter Wright, who had long suspected the existence of a very high-level mole inside MI5, expressed his fears in a report on the case, which he submitted in May 1961 and was read by Hollis.

By yet another coincidence, both White and Hollis should have been especially aware of the extraordinary lengths to which the Soviet intelligence directors would go to protect a penetration agent of a Western intelligence agency likely to remain of exceptional value. Blake's confession in March–April 1961 had exposed yet another staggering betrayal of a secret Anglo-American intelligence operation. In 1954, American and British engineers had driven a five-hundred-yard tunnel under the East-West border in Berlin and, with great technical skill, had tapped into three major telephone cables used by the Soviet forces. For almost a year before the Russians announced the discovery of the tunnel on April 22, 1956, the CIA and MI6 had been able to listen to many thousands of conversations revealing details of military movements and planning. They had also been able to tap into messages being sent and received by the East German Stasi. The effort involved in translating and analyzing the information had probably exceeded its general intelligence value, but it had helped to convince the allies that the Russians had no immediate intention to invade Western Europe, which was of great political value.

Sadly, what had seemed to be an intelligence coup descended into yet another farce when, during Blake's interrogation in 1961, it transpired that the KGB had known about the tunnel and its precise purposes before the first spit of soil had been removed. Blake had been involved in the planning and on January 18, 1954, had given his KGB controller copies of the minutes of an early meeting of CIA and MI6 officers, along with a sketch of what was proposed. Blake had handed over details of the project—known to the CIA as Stopwatch and to MI6 as Gold—two days before the CIA had approved it, as he has stated in his autobiography. It was a massive betrayal of an American intelligence asset by a British traitor, which probably enhanced the satisfaction felt by Blake.

The KGB Center had realized that if they announced their discovery of this "dirty trick" before it could be used, there would be an inquiry, in both MI6 and the CIA, into how the secret had leaked so soon. This might have thrown suspicion on Blake, who was quickly assured by his KGB controller that in the interest of his safety, there would be no interference with the tunnel. Vital secret material would be sent by other routes. "The safeguarding of my position was considered of paramount importance," Blake recalled.

The sacrifice soon paid off because Blake was posted to MI6's Berlin station one month before the tunnel became operational and was quickly betraying scores of Germans and Russians who had been recruited as MI6 and CIA agents. In the London Soviet embassy, only the KGB chief and Blake's controller, Korovin, were allowed to know his identity, and every detail of contact with him was controlled by Moscow. Even at the KGB Center, only three people were aware that such a source existed.

To give Blake further protection, the KGB did not tell even the GRU or the staffs of the Soviet armed forces in Berlin about the tunnel—another example of the strictness of the secrecy, regarding penetration agents, practiced by both Soviet intelligence services. Nor, as Markus Wolf recorded in his memoirs, did the KGB tell the Stasi chiefs, who continued to use the cables for secret work. The KGB cut its losses by diverting some military messages to other lines, but most of the intercepted traffic was genuine and included new facts about the nuclear capability of the Soviet air force and installations in Russia and details about the Baltic fleet.

There is no evidence that the Russians had been able to inject much disinformation into the traffic, mainly because such an attempt would have involved too many people and could have aroused allied suspicions. In fact, *The Mitrokhin Archive* has confirmed that it had all been a genuine sacrifice to protect Blake. As no war was being contemplated at the time, the KGB had considered any short-term military disadvantage well worthwhile if it kept Blake in business, as it did. The FBI officer Charles Bates, who was involved in the tunnel operation, told me that to keep the deception going to preserve Blake, the Russians had even allowed the Americans and British to catch an occasional unimportant KGB agent by feeding the necessary information through the tapped cables. He believed that, if necessary, that was how the GRU would have protected a spy as important as Hollis.

When the Kremlin had decided to end the farce and expose the West's "imperial duplicity" by staging an "accidental" discovery of the tunnel in April 1956, the KGB had even resisted the temptation to make MI6 and the CIA look foolish by stating the truth. As Blake has revealed, the KGB waited until a real fault had developed on a cable so that it had to be inspected, giving the troops who did the digging a genuine reason for discovering the tap. The Americans who were monitoring the cable also knew about the fault, so no suspicions about a leakage were aroused.

When the Russians had shown the tunnel to journalists on April 24, they had also sacrificed the opportunity to make much political capital to avoid any danger to Blake. In this, the KGB had the full support of the two Soviet leaders, Nikita Khrushchev and Nikolai Bulganin, who were on the goodwill visit to London (when the frogman Crabb incident occurred). They had decided to direct all the ignominy arising from the tunnel disclosure at the Americans to show they were abusing their position in Berlin, though it was obvious that most of the equipment in it was British made. They had ruled that no mention of any British part in the enterprise should be made. Meanwhile, even the GRU had been led to believe that the exposure of the tunnel had been accidental. (The GRU's eventual reaction when it discovered the truth is not known. Perhaps it appreciated that it would have behaved the same way itself.)

The KGB sacrifices to protect Blake may be seen as indicative of the lengths to which the GRU would have gone to protect Hollis. It is reasonable to ask why, if Hollis was a spy, he failed to inform the GRU of the existence of the tunnel. I can find no evidence that he knew anything about it before it was publicly exposed. There was no MI5 "need to know," as the British involvement was entirely an MI6 affair. At the relevant time, relations between MI6 and MI5 were cool because of MI5's much resented interference in the Philby case. The MI6 chief, then John Sinclair, did not particularly warm to the MI5 chief, Dick White, and is unlikely to have taken him into his confidence. White appears to have given no indication to his biographer that he knew about the British involvement in the tunnel before being indoctrinated on a visit to Berlin immediately following his switch to head MI6 after the tunnel had been exposed.

When Penkovsky confessed the details of his treachery, under physical as well as mental pressure, General Serov, who had been a drinking companion of the defector's, was demoted and retired. While several books have reported that he committed suicide, his daughter insists that he died a natural death in 1990.

CHAPTER 65

Another Naval Spy

LORD RADCLIFFE AND THE OTHER FOUR MEMBERS OF THE committee set up by Harold Macmillan to investigate security procedures produced their report in April 1962. As a witness before them, I can testify to the depth of the inquiries. The first conclusion wisely overturned the advice of the 1956 Privy Councillors' inquiry that the main threat to security was posed by British Communists. Instead, the committee firmly stated that the situation had changed and the threat was posed mainly by the professional intelligence services of the Soviet bloc. While restraining itself in its criticisms of MI5, at least in the published report, which was heavily expurgated, it clearly indicated that Hollis and his team should have taken the initiative in improving security in other government departments. This may have owed something to my evidence, for as I explained in *Inside Story* in 1978, I alerted the committee to the dangers being posed by trade union officials who were secret Communists and had ready access to defense establishments and to left-wing staff inside them. The committee advised the government to refuse to negotiate with Communist officials, which it did. Clearly, that was a security precaution that MI5 should have recommended but had not. What Hollis thought of the committee's opinion that "irregular sexual or marital relations" indicated a defect of character can only be imagined, but it made no difference to his behavior.

The published version of the Radcliffe report made no mention of the crucial fact that the Soviet Union and its satellites were steadily building up the numbers of intelligence officers far beyond the equivalent numbers of comparable Britons allowed in their countries. The committee could not have missed it, because I stressed it in my evidence to them, but they may have been under pressure from the Foreign Office to avoid offending Moscow on that score.

In April 1962, as the Radcliffe committee reported its findings, Hollis received information from another chance defector to the CIA of the existence of a Soviet spy, and possibly two, in the Admiralty. The informant was Anatoli Golitsin, the KGB officer who had defected in Finland in December 1961, though he was not debriefed by MI5 until the following April. He then provided information leading to the arrest of John Vassall, a clerk in the Admiralty who had been recruited through homosexual blackmail while working in the Moscow embassy in 1954.

I eventually met Vassall twice for long interviews over lunch. An obvious homosexual, he should never have been sent to Moscow, aged thirty, where he would be prey to blackmail, as he soon was. Left alone there, he was quickly spotted by the KGB and set up at a drunken homosexual party, where photographs were taken and shown to him later. Under threat of exposure, and with offer of money, he agreed to spy; he subsequently passed over secret documents and continued to do so when transferred to the Naval Intelligence Division in London in 1957. Vassall was another example of the axiom that in the recruitment of a spy, access is more important than rank. He dealt with the in trays and out trays of naval officers and civilians of the highest ranks, abstracting documents that, with his previous training as a photographer in the RAF, he could copy at his apartment in Dolphin Square during his lunchtime. With money supplied by his controller in the Soviet embassy, he was living far beyond his genuine means, but nobody noticed. During the five years that he worked in sensitive positions, including the military branch of the Admiralty, his massive treachery was never spotted until Golitsin provided his evidence. Even then, MI5 could do no better than put him on a list of four until another defector to the CIA gave further information.

Vassall was arrested on September 12, 1962. His contrite confession has been released into the National Archives, showing that he provided the Special Branch detectives who had been watching him with every detail of his KGB recruiters, controllers, and their methods of contacting him. He even provided the tools to open a secret drawer in a cabinet given to him by the KGB.

Because of the American involvement, prosecution could not be avoided, though the revelation that he had been supplying masses of documents over eight years and regularly meeting Russians in the street was bound to cause further severe criticism of security procedures at all levels. His Soviet controller suddenly left London for Moscow shortly *before* Vassall's arrest, just as had happened with the KGB officer who had controlled the Portland spy Harry Houghton. As usual, once a prosecution became unavoidable, Hollis tried to exploit it as an MI5 triumph. He went to see Prime Minister Macmillan, who told his biographer, Alistair Horne, that Hollis declared with high satisfaction, "I've got this fellow, I've got him!" Macmillan, whose successful handling of the nation's affairs had earned him the title "Supermac" after cartoonists regularly depicted him in the magic garb of Superman, looked glum and forecast that the security service would be not praised but blamed for being hopeless and that with yet another security disaster, the government might fall. He noted in his diary that Vassall had been caught "only by the help of a Russian defector." Perhaps he had not been told that the Russian had defected to the CIA. Hollis's successor, Martin Furnival Jones, was to state, "It is a scandal that a spy has got through the defences." The Vassall case was to prove to be a scandal of appalling proportions.

Macmillan's foreboding was justified. When Vassall was sentenced to eighteen years in prison, it was obvious that he had inflicted great damage over a long period, and the Labour opposition and the media made the most of it. To secure some respite, Macmillan set up yet another investigative committee, headed by Sir Charles Cunningham of the Home Office, on October 23, 1962. Also, to clear the names of ministers who had been accused of negligence by some newspapers, he set up a three-man tribunal under Lord Radcliffe to investigate the Vassall case—in public as far as possible.

In a newspaper article, I had previously disclosed that Vassall had been betrayed by a Soviet defector, and I was therefore required to give evidence to the tribunal. I learned later that Hollis and Radcliffe had ensured that I would not be pressed, when on the witness stand, into revealing any more details about that defector—Golitsin—who was then secretly in Britain. By previous agreement, I was also enabled to identify the Defense Ministry source of my information about the defector Lieu-tenant Colonel Sammy Lohan. Two other journalists who declined to name the sources for their inaccurate press reports found themselves in contempt of court and went to prison, a media disaster that caused fur-ther damage to the government.

Meanwhile, Golitsin had also indicated the presence of another spy recruited in Moscow and alleged to be a senior naval captain. MI5 offi-cers wished to interrogate such a prime suspect, who eventually became an admiral, but Hollis, pursuing his blind-eye policy, refused to allow him to be approached, arguing that he was close to retirement and was by then in a post where he could do little damage. When it was sug-gested that the suspect might be offered immunity to prosecution in re-turn for a confession, Hollis remained adamant, declared the case closed, and ordered that all the papers referring to it should be de-stroyed. This was a further example of "elimination," which was cer-tainly amicable to the suspect.

I know the suspect's name. He seemed to be a most unlikely traitor, and still does, but if he was the man I met while carrying out a high-level assignment, as I believe he was, he could not have been in a more sensi-tive position. Had he been arrested, the scandal would have made the Vassall case look trivial. It would also have been extremely unwelcome to the government, and Macmillan in particular, especially in view of the inevitable American response—a factor no doubt appreciated by Hollis.

The Vassall tribunal, which attracted wide media coverage, pub-lished its findings on April 24, 1963. Hollis, who knew that Macmillan would be required to make a statement to Parliament, where there was sure to be a heated debate on the report, had attempted to limit the dam-age by a preemptive strike. A released cabinet paper is a letter from Hol-lis to Sir Burke Trend, the cabinet secretary, dated April 16, urging him to set up a small group to draft the prime minister's statement for him. Hollis named MI5's representative on the group as Graham Mitchell, his deputy, who would try to ensure that Macmillan would quote statements from the tribunal's report showing how difficult it was to counter the huge effort that Russian intelligence was mounting against Britain.

Though Hollis may have been unaware of it then, in that very month, April 1963, Mitchell came under deep official suspicion, inside MI5, of being a Soviet spy. Small wonder that Macmillan, who was quickly told of the suspicion by Dick White, described MI5 to me as a madhouse when my wife and I last visited him at Birch Grove. He said he had become convinced that Mitchell had never been a spy and that his suspicious behavior was entirely the result of having been "driven mad" because nobody could work for ten years or more in MI5 without losing his reason.

MI5 and the embassy staff in Moscow were severely criticized in the tribunal report. The gross inequality in the number of Russians stationed in London—218, compared with 106 British officials in Moscow—was stressed, as was the strain it placed on MI5's resources.

On April 26, the cabinet's Official Committee on Security met to discuss the tribunal's recommendations, with Hollis and powerful mandarins from the Foreign Office, Treasury, and Home Office present. It was agreed that in future, all the subordinate staff of the service attachés at iron curtain embassies should be married service personnel, who would be more subject to discipline and, hopefully, less subject to sexual temptation and subsequent blackmail. Hollis demanded that every Foreign Office employee returning from iron curtain service, whatever his or her rank, be required to undergo routine interrogation by MI5. He argued that what one diplomat said about another could yield valuable clues. Sir Harold Caccia, for the Foreign Office, was appalled by the plea, rejecting it as "an intrusion into private lives" and a "general invitation to the staff to report on each other" that would have a "disastrous effect on morale."

It is hard to believe that Hollis imagined that his crass demand, which would have included ambassadors, had any chance of success, but if he was Elli, it was no bad thing to appear to be so zealous when the possibility that such traditional mandarins would support him was zero.

Nothing was done to reduce the excessive number of Russian intelligence officers in London. The only eventual constructive result was the setting up of a permanent Security Commission to investigate and report to Parliament on further spy cases, as and when they occurred.

Later conversations with senior naval officers convinced me that the recruitment and running of Vassall had been a major triumph for the KGB, and without the chance information from the defectors, he might have continued for substantially longer, for otherwise there had been no suspicion against him. They agreed that if the second, more senior naval spy indicated by Golitsin really existed, the total damage would have been devastating, had there been a war.

As a result, British security in Moscow continued to be disastrous. The KGB even infiltrated an attractive woman agent as a domestic servant into the residence of the ambassador, Sir Geoffrey Harrison, where she seduced him so that he could be photographed in the act and compromised so deeply that he had to be withdrawn. (His excuse was, "My defenses were down," which inevitably led to obvious ribald comment.)

A recently released MI5 document dated September 21, 1962, throws further light on Hollis's attitude to the Soviet Union around that time. It is a long memorandum written by him of a meeting he had with Sir Roy Welensky, prime minister of the Federation of Rhodesia and Nyasaland (the Central African Federation). He assured Welensky that while Communists were increasing their subversive efforts in Africa, they were not having much success. When Welensky asked whether there was any significance in the fact that so many ministers of the newly independent African countries were visiting Russia, Hollis replied that it was only natural because "the Soviet Union had shown a fantastic development from the backwardness of Russia in 1917 to the present." He thought that the African countries wanted to see how it had all been done because they wanted to develop very quickly themselves. These views seemed to indicate continuing admiration for the Soviet system.

Contemporary comments on those views, which Hollis held in 1962, were sent to me by Basil Spurling, who was commissioner of the British South Africa police from 1958 to 1963. Spurling stated that while he had never been told of the official suspicions concerning Hollis, he had become suspicious himself through his dealings with him. In 1959, when he was visiting London, Hollis had become angry with him, rising from his chair at the suggestion that a Rhodesian security officer should be stationed in London to liaise with MI5.

In October 1962, Hollis had a long meeting with the Chiefs of Staff about positive vetting. There was pressure for MI5 to take over responsibility for the vetting of all Whitehall staff, and he managed to resist it. Not long afterward, in January 1963, Harold Macmillan received a further shock to his Supermac image when Kim Philby, whom he had cleared in Parliament, defected to the Soviet Union from his home in Beirut.

CHAPTER 66

The Strange Escape of an Archtraitor

—

FOLLOWING HAROLD MACMILLAN'S 1955 CLEARANCE OF KIM Philby, who had inflicted so much damage on American as well as British interests, the case was considered closed by MI6, and while many MI5 officers were confident of his guilt, nothing effective was done. Then, astonishingly, in July 1956, MI6 chief John Sinclair—abetted by his deputy George Young and by Nicholas Elliott, who both believed Philby to be loyal—engineered Philby's partial return to secret service under journalistic cover. (It was Sinclair's last gaffe before being dismissed for his dubious role in the Crabb disaster.) On September 6, with the connivance of a newspaper and a magazine, the forty-four-year-old Philby arrived in Beirut to cover the Middle East, under the guise of being a journalist but also carrying out intelligence services. These involved submitting reports and helping to recruit and run agents. The two journals and MI6 shared the payments to him, making the previous elimination even more "amicable." The job kept him in close touch with the MI6 station in Beirut, and being friendly with those who ran it, he resumed his espionage on behalf of the KGB. He was even visited there by Young, a friend of mine who always retained a sneaking admiration for Philby, gleefully retailing stories that the spy had told him about copulating with his future wife, Litzi, in the Austrian snow.

White was later to claim that MI5 was told nothing about this extraordinary return of the MI6 spy to duty, but it was known to the CIA, which had a station in Beirut. From the inception of the idea in MI6, it was also known to the KGB, which was astonished and delighted to have Philby operating for them in the Middle East, at British expense, while consorting with talkative MI6 officers and doing MI6 tasks.

It is possible that this appointment, for which internal talks and negotiations with the journals had begun early in 1956, had been responsible for the reemergence of Guy Burgess and Donald Maclean in Moscow in February of that year. The KGB chiefs had staged their appearance and had some purpose in doing so. Burgess's statement that he and Maclean had never been spies and had moved to Russia voluntarily because they preferred to work there indicated that they had needed no third man to tip them off about anything. This supported the contention inside MI6 that Philby was innocent and perhaps alleviated any doubts in the minds of the two editors about the wisdom of employing a possible traitor.

Philby's move to Beirut effectively put him beyond further action by MI5, because offenses against the Official Secrets Act were not extraditable. He was soon in regular contact with KGB controllers and continued to be of considerable service to the Center, which was extending its Middle East interests, especially in Egypt and Yemen. Those who sent him there had much to answer for.

When Dick White learned that Philby was back on the MI6 payroll, after he became chief there, he was allegedly furious but did nothing, claiming later that as the new man, he had to tread warily. Either this showed feeble leadership or he left Philby there for a purpose. Nor, reportedly, did White inform MI5 about Philby's resurgence, though in view of his closeness with Hollis, this is hard to believe. With their previously warm relationship with Philby, and Hollis's prime role in securing him the plum post in MI6, both had reason to fear him, should he ever choose to talk. So it would seem likely that they discussed the issue at length and agreed that Philby out on a limb with an MI6 job in Beirut was better than Philby jobless and bleating in his cups in London clubs. (Later, President Lyndon Johnson was to immortalize this type of convenience by remarking of a dangerous colleague, "I'd rather have him inside the tent pissing out than outside the tent pissing in!")

In April 1962, the KGB defector Anatoli Golitsin reported the existence of a KGB "Ring of Five"—five British-born spies who had all been at Cambridge when they were recruited. He named Maclean and

Burgess as two of them and knew that a third had alerted them to their danger in 1951. Hollis was advised to have Philby questioned again, but he refused to move without further evidence. This accrued in August 1962 from an elderly woman friend of Philby's, Flora Solomon, who told Lord Rothschild that Philby had always been a Communist and indicated that he had worked for the Russians. Rothschild, who later related the circumstances to me, told White, who alerted Hollis. A decision to try to question Philby was now unavoidable, as Rothschild was expecting some action.

The interrogation should have been conducted by MI5, but Hollis agreed with White's request that MI6 should do it on the mutual understanding that whatever happened, Philby would not have to stand public trial. Without a confession, there was no evidence that could be admissible in a British court. As a traitor and professionally trained liar, Golitsin would have been useless in the witness box, and Flora Solomon's statements alone would not have carried a conviction, especially after Macmillan's public clearance.

Through Philby's past treachery, the KGB had known for eight years what MI6—and much of MI5—was doing in great detail and exactly who was doing it. He had provided insights into the CIA since its foundation. He had stifled important information and betrayed many people to their deaths. Yet White and Hollis were determined to offer him total immunity to prosecution and publicity, whatever he might confess. Ostensibly, in return, he might provide some information about the KGB, but both also appreciated that he could be far too dangerous to them, personally and to their services, in a witness box. Should he reveal that both of them, and Hollis in particular, had been instrumental in securing his promotion in MI6 to a position where he had done so much damage, there would be howls for their resignations. A trial would be extremely unwelcome to Supermac, who along with the attorney general quickly agreed to the immunity proposal. It was like offering immunity to a serial killer.

With Philby judged to be far too wily to be induced back to London, Nicholas Elliott, his closest former colleague in MI6, who had previously been completely convinced of his innocence, was sent to Beirut, arriving there on January 10, 1963. Elliott had seen a great deal of him while serving as MI6 station chief in Beirut from 1960 to 1962. He had used him regularly as a source of Arab politics, gleaned largely during

Philby's clandestine KGB activities in Syria, Iraq, Jordan, and North Yemen, for which MI6 and his journalistic employers had unwittingly paid. So when Elliott volunteered to handle the confrontation, White immediately agreed, seizing the opportunity to keep the case in-house. While Hollis was amenable to White's proposal, there were MI5 officers who would have strenuously opposed it, had they been told. The move was kept secret from the CIA.

White and Elliott discussed in detail, and rehearsed, how Philby should first be confronted. In the process, as White admitted to his biographer, he lied to Elliott regarding the degree of proof about Philby, claiming darkly that MI6 penetration of the KGB on that score was much deeper than it really was. His purpose was to try to strengthen Elliott's hand in dealing with such a formidable opponent who had dominated White in their previous confrontation. As will be seen, White also gave Elliott some further false information.

The MI6 chief in Beirut was then Peter Lunn, who, without being told of the purpose, was instructed to suggest a meeting between himself and Philby to discuss future plans. The rendezvous was to take place in a Beirut apartment, which was then microphoned so the conversation could be tape-recorded. Philby attended, allegedly expecting to meet Lunn or some other local official, only to find Elliott alone in the apartment. According to Elliott, a country neighbor of mine who described the encounter to me more than once, Philby said, "I rather thought it would be you," convincing him that the traitor had been warned of his coming.

When Elliott told him there was new evidence that he had been a long-term spy, Philby protested his innocence, declaring that, as before, the whole idea was ridiculous. Elliott responded by assuring him that he had been betrayed in detail by a KGB source. What were claimed to be precise details of the conversation in the apartment were published in 1994 in *The Philby Files* by Philby's Russian biographer, Genrikh Borovik, who had access to KGB archives and, of course, to the traitor himself. What emerged was that Elliott repeatedly told Philby that MI6 knew for certain that although he had definitely been a Soviet spy, he had broken with the KGB in 1949 and had not spied since. The scenario was strongly reminiscent of the Firs fiasco, when Sonia was assured that MI5 was certain she had ceased to spy when she had arrived in the

United Kingdom and had not spied since. That falsehood, too, had been fabricated by White, assisted by Hollis, or vice versa.

White told his biographer that it was Philby who had raised the 1949 date, but as Borovik stresses, it made no sense to Philby and he could never understand why it was mentioned. In fact, the circumstances offer a simple and sensible solution. It was in 1949 that Philby had been transferred to Washington, where he had remained as liaison officer until recalled in 1951. White knew that he would shortly have to explain the new developments in the Philby case to his counterparts in the CIA and the FBI and that he could expect a roasting, especially from J. Edgar Hoover, for failing to nail Philby in 1951. So it was greatly in his interest to acquire a piece of paper signed by Philby stating that he had ceased to spy before he went to America. It would enable him to claim that Philby had not betrayed any American secrets while in Washington, including details of Venona code breaks, which in fact he had betrayed. Philby's warning to Maclean, through Burgess, in 1951 was not inconsistent with his having given up spying because he would still have been anxious to prevent Maclean from revealing his pre-1949 treachery.

White and Hollis had two further reasons for plugging the 1949 falsehood. If Philby confirmed it in writing, the CIA would have no grounds for objecting to the granting of immunity to prosecution. The date also held an advantage for Philby, though Elliott never reached the stage of pointing it out. If he had not spied in Washington, he could not be prosecuted there. Otherwise, whatever the British government might condone, the U.S. authorities might still wish to try him for crimes committed in their country between 1949 and 1951.

According to Elliott's account of that first confrontation, he offered Philby total immunity from prosecution or publicity for a confession, on the understanding that he would undergo a long debriefing. He also threatened him with the end of his livelihood as a journalist if he failed to comply and gave him twenty-four hours to make a decision.

It is now known that Philby then made contact with his regular KGB controller in Beirut, Petrukhov, who would have been required to contact the KGB Center for advice. Petrukhov eventually warned him that he would have to defect, perhaps because the Center feared that he might be kidnapped by the CIA, if not by MI6. Next day, according to Elliott, Philby returned to the apartment and, without even asking what the new evidence against him might be, agreed in principle and made a partial confession. He admitted that he had become a Soviet agent in 1934, claiming that he had been recruited by his wife, Litzi, which was a lie to cover the real culprit, Edith Tudor Hart. He confirmed that he had been the third man, who had warned Maclean, through Burgess, to defect. He specifically denied that Blunt had been an agent, claimed to know nothing about any fifth man, and, as required, stated that he had broken contact with the KGB in 1949. He produced a two-page type-written statement to those effects, which he signed. Because the windows of the apartment had been left open, the heavy traffic noise outside made much of the tape recording indecipherable, another example of ham-fisted procedure.

The two met again when Philby allegedly handed over more type-written material. White claimed to be elated when he received the cabled news, believing that Philby was finally broken. He was, allegedly, naïvely sure that Philby would never flee to Russia, because now that he had confessed, he would be unwelcome there. Elliott, who eventually returned to London in some degree of triumph, was also satisfied that his old friend would never desert his new wife and defect. He had left Lunn to control the situation without support.

When the admissions in Philby's confession were studied, it seemed they had been carefully contrived, suggesting that he had been prepared for Elliott's arrival. Why had he not continued to deny everything, as he had done so successfully in the past? The view in MI5's counterespionage department was that Philby had been fully briefed both on the new evidence and on the immunity deal before Elliott's arrival. Nevertheless, happy with his piece of paper, White was convinced there was no urgency about the further debriefings, which could be done leisurely in Beirut by Lunn, should Philby be unwilling to return to London. No attempt was made to shadow Philby to see whom he might be meeting for advice.

A firsthand account of what was happening in MI5, meanwhile, was given to me by the FBI officer Charles Bates, who was in London at the time. He told me that Hollis's secretary asked him to see Hollis, who told him that Elliott had been sent to question Philby. Bates queried the wisdom of sending just one man, when in his view the traitor should have been arrested and flown out of the country, as he claimed the FBI would have done. Unimpressed, Hollis asked him to make a list of questions for Lunn to ask Philby at his next interrogation. Bates responded by asking, "What makes you think he will still be there?" to which Hollis replied, "He will be. He isn't going anywhere."

On the night of January 23, 1963, assisted by Petrukhov and others, Philby boarded a Soviet freighter moored in Beirut and disappeared, as Elliott would put it, "into the red." He was fifty-one years old and, having been converted to belief in communism, had served the cause at great cost and danger to himself for more than thirty years.

Next day, Bates, who had prepared several pages of questions, took them to Hollis, who told him blandly that Philby had fled. When Bates said, "That's no surprise to me," Hollis showed no emotion.

These encounters are proof that Hollis was closely involved in the operation. Bates regarded the escape as yet another anomaly affecting the MI5 chief, who seemed totally unsurprised and unconcerned about the outcome. Whether he was displaying coolness in the face of disaster or satisfaction in a mission accomplished remains uncertain.

White, on the other hand, appeared to be horrified, realizing that he had made another major misjudgment for which he could be held responsible. He told Elliott that he regretted having reopened the case at all. There was suspicion in both MI6 and MI5 that White and Hollis had induced Philby to defect and that perhaps his job in Beirut had been kept going to give him easy opportunity should the need arise.

The similarities to the Firs fiasco another White-Hollis extravaganza—are inescapable. The Firs fiasco seemed to have been meticulously planned and rehearsed to induce Sonia to get out of British jurisdiction and stay out. When that had failed, Plan B—the deception that she had done so—was put into highly successful effect. The Elliott fiasco had produced the more desired result. Had it failed, Philby would have been left quietly in Beirut, immune to prosecution or publicity and with no real risk that he would ever return to London to face thorough interrogation. Whether it was intended to keep him on the MI6 payroll for appearances' sake and possibly to provide some degree of control has never been revealed. It seemed implicit in Elliott's offer that there would be no objection to his continuing journalism.

Though the media were full of rumors about Philby's disappearance, neither Hollis nor White wished to be the bad news messenger.

Harold Macmillan did not receive official admission of Philby's disappearance until February 19, when he noted it in his diary, recording that Philby had confessed "in a drunken fit," which, Elliott assured me, was quite untrue.

Macmillan was appalled by the likely political consequences in view of his exoneration of Philby and the now patent falsities of the Whitewash Paper. He agreed that the fact that Philby was obviously in Russia should not be admitted officially for as long as possible. Philby's disappearance was not confirmed until March 29, 1963, when Edward Heath, speaking on behalf of the Foreign Office, which is responsible for MI6, made the bare announcement that Philby had disappeared from Lebanon. Not until July 1 was he forced by American and Russian publicity to admit that the security services were "aware, partly as a result of an admission made by Mr. Philby, that he had worked for the Soviet authorities before 1946 and that in 1951 he had warned Maclean through Burgess." Heath's brief, which had originated in MI5, was deliberately misleading concerning the date 1946 because Hollis knew that Philby had admitted being a Soviet agent since 1934. Putting 1946 into the public mind helped to cover the fact that the traitor had worked against Britain's and America's interests for seventeen years before he was removed from MI6. It also concealed his treachery to both nations during World War II.

There was a further storm in both the British and the American media, as the FBI papers "Philby, Burgess, Maclean" so powerfully recall. The British security and intelligence authorities were rightly lambasted for weeks, and Macmillan had a rough time in Parliament because of his previous clearance of the traitor. Marcus Lipton, the MP who had first named Philby as the third man, received an apology. Fortunately for both White and Hollis, the media were unaware at that stage of Philby's previous post in MI6, as head of anti-Soviet activities, or of the colossal damage he had inflicted. Nor did they know that Philby had been back on the MI6 payroll for eight years, which would have given the Labour opposition a field day.

Meanwhile, White had flown to Washington to try to rectify the damage that the defection had caused there. In spite of the signed confession and the 1949 gambit, which the defection had disproved, the CIA was angry at being kept in the dark about the confrontation, while Hoover—who had heard about it from Bates, but only at the last minute—was furious. White had no excuses and had to rely on his charm to calm things down. He hoped that after the immediate furor, interest would subside, and when Elliott received a letter from Philby suggesting a meeting in Berlin or Helsinki, he ordered him to ignore it. Sadly, in Washington, Philby's defection clearly confirmed that another British traitor who had been given access to some of the most sensitive U.S. secrets had systematically betrayed them to the KGB. The American newspapers were voluble in pointing that out to their readers.

For most of the staffs of MI6 and MI5, the handling of the whole Philby affair had been a disaster, which privately White acknowledged, as his biography shows. Hollis remained inscrutable on the issue.

Far from being welcomed in Moscow as a hero, as Philby expected, he was judged to be an alcoholic who might have been turned into a double agent and was held under tight control for many months, to be "dried out" and thoroughly debriefed. Instead of being a member of an elite force, as he had believed, he discovered that he was not an officer of the KGB, but only "agent Tom," for whom there was to be no KGB post. Nor was he given any rank. He was kept under some degree of surveillance by a security officer, allegedly for his protection, for the rest of his life, while being paid a pension on which he could live in comfort by Soviet standards.

Like Maclean and Burgess before him, he found life in Russia rather different from the ideological dream, in spite of the brave face he showed when interviewed or on camera. He became so depressed that after about five years, he attempted suicide by slashing his wrist.

In 1968, Philby was encouraged to publish a brief memoir, *My Silent War*, which was essentially an apologia for his treachery and contained some KGB disinformation. He mentioned Hollis and their close association, but not in a way that could cast public suspicion on the MI5 chief, then living in retirement. He also ghosted the memoirs of Gordon Lonsdale. As Elliott often told me, MI6 feared a follow-up to *My Silent War*, but it never came. Instead, Philby gave his reminiscences to the Russian writer Genrikh Borovik, who in the 375 pages of his book studiously avoided any mention of Hollis, by that time publicly suspected to have been a spy for the GRU once code-named Elli. Even under its new post-Soviet guise, the KGB would not have wanted to give any credit to the GRU for running a spy perhaps even more valuable than their star had ever been.

After the public exposure of Philby, Maclean, and Burgess, their treacherous reputations were widely exploited in "the busted spy gambit." Past anomalies in MI5 and MI6 could be explained away as due to their activities—a practice also used by some writers to fortify their theories.

In 1970, Philby acquired a Russian lady friend, Rufina, who moved into his eighth-floor apartment in an old building. A year later, they married and lived mutually happy for the rest of his life. The KGB continued to tap his telephone and open his letters. He could not leave the apartment without permission, and when he did he was followed, his every contact recorded. According to Markus Wolf, the Stasi chief who knew him, he complained privately about the poor Communist economy and the gap between rulers and masses.

In 1972, the KGB decided to rehabilitate its small group of Western traitors and improve their living conditions in a futile attempt to encourage more to defect to Russia, as the former KGB general Oleg Kalugin has described in his autobiography. On visiting Philby, Kalugin found a despondent physical wreck, "reeking of vodka." Over the ensuing months, his apartment was improved and his isolation, which had been imposed by the KGB, was ameliorated by social contact with KGB officers, and he was allowed to meet some foreigners. He was weaned from vodka to wine and encouraged to travel to Soviet satellite countries, where he advised on measures for subverting Great Britain.

In 1975, Philby met Colonel Michael Lyubimov, who spoke excellent English, having served in London, and was then in the KGB's Foreign Intelligence Directorate. Lyubimov, whom I met and questioned recently on television, boosted Philby's morale by arranging for him to lecture young KGB officers about Britain. These seminars were held in safe houses, for though Philby had finally been awarded the Order of the Red Banner and the Order of Lenin, he was not allowed to visit the KGB Center, save for one occasion in July 1977 when he lectured KGB officers about his career. In an appendix to Rufina Philby's book (*The Private Life of Kim Philby*), Lyubimov gave a revealing account of their friendship and Philby's mental condition. "Philby could not grasp that he was no longer a valued agent but a problem," he wrote. "The possibility that he was a British plant could not be excluded. No one could predict whether he might do something stupid."

In spite of Rufina's care and affection, Philby's past took its toll, and in 1978, his health began to deteriorate. He died in 1988, aged seventy-six. By then, Maclean, who was also decorated, and Burgess, who was ignored, had also died. Regrettably, none of these traitors lived to see the catastrophic collapse of the monstrous political bubble that they had helped to inflate at so much personal sacrifice and harm to others.

CHAPTER 67

"The Year That the Roof Fell In"

S OME OF ROGER HOLLIS'S COLLEAGUES IN MI5 WERE TO DE-
scribe 1963 as "the year that the roof fell in," and in his retirement,
Harold Macmillan told me that he fully agreed with the remark. Apart
from the Philby disaster, one has only to look at the packed pages of the
Hollis chronology for that year to understand why.

One of Macmillan's many shocks earlier that year was news that
MI5's deputy director general, Graham Mitchell, was under surveillance
on suspicion of being a Soviet agent. The self-appointed MI5 mole
hunters Peter Wright and Arthur Martin had narrowed their search to
two—Mitchell and Hollis. As Mitchell was quickly cleared, the case
against him will be dealt with only briefly, since it was always trivial and
he fitted none of the details ascribed to Elli by Igor Gouzenko.

By the beginning of 1963, without reference to each other, Martin
and Wright had become convinced that so many counterespionage cases
had collapsed that there must still be a Soviet agent at high level in MI5
who was systematically undermining them. In April, having independently narrowed the possible culprits to Mitchell and Hollis, they first
sought the advice of Dick White at MI6 about the general need for an
investigation into Soviet penetration, without mentioning any names.
White advised them to approach Hollis for formal permission for an inquiry. Martin did so, with no names mentioned at that stage, and Hollis's
response was typical: "If Dick agrees, then go ahead."

A few weeks later, Martin gave White the staggering news that the suspects had been narrowed to Mitchell and Hollis. After a day's reflection, White could not bring himself to believe that his protégé could possibly have been a spy, but to protect his position, he professed neutrality. He telephoned Hollis, advising him to permit the investigation of Mitchell as a sensible precaution, and secured his agreement. Next day, he told Martin that he personally dismissed any suspicions against Hollis but had secured support for an inquiry into Mitchell's activities.

Meanwhile, White had fallen under the influence of James Jesus Angleton, the formidable CIA figure who was becoming increasingly convinced that both the CIA and the British agencies had been penetrated by Soviet spies. Angleton had been sympathetic over the Philby case because he himself had been completely duped by him, confiding to that spy CIA information that had gone straight to Moscow. Having been overly influenced by the claims of Anatoli Golitsin, he pressed for a mole hunt, though at no time had that KGB defector pointed a finger specifically at either Mitchell or Hollis. Claims that the case against Hollis derived from Golitsin's wilder allegations are incorrect. The original suspicions dated to earlier events, such as Gouzenko's allegation in 1945 and the Tisler affair arising out of a letter from J. Edgar Hoover in 1958.

White informed Macmillan that he had recommended a secret investigation into Mitchell and kept him informed of progress because of the political and international implications should news of the mole hunt leak to the media. Hollis appeared to be devastated by Martin's suggestion that his deputy, who had been with him at Oxford and had followed him up the MI5 ladder, might be a spy. After the two of them discussed the possibility over dinner at the Travelers Club, Martin claimed that Hollis had behaved "like a broken man who had been found out." Hollis delayed a decision until the following day, when he agreed to a limited investigation, in which he barred telephone taps and full surveillance because he wanted as few people as possible to know about it. Angered by the limitations, Martin sought White's advice again. Accompanied by Wright and Martin Furnival Jones, he had tea with White at his London home and convinced him of the need for a full inquiry. Nevertheless, Hollis, having spoken with Macmillan, who greatly feared that Mitchell might defect and cause a catastrophic spy scandal, had his way. Later, Hollis was to insist that it was Macmillan who had forbidden any interrogation of Mitchell.

As the case progressed, perhaps the most important outcome was the early realization that Mitchell could never have been Elli. As a keen chess player, he played some postal games with various iron curtain enthusiasts, but that was hardly "something Russian in his background." Apart from his habit of taking long, solitary walks in parks, where he might have met a controller or serviced a dead-letter box, the investigators discovered only one real cause for suspicion. When Mitchell had been director of D Branch, he had pursued a policy of shutting down GCHQ's work on the Venona decrypts, which was in the Soviet interest. However, Hollis, who had then been deputy director general, had supported Mitchell in that action and may even have suggested it. In communications with White, Hollis had regarded the work as too time-consuming, as had Philby. It seems that Mitchell soon realized he was being followed and began to take evasive action. He also behaved in other ways indicating that he knew he was suspect.

Tony Henley, an MI5 officer who was involved in the inquiries, told me that he remained suspicious of Mitchell and believed that throughout the case, Hollis had kept Mitchell informed of what was happening. To keep the case secret within the MI5 office, meetings about it were held in a safe house provided by MI6, and Hollis always insisted on attending. Mitchell then virtually ended the case himself by leaving MI5 on early retirement. He had sought Hollis's permission to retire two years early on a reduced pension, and Hollis had agreed to his departure on September 6, 1963. This could have been seen as eliminating the problem amicably, because once he had retired, Mitchell could simply treat the suspicions as beneath contempt and decline any assistance.

After nearly five months, Hollis announced that as the inquiries were getting nowhere, he was closing them down. Martin then wrote a report to Hollis and White, stating that as Mitchell had not been interrogated, the suspicions remained unresolved and that under Anglo-American security agreements, the FBI and CIA would have to be informed. Hollis insisted that the Americans need not be told and then astonished his staff by suddenly deciding to fly to Washington himself. He also insisted on going alone, which his colleagues regarded as odd. His stated purpose was to warn the chiefs of the FBI and CIA, personally, that American secrets might have been compromised. Colleagues, who felt that the damage to Anglo-American security relations might be less if news of the suspicions against Mitchell were fed in at a lower level, saw the occasion as yet another example of Hollis's hands-on determination to deal with dangerous circumstances himself.

Hollis flew to Washington in September 1963, eight months after the Philby defection, which had induced senior officers of the CIA and FBI to suspect that both MI5 and MI6 were riddled with Soviet agents. When the chiefs of the FBI and the CIA asked for details of the Mitchell case, Hollis fazed them by declaring that Martin would bring them later. When Martin eventually reached Washington and revealed that Mitchell had not been questioned because Hollis had forbidden it, the U.S. authorities were even more puzzled by the director general's visit. They regarded the evidence against Mitchell as derisory.

As Hollis's visit had achieved nothing for MI5, Wright suspected that he had rushed to the United States in panic to seek advice from a Soviet controller there. As by then Hollis might have been warned by White that he himself was under suspicion, Wright surmised that he would not have risked contacting a controller in London, in case he was under MI6 surveillance. Wright also suspected that a discussion with a controller in America could explain why he had come back in a calmer frame of mind and why he immediately took action to terminate the Mitchell case, along with any other mole-hunting activity.

On his return, Hollis ordered a new and independent analysis of the evidence of Soviet penetration by another officer, Ronald Symonds, who produced a report in 1964 exonerating Mitchell. Symonds convinced himself that the continuing leaks from MI5 to Moscow had been due to the ongoing treachery of Anthony Blunt, who had gleaned the information through his gossip with MI5 officers who met him socially. This explanation was acceptable only to those anxious to accept it because too many officers would have been involved and some of the leaks were not of a nature that would have been the subject of gossip.

Hollis then wrote to the heads of the FBI, CIA, and RCMP, announcing that Mitchell had been judged innocent. He also drafted a statement declaring that no evidence of any Soviet penetration of MI5 whatever had been found, but under pressure from his staff, he deleted that. Meanwhile, according to Wright, he had destroyed documentary evidence concerning the case.

Shortly before the general election in October 1964, Hollis declared the case closed, observing that even if Mitchell was guilty, he could do no further harm and wanting to avoid having to tell the new, incoming government anything about it. By that time, both Wright and Martin had decided that Hollis was the chief suspect and turned their attention in that direction. The Mitchell case was to be revived later by an investigating committee, code-named Fluency, which also found no convincing evidence against him.

After his retirement from the premiership, Harold Macmillan told me he became convinced that Mitchell's quirky behavior was due entirely to having served too long in MI5, which he referred to in his diary as the "so-called Security Service." Whatever the reasons, the fact that the two top men of the British Security Service were suspected of being Russian spies by some of their own officers was an appalling situation. Had any journalist got wind of it, worldwide publicity with terrific damage to relations with America would have been inevitable.

Meanwhile, earlier in 1963, Hollis had exhibited yet another odd instance of his determination to deal with unusual circumstances himself. An enterprising journalist, John Bulloch, had secured the cooperation of the family of the late Sir Vernon Kell, who had directed MI5 for thirty-one years before being fired by Winston Churchill, to help him write a book entitled *MI5*. It included all that he had been able to discover about the service up to and including the Blake, Lonsdale, and Vassall cases. According to David Hooper, a solicitor who researched the precise circumstances for his own book, *Official Secrets,* as soon as MI5 heard of the project, the D-Notice secretary, then Colonel Sammy Lohan, was instructed to require the publisher, Arthur Barker, to submit the book for security clearance. As publication day was only two weeks away, review copies had already been sent to newspapers. Nevertheless, Lohan returned the text, which had been duly passed to MI5, with a mass of blue-penciled deletions that he insisted be made.

The publisher's solicitors confirmed that the book did not violate the Official Secrets Act and recommended publication without amendment, but three days before the publication date, the publisher was warned in a telephone message that Home Secretary Henry Brooke needed to see him urgently. The publisher, author, and solicitor attended the Home Office on the following day. The home secretary warned them that publication of the book would be a very serious breach of the Official Secrets Act, whereupon he was corrected by a person who insisted on being referred to as "Mr. Rogers." Mr. Rogers, who was really Sir Roger Hollis, said that while the book did not breach the act, its publication would be "against the public interest." He then asked the publisher to agree to deletions and changes involving a number of pages in ways that he would approve.

Reluctantly, the publisher agreed, having secured an assurance that the government—meaning the taxpayers—would pay the costs of unbinding and rebinding the books. Newspapers were then asked by the publisher to return their review copies.

Mr. Rogers's appearance was another instance of personal interference, for traditionally, MI5's relations with journalists had been conducted by the head of C Branch. However, when Hollis had been promoted from that post to become the deputy director general, he had taken that responsibility with him and was still wielding it as the chief. What had been Hollis's motive? When the book appeared, it could hardly have been more harmless. What was removed is unknown publicly, but John Bulloch's lawyers remained convinced that the text had contained no information really damaging to the national interest.

I strongly suspect that Hollis, only too aware of the disasters over which he had presided, was determined to establish a precedent regarding any further books relating to the security or intelligence services. He wanted to establish a general understanding among publishers that all such books should be submitted for official scrutiny and that it should be done indirectly through the secretary of the D-Notice Committee, who would consult directly with MI5. Further, it should preferably be done when the book was in manuscript or in proof pages so that embarrassing deletions could be made more conveniently.

Surprisingly, Hollis's gambit succeeded, and ever since, most authors and publishers have submitted such works, though I have always declined. While it was made to appear that the D-Notice secretary himself would be doing the vetting, copies of any offending pages were quickly sent by him to all interested departments. This enabled them not only to object to statements they did not like, but to prepare rebuttals that, if necessary, could be made by departments or even by ministers in Parliament. It also enabled MI5 or any other department to initiate inquiries into the sources of any leaks. Meanwhile, publication could be delayed by weeks or even months.

It remains the practice for the D-Notice secretary to study publishers' lists for titles and to send a written request for a book to be submitted for scrutiny. In cases where a publisher or author declines to oblige, the security authorities take steps to secure the text by surreptitious means, as I know from personal experience and will describe. In fact, the threat to prosecute is almost invariably hollow, as the details of the Thatcher government's wish to prohibit my book *Their Trade Is Treachery* in 1981, and MI5's fear of the consequences, were to show. In 1993, when I published a book about my country sports experiences, called *Pastoral Symphony*, the D-Notice secretary requested an advance copy from the publisher. He did not get it.

As 1963 progressed, Hollis became embroiled in a scandal in ways that ensured that the roof really did fall in—on his prime minister's political career.

CHAPTER 68

Portentous Liaison

THE PROFUMO AFFAIR HAS BEEN THE SUBJECT OF A NEVER-ending stream of books, television documentaries, comment, and even a musical show. However, while apologizing to the memory of my excessively suffering friend Jack Profumo, who died in 2006 at the age of ninety-one, for raising the issue yet again, I feel the case had such major political repercussions that it cannot be ignored here. It resulted in the rejection of the Conservative government and the installation of a Labour administration much more acceptable to the Soviet Union and quickly penetrated by at least one KGB spy, with several more paid Soviet-bloc agents among its members of Parliament.

Many would say that the downfall of Profumo, then the forty-eight-year-old secretary of state for war, who had been a wartime brigadier at thirty, began with the folly of his liaison with nineteen-year-old Christine Keeler.

The tragedy really began on November 11, 1962, when George Wigg, a Labour backbencher and old soldier specializing in army affairs, was lunching with his political agent in his Dudley constituency. The telephone rang and a muffled voice said, "Forget about the Vassall case! You want to look at Profumo!" The line then went dead. Wigg, who for many years kept me informed almost on a daily basis, became convinced that the caller was Vitali Lui, a KGB agent posing as a freelance Russian journalist calling himself Victor Louis. Lieutenant Commander Eugene Ivanov, a GRU intelligence officer registered as assistant naval attaché in the Soviet embassy, who knew about Profumo's affair, could have tipped off Lui, whom he knew socially, to make the most of it. The vindictive Wigg ran a private intelligence system to gather damaging information about Conservatives and soon learned how Profumo had entangled himself with Keeler, though the war minister had immediately distanced himself when eventually warned of his danger.

Wigg hated Profumo because he felt he had been slighted by him in Parliament, and he reveled in settling scores. So he was keen to expose the "scandal," which had been confirmed to him by a Labour MP, to whom Keeler had confided details of her affair. However, as a married man with a steady mistress himself, Wigg told Harold Wilson, then leader of the Labour opposition, that he knew so many Labour MPs who were having illicit affairs that it would be dangerous to pursue the war minister on moral grounds. Wilson agreed.

The presence of Ivanov in the picture, especially when it was learned that he had also had sexual relations with Keeler, enabled Wigg to claim that national security was threatened. Had he been aware of the extent of Profumo's nuclear knowledge, he would have been more vociferous.

Ivanov, a likable man who loved a good party, had arrived in London on March 27, 1960, to take up his post. In pursuit of his duty, he was required by the GRU Center to establish informative contacts, including journalists, and among them was Sir Colin Coote, editor of the *Daily Telegraph*. Coote had met Ivanov when a party of diplomatic attachés had visited the *Daily Telegraph* building in Fleet Street and wanted to introduce him to one of his special writers. So on January 20, 1961, Coote staged a lunch at the Garrick Club to which Ivanov and the writer were invited.

Coote was a grateful patient of a successful osteopath named Stephen Ward, who was also such a capable portrait artist that he had drawn many distinguished people, including the Duke of Edinburgh. Ward's Communist views were so well-known that some of his patients regarded him as a Soviet agent of influence and may have reported the fact to MI5. In that case, Hollis, who by another coincidence happened to be a golfing friend of Coote's, may have suggested the meeting for some purpose of his own. In any event, Ward and Ivanov became friends, and for that reason, the lunch would acquire historic political proportions.

Hollis was to be required to take special interest in Ivanov three months later, in April, when Oleg Penkovsky, the GRU defector in place, listed the naval attaché among the professionally trained Soviet intelligence officers operating in Great Britain. The information had come from MI6, so Hollis was expected to take some action, which in the final result was to prove disastrous. Watchers from MI5 tailed Ivanov to 17 Wimpole Mews, Ward's home. Inquiries showed that Ward had many distinguished patients, including several prominent MPs and Lord Astor, who had been a wartime naval intelligence officer. The watchers could not help noticing the presence of young girls who lived or visited there, because Ward was a sexual deviant, a voyeur, and procured girls such as Christine Keeler, then working as a hostess in a nightclub, for friends and patients. His consulting rooms were close by, so he often invited patients to have coffee or tea at his home, where they encountered the girls, who would serve it. Keeler has recently claimed that Hollis was occasionally one of them, though there is no other evidence to support that. With his progressive spinal problem, Hollis might have been a patient, having been recommended by Coote to consult Ward. Or they might have met socially through Coote.

Hollis's first overt move against Ward was to send one of his officers, on June 8, 1961, to warn him that his new friend Ivanov might use him to gain access to some of his high-level patients. Ward promised to be careful and to inform MI5 of any developments, but as the officer reported that Ward was not "a person we can make use of" because his political ideas were "exploitable by the Russians," stories that he was recruited as a formal MI5 agent are unlikely to be true. Keeler has always maintained that Ward was serving as an intelligence agent for Ivanov, claiming that she witnessed his delivery of small packages to the Soviet embassy. In her latest version, *The Truth at Last,* she states that Ward was a full-blown Soviet agent. What is certain is that Ward found any involvement in espionage intriguing, even if only on its fringes, and seems to have served both sides when it suited him.

As Lord Astor was another grateful patient, Ward had the use of a cottage on his Thames-side Cliveden estate, to which he could invite his friends and where he had use of the Astors' swimming pool. On the evening of Saturday, July 8, 1961, Keeler and some other girls were bathing in the pool, and Ward dared Christine to remove her bathing costume, which he had then hidden. As she emerged naked from the pool, Astor and Profumo arrived on an after-dinner stroll. Lady Astor, Mrs. Profumo (who was the former film star Valerie Hobson), and other weekend guests then appeared and joined in the amusement. Later, when Christine was dressed, Profumo showed her around the big house, where he had often stayed, and flirted with her.

On the following afternoon, there was a formal bathing party attended by the Astors and their guests and Ward and his guests. The latter included Ivanov, who may well have been summoned by Ward on the chance that he might meet Profumo, an event that the naval attaché would be able to report, with some kudos, to the GRU Center. As a military figure, the war minister would have been a potential GRU target.

During a convivial afternoon, when Ivanov and Profumo swam races, the war minister secured Keeler's telephone number from Ward, who then encouraged her to see him. A sexual liaison developed that lasted, on and off, until the end of 1961. On that same Sunday evening, Ivanov drove Keeler back to London, and they enjoyed what she called "marvellous, passionate love." It was to be widely rumored that subsequently she would be in bed with Profumo and Ivanov on the same day, but later she was to insist that she had intercourse with Ivanov only on the one occasion. Nevertheless, they continued to meet each other at Ward's homes.

During the period of Profumo's illicit affair, the U.S. government was planning to supply the West German army with a medium-range ballistic missile called Sergeant. Its nuclear warheads, designed to blunt an attack by massed Russian tanks, were to be kept under American control until an emergency, when the German troops would be empowered to use them. This plan was open knowledge as part of the deterrent policy, but the date the missiles were to become operational by the Germans was still secret. The Soviet leader Nikita Khrushchev was considering the surreptitious installation of medium-range nuclear missiles in Cuba, and his case for doing that would seem more reasonable if he could prove that the Americans had already placed nuclear weapons in German hands or were about to do so.

Shortly after the Cliveden bathing party, on July 12, Ward told MI5 that Ivanov was trying to find out the delivery date of the Sergeant warheads. He also revealed that he had known Profumo for some time and that the war minister had visited his London home to attend parties there, as was confirmed by Profumo later.

Ivanov would have informed the GRU Center of Keeler's relation-ship with Profumo and they would have seen the possibility, however remote, that if Ward was not prepared to ask him about the date, she might find some reason to do so in the course of their conversations. Had Profumo been foolish enough to reveal it, he could have been a subject for blackmail by the GRU.

The suggestion that Keeler might have been asked to pose the nu-clear question to Profumo has been ridiculed on two counts. Macmillan claimed that, as war minister, Profumo did not know any atomic secrets, but in view of the close operational relations between the German forces and Britain's Rhine army, he would almost certainly have known the date, which turned out to be in the following year, 1962. In fact, the re-lease in 2007 of summaries of cabinet meetings chaired by Harold Macmillan, when sensitive matters concerning atomic weapons were discussed in detail, has revealed that Profumo attended them regularly. Documents reproduced in Peter Hennessy's book *Cabinets and the Bomb* show that he had begun doing so in 1960, when he had been minister of state for foreign affairs, and continued through 1962 and 1963, during which period he learned secrets concerning Britain's acquisition of American nuclear weapons, like Skybolt and Polaris—matters of crucial interest to the Kremlin.

It has also been stressed that Keeler, then nineteen, would have been so ignorant that she would not have known what to ask or how to ask it. Keeler has told several witnesses that she had been requested to discover the date from Profumo. Either she was too frightened to do so or the op-portunity never arose, but a document shown to me by Michael Ed-dowes, a solicitor consulted by Keeler who also met Ward and Ivanov, convinced me that she had been asked to discover it. A statement that Eddowes took from Keeler on December 14, 1962 (of which I have a copy), recorded that Ivanov had asked her directly to "obtain from Pro-fumo the date of delivery of nuclear warheads to West Germany." A young girl could not have invented that terminology, and neither could Eddowes, who eventually made the same statement to the police. The FBI was to take the whole issue as seriously credible in a widespread follow-up to the Profumo affair, code-named Bow Tie.

On August 2, 1961, Lord Astor informed the Foreign Office by letter that if ever an occasion arose when officials there wanted the Russian embassy to be correctly informed about Anglo-American intentions, the relationship between Ward and Ivanov could be a useful channel. He warned that Ivanov was "an absolutely dedicated communist" but also "a nice person." If this suggestion sounds preposterous, the situation then prevailing in Washington shows that it was not. There, a GRU officer, George Bolshakov, posing as a journalist, had become friendly with Robert Kennedy, the president's brother and attorney general, and both Kennedys used him as a private pipeline to Khrushchev. The purpose was to probe the Russian leader's likely reaction to proposals for summit talks, test ban treaties, and solutions to the Berlin problem before they were officially made. The details of this extraordinary relationship, in which Bolshakov and Robert Kennedy even spent weekends together, resulted from access to GRU and Soviet Presidium archives that had been granted to the authors of the book *One Hell of a Gamble*. Alexander Feklisov, the KGB officer who had run Klaus Fuchs after the war and was then serving in Washington, also had a direct link to the Kennedys.

In view of the success in securing such high-level contact by the GRU officers in Washington, it seems likely that Ivanov was required to emulate them in Great Britain, and the first contact with Profumo may have been engineered for that purpose.

CHAPTER 69

The Fall of Supermac

—

As soon as Hollis learned that a senior minister was involved in the extravaganza, he took a hands-on, controlling interest, and on July 31, 1961, he initiated an extraordinary venture. He went to see the cabinet secretary, Sir Norman Brook, and asked him to warn Profumo against confiding in Ward. He then made the suggestion that Profumo might help induce Ivanov to defect to the West. Junior MI5 officers appear to have been planning to trap Ivanov into defecting by compromising him in some way and threatening him with exposure, but they had made no progress. Hollis's suggestion that Profumo might assist them was outrageous, for it meant involvement in a diplomatic conspiracy in which no minister of the Crown, least of all the war minister, who was a secretary of state, should ever be embroiled. Either it was a gross misjudgment unworthy of a director general of MI5 or he intended to cause an international scandal.

It was obvious that, had Ivanov been approached by Profumo and refused to defect, he could then have complained to his ambassador about the attempt to suborn him and the Kremlin could have created a political furor, which the Labour opposition could have exploited. Fortunately, when informed by the cabinet secretary of Hollis's suggestion on August 9, Profumo wisely declined and, unwisely, refrained from reporting the attempt to the prime minister.

Profumo assumed that Brook was also tacitly warning him that MI5 knew of his sexual affair, and he took action to end it by writing to Keeler on the same day. In fact, Hollis had made no mention of Profumo's affair with Keeler when he went to see Brook on that occasion and later assured the judge, Lord Denning, that he had no knowledge of it then, though a six-page report about the relationship between Ward, Keeler, Profumo, and Ivanov had been circulated in MI5 to those needing to know, including Hollis.

When the Cuban missile crisis came to a head in October, Ward telephoned the Foreign Office, using Lord Astor's name, to suggest that it should take the initiative in setting up a summit conference in London to avert nuclear war. At that stage, Khrushchev was trying to find a face-saving way out of the crisis. Through Ward, acting on Ivanov's instructions, the Foreign Office was told that Khrushchev would accept a British invitation to take part in a summit conference with alacrity, when Britain would secure credit for breaking the deadlock.

The Cuban missile crisis was resolved on October 28, as already described. By chance, on that day, Astor gave another party at Cliveden, and both Ward and Ivanov attended it. When news came through that Khrushchev had backed down, Ivanov affected to be furious. All these events make nonsense of Hollis's attitude to Ivanov's activities as being "of little importance."

On January 22, 1963, Keeler signed a contract with a Sunday newspaper to tell her story and provided a letter from Profumo, in which she was addressed as "Darling." Alerted to his danger by Lord Astor on January 28, Profumo asked Hollis to see him immediately, in the hope that some D-Notice might be issued to prevent publication of the story and limit speculation. Hollis told him that was impossible. In the course of the conversation, Profumo told Hollis some details of how he had first met Keeler at Cliveden. Hollis was to state to Lord Dilhorne, the lord chancellor, that they did not include the fact that the relationship had been sexual. Later, when the judge, Lord Denning, was carrying out an official inquiry into the whole Profumo affair, Hollis told him that on that same day, January 28, and on the following day, reports came to MI5 from "a secret source" that confirmed Profumo had been engaged in a long sexual affair with Keeler and that Ivanov was also involved somehow.

With Ivanov, a known GRU officer, in the frame, there was definitely a defense factor in the equation. So Hollis could not have failed to appreciate that the situation was a ticking time bomb under the government. Yet he did not warn the prime minister about it until five months later.

An MI5 secret source had also stated that the Russians were so certain a major scandal was about to break that Ivanov was to be sent back to Moscow prematurely. Ivanov fled the following day, January 29, giving Hollis the excuse to declare no further interest in his case. On February 1, 1963, he prohibited all further inquiries by issuing an instruction to all concerned. It stated, "Until further notice no approach should be made to anyone in the Ward galère or to any other outside contact in respect of it. If we are approached we listen only." This effectively ended all inquiries into Ward or anyone associated with him. If information was volunteered, no questions were to be asked about it or action taken. Later, when an MI5 officer pointed out the dangers of this policy, Hollis reiterated it.

Hollis's policy had always been maximum ponder and minimal action, and he was to explain away this particular decision, which was to lead to disaster for Macmillan, by insisting that further inquiries would be outside MI5's proper scope. Some of his officers, however, foresaw the situation it would cause. One of them warned Hollis, in writing, on February 4, "If a scandal results from Mr Profumo's association with Christine Keeler, there is likely to be a considerable political rumpus. If, in any subsequent inquiries, we were found to have been in possession of this information about Profumo and to have taken no action on it, we would, I am sure, be subject to much criticism for failing to bring it to light. I suggest that this information be passed to the Prime Minister."

Hollis responded to this prophetic advice by repeating his order that no further action should be taken. He particularly forbade any interview of Christine Keeler. His objection to that could be explained by his determination to ensure that his name did not arise in connection with Ward if, in fact, they had met socially, as Keeler was eventually to claim.

On February 7, the commander of Scotland Yard's Special Branch went to MI5 with a report showing that on January 26, Keeler had told police that there had been an illicit association between her and Profumo. She had also stated that she had met Ivanov several times and that Ward had asked her to discover the nuclear warheads' date. Still, MI5 continued to obey Hollis's edict that no action was necessary.

Macmillan had returned from a brief trip to Italy on February 4, and his private secretary warned him of the rumors. By that time, the chief whip—a senior MP responsible for Conservative Party discipline—had confronted Profumo, who had denied the allegations of sexual misconduct. Macmillan accepted the assurances.

On March 21, 1963, Wigg raised the issue in Parliament, in full knowledge of its explosive mixture of high-level politics, sex, and espionage. He referred simply to the widespread speculation about a minister and invited the government to deny it. Next day, after a night during which he had been roused and questioned by fellow ministers, Profumo delivered a statement to a packed House of Commons, declaring that "there had been no impropriety whatsoever." He also threatened to sue for libel if provoked and eventually did so, giving to charity the damages paid by two magazines.

As soon as Profumo made his statement to Parliament, Hollis knew that he had lied, because MI5 had known the truth about the relationship since January 28, at least. Nevertheless, he still did not warn Macmillan. He just sat back and waited for the time bomb to explode.

On March 27, Home Secretary Henry Brooke sent for Hollis to be briefed on the background. Hollis was directly responsible to the home secretary but had previously told him nothing. In fact, he had kept Ivanov's interest in the atomic matter from all government ministers for twenty-one months while the issue festered and presumably would have continued to do so had Brooke not summoned him. (An MI5 officer involved in the case eventually wrote to me describing Hollis's behavior as "a grave dereliction of duty and responsibility.")

A few days later, I received a copy of a long statement that Keeler had made to a *Daily Express* reporter in Spain, where she had fled to avoid involvement in an unsavory court case. From the details she described, there could be no doubt that she was telling the truth, and I felt that Profumo should be warned immediately. My easiest route was through his chief civil servant, Sir Richard ("Sam") Way. After seeing the report over lunch with me, Way agreed that his minister should be warned, but his courage failed him. Instead, he consulted Profumo's chief soldier, General Sir Richard Hull, who agreed with him that to tell their boss he had lied would be too embarrassing. Had they told him, the affair might have been settled more swiftly and with less collateral damage. Way later told me that he had made a bad error of judgment.

A recently released document shows that on May 7, 1963, Hollis and

White visited Macmillan to discuss how to handle yet another espionage disaster—the pending trial in Moscow of Greville Wynne, Oleg Penkovsky's courier. According to White's biographer, Hollis then admitted that he had known about Profumo's sexual relationship with Keeler for five months, having been told about it on January 28. Macmillan's response seems to have been sheer astonishment. For the first time, the prime minister had to face the fact that Profumo had lied to Parliament and that the director general of MI5 had known that and had remained silent. As Macmillan realized at the time, the crisis could have been handled with far less political damage to his Supermac image and the government in general had he known earlier that Profumo was guilty.

On May 19, Ward wrote to the home secretary, complaining that the police were interrogating his patients and ruining his business. He made it clear that he knew Profumo had lied to the House. On the following day, he sent similar letters to Harold Wilson and other MPs. As the tragedy gathered pace, Hollis visited Macmillan again to tell him about the Ivanov complication through his sexual relationship with Keeler. Two days later, Macmillan received information from Harold Wilson about a long statement, which Ward had sent, claiming that Profumo had lied and urging him to take action on the security issue. Realizing that a political scandal was almost inevitable, Macmillan asked his lord chancellor, Lord Dilhorne, to investigate the whole affair and told Wilson that he had done so.

On May 29, Hollis reported to Macmillan in person and told him about the request to Keeler to secure "the date on which certain atomic secrets were to be handed to West Germany by the Americans." When I discussed this with Macmillan in 1980, he asked rhetorically, "What atomic secrets could Jack Profumo have known?" I pointed out that he could well have known the delivery date, with which he agreed. Since then, released cabinet papers have revealed that as late as January 1963, Profumo was attending supersecret cabinet meetings about atomic weapons, with Macmillan in the chair! Hollis denied that Ward was a Russian agent, saying he was just a pimp.

Astonished by Hollis's apparent incompetence, Macmillan asked White, whom he trusted, to visit him at Downing Street. After complaining that he was being ill served by Hollis, he told White that he thought the whole trumped-up security scandal was part of a Soviet plot to drive him from office, and he asked him to search for any evidence of such a conspiracy. Later, as declassified documents have recently disclosed, he even expressed this possibility in a letter to the Queen. Macmillan told White that he rated Hollis as incompetent, and his diaries and biography make clear that he regarded him as having been laxly slow in warning him at all stages of the affair, and especially about the connection between Profumo and Ivanov. White agreed to review the evidence suggesting that the large number of spy cases and MI5's poor performance indicated there might still be spies inside it, though privately he doubted the existence of a plot.

Hollis was to claim that once he had decided the scandal posed no security risk, it was none of MI5's business, in spite of the Russian involvement. The Home Office directive to MI5 had stated that it should not carry out any inquiry on behalf of a government department unless the director general was satisfied that an important public interest bearing on the defense of the realm was at stake. Hollis argued that as soon as Ivanov had fled Britain, the case had ceased to have any defense aspects. However, that implied there had been defense aspects before he left, and it was not usual MI5 practice to drop a case simply because one player had left the scene. Hollis's total ban on further inquiries looked like an excuse for inaction rather than a sound reason.

When White was summoned to see the prime minister again, he agreed that Hollis's omissions were surprising, but as the man who had recommended him for his post, he could hardly say much more.

Meanwhile, Profumo was on holiday with his wife in Venice, their favorite city, where he received a telegram from Dilhorne, summoning him back to London for questioning as part of his inquiry. Profumo then confessed to his wife that there had indeed been an affair with Keeler. He returned to London on June 2. Two days later, he admitted that he had lied to Parliament, which did not happen to be sitting because of the Whitsuntide recess, and he resigned as a minister and as an MP. The *News of the World* began to serialize Keeler's life story, and the media made the most of the scandal, which had everything—sex, espionage, betrayal, and even an atomic aspect, all set in international politics at the highest level.

Parliament reconvened on June 17 and staged a debate on the whole affair, which I attended, noticing the hunched figure of Sir Roger Hollis sitting in the Distinguished Visitors' Gallery. I could see no observable embarrassment as Macmillan blamed him, repeatedly, for failing to inform him of the security aspects of the Keeler-Profumo relationship. To cries of "Oh!" Macmillan declared that MI5 had kept him ignorant about the relationship between Profumo and Keeler and about her requirement to discover the nuclear weapons date. He revealed that Hollis's explanation, on each count, had been that he had not considered the issues "as of great importance"—his favored excuse when cornered. Macmillan was unaware that Hollis had made the same get-out excuse over the Konstantin Volkov disaster and Gouzenko's statement about Elli.

In helping to prepare Macmillan's defense, the law officers had relied on a brief prepared by Hollis. It contained the suggestion that Ivanov had posed no security threat because he was just an accredited diplomat, when MI5 knew from Oleg Penkovsky that he was a professional GRU intelligence officer. Macmillan repeated his regret at Hollis's lack of action and threw himself on the compassion of the House. No sympathy was shown by some of his own MPs, who demanded a new and younger leadership. His reduced majority when the House voted and his admission that he had not known what was going on were extremely damaging, and I watched Supermac leave the chamber crestfallen and dispirited. In Washington, President Kennedy, having received a report on the affair from his London ambassador, David Bruce, on June 15, decided that the British prime minister was effectively finished.

The whole affair was sorry proof, at many levels, that all power corrupts—meaning that it corrupts judgment. To save his ministerial career, Jack Profumo had deceived himself into believing that his word would carry more weight than a young call girl's, and he paid the price.

Once again, Macmillan asked Dick White to find evidence of Moscow's involvement. White assured him that "the Russians had no assets to organise a plot involving Profumo." In fact, if Hollis was Elli, they had the perfectly placed GRU asset, and there can be no doubt, as Macmillan was eventually fully aware, that, whether deliberately or not, Hollis had expedited his downfall.

On June 21, Macmillan appointed a judge, Lord Denning, to investigate and report on the whole Profumo affair and especially on the security aspects. He knew that if the report exposed further ministerial scandals, he would have to resign. In the following month, Philby surfaced in Moscow and the Mitchell case was still in secret progress, with Macmillan beginning to fear, as he noted in his diary, that somebody at a high level in MI5 was a Russian spy.

As sympathy for Macmillan began to restore his public popularity, interest in the Profumo affair was regenerated on July 22 by the trial of Stephen Ward on a charge of living on the immoral earnings of his call-girl friends. He was found guilty and compounded the whole tragedy by committing suicide on August 3.

Macmillan received Lord Denning's long report on September 17. It stated that MI5 did not know Profumo had been involved sexually with Keeler until January 29, 1963. This information, which was supplied by Hollis, was described to me by an M5 officer as "a brazen lie." Over-borne by the mystique attached to the office of director general of MI5, Denning made judgments that were flawed and excused officials who should have been censured. The entire report also seemed intent on di-minishing the importance of Ivanov, with respect to both Keeler and his attempt to secure the date about the Sergeant warheads. As the report progressed, the date again became "atomic secrets."

It was suggested to Denning that Ivanov's function, set by the naval GRU, had been to divide Britain from America by undermining Wash-ington's trust in British security. If so, he had considerable success, be-cause the whole affair made Britain a laughingstock worldwide in the media, on stages, and in cabarets.

Publicly, Macmillan expressed sorrow for Profumo, who thereafter devoted his life quietly to good works, but he did not forgive him, and privately, he would express his bitterness at his behavior, as he did in my hearing. Coming on top of the many spy scandals, the Profumo affair left Macmillan mentally shattered. Suddenly stricken by prostate prob-lems, he underwent surgery, and the consequent weakness induced him to retire from the premiership on October 18, 1963.

In October 1964, after the brief premiership of Sir Alec Douglas-Home, the Conservatives were defeated and a Labour government led by Harold Wilson came to power. Later, when I questioned Macmillan and Wilson in private, both said they were convinced that the scandal of the Profumo affair had decided the election, which Labour won by an overall majority of only four seats. Macmillan was in no doubt that Hol-lis's inaction had contributed to his personal predicament.

Under the guise of being a consultant for a timber merchant, Wilson had been ingratiating himself with leading Soviet politicians during vis-its to Moscow, to the consternation of the British embassy there. So when he became prime minister, the Kremlin received a massive trade credit arrangement. Wilson's MPs were permitted to support Communist front organizations, which had previously been proscribed. Any form of surveillance of MPs by MI5, however suspect they might be, was forbidden by Wilson, save with his express permission. Eventually, Labour's manifesto was to include commitments to unilateral nuclear disarmament and the elimination of American bases in Britain, though both potential political disasters were quietly abandoned as Wilson was forced to face the facts of cold war life.

Many years later, in Venice, my wife and I encountered Jack Profumo and his wife, who stood by him so splendidly. They were having dinner in Harry's Bar, and we joined them. I had recently published *Their Trade Is Treachery,* describing how Hollis, who had died in 1973, had been suspected by his own officers of being a Russian spy. Though Hollis had handled the security aspects of the Profumo affair in ways that had done the whole Conservative Party catastrophic disservice, Jack rounded on me for impugning the loyalty of a dead man. "You are entitled to criticize living people, like me, but not dead people," he argued. His wife gently pointed out to him that most warts-and-all biographies are about dead people.

Later, whenever I alluded to any aspect of the affair, he would smile and say, "Oh, it's all so long ago." Indeed it was, but the mixture of high politics, high society, sex, espionage, deception, and exposure made it explosive and continues to do so. Save, perhaps, for the wistful sadness for his lost career and the pain he inflicted on others, Jack Profumo, with whom I lunched not long before his death, seemed at peace with his predicament. His luncheon companion on that intimate occasion was the late Queen Mother.

CHAPTER 70

Irish Interlude

—

MEANWHILE, IN AUGUST 1963, CLAUD COCKBURN, WHO HAD been based near the remote town of Youghal in Irleand since 1949, had been invited by the editor of the satirical magazine *Private Eye* to take over for a brief period while he went on holiday. As a writer for magazines, Cockburn visited London frequently, and though he had professed to have "fallen out of love with communism," MI5 had continued to monitor his visits from Ireland, with his baggage being searched. With *The Week* having been something of a precursor to *Private Eye*, Cockburn had accepted the invitation and, ever mischievous, as he described in his autobiography, *I, Claud,* had promptly made his mark by publishing Sir Dick White's identity as "C" of MI6. He did so in a small paragraph under his own name, headed, "Note to Foreign Agents" and naming White as "the head of what you so romantically term the British Secret Service." This was uncommon knowledge at the time, when newspapers had agreed not to name any members of the secret services, and it caused consternation in Whitehall and Westminster, as cabinet papers released in 2000 revealed. Powerful people, led by Sir Burke Trend, the cabinet secretary, were considering Cockburn's arrest.

In his book, Cockburn then described how, following telephone calls warning that he might face prosecution, "a source" whom he considered well-informed on the issue had agreed to meet him. The meeting was to be in "an open space without microphones." The unnamed source had told him that there was "a terrible row" going on about his naming of C and that important people were insisting he should be arrested. The source had then urged Cockburn to return home to Ireland immediately to avoid arrest, though he had merely breached a D-Notice, which was not a legal offense.

There is witness evidence that this unnamed source was Sir Roger Hollis. According to W. J. West, an assiduous researcher, Cockburn had told Alan Brien, then assistant editor at *Private Eye,* that he was going to fix a meeting with an old contact "high up in MI5." The contact insisted the meeting take place outside the offices of the magazine in Soho. Brien, a well-known journalist who confirmed the substance of the story to me in 1991, witnessed the meeting, as he was standing in the street with Cockburn, but he could not recognize the visitor as Hollis, as he had never met him or seen a picture of him. Cockburn's use of the word *source* for his visitor is significant because there is no evidence that he knew anybody else who was still serving in MI5, and Hollis may have used him in the past to publicize information, as he had occasionally used me.

According to Brien, when the MI5 contact saw that Cockburn was not alone, he walked past them without a word. Cockburn then followed and caught up with him. The two then went to lunch together at a pub. Years later, when Brien saw photographs of Hollis, he realized who the visitor had been. (In a report in the *Spectator,* W. J. West claimed that Cockburn had later referred to his source as Hollis.)

The situation had been something of a crisis for Hollis. Cockburn's act was seen as threatening the whole D-Notice system of agreed censorship, and if an arrest had to be made, it would have been carried out by Scotland Yard's Special Branch, as would the subsequent interrogation. That could have led to an admission by Cockburn that he was an old friend of Hollis's, a fact that the director general was most anxious to avoid, as subsequent events would prove. The admission would inevitably have been leaked to some newspaper, because, as Hollis was aware, there was no love lost between Special Branch and MI5. So there was urgent need to induce Cockburn to lose himself back in Ireland, from which extradition was not possible under the Official Secrets Acts.

Clearly, it had been a situation demanding the direct treatment—personal action to douse the fire—and "Hands-on" Hollis apparently took it before the maverick journalist, who obviously could not be trusted, did even more damage. Cockburn was an eccentric character who seemed unable to resist any opportunity to create mischief. As he described in his autobiography, "the source" urged him to return to County Cork with all speed.

As *Private Eye* was dealing with the seamier aspects of the Profumo affair, it would also have been in Hollis's interest to use the opportunity to mark his old friend's card about the case, especially as he had assumed personal control of it. All in all, it was a situation that only he could have handled safely, because any other MI5 officer sent to advise Cockburn might have learned of his past association with the director general, who had also been his case officer. As will be seen, there may have been an even more pressing reason for Hollis's pressure on Cockburn to return to Ireland.

Cockburn, as stubborn as he was unpredictable, had nevertheless lingered in London, as deliberate evidence of his journalistic courage and perhaps to let Hollis know that he could safely take liberties with him. He suffered no known consequences, indicating that Hollis's warning had been an ill-founded excuse to try to frighten his old friend out of the country. The next edition of *Private Eye*, on August 9, 1963, even printed aspects of the Profumo case involving rivalry between MI5 and Special Branch, which Cockburn, like the able reporter that he was, may have gleaned from his lunch date.

At that time, nobody was likely to question Hollis had he been spotted with Cockburn, and he could have explained the meeting as being in the line of duty. Meanwhile, Cockburn's files were inaccessible because Hollis had taken the precaution of removing them from the registry and storing them in the private safe in his office.

Many years later, when questioned by the *Daily Mail*, Cockburn claimed that he had known Hollis only at Oxford, where he had been "a pleasant non-entity" and totally apolitical. However, another source (James Hanning, then of the *Evening Standard*) stated that Cockburn had remained friendly with both Roger Hollis and his brother Christopher. By that time, the much mellowed old campaigner seemingly regretted his Communist past and had no wish to exacerbate a situation that might reveal the truth about his involvement with Soviet espionage, which is now on record in the National Archives for all to see.

After a charmed, roller-coaster life without retribution, Cockburn, a chain-smoker as well as heavy whiskey drinker who suffered from both tuberculosis and throat cancer, died in 1981, aged seventy-seven, outliving Hollis by eight years.

CHAPTER 71

A Sordid Deal

Harold Macmillan was spared the next espionage horror because it did not come to light until after he had resigned and Sir Alec Douglas-Home was, briefly, prime minister. This was the official, but totally suppressed, exposure of Sir Anthony Blunt as another long-term and particularly virulent Soviet agent—the first MI5 officer to be unmasked as a spy.

The KGB had urged Blunt to defect in 1951, along with Donald Maclean and Guy Burgess, but he had been so confident of dealing with any inquiries by MI5 that he had declined. The basis for that nonchalance is worthy of study and may have resided in his detailed knowledge about MI5's role in the double defection.

With the ending of the war in 1945, Blunt was keen to return to his work at the Courtauld Institute, a major London center for the study of art, especially as he had also been offered the unpaid post of surveyor of the king's pictures. The KGB permitted him to quit MI5, though he could have been forced to remain under threat of exposure.

When he was leaving, he induced a stupid colleague to give him a list of all MI5's agents operating inside various embassies in London. He had regularly handed over copies of the MI5 directory to the KGB, and such was his arrogance that as he departed, he remarked to his senior colleague Colonel T. A. Robertson, "It has given me great pleasure to pass on the names of every MI5 officer to the Russians." Robertson, who told me the story, said that he thought it was a joke but passed on the information to those who should have reacted. Nothing was entered in Blunt's file.

Hollis remained friendly with Blunt and invited him to his home. So, counting Kim Philby, he had been on close terms with two ardent spies, and through Blunt, he had also met Burgess socially. Occasionally, Hollis attended Blunt's art lectures at the institute. Professor James Joll confirmed to me that they were friends, remarking that "Roger saw Anthony as the intellectual, which he was not."

Almost unbelievably, Blunt's KGB file shows that on January 9, 1949, he had informed the Moscow Center that MI5 had sought his permission to use a room at the Courtauld for meetings with foreign agents who had been recruited in Soviet-bloc countries! Blunt agreed and gave MI5 a key to it. He also used his apartment at the Courtauld to photograph documents temporarily removed from the Foreign Office by Burgess and sometimes delivered them to a KGB controller from the Soviet embassy. His KGB file records that on January 21, 1949, he and his controller, Nikolai Korovin, were stopped in the street by two detectives, who searched his briefcase. Apparently, they failed to see photographs of Foreign Office documents, which had been supplied by Burgess, and no action ensued. So there is no doubt that while serving at Buckingham Palace, Blunt continued to serve the KGB.

White went through the motions of having Blunt interrogated after the Maclean-Burgess escape, but as had happened with Philby in MI6, he was questioned gently by old colleagues in what were to be described as "comfortable conversations." During eleven interviews, nobody, including William Skardon, reported anything but vehement denials, though the suspicions that he had been a spy were strengthened. He felt so confident that he continued to see Philby, and the two discussed their chances of surviving exposure. They met again in Beirut in 1961.

In June 1963, a chance event in Washington was eventually to expose Blunt. The American Michael Straight, whom Blunt had recruited to the KGB at Cambridge, was offered an arts advisory post by the Kennedy government. Fearing the routine FBI investigation, and having done little to help the KGB, Straight reported his recruitment by Blunt. Straight was not interviewed by MI5 until January 1964, when he repeated his story and also stated that he was prepared to face Blunt in a British court. He also named Leo Long as another Cambridge spy recruited by Blunt. So once again, the clues about three more Soviet spies had come via an American agency, and without that initiative, one of Britain's most damaging traitors, who had been knighted in 1956, might have gone to his grave full of honors and respect.

Hollis's outward reaction to Blunt's exposure was one of "dreadful embarrassment," according to Peter Wright, who witnessed it. So was White's when Hollis visited him to give him the news. They both wished that the FBI tip had never arrived, realizing that if it became public, their incompetence for having failed to detect a spy literally in their midst would be so manifest that they might have to resign. Both were widely known to have been personally friendly with Blunt and to have trusted him completely. If Blunt had given Hollis and White a helping hand in facilitating the Maclean and Burgess defections, a trial was the last thing they would have wanted, on that score alone. The delay in questioning Blunt, imposed by Hollis, could have given the traitor time to defect, but it is now known that he had no intention of ever living among the Russians, whom he had affected to admire so much. So between them, Hollis and White devised a way of keeping the exposure secret—hopefully for all time—quickly convincing each other that it would be "in the national interest."

The solution was simple: In return for the promise of a full confession, with details of all his crimes and of everyone associated with them, including all Russian controllers, Blunt was to be offered immunity from prosecution and from publicity, however appalling the crimes he had committed. That way, the whole of his treachery could be buried without repercussions—an extreme example of "amicable elimination." It was nothing less than a bribe to one of the most dangerous spies in British history. Perhaps the fact that the monetary bribe to prevent Alan May's defection had never leaked fortified Hollis's confidence.

In the process, White, who apparently understood little about the lure and grip of communism, was particularly curious to hear Blunt's explanation of how he had become embroiled. As Tom Bower reveals in his biography, White had convinced himself that the Cambridge spies' treachery had all been "self-inspired" and was not the result of skillful

Soviet recruitment and control—a crass error for a man so long involved in counterespionage.

White and Hollis assured each other that sufficient evidence could never be found to prosecute Blunt, which was a false assumption. As the person who eventually exposed Straight publicly, along with his exposure of Blunt, I interviewed him several times, and he confirmed that he had been fully prepared to be a firsthand witness of Blunt's allegiance to the KGB. He reiterated that on a BBC radio program in which we appeared together. Long might also have been prepared to testify, even more devastatingly.

It was left to Hollis to pursue the immunity bribe, which if he was Elli would create an insurance precedent for himself, should he ever be exposed. He could not safely make the offer without the collusion of the attorney general, and to secure that, he devised the claim that Blunt would never confess anything if he was prosecuted. He saw the home secretary on March 2, 1964, as this was a legal requirement before he could approach the attorney general. Hollis had to tell him about Straight's information, but whether he mentioned the American's willingness to appear as a witness is unknown. The possibility of using Long, who was living in London, was never considered, though he could have proved that Blunt had been his controller and courier as well as his recruiter, with details of their joint treachery over several years. Instead, Hollis ensured that Long was not questioned before the immunity deal was fixed.

At Hollis's behest, legal officials of MI5 then went to secure the support of the director of public prosecutions for an immunity deal but saw only his deputy, who gave me a firsthand account of what happened. The deputy director of public prosecutions agreed that the evidence supplied was insufficient to warrant a prosecution, but no mention had been made to him of Long as a regular witness of Blunt's five years of treachery. He was also assured that in return for immunity, Blunt would provide vital intelligence, though the MI5 men had no reason to be sure of that, unless the traitor had already been approached surreptitiously by Hollis.

Foreseeing the political damage should news of the deal leak, the attorney general was more cautious. He insisted that Blunt would first have to give an assurance that he had ceased to spy after 1945, when the wartime alliance with the Soviet Union had ended. The fact that he might have spied while Russia was Hitler's ally, in 1940 and 1941—a possible capital offense at the time—as he certainly had, was set aside. Hollis further abused his position by avoiding any mention of Long to the attorney general, who might have insisted that he should be approached first.

CHAPTER 72

Playing the Royal Card

—

IN HIS DETERMINATION TO CONCEAL BLUNT'S TREACHERY IN-
side MI5, Hollis claimed that it was vital the Russians not learn that the
traitor had been exposed, though that was really of small consequence,
since all that he could tell them was already old history and the KGB
controllers who had served him had long left Great Britain. Hollis was
greatly assisted by the complication of Blunt's exalted position as surveyor of the queen's pictures, which he had held in succession to his appointment as surveyor of the king's pictures in April 1945. He had not
formally left MI5 for seven more months, so he had been an active spy
while in service to the palace, but that enormity was also to be set aside.

The home secretary and attorney general both agreed that public exposure of Blunt would be embarrassing to the Queen and felt that they
had no option but to accept the MI5 chief's advice on the overriding importance of the intelligence aspects. They therefore confirmed the offer
of immunity, which would be binding in law whatever Blunt might or
might not confess. There may have been no other occasion on which the
mystique attaching to Hollis's position had served him so well.

Hollis also wanted to ensure that Blunt could be told that as part of
the deal, he could continue in his royal post, as otherwise he might not
agree to it, especially when it became apparent to the wily traitor that he
was never going to be prosecuted anyway. So the MI5 chief faced the
question of whether the palace should be informed of Blunt's treachery.

He therefore called the Queen's private secretary, Sir Michael Adeane, to a meeting at the Home Office in April 1964. Adeane was told that in Hollis's view, Blunt should be allowed to continue in the Queen's service, with the retention of his knighthood, because otherwise he might not be helpful. Further, the Russians might become suspicious if he left suddenly and might then learn what had happened and exploit it. In fact, Blunt could easily have been required to retire on grounds that would not have raised suspicion anywhere. Swayed by Hollis's professional assertions, Adeane agreed to pass the outrageous advice to the Queen.

These known facts suggest that Hollis may have secretly approached his friend Blunt in advance, to discover the terms on which he was prepared to admit his guilt and that retention of his royal post was one of them.

The new prime minister, Alec Douglas-Home, was deliberately excluded from the whole process and knew nothing about the immunity. Amazingly, Hollis persuaded the home secretary and the attorney general that Sir Alec might refuse to compromise the Queen and that it would be essential for Blunt to maintain his status at the palace if he was to cooperate. Hollis also feared that Sir Alec might insist on referring the case to the Standing Security Commission set up to carry out independent inquiries into serious security breaches. In that case, a report to Parliament would have been required.

Again, Hollis failed to warn his prime minister of an intelligence situation that could have serious political consequences for him if news of the immunity leaked. Hollis's silence about Jack Profumo and Eugene Ivanov had saddled Harold Macmillan with the damaging title "the Man Who Did Not Know." The same could have happened to Douglas-Home, who with his honest, commonsense approach might have required Hollis to try first to secure a confession from Blunt without offering any bribe. Such a course had proved successful with George Blake, even though there were no available witnesses against him, as there were against Blunt.

After Hollis's experience of his public condemnation in Parliament for having failed to warn Macmillan about Profumo's problem, his quick repeat of similar treatment to his new prime minister certainly demonstrated a degree of brass nerve, if not controlled panic. Perhaps he appreciated that the exposure of an active spy as well bred, well connected, well trusted, and well placed inside MI5 as Blunt had made the unthinkable about himself very thinkable indeed. Whatever his motive, he was risking his career, as Sir Alec could have been furious enough to require some retribution had he discovered that he had been so studiously excluded.

The deal was actually far worse than Sir Alec might have appreciated. From the start, Hollis realized that the immunity would have to be extended to Long and any other spies Blunt might identify, however many and however villainous they might have been, because to expose them in court would inevitably expose Blunt. As a result, several traitors, including the nastiest of all, John Cairncross (until I exposed him in 1981), escaped punishment and disgrace.

I had discovered that the Queen had been told about Blunt's treason before I published *Their Trade Is Treachery* in 1981, as I indicated there. Her Majesty had admitted it in front of a friend of mine attending a shoot lunch at Broadlands, where the Queen had been pursuing her hobby of working her gundogs. In 1987, Peter Wright confirmed that after he took over the interrogation of Blunt, Michael Adeane had called him to the palace and assured him that the Queen had been fully briefed about Blunt. Her Majesty had asked what the professional advice was and, when told, agreed to take it, feeling that she had no option but to accept the argument put forward by the director general of her security service. As usual, she behaved impeccably, maintaining the pretense, obnoxious though it was, that all was normal whenever she encountered the traitor. She knew that Blunt was not only a spy, but dedicated to overthrowing the monarchy and replacing it with a dictatorship. Her Majesty even agreed to attend the opening of the Courtauld's new galleries, which Blunt directed, in 1968. As Hollis—and Blunt—could not have failed to appreciate, once the Queen had become embroiled, the necessity to keep the deal secret for all time became absolute.

The Queen had been subjected to an MI5 deception in a ruthless display of secret power, which kept a vile traitor in her service for a further fourteen years to save MI5, and Hollis in particular, from public embarrassment. Had any other department of state fixed such a deal with a major criminal, as Blunt was, it would surely have been censured.

By his determination to conceal and effectively condone Blunt's duplicity, Hollis had reinforced the belief inside MI5 that it could safely manipulate the legal system if its reputation was ever threatened again by exposure of its crass incompetence or further treachery. Not until

2000—thirty-six years later—would MI5 be properly castigated by Parliament for pursuing this monstrous assumption, following the exposure of a series of willful cover-ups concerning the case of Melita Norwood.

On April 23, 1964, Arthur Martin visited Blunt's apartment and wasted no time in telling him that MI5 had acquired proof that he had been a Soviet spy during the war. He said that he had been authorized by the attorney general to offer him immunity from prosecution. There was no mention of the requirement that he had ceased to spy in 1945, which was a breach of the attorney general's express demand. The offer was like saying to a mass murderer, "If you confess to one murder and then tell us all about the rest, you can go free without any censure. So can any of your accomplices."

After a dramatic pause, during which he poured himself a large gin, Blunt said, "It is true," and accepted the deal, in which he appeared to have immediate confidence. Later, Martin told John Costello that he was convinced Hollis had warned Blunt in advance that he had been blown by Straight and that immunity would be forthcoming, hopefully with the further bribe of no threat to his job or his knighthood. The fact that Blunt did not ask Martin for any details of the immunity deal suggests that he already knew them.

He was never given anything in writing and did not ask for it, indicating that he was completely confident of Hollis's power to deliver. He also quickly volunteered a statement that he had not been a Soviet agent after 1945—which was a lie—showing that he knew of that requirement.

As both Hollis and White desperately wanted Blunt to agree, it would be surprising if he had not been instructed, in some detail, how to behave when confronted. The delays had provided ample time. Hollis had ruled that Blunt should not be placed under any surveillance, so if he had seen him, the meeting would have gone undetected.

Under British law, from the moment of Blunt's acceptance, no legal action could be taken against him whatever he might confess or whatever might be discovered about him, even if he had been actively spying inside the royal household. He could also decline to incriminate particular friends, as he did repeatedly. The details of his treachery, now exposed by his KGB files, reveal what a sordid deal Hollis had secured. Guy Liddell's diaries have recently confirmed the degree of Blunt's wartime access. In March 1941, Blunt had induced Liddell to transfer him to B Division as his assistant, giving him access to almost everything about counterespionage, both German and Soviet.

On August 14, 1941, Liddell had suggested that Blunt go to the codebreaking Station X at Bletchley periodically and "make notes" for MI5 about the methods and findings there. He had become involved in the deception operations being devised in support of the D-Day landings in Normandy and had given the Russians a copy of the entire plan. He had also previously supplied all the details he knew of the plans for the landings in Italy. Had there been a German spy in the Kremlin or had it suited Stalin to leak them, as it might with the Germans in full retreat in Russia, the landings could have ended in bloody defeat, leaving the Soviet Union in full control of Europe.

Keen to begin a tough interrogation, Martin immediately saw Hollis, who said that there was no need for haste and that Blunt should be handled gently. Arguments ensued, and two weeks later, Hollis suspended Martin from all duty and Blunt was given a free run for two more weeks, an event that raised suspicion among some MI5 officers who wondered whether the traitor was being briefed on what to confess and on what to remain silent. The hiatus also gave Blunt time to warn any friends who might be at risk. When Blunt had been in MI5, he had never needed a protective hand, but Hollis provided one the moment he was in danger of exposure.

A series of interviews in Blunt's apartment spread over eight years—first with the reinstated Martin, with Courtney Young, and then with Peter Wright—produced what appeared to be a mass of admissions, without remorse but with much self-justification. I discussed the case for many hours with Wright at his home in Tasmania. He said there was no evidence that Blunt's conscience was pricked at all by the Soviet supplies of oil and other strategic materials that during the Stalin-Hitler pact had assisted the Germans to bomb London, overrun Poland, France, and the Low Countries, and round up countless Jews for the concentration camps.

Blunt identified his Russian case officers from photographs, but they were all safely out of Great Britain, as he knew. He confessed that he had betrayed every detail about MI5 that he knew, including the names and functions of its staff. His KGB file shows that he had submitted numerous profiles of his MI5 colleagues, including White and Liddell, but had never sent one on Hollis.

For several months, he had been in charge of the Watcher Service and had told all he knew about that. He revealed that he had told the KGB that MI5 had bugged Communist Party headquarters in London. In his various posts, documents of the highest secrecy had crossed his desk. About once a week, he had met a Soviet controller in the late evening to hand over his cache, which he took out in his briefcase. The Russians would photograph them and return them to him early next morning for replacement in the MI5 files.

Blunt named Edith Tudor Hart as a Soviet agent, and MI5 approached her, but she simply declined any assistance. (After working many years as a commercial photographer, she ran a small antiques shop in Brighton, where she died in 1973.)

The traitor admitted he had known that Philby, Burgess, Maclean, and Cairncross had been Soviet spies and that he had recruited Straight and Leo Long. He named various friends who were deeply or marginally involved in espionage, but none was ever prosecuted, though some were moved from secret work. His interrogators were convinced that he concealed his knowledge about several other spies, whom Wright referred to as "his fine friends." He recalled how after he had left MI5 in 1945, he had continued to meet Burgess, Liddell, and Hollis and had kept in touch with office gossip. He did not confess his role in the escape of Maclean and Burgess, which has now been fully confirmed by Russian publications.

Blunt described how he had collected a wad of banknotes and a message left by the KGB for Burgess in a hiding place under a tree on a common in the East End of London. Those who find it difficult to imagine that the director general of MI5 could possibly leave his Curzon Street office to meet some Soviet contact in a distant part of London need reminding that when Blunt did that service for Burgess, he was based in Buckingham Palace!

According to Wright, one of Blunt's controllers had urged him to avoid joining F Branch, which handled Soviet espionage and was run by Hollis. Blunt eventually agreed that this might imply the Russians already had a source there. He also agreed that he himself could not possibly have been Elli.

Recently, his KGB record has shown that he had given the Russians 1,771 MI5 documents, some of them entire files, confirming the extent to which we could all have suffered at his thieving hands. He had been twenty-nine at the time of his recruitment—not an adolescent, starry-eyed, idealist undergraduate. Yet he had made a deliberate choice to undermine his own country's security at a time when Britain was in danger of invasion by Stalin's ally Hitler. He had believed that revolution in Britain was inevitable and that "the happiness of humanity" would be accomplished only in the wake of a world revolution. He had stated that when revolution came to Britain, he "fully expected to be made Commissar for the Arts."

The known details of the recruitment of Blunt and Blake enable us to accept that an intelligent man, without pressure from outsiders, could delude himself and dedicate himself to the Soviet cause at daily risk to his freedom. Blunt also demonstrated how it was possible to have been an active spy and then lead a normal life in retirement.

The whole interrogation of Blunt satisfied the personal curiosity of Hollis and White about old spies and swelled and tidied up the MI5 files, but it produced nothing of much value to the state or to its people.

Hollis had insisted on being consulted before anyone was approached as a consequence of Blunt's leads. As a result, Martin repeatedly complained to his immediate superiors about limitations imposed on some of them. Since Hollis also knew by then that Martin suspected that he and his deputy might be Soviet agents, he seized the opportunity to get rid of him. After consulting White, he called a meeting of his directors and declared that Martin was the ringleader of a "Gestapo" that was threatening MI5's morale. Martin was offered a transfer to MI6, where White was keen to acquire him, or dismissal with no pension. Martin joined MI6, and Wright then took over as Blunt's interrogator, amassing many hours of taped conversation over a long period lasting into 1972. Wright illicitly took them with him when he left MI5 in 1976 and immigrated to Tasmania, or so he told me and Lord Rothschild.

Again, there can be little doubt about which cold war adversary benefited more from Hollis's handling of the Blunt case. MI5 secured historic information for its files, and a few minor spies were named but never shamed, Leo Long having first been exposed by Straight, not Blunt. The KGB and GRU, on the other hand, received the welcome message that their British moles, however successfully treacherous, would be neither prosecuted nor exposed.

In November 1981, the prime minister, then Margaret Thatcher, was to tell Parliament that "prior to 1964 no records exist anywhere of immunities and inducements offered to spies to secure their confessions." She had been given that information by the cabinet secretary after consultations with MI5, MI6, and the Office of the Attorney General. What it implied was that all the records covering the immunities offered to Philby, Blunt, and, effectively, Long, Cairncross, and any other traitors Blunt exposed had been deliberately destroyed. There can be little doubt that the original initiative for this destruction came from MI5, where the records were stored. The cutoff date of 1964 just covered the really embarrassing cases, with all of which Hollis had been deeply involved.

Mrs. Thatcher gave no indication of the date the destruction had been ordered. It may be yet another coincidence, but if it was done in 1965, it was in the last year of Hollis's service. Peter Wright told me that before departing, Hollis had ordered the destruction of many documents, including all twelve volumes of Liddell's diaries, which Wright managed to prevent.

CHAPTER 73

Still More Cover-ups

—

WHEN BLUNT HAD BEGUN WORKING IN MI5 IN JUNE 1940,
one of the agents he had recruited at Cambridge, Leo Long, a fluent
German speaker, was already installed in a separate intelligence branch
called MI 14(b). This had been set up to provide continuing intelligence
assessments of Germany's armed strength and future actions. At that
time, and for a further year, the Soviet Union and Nazi Germany were
virtually allies, both being keen to expedite the defeat of Great Britain
and the dissolution of the British empire. Yet when Blunt told Long that
he must supply him with all the secret information he could for onward
passage to Moscow, Long obliged. Throughout Long's espionage career, Blunt acted as his courier and controller, meeting him about once a
fortnight during the three years that Long was based in London and, on
occasion, in Germany, when Long moved there after the war. Long had
no separate Soviet controller, relying entirely on Blunt—a particularly
safe situation, as it was normal for Blunt of MI5 to be seen meeting Long
of MI 14(b).

KGB releases have shown that Long was an agent of that organization, known to them as an informant of Blunt's, and was given the code
name Ralph. When questioned, Blunt revealed that the GRU had attempted to recruit Long but had held off when they discovered he was
already working for the KGB. So there is no way that Long could have
been the GRU spy Elli, who, according to Igor Gouzenko, was working

inside MI5 and was serviced by a GRU controller who emptied *duboks*. Long fulfilled none of the other features of Elli described by Gouzenko.

At the end of the war, Long had moved to the Control Commission in Germany, later becoming deputy chief of British intelligence there, and was referred to in Genrikh Borovik's biography of Kim Philby as "General Long." He continued his treachery, showing that a man recruited young as a Soviet agent could achieve high rank and remain an active spy. He was serviced in Germany by Blunt, who visited there in connection with royal affairs and looted paintings. At KGB instigation, Blunt saw Long there to suggest that he should recommend him for a full-time senior post in MI5, with which he agreed, but the selection board turned him down by a narrow margin. When Long left the Control Commission in 1952, he ceased to have access to secret information. Clearly, the KGB had wanted Long inside MI5, where, once installed, he could have been required to continue his treachery whether he wished to or not. The odds are that Blunt would also have been required to continue as his courier, with his palace position providing perfect cover.

In 1964, Hollis delayed any questioning of Long until he had fixed Blunt's immunity deal, so whatever happened, Long was safe from prosecution and, in theory, public censure. The circumstances of MI5's approach to Long are extraordinary, even by the strange standards of the secret world. In agreement with MI5, Blunt telephoned Long to say, "Something has come up," and that he should make his way to Blunt's apartment for a drink and a chat. Blunt's sitting room had been wired by MI5 so that the conversation could be overheard and recorded. Long was briefly told what had happened and was then urged by Blunt to "come clean" on the understanding that if he made a confession, he would not be prosecuted. Long quickly agreed, and the MI5 officer Arthur Martin was telephoned. Two days later, the two traitors met Martin at a safe house. After Blunt left, Long formally asked for immunity, but this was refused because only the attorney general could grant it, and he had been told nothing by Hollis about Long. Hollis may have been reluctant to admit the existence of yet another traitor in the secret services and may also have wanted to conceal the fact that a witness against Blunt had been conveniently available. All Martin could do was assure Long that in view of Blunt's unassailable position, any action against him was most unlikely. Long accepted the arrangement, which was as good as immunity, because under British law, the verbal inducement alone could have been binding in that respect.

In several conversations, Long admitted to conduct that he later described as "frankly treasonable" and gave details confirming that Blunt had acted as his courier. Again, Hollis's action benefited the KGB, with another of its dedicated agents escaping without legal or public censure.

Peter Wright first exposed the Long case to me when I visited him in Tasmania in October 1980, and I gave some details about him in my book *Their Trade Is Treachery*. For legal reasons, as Long was still alive, the publisher's lawyers deleted his name, which I then gave to newspapers, hoping that they would take the risk and "doorstep" him. None did so, and his name did not become public until the following year when he was exposed in *The Sunday Times*, his treachery being confirmed by the prime minister, Margaret Thatcher, in Parliament.

Mrs. Thatcher realized that in sanctioning the effective extension of Blunt's immunity to Long, Hollis had dispensed justice without reference to the law officers. She took steps to ensure that in future, inducements to confess could not be offered to suspect spies without reference to the attorney general.

Blunt had also pointed a finger at John Cairncross, the Cambridge Communist whom he had talent-spotted for the KGB and happened to dislike. MI5 had previously become suspicious of Cairncross, by then a civil servant who had held several Whitehall posts giving him access to the most sensitive information. When MI5 officers had searched Burgess's apartment, following his disappearance in 1951, they had found some old handwritten notes about Whitehall officials, clearly penned by a Soviet talent scout, along with an account of British policy on Poland. The handwriting was recognized as that of Cairncross, who was then working in the Treasury. He was put under surveillance without result, probably because the Soviet controller he had agreed to meet by telephone either had been warned or had spotted the watchers. He was interviewed by William Skardon in 1952 and denied being a spy but, later, agreed to resign with a cash payment in lieu of pension and moved abroad, filling a succession of posts. In a further display of "amicable elimination," another extremely damaging traitor had been spirited out of danger of exposure on Hollis's instructions.

In the files of MI5, according to Wright, Cairncross was dismissed as small fry of no further interest, but his KGB record would eventually show that he was one of the biggest fish ever landed by Soviet intelligence. Once again, MI5 had blundered over a major spy, who had betrayed atomic secrets and Enigma codes in addition to more than five thousand secret documents, or else it had deliberately "kicked the case into the long grass." Hollis had ensured that a really major spy remained unpunished without any shaming publicity until I exposed him in 1981.

Cairncross had been recruited to KGB service in London in April 1937 but, as was common practice, was introduced to his controller in Paris. He was given the code name Molière and, later, List or Liszt. Once installed in his first appointment in the Foreign Office, he passed on everything he could, including details of the government's position in the Munich crisis with Hitler. He handed over a copy of a report showing that a senior official in the Soviet Foreign Ministry was a British agent.

In 1940, at the KGB's suggestion, he managed to secure the position of secretary to Lord Hankey, a government minister who then chaired the cabinet's Scientific Advisory Committee, involved with intelligence work, radar, and atomic research. Papers on every aspect of the most secret defense research crossed Cairncross's desk, and he transmitted them to the KGB, including deliberations of the Chiefs of Staff about the conduct of the war. He also saw the daily War Cabinet Record of Operations and Intelligence and betrayed all he could about them.

In September 1941, as already stated, he gave the KGB its first detailed information about the atomic bomb project—that a uranium bomb was technically feasible and that the Chiefs of Staff had urged that it should be made.

After transfer to the Treasury, he betrayed details of arrangements to intercept illicit communications and the plans for Station X, the supersecret establishment at Bletchley to be devoted to the breaking of German codes. He provided War Office directories. Then, in August 1942, because of his fluency in German, he insinuated himself onto the staff of Station X, where he dealt with air intelligence. Winston Churchill called the code breakers there "the geese who laid the golden eggs but never cackled." In fact, Cairncross cackled continuously throughout his two years there. Just two weeks after his arrival, he told his KGB controller exactly what Station X was about and agreed to hand over bundles of intercepts every week. He provided manuals for reading German codes and documents taken from the disposal box where they had been placed for burning. One batch of intercepts, which he handed over in 1943, contained details of Luftwaffe dispositions before the crucial tank battle of Kursk. They helped the Russians to destroy several hundred Luftwaffe aircraft on the ground, and the Germans were decisively defeated. The information had already been officially fed to the Russian commanders by another route, to preserve the secret of the code breaks, but Cairncross's copies of the intercepts provided confirmation. As a result, when he learned of this achievement by reading *Their Trade Is Treachery,* he was later to call himself "the man who changed the course of World War Two."

He moved from Bletchley in the autumn of 1943, joined an MI6 outpost at St. Albans, and soon moved to London, along with Philby, continuing his espionage inside MI6 headquarters and accepting occasional gifts of money from the KGB. In June 1945, when Germany had surrendered, he provided the KGB with the identities of MI6 agents in several countries.

He then rejoined the Treasury, which received many defense and intelligence documents because of its responsibility for financing all government departments, and continued his treachery until the KGB Center broke contact with him in October 1945, following the general alarm caused by Igor Gouzenko's defection. According to Oleg Tsarev, the KGB ignored him until June 1948, though the spy himself told a different story, as will be seen. He had certainly resumed spying in 1948 when he had access to documents about Britain's defensive strategy for the cold war, including atomic aspects. He was still meeting his controller in February 1950 and continued to provide parcels of defense documents, especially after he was transferred to the Supply Ministry in May 1951. Had there been a war, Cairncross's material could have been devastatingly damaging to the British forces. In total, KGB records credit him with the delivery of 5,832 classified papers, including entire files, for copying—proof of massive security incompetence by various Whitehall departments and by MI5 and MI6.

For a short spell, Cairncross was in America teaching at Cleveland University, where Arthur Martin warned him to get out, as he was about to be expelled from the United States following action by the FBI. He then moved to Rome, where in 1964, long after he had ceased to be of any value to the KGB, he was questioned by Martin and Peter Wright, who secured a further confession containing details of his recruitment. The findings were reported to Hollis, who took little personal interest in the case, regarding it as closed as long as Cairncross, who knew too much about Blunt, remained abroad. In the course of the discussions, he had been given a qualified grant of immunity and, in 1981, the attorney general was to tell Parliament that Hollis, then dead, had overstepped his rights in that respect. He had done far more. He had ensured that a most damaging spy who regularly took Soviet money for his treachery escaped punishment, to the KGB's delight.

Cairncross returned to England several times without entry or exit problems. In 1981, on evidence provided by Peter Wright, I described his activities in *Their Trade Is Treachery* and mused on the possibility that he might be the so-called fifth man of the Cambridge group. He was never friendly with the other four and had operated quite separately, but because of his vast output, the KGB sometimes included him among the five most productive British spies, when driven to limit the number with which the Center's analysts could cope. The former KGB officer Colonel Michael Lyubimov has recently assured me that the term *the Cambridge Five* was never used in official Soviet circles. He also insisted that there is no foundation to the story that they were referred to as "the Magnificent Five" (following the appearance of the American film *The Magnificent Seven*), though MI5 has used the phrase on its website.

After the publicity, Cairncross went to live in France, where, according to his old controller Yuri Modin, he appealed to the KGB for financial support but received no response. Eventually, not wanting to die in exile, he crept quietly back to a pleasant cottage in West Herefordshire. He wrote a self-justifying autobiography entitled *The Enigma Spy*, in which he struggled to convince himself that he had been not a traitor but a patriot braving great danger. He denied having supplied any atomic information, but his KGB file, which became available in 1998, confirmed that he was a liar. Among his fantasies, he claimed that he had intended to sue me for libel. A pity he did not! How I would have relished taking on in open court such a willful and whining traitor, who claimed that both the KGB and MI5, to which he had made an incomplete confession only when cornered, had "let him down."

In his book, Cairncross devoted a whole chapter to the Hollis riddle under the title "The Superspy." With the insight of a long-term Soviet agent, he spotlighted the stupidity of those who had tried to ignore the evidence against Hollis by stating that, as Cairncross was the fifth man, Hollis could not be and was therefore totally innocent. He appreciated the rather obvious truth that Hollis, who had been in Oxford in the 1920s, could not possibly have been the fifth member of a treacherous group who had all been at Cambridge in the 1930s.

He also brought the mind of a practiced intelligence officer and spy to consider the identity of Elli, who, he appreciated from the evidence, had definitely been inside MI5 in the 1940s and whose existence had been deliberately smothered by Hollis and others. On this subject, he was particularly scathing about the evidence of the KGB defector Oleg Gordievsky, which had carried such weight with the MI5 management. After researching all Gordievsky's statements, he stated that the defector had first indicated that he did not know whether Hollis was a spy or not but believed him innocent because nobody at the Center had ever mentioned a spy at such a high level. Gordievsky had worked at the British desk in the KGB Moscow Center in 1981 and 1982, where, he claimed, he had access to files. Yet he admitted that he knew nothing about Geoffrey Prime, who had been a highly productive KGB spy inside GCHQ from 1968 to 1977 and was not unmasked until 1982.

Later, Gordievsky claimed that the KGB's London residency files indicated that the KGB had no high-level source inside MI5 after 1954, but that could be irrelevant regarding Hollis. Gordievsky would not have been allowed access to the GRU files, and as Cairncross pointed out in his book, twenty years had elapsed between Hollis's retirement from all intelligence activities and Gordievsky's appointment as acting KGB chief in the London embassy in 1985. So the likelihood of any record of such an important agent being still in overseas files was nil.

Cairncross died in 1995 at age eighty-two, two years before his book appeared. Like the other four, he had ruined his life, sacrificing his considerable abilities in pursuit of a spurious ideal and showing no remorse for his treachery.

The disgraceful cover-ups of the activities of both Cairncross and Long had been in the interest of the reputation of MI5 and were also in the interest of Soviet intelligence, which could reassure any new penetration agents in the British secret services that even if they were ever caught, their risk of prosecution or public exposure was minimal.

This benefit was underlined by MI5 yet again at the end of 1964, when a particular coded KGB message was deciphered during the ongoing Venona program. Originally dated September 15, 1945, it was a message from the KGB director, General Pavel Fitin, asking the London GRU chief to tell Tina that her "material on Enormoz" represented "a valuable contribution." MI5 soon realized that Tina was one of the code names for Melita Norwood, who was then only fifty-two and was still working inside the British Non-Ferrous Metals Research Association. After a detailed investigation in 1965, the MI5 management, led by Hollis, concluded that she had been a spy in the 1940s but decided against interrogating her because, "as a committed communist she would be unlikely to incriminate herself."

Hollis went through the motions of referring this decision in writing to the home secretary, Sir Frank Soskice, with whom he was friendly. It was the same argument that had been used to avoid questioning Brigitte Kuczynski. Hollis and his lieutenants consoled themselves that Norwood's security clearance had been revoked in 1951, when known Communists were being refused access to secrets, and in 1962, when clearance had again been refused. Somehow, however, she had continued to supply her Russian masters until she retired eight years later, being awarded a KGB pension, though presumably Hollis and company were unaware of that. At that stage, they were also unaware that in 1958 she had been awarded the Order of the Red Banner.

The roll of dishonor may prove to have been much longer, because other traitors, especially some of those secured by the GRU, remain unknown, as Markus Wolf, the Stasi spymaster, and GRU archives have confirmed. Until very recently, the GRU refused to release any details of the foreign spies who assisted it, following a ruling in the 1960s by General Peter Ivashutin, then the commander in chief, who decreed, "Intelligence work does not need publicity!" In response to claims made by former KGB officers seeking to hog all the honor for securing the secrets of the atomic bomb, the GRU has declassified some archives, allowing its side of that extraordinary saga to be revealed in books published in 2002. However, the GRU is still very much in business, with extra responsibilities for signals and satellite intelligence, and is averse to doing anything that might discourage new agents. So, like the former KGB, it is restricting its disclosures to proven, well-publicized cases, like those of Fuchs and Sonia, remaining reluctant to release any information about Elli or any other of its officially unidentified spies.

The GRU is also genuinely concerned about the effects that such releases might have on surviving relatives of agents who served them well. This was recently confirmed to me by Colonel Michael Lyubimov, who warned that the number of British Soviet agents so far exposed is "only the tip of the iceberg."

CHAPTER 74

Suspect Finish

—

IN NOVEMBER 1963, THE NEW CHIEF OF THE CIA'S SOVIET DIVI-
sion in Washington, David Murphy, passed through London, where he
was welcomed by the resident CIA liaison officer there. He complained
about MI5's poor performance and lax security. MI5 seemed paralyzed,
with London having become a major Soviet spy center for the ideological drive into the West.

The pattern of events in which serious traitors were detected only
through chance leads provided by American agencies continued into
Hollis's last year. Late in 1964, a GRU officer working in New York informed the FBI that information about British naval missiles was leaking to Moscow, and the tip was passed to MI5. The officer, code-named
Nick-Nack, gave details leading to the conviction of Frank Bossard, a
Briton who worked in the Aviation Ministry and spied purely for money.
When he had been positively vetted, inquiries had shown that he had a
criminal record, but his claim that he had forgotten about that had been
accepted. He had even worked as an intelligence officer in a branch of
the Joint Intelligence Bureau in Germany, where he had been talent-
spotted by the GRU and recruited on his return to London, allegedly in
1961. Bossard had been spying for at least four years before he was arrested, after long surveillance, in March 1965. He was yet another active
Soviet spy operating in London who was detected only because of a tip
from the United States.

Michael Goodman's research has shown that the Bossard case may have been far more serious than MI5 cared to realize or admit. Previously, Bossard had been a senior figure in the Scientific and Technical Intelligence Branch, charged with surveillance of the Soviet nuclear weapons program and assisting in the assessment of Russia's capability to wage atomic war. Its findings were shared with the United States. So if in reality Bossard had been recruited earlier by the GRU than he admitted, he could have been a far more damaging spy to both British and American defense interests.

In October 1964, when Harold Wilson became prime minister of a Labour government, he took an early opportunity to summon Hollis to Downing Street. Wilson and his friend George Wigg, the new paymaster general, had been staggered by the way Hollis had kept Harold Macmillan in ignorance of the Profumo affair. So Wilson told Hollis that Wigg would be serving as his personal liaison with him, with regular access to MI5 headquarters, the prime purpose being (as Wigg told me) to secure the earliest possible warning of any scandal affecting Labour ministers. He also told Hollis that he must seek his personal approval before carrying out any investigation involving members of Parliament—in the Commons or the Lords. The ban covered telephone tapping, bugging, the opening of letters, and the examination of bank accounts. Wilson also warned Hollis that he regarded the evidence of defectors as unreliable and would be unlikely to accept it as a basis for MI5 investigations of MPs.

Though Wilson could not have foreseen it, his bans were to cover up the serious espionage of John Stonehouse, whom he appointed to the post of parliamentary secretary inside the Aviation Ministry. There, with access to airplane and weapons secrets, the traitor inside the Labour government was quickly taken over by the KGB, and there is evidence, from the senior KGB officer Valdimir Barkovsky, that he provided details of the Concorde supersonic airliner, assisting the Russians to build their "Concordski" near replica.

When, in 1969, two Czech intelligence officers defected to the CIA and named Stonehouse as their spy, Wilson was able to obstruct MI5's efforts to induce him to confess, and the case was hushed up until 1974, when it was exposed in the American press. Wilson then told Parliament that Stonehouse had been investigated and had proved to be innocent. The truth was not to emerge until 2006, when, in a media investigation I initiated, a copy of Stonehouse's Czech intelligence file was found in Prague. Its one thousand pages showed that the traitor, code-named Kolon and then, more aptly, Twister, had taken money for ten years. Though Stonehouse committed his most serious treachery after he became aviation minister in 1967 and, later, minister of posts and telecommunications, with links to GCHQ, he spied for five years during Hollis's reign without being inconvenienced by MI5.

Wigg, whom I was still consulting regularly, told me that he was captivated by the prospect of his entry into the secrets world, but in short order, he was captured by it. He brought occasional information of use to Wilson but also informed MI5 about the new inhabitants of Number 10 and its peculiar visitors, who were so numerous that he described it as "like a bloody railway station." Like MI5, he was particularly perturbed by some of Wilson's friends who were of Eastern European origin.

In view of the castigation that Hollis had received in Parliament from both Wilson and Macmillan during the Profumo debate, it is remarkable that he survived in his post. The explanation probably lay in Wilson's frustrated desire to emulate Clement Attlee and bring in another "honest copper," who was not immediately available, to replace him. This was Sir Eric St. Johnston, then chief constable of Lancashire, whom Wilson admired, his own constituency being in that county. However, as Sir Eric explained to me while we were fishing together, under pressure from his newfound friends in MI5, Wigg ensured that another MI5 man was appointed.

For Hollis, it was effectively the end of his career, as during much of 1965, he was abroad on the customary farewell visits to allied security organizations.

When the Wilson government was installed, Hollis should have ensured that the new home secretary or the attorney general was informed about the Blunt situation. Being so recent, it could have leaked, but he told nobody, and Wigg also remained ignorant of the immunity deal. So another sensitive situation involving a Soviet spy, fraught with political considerations, never reached the ears of the prime minister while Hollis remained director general. Not until 1966, after Hollis's retirement, did MI5 acquaint Wilson about the Blunt affair. By then, the investigation into Hollis himself was under way. Perhaps the possibility that he, too, might have to be offered immunity to save MI5's face induced the new MI5 management to inform the Labour leader about the allegedly "highly productive precedent" set by the Blunt case.

In May 1965, a report by London-based CIA officers claimed that MI5 was "poorly managed, poorly organized and poorly led, even though it employed many talented officers." The report was welcomed warmly by the CIA counterintelligence chief, James Jesus Angleton, who secured White's agreement that there was urgent need to identify the mole in MI5. Meanwhile, Angleton (with whom I corresponded, though mainly about fishing) and some other CIA officers recommended that Hollis should be dismissed but failed to apply sufficient pressure because he was due to retire shortly anyway.

MI5's deputy director general, Martin Furnival Jones, while regarding the suspicion of Hollis as grotesque, agreed that a proper inquiry was necessary, and White concurred. The prospect that his protégé might prove to be a Soviet agent was appalling for White, but he was in the habit of saying, "One of the only things to be learnt from spying is that the least likely is the most probable." Anthony Glees, in his dealings with White, found him "a bit equivocal about Hollis." He would refute particular allegations but cover himself by saying, "But you can't ever be sure about anyone."

Also, in May 1965, a former U.S. defense secretary, Gordon Gray, accompanied by Gerald Coyne, a former FBI officer, arrived in London to carry out a surreptitious investigation of the efficiency of the British secret services. They had been commissioned by an advisory board working for President Lyndon Johnson. According to Wright's account, the Gray-Coyne report, submitted to the U.S. government, claimed that both MI5 and MI6 were afflicted by poor organization, poor management, and (especially) poor leadership, Hollis being singled out for particular criticism. It stated that Hollis had lost the confidence of his senior colleagues and of the chief civil servants in Whitehall. Had the American investigators been aware of the many anomalies presented in this book, they are likely to have been even more censorious.

While visiting Washington, Peter Wright saw Angleton, who told him about the report, saying that the CIA wanted Hollis to be dismissed in joint American and British intelligence interests. This was ostensibly on the grounds of incompetence, but Angleton also believed in the existence of a high-level mole inside MI5. He pointed out that although there had been no legal proof against Kim Philby in 1951, MI6 had still fired him because of the excessive anomalies in his record.

White had already been informed of the Gray-Coyne report by the MI6 resident officer in Washington, and according to White's biographer, Angleton wanted the U.S. ambassador in London to approach the British government to suggest Hollis's dismissal. The ambassador declined to interfere. Meanwhile, with Hollis just a few weeks from retirement, Wright told him of the machinations. Hollis was so shocked that he complained personally to the foreign secretary.

Meanwhile, yielding to the pressure from his own officers, Hollis would have preferred a one-man inquiry into specific issues, arguing that the existence of a standing committee to check on apparent leaks was "intolerable and would break morale." Eventually, however, under further pressure from White, who was anxious to please Angleton, there was agreement that a joint MI5-MI6 committee, eventually code-named Fluency, should be established to investigate all the security anomalies and suggestions of penetration affecting both services. White's biography suggests that while he consulted Cabinet Secretary Burke Trend, he took the decision without first consulting Hollis, who reluctantly deferred to him. Nobody was to be above suspicion, and at one stage Wright is said to have suspected even White, who had observed casually to another MI5 officer that "communism was likely to win, eventually."

The Fluency committee, set up in the autumn of 1964, had seven regular members, three from MI5 and three from MI6, plus a chairman, operating in such secrecy that their colleagues would be unaware of its existence. Throughout the inquiries, Furnival Jones, who succeeded Hollis, was horrified at the prospect of a leak, especially to the media, so the number of people in the know was kept to a minimum.

Fluency would be expected to reexamine every apparent discrepancy, but as all its members were also required to continue with their normal work, no great sense of urgency attached to it. It met weekly, after office hours at Leconfield House, under the chairmanship of Wright and, later, of Christopher Phillpotts of MI6. It was therefore essentially a spare-time effort with limited financial and technical resources for investigations. As officers retired or moved to different positions, more than a dozen senior men and women served on the Fluency committee at various times.

Shortly before Hollis retired in November 1965, just short of his sixtieth birthday, Peter Wright complained that he was prohibiting the most elementary precaution against penetration—positive vetting of the staff. Reluctantly, after Wright's complaint, he ordered the introduction of positive vetting but left before he was vetted himself. This meant that when he came to be interrogated, there was no PV statement about which to question him.

A few days before Hollis retired, he summoned Wright to his office and, after some friendly banter, smilingly asked him, "Why do you think I am a spy?" Taken aback, Wright admitted the suspicion and explained that it was based on the old allegations and that everyone else had been eliminated. According to Wright, they had talked for about an hour when Hollis remarked with a laugh, "Well, Peter, you have got the manacles on me, haven't you?" He then said, "All I can say is that I am not a spy."

It was perhaps odd that Hollis's attitude to Wright should be so mild when many innocent men would have expressed anger at being accused of treason, especially by a subordinate. Some have viewed this story as due to Wright's imagination in creating copy for his book. However, he did tell it to me when I was with him in Tasmania, some seven years earlier, in 1980, when he had nothing to gain by lying. In Wright's time, there were always too many links missing in the chain connecting the manacles for Hollis to be unduly concerned.

Originally, Hollis had refused to visit Washington on his farewell tour because of the Gray-Coyne report, though he was eventually persuaded by the CIA chief, Richard Helms, to go. He did so, but Helms stayed away from the CIA party in his honor, as did Angleton, who still suspected him. The situation at the retirement dinner given for him in Ottawa was also tense. The RCMP commissioner who hosted it and one or two others knew that he was under suspicion of being a spy, and the occasion was awkward for them. This information from a Canadian source, Kim Abbott, clearly shows that Hollis was under suspicion before he retired and not afterward, as Margaret Thatcher was to allege.

While I was still forbidden under the D-Notice agreement to mention Hollis's name on his retirement, I tried to secure permission for a photographer to take a picture of him from behind, showing this once powerful and mysterious figure walking into what he hoped would be private oblivion. It was refused.

One early MI5 contemporary of Hollis's who put an impression of his work on record was the writer Derek Tangye in his autobiography, *The Way to Minack*. In 1940, Tangye had been transferred to MI5 from the army to serve in the rather unproductive post of press relations officer because he had been a reporter. During the ten years that he remained on the payroll, part of it in Blenheim Palace but frequently in London hobnobbing with politicians, war correspondents, and other journalists, he formed a dim view of MI5's attempts to counter Soviet espionage. "The impression I had was that counter-espionage was in the doldrums," he stated. He recorded that as the "recruitment of university undergraduates by Soviet Intelligence was a known fact in some quarters, it was difficult to understand how Maclean, Burgess and Philby got through the net and, having done so how they disposed of the information they acquired." Clearly, he thought that Hollis and his departments had been incompetent.

The only other MI5 contemporaries to have their opinions of Hollis published were Peter Wright and Dick White. Wright believed that the Russians had been so successful because Hollis was a Soviet agent. In White's account of Hollis's career, which he wrote for *The Dictionary of National Biography,* he claimed that his old colleague's name and reputation had been cleared by Prime Minister Thatcher. He still left room for doubt, however, in his final sentence: "The balance of opinion appears to suggest that Sir Roger was indeed innocent of the accusations leveled against him."

Later, White told his biographer that Hollis had "no real interest in Soviet operations, was regarded as ignorant, and had no true taste for the job." Considering that "Soviet operations" had been Hollis's prime target during his entire career, that was a damaging admission by the man who had consistently promoted him when they were all-important to the survival of democracy. White claimed to be convinced that Hollis could not possibly have been a Soviet spy because, in that case, "almost everything would have gone to the other side." Whether Hollis was a spy or not, it now seems, as more and more Soviet archival material becomes available, that almost everything did go there.

Hollis went back to his roots in Somerset, residing with his wife in Beaumont House in New Street, Wells, from which, on January 10, 1966, he wrote to his recent political master, Sir Frank Soskice, the Labour home secretary, inviting him to visit them. The letter indicates that he had just retired, so he had ended his MI5 career at the end of

1965, completing nearly twenty-seven years. Now that he was away from London and his mistress, who continued in MI5, soon achieving officer status, his wife hoped that they would stay together. Hollis became a member of the Bridgewater Rural District Council and captain of the Burnham and Berrow Golf Club, rarely visiting London and never attending MI5 functions. He was photographed joyfully holding his baby granddaughter. Such a picture of contented rural retirement may not seem to accord with a history of active treachery, but even after his public exposure as a most damaging Soviet spy, the traitorous John Cairncross ended his days quietly, and apparently contentedly, in a country cottage in Herefordshire.

If Hollis had been Elli, would he in retirement have regarded his professional life as a success? At that time, communism appeared to be working in the Soviet Union, which had firm control of its satellite countries, where sovietization had been enforced. The Soviet Union was an acknowledged superpower, achieving nuclear parity with the United States, and there had been no nuclear war. He could have consoled himself by believing that his actions and information, down the years, had been instrumental in preventing any preemptive strike by the United States, as they may have been. He could also be confident that the solidly professional GRU would never expose his assistance. Nor would it ever be likely to trouble him again once he was of no further use.

Like Philby, Hollis would die before the Communist system imploded, quite suddenly, under the weight of its human, economic, and political deficiencies.

CHAPTER 75

Kid-Glove Showdown

—

ETER WRIGHT AND ARTHUR MARTIN HAD SET THE FLUENCY COM-
mittee off to a good start by compiling a list of about forty instances suggesting that MI5 had been penetrated. The committee paid attention to
the evidence of Soviet-bloc defectors and took special note of the fact
that there had been *none* to MI5 during the twenty-seven years that
Roger Hollis had been a member. Hollis, who was given a code name,
Drat, quickly proved to be the common factor in many suspicious situations and was linked to many anomalies. A chart of MI5 operations that
had collapsed and of Soviet operations that had succeeded was dominated by Hollis's hand to an extent difficult to explain by coincidence.

Wright and the other MI5 researchers had failed to find Hollis's
Russian connection with Peter the Great that had satisfied Igor Gouzenko's revelation so specifically. Initially, the committee made the
major mistake of failing to question Gouzenko, who had been wrongly
dismissed by Wright as an "irretrievable alcoholic."

As Wright had failed to discover that Arthur Ewert was such an important Communist figure, though much of his record was in the registry files, the significance of that connection was entirely missed. Dick
White did not inform the Fluency committee about Hollis's expulsion
from Oxford, revealing it only shortly before he died.

In spite of the ready availability of the early history of MI5, the committee appeared to be unaware of the crucial role that Hollis had played

in placing Kim Philby in his prime position in MI6. Nor did it pay much attention to Hollis's generally close relationship with Philby and the extent to which they had worked together. The same applied to his relationship with Anthony Blunt.

After further consideration, the Fluency committee recommended, early in 1966, that Hollis be given full investigative treatment, but Martin Furnival Jones continued to regard the suspicions as "too grotesque" in spite of the almost equally unlikely cases of Philby, Blunt, Cairncross, Long, and Blake inside the secret services.

In 1966, White was in Washington for consultation with the CIA chief and also called on J. Edgar Hoover at the FBI. He told them that Hollis was under investigation. According to White's biographer, Hoover showed no surprise.

In its first formal report to Furnival Jones, and to Dick White at MI6, in 1967, the Fluency committee concluded that MI5 had been penetrated by one or more Soviet agents during many years since the departure of the proven spy Anthony Blunt. It listed twenty-eight anomalies that could not be attributed to any known spy. It highlighted the continuous nature of the apparent treachery over a long period and suggested that the "preponderance of probabilities" indicated that Hollis had been the most likely suspect.

At the end of 1967, it was agreed that Graham Mitchell should be recalled from his retirement for interrogation. He had no difficulty in answering every question. Nor did he plead faulty memory due to age. As White told me in writing, the case against him "collapsed like a house of cards."

One of the first important Furnival Jones reforms was to end the long-established MI5 practice of destroying files deemed out of date of which Hollis had made regular use, according to the evidence of Peter Wright. Under the new system, the older files were stored on microfiches.

In 1969, the Fluency committee was dissolved when it was decided to set up a small, permanent section inside MI5 with the full-time, ongoing remit of investigating possible penetrations of MI5, MI6, and GCHQ. It was called K7 and was headed by John Day, a former Royal Marines officer with a reputation for being tough. Fluency members such as Wright were barred so that the K7 members could all view things with fresh eyes and without prejudice.

The new group quickly agreed with the suspicion that there had been substantial penetration of MI5 after all allowances had been made for the activities of known spies. The evidence also pointed toward a single guiding hand over many years. After reconsidering the old evidence and making new inquiries, the K7 officers decided that the seriousness of the situation warranted a hostile interrogation of Hollis, especially as the problems appeared to have ceased on his retirement. All that K7 required was a confession so that an internal damage assessment could be made and the supermole saga could be consigned to supersecret files.

The director general, Furnival Jones, was strongly opposed to the embarrassing duty of dragging in the man who had recommended him as his successor, especially as he knew there was no probability of a prosecution, whatever admissions Hollis might make. However, unable to reject the requirement of the section, which he had established, Furnival Jones sent Day to see White, who by then had retired from MI6 and had a new post as coordinator of intelligence in the Cabinet Office. In principle, White was opposed to any interrogation of his old friend, but he reluctantly agreed that the mole hunt had to be completed, satisfied that Hollis would weather any questioning.

The K7 officers wanted Hollis to have no warning and to be placed under surveillance, with telephone and letter checks, in case he tried to reestablish contact with a controller to warn Moscow or seek advice. He should be picked up from home without warning. Furnival Jones, however, totally opposed such actions, claiming that the employment of watchers and bugging technicians would greatly increase the chance of a leakage to the media. He appreciated that the situation was so serious that MI5 could hardly survive if Hollis's guilt was proved and became known. So he restricted the conditions as far as he could and, late in 1969, wrote Hollis to ask him to visit his old office on a day convenient to him.

By that time, Hollis was living in a cottage in the small Somerset village of Catcott, as he had decided to resume his relationship with his former secretary. He had written to a friend, stating, "People will think I'm a shit but it has to be done," but he had not explained why. Ever the opportunist, he had not risked divorce while still in MI5 to avoid prejudicing his position. His wife had divorced him in 1968 on grounds of adultery, for which he had offered no defense and had moved to London. Then, at age sixty-two, he had married Val Hammond in that year.

Furnival Jones received his old chief in the privacy of his office, where he explained that there were allegations and circumstances in need of clarification, adding that he was confident Hollis would easily do that.

Hollis was questioned by Day, who had a thick, imposing brief. It was conducted in a safe house that was microphoned so the conversation could be taped, while Wright and another officer, Ann Orr-Ewing, listened in from an office some distance away to make notes and detect any discrepancies or faltering. The possibility of offering Hollis immunity for a confession did not arise, if only because, under new rules, it would have entailed application to the attorney general for permission, and Furnival Jones was averse to informing him or anyone else outside the agency. The prime minister was told nothing about the interrogation.

Day began by taking Hollis through his early life. The suspect claimed that he had no political interests at Oxford and made a point of saying that he had little in common with his known left-wing friends. He described Claud Cockburn as being only "pink." When asked why he had not recorded his friendship with Cockburn in the files about him, he said that he had simply forgotten to place a note there, which was a lie he was later to admit. Knowing nothing about his association with Ewert because of Wright's gaffe, Day did not ask him why he had failed to record that, too.

When asked why he had gone down from Oxford to travel to China, he said it was to "get away from the Church and from the family." According to Wright, he then explained that he had left home because he realized he was not religious and claimed that the Far East had always attracted him. As White had failed to give K7 his knowledge that Hollis had been rusticated or sent down from Oxford, Hollis was able to give a false reason for his abrupt departure.

Though only sixty-four, Hollis claimed poor memory for events and contacts relating to his journalism in China and was never asked for any documents, such as diaries, about his time there or anywhere else. He admitted knowing the Communist Agnes Smedley but was not asked about Sonia, since at that stage, K7 did not make any connection between her and Hollis's proximity in Shanghai. Nor was there any appreciation of the implications of Sonia's presence so close to Hollis in and around Oxford. Day knew nothing about Sonia's coup in securing the Quebec Agreement. Nobody in MI5 appears to have made any chronology of Sonia's activities relevant to the moves of MI5 to and from Blenheim.

The part that Hollis may have played in ensuring that Sonia's transmitter was never located was not considered. MI5 officers such as Kenneth Morton Evans who could have volunteered impressive evidence played no part because the interrogation of Hollis was kept completely secret from the rest of the staff, past or present. His controlling influence in the Fuchs case was also ignored.

Hollis was particularly vague concerning his recollection of events immediately prior to his entry into MI5, which his interrogators were anxious to probe to discover his reasons for joining. So much so that Wright was to state on television in July 1984, "We were of the opinion that he was hiding something. He avoided telling us exactly whom he was meeting at the time or what he was doing." The only explanation Hollis offered for wanting to join MI5, and then MI6, was that he must "simply have thought the work would be interesting."

Knowing nothing about the strange trip to Paris, which Hollis never mentioned, Wright set off later on an unproductive inquiry into what he called the suspect's "two missing years"—his period of alleged poor memory after his return from China. Wright said, "It could well have been that either he was recruited in that period or reactivated as a spy." Wright should have been concentrating on one missing month.

When asked why he had been so dismissive of the Elli allegations, Hollis claimed that he could not remember the details, doubted that Elli existed, and had simply believed that any penetration of MI5 was impossible. The information indicating that he had faked his report on Igor Gouzenko did not become available until 1973. Hollis could give no explanation of the long list of case deaths and the lack of defectors.

On a second day of interrogation, he was asked again why he had never declared his friendship with Cockburn. Under repeated questioning, he finally admitted that as Cockburn had become so well-known as an active Communist and Comintern agent, he did not want to prejudice his own career prospects by letting their past association be known and had therefore kept quiet about it. This change in his story was accepted as a reasonable, candid admission, but his behavior over his association with Cockburn had been frankly dishonest.

The total interrogation time was about ten hours, spread over two days, which was short when so many years of service and so many blind-eye incidents were being considered. Hollis had remained calm and unruffled throughout it, behaving very much as Philby had done so successfully. According to Wright, Hollis had been given an easy ride because the interrogators had been forbidden to question him as toughly as they would have treated a suspect of lower rank. He returned to Somerset relatively unscathed.

The K7 group then made an analysis of Hollis's responses and interviewed a few witnesses, but they yielded little. A further interrogation is said to have taken place some time after K7 had been able to check his answers and wished to ask supplementary questions, but if so, it yielded little of significance.

A formal report was submitted to the MI5 management early in 1972. It concluded that MI5 had almost certainly been penetrated by Soviet intelligence in the 1950s and 1960s and noted that there was no evidence of serious penetration in the six years since Hollis had retired. A KGB defector named Oleg Lyalin, recruited in 1970, had provided valuable information for six months while remaining "in place" in London without being detected by the Russians.

The report noted that Hollis had repeatedly avoided, or even prevented, action that could have been damaging to Soviet interests, but K7 had been unable to produce the kind of evidence that could have secured a conviction against him in a court of law. That was interpreted by Furnival Jones, a lawyer, and by White as a clearance amounting to a verdict of not guilty. Both had already held the view that Hollis could not possibly have been a spy, because if he had been, so much more would have gone wrong or been compromised.

It was generally agreed that a damage assessment exercise in case Hollis had been a spy was pointless. The injury he would have inflicted through his membership of the Joint Intelligence Committee alone would have been so enormous, with intrusions into the operations and planning of MI6, GCHQ, and even NATO, that efforts to limit it all would have been too monumental to attempt.

When Furnival Jones retired at the end of April 1972, he could comfort himself in believing that the Hollis affair had been laid to eternal rest. Instead, as new evidence emerged from the successful decoding of more wartime Soviet messages, his successor, Michael Hanley, who had been involved with the Elli inquiries and was not convinced of Hollis's innocence, agreed to a reexamination of the case by K7.

Sonia's significance was finally appreciated, and the probability that Hollis had been recruited by the GRU and not the KGB led to the belated questioning of the GRU officer Igor Gouzenko. When K7 summarized its new findings, it concluded that Hollis had done all he could to prevent any action on Gouzenko's allegation about the GRU spy called Elli.

The second formal report of K7 regarded the case against Hollis as being strengthened by the new evidence, but the possibility of questioning him again was ruled out by his ill health, caused by a light stroke. On October 26, 1973, Hollis suffered a further stroke and died at the Catcott cottage a little short of his sixty-eighth birthday. He had been under treatment for high blood pressure. Still security-conscious, his widow, Val, stated his profession on the death certificate as "Civil Servant— Executive Officer (retired)." His funeral was well attended, but (unusually) there was no memorial service. His obituary in *The Times* noted that "the hotter the climate of national security, the cooler he became." Hollis's will showed that he had left £40,000, which was enough in those days to warrant the headline SPY BOSS LEFT A FORTUNE.

The way that the Hollis case had been disposed of continued to bother some MI5 and MI6 officers, and in June 1974, one of them, Stephen de Mowbray, a former MI6 member of the Fluency committee, presented himself at Downing Street. He had gone there at the suggestion of his MI6 chief, Sir Maurice Oldfield, hoping to see Prime Minister Harold Wilson, but instead he saw the new cabinet secretary, Sir John Hunt (later Lord).

After hearing de Mowbray's allegations, Hunt was not too surprised about the suspicions concerning Hollis, because a few months previously, in Edward Heath's premiership, there had been discussions about the dangers of KGB penetrations. As an extra precaution, it had then been decided to appoint a Privy Councillor of unquestionable integrity to whom allegations of possible treachery might be referred for quick investigation, and Lord (Burke) Trend, the previous cabinet secretary,

had agreed to take on the task. Hunt consulted White, who had been retired for two years. According to Tom Bower, White gave Hunt the impression that although he would be surprised if Hollis had been a spy, he
believed it possible. Hunt informed Prime Minister Wilson, who remarked to his political secretary, Marcia Williams (now Lady Falk-
ender), who later retailed it to me, "Now I've heard everything! I have
just been told that the head of MI5 itself may have been a double agent!"

With Wilson's agreement, Hunt decided to ask Trend to reexamine
the existing evidence considered by Fluency and K7 and to report to
him. Contrary to common belief, Trend's task was not to declare Hollis
or Mitchell guilty or innocent, but to decide whether MI5 had pursued
the cases properly and thoroughly and reached the right conclusion
based on the evidence available. While Trend would be able to call witnesses, if they were willing, he was not required to look for any new evidence or make any new inquiries and was given no investigative staff.

Trend was another archetypal Whitehall mandarin, who had known
Hollis personally and, while being cabinet secretary, had been the chief
accounting officer for the secret services. So he was in an invidious position in that he had a personal interest in giving MI5 a clean bill of
health. He was also aware that an inability to clear the former director
general could have disastrous consequences in Washington, where there
was always the additional danger of a leak to the media.

He arrived at MI5 headquarters, which had moved to Gower Street
in late 1974, and was set up on the fifth floor with a secretary and all ten
volumes of the Fluency working party. For about a year, usually working one day a week, he browsed among those files.

Called to give evidence, Peter Wright, the former MI5 chairman of
the Fluency committee, told Trend he was convinced that Hollis was
Elli, but Trend was unimpressed because there was so little on file.
Wright weakened his case by stating his ill-founded belief that Gouzenko had become an irretrievable alcoholic. That enabled Trend to
conclude that there was no reliable defector evidence and that none
could be obtained. The more balanced former MI6 chairman Christopher Phillpotts supported Wright's stance, as he told me, but to no avail.

White, who had a major interest in proving Hollis's innocence, had a
great influence on Trend, who was particularly impressed by his statement that no defector had put a finger on Hollis, though that was exactly

what Gouzenko seemed to have done. The Cockburn connection carried little weight with Trend, who knew nothing of the even more suspicious Ewert connection.

Like some other witnesses, Wright left Gower Street believing that Trend had been impressed by the weight of the evidence. They were never officially told the results of his conclusions, however. As a result, Wright informed me in 1980 that he was sure Trend had concluded there was a prima facie case for suspecting that there had been a spy at high level in MI5 and that the evidence extended from the entry of Hollis in 1938 to his retirement in 1965. Christopher Phillpotts told me the same.

In the early summer of 1975, Trend submitted his report to Hunt, who passed it to the prime minister. So far, it has been held tightly secret. Nevertheless, two people who have read it—Sir Michael Havers (when attorney general) and Lord Chalfont—have briefly described its contents to me. Both agreed that all Trend had been able to do, with respect to Hollis, was to give him the benefit of the doubt—the only decision he could reach in the absence of proof. He reported that all the available evidence had been fairly and properly examined. He pointed out that none of it definitely implicated Hollis. While admitting that his innocence could not be proved, there could be no certainty that he had been a spy. In his view, evidence was lacking, and what there was could be attributed to the activities of others, such as Blunt and Philby, though the KGB archives have since shown that to be incorrect.

The Trend report, therefore, indicated that until and unless further evidence emerged, MI5 could continue to assume that Hollis had not been an agent of the Soviet Union. Nevertheless, as former cabinet secretary Lord Armstrong confirmed to me, Trend worded his report so that he, and those making use of it, would be covered if new evidence did come to light, as it has. He was at pains to point out that in no way had there been any kind of cover-up, but he was entirely in favor of continuing to keep the whole matter secret from other government departments, Parliament, and the public. Until *Their Trade Is Treachery* appeared in 1981, nobody outside a small circle knew of the Trend report's existence. It had been very effectively concealed.

Though the Trend report was no more than a third umpire's verdict of "Not out!" it remains one of the two reasons for the discrediting of the whole modern case against Hollis as "a myth" given by the MI5 management. Their website stated, "The Trend Inquiry of 1974 cleared

Hollis of that accusation. Subsequently, the evidence of the former KGB officer, Oleg Gordievsky, confirmed the judgment." More recently, this has been modified to "In 1981 allegations were published claiming that Sir Roger Hollis had been a Soviet agent. These were investigated and found to be groundless."

Eventually, de Mowbray was invited to the Cabinet Office to be briefed on Trend's finding, but he was not allowed to see the report. Like Wright and others, he was not impressed. He agreed with the comment of *The Times* after Mrs. Thatcher made her statement about the report in 1981: "There were serious professional suspicions about Sir Roger Hollis which do not seem to have been dispelled but merely disposed of, as it were, by majority verdict." After reading the Trend report, Michael Havers rated Hollis as "a buffoon" and "a poor spy for Britain."

While Trend was still laboring away, a meeting of an organization called CAZAB had been held in May 1974. CAZAB was a secret conference of senior counterintelligence officers from Canada, Australia, New Zealand, America, and Britain that had first met in November 1967 and had continued to exchange information and ideas about every eighteen months. At the 1974 session, Michael Hanley, who still considered the Hollis case unproven either way, gave the delegates an account of the investigations, with no conclusions as to innocence or guilt. He did this so that they could consider any consequences to themselves if Hollis had, in fact, been a spy, in view of his intimate past association with them all. Canada took the matter especially seriously, because of Hollis's close connections there, but in the tightest secrecy. Not until March 1981, after *Their Trade Is Treachery* had appeared, did the Canadian solicitor general reveal that "in the mid-1970s, the RCMP security service was warned by British authorities that Sir Roger Hollis might have been a Soviet agent." He said that security officials had "governed themselves accordingly," meaning that action was taken to limit any possible damage.

Similar action was taken in Australia and New Zealand. The CIA and the FBI, which had known of the suspicion from an early stage, had already taken action. No such operation was attempted in Britain because it was decided that the damage would have been so far-reaching that no assessment of it would be practicable. Yet as late as 1977, MI5 asked the American intelligence authorities to review their deciphered

Venona traffic because of the possibility that a wartime Soviet agent known to have been operating in London might have been Hollis. These events show that in spite of the clearance of Hollis by Trend, considerable doubts about his loyalty still existed and make nonsense of official claims that the whole inquiry into his past had simply been a routine business to clear him off a list of suspects.

In February 2006, Dr. Michael Goodman of King's College, London, tried to secure the report of the Trend inquiry under the Freedom of Information Act. He received a quick response from the Cabinet Office stating that it remains classified "on grounds of national security."

CHAPTER 76

Overdue Cull

—

BY 1960, THE NUMBER OF KGB AND GRU OFFICERS IN LONDON who were agent runners posing as diplomats, trade delegates, chauffeurs, and journalists had become so swollen that they were saturating the MI5 and Special Branch police defenses, especially those involved in surveillance. That this had been a deliberate policy by the Kremlin was recently confirmed to me by retired KGB officers, who also told me that what they hated most about my reporting was my determination, whenever opportunity offered, to draw public attention to the situation. Hollis took no positive action to remedy it in spite of warnings from some of his officers.

In sharp contrast, as soon as Martin Furnival Jones succeeded Hollis as director general, he did all he could to redress the balance. First, he tried to induce the Treasury chiefs to increase the number of MI5 counterespionage officers, but they declined on cost grounds. He was unable to make any progress in securing a reduction in numbers of Soviet intelligence officers because Harold Wilson's Labour government was determined to appease the Kremlin in the interest of "better relations" and détente. Those of us who continued to press for action were branded as anti-Communist hysterics. So it was a situation that the KGB and GRU continued to exploit, with the extra bonus that the "special relationship" with the United States had made Great Britain a prime source of American intelligence and defense secrets.

Then, in 1970, with Labour gone and the Conservative Edward Heath in power, Furnival Jones, assisted by MI6, tried again to secure a reduction in the offending Russians. Heath was keen, if only because Britain was being treated with such contempt, but it took until March 1971 for the Foreign Office's top officials to agree in principle, because they, too, were anxious to avoid upsetting the Kremlin for fear of reprisals against the much smaller number of their own diplomats in Moscow, some of whom were MI6 officers.

Coincidentally, around that time, MI5 had secured the defection of Oleg Lyalin, a young KGB officer who was in the Sabotage Department, which was concerned with plans to destroy military targets in Britain in the event of a surprise attack by the Soviet Union. His confirmation that the Russians had about 450 intelligence officers based in London and that at least half of them were agent runners strengthened Furnival Jones's case. Heath and his foreign secretary, Alec Douglas-Home, agreed to resolute action.

A plan, code-named Operation Foot, was initiated on May 25 at a meeting attended by Furnival Jones, who robustly urged the expulsion of all KGB and GRU suspects whose names and activities had been recorded. After much argument, it was agreed that 105 of the most dangerous and most blatant Russians should be expelled. A list of a further 200 was to be kept in reserve so the Kremlin could be threatened with their expulsion should the reaction be severe.

As Lyalin was bravely prepared to remain "in place" in London while reporting regularly to MI5, action on Operation Foot had to be delayed. Meanwhile, MI5 took comfort in the KGB's failure to get any whiff of his defection, convincing Furnival Jones that whatever the situation may have been in Hollis's time, there was no spy inside his MI5. As Peter Wright recalled, "From 1966 onwards we had no evidence of Russian interference with our operations."

Lyalin's chance arrest in London on August 31 for drunken driving precipitated his need to defect completely, as the KGB would have sent him back to Russia in disgrace. The implementation of Operation Foot could therefore go ahead, and expulsion orders were issued on September 24, 1971. The Russians were given two weeks in which to remove 105 named diplomats and trade officials, including some from the Narodny Bank. They were also informed of the second-strike list if they attempted to retaliate against British officials serving in Moscow. A published Foreign Office statement pretended that the action was due to new information from a defector, who remained unnamed, though his identity was quickly leaked to the media, Lyalin by that time being in safe custody.

There were howls from the Kremlin, but there was no effective riposte. Several high-ranking KGB officers such as Michael Lyubimov have since admitted to me, and to others, that their organization never recovered from the long-overdue cull. Within MI5, there was a comforting sense of revenge for the many humiliations inflicted during Hollis's reign, and it was generally appreciated that it should have happened much sooner. Though it had taken Furnival Jones five years to trigger the clear-out, it contrasted with Hollis's inaction during his nine-year stint as chief, when MI5's counterespionage resources were progressively saturated.

Shortly afterward, in 1972, MI5 and the Cabinet Office were greatly disturbed by the news that the amicably eliminated Anthony Blunt was to undergo emergency treatment for cancer and by fear that, for spite or to salve his conscience, he might leave an account of his espionage—and his immunity—for posthumous publication. With the agreement of Prime Minister Heath, and with palace approval, a document marked "If Blunt Dies" was prepared to counter any embarrassing incidents, especially the details of his secret immunity deal, which the old traitor might expose. The apprehension in high places was certainly severe.

Appallingly, Blunt, who survived his surgical ordeal, had just been appointed adviser for the queen's pictures and drawings on relinquishing his previous position. This appointment, which the confessed traitor would hold until 1978, had been made by the lord chamberlain, who apparently knew nothing about his treachery. Save for the activities of an investigative journalist, the late Andrew Boyle, Blunt would have been honored at his death. His public exposure in 1979, through Boyle's book *The Climate of Treason,* was sensational, though the extent of his treachery throughout his years in MI5 was not to be fully known, even by MI5, until his KGB records became available after the collapse of the Soviet Union. The media and the public were shocked by what was revealed in 1979, but even more so by the way the traitor had been spared prosecution and allowed to retain his position and his honors. They would have been even more appalled by what has emerged from Russian records since.

Before Boyle's book was published, Blunt heard about it and threatened to sue for £100,000 libel damages in a bid to suppress it. His old friends had assured him that MI5 would keep its bargain and would not provide any witnesses. Further, if Boyle tried to subpoena any of them, MI5 would plead Crown privilege, and they would be exempted. Michael Havers, then attorney general, told me he had been horrified by the situation, and when MI5 had refused to change its position, he had induced Prime Minister Margaret Thatcher to expose Blunt in Parliament. She had immediately realized the political implications if the old rogue pocketed libel damages while MI5 had stood aside. In November 1979, Mrs. Thatcher gave what she believed to be a frank account of the sordid story, though without revealing how Blunt had been secretly exposed in 1963, and the palace announced that he would be stripped of his knighthood and other honors.

Speaking from a brief supplied by MI5, she told Parliament that the information that had implicated Blunt had not been usable as evidence on which to base a prosecution, which was untrue. She claimed that as Blunt had previously denied being a spy over eleven interviews, MI5 had "no reason to suppose he would do otherwise at a twelfth."

At the suggestion of the MI5 management, Mrs. Thatcher then went out of her way to stress that Hollis had gone through all the proper Whitehall motions in securing Blunt's immunity. In contrast, Michael Havers confided to me more than once that he had been appalled at the way Hollis had used the mystique attached to MI5 to bamboozle ministers and palace officials into securing immunity for a villain.

After consultation with MI5, Blunt gave one news-managed interview to *The Times* in which he made misleading statements and, as Philby had done, hid behind the Official Secrets Acts, while claiming that he had only followed his conscience.

Wright and other MI5 officers were shocked by Mrs. Thatcher's confirmation of Blunt's treachery. Wright was to complain to me that it meant that MI5 had failed to keep its word and that future spies would be unwilling to make such a deal. Some of the undercover brotherhood even declared that Boyle was legally at fault because he had flagrantly violated the "fiduciary relationship" between Blunt and the government!

CHAPTER 77

A Crucial Call

—

PETER WRIGHT HAD RETIRED FROM MI5 IN JANUARY 1976, signing the usual Official Secrets Act form (of which I have a copy) accepting that he must never reveal anything about his work. As he had joined the service late and held modest rank, his pension was only £2,000 a year, so he and his wife emigrated to the tiny village of Cygnet in Tasmania, where their married daughter was domiciled. There, living in a converted shack, he set up a small Arabian horse stud farm and soon fell into debt. In 1979, his resentment about his meager pension was intensified by his belief that Andrew Boyle would be a millionaire from the sale of his book about Anthony Blunt, about whom he knew so much more. With his wife doing the typing, he began writing what he hoped would be a revealing—and lucrative—account of what had really happened inside MI5.

On the sunny afternoon of September 4, 1980, about eighteen months after my retirement from Fleet Street, I answered a totally unexpected telephone call at my home in the village of Kintbury in Berkshire. I recognized the caller as Lord (Victor) Rothschild, with whom I had been in regular touch, especially since the public exposure of Blunt in the autumn of 1979. As they had been at Cambridge University together, shared intellectual interests, and remained close friends, Blunt's disgrace had ignited media speculation that Rothschild, too, had been a Soviet agent. This had been fortified by the revelation that in 1940,

Rothschild had been responsible for first suggesting to the MI5 management that it should recruit Blunt and so might even be the elusive fifth man of the Cambridge spy group, Blunt then being known to have been the fourth.

In consequence, Rothschild, then aged sixty-nine, had been collecting evidence for a possible libel action on which I had been giving him advice concerning the media.

Rothschild had been chairman of the famed N M Rothschild & Sons bank, where he retained an office that I often visited, and we had been friends for thirteen years, after we had met socially. Intelligence affairs were our main mutual interest, because he had served in MI5 throughout the war and had remained in touch with former colleagues, who kept him informed about secret matters, in which he reveled. As former biologists, we also shared scientific interests.

With his usual economy of words on the telephone, Rothschild told me that he had an overseas acquaintance at his home in Cambridge and urged me to drive over to meet him. When I balked at the distance, he offered to send a chauffeured car and to put me up for the night. The call, which I could so easily have missed because my wife and I were preparing to go trout fishing on our local stretch of the Kennet, had been one of those mutation moments that change one's life. Its long chain of consequences was to ensnare some of the greatest names in the land, engage the attention of the media for years, and lead to major changes in the law and regulations governing official secrets.

I arrived at Cambridge before eight p.m., and, alone with me in his study, Rothschild explained that the visitor, whom he called Philip, was a former member of MI5 domiciled in Australia. He showed me a slip of paper bearing the names of all the Cambridge spies plus Hollis, Driberg, Mitchell, Blake, and others unknown to me and asked me if I would be interested in talking to Philip about them. Philip then entered—a slim, smiling, white-haired man of medium height leaning on a cane. I had never met him before. He explained that he had become so worried about the Soviet penetration of MI5 that he had started writing a book about it but, being ill, sixty-four, and overworked on his stud farm, could not finish it. He had completed only ten short chapters and urgently needed £5,000 to prevent his bankruptcy. So he suggested that I should write the book on some profit-sharing basis. Though there was truth in his claim that his original purpose was to expose security scandals, there was no doubt that his immediate motive was money.

While unwilling to tell me much at that stage or to let me see any of the ten chapters he had brought with him to show Rothschild, he whetted my appetite with a few exciting details and new names, such as Michael Straight. He also made it clear that the book would concentrate on the case against Hollis, about which I had already been informed by Jonathan Aitken, the Conservative MP. Aitken had been briefed by the former MI5 officer Arthur Martin and had written to Mrs. Thatcher on January 31, 1980, to warn her that the details might become public. After the prime minister responded simply by saying that she had heard of the allegations, Aitken had shown me a copy of his letter. I had then asked Rothschild for any information about the Hollis case, but he had replied in a way suggesting that I should not pursue it. Now, through Philip, whose real name was soon revealed as Peter Wright, he had offered me the opportunity to do just that.

Rothschild had first met Wright in 1961 after joining the Shell Oil Company as a science adviser. On the outbreak of war in 1939, he had joined MI5, which was searching for talent, and had served there with distinction, being awarded the George Medal for his bravery in dismantling German booby traps. He had even been responsible for examining cigars, food, brandy, and other presents given to Winston Churchill to ensure that they had not been loaded with poison. After leaving in 1945, he had remained close to Dick White, and on realizing that one of the Shell scientists had special qualifications that might be of use to MI5 in the preparation of new secret inks, he informed him. White arranged for Wright, then MI5's only scientist, to visit him.

Rothschild had greatly missed the intrigue of the undercover life, which suited his devious, introverted nature, and he cultivated Wright, who kept him informed of MI5's activities by regularly visiting his apartment in St. James's Place. In return, Wright used his clever new friend as a sounding board for judging the feasibility of technical deceptions and other operations. Rothschild, who had influential political friends, supported Wright's plans for the scientific modernization of MI5.

After Wright had moved to Australia, they had remained in touch by letter, with Rothschild even trying unsuccessfully to induce the government to increase Wright's pension. He had told Wright about the media's "fifth man" allegations and, in preparation for his possible libel action, had asked him to make a list of the anti-Communist services he had accomplished for MI5, with which Wright was familiar.

I was immediately attracted by the book project. I had been looking for someone like Wright for forty years, because nobody from MI5 had ever told its secrets before—except to the Russians. Nevertheless, I did not relish the necessity of visiting Tasmania to be fully briefed, because Wright claimed that he dared not do it in Britain. I finally agreed, but only on condition that I would not be responsible for paying money to him under any circumstances. Nor would I sign any agreement that might involve me in a charge of bribery. Wright would have to be paid directly by the publisher, if one could be found.

To my astonishment, the normally ultracautious Rothschild then volunteered to set up some private banking arrangement so that Wright's name could be kept secret from the publisher and from everyone else. The publisher would pay Wright's share of the royalties into a small company that would forward it to him.

After dinner with Rothschild, his wife, Tess (also a friend), and Wright, I retired to my bedroom, making notes of everything that Wright had said. I did not see him again until I visited him in Tasmania, as he did not appear for breakfast.

I arrived in Cygnet in mid-October to find Wright smoldering with resentment at his treatment by MI5, both financially and by the management's dismissal of his claims about Soviet penetration. Clearly, he had convinced himself that he was justified in selling his secrets through me. Though he was taking many pills for a blood disorder, there was no sign of the walking stick, and it soon seemed that he had been exaggerating his infirmity during our meeting in Cambridge, perhaps to stress his difficulties in finishing his book himself.

He showed me nine of the ten short chapters. The missing one had dealt with Rothschild's career in MI5, with other details about his private life that he had discovered, and he had undertaken to omit it at Rothschild's request. There was disappointingly little meat in the chapters I saw, all but one of which—called "The Klatt Affair"—I quickly decided to scrap. There was no mention whatever of the Hollis case, as he had not reached that far in his narrative. I had to make notes from the chapters because Wright would not let me take away anything that might be traceable to him.

I had always understood that MI5 officers were told only what they needed to know for their specialized work, but I was astonished by the breadth of Wright's knowledge. As MI5's technical expert, at which he had demonstrated virtuosity, especially in the field of illicit eavesdropping, he had been involved in most of the major cases at some stage. Then, through his chairmanship of the Fluency committee, he had learned almost everything.

After nine long days, I felt that I had relieved Wright of his main admissions, including all he knew about Hollis. Wright felt sure that if MI5 got wind of the venture, they would find some means of prohibiting it, but if the publisher could achieve a fait accompli, they would take no action. I arrived home on October 24 and started work on the book immediately, having already decided on its title. Wright had called his limited effort *The Cancer in Our Midst,* but I much preferred *Their Trade Is Treachery,* which was the title of an insider MI5 booklet written for government officials to warn them of the wiles of the KGB. The "authorities" had gone to great lengths to prevent me from publishing parts of it when I had secured a copy some years previously, so it would be rather satisfying to use their title and publish a more entertaining version.

I confirmed what I could from various MI5, MI6, and Whitehall sources. I was in regular touch with Nicholas Elliott and am fairly sure that he had alerted his old office, MI6, about my activities even before I had left for Tasmania, though I had told him nothing about Wright. Meanwhile, I had made a provisional publishing deal with William Armstrong, the managing director of my existing publisher, Sidgwick & Jackson, with an advance, which secured a rapid payment of £5,000 for my unnamed collaborator. Armstrong had the courage to accept the Official Secrets Act risk but insisted on vetting by a lawyer for libel danger, and as a result, various names such as Leo Long, Flora Solomon, and Michael Straight had to be omitted from the hardcover edition, which saddened me.

Armstrong told me that because the book would obviously cause a political sensation, he would have to discuss it with his proprietor, Sir Charles Forte, the catering industry entrepreneur who had bought Sidgwick & Jackson to help the owner. Sir Charles, who was a long-

established shooting companion of mine, had soon found himself fascinated by the publishing business and took such a personal interest that
Armstrong rightly felt it necessary to tell him about the project. I was
aware that he could reject the book, in which case I would have to scrap
it or seek another publisher.

Sir Charles numbered leading politicians—including Prime Minister
Margaret Thatcher; William Whitelaw, the home secretary; and Whitehall mandarins—among his friends, and he was perturbed by the security, legal, and political implications. He decided that he needed
confidential advice before agreeing to publication. He telephoned me to
discuss his concerns, which I did my best to allay, telling him that the
book would contain no criticism of the current state of MI5 and MI6 because I had been assured—as I had been, by Wright—that the problems
seemed to have disappeared with the retirement of Hollis.

Armstrong then asked me to prepare a synopsis to show to Sir
Charles, with no indication of the sources. On seeing it, Sir Charles still
felt he needed assurance that the book would not be damaging to the interests either of the nation or of the government. He was also concerned
about the possibility of legal action against me and his company. So as he
happened to be golfing friends with Sir Arthur ("Dickie") Franks, the
chief of MI6, he showed him the synopsis to secure his opinion. Neither
I nor Armstrong knew that he had done so. Later, when explaining his
action to me, he said, "You are a dear friend of mine, but my country
comes before my friends."

Sir Arthur, with whom I was eventually to discuss the episode, was
shocked by what he read, and he alerted senior colleagues in MI6 and
MI5, but without mentioning the source. He told Sir Charles that he
could not offer a worthwhile view without seeing the full text of the proposed book. Before he agreed to supply the text, Sir Charles had secured
some firm undertaking that neither I nor the publisher would be at personal risk if any objection was taken to it. It was an agreement that was
to serve us both in excellent stead and save Rothschild and myself from
possible arrest and prosecution in 1987. Sir Charles also secured a
solemn agreement that nobody else should know how and from whom
Franks had received the typescript. The arrangement meant that because the secret service was involved, he could not tell either William
Armstrong or me what had occurred.

I wrote the book in less than four months and delivered the typescript on January 13, 1981. Having read it, with growing concern, Sir Charles passed a copy to Franks in the following month via an intermediary who called for it. Again, neither I nor Armstrong knew what was happening.

There was a clear understanding, on Sir Charles's part, that if there were serious security objections to the book, he would ensure that Sidgwick & Jackson would not publish it. I also feel certain that he would have advised me against publishing the book, and being by then a freelancer with no financial backing, I might well have taken that advice, as I valued his judgment on any issue so highly. So all the government had to do to prevent publication of *Their Trade Is Treachery* was to convince Sir Charles Forte that it could do serious damage.

Copies of the manuscript handed to Franks were quickly made and distributed to MI5 and the Cabinet Office, which would later be accused of obtaining it by theft or some other nefarious means. Wherever it was read it caused consternation, mainly because of its revelations about the Hollis case, which the few who knew about it had tried so hard to conceal.

A summary of documents produced in December 1986 at an Australian trial—which will be described later—showed that the crucial advice about action or inaction about my book had been left to the legal advisers of MI5. They agreed that there was no point in seeking any specific deletions or other changes in the text because the whole book offended the Official Secrets Act, with breaches on every page. Surprisingly, they then decided—in agreement with the Treasury solicitor— that it was not in the interests of MI5 or MI6 that the book should be restrained in any way.

The prime minister, the home secretary, and Sir Robert Armstrong, the cabinet secretary, all wanted the book suppressed when they met with the director general of MI5 and his legal adviser for the final consideration at Number 10 Downing Street. Nevertheless, they felt constrained to agree with the MI5 legal advice while being fully aware that the book, which Sir Robert later publicly described as "a bombshell," would cause a furor.

The whole scenario was like a tale told by an idiot, because the decision was to lose the government its eventual costly court case against Wright and lead to the publication of his even more damaging book, *Spycatcher*, six years later in a blaze of adverse publicity and legal troubles. Clearly, neither Mrs. Thatcher nor any of the others present had been told that all that was needed to stop the book was a telephone call to Sir Charles. Otherwise, I am convinced that one of them—perhaps Mrs. Thatcher herself, since she was so close to the Forte family, with whom I have seen her many times—would have made the call. Instead, Sir Charles himself was treated as a secret MI6 source whose identity could not be revealed to anyone.

This decision that the book could be published without deletions was passed, verbally and without explanation, to Sir Charles, who naturally assumed there were no security objections to it. Later, he was to tell me that he had been "very surprised" by the verdict and that he would certainly have vetoed the book had there been any serious objections. With a clear conscience, he instructed Sidgwick & Jackson to press ahead. Still knowing nothing of the Whitehall machinations at that stage, I had assumed that his decision had been based on his own assessment that the book would not damage the national interest.

Many people have asserted that MI5 and MI6, with the government's blessing, simply decided to take the opportunity of disposing of all the skeletons in MI5's closet to get rid of them because other investigators were on their trail. The true reasoning behind the government's decision is very different and almost farcical in view of the eventual consequences.

The main reason the book was cleared was that the MI5 legal advisers did not themselves know the name of the person who had supplied the script. They had been told that the source had been assured that its name would never be revealed to anyone under any circumstances. Nor did they know that he had offered to scrap publication if requested to do so, because this would have given a clue to his identity. They therefore assumed—quite wrongly—that an injunction would be needed to restrain the book, that I and the publisher would fight it, and that in the process, legal argument might require the source of the text to be exposed. At that stage, even Robert Armstrong was told by an MI5 official that the script had been obtained "on conditions which made it impossible to take any action about it," as was to be revealed in the summary of relevant documents submitted to the Sydney court in the *Spycatcher* trial. Much later, Sir Robert was to tell me that he had eventually learned the identity of the source.

When Lady (Val) Hollis disappeared from her cottage at Catcott on the eve of the book's newspaper serialization in March 1981, it became clear that security authorities had gotten wind of its contents. MI5 had organized her removal to a safe house for an indefinite period so that she would not be troubled by reporters pursuing the revelations about her late husband. The next event was a deception operation by Robert Armstrong (now Lord and no relation to William Armstrong). On the day that the *Daily Mail* began to serialize *Their Trade Is Treachery*, William Armstrong was telephoned by Sir Robert, who said that he urgently needed a copy of the book because the prime minister would be required to make a statement to Parliament about it. In fact, a statement had already been prepared for her based on the script in his possession. My advice to William was to supply a copy only if Sir Robert would give a written guarantee that the government would not prevent its publication. To our delight, he agreed to do so, immediately sending a letter by hand.

In 1986, during the *Spycatcher* trial in Australia, Sir Robert was to admit that the letter was a deception to cover the government's possession of the script, and while denying that it was a lie, he made the comment (which was to haunt him) that he had been "economical with the truth." All he had needed to do, had he been better advised, was to tell the court that he had required the book because it might have been different from the script as a result of possible redrafting by me. That would in fact have been correct because of the omissions demanded by the publisher's lawyer.

In Prime Minister Thatcher's brief statement to Parliament on March 26, she attempted to suggest that *Their Trade Is Treachery* was speculation and insinuations when an urgent inquiry had been set in train to discover my MI5 sources and had already identified Wright. She stated that the investigations I described had been undertaken "following the defection of Burgess and Maclean," which was nonsense. Using the "busted spy gambit," she claimed that security disasters attributed to Hollis could be debited to Philby or Blunt and by referring to "the war years" gave the impression that it was all ancient history. Regarding the undoubted leaks from MI5 to the Soviet intelligence services during the 1950s and 1960s, the suggestion seemed to be that they had come from Blunt, who maintained links with his old colleagues and gossiped with them.

In fact, the leaks involved many cases that were being overseen by several different officers, and most were of such a detailed nature that it is not feasible they could have been inadvertently revealed during occasional gossiping sessions with Blunt.

While admitting that the internal investigations did not prove Hollis's innocence, the prime minister claimed it had been concluded that he had not been a Russian agent, which was not the view of the Fluency committee. She added that Lord Trend had reached a similar opinion, when all he had done in his report was to state that in his view, the investigations into the possible existence of a high-level spy inside MI5 had been properly conducted without firm result and that Hollis should be given the benefit of the doubt.

Some historians still dismiss the whole case against Hollis by stating, "He was cleared by Mrs. Thatcher," but when questioned in the Australian court about Hollis in November 1986, Robert Armstrong stated, "It is possible further information will come to light which would prove guilt. It has not. If there was more information the investigation would have to be re-opened."

Whenever a secret department is in difficulties and questions have to be answered in Parliament, the information about that department can come only from the department itself. The opportunity for deception is unrivaled, and MI5 did its best for itself when helping to prepare Mrs. Thatcher's eventual statement about *Their Trade Is Treachery*. She therefore concentrated on minor errors that Wright had made in his statements to me about the still secret Trend report, to suggest that the whole book was ill founded. MI5 was also responsible for her claim that the leakages could be attributed to Philby or Blunt, though many had occurred long after they had left the scene.

The prime minister preempted further parliamentary curiosity by announcing the first independent inquiry in twenty years into the efficiency of the safeguards against further penetration of the secret services by foreign powers. It meant that no more questions could be asked in Parliament before the report was published.

Mrs. Thatcher's independent inquiry, carried out by the Standing Security Commission, did not produce its thick report until May 1982, when she failed to keep her promise to publish it. A brief statement listed a large number of improvements while referring to others so secret that they could not be described. It seemed crazy that major changes in the running of MI5, MI6, and GCHQ should have had to wait on the chance publication of a book by an investigative writer and especially one that had been dismissed as speculation.

When I came to describe all these events in detail in a later book, *A Web of Deception,* my publisher, Lord Forte, as he had become when ennobled in 1982, wanted no personal publicity or diversions, being totally involved in his huge catering business. Nor did he wish to embarrass Sir Arthur Franks. I therefore referred to him in the text just as "the Arbiter," and astonishingly, though many journalists were keen to discover his identity, none did so. I reveal it now only because Lord Forte died in 2007, aged ninety-eight.

CHAPTER 78

Two Turncoats

THE HOLLIS AFFAIR WAS RESURRECTED PUBLICLY IN JULY 1984 when Peter Wright appeared in an hour-long BBC television feature in which he claimed to be 99 percent certain that Hollis had been a spy and accused Mrs. Thatcher of having given false information to Parliament about the case. By that time, Wright knew that MI5 had established him as my major source for *Their Trade Is Treachery*, but the program had been filmed in Tasmania, where he remained free from prosecution under the British Official Secrets Act. Wright's aged appearance, diffident manner, odd diction, and tatty, casual clothes gave a poor impression of an intelligence officer. The program did not carry conviction and produced no political impact because Parliament was not in session. It did, however, stir up concern inside MI5.

As had happened with my book, MI5 had advised against an injunction to prohibit the showing of the feature, because in any court case, it might be cornered into making damaging disclosures. However, the program was taken as a clear sign that Wright might publish a book under his own name, and serious thought was given about the action, which might then be unavoidable. In the following month, this fear was fortified by the arrival on Sir Robert Armstrong's desk in the Cabinet Office of a 160-page report by Wright, entitled *The Security of the United Kingdom Against the Assault of the Russian Intelligence Service*. It was little more than a rerun of what he had told me and I had already published, but he had sent it in the hope of forcing a parliamentary debate on the subject. That was cleverly foiled by Mrs. Thatcher, and the report was returned to Wright, the only immediate result being a private statement by the attorney general, widely leaked to the media, that Wright would be prosecuted if he ever visited Britain.

A few weeks later, the Hollis case received international publicity with the appearance of my book *Too Secret Too Long*, which was serialized in *The Sunday Times*, published in America, and widely reviewed. It was essentially a plea for some degree of independent oversight of the secret services but included new material about Hollis of which Wright had been ignorant.

In September 1984, though Wright had severed his connection with me without giving any reason, I learned that he was well advanced with a substantial book under his own name and, a few months later, was told that he had found an American publisher. He also soon found a tentative publisher in Britain and one in Australia. To avoid an expensive court action, a copy of Wright's long and rather technical typescript was sent to the attorney general, Sir Michael Havers, who was keeping me informed of the situation. He described it as "dull and very repetitive" but also damaging because it contained details of secret radio surveillance methods used by MI5 and accounts of spying on friendly nations. The publisher's offer to remove any offensive passages was declined because Havers, backed by Mrs. Thatcher, took the view that Wright was in breach of his solemn undertaking to publish nothing whatever. MI5 also assured Havers that in order to make the book different from *Their Trade Is Treachery* and to increase its sales, Wright had introduced false anecdotes, such as a story that a substantial groups of MI5 officers had been plotting to undermine Harold Wilson and the Labour government.

In the six years that had elapsed since I had visited Wright in Tasmania, he had deteriorated, physically and mentally, into a self-deluding pantomime character sporting a ridiculous drover's hat, ravaged by illness, greed, and lust for revenge. Unlike the coldly analytical man who had briefed me to expose serious defects in MI5 (while also hoping to make enough to save himself from bankruptcy), he was prepared to fake evidence and commit perjury to ensure publication of his own book, to make himself a millionaire. Though he had never caught a spy, he agreed to call it *Spycatcher*.

A court case to secure the right of publication was begun in Sydney in November 1986 and was to prove of great political consequence. It was based on the argument that as the British government had failed to ban *Their Trade Is Treachery,* it had no grounds for banning *Spycatcher,* which covered the same facts. This argument was backed by the totally imaginary concept of a secret deception operation in which MI5 had conspired with Rothschild and myself to induce Wright to part with official secrets so that my book could be written and published. Its alleged purpose was to allow MI5 to dispose of all its "skeletons" in one burst!

Wright knew that there was no truth whatever in this crackpot conspiracy. Nevertheless, his lawyer warned me by telephone that certain Labour MPs would be calling for the prosecution of Rothschild and me for corrupting Wright. Prolonged inquiries by Scotland Yard detectives were to prove that neither of us had done any such thing.

Wright had readily agreed to this courtroom gimmick, which would inevitably discredit his old friend Rothschild, whose involvement in my book had not been mentioned by me or anyone else. When it had been suggested to Wright that he should expose Rothschild's part in introducing him to me and setting up the secret banking arrangement, he had put down his whiskey glass and said, "Oh well! Poor dear Victor! Throw him to the wolves!"

In the continuing deception campaign, masterminded from Australia, various MPs in London swallowed lie after lie and regurgitated them in Parliament as a means of attacking the Thatcher government. At the same time, sensational claims alleged to be in *Spycatcher,* though they never appeared there, were leaked to British and American newspapers. Throughout the case, Wright was projected as an old man so frail that it would be dangerous to subject him to cross-examination. Had he been intensively questioned, the statements he gave in a thirty-page secret affidavit could have been demolished, as they were later by a Scotland Yard inquiry. The police report showing that Wright had given so many false statements shocked the attorney general, who realized that the British failure to insist on cross-examining Wright had been a major blunder.

Publication of *Spycatcher* in America was timed to do maximum damage to the government's legal appeals in the Australian courts by showing that as the horse had bolted, any action to restrain it was pointless. The government lost the case, its legal costs being £2 million, though I understand that secretly it managed to claw back a substantial portion of the royalties paid by the publisher.

Spycatcher was only 382 pages long, because the American publisher required the removal of material considered unsuitable for the U.S. market. The cover deceptively described Wright as "Former Assistant Director of MI5," giving the impression that he had been number two when, in fact, it was a modest rank in the service and hardly accorded with his bleat that he had retired with such a small pension. The book became a bestseller, and though it could not be printed in Great Britain, it was imported in huge numbers.

The publicity attached to the *Spycatcher* trial promoted the case against Hollis, worldwide, over many months, especially after the government's lawyers formally accepted all Wright's allegations in the book as being true. Havers told me that this had been simply a legal device to avoid having to make damaging admissions in court. It was offset by a leak to journalists, including me, that the KGB defector Oleg Gordievsky had provided evidence indicating Hollis was innocent. However, it transpired that when he was first questioned, Gordievsky had simply stated that he did not know whether Hollis was a spy or not, but he believed that if such a high-level spy had existed, he would have heard gossip about him. That information may have been available to Mrs. Thatcher five years previously and could have reinforced her statement to Parliament about Hollis. At that stage, however, Gordievsky was still serving in the KGB as an MI6 spy in place so no mention of his evidence was possible then. So much has since been made of this evidence by MI5 that a critical examination of it is essential.

Now a British citizen, Gordievsky, who had joined the KGB in 1962, has claimed that he had gradually decided to break with the Soviet regime, but the opportunity to do so did not present itself until he had been posted to Copenhagen in 1972 for a second term of duty there. Danish intelligence advised MI6 that he was a likely defector, and he was recruited in 1974. During 1981 and part of 1982, he was on the British desk at the Moscow headquarters, feeding information to MI6 when he could. In the summer of 1982, he was transferred to the Soviet embassy in London. Three years later, in September 1985, Gordievsky defected physically, having spied for Great Britain for eleven years.

He has since revealed the extent of his knowledge of the Hollis affair in his autobiography, *Next Stop Execution*, published in 1995, where he stated that before leaving Moscow for the KGB cover job of counselor in London, he discussed with colleagues "the totally fanciful claims by British authors that Sir Roger Hollis had been a KGB mole." It has always been clear that if Hollis was a Soviet agent, he operated for the GRU, and at no time in his career did Gordievsky have any access to GRU records. Further, these "fanciful claims" had been made by Hollis's own colleagues.

At several points in his autobiography, Gordievsky confirmed that the GRU operated entirely separately from the KGB. When describing the London embassy's GRU section of fifteen officers as "a smaller but more highly disciplined organization than the KGB," he added, "I never had any idea who its contacts were."

Sir Michael Havers, when attorney general, told me that following his defection, Gordievsky was questioned about the Hollis case and his answers were all negative. He said he had never heard that Hollis had been a Soviet agent. When Hollis had retired in 1965, Gordievsky was only twenty-seven and had held only low-ranking posts in Moscow, unlikely to have given him access to any information about topflight foreign agents. The degree to which "need to know" was practiced in the KGB was stated to me recently by Michael Lyubimov, who had been Gordievsky's superior officer in Copenhagen. When Lyubimov was serving in the Soviet embassy in London, the spy John Vassall was being run by a close KGB colleague, Nikolai Korovin. Yet the first that Lyubimov knew of the case was when news of Vassall's arrest appeared in the newspapers. This was not just sound tradecraft. There were severe consequences if "need to know" was breached.

To prepare himself for his posting to London, Gordievsky read files kept in the KGB's British section, but he admits in his autobiography that he never had access to the most secret files, which were stored elsewhere. He alleged that there was no file on Hollis, but Kim Philby received so much MI5 information from Hollis in their regular liaisons that he reported on him regularly via his controller. Indeed, one of his letters about him was reproduced on the cover of the book *Crown Jewels*. The MI5 reports on the Gouzenko case prove that letters passed between the two and that Philby reported on them. It is therefore inconceivable that the KGB had no routine file on the man who also headed MI5 for nine years and should have been one of their main opponents. It is also on record that the KGB had cobbled together what it could discover about Hollis for an in-house history of the organization, completed in 1978 under the direction of General Grigori Grigorenko. The odds are that Hollis had a KGB code name that was used regularly by Philby's controllers.

While the MI5 management has gratefully accepted Gordievsky's argument that if Hollis had been a spy, he would have heard of him, senior British military intelligence officers who have served in Moscow have assured me that the existence of any Soviet agent in such a powerful position would be known to only a few at the highest level. Even within the GRU itself, the existence of such an asset would have been held closely secret, and there would be no files about him in circulation, even after he had ceased to function.

After Gordievsky had provided MI6 with his full list of Soviet agents known to him and their British targets, some of the officers who interrogated him were deeply disappointed. Nicholas Elliott, who was especially friendly with Gordievsky, told me there was not a name on it that would surprise me.

In February 1990, on a BBC *Panorama* program, Gordievsky, heavily disguised, told a sanitized version of how he had escaped from the clutches of the KGB in Moscow to safety in Britain. The program was then used to allow him to rebut publicly the allegation that Hollis had been a Soviet agent. Gordievsky's evidence was critically examined by the Soviet agent John Cairncross in his book *The Enigma Spy*, published in 1997. He drew attention to the fact that by the time of the *Panorama* broadcast, Gordievsky and Christopher Andrew, the Cambridge historian, had written a book, with the blessing of MI6 and MI5, called *KGB: The Inside Story*, which was to appear six months later and in which Hollis's innocence would be stressed. Following that broadcast, the Soviet embassy in London held a press conference and claimed that Gordievsky was small fry and had never been senior enough to warrant access to the kind of information he was claiming to know.

Nevertheless, when *KGB: The Inside Story* appeared, the introduction stated that in 1980, Gordievsky had been "responsible for preparing the sections of a highly classified in-house history of the First Chief Directorate dealing with KGB operations in Britain." This allegedly had given him access to files about Soviet agents. Some MI5 officers were as bemused as I was by the idea that the KGB allowed him full and free access to its files about secret sources and then posted him abroad, where he might reveal all to its adversaries. Such sensitive historical jobs were usually reserved for much older men who would never be sent abroad.

The extent of Gordievsky's access to the names of British KGB agents was further put into question by his ignorance of the existence of Geoffrey Prime, the KGB agent in Britain who provided Moscow with a stream of information, mainly from inside GCHQ, from 1968 to 1977. Prime had still been inside GCHQ, inflicting damage to the U.S. spy satellite system eventually estimated at costing $1 billion, when Gordievsky had been recruited by MI6 in 1974. Nor, apparently, in his perusal of the KGB files had he encountered Kitty Harris or the London atomic spy Melita Norwood. Their names were not mentioned in *KGB: The Inside Story*, where they would have provided considerable scoops, had the authors known them.

Since then, Oleg Tsarev, who had regular recourse to the KGB archives, has commented on Gordievsky's claim that he had wide access to them, pointing out that under stringent KGB rules, which it would have been dangerous to disobey, Gordievsky would have been required to place his signature on those he consulted. Tsarev has examined the files concerned, and has recently confirmed to Dr. Svetlana Chervonnaya that the defector's access was limited because on some of the files of the Cambridge group spies, such as Leo Long, his signature is not there.

In October 2007, MI6 secured Gordievsky a British decoration—the CMG (Companion of the Order of St. Michael and St. George). In the following month, aged sixty-nine, he was rushed to the hospital after collapsing at his country home and was allegedly "close to death" for many hours. After regaining consciousness, he recuperated in a private clinic paid for by MI6. Then, in April 2008, he was quoted in newspapers as claiming that he had been poisoned on KGB orders. Police investigated his allegation, but forensic tests failed to find any poison in his system. The police view was that there was nothing suspicious about the illness. Gordievsky was then reported as claiming that MI6 had forced Scotland Yard's Special Branch detectives to drop their investigation and had then tried to cover up the case. He had allegedly then contacted the MI5 chief and would later be quoted as claiming that he was "caught between MI5, MI6, and Special Branch."

Gordievsky suspected that a Russian friend who visited his house had administered the poison thallium, but the friend, who was questioned by the police, dismissed the statement, saying that the defector had been ill for many months.

While Gordievsky is a brave and resolute man who has served British intelligence well, his saga reminds me of wisdom imparted to me by the late MI6 chief Sir Maurice Oldfield: "Defectors are like grapes—the first pressings are the best."

CHAPTER 79

Brush with the Police

―

AFTER PETER WRIGHT AND HIS LAWYERS AGREED TO "THROW Rothschild to the wolves," Rothschild's part in initiating *Their Trade Is Treachery* was leaked for the first time to British journalists covering the case in Australia. As agreed, I had never divulged that either Rothschild or Wright had been involved. The naming of such a distinguished figure in such a comprehensive leak of MI5 secrets received massive publicity. Inevitably, it resurrected the allegation that Rothschild had been the fifth man of the Cambridge spy group. This was hyped up by the ludicrous suggestion that Rothschild had encouraged Wright to give me the information about Hollis so that the former MI5 chief would be exposed as the fifth man. He had done this, it was argued, to draw suspicion away from himself in that respect.

The whole concept was nonsensical, because as Wright well knew, Hollis was at Oxford in the 1920s and could not possibly have been the fifth man of a group recruited in the 1930s.

Rothschild had known all about the Hollis case as it unfolded in MI5, because Wright had kept him informed about it. So if he had wanted publicity to suggest that Hollis was the fifth man, he could simply have given the information to me, without having to bring Wright from Australia. In fact, when I had asked him about the case, he had refused to tell me anything and had sent me a letter suggesting that the allegations were untrue.

While the exposure of Rothschild in Australia generated a tide of damaging innuendos in the British media and in Parliament, where Labour MPs made the most of their privilege to make wild charges without fear of libel action, the MI5 managers remained silent. Their former George Medalist was besieged by reporters and photographers, with one group even trying to bribe a milkman to let them drive his vehicle past the security arrangement to the front door of Rothschild's Cambridge home. At the age of seventy-six, he was knocked down in a media melée outside Rothschild's Bank.

Through intermediaries, he asked MI5 to assist him with some sort of statement, but without response. His comment on the behavior of the MI5 management, when those who have helped them are in difficulty, was, "They will see you dead before they will help you." Eventually, in desperation, he tried to force MI5's hand with a statement in the *Daily Telegraph* urging the director general of MI5 to declare publicly that "it has unequivocal evidence that I am not, and never have been, a Soviet agent."

The MI5 management did nothing except bleat to the Cabinet Office about the difficult position in which they had been placed. Two days later, Prime Minister Margaret Thatcher issued a press notice saying only that the government had no evidence that Rothschild had ever been a Soviet agent. Worse was to come. The demands by publicity-seeking Labour MPs for the prosecution of Lord Rothschild and myself for corrupting Wright eventually overbore the attorney general, Sir Michael Havers, who was not well and had been subjected to a barrage of shameful allegations about his own integrity in the Australian court. Sheepishly, at a pheasant shoot, he warned me, "I'm afraid I might have to do something." He consulted the director of public prosecutions and on December 17, 1986, instituted inquiries by the Serious Crimes Squad of the Metropolitan Police Service.

A more robust minister would have resisted the demands for an investigation, as Rothschild was then far too ill with severe arterial sclerosis and a throat problem to appear in court. Further, there could be no fair case without the cross-examination of Wright, who dared not return to Britain and could not be extradited.

The remit of the two senior officers of Scotland Yard allotted to the task was to investigate the allegations involving Rothschild and myself, which Wright had made in a long affidavit to the Australian court, part of which was classified secret. They told me that Wright had stated in camera that I was not only an agent of MI5, but a double agent—also working for the KGB!

One by one, Rothschild and I, who voluntarily agreed to be interviewed separately in our homes, demolished Wright's statements with indisputable documents and facts.

My three interrogation sessions, which began on February 12, 1986, totaled about twelve hours. I gave the police a substantial advance statement and predicted to the detective chief superintendent who asked the questions and the inspector who made the notes that they would reach a point in their inquiries when they would be called off. They disagreed, but it was clear to me that they could not complete their task without interviewing Sir Arthur Franks, the former MI6 chief, and I was confident that would not be permitted. They interviewed my publisher and Lord Forte, who answered all they asked. Shortly afterward, they telephoned me to say that my prediction had been correct. To their great annoyance, because the whole exercise had been a monstrous waste of police time, they had indeed been called off.

At the end of my interrogation, the detective chief superintendent had suddenly produced a search warrant and demanded to see my private files. Though rather angry, I helped the police to make a selection, including some marked "Hollis," and ensured that they also included files containing information about certain individuals of such eminence that it would make any prosecution impossible. In particular, I made sure they left with the rather fat folder marked "Havers," concerning the former attorney general. Those who had to read the documents would realize that I would be likely to divulge the information in my defense and the damage to the government would be catastrophic, with at least one high-profile resignation inevitable and Labour having a field day. When my documents were returned, I was told that some of them had been copied and suspect that they resulted in one major political action, for which I have no regret.

I confess to having enjoyed the whole episode. I was appalled by the extent of the perjury committed by Wright in his attempt to appear as a poor old man who had been corrupted with money, and I had no difficulty disproving his statements concerning me. I had documents that proved I had never offered or paid him a penny when he had claimed that I had. Had I been prosecuted simply for being in possession of secret information, I had decided to ask for ten thousand previous offenses to be taken into consideration, the evidence being in my thirty volumes of press cuttings and in the numerous cabinet papers detailing the official inquiries that had attempted (always unsuccessfully) to discover my sources. The witnesses I would have been required to try to subpoena would have included the prime minister, Sir Robert Armstrong, Sir Arthur Franks, and above all, Lord Havers, as he then was, having been promoted to lord chancellor (for a brief reign that ended in his sudden resignation on health grounds).

Rothschild was also able to rebut all Wright's attempts to "throw him to the wolves," but he suffered medically from the ordeal. He became depressed about the publicity damage to the family name and especially to that of his wife. During the investigation, he underwent a "scrape-out" of one of his carotid arteries, a serious operation that can lead to brain damage.

Though the case against both of us had collapsed by April 1987, the government wanted to defer any clearance until after the coming general election in the autumn, because their abject defeat in the Australian court had been bad publicity, which they did not want to resurrect. On May 7, the attorney general told Parliament that the director of public prosecutions was considering the report by the police, who might have to make further inquiries, when they had already been taken off the case. The government's hand was forced, however, by Rothschild's MP, who let it be known that his distinguished constituent was suffering distress. On July 8, 1987, the attorney general therefore told Parliament that there was no evidence to justify any proceedings against Rothschild or me.

Rothschild died suddenly from a massive heart attack in March 1990. His memorial service was attended by three prime ministers—Margaret Thatcher, James Callaghan, and Edward Heath—along with many former ministers, service chiefs, civil servants, and Sir Dick White, representing MI6 and MI5.

Wright made more than £1 million from his book, but he remained in his shack and died in 1995—nearly nine years after he had been judged too ill to be cross-examined. While he was regarded as something of a folk hero in Australia because he had "bashed the Brits," inside MI5 today he is the example to recruits of everything a secret service officer should not be. Although the British public had some sympathy for Wright, they did not approve of their security secrets being sold by one of their salaried servants for private gain after he had signed a pledge not to do so.

One major mystery that has puzzled some of the greatest in the land, including several prime ministers, remains: Why did the ultracautious and security-minded Rothschild go to such pains to put me in touch with Wright? Evidence indicates that the answer lies in the close relationship between his second wife, Tess, and Anthony Blunt.

Rothschild had become friendly with Blunt when both were at Cambridge in the 1930s and shared intellectual interests. Another contemporary was Teresa (Tess) Mayor, said to be the most beautiful of her generation at Cambridge. As he records in his book *After Long Silence*, Michael Straight was infatuated with her but failed to seduce her because she was infatuated by Blunt, who, though essentially homosexual, had occasional affairs with women. Describing the relationship between Blunt and Tess, Kenneth Rose, a close friend of Rothschild's and his official biographer, told me that "they certainly went to bed when they were young, but what happened there is anybody's guess."

Tess remained friendly with Blunt after she had become Rothschild's second wife in 1946. She had started working for Rothschild in MI5 in 1941 as his personal assistant. A few days after Blunt had confessed in 1964, Wright was summoned to Hollis's office to find Rothschild there. Hollis explained that he had just told Rothschild about Blunt's exposure as a Soviet spy by Straight. To save himself emotional difficulties, Rothschild asked Wright to break the news to Tess at their apartment, where she exclaimed, "All those years and I never suspected a thing!" As I was to learn, Tess insisted on maintaining her friendship with Blunt even after his exposure as a traitor.

I am now as sure as I can be that Rothschild involved me in desperation because Wright effectively blackmailed him into doing so. During Wright's interrogation of Blunt, spread over many months, he had learned what he believed to be damaging information about Tess. He told me that when interrogated, Blunt had admitted to many homosexual affairs and had also revealed that he had enjoyed at least two liaisons with women who remained close to him throughout his life. Allegedly, Tess was one of them.

According to Wright, Rothschild had been nervously concerned when it had been feared that Blunt might die from cancer and leave a spiteful statement about his private life. Wright may have included that in the chapter I was never allowed to see or had threatened to do so. It would seem significant that Wright made a point of telling Rothschild that he not only had all his notes of his talks with Blunt, but still had all the tape recordings of them.

So the question poses itself: Had Tess been the standard confidante to whom Blunt had been driven to confess his treachery to ease the constant stress of his conspiratorial life? And had her affection, sympathy, and perhaps a solemn promise extracted from her driven her to protect him?

Tom Bower confirms that, according to White, Rothschild's "sensitivity about his wife's friendship with Blunt emerged in the aftermath of the art historian's exposure in 1979." Public allegations of a long sexual relationship with Blunt alone would have also raised the suspicion that she had known he was a spy and had kept quiet about it. I can think of nothing else that would have induced the ultracareful Rothschild to behave so uncharacteristically, in exposing himself and the family name to such risk in introducing Wright to me, that friends like Lady Thatcher, Sir Edward Heath, Sir Dick White, and Sir Robert Armstrong were amazed when they learned what he had done. They found it particularly hard to believe that the former chairman of N M Rothschild & Sons, with its international reputation for integrity, had set up deviously secret banking arrangements to funnel Wright's share of the book royalties to him.

So it would seem that in return for Wright's deleting the offending chapter and giving it to Rothschild—as definitely occurred—Rothschild undertook to find a professional writer to complete Wright's book and so provide the money he urgently needed to prevent his bankruptcy. Rothschild knew that I was already on the trail of the Hollis case, and because of our friendship and his confidence that I could be trusted, I was his first choice as an author. The timing of the fateful telephone call to me, without any warning, shows it had clearly been made on the spur of the moment, for the odds were that my house would have been empty. Rothschild knew that I was usually away in North Yorkshire shooting grouse in early September and simply took a chance that I might be at home. The concept that my meeting with Wright was planned in advance by the KGB, by Rothschild, or by MI5, which have all been seriously suggested by conspiracy theorists, is ruled out by the time scale. The trigger was something that had happened between Roth-schild and Wright on that day.

Unless he had been under duress, Rothschild would not have made the call, for normally he never did anything—especially over the tele-phone—without deep thought for the consequences, which were to prove disastrous to the government, to MI5, and to himself. Such an an-alytical man could not have failed to realize that he was creating a hostage to fortune, especially with such a twisted character as Wright, so the impetus must have been imperative. His behavior seems to have been that of a cornered man with something shattering to hide.

Had I been out, he would have been driven to find some other solu-tion, which might have been money. Wright's lawyer was to ask me why Rothschild had not resolved the problem simply by giving Wright the £5,000 he so desperately needed. Knowing his man, Rothschild may well have realized that the sum would solve only his immediate problem and that Wright would be back for more. He may also have wanted to avoid any future charge of having literally paid off Wright to silence him. Our projected book would be likely to bring Wright much more, as indeed it did—more than £40,000, a substantial sum in those days.

Rothschild certainly abstracted the offending chapter and, as was his wont, probably shredded it. It is significant that after my meeting with Wright in Cambridge, neither Victor nor Tess ever communicated with him again. Before Wright left, Rothschild made it plain that he wanted never to see him again, as Wright himself confirmed on BBC television. Nor did Wright ever try to get in touch with them. In later conversations with me, Tess was particularly bitter about him. Clearly, on the evening when I was there, they had staged an effective pretense of liking him.

CHAPTER 80

Missing Link?

—

OVER CHRISTMAS 1990, WHEN THE SOVIET UNION WAS IN ITS death agonies, I received a brief note from a Michael J. Butt, of whom I had never heard, stating, "If you should require further information relating to Roger Hollis you can contact me." He gave me his address and telephone number, which I duly rang. After that, we met on several occasions and kept in touch by letter and telephone for twelve years, during which time he proved to be informative and—so far as I could check his statements—truthful, accurate, and certainly no crank. Though his income as a security guard at a factory was modest, he never asked for money or any other favor and wanted no publicity. He had been married since 1968, and he and his wife lived quietly in Gloucester.

Butt, who was born in 1936, told me that when living in Hampstead during his early twenties, and coming from a working-class family—he had left school at fourteen to train as a silk-screen printer—he had been recruited to the Young Communist League. He had then joined the Communist Party in 1960, having been assured that "revolution and a better life for all were just round the corner." He said that he had contacted me because, with the collapse of Soviet communism and the revelation of what life was really like behind the iron curtain, he had been angry at having been duped into hitching his ideals to a star that had proved to be so false. He wanted to make some amends to society for the mistake he had made, and especially for his involvement in converting others, but apart from personal satisfaction, he had nothing to gain.

In the summer of 1959, another young Communist, who had needed to move from the Hampstead area, had suggested that Butt might like to take over his one-room accommodation at 62a Belsize Park Gardens. This was the home of a dedicated woman Communist widely known as Comrade Bridget, who had been the long-serving secretary to the Adelaide ward of the Hampstead branch of the Communist Party (being listed as such in an MI5 document dated December 1, 1947). This branch was regarded as special because it contained so many important members who happened to live in its area. Bridget was married to Jock Nicolson, a Scottish railwayman who was to stand as a Communist candidate for St. Pancras North. There were three young children living with them.

Butt agreed, was interviewed, and was accepted as a lodger. He moved in during October 1959 and found that as his single-room apartment was at the front of the house, while the Nicolsons lived at the back, he was required to answer the door to callers, as his predecessor had been. Further, on certain nights when there were likely to be several visitors, he was required to stay in. Being impressed by Bridget, whom he described as "pleasant, with Jewish features, smartly dressed, with a slight German accent, but formidable and not open to argument," he agreed. As many of the visitors were well-known Communists, whom he was proud to encounter, he found this chore a privilege. "I liked the job as doorman because it meant that I saw so many leading figures, and it made me feel important," he told me.

Officials of the prestigious Adelaide ward and others, such as St. Pancras, sometimes met at the house. In that way, over the four years that he lived there, he told me he had met so many Communist luminaries, including Bob Stewart, the avuncular Communist Party official, that he had felt he was rubbing shoulders with the great. Butt remembered that on many occasions during his tenancy, Stewart, now known to have been a KGB courier between British spies and the Soviet embassy, returned to the house with Bridget after meetings elsewhere.

He told me that with one exception, all the callers he did not know tended to give their names before he let them in. The exception was a slim, round-shouldered, clean-shaven, tallish man who wore dark clothes and a large black hat on his rare visits. Butt recalled that whenever this man had visited, which was always in the evening, Bridget had forewarned him by saying, "Someone will be calling tonight," which was the signal for him to stay home, answer the door, and admit the visitor, who was always alone. She never did this with any other caller. The mystery man would usually say nothing when the door was opened and would make his own way to her room. This had happened on the first occasion Butt had admitted him, so clearly he had been visiting before that.

Butt never had the courage to ask his formidable landlady the man's name and assumed he was just another comrade, though he was clearly English, not German, as some of her visitors were, and seemed to be a cultured person from the few words he heard him utter. He remained intrigued by the mystery man but was never able to discover his identity until 1984, when, while browsing in a public library, he found my recently published book, *Too Secret Too Long*, which contained photographs of Sir Roger Hollis. Butt told me—on several occasions and in writing—that he was absolutely certain, from the facial features alone, apart from the hunched shoulders, that the caller had been Hollis. The recognition came after a long interval, but the caller had taken off his hat when entering the house, and Butt had been face-to-face with him. He remained sure that it was Hollis, whom he described as "very recognizable," and I was never able to shake him on that conviction.

While intrigued by his discovery, from which at that time he could have earned a great deal of money from newspapers that wanted follow-ups to the Hollis story, he said nothing because he still felt loyalty to Bridget, though he was out of touch with her by then. It was only when the Berlin Wall came down and the horrors of the East German regime and the Stasi were fully exposed that Butt realized he had been involved in promoting an evil system.

The few visits by "the mystery man" that Butt had observed had taken place between 1960 and 1964, when Hollis was director general of MI5. These were crucial years in East-West security relations involving the Berlin Wall, the navy secrets spy cases, the Blake case, the Penkovsky affair, the Cuban missile crisis, the Vassall spy case, the Philby defection, the Profumo affair, and the exposure of Blunt. If Hollis had been an active spy or, more likely, a Soviet confidential contact at that stage of his career, any face-to-face meetings between him and his courier would have been restricted to such important situations. So the rarity of the occasions on which Butt encountered "the mystery man" conformed with GRU practice. As Bridget remained silent about this visitor, Butt never found out for how long he had been calling there. It is, of course, possible that originally Bridget may not have known her caller's true identity or his profession, for she could never have seen a picture of Hollis before my books were published. She may well have known him under another name.

Butt's allegation that Hollis was in the occasional habit of paying surreptitious visits to a well-known Communist was intriguing enough, but it was only when he confirmed the identity of his landlady that I appreciated the full significance of his claims. Mrs. "Bridget" Nicolson was Sonia's younger sister Brigitte!

Butt had quickly discovered that Bridget's maiden name had been Kuczynski because she had a collection of books by Jurgen, who, she had explained, was her distinguished brother. However, it was not until he had read *Too Secret Too Long* years later that he had realized she belonged to a family of Soviet GRU spies and had been one herself.

I quickly established the truth of the background details. In May 1949, she had married Nicolson, whom she had met at a Communist Party summer camp two years earlier, continuing her propensity for mating with younger men she could dominate. She was thirty-eight while he was twenty-seven and a bachelor. He gave his profession as a journalist—he occasionally wrote for the *Daily Worker*—but was essentially a railroad man.

By 1990, they had moved to a smaller apartment at 15F Bickerton Road but were still reasonably well and active. Marriage and birth certificates showed that Bridget was without question Sonia's sister and the GRU agent mentioned in the CIA handbook *The Rote Kapelle*. It seemed that she could be the missing link in any connection between Hollis and Moscow—his contact and courier in London, as opposed to the service he may have received in and around Oxford from Sonia.

When Butt knew her, Brigitte had a connection with the London branch of the Moscow Narodny Bank, which gave her a legitimate excuse to visit it. The Narodny Bank was regularly used by the GRU and KGB for espionage and subversion purposes, as was proved in 1971 when members of its staff figured among the many Russians expelled then for espionage. So Brigitte was perfectly placed for delivering documents to the GRU or for picking up instructions. Her avowed open communism could be viewed as a reasonable explanation for any visits to the Narodny Bank or to the Soviet embassy, which might have attracted MI5 attention.

Brigitte, whose code name has not yet been revealed, was listed in the CIA handbook in her previous name of Brigitte Lewis, being described as Sonia's sister and as a "recruiter for Soviet espionage." It specifically stated that she recruited Len Beurton and "turned him over to her sister Ursula (Sonia) on 13 February 1939." There can now be no doubt, after the release of MI5 documents, that it was Brigitte who gave Alexander Foote GRU instructions for contacting Sonia in Geneva. Could it be just a stupid error that the 1964 edition of Foote's *Handbook for Spies,* which was ghosted by MI5, went out of its way to state that the woman who had recruited him—Brigitte—was beyond reach behind the iron curtain when she had never moved from London? Or was the false statement calculated to deter any search for Brigitte in and after 1964, just when Hollis knew that he was under suspicion?

Was it another coincidence that Brigitte was never subjected to the interrogation urged by MI5 officers? Had the protective hand inside MI5, which Sonia suggested in her memoirs, been at work with Brigitte, as it also appeared to have been with Jurgen? Had Brigitte remained in London, confident of her safety and flaunting her communism, because she had been assured that she was in no danger?

Brigitte made no known effort to deny any of the GRU agent charges when they were published, first in *Handbook for Spies* in 1949 and 1964, then by the CIA in 1982, and then given international exposure two years later in *Too Secret Too Long.* The only occasion on which Butt had heard her privately refer to espionage was when she had expressed her horror at the forty-two-year sentence imposed on George Blake, the MI6 spy, in 1961. As Butt himself realized, Blake would have been summarily shot for his crimes in the Soviet Union.

Years later, while in touch with me, Butt was told by one of Brigitte's family that she had been "very active in the 1960s" and "had dealings with the Profumo affair." So, was Hollis receiving GRU instructions on the Profumo case, given to him perhaps in code or in sealed envelopes, through Brigitte? Had Hollis been a confidential contact, the stakes were high enough for him to have been consulted, and Butt said that he remembered a visit by "the mystery man" at the relevant time in 1963.

For good measure, Butt showed me a Soviet-made photographic enlarger and reducer, which Brigitte had given him to dispose of in some refuse bin because she wanted it out of the house in a hurry. It was so elegant in its thin, compact case that he had kept it without telling her. Beautifully designed, it seemed to me to be an instrument that could be used for preparing or enlarging the microdots used by spies for sending written messages. It was stamped as made in the CCCP (USSR), and the instruction book was in Russian. Butt had seen no evidence that Bridget had been interested in photography, so she may have used the device, of which I possess a photograph, solely for reading microdots or may have been housing it for somebody else's use. Sonia admitted in her memoirs that she had been instructed in microphotography in Moscow. So the apparatus may have previously belonged to her before she fled to East Germany in 1950.

Later, Butt recalled that Bridget had given him the device, with some degree of urgency to get rid of it, at the end of 1960 or early in 1961. This was precisely the time of the arrest of the two Soviet agents Peter and Helen Kroger. The discovery by the police of a Soviet-made transmitter and other incriminating evidence in their house in Ruislip had been widely reported in the newspapers.

As Brigitte remained in London, Sonia revealed nothing about her sister's GRU activities in her memoirs, but it would seem most unlikely that the Center would have allowed such a dedicated Communist and willing agent as Brigitte to lie fallow. If Hollis was in the habit of visiting Brigitte, then the suspicion that he also knew Sonia, and was serviced by her in and around Oxford, is strengthened.

If Butt's information is correct, what degree of risk would Hollis have been taking? Hollis had developed a habit of working late, frequently until eight p.m., and of walking home across Hyde Park, though a chauffeured office car was always available. On the rare occasions when contact was essential, all he would have needed to do was take a taxi to within easy walking distance of Brigitte's house and knock on her door, having first taken steps to ensure that she would be at home and without visitors. He could safely do this by phone from a telephone booth because he would know that she was no longer under any other kind of surveillance by MI5. It is therefore difficult to imagine a more secure safe house. The arrangement would have been far safer than any meeting outside. He could have handed her a document in a sealed envelope and received one in return or, if no contact was necessary, could simply have slipped an envelope through her mailbox. Her live mailbox would have been safer than any dead-letter box serviced surreptitiously, because nobody could find the envelope by accident.

In the morning following a visit, Brigitte could have delivered any message or document to the right recipient in the Narodny Bank or the Soviet embassy and it could have been quickly on its way to the GRU Center in Moscow. On occasion, she could even have used her ubiquitous friend Bob Stewart as a cutout for delivery to the embassy, as he is known from KGB documents to have worked for Blunt that way.

Hollis would have been at virtually no risk of being spotted. In those days, the MI5 chief did not have a bodyguard, as the terrorist threat did not exist. He also knew that his identity was so secret, no ordinary citizen would recognize him: No photographs of him had been published since he had entered MI5 because of a blanket D-Notice ban, accepted by the media. If by the remotest chance anyone did so, he could explain any such visit as being in the line of secret business. Because of his previous responsibility for securing intelligence about alien Communists resident in Great Britain, he had a ready-made explanation, if ever detected when seeing one of them surreptitiously. He could claim to be maintaining contact with a valuable source who declined to deal with anyone else. This would not have surprised his colleagues, who were aware that he was an unusual director general in that, when it suited him, he would take hands-on actions normally carried out by his staff. Regarding his wife and family, a secret service officer is advantaged as a spy because any telephone call or sudden assignation can be attributed to the line of duty. Almost any suspicious activity can be explained away as too secret to discuss.

Such a safe and simple arrangement could explain why, if Hollis was an active spy for twenty-seven years, he had never been caught in contact with a courier. Such an early role would also help to explain why Sonia, who was serving the GRU so effectively in Switzerland, was switched to Oxford as soon as the GRU learned—perhaps from Brigitte—that Hollis was being moved to Blenheim. Independent transmitting facilities were needed there when quick access between Oxford and London could not be guaranteed while Britain was being bombed. There was also the coincidence that by December 1940, and maybe earlier, the Center knew that Brigitte would no longer be available for service in or near London for an indefinite period, as her husband had been posted to Bristol and needed her to be with him.

With the services of two such dedicated and experienced couriers as skilled in conspiratorial life as Sonia and Brigitte, Hollis could have felt far more secure than most spies. With such a simple arrangement, he would never have needed to meet a Russian conspiratorially, which would have greatly reduced the risk of betrayal by a defector. The GRU would not have disturbed such a cozy courier system, if it had worked faultlessly over so many years.

Readers may wonder why I delayed publicity about Brigitte after receiving Butt's information. I was hoping to question her, but because of my well-known books and their disclosures about Sonia, there was no way that Brigitte would see me. My several attempts to contact Sonia had also failed, and she made no secret of the family hatred for me. Butt was hoping to question Brigitte on my behalf, as his letters show, and after talking to her by telephone in 1991, he made an appointment to do so at the smaller accommodations at 15F Bickerton Road to which she had moved. However, she chose to be out when he arrived, and her husband was noncommittal. I received polite replies from Jurgen but no answers to questions.

Shortly afterward, Butt became seriously ill with Hodgkin's disease, a form of cancer, and I thought he was unlikely to recover. Understandably, he did not want mention of his name, as the tough treatment was making him feel so weak that he could not face questioning by other journalists or possibly by MI5. Then Brigitte died in 1997, aged eighty-seven. Unlike the more notorious Sonia, she died unsung. Butt, who maintained his wish for anonymity during the recession of his illness, which he foresaw as brief, died in May 2002, aged sixty-five.

Some may think that it was my duty to report Butt's information to MI5 so that Brigitte could have been questioned. However, apart from Butt's tragic illness, the information reaching me clearly showed that MI5 wanted no part of any further examination of the Hollis case, which it had decided to abandon as a myth. No effort seems to have been made to question Sonia when, as will be seen, she visited Great Britain in 1991.

CHAPTER 81

Sonia Resurgent

—

SONIA HAD LEFT GREAT BRITAIN FOR WEST BERLIN, OSTENsibly for a visit to her brother, on February 28, 1950—immediately before the trial of Klaus Fuchs, twenty-five days after the public announcement of his arrest. Perhaps it had taken that long to secure GRU agreement for her departure, or she may have been informed that she had no reason to rush. According to her son Michael Hamburger, she had shown no signs of apprehension as she flew out with her two younger children.

In Berlin, Sonia's brother, Jurgen, supported her financially until the end of April, when she heard from the GRU Center, which offered her more conspiratorial work. After twenty years' service, Sonia opted for a quieter time, serving the German Democratic Republic. The GRU agreed to the final closure of Sonia's Station and found her a retirement apartment in East Berlin. They then put her in touch with the GDR Communist Party, which secured her a post in the press section of the Office of Information, where she produced the fortnightly *Bulletin Against American Imperialism*.

In June 1950, she was joined by Len, who was given a job by the GDR news service analyzing the British and American press. He was to remain in East Germany for forty years but, according to Sonia's children, remained essentially English. Michael decided to rejoin the family a year later, having completed his British education. Sonia's first husband, Rudi Hamburger, was allowed by the Soviet government to move to East Germany in 1955, probably with her assistance. Only then did her eighteen-year-old daughter, Nina, learn that he was not her father. She was the result of her mother's affair with Ernst, who had been Rudi's superior in the GRU. Rudi moved to Dresden to work as an architect and died in 1980.

In 1956, Sonia became a full-time writer under the name of Ruth Werner, which may have been a GRU requirement to hide her identity. She was successful with Communist-slanted books, including novels, and eventually became a political figure drawing large audiences when lecturing at schools and factories. She also gave confidential lectures to Stasi officers, and Markus Wolf suggested that she should write her memoirs for purely internal use, but even that was forbidden. Wolf had been instructed by the KGB not to approach Klaus Fuchs and told the BBC that during the many occasions he and Sonia met in privacy, they never mentioned him! Such was the discipline and fear of reprisal behind the iron curtain that they never named any agents in their private conversations. For the same reasons, Sonia would not have mentioned Roger Hollis, had he been one of the spies she had serviced. Wolf doubted that she had been a courier for Hollis but admitted that he could not be sure about it. He did confirm, however, that Sonia could not possibly have been a double, working for MI5 as well as the GRU. Wolf also stated that Sonia had to be careful not to incriminate the British Communist Party or anybody in it. This applied especially to Sonia's sister Brigitte.

On December 29, 1969, she was awarded the Order of the Red Banner, thirty-one years after her previous decoration, receiving it from the ambassador at the Soviet embassy in East Berlin. That was one of the highest decorations of the Red Army, usually awarded to those who had operated in extreme personal danger. It seems unlikely that it was for her wartime work with Fuchs, as that lasted only one year of the twenty that she served the GRU. Further, it had been nineteen years since his public exposure. So it may have been for her service to other spies.

Later, Wolf was to record in his memoirs that Sonia was also awarded the rare honorary title of colonel in the Red Army—the only woman to receive it. She also came to be held in such esteem in East Germany that she was awarded the Order of Karl Marx there. In the book *Inside Soviet Military Intelligence,* published in 1984, the GRU defector Victor Suvorov would name Sonia as among the outstanding intelligence officers of the service.

In 1970, Sonia attended a reception for veteran Soviet agents in Moscow. She was then permitted to visit Fuchs in Dresden and renew their friendship. At that time, he was still a nonperson in Soviet eyes because he had identified his American courier, Harry Gold, which had led to the arrest of other Soviet spies, including the Rosenbergs. Michael Hamburger has revealed that Fuchs and Sonia became really close friends, as possibly they had been before.

Through Wolf's persistence, Sonia was permitted to write her memoirs, for Stasi use only. Then, in 1977, she was allowed to publish a sanitized version of them in German, under the title *Sonya's Rapport*, still by "Ruth Werner," though by that time, according to her son Michael, it was common knowledge that she was Ursula Beurton, formerly Kuczynski. While she recalled her espionage work in and around Oxford, there was no reference whatever to Fuchs, who was still alive. Michael has recently confirmed to me that "a number of cuts were ordered" after her draft had been read by the GRU and by East German authorities, including the Communist leader there, Erich Honecker.

The GRU and the Atomic Bomb has confirmed that Sonia obeyed the rules in omitting her contact with Fuchs in the first edition of her memoirs because "the subject was still completely secret." Presumably, had she been questioned by journalists about Fuchs at that time, she would have been required to deny having serviced him or having ever met him. Nor was she allowed to reveal her Quebec Agreement coup, presumably because of continuing need to protect its source. She also made no mention of Melita Norwood, whom she had serviced when that spy was still under GRU control. Colonel Sonia obeyed orders to the letter.

In February 1985, Sonia was interviewed in East Berlin for a Soviet television program, mainly about Richard Sorge. In it, she confirmed that she did not leave Great Britain for Germany until 1950. She said that she had begun her espionage career in China in 1930, and it had lasted twenty years, implying that her clandestine operations had continued until her departure from Britain. During the whole of that time, she believed that her life had been "in mortal danger, daily." This indicates that she had continued to service some spy or spies after Fuchs's departure at the end of 1943.

She maintained the myth that she had chosen to move to Oxford for the sake of her children and because her parents were there, which they were not. However, whether by accident or design, she specifically stated that her husband, Len, had eventually received the same GRU *order* she had: "Go to England!"

In 1988, she was part of a delegation to a gathering of veteran Communist spies in Shanghai, recalling the days when she had served Sorge, who by that time had been publicly recognized as a Soviet hero. She had to travel there alone because her husband and co-conspirator, Len, had died the previous year.

Two years later, in July 1990, on another television program, she was finally allowed by the GRU to admit her part in serving as a courier for Fuchs, who had died in 1988 and was beyond being interviewed by probing journalists.

This admission was followed a year later by an expanded version of her memoirs published in English and including details of her operations with Fuchs. She recalled with relish how on one occasion alone, the traitor had given her more than a hundred pages of drawings and formulas for passage to Moscow—a fact since confirmed from the GRU archives. She still refrained, however, from mentioning Melita Norwood, who was alive in London.

Strangely, the reference to her second Order of the Red Banner was cut from the English edition. In fact, she went out of her way to suggest that the second award was simply the delivery of her original medal, which had been held in the Soviet Union for thirty years. As she was so proud of the awards and was still permitted to mention the first one, with its photograph, she would have been less than human had she not felt frustrated by the deliberate omission of the second. Her son Michael has confirmed to me that she did win two orders, which is also stated in the latest book about her—*Funksprüche an Sonja*—a collection of tributes from many sources published in Germany in 2007. As Sonia admitted, and her son has also confirmed, the GRU continued to exercise close control of the contents of her memoirs, so it would seem probable that it insisted on the cut.

With GRU agreement, her final additions to her life story included a brief but firm denial that she had ever known Roger Hollis, claiming that, had she serviced him, she would have been proud to admit it. This was an unusual concession, because normal GRU practice would have been to admit nothing on that issue, leaving the British and American opposition to remain unsure about it. So presumably the GRU had some purpose in requiring or permitting the negation, which of course did not deny that Hollis had been a spy. Perhaps, in view of her age, the Center wished to spare her from harassment by journalists on the Hollis issue. Her son Michael remembers how her house was besieged by journalists, with Len fighting them off with his crutches! There remains the possibility that Sonia was telling the literal truth in that she may always have serviced Elli impersonally, by means of *duboks,* without meeting him or knowing his identity—as Igor Gouzenko's original information had indicated. It may be significant that Sonia was permitted to raise the possibility that, as she put it, "there was someone in MI5 who was, at the same time, working for the Soviet Union and had protected us."

Understandably, Sonia's British publisher wanted her to visit London to promote her book on television, and angry MPs called for her arrest, as there is no time limit on such criminality and the government had ruled that decrepit old Nazis could still be prosecuted for war crimes. The attorney general, who had consulted both MI5 and the director of public prosecutions, ruled against any interference with her visit. Her age—eighty-four—and the belief that she posed no danger were given as the reasons. However, the real problem was that, had she been arrested, interrogation by MI5 or Special Branch police could not have been avoided, and MI5's treatment of the Sonia case is one of the worst security scandals of all time. The MI5 management did not want to antagonize her or see her in the witness box in a trial, which would generate international publicity, especially in the United States, where Fuchs had inflicted so much damage.

So the old traitor to her adopted country was allowed to visit London and exult in her achievements, revealing only the facts that suited the Russians. In particular, she had been forbidden to explain why the Moscow Center posted her to Oxford early in 1940, when she was a prime member of an important spy ring in Switzerland. Perhaps, after her broadcast, she and her husband could even have safely returned to live in Britain! Instead, she simply extended the expenses-paid visit to London to contact relatives, including Brigitte. Jurgen, who was known to have assisted in the recruitment of Fuchs, had never been questioned during his several postwar visits to Britain. MI5 knew about them but preferred to let its failures lie. In newspaper articles, I raised the possibility that even the aging Kim Philby might be allowed a brief return to promote a book or that George Blake might eventually be permitted a visit to exult on television about having sent four hundred Western agents to their deaths.

In a further television program in February 1999 called *The Spy Game*, Sonia confirmed that she had been a Communist dedicated to serving the Soviet Union by 1924, when she was only seventeen. This vitiated her claim that she had been motivated by the fight against Hitler, who was of little consequence then. She showed how she had made her first transmitter using a slab of metal and a ruler with a bobbin and screw to make her tapping key. She said that MI5 "stinks to heaven" for its inefficiency—which could only have delighted the GRU, while at the same time MI5 would have preferred that ignominy to a charge of internal treachery.

Meanwhile, in 1992, the seventy-year-old former KGB officer Vasili Mitrokhin had been "exfiltrated" out of Russia by MI6, along with a mass of notes he had made about KGB documents that he had examined before his retirement in 1984. When these were being processed in 1993, they exposed the long-term espionage of Melita Norwood in a manner that MI5 could no longer ignore. She was eighty, in good health, and with her memory remarkably intact, as her future biographer, Dr. David Burke, was to testify. She was also living handily in southeast London. Nevertheless, the MI5 management decided against any interrogation—even to fatten the files—because of the alleged fear that they could be criticized for harassing an old lady and that "as a communist, she would be unlikely to incriminate herself." Spread over nearly forty years, as her espionage proved to have been, it was, of course, a "stinking fish" case to be suppressed if it could be. Nothing was to leak for a further six years until the main items of the whole Mitrokhin archive were published by Christopher Andrew and Vasili Mitrokhin, with full MI6 collaboration. It publicly exposed Norwood, then eighty-seven, as Britain's longest-serving Soviet spy, known by the code name Hola (previously Tina).

When interviewed by the media, the old traitor admitted her espionage almost proudly, expressing no remorse and stating that she had thought she "had got away with it." Again, the MI5 management declined to interrogate her, wanting to limit the embarrassment of having failed to spot any of her numerous meetings with Sonia or any other Russian controllers in various London suburbs over so many years. In

Parliament, Ann Widdecombe called for Norwood's prosecution, but after talks with MI5, the home secretary refused any action. Nevertheless, the Commons Intelligence and Security Committee investigated her case, calling witnesses, and concluded that MI5 had made a series of "serious failures."

According to David Burke, shortly after her public exposure, Norwood received a signed copy of *Sonya's Report* with a card bearing Sonia's photograph and a message: "To Lettie. Sonia salutes you!" However, Norwood was quoted as saying that the contact who had helped her was dead. Sonia was alive, but Brigitte had died in 1997. Whoever had serviced her, and there may have been several, Norwood had continued to spy long after the war and throughout Hollis's time in MI5, with never a whiff of suspicion. Her most damaging espionage had been committed on Hollis's watch.

On Sonia's birthday in May 2000, the military attaché from the Soviet embassy visited her, in uniform, and told her that she would be receiving yet another Russian honor. As her children recall, he bowed and said, "I honor you very much." (That award proved to be a modest medal for promoting friendship between Germany and Russia.)

Like many who had committed their lives to international communism, Sonia was shattered by the collapse of the Soviet Union, and she suffered from "political depression," as her son Michael Hamburger confirmed in a BBC program, in which I took part, in October 2002. He said that after 1989, his mother had been very depressed by the turn of events, as "her life's purpose had been destroyed." She pleaded sincerity and "conviction" as legitimate excuses for her behavior. She also claimed that she had serviced Fuchs so that America would not have a monopoly of atomic weapons, ignoring her previous assurance that she had not known what Fuchs was doing.

In June 2000, Sonia, aged ninety-three, was in a wheelchair when interviewed for a German television program about her life, in which I also appeared, but she died on October 7, 2000, before the program was completed, so it contained shots of her funeral in Berlin. The video showed a large turnout of some three hundred friends and admirers, who joined her three children. They included former Communist associates, among them Markus Wolf, who wished to pay their respects to an exceptional woman who, through her brief services to Fuchs alone, had helped to change the course of world history over almost half a century.

A representative of the Russian embassy announced that his government would be awarding her yet another high decoration. Vladimir Putin, president of the Russian Federation and a former KGB officer, then awarded Ursula Kuczynski the posthumous title of "Superagent of Military Intelligence," emphasizing that she had worked for the GRU.

Michael Hamburger has confirmed to me in writing that his mother went to her grave without revealing her coup in securing the details of the Quebec Agreement in 1943. The GRU had been unwilling to release that secret while she was alive and did so only in a one-upmanship clash forced on it by old KGB officers. Ever the dedicated professional, Sonia had remained tight-lipped and left no telltale papers. The full story of her career may hold further surprises.

In 2002, the GRU publicly paid its respects to Sonia by permitting publication not only of *The GRU and the Atomic Bomb*, but of a book solely about her career called *The Superfrau in the GRU*, described as a biography of Colonel Ruth Werner. It was written by the Russian authors Victor Bochkarev, a former GRU officer, and Alexander Kolpakidi, who had been given some, but strictly limited, access to secret GRU records. They were restricted to already "exploded" cases; even access to the files on Melita Norwood, who then had been fully exposed in Great Britain, was still forbidden.

Surprisingly, in 2006, the original German publisher of *Sonya's Rapport* reissued it with the cover marked "First complete edition." It included the admission she had made in the English edition to having serviced Fuchs but excluded her denial that she had ever had any connection with Roger Hollis. This omission supports the contention that her reference to Hollis was not in her manuscript and had been specially written in to ease her return to London in 1991 to promote her book without risk of prosecution.

The new edition ends with a series of interviews with her three children, who state that they had no knowledge of their mother's activities beyond noticing that she was obsessively secretive but, later, realized that they were part of her cover. They had all been amazed when she let them read the manuscript of her book, twenty-seven years after she had finished spying. Disciplined to the end, there were many secrets that she never revealed to them.

CHAPTER 82

The Sanden Saga, Part 1

—

BOOKS ON MANY SUBJECTS THUMP THROUGH MY MAILBOX, and one that engaged me during 1996 had a most unpromising title: *An Estonian Saga*. On seeing that it was a biography of a famous Estonian footballer, I went through the routine motions of running through the index before consigning it to the bin and was astonished to see that one of the players in this story had been Roger Hollis.

There were several other names well-known in the history of espionage that also engaged my curiosity. One of them was a woman usually referred to in the literature as Luise Rimm, though she was better known in her native Estonia by her maiden name of Lyubov Mutt. For convenience, I will refer to her as Luise, as she appears in several other books by that name.

The author of *An Estonian Saga*, who was then unknown to me, was Dr. Einar Sanden, a sixty-four-year-old resident of Cardiff, where he had a small publishing company. Born in Estonia, he had fled from that sad country at the age of twelve, with his parents, in September 1944. Before 1940, Estonia had been an independent Baltic republic, but after the Hitler-Stalin pact, it was compelled to join the Soviet Union. The occupying Red Army troops and the puppet Communist government were so deeply resented that when the Germans invaded the Soviet Union in June 1941, they were regarded as liberators, and Estonian partisans helped to drive out the Russians. Inevitably, when the Germans were forced to retreat after Stalingrad, the Red Army reoccupied Estonia and took its revenge on the indigenous population. The Sanden family had managed to escape after the Red Army had reached the Estonian border in 1944. Estonia then remained enslaved for a further forty-seven years until the collapse of the Soviet Union, when it regained its independence.

Einar Sanden's research into the footballer's past had led him to a study of espionage in Shanghai from the period 1927 to 1937, because several Estonian Communists had been sent there for conspiratorial training and duties by the GRU Center in Moscow. The most senior was Karl Rimm, a well-documented senior figure in Soviet espionage and subversion. Rimm was part of the Shanghai spy ring controlled by the major GRU agent Richard Sorge, whom he served as deputy, while Luise, who posed as his wife, was a Moscow-trained cipher expert. When young, pretty, intelligent, and eager to improve her education, Luise had been a nanny to a rich Russian family who had a holiday home in Estonia, and in 1913, she had followed them to Moscow as a maid in their main house there. The family was liquidated after the revolution in 1917, but, favoring Bolshevism, Luise managed to secure training as a nurse. She also joined a political club in Moscow, where she was spotted by the GRU. After basic training, the GRU ordered her to become Rimm's "operational wife" for his cover in Shanghai, where he was to pose as a Jewish entrepreneur owning shops and a restaurant. She was shipped out to join him there in 1933, having been trained at the GRU spy school. She was told that her name was now Luise Klas and that she, too, was Jewish.

In Shanghai, Luise was introduced to Sorge, whom she was to serve as a cipher clerk, to Agnes Smedley, and to Sonia, who worked with Luise in the Sorge ring and mentions her with affection in her memoirs. When Sorge was posted to Tokyo in 1932, Rimm replaced him as chief in Shanghai.

Around Christmas 1935, Rimm sold his businesses and left for duties in Moscow with Luise, who became a cipher clerk at the GRU Center. She was also given the task of trying to ensnare the wives of foreign diplomats at cultural and social circles in the Soviet capital set up and managed by the GRU. Then, after so many years of selfless service, Rimm was arrested by the KGB on December 11, 1937, and taken to the

Lubyanka for interrogation and was eventually executed in 1943, having made an enforced confession to spying for Great Britain. He was a victim of Stalin's manic purge of GRU and KGB stalwarts, which included some of those who had recruited the Cambridge group. It would seem that many were liquidated because they knew too much about valuable spies, whose identities they might reveal under pressure or if they defected.

In her memoirs, Sonia lamented the execution of Karl Rimm but said nothing about the fate of Luise. She was, in fact, imprisoned in the Lubyanka for eighteen months and was then sent to the Vorkuta labor camp in the Arctic, where she remained for more than eighteen years. She survived because her training allowed her to do medical work, which gave her favored treatment.

Luise was released in 1957 and moved back to Estonia, then part of the USSR, living with relatives in a desolate area, and was warned that she was forbidden to talk about her past to anybody. Later, she moved to the town of Viljandi and was readmitted to the Communist Party, to which she remained faithful in spite of her appalling treatment and the execution of her partner.

When Luise developed a serious liver problem, she agreed that Vello Lattik, a local journalist, writer, and law graduate, should tape-record her biography. There were many interviews over a period of months, resulting in six tapes, each ninety minutes long. I have contacted Mr. Lattik, who still lives in Estonia. He confirmed that he had made the tapes but would not comment on the contents, not wishing to be involved in publicity about them. Luise died in July 1976, aged eighty-two, and photographs of her funeral appear in Sanden's book.

All the above is well documented, especially in the book *Dr.-Sorge-Report* by the East German writer Julius Mader. And there is no doubt, as I have checked with Mr. Lattik, that in 1992, Sanden secured Luise's tape recordings from him in the course of his extensive research. Sanden brought them to my house in November 1997, after I had read his book and written about it in the *Daily Mail*.

Dr. Sanden's main assertions regarding Luise are as follows:

First, that the Rimms, who were always on the lookout for possible recruits among the young men and women they met, encountered Roger Hollis on the social round of the Shanghai international community. Luise already spoke German and French but needed to learn English. So the young Hollis, whose accent, as a bishop's son, was judged to be excellent, taught her for a fee, being short of money.

Unhappy with her stern, enforced partner, she started a long love affair with Hollis in 1932 after the GRU Center encouraged her to do so. Though he was ten years younger, it continued for almost three years, with intervals when he was in other parts of China on BAT business. (Information given to me by the MI6 officer Nicholas Elliott may be relevant in this respect. After the defection of his friend Kim Philby, Elliott consulted a psychiatrist in the hope that he might shed light on the reasons for the traitor's treachery. The psychiatrist said, "In such cases, I always look for the mother figure." In Philby's case, it was deemed to be the much older Flora Solomon, who eventually betrayed him. Possibly, Luise was the mother figure in the Hollis case, for according to Sanden's account, he remained smitten.)

Second, that allegedly, according to the tapes, Karl Rimm did not like Englishmen but approved of any way of ensnaring a promising recruit to the cause, as he believed a bishop's son to be. Hollis's father had become a bishop in 1931, shortly before he is alleged to have met Luise, and it would have been natural for him to have mentioned the promotion to friends. (When Harriet Sergeant was researching at the military reference branch of the National Archives in Washington for her book *Shanghai,* published in 1991, another researcher told her that he had heard of a document proving that Hollis had shared a house with Comintern agents. She found nothing and the document may not have existed, but it was an unusual statement for a stranger to have made to her, had there been no grounds for it.)

And third, that Luise's familiar name for Hollis was Bobby, which Sanden alleges was an official code or cover name. In the tapes, she often referred to him by that name and as "the bishop's son." She also said that he had eventually become head of security in Great Britain, so her alleged lover could hardly have been anyone else.

Sanden told me, in a letter, that the tapes state that Luise was convinced that in 1957, Hollis had assisted in her release from the Vorkuta labor camp. Allegedly, on her release, she was told that "influential friends in the West" had interceded on her behalf, and many years later, when she learned about Hollis's career, which astonished her, she believed that it was he who had intervened. According to Sanden, she even came to suspect that she and Rimm had been victimized because they both knew about Hollis and the GRU was desperate to protect him, having just assured his intrusion into MI5. The Rimms were, in fact, both arrested in December 1937, which could be the time, immediately after his return from Paris, that Hollis was confident he had secured a post in MI5 or would do so.

Whatever the truth about such details, if Hollis had been involved in a sexual affair with a GRU officer, it would certainly have barred him from MI5, had he declared it. The Luise tapes would also seem to increase the likelihood that Sonia met Hollis, as Sonia and Luise were unquestionably close friends in Shanghai.

I have only Dr. Sanden's statements for these allegations, but the fact that he had been prepared to make the tapes available to MI5 carries some weight. Though dispensable, meanwhile, in the general buildup of the evidence, the tapes certainly fortified my interest, as did the even more specific statements that Sanden claims he secured from a much more detailed documentary source.

CHAPTER 83

The Sanden Saga, Part 2

———

IGNORED BY THE BRITISH AUTHORITIES, NEW EVIDENCE HAS come to light about a complicated chain of relationships that offer confirmation of Hollis's Communist recruitment in Shanghai.

When Red Army soldiers marched into Estonia in June 1940, they were welcomed by homegrown Communists who were part of the political conspiracy to force the country into the Soviet Union. Prominent among these, waving from a balcony alongside Kremlin representatives, was Karl Säre, a short, bespectacled apparatchik who is vilified today in free Estonia. Born in 1903, Säre had been sent to Leningrad when only eighteen to be trained in a GRU spy school, his main foreign language being English. He returned to Estonia in 1925 to reorganize the subversive underground movement there and was then posted by the GRU to Shanghai for conspiratorial work. While posing as a journalist, Säre was required to recruit young Europeans to communism, especially those from well-placed families who were in Shanghai hoping to make their fortunes before returning home. His method was to spot their weaknesses, curry their friendship, and help them with loans of money.

After a succession of conspiratorial duties in other countries, including Great Britain, Säre visited New York and Canada on GRU business, was posted to Stockholm in 1937, and returned to Estonia in 1938. When the Soviets occupied Estonia in 1940, he was made first secretary of the Estonian Communist Party. His reign was cut short in June 1941 when the Germans drove out the Russians. Ordered by the GRU to remain in Estonia, he went into hiding in Tallinn, the Estonian capital, but was arrested on September 3.

The Estonian-speaking man chosen by the Germans to interrogate Säre was Evald Mikson, the former footballer who became the subject of the biography written by Einar Sanden. In 1936, he had joined the Estonian political police, set up to oversee Communist subversion. In his spare time, he played as goalkeeper for the national football team.

When the Soviets invaded Estonia in 1940, Mikson had joined a partisan group that welcomed the Germans as liberators in the summer of 1941. He had then rejoined the political police.

Mikson's interrogation of Säre was spread over several weeks, during which, in the hope of saving his skin, the captive appeared to tell all he knew about the Communist network in Estonia, implicating his associates without reserve. A statement by Mikson about the interrogation, signed by him in April 1992, indicates that he conducted ten interviews with Säre, each lasting about two hours, between September 3 and November 2, 1941. It records that, among other things, Säre had confessed to having been a Soviet recruiting agent in Shanghai from 1925 to the end of 1927, in Estonia in 1928 and 1929, and on the Trans-Siberian Railway, which was much used as a recruiting medium for foreigners.

The Germans flew Säre to Berlin on November 2 to interrogate him, particularly about Richard Sorge, whom he had named as a GRU agent. By that time, posing as an ardent Nazi, Sorge had established a highly successful GRU spy ring in Tokyo, delivering a stream of secret information to Moscow. In March 1943, Säre was produced by the Nazis as a witness in a murder trial in German-occupied Copenhagen, but his subsequent fate is unknown.

My research has shown the facts about Säre stated above to be well-documented history. Photographs of him with his Russian friends appear in Sanden's *An Estonian Saga.* Sanden had originally written to Mikson when researching a historical book about Estonia and discovered he had led such an extraordinary life that he conceived the idea of a biography about him.

When the Russians returned to Estonia in 1944, Mikson escaped to Sweden by ship, was interned there, and in November 1945 was told that the Soviets were applying pressure for his extradition as a war criminal. I have a copy of a record of Mikson's hearing in the Stockholm Municipal Court in the spring of 1946. After being refused refuge, he left Sweden on a ship in December 1946, serving as a deckhand on what he thought was his way to Venezuela, but it ran aground off Iceland, which granted him refuge. He made a new career there and married an Icelandic girl.

In June 1986, Sanden met with Mikson at his home in Reykjavík. They talked for a week, and Mikson made all his papers available. Later, Mikson sent Sanden fifteen tapes of his life story.

Sanden states that Mikson's seventy-page report of his interrogation of Säre contained numerous references to Roger Hollis, whom Säre claimed to have met in Shanghai and recruited to Communist service. It also stated that Säre had introduced Hollis to Luise Rimm. If correct, this would be crucial evidence, because Säre's statement was supposedly made in 1941, many years before Hollis became suspected of being a spy. There is no conceivable reason why or how Säre could have concocted it.

Sanden told me that Säre's report mentioned Hollis by name several times as Luise's lover. His book states that in 1934, Säre was told that Hollis wanted to stay a few days in Moscow while returning to Shanghai from leave in England, via the Trans-Siberian Railway, and that they met there. It also alleges that two years later, Hollis visited Moscow again on his final journey back to England and met up with Luise, who entertained him in one of the GRU "love nests."

In December 1936, Sanden states, Säre left Moscow for Britain, posing as a Canadian journalist on his way to the United States, and met Hollis in London, spending several days in his company. Mikson's witnessed statement declares that Säre was on recruiting missions in Great Britain, the United States, and Canada in 1936 and 1937.

Sanden claims that the report of Säre's interrogation also stated that when Hollis joined MI5 in 1938, the GRU Center knew immediately, ordering Säre to sever all communications and connections with him. All possible measures had to be taken to safeguard the Englishman's prospects.

The total material about Säre assembled by Sanden as fact in his book would set the seal on the Hollis case, but I have so far been unable to verify it, in spite of much patient effort. Regrettably, Sanden has no copy of the report of Säre's interrogation, because, he insists, Mikson would not part with it, though he promised to leave it to him, along with other papers, in his will.

According to Sanden, the report of Säre's interrogation, along with a translation of it into German, still resides in Reykjavík with Mikson's son, Atli Edvaldsson, who is a famous footballer, having played for several major German teams. I have been in contact with Atli over several years, and he has confirmed that he still has many of his deceased father's papers. He also emailed, "In my father's file the name Karl Säre is mentioned many times," a statement that supports the claim that Mikson had interrogated him. To date, however, I have been unable to extract a copy of the interrogation report from Atli.

I have verified beyond doubt that the Soviet government did all it could to lay hands on Mikson, claiming that he was a war criminal who had assisted the Germans and was guilty of atrocities against Jews and others. These charges are well-known in Iceland because of newspaper publicity there. The Soviet Union accused the Western allies and other governments of hiding Mikson. However, I have a copy of a document from the Estonian Ministry of Foreign Affairs, dated February 1992, which declares that, following inquiries, "it has become clear that Mr. Mikson is not guilty of any crimes, least of all against the Jewish people." Additionally, it states that Mikson had interrogated Säre and that Russian officials had blackened his character because they feared that Säre had revealed too much to him.

Soviet attempts to extradite Mikson from Iceland were bravely rebutted. Having failed to secure him, the Russians continued to plant false stories about him, even after the collapse of communism and after his death in 1993, which has caused Atli much embarrassment. So it is understandable that, being such a prominent figure in a small country, Atli may wish to avoid further unpleasant publicity.

Why had the Russians hated Mikson so much for so long? Was it because he had interrogated Säre and found out about Hollis, who had become all-important to the Soviets? Dr. Sanden thinks so, and the cover of his book states, "Mikson carried with him a dangerous secret about an Englishman who, in later years, rose to the top of MI5."

Sanden's first intention had been to publish the Mikson biography in Iceland, and that edition, entitled *Úr Eldinum til Íslands* (*From the Fire to Iceland*), was published in 1988, sold well there, and was well reviewed.

Mikson's witnessed statement in 1992 declares that he had vetted the text for accuracy.

While there was much about Säre in that book, there was no mention of Hollis by name. However, it briefly states, in translation, "One of the very last persons Säre recruited in Shanghai was a young upper middle-class English gentleman, a dropout from Oxford, a member of a family of Anglican bishops. He arrived in Shanghai in the summer of 1927 with very little money but with a big thirst for sex and alcohol. Säre was able to help him in a number of ways, including giving him valuable advice on how to become a respected freelance journalist."

Sanden claims that he omitted naming Hollis or giving any more details at the insistence of Mikson, who, as a grateful immigrant, did not want to offend the Icelandic Foreign Office. Sanden had told him that following the publication of my book *Their Trade Is Treachery*, the British government had indicated that Hollis had not been a spy, and Mikson feared that the Icelandic government could find itself embarrassed by the new revelations.

There were no such qualms about the expanded English edition, which appeared in 1996. Mikson read it chapter by chapter as Sanden wrote it and left a witnessed statement declaring that he had vetted the text of the English edition and that he agreed with its contents. The statement says that during his interrogation, Säre identified some of the agents he had recruited and that those named by Sanden in *An Estonian Saga* are correct. Mikson had no objection to Säre's claims about Hollis appearing in a British book, as he believed that the Icelandic authorities would not be concerned about that. As Sanden had secured the tapes made by Luise by that time, he also included the information he gleaned from them.

Meanwhile, in Great Britain, Einar Sanden's claims, which could clinch the Hollis case, remain ignored.

CHAPTER 84

Censure Deferred

I N APRIL 2000, HOLLIS AND MI5 IN GENERAL FINALLY RECEIVED public censure for their appalling handling of the case of the traitor Melita Norwood. This resulted from a government decision to require Parliament's Intelligence and Security Committee to examine the handling of the mass of information supplied by the KGB defector Vasili Mitrokhin in 1992. The committee concentrated on the Norwood case, which Mitrokhin had exposed, as an example of a "Soviet atom spy" who had operated for so many years under MI5's nose and had escaped prosecution even when Mitrokhin had exposed her and she had confessed publicly on television!

Originally, the authorities, advised by MI5, had decided not to name her in the *The Mitrokhin Archive,* a book produced jointly by Mitrokhin and Christopher Andrew, but to give only her code name, Hola; but their hand was forced when a BBC journalist identified her and intended to expose her in a television program. The committee noted that MI5 had decided against prosecution without consulting the prosecution authorities, as had nearly happened in the Fuchs case. It also noted that MI5 had used "public interest" reasons to justify its lack of action.

In 1993, without consulting the law officers, MI5 decided that because Norwood was so old and her spying had happened so long ago, police action was inappropriate. The MI5 management told the commit-

tee that the Norwood case had "slipped out of sight," so no further action was taken.

In 1999, knowing that the government had decided to permit publication of a book about the Mitrokhin archive, the MI5 managers consulted the law officers to see if they could still take action against
Norwood. They were told—to their relief—that since an opportunity
to do so had been rejected in 1992, successful prosecution was no longer
possible under the law.

The parliamentary committee finally judged that "it was a serious
failure by the Security Service" not to refer Mrs. Norwood's case to the
law officers in mid-1993. Its report indicated that the committee believed
that MI5 had been acting in its own interest—to cover up exposure of its
failures—and that this further failure meant that Mrs. Norwood could
never be prosecuted.

The committee deplored MI5's failure to interview Norwood at any
time and questioned its reasons for it. The MI5 management was also
castigated for allowing the Norwood case to slip out of sight instead of
being kept under review.

MI5 had been required to supply all the relevant details known about
Norwood, and though these clearly showed that her atomic espionage
had all happened under Hollis's watch, the committee's terms of reference restricted its criticisms to post-1992 events. Though MI5 continued
to try to excuse its failures on operational grounds, it assured the committee that such "mistakes" would not happen again.

MI5 did its best to convince the committee that Norwood's espionage had never been important. An assessment of her case passed to
the committee stated that "her value as an atom spy must have been, at
most, marginal." MI5 did not seem to know that Norwood had sat in on
Tube Alloys meetings, taking notes for her boss, the liaison officer with
that ultrasecret body, and had passed on carbon copies to her Soviet
masters, as she would tell her historian friend Dr. David Burke. Nor was
MI5 aware that she had been awarded the coveted Order of the Red
Banner, which was not given for marginal services, and a KGB pension.
She has since been given honorable mention in an official history of the
GRU, *The GRU: People and Deeds,* which restricted itself to publicly
known cases.

In May 2005, Melita Norwood died at the age of ninety-three, still
committed to communism in spite of its abject collapse. Her espionage

career had been one of MI5's worst cases, its most significant phases having occurred unchecked during Hollis's watch.

As a result of its gross mishandling of the case, MI5 has been forced to introduce checks that will make it more difficult to conceal its failures from ministers, but governments tend to be so averse to bad publicity from spy scandals that the continuing abuse of "the national interest" can be guaranteed. Most secret operations come and go, but Operation Cover-up goes on forever.

CHAPTER 85

Conclusion

—

IN 1988, WHEN GIVING EVIDENCE AT A MOCK TRIAL OF ROGER Hollis on British television, Ray Cline, who had been the CIA's deputy director of intelligence from 1962 to 1966, said that he had made a study of the case. He had concluded that there was "a high percentage of probability that MI5 had been penetrated at a high level and that, among the possible candidates to be a Soviet agent in that category, Roger Hollis was the best fit to be matched with all the evidence concerned." He stated, "I would say that it was about three chances out of four that Roger Hollis was indeed the agent mentioned by Gouzenko." Cline had been impressed by the sequence of coincidences. He said that the fact that Oleg Gordievsky had no information about Hollis was "of almost no consequence," particularly as his claim was made so many years later.

Robert Lamphere also appeared on the program as a witness. He told how the FBI had established that Soviet agents in America, like Harry Gold, David Greenglass, and the Rosenbergs, were receiving warnings about their danger from Moscow. These had ceased between February and late May 1950, and between those exact dates, J. Edgar Hoover had forbidden his counterintelligence men to give any information to MI5. When the ban had been lifted in late May, the warnings to Soviet spies had resumed. Lamphere said that he became convinced the leaks had come from MI5 and also stated, "To me, there now remains little doubt that it was Hollis who provided the earliest information to the KGB that the FBI was reading their 1944–45 cables. Philby added to this knowledge after his arrival in the U.S., but the prime culprit in this affair was Hollis." Charles Bates of the FBI and other professionals also gave evidence of their belief that Hollis had been a spy. Several other witnesses gave evidence in Hollis's defense.

I had agreed to take part only on the understanding that the jury would not be asked to make their judgment as they would in a proper trial. It was obvious that without proof of Hollis's espionage, which did not then exist, and without his testimony, he would be pronounced not guilty in a real trial. The only sensible way of reaching a verdict in a mock trial of a dead man based on intelligence information was to ask the jury to come to a conclusion based on the balance of probabilities, and I understood that they would be asked to do that. Instead, the judge and the jury conducted themselves as they would have done at a proper trial, and the inevitable verdict was not guilty. (A few weeks after the trial, the real-life retired judge who had controlled the proceedings telephoned to urge me to continue with my inquiries about Hollis, clearly having been impressed by the evidence against him.)

In that same year, 1988, an even more impressive American opinion—that of a distinguished chief of the CIA—reached me from an impeccable American source, who happened to be an occasional acquaintance for whose integrity I had great regard. The source was Senator Malcolm Wallop, the long-serving member of the Senate committee in charge of the U.S. intelligence budget, as a consequence of which he had intelligence contacts at the highest levels.

Senator Wallop was the brother-in-law of the late Earl of Carnarvon, an old friend of mine who often invited me to his excellent pheasant shoot in Hampshire, where the three of us shot together several times. Malcolm informed me that William Casey, the CIA chief from 1981 to 1987, appointed by President Ronald Reagan, had told him that he was convinced Hollis had been a spy.

Casey had examined Hollis's record and found too many anomalies. Both the FBI and the CIA were suspicious of any focus of anomalies— coincidences, counterproductive actions and inactions. Relatively few known anomalies in Kim Philby's record had correctly alerted the U.S. authorities to his treachery, while those attached to Hollis were far more numerous and persisted over a much longer period. So, as Casey had pointed out, had the MI5 chief been a Soviet agent, his impact on American security and intelligence affairs could have been infinitely greater than that of Philby, who has been generally accorded the dubious accolade of "Spy of the Century."

Casey had been particularly impressed by the extraordinary chain of events that had made Hollis the king of coincidence. He had found them way beyond his belief for an innocent man. Since then, my research has produced a scroll of fifty-two anomalies, which I list in chronological order as an appendix. Further, with the steady release of formerly secret information from British and Russian sources, each item of scaffolding erected in support of Hollis's innocence by his supporters has been toppled as new evidence has relentlessly accrued.

. In summary, if one imagines a magic compass that could be placed over any suspicious set of circumstances affecting MI5's countermeasures to the Soviet intelligence assault, the needle almost invariably points to the man who served in the agency for twenty-seven years and became its chief. The extraordinary concatenation of dates and circumstances all fit. Hollis's serial culpability for security disasters, whether due to treachery or to sheer incompetence, can no longer be in doubt. Except when events outside his control took command, almost every recommendation he made and almost every decision he took benefited Soviet intelligence. Whatever his motives, his record of uncontrolled power, deriving from the singular mystique attached to secret service and influencing politics at the most sensitive levels, reiterates the need for effective political oversight.

The whole array poses one question in particular: Could any individual have attracted so many suspicious circumstances over so many years and be judged innocent now? One might have expected that some of the documents released by MI5 would support Hollis's innocence, but they do the reverse. His serious failures were major victories for Soviet intelligence and major disasters for the Anglo-American alliance.

Some of Hollis's old colleagues thought it monstrous that he should ever have been suspected, but the scroll showing such a multitude of anomalies asks a different question: Why had it taken so long for him to become suspect? Hollis's fingerprints are all over the relevant evidence, and there are no others. I have not been selective with the evidence, and I have no personal animosity against Hollis, with whom I had a mutually productive working relationship when in national journalism.

There is simply no instance in twenty-seven years when Hollis initiated any effective action that he could not avoid. He pursued traitors only when forced by circumstances to do so.

While Wright and Martin were castigated for suspecting Hollis in the 1960s, it is remarkable, in view of his consistent record, that he was not suspected sooner. As Philby had been forced to resign from MI6 on the evidence of a few known anomalies, without proof of guilt, Hollis should surely have been required to resign from MI5, had the multitude associated with his career been more widely appreciated.

Some of his supporters have tried to explain his deficiencies as due solely to ineptitude, but consistent incompetence on that scale over such a long period is inexplicable unless it was contrived. Others continue to dismiss all the anomalies and other evidence against him as circumstantial, but circumstantial evidence can become so weighty that it tips the scales of justice and in some cases slams them down. Unless a confession is obtained, intelligence evidence against professional spies is almost always circumstantial, as it was against Philby until he defected and against Blunt, Cairncross, and others until they were "blown." All the evidence that has been put forward in favor of Hollis is similarly circumstantial and has been systematically demolished as various windfalls have accrued.

It may reasonably be asked why, if Hollis was such a successful spy, the GRU has not claimed prestigious credit by admitting it. A GRU general has recently gone on written record stating that there are indeed important spies whose identities cannot yet be safely exposed, while the former KGB controller Alexander Feklisov referred to well-placed sources "whose names the Russian government continues to protect." Russian penetration agents were always given "special source" protection, with extraordinary precautions and intelligence sacrifices to conceal their identities. Knowledge of their existence was restricted to their handlers, with their KGB or GRU file being accessible to very few, and even then—according to the research of the American counterintelligence officer Pete Bagley—only with the special permission of the directors. The concealment has continued long after their deaths, with concern for close relatives being a major factor. Currently, when the GRU is trying to recruit new British and American spies, it would hardly be good for business to be seen exposing old ones whose identities have never been officially confirmed.

The case of John Stonehouse, the traitor inside the Labour government, is instructive in these respects. In 2006, though Stonehouse had been dead for eighteen years, the Czech Intelligence Service declined to provide his file. Evidential proof of his guilt was discovered only through the enterprise of journalists who found a Czech who had secured a complete copy of the file. Until then, the Stonehouse case was regarded as nonproven, with his innocence therefore assumed.

Soon after the collapse of communism in the Soviet Union, the MI5 chief, Stella Rimington (later Dame), traveled to Moscow with another MI5 officer and a civil servant from the Home Office. As she revealed in her autobiography, *Open Secret,* she had proposed a meeting with the chief of the KGB in the hope of reducing the intelligence activity between them and to "clear up some of the old cases." During several meetings at KGB headquarters, all she got was an outsize KGB flea in her ear. She was faced with an array of hard-nosed Russian intelligence officers who made it clear that spying in Great Britain would continue—as it has. She did not see anyone from the GRU, which alone could have told her much about the Hollis case. Nevertheless, in her book she dismissed the suspicions against Hollis as "discredited" but gave no reasons. If MI5 had possessed any more solid evidence, the book, with its heavy publicity and newspaper serialization, would have been an ideal medium in which to deploy it.

Whatever his motives, Hollis was such a disastrous counterespionage officer that only three possible explanations for his behavior present themselves. The first is that he was consistently incompetent. Yet making all allowances for an admittedly difficult profession with limited resources, continuous ineffectiveness on such a scale over twenty-seven years is so difficult to credit that to brand him a spy would almost be paying him a compliment.

The second is that he was a secretly dedicated devotee of the Soviet system, without any actual contact with Moscow, and simply did all he could to serve its interests by his actions and inactions. That charitable scenario, however, ignores the Elli evidence and the fact that no other feasible MI5 candidate for Elli has ever emerged.

The third is that when the MI5 *Official History* listed Hollis as in charge of "Soviet espionage," it was inadvertently stating the literal truth.

Whatever the reasons for his disasters, and those of MI5 and MI6 in general, the American authorities and people, who were as ill served as the British, are clearly owed an abject apology for his appalling stewardship. An opportunity for honesty and contrition arose in 1997, when the MI5 leadership decided, under governmental pressure, that it would be politic for its image to begin making some of its secret documents public. Instead, one of its first moves in its published brochure and on its website was to dismiss the suspicion against Hollis as "a myth," hoping to dispose of it for all time. That the myth had originated inside MI5, following several years of official investigation by its own serving officers, was not stated, thereby encouraging the totally false beliefs that it had been invented by writers or planted on the public by the KGB.

The brochure and website also depict the official badge of the service with its motto, *Regnum Defende*—"In Defense of the Realm." There is an MI5 insider joke that alleges the effective motto is *Rectum Defende*— regularly translated as "Defending Your Ass." That objective now seems so firmly set in concrete that, as a veteran investigator who has always operated on the principle that the exposure of unpleasant truths is good for the national soul, I strove to assemble this public record, with the many lessons it poses, while I still had time. With the current, unexpected Kremlin threats to restore a cold war situation to reestablish Russia as a superpower, which will assuredly demand a major resurgence of espionage, particularly inside the United States, the timing would seem to be singularly propitious.

Acknowledgments

I would like to express my grateful thanks to my son, Michael Chapman Pincher, and to his son, Edward, for their arduous and successful researches on my behalf, especially in the U.K. National Archives. The critical advice of my daughter, Pat, has been most helpful. The generous assistance of computer expert John Maher, often at short notice, has been essential. Others who have kindly assisted me with research and shared information are named, with gratitude, in the Note on the Sources.

My wife, Billee, merits special mention for her unflagging encouragement and patient understanding throughout the lengthy haul.

I am deeply indebted to our friend Stella Shawzin for putting me in touch with the legendary Robert L. Bernstein, whose son, Peter, became my very helpful literary agent and introduced me to Random House New York. My editor there, Robert Loomis, has been of splendid professional assistance to me, as have his colleagues Dana Isaacson, Dennis Ambrose, Abigail Plesser, Heidi Luedemann, and, indeed, all those with whom I have been, so pleasantly, in contact. No author could have been better served, especially in view of the geographical distance between us.

The Scroll of Anomalies

1. Roger Hollis left Oxford, prematurely and under some compulsion, in 1926 at the exact time of a clampdown on Communists there.

2. In the early 1930s, Hollis and Sonia (Ursula Kuczynski) were in Shanghai and other Chinese cities simultaneously and had mutual Communist friends who were avid recruiters to Soviet espionage, particularly to the GRU.

3. Among the targets where Soviet intelligence urged new recruits to obtain employment were *The Times*, MI6, and MI5. Hollis applied for a post at all three.

4. Though unemployed and short of money, Hollis made a mysterious trip to Paris, a GRU base for recruitment, in November 1937. Either before or shortly afterward, he had applied for entry to MI5 and MI6 and may already have been told that he had been successful with MI5.

5. In December 1937, the GRU agents Karl and Luise Rimm, who were allegedly involved in the recruitment of Hollis to the Soviet cause in China, were arrested and silenced by the GRU.

6. Immediately after Hollis was officially confirmed as an MI5 officer in June 1938, Sonia made a potentially dangerous visit to London.

7. An operation in which radio traffic between Moscow and Comintern agents in Europe had been successfully decoded for several years ceased abruptly soon after Hollis entered MI5 in 1938.

8. Hollis soon discovered that MI5 had files on two of his former associates who were listed as dangerous Communists—Claud Cockburn and Arthur Ewert. A strict office rule required him to disclose his relationships and to pro-

vide any relevant information he knew about them. He decided to remain silent about both.

9. When the senior GRU defector Walter Krivitsky was being debriefed by MI5 during January and February 1940, the KGB Center behaved as though it had suddenly been warned that he was revealing leads to some of its British spies. Hollis knew the details and was in charge of anti-Soviet operations when no effective action was taken about them.

10. In August 1941, two GRU spymasters took the risk of traveling to Birmingham to recruit the atomic spy Klaus Fuchs. That was precisely after Hollis had taken full control of Soviet counterespionage and was in a position to assure the GRU that none of the three was under surveillance of any kind.

11. In May 1941, Hollis learned of the existence of the atomic bomb project. Soon afterward, the KGB instructed its officers serving in Great Britain to secure any available atomic intelligence.

12. It was through an initiative by Hollis that Kim Philby secured the promotion that enabled him to betray so many prime secrets to the KGB Center in Moscow. Philby and Hollis were then able to work in tandem concerning Soviet counterespionage.

13. The situation that Hollis's initiative had created put him in command of any action or inaction against British-based Soviet agents contacting Moscow through illicit radio transmitters. This meant that if he was a spy, he could ensure protection for his own couriers.

14. Soon after Hollis had initiated the action that ensured Philby's prime position in MI6, the Soviet agent Sonia received special congratulations from the director of the GRU Center for her work.

15. Sonia was ordered to obtain British nationality and to move from Switzerland to the Oxford area at the time Hollis was due to go there with the evacuation of MI5 from London.

16. At exactly that time, Sonia's sister Brigitte, an established GRU agent who may have been servicing Hollis in London, was forced by domestic circumstances to move to Bristol, thereby depriving the GRU of her services in the capital. The timing suggests that Sonia was her replacement.

17. With the German bombing of London likely to continue, and making a rail journey to the capital uncertain, it was essential that the new courier in Oxford should have an independent transmitting and receiving link with the Center. Sonia had that qualification.

18. When Sonia was in transit by train and boat from Switzerland to Oxford in late December 1940, the FBI asked MI5 for a list of German Communists liv-

ing in Great Britain who were considered dangerous. The list was supplied by the section of which Hollis was then in charge, and though Sonia's brother, Jurgen, Brigitte, and their father, Robert, had all been described in the MI5 files as dangerous, they were not mentioned on the list. Any FBI investigation of any of the Kuczynskis at that time would have been most unwelcome to the GRU.

19. Sonia secured lodgings and then a bungalow close to where Hollis worked in Blenheim and then closer to where he lived in Oxford.

20. The time when Sonia moved into Oxford and became the courier for Klaus Fuchs coincided with Hollis's return to duty from his stay in a sanatorium in Cirencester, where he would not have been easily available for assistance. During the several months Hollis was in the sanatorium, the GRU cut off contact with Fuchs, who made no effort to restore it until Hollis was ready to return to duty—and to access to knowledge of who was under surveillance.

21. Shortly after Hollis returned to his MI5 office early in October 1942, when he could have checked that neither Fuchs nor Sonia was under surveillance, Sonia traveled to Birmingham to meet Fuchs.

22. Sonia was a GRU agent runner. Elli was a GRU spy. The circumstances of Sonia's coup in securing a copy of the Quebec Agreement were particularly suspicious in that respect.

23. Several of Sonia's illicit radio messages that were intercepted were passed to Hollis for action, but nothing was done to have them deciphered. No effort was ever made to trace her transmitter during the nine years she was active, though the Radio Security Service had reported illicit transmissions in her area.

24. The consistently charmed lives of the Kuczynski troika—Jurgen, Sonia, and Brigitte, who had all generated security concern in the Home Office, MI5, MI6, and the FBI—constitute a major anomaly. While serving as active GRU agents over many years, they were never detected in contact with a spy, leading Sonia in particular to suspect that they had survived unscathed because of a protective hand in MI5.

25. In the summer of 1945, when Sonia had to move from her cottage in Oxford at the end of the war in Europe, she rented a house in a remote village twenty miles away, from which it would have been impracticable to have served a spy in MI5. This was just the time MI5 was returning from Blenheim to London.

26. Hollis cleared Fuchs six times, enabling him to pass the basic secrets of the atomic bomb to Russia. As declassified MI5 documents have proved, he did so often in the face of warnings by colleagues that Fuchs could be a spy.

27. During the time Fuchs was under surveillance by MI5 on Hollis's reluctant instructions in 1947, he made no suspicious contacts. Hollis was instrumental in terminating the surveillance, and shortly after it ended, Fuchs made contact with his new Russian controller.

28. When Sonia's cover was blown, MI5's attempts to interrogate her were superficial and effectively assured her that she was in no danger. No attempt was made to watch her, and her interrogators had been ordered not to question her about any activities in Great Britain. Immediately after MI5 closed its file on Sonia, who might have been induced to betray Fuchs by more persistent tactics, Fuchs resumed espionage contact with his new Soviet controller.

29. Immediately before Fuchs's trial in 1950, Sonia defected without hindrance or effective follow-up.

30. When the FBI sought permission to interrogate Fuchs in prison, Hollis insisted on imposing a technical restraint that was calculated to cause offense at the highest levels in the United States and did so, inflicting serious damage on Anglo-American relations.

31. The GRU defector Igor Gouzenko gave six features about a spy inside MI5 called Elli, whose existence there has since been proved from a deciphered Soviet message. Hollis was the only MI5 officer who fitted them all, including the rare feature of "having something Russian in his background"—a possible family connection with Peter the Great.

32. It was Hollis's associate, the spy Philby, who suggested that Hollis should be the officer sent to interrogate Gouzenko. If Hollis was Elli, it was urgently in his and the Soviet interests that he should handle and manipulate the case.

33. Exactly at the time Elli would have feared he might be under surveillance, following Gouzenko's revelations about him, Hollis sent a gratuitous letter to the Foreign Office. This would have given him an explanation had he been spotted contacting his controller, as he may have been forced to do with some urgency.

34. Hollis derided Gouzenko as a source of information, just as Philby had previously derided another valuable defector, so that his statements would be ignored, as they were. As long as Hollis remained in MI5, Gouzenko's claim about Elli was never seriously investigated. Though most of MI5's papers on the Gouzenko case have been released, Hollis's reports on it have been withheld—if they still exist—after sixty years!

35. The Cambridge group spies and several others operated throughout the war blatantly, without hindrance, Anthony Blunt being inside MI5 itself. Hollis was responsible for countering such agents and their couriers and controllers.

Save for minor anti-Fascist activity during the war, Hollis had been required to counter only one main opponent, the Soviet Union, which operated almost with impunity throughout his long career.

36. When Hollis was sent to Australia following code breaks of KGB traffic to and from that country, the KGB quickly changed the codes. Fuchs also suspended his espionage when Hollis was in Australia and resumed it on his return, suggesting that he had been warned to do so until the GRU Center had been assured by a source inside MI5 that he was not under surveillance.

37. Throughout Hollis's career, MI5 secured no Russian defectors of consequence, and there is evidence that some who wished to defect to Great Britain were afraid to do so because they believed the British secret services to be penetrated. After Hollis left in 1965, evidence of penetration ceased and important defectors were secured.

38. All prosecutions of major spies, which were presented as MI5 triumphs, arose out of information originally supplied by American security agencies that could not be ignored.

39. Anatoli Golitsin, a defector to the CIA, gave a lead about a Soviet agent in the Royal Navy alleged to be operating at such a high level that his information could have inflicted catastrophic damage in the event of war with the Soviet Union. Hollis frustrated all attempts to pursue it, though MI5 officers were confident that they had identified the officer.

40. In January 1963, Philby behaved as though he had been forewarned that he was to be approached and interrogated in Beirut. Hollis was one of the few who knew about it and did not appear to be surprised when Philby disappeared.

41. When MI5 officers began to suspect that Graham Mitchell, their deputy director, was a Soviet agent, Hollis seemed to panic and rushed to Washington, insisting on the unusual course of going there alone. Having arrived there, he told the FBI and CIA chiefs that he did not know the details of the case, which would be supplied later. Officers investigating possible Soviet penetration of MI5 suspected that Hollis had gone to America to seek firsthand advice from a controller.

42. Hollis indisputably controlled the Profumo inquiries, which effectively ended Harold Macmillan's political life and installed a Labour government far less hostile to the Soviet Union.

43. Hollis did all he could to ensure that Blunt, Long, Cairncross, and other exposed Soviet agents would never be prosecuted, and their legal immunity extended to anybody else they named as agents or assistants. In doing so, Hollis knowingly overstepped his rights, as Parliament was eventually told.

44. Blunt seems to have been warned about his exposure and the coming offer of immunity. His friend Hollis was the likeliest source of that leak.

45. When Hollis knew that he was under suspicion in 1964, a second edition of *Handbook for Spies,* which had been ghostwritten by MI5 officers, appeared for no apparent reason. It contained a newly inserted introduction containing deliberate false statements concerning the whereabouts of Sonia and her sister Brigitte that would deter anyone from trying to find and question either of them.

46. When the Fluency committee prepared a chart of MI5 operations that had collapsed and of Soviet operations that had succeeded, it seemed to be dominated by Hollis's hand to an extent difficult to explain by coincidence.

47. After Hollis retired, the debacles ceased.

48. During Hollis's reign, no sustained effort was made to reduce the excessive numbers of KGB and GRU officers operating in Great Britain. When this was achieved in 1971, Soviet espionage in Britain was greatly curtailed, as retired KGB officers have confirmed.

49. When Sonia published her memoirs in English in 1991, the fact that she had been awarded a second Order of the Red Banner in 1969, not long after Hollis's retirement, was deliberately cut. The edition had been vetted by the GRU, which may have been anxious to prevent speculation about the reasons for the award.

50. The number of proven Soviet spies and active agents who operated for years under Hollis's aegis is perhaps the most impressive anomaly of all—*more than thirty,* not counting the KGB and GRU officers operating out of the Soviet embassy. The number of unidentified spies is increasing steadily as Russian archival information is being released.

51. The serial promotion of Hollis when it was on record in the MI5 files that he had been responsible for the failure to act against the persistent espionage activities of Sonia, Jurgen, and Brigitte Kuczynski, Klaus Fuchs, Hans Kahle, and others is yet another major anomaly.

52. Hollis was deeply involved with the further disasters of the Maclean-Burgess and Philby defections, which inflicted dreadful damage on Anglo-American intelligence relations.

Note on the Sources

Regarding archival sources, I have dispensed with the customary source notes for several reasons. First, because chronology has been so important in untangling such a complex web of deception, it has been essential to insert the dates of the many events recorded in the text as they arose. Second, the declassified MI5 files in the National Archives, which have been major sources, are presented there simply as continuous running commentaries consisting of short, dated minutes or letters supplied by the officers involved. To consult them, the researcher needs only the file number and date of the event concerned. With the dates already in the text, all else required are the titles and file numbers of the accessible papers given in the list of archival sources supplied at the end of this note. The file codes for other recorded documents are given in full there. Third, as there was nothing more to add to the statements made in the text, I soon appreciated that to repeat all the dates in the customary appendix of source notes would unnecessarily bulk an already large volume while serving little purpose.

Regarding Russian sources, which are very difficult to access in Moscow, the file numbers of those documents in the KGB archives that were temporarily released in the 1990s are given in the archival sources under the name of the individual concerned (for example, Donald Maclean file no. 83791). The relevant Molotov documents are also listed there. At a personal level, the retired KGB official Oleg Tsarev has confirmed several significant events. The former KGB officer Michael Lyubimov, who had served in London and with whom I spent a whole day, was helpful regarding the true scope of the Soviet espionage effort.

I am indebted to Dr. Svetlana Chervonnaya, the independent Russian researcher based in Moscow, for information about her many discoveries in the

Molotov Papers and otherwise inaccessible documents and books and for her translations. These include extracts from the continuing works of Vladimir Lota, a former GRU official who appears to be the only person granted any access to GRU records. His books, published only in Russian, are listed in the bibliography. Regarding the behavior of the GRU to its agents, Michael Hamburger, Sonia's distinguished son, domiciled in Berlin, has assisted me over several years with information and a supply of relevant books published only in German.

Nigel Bance, who has built up remarkable Russian contacts over many years on his regular visits to Moscow, has shared some of his documentary findings with me, as did the late John Costello, who pioneered the original release of the KGB documents with Tsarev and was a regular visitor to my home. The academic intelligence specialist Dr. Michael Goodman of King's College, London, has shared relevant findings with me, as I have with him. The former Estonian Dr. Einar Sanden has unselfishly shared all his archival information with me. I am also indebted to Dr. David Burke for advance information about his personal knowledge of the long-serving spy Melita Norwood, prior to the publication of his book *The Spy Who Came in from the Co-op*.

While documental sources are vital evidence, any investigative writer on intelligence affairs is only as good as his human sources, and so many of mine were so prime and highly placed that I owe the reader an explanation of how I acquired, cultivated, and kept them over so many years. One requirement was their trust that I would not reveal their identities in their lifetimes without their permission, whatever the pressures on me to do so. That I kept my word in many circumstances, some public but most known only within the secret world of Whitehall, assured their continuing confidence and secured new sources.

When compiling this account of so many shadowy events, I quickly realized that it would be more convincing if I could identify such sources. After such a long passage of time, I eventually found myself released from my restriction, as my instructive friends have almost all expired. I welcome this opportunity to pay tribute to them and to name those who helped to keep me accurately informed, regularly giving me guidance on request, even about sensitive intelligence and security affairs. They included Sir Frederick Brundrett, Lord Mountbatten, Sir Solly Zuckerman, and John Drew from the Defense Ministry. Sir Maurice Oldfield, the MI6 chief, and George Young and Nicholas Elliott, former MI6 officers who retained close contact with their old office, were regular informants—especially about MI5. Oldfield occasionally funneled information to me through a mutual friend, Bruce Mackenzie, whose close connections with

Mossad (which I sometimes shared) deeply involved him in the Israelis' famed Entebbe raid and, eventually, occasioned his assassination at the behest of Uganda's Idi Amin.

In his later years, Sir Dick White, formerly chief of both MI5 and MI6, was informative by letters. The results of my close association with the renegade MI5 officer Peter Wright are now fully on record. Former attorney general Lord Shawcross, who had been so heavily involved in the Fuchs case and others, was also helpful to me on those and other matters.

Among politicians, Defense Ministers Duncan Sandys, Harold Watkinson, and Peter Thorneycroft kept me topped up, as did Julian Amery, the air minister, and John Profumo, the war minister, along with his chief administrator, Sir Richard ("Sam") Way, a trusting friend over many years. Lord Lambton, when minister for the RAF, assisted me (in return for sometimes vetting his speeches), while Lord Jellicoe, when involved with the Admiralty, alerted me with exclusive results.

The former MP Jonathan Aitken was regularly instructive through his friendship with the MI5 officer Arthur Martin. John Stonehouse, when technology minister, was a frequent source, while Sir Michael Havers, when attorney general and, later, lord chancellor, was a mine of secret information. On the atomic front, Sir Willam Cook and Victor Macklen kept me up-to-date.

Casting my net wide, I soon encountered the Institution of Professional Civil Servants, which was the trade union for the upper levels of the Civil Service, including all the scientists at the defense research establishments. Its chief, Stanley Mayne, a charming and highly intelligent operator who became a close friend, had regular entry to all the secret stations where his representatives kept him informed far beyond his proper requirements. We met regularly, and I was first to know of any security problems facing his members, usually because of the discovery that they were secret Communists and possible spies. He gave me scoop after scoop, and it was only when he was close to retirement that I discovered he was a secret member of the Communist Party, a fact unknown to the government.

Among many ancillary sources, I am indebted to Major General Gilbert Monckton, Brigadier Godfrey Hobbs, and Brigadier John Stanier, all chiefs of army public relations. Augustus Walker and John Barraclough, later air chief marshals, gave me similar service at the Air Ministry.

The two D-Notice secretaries, Rear Admiral George Thomson and Colonel L. G. ("Sammy") Lohan, were of inestimable value both as sources and for advice on how to publish information without risking prosecution. While Lohan was previously on the press relations staff of the Defense Ministry, he fed major scoops to me, often involving secret intelligence, sometimes out of friendship but more often at the request of some minister or official who wanted publicity for a personal reason. Lohan had close relations with MI5, being on its payroll.

Air Marshal Sir Geoffrey Tuttle and Lord Weinstock were among many in the defense industry whose knowledge of secret matters was surprising.

Among American sources, the FBI officers Charles Bates and Robert Lamphere were informative about certain British espionage cases and the FBI's relationship with both MI5 and MI6. Michael Straight, whom I met several times, shared his firsthand knowledge of the Soviet espionage scene.

Entertaining so many sources, usually to regular lunches or dinners in London restaurants, was expensive, but I had the backing of a successful newspaper and owned an impressive Tudor house in delightful country often enjoyed by many of those mentioned above.

The documentary products of these sources and many other clandestine associations lie in the thirty thick volumes of cuttings (clippings) of my newspaper coups and in recently released cabinet papers concerning the many official "leak procedures" to uncover my sources. These papers, samples of which are listed in the archival sources, have been discovered by academics, in particular Dr. Christopher Moran of Warwick University, who has made much use of them in his PhD thesis. There were delicious occasions when some of those involved were the very sources themselves.

So much time was wasted interrogating senior personnel, including British Armed Forces and Civil Service chiefs, about my reports—with never a positive result—that on November 27, 1958, Sir Richard Powell, the Defense Ministry's permanent secretary, wrote to his minister in response to a suggestion that I should be put under surveillance. He advised, "Pincher will have covered up his tracks so adeptly that nothing will ever be discovered. I believe that we must learn to live with the man and make the best of it." However, that did not deter Prime Minister Harold Macmillan from asking the Defense Ministry, on May 4, 1959, "Can nothing be done to suppress or even get rid of Mr. Chapman Pincher? I am getting very concerned about how well informed he always seems to be on defence matters. It is really very serious if a Cabinet secret cannot be kept for more than two days."

Whenever the leak procedure—the subjection of all possible suspects to a long, interrogatory questionnaire—had been ordered, I was usually warned and lay low for a decent interval. I was always confident that I would never be prosecuted precisely because of the eminence of my sources. Involving any of them in a court case would have been far too damaging to the government. The reluctance of officialdom to include me in their interrogations, because they feared that I would make another news story out of it, appears repeatedly in the released documents. Eventually, the Defense Ministry expressed its acceptance of my activities by ensuring that when defense reporters were issued with passes for entry into its buildings, mine was numbered 007.

To explain my private access to so many important figures, I need to describe the flukes of fortune that so peculiarly equipped me for dealing with secret affairs, particularly in the atomic field, where so much espionage has been concentrated, then pushed me into that unusual specialty and kept me there for so long. I apologize if my CV sounds immodest and involves so much name-dropping, but this is how it really was.

I began my professional life as a biologist at King's College, and the scientific approach to problems was suited to what would be, to a large extent, detective work. While teaching science at the Liverpool Institute, pending a return to King's to research genetics, I enhanced the pittance salary by freelance writing for technical magazines, learning much about the art of journalism. Hitler then intervened, and in 1940, I joined the Royal Armoured Corps for training as a tank gunner, became a gunnery instructor, and, on being commissioned, served a year of regimental duty, during which, through chance friendship with RAF pilots, I was able to fly surreptitiously in Lancaster bombers. As the army needed a group of scientifically qualified officers to liaise between the weapons scientists in the laboratories and the users in the field, I was posted to the Military College of Science, where I completed the six-month advanced class in ammunition and explosives. Until 1946, I was then involved in the development and field testing of rocket weapons and other devices, which involved firing trials on RAF fighter planes and warships as well as with army units. That not only familiarized me with all three services, but introduced me to the secrets world. As I served on secret committees, I also became friendly with several officers and civil servants who would later become very senior in the defense establishment, Solly Zuckerman and William Cook being notable examples.

While stationed in London, I met the editor and other senior figures of the *Daily Express*, then a broadsheet newspaper with the world's largest circulation. When the German flying bombs and V-2 rockets began to strike, I was able to help the paper make accurate diagrams of their structure because I had seen the mock-ups made from recovered parts at the Farnborough Royal Aircraft Establishment. Secrecy was not involved, because the newspapers had been told officially that they could speculate. Shortly after the defeat of Germany, I met an officer who had just returned from Garmisch-Partenkirchen, where, he informed me, the entire team that had produced the V-2, including its inventor, one Wernher von Braun, had been rounded up by the Americans and were being heavily debriefed by intelligence officers. I contacted the *Daily Express* editor, who speedily dispatched a reporter there, with enviable result.

With my usual luck, I was then posted to a military office in the Mansion House, near the *Daily Express,* to await my release to civilian life and so happened to be close at hand when news of the atomic destruction of Hiroshima arrived. I telephoned Marcus Oliphant (later Sir), who had been involved in the atomic bomb research, and he told me that the Americans had produced a thick report (the Smyth report), which was about to be published, and that the Tube Alloys headquarters in London had an advance copy. I presented myself there and was allowed to see the report in advance of publication and, amazed at the revelations, took so many notes that I was able to produce a string of scoops. These were especially welcome to the *Daily Express* editor, who had been instructed by his proprietor, Lord Beaverbrook, to keep the atomic bomb story on the front page for a fortnight. Beaverbrook had been the minister responsible for the early years of the British atomic effort and foresaw its political consequences so clearly that he dictated the astutely prophetic headline THE BOMB THAT CHANGED THE WORLD.

For my exclusive contributions I was offered, and accepted, the post of defense and scientific reporter, which meant that I would be entering national journalism in a specialist role at the start of the atomic age, the missile age, the space age, and the computer age and was qualified to deal with them all. On the day after my discharge from the army in 1946, I was at my desk in Fleet Street.

A spy can be defined as someone who uses surreptitious means to secure information to which he or she is not legitimately entitled, and I quickly became one for my newspaper, finding that the acquisition of information withheld from the public suited an odd streak in my temperament. Through the gentle art of the leisurely lunch, I began by consulting wartime friends who had remained in secret business, mainly in government departments or in industry, and through them I gradually expanded my contacts. Then another fluke circumstance provided me with a new source of such eminence and influence that he ensured my success for many years.

While teaching in Liverpool, I had written and illustrated an easy guide to genetics for farmers, *The Breeding of Farm Animals,* which was published in 1946 as a Penguin handbook. Shortly afterward, at the end of a press facility visit to a government research station, I boarded a bus to take me to the main gate and sat opposite a small man in a black pin-striped suit and bowler hat. He introduced himself as Fred Brundrett, explaining that while he worked in Whitehall, his hobby was farming and that he had enjoyed my book. He invited me to see his herd of Redpoll cattle and, when I accepted, told me that he was deputy to the chief defense scientist, Sir Henry Tizard (whom he would soon succeed).

Fred and I became close friends, meeting regularly for long lunches until and after his retirement. He was on numerous secret committees, including one with MI5, and little about defense intelligence and security escaped him. Unusually, he believed that the taxpayers who would be funding the heavy peacetime defense costs were entitled to be kept reliably informed about their investments, and the reasons for them, as projects proceeded. He chose me as his medium for imparting what his more traditional colleagues regarded as most secret affairs of state. I was even able to visit him in his Defense Ministry office, where he introduced me to his chief minions who were specialists on various aspects of defense and were all assured that I could be trusted. They included the ministry's atomic weapons specialist, Victor Macklen, and its intelligence liaison and deception operations officer, John Drew. Their assistance in ensuring that what I wrote was accurate continued long after Fred had retired.

Being so well-informed in print attracted the curiosity of some astute politicians who were quick to appreciate that anyone with such access to publicity could be useful in the coming defense revolution occasioned by the impact of the atomic bomb and the guided missile. The Chiefs of Staff were already aware that the cold war had started and knew they would have to compete for scarce resources to construct atomic weapons and new bombers and missiles to carry them. Clearly, a trusted former insider keen to support them and their projects through mass publicity would be useful in the coming political struggles in Whitehall and Westminster. This applied even more so to those ministers charged with pushing through Parliament the new postwar defense policy, which was based largely on the controversial principle of nuclear deterrence.

My relationship with Fred Brundrett was much resented in the higher Whitehall echelons and in MI5, but Fred was his own man and had the backing of ministers, such as Duncan Sandys, who also became such a trusting friend that on the day before presenting his 1957 defense white paper containing so many revolutionary proposals, he called me to his office to read it. He wanted my views on how it would be received by the media. Had my preview before its presentation to Parliament become known, there would have been calls for his resignation.

Through such contacts, with most of whom I topped up my knowledge over lunches or their visits to my country home, I became the recipient of a steady stream of classified information, which eventually occasioned my most cherished compliment in Parliament—the Labour Party gibe that I was "a public urinal where ministers and officials queued up to leak!" Though initially unaware of it, I was pioneering a system of reporting through eliciting high-level leaks, because previously in Britain, senior civil servants and forces chiefs had been regarded as leak-proof. Critics claimed that I was allowing myself to be used, to which my response was—and remains—if the information is true, exclusive, and newsworthy, I am open for use at any time.

I quickly learned that specialist reporters in Fleet Street zealously guarded their turf and resented any intrusion by colleagues, which severely limited my contribution to the coverage of my first spy case—the arrest of Alan Nunn May in 1946. Spies were classed as criminals and dealt with by the crime reporter. In 1950, however, when Klaus Fuchs was exposed, the *Express* crime reporter assumed that the evidence would involve scientific matters beyond his expertise and asked me to cover the Old Bailey trial. I did so with relish, and armed with background information from friends in the Harwell atomic research station, where Fuchs had worked, I produced a front-page account headlined FUCHS GAVE BOMB TO RUSSIA, which British and Russian documents have confirmed.

From then on, I was also the *Daily Express* "spy man" and became the only journalist to have covered all the spy cases, as they occurred, from Fuchs, Maclean, Burgess, Philby, Cairncross, Blunt, Houghton, Londsale, Vassall, and Blake to the GCHQ traitor Geoffrey Prime and others. There were also espionage aspects to the Profumo affair, the Penkovsky-Wynne case, and especially the Hollis affair, about all of which I had inside knowledge from prime sources, eventually including Peter "Spycatcher" Wright. The friendship that I established with the GRU defector Igor Gouzenko was to be unusually helpful in my pursuit of the Hollis affair.

My lengthy specialization was due to my resistance to all efforts to promote me to executive status, even by Lord Beaverbrook. I was not interested in newspaper management and enjoyed the chase so much, with each day offering a new challenge, that I was determined to remain in active investigation. It may be that as a lifelong countryman, the chase was in my blood, with particular addiction to game shooting and fishing, which quite unexpectedly hugely advantaged my investigative efforts. That aspect of my continuing good fortune began with my entry into the Marks & Spencer shooting syndicate, which pursued pheasants and partridges on the estate of that great company's chairman, Israel Sieff (later Lord), in Berkshire. My ensuing friendship with him and his family quickly resulted in an invitation to accompany him to Israel, where I was introduced to the major political and military figures, including one from the Israeli Intelligence Service, Mossad. That was to secure me some notable scoops, such as the long-term closure of the Suez Canal, and would even enable me to play a cameo role in the famed Entebbe raid, for which Mossad expressed its gratitude.

Game shooting, as organized in Great Britain, can be an exceptional fount for meeting eminent people who are attracted by its difficulty, its rituals, and its wonderful environments. At the Sieff shoot I met Lord Forte, the hotel and restaurant tycoon, who invited me to his shoots, where, as a frequent guest, I met ambassadors and politicians, such as the gloriously indiscreet Sir Michael Havers, Reginald Maudling, the home secretary, and other cabinet ministers. Through shooting—and later salmon fishing—with Sir Thomas Sopwith, the aircraft pioneer, I developed a regular friendship with Lord Dilhorne, the lord chancellor, who was deeply involved with security and intelligence affairs. Other sources I encountered there included Duncan Sandys and Lord Mountbatten, when he was first sea lord and, later, chief of the defense staff.

I even became friends with Harold Macmillan, then retired from office, who could be delightfully indiscreet around the shoot lunch table.

It is extraordinary how a day's shooting together can break down barriers of reserve. I had met "Dickie" Mountbatten through formal interviews and Defense Ministry parties, but he had always been aloof and rather grand. Then, at a shoot lunch, the hostess, Lady Sopwith, said, "Dickie, sit next to Harry, and don't mumble." From then on, as I was the Harry referred to, Mountbatten was just another human being. He invited me to shoot on his Broadlands estate and insisted on having me with him in his vehicle. He was keen to impart his own views about defense so that they would color my reporting—even dictating one naval scoop to me. He also wanted to know what might be going on in the Defense Ministry behind his back, and I was always happy to repay his confidences. Between them, Mountbatten and Zuckerman built up a fearsome partnership in the defense field that exerted such influence, I referred to it repeatedly in my writing as the "Zuckbatten Axis." Both were delighted.

Shooting also cemented my friendship with Julian Amery, to the extent that when he became air minister, we would meet, usually at his home, to discuss ways in which I might promote the RAF. Once, when we were stumped for an idea, I suggested, almost in jest, that a photograph of me leaning against an H-bomb, which no outsider had ever seen, would be newsworthy. Julian grinned dismissively but a few days later asked me to attend an airfield where an official photographer would be waiting. On arrival, I was taken to a hangar from which was wheeled a trolley bearing the RAF's biggest-megaton bomb, and the photograph duly appeared. The incident underlined that much of official secrecy was bogus and strengthened my resolve to reveal whatever I could.

I had quickly realized that it was wise to be on equally good terms with the junior as well as senior press officers of the various ministries—mainly Defense and Supply—with which I was in daily contact, and many of them were regular guests at my lunch table. There were many instances when they had been forbidden to volunteer information but were empowered to supply it if asked about it. So tips about what to ask could be highly productive. It could also be profitable to ask senior officials about areas worth probing, and one such request was to lead to what many regarded as potentially my most damaging intelligence leak—an event that was highly instructive about the many motives that induce indiscretion.

In 1953, Sir Archibald Rowlands, the highly respected permanent secretary of the Supply Ministry, retired, and while at lunch with him one day, I asked if he could remember any area where I might profitably dig—to which he replied mysteriously, "Ask the Ministry of Supply about Nomination." Realizing that it was a code word, I questioned the Supply Ministry's public relations chief, who eventually assured me that the name was unknown. Other evasive responses convinced me that there was a cover-up, so I eventually printed a small report, which appeared to arouse no interest. In fact, my inquiry had caused such an upheaval that I was subjected to surveillance to discover the source. Rowlands's successor, Sir James Helmore, then called me in to say, "I must tell you that whoever gave you that information is a traitor, and it is your duty to give us his name." After declining to oblige, I assured him that the source could not possibly be a traitor and that had the ministry been honest with me, instead of burying its head in the sand, I would never have mentioned Nomination.

Years later, when lecturing to the War Course at Greenwich, I was seated at lunch next to Professor R. V. Jones, whose wartime intelligence adventures have been recorded in his classic *Most Secret War*. "However did you find out about Nomination?" he asked. "It was more secret than the bomb itself." He then explained that it had been an MI6-CIA group set up to exchange intelligence about Russia's atomic activities and, on the day after my report appeared, was about to hold a meeting in Washington with luminaries like Sir William Penney and Sir John Cockcroft in attendance. The American reaction had been fierce. Why had Rowlands been so mischievous? Simply to cause grief to his successor.

Usually, there is a more sensible purpose behind a loose tongue. Many leaks were given to me to smite opponents in the various struggles invariably in progress within the government machinery. Others, especially from politicians, were designed to inflate their public reputations or deflate those of parliamentary opponents. For that and other reasons, I cultivated Labour Party luminaries against the day they might be in office, the most productive of these being George Brown, an ambitious extrovert destined to become foreign secretary.

In August 1961, Brown sought my help in contacting MI5 and MI6 in the hope of discovering how many Labour MPs were really Communists. He and other Labour leaders were deeply worried about newspaper claims that their party was riddled with such crypto-Communists, and any named by MI5 were to be expelled in a cleanup drive before the next election. Upon hearing this, the Conservative prime minister, Harold Macmillan, forbade MI5 to reveal the names, and Brown was told that none had been found, though he was given the name of a Labour Party official who was a Soviet-bloc agent and was duly fired. Brown wanted me to publish this as evidence of the cleanup, and I obliged.

In the same year that George Blake, the KGB spy inside MI6, was sentenced to forty-two years' imprisonment, the Conservative government blanketed all details of his crimes, being anxious to avoid revealing even that MI6 was run by the Foreign Office. Rightly, sensing a scandal, the Labour opposition kept demanding the facts so volubly that Macmillan offered to reveal them to three Labour Privy Councillors who, while maintaining absolute secrecy, could assure their colleagues that silence was being imposed only for genuine security reasons. Brown was one of the three, and a few days later, while lunching with him, he told me the whole story of how Blake had betrayed the names of at least forty agents working for MI6 abroad and had disclosed details of a tunnel that the Americans had dug under the Russian sector of Berlin to plug into Soviet telephone cables. Brown made it clear that he wanted me to publish everything, without reference to him, and it all appeared on the *Daily Express* front page. Later, Brown assured me that he felt no qualms about breaking his Privy Councillor's oath of silence, as it had made the Conservative government look inefficient.

Leaks to me from the Foreign Office were rare, but one I treasure concerned the dramatic exchange in 1964 of Kolon Molody, the KGB officer operating under the name Gordon Lonsdale, for the British MI6 agent Greville Wynne, held captive in Russia. The Russians released photographs of Wynne, showing that he was being treated so badly that the British authorities had no option but to offer Lonsdale in exchange. To preempt any Soviet attempt to secure international kudos from the deal, the authorities decided to leak it in such a way that it would become public shortly after the two spies had reached Berlin from their respective prisons, when it was felt the Russians would be unable to retract. In choosing me as the medium, Michael Hadow of the Foreign Office news division, which controlled the exercise, paid me the compliment of assuming that, as I had a reputation for accurate leaks, the other media would publish the story—as indeed they did, worldwide.

Many leaks were occasioned by sheer vanity. I quickly realized that great men do not obey the laws of optics—the nearer you get to them, the smaller they become. Most display what I call "the peacock factor," meaning that they derive pleasure from letting someone else know that they have access to secrets denied to most mortals. This pleasure seems to intensify when the leak duly appears and causes a commotion.

Though newspaper readers claiming to have secret information were usually time wasters, one of them, in 1967, was to occasion the most bitter and politically charged intelligence incident of my career—the so-called D-Notice affair. The informant claimed that every day, all telegrams sent from the Post Office and private cable companies were being made available for scrutiny by the security authorities (which turned out to be GCHQ, looking for coded messages to and from intelligence agents). While the Defense Ministry denied the allegation, a fishing companion, who headed the Post Office press department, confirmed it, and my front-page disclosure caused a public collision between Prime Minister Harold Wilson and the entire media, lasting six months. It led to a tribunal and a white paper designed to discredit me and Colonel Lohan, who as D-Notice secretary stood accused of failing to veto the story, true though it was. As a result, I and my paper were vindicated by the tribunal, as is described in *The Official History of the D-Notice System*, recently completed by Rear Admiral Nick Wilkinson.

The full reason for the intensity of the government's response has never been officially admitted but undoubtedly involved a highly sensitive American aspect. Selected cables were being supplied to U.S. security in contravention of the American Constitution. Years later, Wilson went out of his way to apologize to me in person for what he described as "his worst self-inflicted wound."

When it seemed that Margaret Thatcher, who had been elected leader of the Conservative opposition, might well become the first woman prime minister, Maurice Oldfield (later Sir), who had become the chief of MI6, asked me if I knew her. On hearing that I did, he asked me to tell her that should she wish, he would keep her briefed on intelligence matters so that she would be already well-informed on assuming office. I did so, and they then met regularly.

Sadly, it would fall to me to expose the fact, which I learned only after Sir

Maurice's death in 1981, that he had repeatedly faked his positive vetting by denying that he was a practicing homosexual, which during his time would have barred him from service in MI6. How this occurred is illuminating regarding the ways in which supersecret information becomes public news. Oldfield's behavior was unknown until after he had retired in 1978. Courageously, in 1979, he had come out of retirement at Mrs. Thatcher's request to become coordinator of intelligence in Northern Ireland. As he was often in London and had retained his bachelor apartment in Westminster, he required protection because he was a prime target for the IRA, which had previously attempted to assassinate him in 1975 with a bomb in a carryall slung on railings below the apartment. Protection officers supplied by Scotland Yard became suspicious of the type of men who visited the apartment, and some, who were traced, proved to be homosexuals of the kind known as "rough trade." A close watch was kept, and eventually, the Metropolitan Police commissioner, Sir David McNee, felt it his duty to warn the home secretary (who informed the prime minister) that Oldfield might be a security risk.

Oldfield was recalled to be formally interviewed by MI5. When confronted by the evidence, he confessed. As inquiries by the Standing Security Commission produced no evidence that he had been compromised in any way, and as he had only three months to serve in Northern Ireland, he was allowed to return there. He was seen by the attorney general, Sir Michael Havers, and gave an undertaking not to misbehave. The whole sorry business was kept secret, of course, hopefully for all time. In 1984, when I was researching *Traitors*, a book I was writing about the motivations for treachery, I heard of moves to expose the Oldfield case from McNee. I raised the matter in Havers's hearing at a pheasant shoot, and he confirmed it, with details of his part in it. I then decided that it would be professionally dishonest to suppress the case in *Traitors* just because Oldfield had been a friend. Some of his colleagues disbelieved my statements, but Mrs. Thatcher shot them down by confirming in Parliament that in March 1980, Oldfield had admitted that from time to time he had engaged in homosexual activities and that his positive vetting had been withdrawn because his behavior had made him a security risk.

It is satisfying, at the age of ninety-four and with near total recall, to look back on a career in investigative reporting spanning more than sixty years—in various media—and to know that, given the chance, I would elect to repeat it in preference to any other profession. It continues to excite and entrance, with new material continuing to reach me from sources in Russia and elsewhere.

Archival Sources

NA: National Archives (U.K.)

KV: MI5

CAB: Cabinet Office

PREM: Office of the Prime Minister

DEFE: Defense Ministry

ADM: Admiralty

AIR: Air Ministry

AVIA: Aviation Ministry

FO: Foreign Office

HO: Home Office

Hansard: proceedings of the Parliament (U.K.)

Aitken, Jonathan. For the full text of his warning letter to Margaret Thatcher about the Hollis case, see Appendix A in *A Web of Deception,* Chapman Pincher, 1987.

Armstrong, Robert. For the text of his letter to the publisher of *Their Trade Is Treachery,* see Appendix C in *A Web of Deception.*

Barkovsky, Vladimir. *Notes for Confidential Lecture on Soviet World War II Atomic Espionage.* Delivered at the Los Alamos laboratory. November 1994.

Bishop, Edgar, ed. *Ten Singers.* Fortune & Merriman, London, 1925.

Bishop, Reginald Thomas. NA KV2/1600.

Blunt, Anthony. KGB file 83695 and his KGB biography.

————. *Hansard,* November 21, 1979, col. 402.

————. *Hansard,* November 9, 1981, col. 40.

————. On-record interview. *The Times,* November 21, 1979.

Bossard, Frank. Report of the Security Commission. Cmnd. 2722. June 1965.

Bridges, Sir Edward. *Report of an Enquiry on an Intelligence Operation Against Russian Warships.* Released by Cabinet Office in 2006 (with many deletions).

Broda, Engelbert. NA MI5 file KV2/2349.

Burgess, Guy. KGB file 83792.

————. *Report Concerning the Disappearance of Two Former Foreign Office Officials.* Cmnd. 9577. September 23, 1955.

————. *Hansard,* November 7, 1955, col. 1599.

Cairncross, John. KGB file 83896.

Canada (Espionage). *Report of the Royal Commission.* Ottawa, 1946.

Cockburn. NA MI5 files KV2/1546–1555.

Comintern. NA MI5 files KV3/127–136.

Communists and suspected Communists. NA MI5 files KV2/2317–2374.

Conference of Privy Councillors Report on Security. Cmnd. 9715. March 1956.

Crabb, Frogman Lionel. NA papers CAB 165/207, Admiralty papers ADM 1/29240.

————. Parliamentary debate. *Hansard,* May 14, 1956.

Day-Lewis, Cecil. NA MI5 file KV2/1385.

Delmer, Sefton. NA MI5 file KV2/2586.

Dilhorne, Lord. *The Stephen Ward Case.* NA CAB 129/113.

D-Notice Affair. *Report of the Committee of Privy Councillors Appointed to Inquire into D-Notice Matters.* Cmnd. 3309. June 1967.

Ewert, Arthur. NA MI5 file KV2/2336.

Foote, Alexander. NA MI5 files KV2/1611–1616.

Fuchs, Klaus. NA MI5 files KV2/1257, KV2/1259, KV2/1263.

————. FBI papers (Foocase). *Rosenberg et Alia,* vols. 1–43.

————. Miscellaneous papers in the Stasi files.

Glees, Anthony. "The Hollis Letters." *The Times,* April 3, 1982.

Goodman, Michael S. "British Intelligence and the Soviet Atomic Bomb 1945–50." *Journal of Strategic Studies* 26, no. 2.

————. "MI5-FBI Relations and the Klaus Fuchs Case." *Journal of Cold War Studies* 7, no. 3 (2005).

Goodman, Michael S., and Chapman Pincher. "Research Note Clement Attlee, Percy Sillitoe and the Security of the Fuchs Case." *Contemporary British History* 19, no. 1 (2005): 66–67.

Gordievsky, Oleg. *Daily Mail* (London), April 7, 2008.

Gouzenko, Igor. Gouzenko papers. NA MI5 files KV2/1419–1423, 1425–1426.

————. Memorandum to the RCMP made at request of MI5. May 6, 1952. (Reproduced as Appendix A in *Too Secret Too Long*, Chapman Pincher, Sidgwick & Jackson, 1984).

————. Report of Canadian Royal Commission. Ottawa, June 27, 1946.

Green, Oliver. MI5 papers. NA KV2/2203–2206.

Hamburger, Rudolf. MI5 papers. KV2/1610.

Hollis, Roger. "The Conflict in China." *Transactions of the Royal Central Asian Society* 25 (1938).

Kahle, Hans. Brief biography in Stasi files.

KGB. History of the London *rezidentura*. KGB file 89113.

Khariton, Yuli, and Yuri Smirnov. "The Khariton Version." *Bulletin of the Atomic Scientists* 49 (1993).

Klugman, James. NA MI5 files KV2/788 (1937–47).

Krivitsky, W. G. NA MI5 files KV2/802–805.

————. FBI papers. File 100-11146.

Kuczynski family. NA MI5 files KV2/1871–1880.

Long, Leo. *Hansard*, November 9, 1981, col. 40.

Lota, Vladimir. *Tehran 43 Red Star* (Moscow). November 1, 2003.

Maclean, Donald. KGB file 83791.

————. *Report Concerning the Disappearance of Two Former Foreign Office Officials.* Cmnd. 9577.

————. Parliamentary debate. *Hansard*, November 7, 1955, col. 1599.

May, Alan Nunn. NA MI5 files KV2/2209–2226, KV2/2553–2555.

————. For final confession, see *Sunday Telegraph*, January 26, 2003.

McDonald, D. *Commission of Enquiry Concerning Certain Activities of the RCMP.* 1981.

Mitrokhin Inquiry Report. Intelligence and Security Committee. Cmnd. 4764. June 2000.

Molotov, Vyacheslav. Molotov Private Papers. Fund 82. Russian State Archive of Social and Political History.

————. Operation Overlord. Reel 100 (815).

————. Fuchs arrest. File 1146.

————. Operation Red Socks. Files 5372 and 5147.

Moorehead, Alan. NA MI5 files KV2/1257, KV2/1259.

Murphy, Philip. "Creating a Commonwealth Intelligence Culture." *Intelligence and National Security* 17, no. 3 (2002).

Ohmann, Valdur. "The Secret Lives of Karl and Artur Säre." *Tuna* (Estonia) 3 (2003): 64–77.

Peierls, Sir Rudolf. NA MI5 files KV2/1658 and 1659.

————. See Sabine Lee, "The Spy That Never Was," *Intelligence and National Security* 17, no. 4 (2002): 77–99.

"Philby, Burgess, Maclean." FBI files BU100-374183.

Philby, Harold ("Kim"). *KGB Memoir* and eighteen other volumes in the KGB archives.

————. Parliamentary statement about Philby's disappearance. *Hansard,* July 1, 1963, col. 33.

Pincher, Chapman. Sample papers concerning "leak procedure" investigations in NA:

> CAB 126. Telegram to Cabinet Office from U.K. embassy, Washington, D.C., reporting that General Leslie Groves (chief of Manhattan Project) seriously disturbed by Chapman Pincher report printed November 2, 1946.
>
> AVIA 65/2340. Various articles by Chapman Pincher. 1947–51.
>
> DEFE 13/58. Letter to defense minister from air minister about installation of U.S. Thor missiles in United Kingdom. February 5, 1958.
>
> DEFE 13/123. Letter from prime minister to president of the United States about Thor missile leak. February 28, 1958.
>
> PREM 11/2633. Letter from prime minister to Defense Ministry. August 29, 1958.
>
> DEFE 13/169. Letter to defense minister from air minister. November 4, 1958.
>
> DEFE 13/169. Letter to defense minister from Sir Richard Powell. November 27, 1958.
>
> PREM 11/2800. Letter from prime minister to defense minister. May 4, 1959.
>
> AIR 8/2239. Letter from defense minister to prime minister. November 3, 1959.
>
> CAB 21/4979. Letter about Blue Steel missile. June 23, 1960.
>
> PREM 13/1816. Disclosure of information about alleged inspection of overseas telegrams ("D-Notice affair"). February–April 1967.
>
> CAB 164/520. Letters to cabinet secretary and director general MI5 from Treasury. November 1967.
>
> CAB 164/1520. Letters from cabinet secretary concerning MI5's involvement into inquiry regarding Chapman Pincher's sources. February 1968. Admits inquiry failed.

PREM 13/2367. Letter to prime minister about "satellite spies." May 1, 1968.

PREM 15/174. Letter from MI6 to Cabinet Office about intelligence affairs. August 3, 1970.

PREM 15/174. Letter to cabinet secretary from MI6. August 6, 1970.

DEFE 68/143. Letters from Defense Ministry to thirty-six government departments and MI5 concerning leakage of an admiral's secret report. November 1971. Result negative.

HO 292/22. Details of Mr. Chapman Pincher. 1972.

PREM 15/1898. Letter from Defense Ministry to Civil Service chief saying that 171 people were interrogated without result after leak about Polaris missiles. Leak questionnaire attached. October 1, 1973.

PREM 16/270. Letters re defense review and intelligence activities. November 23, 1974.

DEFE 68/223. Inquiry into leak of information on proposed supply of arms to Kenya. July16, 1976.

Pontecorvo, Bruno. NA FO 371/184837, AB6/798.

Positive vetting papers. NA CAB 130/20.

Profumo, John. *Report by Lord Dilhorne*. NA CAB 129/113. June 14, 1963.

———. Parliamentary debate. *Hansard*, June 17, 1963, col. 34.

———. Lord Denning's report. HM Stationery Office. Cmnd. 2152. September 1963.

———. Security and the Denning report. *Hansard*, December 16, 1963, col. 974.

Quebec Agreement. NA papers. FO 800/540, FO 115/4527, PREM 8/1104.

Radcliffe report. *Security Procedures in the Public Service*. HM Stationery Office. Cmnd. 1681. April 1962.

Romer report. *Committee of Enquiry into Breaches of Security 1961*. CAB. June 2007.

Rote Kapelle. NA MI5 files KV3/349–351.

Rust, William. NA M5 file KV2/1050.

"Sonia" papers. NA MI5 files KV6/41–45. Includes Beurton file.

Springhall papers. NA MI5 file KV2/1594.

Stewart, Robert. NA MI5 files KV2/1180–1183 KV2/2787–2792.

Stonehouse, John. *Daily Express*, January 2 and 10, 2006. *Mail on Sunday*, January 15, 2006.

Straight, Michael. FBI documents. "Michael Whitney Straight." File 100-61929.

Thatcher, Margaret. Statement about *Their Trade Is Treachery. Hansard,* March 1981, col. 1079. (Reproduced as Appendix B in *Too Secret Too Long,* Chapman Pincher, Sidgwick & Jackson, 1984.)

Tripartite talks document (U.S.). June 19–21, 1950.

Tsarev, Oleg. *Soviet Intelligence on British Defence Plans, 1945–1950.* Norwegian Institute for Defence Studies. 2001.

———. Paper in *Agents for Change.* Edited by Harold Shukman. St. Ermin's Press, 2000.

Tudor Hart, Edith. NA MI5 files KV2/1012–1014.

Vassall, John. Vassall papers. NA CRIM 1/4003. Report of the tribunal appointed to inquire into the Vassall case and related matters. Cmnd. 2009. 1963.

Vassall Tribunal. Message from Roger Hollis to Burke Trend. CAB 21/6028, April 16, 1963.

———. *Hansard,* May 7, 1963, col. 240.

West, W. J. "Proven Connection." *The Spectator,* London, October 14, 1989.

Whomack, George. NA MI5 file KV2/1237.

Woolwich Arsenal case (Glading, etc.). NA MI5 files KV2/1004–1007.

Bibliography

Abend, Hallett. *My Years in China, 1926–41*. Bodley Head, London, 1944.

Albright, Joseph, and Marcia Kunstel. *Bombshell*. Random House, New York, 1997.

Aldrich, Richard J. *British Intelligence Strategy and the Cold War, 1945–51*. Routledge, London, 1992.

———. *Espionage, Security and Intelligence in Britain, 1945–1970*. Manchester University Press, Manchester, UK, 1998.

———. *The Hidden Hand*. John Murray, London, 2001.

Andrew, Christopher, and David Dilks. *The Missing Dimension*. Macmillan, London, 1984.

Andrew, Christopher, and Oleg Gordievsky. *KGB: The Inside Story*. Hodder & Stoughton, London, 1990.

Andrew, Christopher, and Vasili Mitrokhin. *The Mitrokhin Archive*. Allen Lane, Penguin Books, London, 1999.

Arnold, Lorna. *Britain and the H-Bomb*. Palgrave, Macmillan, London, 2001.

Atomic Project of the USSR (1938–1945). 3 vols. Minatom, Moscow.

Badash, Lawrence, Joseph O. Hirschfelder, and Herbert P. Broida, eds. Reminiscences of Los Alamos, 1943–1945. Reidel Publishing Co., Dordrecht, Holland, and Boston, 1980.

Bagley, Tennant H. *Spy Wars: Moles, Mysteries, and Deadly Games*. Yale University Press, New Haven, CT, 2007.

Bance, Nigel. See Jerry Dan (pseudonym).

Bethell, Nicholas. *The Great Betrayal*. Hodder & Stoughton, London, 1984.

Blake, George. *No Other Choice*. Jonathan Cape, London, 1990.

Bochkarev, V., and I. A. Kolpakidi. *Superfrau iz GRU*. Olma Press, Moscow, 2002.

Born, Max. *My Life and My Views*. Charles Scribner's Sons, London, 1968.

Borovik, Genrikh. *The Philby Files*. Little, Brown & Co., London, 1994.

Bothwell, Robert, and J. L. Granatstein. *The Gouzenko Transcripts*. Deneau, Ottawa, 1982.

Bower, Tom. *The Perfect English Spy*. Heinemann, London, 1995.

Boyle, Andrew. *The Climate of Treason*. Hodder & Stoughton, London, 1980.

Branson, Noreen. *History of the Communist Party of Great Britain, 1927–1941*. Lawrence & Wishart, London, 1985.

Bristow, Desmond. *A Game of Moles*. Little, Brown & Co., London, 1993.

Brook-Shepherd, Gordon. *The Storm Birds*. Weidenfeld & Nicolson, London, 1988.

Brown, Anthony Cave. *Treason in the Blood*. Jonathan Hale, London, 1995.

Bulloch, John. *MI5*. Arthur Barker, London, 1963.

Burke, David. *The Spy Who Came in from the Co-op*. Boydell & Brewer, London, 2009.

Cain, Frank. *The Australian Security Intelligence Organization*. Frank Cass, London, 1994.

Cairncross, John. *The Enigma Spy*. Century, London, 1997.

Carter, Miranda. *Anthony Blunt: His Lives*. Macmillan, London, 2001.

Cecil, Robert. *A Divided Life: A Biography of Donald Maclean*. Bodley Head, London, 1988.

Chang, Jung, and Jon Halliday. *Mao: The Unknown Story*. Jonathan Cape, London, 2005.

CIA Handbook. *The Rote Kapelle*. 2 vols. University Publications of America, Washington, DC, 1982.

Clark, Ronald. *J.B.S.: The Life and Work of J. B. S. Haldane*. Hodder & Stoughton, London, 1968.

Cockburn, Claud. *I, Claud*. Penguin Books, London, 1967.

———. *Crossing the Line*. MacGibbon & Kee, London, 1958.

Cockburn, Patricia. *The Years of The Week*. Comedia, London, 1968.

———. *Figure of Eight*. Chatto & Windus, London, 1985.

———. *The Broken Boy*. Jonathan Cape, London, 2005.

Cole, D. J. *Geoffrey Prime*. Jonathan Hale, London, 1998.

Connolly, Cyril. *The Missing Diplomats*. Queen Anne Press, London, 1952.

Costello, John. *Mask of Treachery*. William Morrow & Co., New York, 1988.

Costello, John, and Oleg Tsarev. *Deadly Illusions*. Century, London, 1993.

Courtney, Anthony. *Sailor in a Russian Frame*. Johnson, London, 1968.

Cradock, Sir Percy. *Know Your Enemy*. John Murray, London, 2002.

Damaskin, Igor. *Kitty Harris: The Spy with Seventeen Names*. St. Ermin's Press, London, 2001.

Dan, Jerry. *Ultimate Deception*. Rare Books and Berry, Porlock, Somerset, UK, 2003.

Day-Lewis, Cecil. *The Buried Day*. Chatto & Windus, London, 1960.

Day-Lewis, Sean. *C. Day-Lewis: An English Literary Life*. Weidenfeld & Nicolson, London, 1980.

Deacon, Richard. *The British Connection*. Hamish Hamilton, London, 1979.

Driberg, Tom. *Guy Burgess: Portrait with a Background*. Weidenfeld & Nicolson, London, 1956.

Elliott, Nicholas. *With My Little Eye*. Michael Russell Publishing, London, 1993.

Feklisov, Alexander, and Sergei Kostin. *The Man Behind the Rosenbergs*. Enigma Books, London, 2001.

Foote, Alexander. *Handbook for Spies*. Museum Press, London, 1949 and 1964.

Frisch, Otto. *What Little I Remember*. Cambridge University Press, Cambridge, 1979.

Frolik, Josef. *The Frolik Defection*. Leo Cooper, London, 1975.

Fursenko, Alexsandr, and Timothy Naftali. *One Hell of a Gamble*. John Murray, London, 1997.

Glees, Anthony. *Exile Politics During the Second World War*. Clarendon Press, Oxford, 1982.

———. *The Secrets of the Service*. Jonathan Cape, London, 1987.

———. *The Stasi Files*. Simon & Schuster, London, 2003.

Goncharov, G. A. *American and Soviet H-Bomb Development Programmes*. History of Physics, Russian Academy of Sciences, Moscow, 1996.

Goodman, Michael S. *Spying on the Nuclear Bear*. Stanford University Press, Stanford, CA, 2007.

Gordievsky, Oleg. *Next Stop Execution*. Macmillan, London, 1995.

Gottlieb, Amy. *Men of Vision*. Weidenfeld & Nicolson, London, 1998.

Gouzenko, Igor. *This Was My Choice*. Eyre & Spottiswoode, London, 1948.

Gouzenko conference, 2004. *The Gouzenko Affair*. Penumbra Press, Canada, 2006.

Gowing, Margaret. *Britain and Atomic Energy, 1939–45*. Macmillan, London, 1964.

———. *Independence and Deterrence (Britain and Atomic Energy)*. 2 vols. Macmillan, London, 1974.

Granatstein, J. L. *A Man of Influence*. Deneau, Ottawa, 1981.

Haldane, Charlotte. *Truth Will Out*. Weidenfeld & Nicolson, London, 1949.

Haynes, John Earl, and E. Harvey Klehr. *Venona*. Yale University Press, New Haven, CT, 1999.

Hennessy, Peter. *The Secret State*. Allen Lane, Penguin Press, London, 2002.

———. *Cabinets and the Bomb*. Oxford University Press, Oxford, 2007.

Hollis, Christopher. *Lenin: Portrait of a Professional Revolutionary*. Longmans, Green & Co., London, 1938.

———. *Along the Road to Frome*. Harrap, Edinburgh, 1958.

———. *The Seven Ages*. Heinemann, London, 1974.

———. *Oxford in the Twenties*. Heinemann, London, 1976.

Holloway, David. *Stalin and the Bomb*. Yale University Press, New Haven, CT, 1994.

Hood, William. *Mole*. Weidenfeld & Nicolson, London, 1982.

Hooper, David. *Official Secrets*. Secker & Warburg, London, 1987.

Horne, Alistair. *Macmillan*. 2 vols. Macmillan, London, 1989.

Hyde, Douglas. *I Believed*. Heinemann, London, 1951.

Jordan, Philip. *Russian Glory*. Cresset Press, London, 1942.

Kalugin, Oleg. *Spymaster*. Smith Gryphon, London, 1994.

Kavchak, Andrew. *Remembering Gouzenko: The Struggle to Honour a Cold War Hero*. Mackenzie Institute, Toronto, 2004.

Keeler, Christine. *The Truth at Last*. Sidgwick & Jackson, London, 2001.

Kern, Gary. *Walter G. Krivitsky MI5 Debriefing*. Xenos Books, Grand Terrace, CA, 2004.

———. *A Death in Washington*. Enigma Books, London, 2003.

King, Mackenzie. *Diaries*. Canadian National Archives, Ottawa. Also online at www.archives.ca.

Kramnick, Isaac, and Barry Sheerman. *Harold Laski: A Life on the Left*. Hamish Hamilton, London, 1993.

Krivitsky, W. G. *I Was Stalin's Agent*. Hamilton, London, 1939.

Kuczynski, Jurgen. *Memoiren*. Aufbau-Verlag, Berlin and Weimar, 1983.

Kvasnikov, Leonid. See Nigel West and Oleg Tsarev, *Crown Jewels*, pp. 227–228. HarperCollins, London, 1998.

Lamphere, Robert J. *The FBI-KGB War*. Random House, New York, 1986.

Lewis, Julian. *Changing Direction*. Frank Cass, London, 2003.

Lota, Vladimir. *GRU I atomnaia bomba* (*The GRU and the Atomic Bomb*). Olma Press, Moscow, 2002.

————. *Sekretnyi Front General'nogo Shtaba* (*The Secret Front: The General Staff's Eyes and Ears*). Moldaia Gvardiia, Moscow.

————. *Military Intelligence in the Far East, 1918–45.* Kuchkovo Pote, Moscow, 2008.

Lyubimov, Mikhail. *Martyr to Dogma.* See appendix to *The Private Life of Kim Philby,* Rufina Philby.

MacDonald, Malcolm. *People and Places.* Collins, London, 1969.

MacKinnon, J. R., and S. R. MacKinnon. *Agnes Smedley.* Virago Press, London, 1988.

Maclean, Alan. *No, I Tell a Lie, It Was the Tuesday.* Kyle Cathie, London, 1997.

Mader, Julius. *Dr.-Sorge-Report.* Militarverlag der Deutschen Demokratischen Republik, Berlin, 1984.

Mather, John. *The Great Spy Scandal.* Daily Express Publications, London, 1955.

McKnight, David. *Australia's Spies and Their Secrets.* Allen & Unwin, London, 1994.

Miller, Joan. *One Girl's War.* Brandon, Dingle, Ireland, 1986.

Mitrokhin, Vasily. *KGB Lexicon.* Frank Cass, London, 2002.

Moberly, C. A. E. *Dulce Domum.* John Murray, London, 1911.

Modin, Yuri. *My Five Cambridge Friends.* Headline Book Publishing, London, 1994.

Moorehead, Alan. *The Traitors.* Hamish Hamilton, London, 1952; Harper & Row, New York, 1964.

Moss, Norman. *Klaus Fuchs.* Grafton Books, London, 1987.

Murphy, Donald, Sergei Kondrashev, and George Bailey. *Battleground Berlin.* Yale University Press, New Haven, CT, 1997.

Murphy, Philip. "Creating a Commonwealth Intelligence Culture." *Intelligence and National Security* 17, No. 3 (September 2002): 131–162.

Newman, Michael. *Harold Laski.* Macmillan, London, 1993.

Norris, Robert S. *Racing for the Bomb.* Steerforth Press, South Royalton, VT, 2002.

Norwood, Melita. See *Mitrokhin Inquiry Report.* Also see David Burke, above.

Panitz, Eberhard. *Treffpunkt Banbury.* Das Neue Berlin, Berlin, 2003.

Pavlov, Vitaly. *Dela Sneg* (*Operation Snow*). Geya, Moscow, 1996.

Peierls, Rudolf. *Bird of Passage.* Princeton University Press, Princeton, NJ, 1985.

Pelling, Henry. *The British Communist Party.* A&C Black Publishers, London, 1975.

Petrov, Major General Ivan. *Radio Communications Facilities and Service with Military Intelligence*. L. Military Parade JSC, 1998.

Philby, Eleanor. *Kim Philby: The Spy I Loved*. Hamish Hamilton, London, 1968.

Philby, H. *My Silent War*. Macgibbon & Kee, London, 1968.

Philby, Kim. *Autobiographical Reminiscences*. See appendix to *The Private Life of Kim Philby*, Rufina Philby.

Philby, Rufina. *The Private Life of Kim Philby*. St. Ermin's Press, London, 1999.

Philby's lecture to the KGB, July 1977. See appendix to *The Private Life of Kim Philby*, Rufina Philby.

Pickersgill, J. W., and D. F. Forster. *The Mackenzie King Record*, Vol. 3. University of Toronto Press, Toronto, 1960–1970.

Pincher, Chapman. *Inside Story*. Sidgwick & Jackson, London, 1978.

———. *Their Trade Is Treachery*. Sidgwick & Jackson, London, 1981; paperback (rev. ed.), Bantam Books, New York, 1982.

———. *Too Secret Too Long*. Sidgwick & Jackson, London, 1984; St. Martin's Press, New York, 1984; paperback, Sidgwick & Jackson, London, 1984.

———. *A Web of Deception*. Sidgwick & Jackson, London, 1987. (As *The Spycatcher Affair:* St. Martin's Press, New York, 1988.)

———. *Traitors*. Sidgwick & Jackson, London, 1987; St. Martin's Press, New York, 1987.

———. *The Truth About Dirty Tricks*. Sidgwick & Jackson, London, 1991.

Popov, F. D. The Atom Bomb and the KGB. Moscow, 2003.

Rees, Goronwy. *A Chapter of Accidents*. Chatto & Windus, London, 1972.

Rhodes, Richard. *Dark Sun: The Making of the Hydrogen Bomb*. Simon & Schuster, London, 1995.

Rhodes James, Robert. *Anthony Eden*. Weidenfeld & Nicolson, London, 1986.

Riddel, J. N. *C. Day Lewis*. Twayne Publishers, London, 1971.

Rimington, Stella. *Open Secret*. Hutchinson, London, 2001.

Rose, Kenneth. *Elusive Rothschild*. Weidenfeld & Nicolson, London, 2003.

The Rote Kapelle: MI5 History of Soviet Intelligence and Espionage Network in Western Europe (1936–1945). 3 vols. NA MI5 files KV3/349–351, released 2008.

The Rote Kapelle: The CIA's History of Soviet Intelligence and Espionage Networks in Western Europe, 1936–1945. 2 vols. University Publications of America Inc., Frederick, MD, 1979.

Rothschild, Lord. *Random Variables*. HarperCollins, London, 1984.

The Report of the Royal Commission (Canadian) (on the Gouzenko affair). Ottawa Stationery Office, Ottawa, 1946.

Sanden, Einar. *Úr Eldinum til Íslands*. Almenna Bokafelagio, Reykjavík, Iceland, 1988.

————. *An Estonian Saga*. Boreas, Bristol, UK, 1996.

Sawatsky, John. *Gouzenko: The Untold Story*. Macmillan of Canada, Toronto, 1984.

Schecter, J. L., and P. Deriabin. *The Spy Who Saved the World*. Brassey's, London, 1995.

The Security Service, 1908–1945: The Official History. Public Record Office, London, 1999.

Sergeant, Harriet. *Shanghai*. Jonathan Cape, London, 1991.

Shukman, Harold, ed. *Agents for Change*. St. Ermin's Press, London, 2000.

Sillitoe, Sir Percy. *Cloak Without Dagger*. Cassell & Co., London, 1955.

Skidelsky, Robert. *Oswald Mosley*. Macmillan, London, 1975.

Smith, Michael, and Ralph Erskine. *Action This Day*. Bantam, London, 2001.

Soviet Atomic Espionage. U.S. Government Printing Office, Washington, DC, 1951.

Stafford, David. *Churchill and the Secret Service*. John Murray, London, 1997.

————. *Spies Beneath Berlin*. John Murray, London, 2002.

Stanford, Peter. *C. Day-Lewis: A Life*. Continuum International Publishing Group, London, 2007.

Straight, Michael. *After Long Silence*. Collins, London, 1983.

Sudoplatov, Pavel, et al. *Special Tasks*. Little, Brown & Co., London, 1994.

Suvorov, Viktor. *Inside Soviet Military Intelligence*. Hamish Hamilton, London, 1984.

Szasz, Ferenc Morton. *British Scientists and the Manhattan Project*. Macmillan, London, 1992.

Tangye, Derek. *The Way to Minack*, Michael Joseph, London, 1968.

Taubman, William, Sergei Khrushchev, and Abbott Gleason. *Nikita Khrushchev*. Yale University Press, New Haven, CT, 2000.

Tschikov, Vladimir. *Perseus: Espionage in Los Alamos*. Verlag Volk & Welt, Berlin, 1996.

Wasserstein, Bernard. *Secret War in Shanghai*. Profile Books, London, 1998.

Waugh, Evelyn. *The Diaries of Evelyn Waugh*. Edited by Michael Davies. Weidenfeld & Nicolson, London, 1976.

Weinstein, Allen, and Alexander Vassiliev. *The Haunted Wood*. Random House, London, 1999.

Werner, Ruth. *Sonya's Report*. Chatto & Windus, London, 1991.

————. *Funksprüche an Sonja*. Edited by Rudolf Hempel. Neues Leben, Berlin, 2007.

West, Nigel. *Venona*. HarperCollins, London, 1999.

————, ed. *The Guy Liddell Diaries*. Vol. 1, *1939–42;* Vol. 2, *1942–45*. Routledge, London, 2005.

————. *Mask*. Routledge, London, 2005.

West, Nigel, and Oleg Tsarev. *Crown Jewels*. HarperCollins, London, 1998.

West, W. J. *Truth Betrayed*. Duckworth, London, 1987.

————. *Spymaster*. Wynwood Press, New York, 1990.

————. *The Quest for Graham Greene*. Weidenfeld & Nicolson, London, 1997.

Whymant, Robert. *Stalin's Spy*. Tauris, London, 1996.

Williams, Francis. *Nothing So Strange*. Cassell, London, 1970.

Williams, Robert Chadwell. *Klaus Fuchs: Atom Spy*. Harvard University Press, Cambridge, MA, 1987.

Wolf, Markus. *Man Without a Face*. Jonathan Cape, London, 1997.

Wright, Peter. *Spycatcher*. Viking Press, New York, 1987.

Index

CHAPMAN PINCHER is perhaps the best-known British espionage writer. Born in 1914, he was educated at King's College London, of which he is a Life Fellow, and the Royal Military College of Science. His book *Their Trade Is Treachery*, which revealed the official suspicion that Sir Roger Hollis, chief of the British Security Service (MI5), had been a Soviet agent, was a sensation. For decades he has been the most effective critic of the British security system, and he has broken scores of stories that have created major headlines. He lives in Berks, United Kingdom.

This book is set in Fournier, a typeface named for Pierre Simon Fournier, the youngest son of a French printing family. Pierre Simon first studied watercolor painting, but became involved in type design through work that he did for his eldest brother. Starting with engraving woodblocks and large capitals, he later moved on to fonts of type. In 1736 he began his own foundry, and published the first version of his point system the following year. He made several important contributions in the field of type design; he cut and founded all the types himself, pioneered the concepts of the type family, and is said to have cut sixty thousand punches for 147 alphabets of his own design. He also created new printers' ornaments.

Pierre Simon Fournier is probably best remembered as the designer of St. Augustine Ordinaire, one of the early transitional faces. It served as the model for the Monotype transitional face, Fournier, which was released in 1925.